Dear Valued Customer,

We realize you're a busy professional with deadlines to hit. Whether your goal is to learn a new technology or solve a critical problem, we want to be there to lend you a hand. Our primary objective is to provide you with the insight and knowledge you need to stay atop the highly competitive and ever-changing technology industry.

Wiley Publishing, Inc., offers books on a wide variety of technical categories, including security, data warehousing, software development tools, and networking — everything you need to reach your peak. Regardless of your level of expertise, the Wiley family of books has you covered.

- For Dummies® – The *fun* and *easy* way™ to learn
- The Weekend Crash Course® –The *fastest* way to learn a new tool or technology
- Visual – For those who prefer to learn a new topic *visually*
- The Bible – The *100% comprehensive* tutorial and reference
- The Wiley Professional list – *Practical* and *reliable* resources for IT professionals

The book you now hold, Mastering Jbuilder®, shows Java™ developers how to get the most from JBuilder to create enterprise-strength applications. This comprehensive tutorial and reference guide tackles the tough issues developers face when creating large-scale applications with JBuilder, including:

- Rapid Application Development with JBuilder
- Developing, testing, and deploying EJBs
- Local and remote debugging
- Web development with servlets, JavaServer Pages, and Struts
- Database development with JDataStore, DataExpress, and DBSwing
- Distributed computing with CORBA, RMI, and Web services

The lead author of this book is the Chief Technical Architect for Borland, so you can be assured that this book is authoritative, comprehensive, and up-to-date. Be sure to check out the companion Web site for all of the source code in the book as well as links to updates on JBuilder.

Our commitment to you does not end at the last page of this book. We'd want to open a dialog with you to see what other solutions we can provide. Please be sure to visit us at www.wiley.com/compbooks to review our complete title list and explore the other resources we offer. If you have a comment, suggestion, or any other inquiry, please locate the "contact us" link at www.wiley.com.

Finally, we encourage you to review the following page for a list of Wiley titles on related topics. Thank you for your support and we look forward to hearing from you and serving your needs again in the future.

Sincerely,

Richard K Swadley

Richard K. Swadley
Vice President & Executive Group Publisher
Wiley Technology Publishing

15 HOUR WEEKEND CRASH COURSE

Visual

Bible

FOR DUMMIES

Wiley Publishing, Inc.

# Advance Praise for *Mastering JBuilder*

"Without a doubt, the seminal work on JBuilder. Previous JBuilder books teach Java using JBuilder. This book teaches JBuilder, its history, how to configure it and how to get the most out of it. It is filled with insights only a Borland insider would know. An absolute must for JBuilder developers and those wishing to be JBuilder certified. JBuilder has a new owner's manual!"

*Ken Sipe*
*CEO, Code Mentor, Inc.*

"Finally a comprehensive book that walks through the great features of JBuilder. Mastering JBuilder targets both the novice and expert. It provides a HOW-TO approach dividing up features into usable segments. The chapters try to avoid assumptions while still giving enough details to cover topics in an easy to understand fashion. Every JBuilder user will want this as a quick reference."

*David Lucas*
*President and Software Architect,*
*Lucas Software Engineering, Inc.*

"This book has a significant amount of detail, enough to prove that the name is appropriate! I was particularly impressed with the chapters on unit testing and team usage — the depth was good and gives a very solid foundation from which to work from. When my team gets a hold of this, it will not only help the newer developers get up to speed, but the more advanced people can certainly learn a thing or two!"

*Angelo Serra*
*Information Technology Manager, COJUG*

"Mastering JBuilder is full of useful information and valuable tips. It starts with giving you complete instructions on configuring JBuilder then expands to focus on utilizing the power of JBuilder to accelerate development. I especially enjoyed the chapters on debugging, EJB development and Web Services. I would recommend this book for anyone looking to take his or her JBuilder development skills to the level of 'Master'."

*Jerry Jones*
*Consultant, Enterprise Developer*

# Mastering JBuilder®

# Mastering JBuilder®

Mike Rozlog
Geoffrey L. Goetz
Sung Nguyen

Wiley Publishing, Inc.

Publisher: Joe Wikert
Executive Editor: Robert M. Elliott
Assistant Developmental Editor: Emilie Herman
Editorial Manager: Kathryn Malm
Managing Editor: Pamela M. Hanley
Media Development Specialist: Brian Snapp
Text Design & Composition: Wiley Composition Services

This book is printed on acid-free paper. ♾



Published by Wiley Publishing, Inc., Indianapolis, Indiana

Published simultaneously in Canada



*Library of Congress Cataloging-in-Publication Data:*

Rozlog, Mike, 1968-
Mastering JBuilder / Mike Rozlog, Geoffrey L. Goetz, Sung Nguyen.
p. cm.
Includes index.
ISBN 0-471-26714-7
1. Java (Computer program language) 2. JBuilder. I. Goetz, Geoffrey L., 1970- II. Nguyen, Sung, 1971- III. Title.
QA76.73.J38 R695 2003
005.13'3--dc21

2002156130

Printed in the United States of America

10 9 8 7 6 5 4 3 2 1

***Mike Rozlog:***

*I dedicate this book to my wife, Leigh Ann, and Michael Jr. I'm sorry for all of the nights and weekends I sat in front of the computer working on the book instead of spending them with you. But, now it is done, time for a vacation!*

*Special thanks to Michael Jr., my 2-year old, for understanding daddy has to work and shutting the door behind him.*

***Geoffrey L. Goetz:***

*I dedicate this book to my loving wife, Allyson, for all of her patience, understanding, and support as I spent many an evening and weekend working on the book.*

***Sung Nguyen:***

*My dedication is to my Grandma, her endless love built the best I can be; and to my mother and her unconditional supports.*

*Specially, to my loving wife, Mimi, who makes all things possible by putting up with me on my book activities. I love you. Now, my nights and weekends are yours; that's my commitment to you and our son.*

*To my little BaoNghiem, who always wants to play with his daddy. And here he is.*

# Contents

# Foreword

I'd like to thank the publisher and authors who are willing to rise to the challenge of helping people make the most of JBuilder. This is a tremendous task when you consider the pace of change in the Java development arena and the number of new features appearing in Jbuilder with every release. JBuilder 8 is the latest incarnation of a product with over five years of history, and is an invaluable tool for the Java developer, but it is inevitable that we will continue to improve on it. The great news is that the majority of the information here will continue to be relevant for future releases of JBuilder as well.

The development teams here at Borland are always looking to share their enthusiasm for what they've created. The members of the JBuilder team have slaved to make things easier for the Java developer, and are eager to spread the word about the product. The most common response from audiences that see firsthand how the creators of JBuilder use their own product is "wow, I didn't know it could do that!" If we could package their experience and enthusiasm, we would, but instead we need to find other ways to distribute that knowledge.

We deliver the best documentation we can with the product but schedules are tight and there are always additional angles to be covered. Mike, Geoffery, and Sung have seen the product evolve through early access to the technology and discussions with Borland engineers. They can give you the extra edge because they know why JBuilder works the way it does — and do their best to draw on this background to show you the most productive ways of working with JBuilder.

It may seem daunting at first, but really the material in this book covers a wide range of topics that you'll draw on over time. Some projects will focus on client-side development, others on the server. Developers creating distributed applications may work directly with CORBA, or they may rely on EJB to hide the infrastructure and allow them to focus on business logic and a transaction model. Take things a step at a time and it will all fall into place.

You may be tempted to rush through the early material to get to these powerful technologies, but some of the real gems are introduced early on. Every Java developer can benefit from a deep understanding of the basic code editing and browsing technology in JBuilder, no matter what problem they're solving. It is part of the true spirit behind each of Borland's products: Keep the developer in touch with their code and give them a toolkit that helps make each and every day that much more productive.

I hope this book gives you deeper insight into a product we're extremely proud of here at Borland. With the most popular Java development environment available and the knowledge of how to put it to work, you'll have what it takes to put Java to work for you.

# Acknowledgments

First of all we would like to thank those people who were involved with this project from the beginning and helped immensely on getting the book completed. They include the editors at Wiley Publishing, Inc., Robert Elliott and Emilie Herman. Also, thanks to Ted Shelton at Borland for proposing the Book to Wiley with us in mind to help write it.

We would like to thank Borland for producing a world-class product for Java development.

We sincerely appreciate the efforts of our reviewers, Christopher Judd and Andy Tran. Under incredibly short timelines, these guys scrutinized every page for accuracy and completeness and I don't think Sung, Geoff or myself can thank them enough for their hard work and dedication.

Each of us strongly feels that the effort set forth to forge this book from our collective experiences at Borland has only strengthened our friendship. Without the friendly competitive nature we all share, this book may not have come to fruition. Many a day and night were spent discussing the finer details of a function or feature found inside JBuilder. These tireless discussions resulted in a clearer understanding of the technologies by all, and better explanations throughout the book.

# Introduction

Borland has a long-standing tradition of making award-winning, highly productive tools that free developers from the tedium of day-to-day development. Java has evolved into a proven, industry-standard, object-oriented development language that has been used to build many of the frameworks that companies have come to depend on. Bring Borland and Java together and you have JBuilder.

From its inception, JBuilder has been a tool designed by Java developers for Java developers. To this end, JBuilder looks at the various frameworks implemented in Java, from the language's point of view. The lessons learned about Java frameworks, best practices, and design principals were encapsulated in this one tool. Beyond the major frameworks that are used to build many of today's mission-critical systems, JBuilder allows almost any Java technology to be integrated into its environment. JBuilder exposes these technologies through generic interfaces that include wizards, templates, frameworks, refactoring, and two-way tools. Learning how to use JBuilder to accomplish simple tasks is easy enough given JBuilder's intuitive and easy-to-learn user interface, but *Mastering JBuilder* is another matter entirely.

## Overview of the Book and Technology

JBuilder can be divided into two major disciplines, the development of Java source code and the management of Java source code. JBuilder uses various technologies and frameworks to help developers manage the code they are developing. These technologies and frameworks include Ant, UML, JUnit, and CVS. JBuilder also helps developers work with Java technologies and frameworks. One of the strengths of JBuilder lies in its approach to help developers tame these technologies. Without playing favorites, JBuilder allows the developer to choose from several different technologies and frameworks including Swing, JDBC, servlets, Java Server Pages, Struts, EJB, RMI, CORBA, and Web services.

Technologies and frameworks used to help manage development include the following:

- Version Control with CVS in Chapter 9
- Jakarta Ant in Chapter 10
- Extreme programming with JUnit in Chapter 11
- Refactoring using The Object Management Group's UML in Chapter 12

Technologies and frameworks for developers to develop with include the following:

- Sun Microsystem's J2SE in Chapters 7 and 8
- Borland's JDataStore Database in Chapter 13
- Sun Microsystem's J2EE in Chapters 15–20
- Jakarta Tomcat in Chapters 15–18
- Jakarta Struts in Chapter 18
- Borland Enterprise Server AppServer Edition in Chapters 19, 20, 22, and 23
- The Object Management Group's Common Object Request Broker Architecture in Chapter 22
- Jakarta Axis in Chapter 23

# How This Book Is Organized

*Mastering JBuilder* is also divided into these two major disciplines. Parts I, II, and III define JBuilder as a development tool that helps developers manage their code in terms of an Integrated Development Environment (IDE), a Rapid Application Development (RAD) tool, and finally as an Application Lifecycle Management (ALM) tool. Parts IV, V, VI, and VII take a look at different types of applications that a Java developer would create; from traditional two-tier client/server-based applications, to n-tier-based solutions using servlets, Java Server Pages, and Enterprise JavaBeans (EJB), to using various distributed technologies such as RMI, CORBA, and Web services.

**Chapter 1, Installing JBuilder.** This chapter shows you how to install and configure JBuilder on any machine. Details of where the files are loaded, memory utilizations, and overall configuration of the JBuilder system are covered.

**Chapter 2, Customizing the AppBrowser.** This chapter reviews the basics of configuring the AppBrowser, which is the interface to the Java language that can be customized to best meet the needs of the developers. Special attention is given to Java Look and Feels and configurations for limited machines.

**Chapter 3, Controlling Java Configurations.** This chapter focuses on using multiple JDKs and how JDK switching can be used in a project. Java API management in the JBuilder environment is also discussed.

**Chapter 4, Project Properties and Configurations.** This chapter defines projects, project properties, and their configurations. Also covered is the concept of configurations that can be used for running, debugging, and optimizing code.

**Chapter 5, Debugging with JBuilder.** This chapter focuses on the basic, intermediate, and advanced concepts of debugging Java code. This chapter helps you understand how the interface can be used and interacted with and how to debug threads, multiple-processes, and even remote debugging using the tools provided by JBuilder.

**Chapter 6, Using the JBuilder Help System.** This chapter looks at the enhanced context-sensitive help, integrated error help in the editor, and even the tip-of-the-day capabilities that JBuilder now has. The chapter covers how to get the most out of the JBuilder help system and even how to extend some of its features.

**Chapter 7, Creating Classes.** This chapter covers the basic wizards that are included with JBuilder. These wizards are focused on all points in the development process, from creating a simple framework to generating test clients, unit tests, and to even creating and working with deployment features.

**Chapter 8, Modifying Classes.** This chapter covers the basics of creating Java classes that use all of the tools available in JBuilder to make the effort as painless as possible.

**Chapter 9, Integrated Team Development.** This chapter covers JBuilder integration with team development and illustrates the uses of team development via JBuilder-CVS integration.

**Chapter 10, Using the Build Systems.** This chapter covers what the JBuilder build system is and how to best use it. The chapter also introduces the integration of JBuilder and Ant Builder.

**Chapter 11, Unit Testing with JUnit.** This chapter covers JBuilder-JUnit integration, which is best for programmers doing unit test synonymously with their coding. Chapter 11 guides you through the creation and run unit tests for the Java component using JUnit framework in the JBuilder.

**Chapter 12, UML Visualization.** This chapter shows that JBuilder uses UML structural diagrams to help developers visualize and traverse Java classes and packages.

**Chapter 13, Building the Database with JDataStore.** This chapter covers the product from beginning to end. It shows how to use the graphic tools included with JBuilder and how to do the exact same tasks using regular programming techniques.

**Chapter 14, DataExpress and DBSwing Applications.** This chapter brings attention to the frameworks included in JBuilder that can help developers develop great client/server applications without a lot of fuss. The tools included with JBuilder can literally generate a complete application with no coding that will allow for manipulation of generic data sources, JDBC or not.

**Chapter 15, Server and Service Configuration.** JBuilder itself does not provide the technologies that are compliant with the various specifications that make up J2EE. To develop solutions within J2EE, an application server will need to be configured. This chapter goes over the setup and configuration principles common to all servers.

**Chapter 16, Web Enablement with Servlets.** Developing servlets that will be packaged in a given Web application's Web archive is the focus of this chapter. In addition, basic edits to the Deployment Descriptor specific to servlets is also discussed.

**Chapter 17, Moving from Basic Servlets to Java Server Pages.** Expanding on the servlet technology, JavaServer Pages allow developers to separate presentation from Java code by using tags within HTML. Developers can also create their own tags by developing Tag Libraries.

**Chapter 18, Developing with Struts.** Taking full advantage of the servlet, JavaServer Page, and Tag Library capabilities outlined in the previous chapters, the struts framework provides a Model View Controller architecture for developing dynamic Web applications.

**Chapter 19, Developing EJB 1.1.** Focusing on version 1.1 of the Enterprise Java Bean specification, this chapter outlines the steps necessary to develop Enterprise Java Beans compliant with the EJB 1.1 specification. In addition, Deployment Descriptor edits and configuration are discussed for Session Beans and Entity Beans.

**Chapter 20, Developing EJB 2.x.** Not only are there new capabilities within the EJB 2.0 specification, but JBuilder has also introduced a new way of developing EJBs with the EJB 2.0 Designer. This chapter covers the development of EJBs using all of the features and capabilities of this designer.

**Chapter 21, RMI Development with JBuilder.** The chapter discusses how JBuilder facilitates the development with RMI.

**Chapter 22, CORBA Development with JBuilder.** The chapter discusses how JBuilder facilitates the development with CORBA.

**Chapter 23, Web Services Development with JBuilder.** In this chapter, you will learn to consume and construct Web services with the Apache Axis toolkit and Borland Application Server. JBuilder provides wizards to create Web services from any Java class and EJB components. Also, the chapter shows the Web Services Explorer for searching and publishing Web services to a UDDI registry.

## Who Should Read This Book

This book teaches you how to use the tools in the best way possible to make development of Java programs as easy as possible. You should read this book if you are doing any of the following:

- Developing with Java not using an IDE
- Developing with Java using a generic IDE
- Developing with Java using JBuilder
- Working on an Open Source project and want to understand a great implementation

## Tools You Will Need

This book is based on JBuilder Enterprise version 8. The JBuilder family of products, however, consists of the following editions that may have some limited practical use:

**JBuilder Personal.** With this entry-level product offering from Borland, it supports the basic ideal of what an IDE is, and it allows you to run, compile, and debug from within a single environment. This product is available from Borland at no charge and is not for commercial use. It is a great teaching tool, which is covered in Chapters 1–6.

**JBuilder SE.** With the SE edition users increase the capability of the Java IDE. This product allows for a complete RAD environment including refactoring, JavaDoc tools, team development, and BeansInsight technologies. This edition is for commercial use, and most of its functionality is covered in Chapters 1–10.

**JBuilder Enterprise.** With the Enterprise Edition users of this product have the leading Java IDE in their hands. JBuilder 8 Enterprise is the product that this book is based on, and it is covered thoroughly throughout its contents. JBuilder 8 Enterprise includes all of the technology in the other editions, plus it adds a full testing environment, UML visualization, code formatting, HotSwap debugging, J2EE support, Web services, CORBA, database application development, and deployment to most major application server vendors.

This book covers major portions of J2EE and advanced distributed technologies like RMI, CORBA, and Web services, so it relies on the latest features of JBuilder 8 Enterprise. This level of product will give the most complete set of Java development tools.

JBuilder Enterprise Trial edition can be downloaded from Borland at www. borland.com/products/downloads/download_jbuilder.html and gives a 30-day free trial. Alternatively, a trial edition can be purchased at http://shop.borland.com under trial software.

## What's on the Web Site

The companion Web site for this book includes additional product information, the source code for examples in the book, and updates to both the book and the technology. The URL is www.wiley.com/compbooks/rozlog.

PART

# One

# JBuilder as an Integrated Development Environment

When Jbuilder—then called Latte—was first discussed as a new Integrated Development Environment (IDE) for Borland, desktop development was coming to an end, object orientation was finally starting to become mainstream, and development tools were getting better. Borland's Delphi product, which is based on the Object Pascal language, was one of the first Integrated Development Environments to improve developer productivity. This was due, in large part, to the fact that it was well conceived and easy to work with. These same principles were needed for a Java environment.

The first plan was to integrate Java into C++ 4.5.1, an early predecessor to the C++ Builder still in production today. The program allowed the creation of a Java source file and could run the compiler, but errors and debugging were a challenge because of limited support. Borland scrapped the integration idea and instead decided to create an environment based on the Delphi language and interface. Latte, as it was called, supported the basic Java 1.0 features and used the established Delphi IDE as a framework to make development simpler and less time-consuming. Because Borland wouldn't own the Java language the way it did the Pascal language, it was thought that the underlying programming support could be provided as a language plug-in to an existing IDE framework. Later, in the product cycle when Borland tested the name "Latte" around the world, other countries could have been offended by the name because of translation issues.

Java was progressing quickly, and it was decided that building on top of an existing framework might really hinder support for the language in the long term. The new JDK 1.1 included new features, so maybe an underlying framework built in Java would better support the rapid changes over time. Java could not handle the tasks being asked of it, though, leading to the creation of Open JBuilder. It used about 20 percent C++, 50 percent Delphi, and 30 percent Java. "Open" was later dropped from the name when it was officially released. These percentages continued to favor the Java side as each new release of JBuilder hit the streets; finally, when JBuilder 3.5 was released, it was 100 percent Java.

When JBuilder was released, it was a fairly good attempt at a Java IDE. Remember that an IDE is basically the editor, compiler, and debugger wrapped into one interface. A base-level IDE requires that an environment be configurable enough that most developers can create a suitable place to work with all of the known creature features. Over the life span of JBuilder, these features and their ability to be customized have grown rather significantly.

Part One shows you how to customize your JBuilder IDE and helps you understand some of the advanced features of JBuilder:

**Installing JBuilder.** Chapter 1 shows you how to install and configure JBuilder on any machine. Details of where the files are loaded, memory utilizations, and overall configuring of the JBuilder system are covered.

**Customizing the AppBrowser.** Chapter 2 reviews the basics of configuring the AppBrowser, which is the interface to the Java language that can be customized to best meet the needs of the developers. Special attention is given to Java Look and Feels, as well as configurations for limited machines.

**Controlling Java Configurations.** Chapter 3 is focused on using multiple JDKs and how JDK switching can be used in a project. Java API management in the JBuilder environment is also covered in detail.

**Project Properties and Configurations.** Chapter 4 defines projects, project properties, and their configurations. Also covered is the concept of configurations that can be used for running, debugging, and optimizing code.

**Debugging with JBuilder.** Chapter 5 focuses on the basics, intermediate, and advanced concepts of debugging Java code. It will help the reader understand how the interface can be used and interacted with and how to debug threads, multiple-processes, and even remote debugging using the tools provided by JBuilder.

**Using the JBuilder Help System.** Chapter 6 looks at the enhanced context-sensitive help, integrated error help in the editor, and even the tip-of-the-day capabilities JBuilder now has. The chapter covers how to get the most out of the JBuilder help system and even how to extend some of its features.

CHAPTER

1

# Installing JBuilder

Understanding the installation process, file locations, configuration files, and advanced settings can help a developer establish a stable and usable environment that will support the development effort. Borland JBuilder uses the InstallAnywhere installation program from Zero G to handle the install process; so many typical installation problems are minimized. The most daunting task removed was installation on multiple platforms. InstallAnywhere provides easy installation on the Mac, Windows, Linux, and Solaris platforms. Installation can be attempted for unsupported platforms, but it requires additional work and is not supported in any way by Borland.

The installation process itself is fairly painless, but developers installing the product should follow up with the following tasks:

1. Install everything first: Web services, Borland Enterprise Server, MobileSet, OptimizeIT.
2. Review what was installed and where it was installed.
3. Review the configuration files.
4. Set the user.home.
5. Review the licensing procedure.
6. Set additional switches.
7. Perform troubleshooting.

# Installing JBuilder

Because JBuilder is a Java program, it is always recommended that it be installed on a noncompressed drive with ample free space. JBuilder should be installed and used on a machine with as much memory as can be afforded. A fast processor is important, but when using Java-based programs, memory is even more critical. The base machines that Borland recommends will allow JBuilder to run fairly decently; however, if at all possible, having a machine with 512MB more memory will really make the product perform like native development environments. Later in this chapter, we recommend the proper levels of JVM switches to get the most out of your environment.

The installation process itself is rather painless and will require the standard information about what components are to be installed and where the files should be located. The installation process normally will be started from a CD; the appropriate executable on Windows or the script on other platforms should be executed to begin the installer program. The install process will then proceed to load a JVM into memory and start a step-by-step wizard to complete the process. Once the install process is complete, the developer will have an opportunity to install additional programs from the installer, if necessary. Once all programs have been installed, the developer can exit the installer program.

Make sure to install all programs that may be part of the JBuilder system first before starting the program because of the licensing procedures that Borland is now using to register the products, which is covered later in the chapter. Additional features can be added to the JBuilder environment from the Borland Enterprise Server, Web Services pack, MobileSet, and OptimizeIT; however, they do not need to be installed for JBuilder to work. For example, if the developer were not going to be programming J2ME, the usefulness of JBuilder's MobileSet would be limited.

JBuilder was designed to be completely extensible, meaning that if a function or feature was missing inside JBuilder, then any Java developer could add an OpenTool without having to recreate the entire product. The concept of OpenTools is not new; it is nothing more than a standardized plug-in for the environment. JBuilder's implementation of an OpenTools framework is much more complete and documented than other OpenTools frameworks. In fact, the JBuilder program itself is only about 3K in size, with its major responsibility being to understand how to load and run OpenTools, meaning that everything in JBuilder is an OpenTool. Tools like MobileSet are nothing more than a set of OpenTools that give new functionality to JBuilder.

Borland uses this framework to introduce new products and features to JBuilder. Most of these new features can be found at www.borland.com/jbuilder and are available for free download. Two examples given thus far have been MobileSet and the Web Services pack OpenTools, each giving distinct functionality. When it came to Web Services, Borland wanted to give the users of JBuilder a preview of what features it was planning to add to the product. The standards that were going to be used were not yet complete from a specification standpoint, though, so Borland could not add the features to JBuilder because it would have been introducing a nonstandard implementation that could have made JBuilder unstable. Borland still wanted the feedback from developers to make sure that what was being developed was on target, so it made the Web Services pack available from the download site to let developers interested in Web Services to download it and try it out. Once the specifications were completed, the Web Services pack was then added to the standard build of JBuilder Enterprise. This gives Borland the best of both worlds, exposing new technologies that might not be ready for the real world or of interest to only a small portion of developers while still getting valuable information.

Other programs that may be installed include Borland's Enterprise Server (J2EE 1.3 compliant server) included in the Enterprise Edition, Together, StarTeam, and OptimizeIt, which is included in the Studio product. Because these are additional technologies, they may need to be registered with Borland, so installing all of them can save time in the registration process. Plus, the installer may want to control where licenses are located on the machine.

## Review the Installation

After everything has been installed, understanding file locations and their meanings helps the developer understand how JBuilder works. Understanding the directory structure or file extensions will help a JBuilder developer understand what is being held in each file and where. As the developer becomes more knowledgeable with the product, this underlying information will become more important. Projects will continue to get larger and more complex, so having a firm understanding of the environment will allow the developer to understand how to configure JBuilder to handle these situations better. Understanding the configuration files that JBuilder uses to load itself into memory can help developers create advanced configurations for resource-starved machines or set switches so that the painting mechanism that JBuilder uses works better with the underlying hardware and operating system.

Figure 1.1 shows the directories located under the JBuilder directory. This directory structure will be the same no matter what OS you install JBuilder on. All versions of JBuilder will follow this directory layout; some older versions of JBuilder may not include all of the ones listed in Figure 1.1. Most of the directory structure is explained throughout this book; however, this chapter focuses on the bin and .jbuilder directories because they have the most to do with installing JBuilder.

The *bin* directory is where the JBuilder executables are located. Notice that all the files are either executables or configuration files. The executables .exe on the Windows OS and a single name with a MOD of 777 on Unix are nothing more than bootstrap programs that use the configuration file to define what should be run. This type of executable is the same that Native Executable supports in the build system, which is fully covered in Chapter 10. Inside this directory, notice that most executables have a corresponding .config file; this is where program specifics like classpath and memory setting are located. Now, there are three files in this directory to make note of. The first is config_readme.html, which is nothing more than an HTML page that explains how the configuration files are defined and what each switch means.

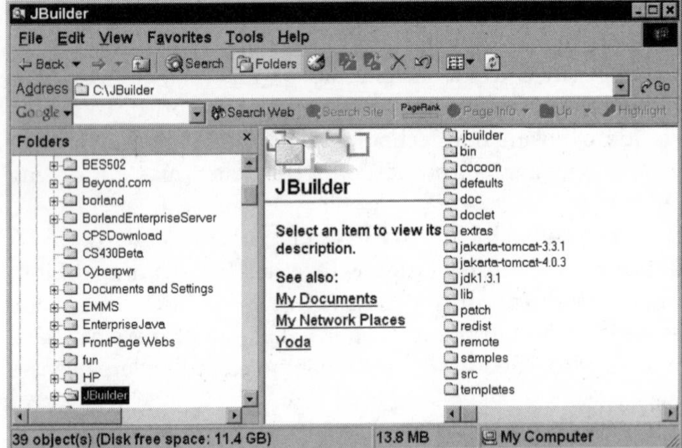


**Figure 1.1** Directories installed on the Windows OS.

The next file is the jbuilder.config; it is responsible for holding all the settings for launching JBuilder using the bootstrap program called jbuilder.exe or jbuilderw.exe on the Windows OS. The only difference between jbuilder.exe and jbuilderw.exe is that if you call the jbuilder.exe, it will launch from a command or terminal window, and if jbuilderw.exe is used, it will not spawn a window. This becomes important if you need to see what JBuilder is loading or doing when executing; this topic is covered later in this chapter.

# Review the Configuration Files

The last file of interest in the bin directory is the jdk.config. It is one of the most important files in the directory because it is called by all the other configuration files. It can be thought of as an include file, which means that jdk.config can be used to make global settings for all JBuilder executables.

The jdk.config file includes the two following lines:

```
vmparam -Xminf0.2
vmparam -Xmaxf0.2
```

The -Xminf0.2 represents the minimum ratio of free memory used in heap after Garbage Collection (GC), and the -Xmaxf0.2 represents the maximum ratio of free memory used in heap after GC. The two settings can be found in the documentation for the Hotspot JVM. They also have long names associated with them. -Xminf also can be denoted as -XX:MinHeapFreeRatio=<minimum on the command line and -XX:MaxHeapFreeRatio=<maximum>, respectively. These two settings are bound by the -Xms and -Xmx VM switches. The -Xms represents the initial memory size (heap) available to the program's memory pool. The -Xmx represents the maximum size the memory pool can get for a given program. This then means that -Xminf and -Xmaxf are percentages of the values found in the -Xms and -Xmx switches. These two can be worked with, depending on the amount of memory a given machine has available to it.

The current settings are for 20 percent both min and max. Documentation states that the max can be as high as 70, but this has not been tested. They are currently set in a generic form and are good for most machines. Machines with more memory may want to set these settings higher to get better performance. If performance becomes an issue, this is one area to keep in mind. You should also keep in mind that these switches are located in the jdk.config and will be used by all the executables found inside the jbuilder/bin directory. Setting these switches to optimize JBuilder performance may have adverse effects on the other programs that use these settings.

The jbuilder.config file also has memory switches defined; they are the -Xms and the -Xmx switches, and these should be set according to the amount of memory on the particular machine on which JBuilder will be executing. The defaults are as follows:

```
vmparam -Xms32m
vmparam -Xmx256m
```

Reviewing the definitions defined previously, these vmparams represent the base starting memory pool, which will be started with 32 megabytes and has a maximum of 256 megabytes. Because the machine being used for this book includes 512 megabytes of memory, the -Xms switch could be set to 128 and the -Xmx switch could be set to 384. The last character is important when using these switches:

- "m" represents megabytes
- "k" is used for kilobytes
- "g" represents gigabytes

More information on memory management can be found at the following sites:

- http://java.sun.com/docs/hotspot/gc/index.html
- http://java.sun.com/docs/hotspot/VMOptions.html
- http://community.borland.com/article/0,1410,23022,00.html

These are just some of the more useful links. JDK versions noted in the links are still valid for JDK 1.3.x and beyond. These techniques can be used with all Java programs, not just JBuilder.

Another set of switches found in the jdk.config file that can be very important to the way JBuilder performs are these:

```
# vmparam -Dsun.java2d.noddraw
# vmparam -Dsun.java2d.d3d=false
```

On certain hardware, notably machines with ATI graphics cards or machines using the Windows XP operating system, the preceding switches can be uncommented to fix the problem. Do not change these settings unless problems are occurring with JBuilder. A line beginning with "#" is a commented line; removing the "#" will make it uncommented. Normally, the –Dsun.java2d.noddraw is the switch most used with the ATI graphics card. The –Dsun.java2d.d3d=false switch is the one used for the XP operating system. Uncomment only one line at a time, then test the configuration by restarting JBuilder; if the results do not change, recomment the line, uncomment the other line, and repeat the process.

**NOTE Always exit JBuilder when making changes to one of its configuration files, as JBuilder will rewrite them on exit. Always save the file, exit, and restart JBuilder for changes to take effect.**

## Set the user.home

When you start up JBuilder, the first thing that will pop up is a request to enter the license key. The license key will allow the program to be properly registered, so Borland can refine the product and contact the user if issues arise. Starting with JBuilder 5, Borland has taken steps to ensure that, at a very minimum, a registration process is followed to activate the product.

The location of the license information on a machine can be set manually. This helps long-term maintenance and ensures that the installer has complete control over the process. This also allows the installer to have all the needed files in one defined location. JBuilder and the tools included with it use license files to validate users; some tools like JDataStore need to have a license file with a valid key before it will work in a deployed situation, so knowing the location of these files can eliminate the guesswork of where they are located. Then, by placing the license files on the classpath, JBuilder and its tools will be able to find and execute without asking for revalidation. The switch that should be added to the jbuilder.config file is the following:

```
vmparam -Duser.home=[location]
```

The [location] part is important because this is where all the default files will be located for JBuilder, including the licensing file. The default project file and the internal configuration files are also held there after the initial install. The [location] could look like the following:

```
vmparam -Duser.home=\JBuilder\.jbuilder
```

This means that all files would be located in the .jbuilder directory under the JBuilder directory. Once this location has been set, it cannot be moved or changed unless the JBuilder licensing process is followed again. This is another reason for making sure that the directory is where the installer needs it to be, and this is also why it is better to change the configuration files first before running and then having to reregister after the directory has been set.

## Review the License

JBuilder has a fairly simple licensing process. It can be changed or updated anytime to show additional programs that have been registered. The Licensing Information program has an icon on the Start menu in Windows, or its icon can be found in the JBuilder shortcut list in Unix. Typing the following line also can start it:

```
C:\JBuilder8\bin\JBuilderW.exe -license
```

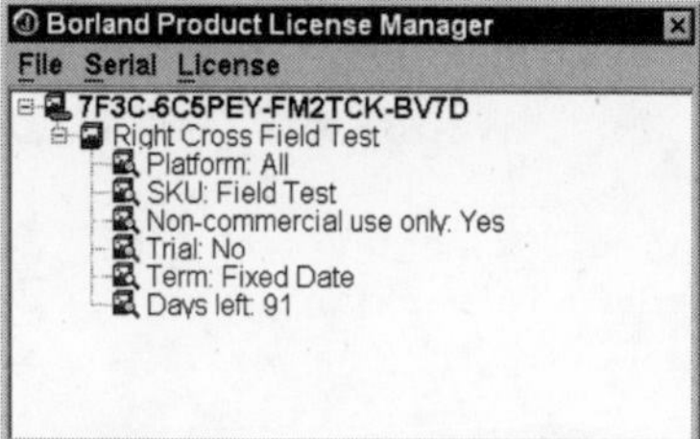


**Figure 1.2** Licensing manager.

This can be done at the operating system command prompt, so make sure to have a defined JDK in the path. Figure 1.2 shows a license file for a Field Test product, which explains exactly what the program is supposed to be used for. Licenses come in many forms; normally the license is found on the CD case that holds the JBuilder product. License strings can be emailed or loaded from a file, so remember that anytime a license is changed, a connection to Borland through the Internet will most likely be needed. If an Internet connection is not available, then other licensing schemes can be used like email or even postal mail; these options can be discussed with Borland Technical Support if issues arise. Borland Product License Manager can be used to change or update licenses of Borland products. It is available in the JBuilder Program menu list.

# Set Other Switches

Most Java and VM switches can be used with JBuilder. Another often used switch is this one:

```
vmparam -Djava.io.tmpdir=\jbuilder\tmp
```

This is useful if a lot of IO is going to be done. This also helps JBuilder put in a Java caching area when it needs to find space. This is normally added to the jbuilder.config file; however, it could again be added to the jdk.config if the setting was going to be used by all the executable programs found in bin directory.

Another reported problem is that sometimes developers use multiple versions of a program. This is especially true when dealing with the Borland Enterprise Server. There are many ways to solve the problem; one is to change the classpath found inside the jbuilder.config file and use the addjars command to add any specific jars needed. This will mean, though, that each JBuilder configuration will have to be modified for each version of the software being used. In the older editions of JBuilder, before JBuilder 6 (that is, JBuilder 5 and below), the quickest and easiest way is to create a .bat, .cmd, or script file that will set all the settings for that particular version. The following is a script file used to point JBuilder to the latest .jar files to be used when using the Borland Enterprise Server:

```
set path=
set classpath=
set path=c:\JBuilder\jdk1.4\bin;c:\JBuilder\jdk1.4\jre\bin;C:\
BorlandEnterpriseServer\bin
set classpath=%classpath%;c:\JBuilder\jdk1.4\jre\lib\rt.jar;c:\
JBuilder\jdk1.4\lib\tools.jar;C:\BorlandEnterpriseServer\lib\
vbjorb.jar;C:\BorlandEnterpriseServer\lib\vbejb.jar
jbuilderw
```

This code sets the current path and classpath so that JBuilder uses the latest Borland Enterprise Server. This is critical when you want to point to one version of the Application Server and at another time point to a different version of the VisiBroker technology, as it ensures that JBuilder will not get confused.

**WARNING The preceding technique works only with JBuilder 5 and below. Starting with JBuilder 6, these limitations were solved using the configuration files.**

Two other switches that can be very helpful when trying to figure out why a problem is occurring when the JBuilder program loads are these:

```
-verbose
-info
```

These switches can be placed on the JBuilder command –line, and they will give additional information on configuration, classpath, and OpenTools being loaded during the load process.

## Perform Troubleshooting

Whenever you make changes to any files, be sure to create a backup and exit JBuilder first. Any changes made while the JBuilder program is open most likely will not be saved.

When changing memory switches, make sure to test the configuration before beginning real programming. Nothing is more irritating than getting knee-deep in a problem and having JBuilder just crash or lock up with no warning.

Also keep in mind that custom configurations are probably not supported by Borland. It is good practice to make copies of the standard files so that the system can be reset to a default setting if problems arise.

## Summary

This chapter gave an overview of the process for installing the JBuilder product. It covered the proper steps to ensure a good install and highlighted some of the areas that can cause long-term problems with license files. The chapter also covered memory allocation, switches, and startup parameters to ensure that JBuilder works the best it can from the install point forward.

The next chapter discusses customizing the AppBrowser, which is JBuilder's main interface to the developer.

CHAPTER

2

# Customizing the AppBrowser

The Integrated Development Environment (IDE) includes three standard tools: the editor, compiler, and debugger. Before Borland invented the IDE, building programs consisted of using an editor for editing code and command-line tools for compiling and debugging. Once tools like JBuilder became available, they increased developer productivity by reducing the edit, run, compile, and debug cycle. Borland is now continually upgrading and adding new tools and functions by adding tools specifically for Java with the JBuilder IDE. The AppBrowser applies the concepts of the older IDE and adds views into the projects. Views can be thought of as different ways of looking at a project to get new meaning. A project may be looked at from a GUI standpoint, or from a documentation standpoint, or an object standpoint. The AppBrowser allows all those views to be shared inside a single interface. Plus, no matter in which view the code is changed, all the other views will be kept synchronized. Some IDEs use views to represent –project-level, hierarchical-level, and code-level interactions, which is great but very limited. The AppBrowser exposes the complete Java language and its features of object orientation, package development, GUI development, and integrated documentation into one standard interface, thus eliminating the need to use multiple programs to understand the code or project being worked on.

This chapter outlines the features of the AppBrowser, which is the integration point for all development using JBuilder. It covers the options based on layouts inside the AppBrowser and how each one interacts with the other. It provides quick hit lists to speed the setting up of a generic AppBrowser. It also will provide detailed information on the editor, the options associated with it, and how to make the most out of those settings.

## Generic AppBrowser Components

The AppBrowser is really broken into seven major panes:

- The Main menu line lists the major features found in the AppBrowser.
- The Main toolbar includes a set of icons that handle the most common tasks inside the AppBrowser with a click of the mouse.
- The Project pane, located in the top left-hand corner of the screen, is responsible for managing the project's default properties (covered in Chapter 4, "Project Properties and Configurations") and the files to be included in the project or projects.
- The third pane is located at the bottom left-hand corner of the screen. Its contents change; depending on the view being used by JBuilder, and it has two purposes (discussed later in this chapter):
  - Show the structure of the file being viewed, which could include Java, XML, JSP(s), or other file types
  - View a Component Hierarchy pane when in the designer
- The Content pane is the integration point to the file being worked on. This pane also has the ability to work with other views of a file and additional tools to make it tie together with the rest of the AppBrowser.
- The Message pane, like the Structure/Component panes, can have multiple roles depending on the context occurring in the AppBrowser — for instance, it can be the view into the integration of JUnit or a testing framework included with JBuilder (covered in Chapter 11, "Unit Testing with JUnit"), or it could be the view into the advanced debugger (covered in Chapter 5, "Debugging with JBuilder"); finally, it could be just a great Message pane to tell the developer what is going on within the context of the JBuilder IDE.
- The Status Bar is a great source of context information, usually generated by either pointing to an object on the AppBrowser or as a standard message from it.

Figure 2.1 shows a basic AppBrowser with all seven standard panes active. This raises the following question: Why is the Status Bar currently displaying information? The mouse pointer at the moment the screen shot was taken was pointing at the Untitled1 object under the Imports folder in the Structure pane, and JBuilder is reporting that the object being pointed to is a public constructor. This is an example of how the AppBrowser is completely aware of the Java language as a whole; almost anywhere the mouse pointer is used inside the AppBrowser, it will return current information on that subject. Each pane located inside the AppBrowser is configurable; its view can be toggled from hide to unhide, depending on the developer's desires.

Table 2.1 shows the hot-key and menu item to use to toggle the hide and unhide settings. This list assumes that this is not a customized AppBrowser and that the Message pane has been turned on.

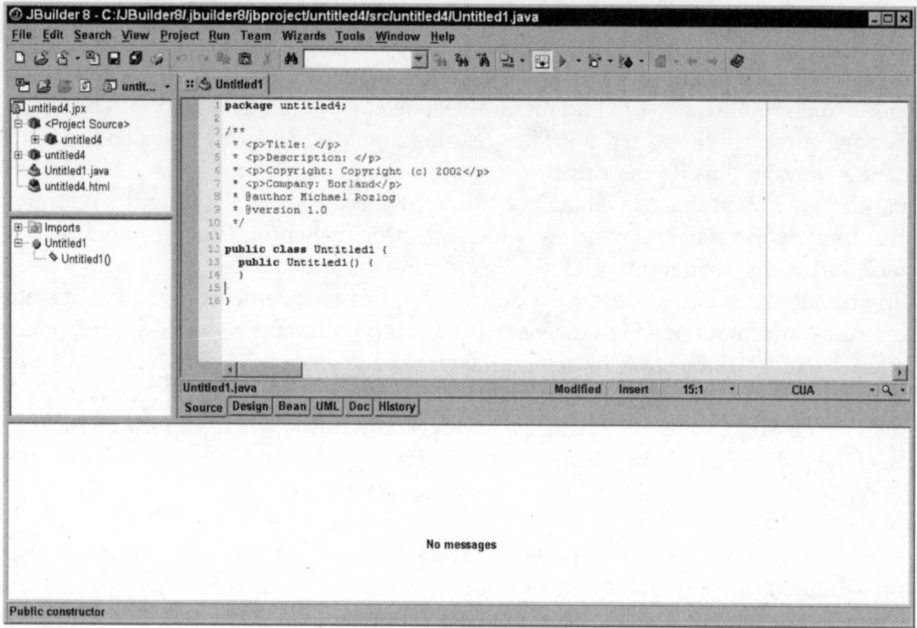


**Figure 2.1** Basic AppBrowser (all panes showing).

**Table 2.1** Show/Hide AppBrowser Basics

| ACTION HOT-KEY-COMBINATION | MENU COMBINATION |
|---|---|
| Hide/unhide Project pane | Ctrl-Alt-P<br>Alt-V-P |
| Hide/unhide Structure/Component pane | Ctrl-Alt-S<br>Alt-V-S |
| Hide/unhide Content pane | Ctrl-Alt-C<br>Alt-V-C |
| Hide/unhide Message pane | Ctrl-Alt-M<br>Alt-V-M |
| Hide/unhide status bar | Alt-V scroll to Status Bar menu item |
| Hide/unhide toolbars | Alt-V scroll to Toolbars |
| Expand content/hide Project and Structure panes | Ctrl-Alt-Z<br>Alt-V scroll to hide all menu items |

## Message Pane

The Message pane is a special pane, one that is unique to JBuilder. It can be turned on or off by the standard got-key and menu selections or by a Toolbar button. This is the only pane currently supported with this feature. The Message pane can also float as a separate window outside the AppBrowser confines, as shown in Figure 2.2. This will maximize the screen space available for the AppBrowser while allowing the information to be seen on a separate window, which is especially helpful in a two-monitor system or during the debugging process.

To activate the floating Message pane, the AppBrowser context must be in a state that returns information, which means that compiling, running, version control, refactoring, searching, unit testing, or debugging must be in progress. There is currently not a hot-key or menu combination to set the Message pane to float; a small icon is located at the bottom far right-hand side of the Message pane that, when pressed or clicked, will set the pane afloat. If the Message pane is closed using the "X" window close button or if the Float icon is pressed, the Message pane will be docked back into the AppBrowser.

The Message pane not only reports on the standard in, out, and err streams, it also returns valuable information to the developer. In Figure 2.2, the Message pane shows a running process that appears to be a standard command-line invocation. JBuilder always displays the command line used to start a process. Copying the command-line output makes it easy to create scripts or command programs to execute the Java process. The command line is the exact Java execution line needed to run the program in question. It includes the Java keyword, classpath settings, and the class to be called. The complete technique for making that command –line is covered in Chapter 3, "Controlling Java Configurations."

You can access the Context menu for the Message pane available by either right-mouse clicking inside the pane or, when the context is inside the Message pane, pressing Shift-F10. The Message pane has three options:

- Clear All from the pane
- Copy All from the pane
- Word Wrap setting

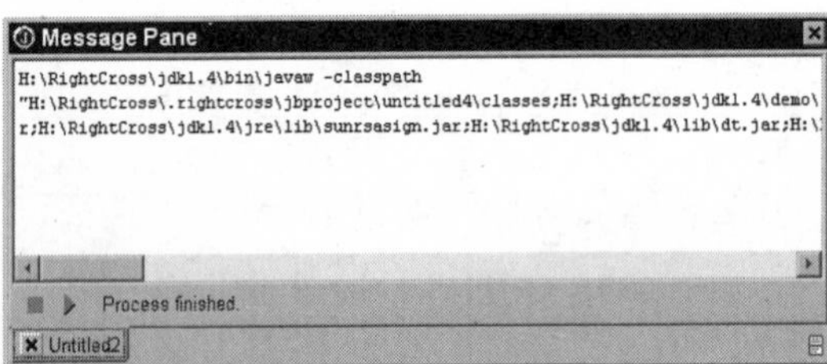


**Figure 2.2** Floating Message pane.

When viewing standard in, out, and error, the preceding features become especially important if limited screen space is available. Using the Word Wrap option can make hard-to-read displays easier by not having to scroll every time a line is displayed. Another feature about the Message pane is that it allows for the standard out display to have full interaction between the pane and the keyboard, thus making it easy to work with programs using standard in as an input device.

The final feature of the Message pane that we cover is the tab named *Untitled2* and "X," located to the left of the name. This "X" can be used to close the tab at the click of a button, and it is found on all tabs inside the AppBrowser regardless of their location. Tabs can be removed or hidden using the Context menu either by right-mouse clicking on the tab or by having focus on the tab and pressing the Shift-F10 hot-key combination. The Context menu gives finer granularity of functions, including removal of a single tab or all clear messages, plus hiding the Message pane completely.

# Configuring the AppBrowser Using IDE Options

The AppBrowser configuration does not directly affect the Java code being produced, but you will probably increase your productivity because the environment is best suited to your needs. The first dialog, the IDE Options, can be viewed by selecting the Tools | IDE Options... menu item. This section covers all of the tabs available from the IDE Options dialog. Customizing these options can make the generic JBuilder feel like a tool that has been used for many years.

## Browser

In Figure 2.3, the IDE Options dialog shows the general layout of the AppBrowser, which has been updated to include new features such as error text color, message timeouts, and additional VCS options. One of the first decisions that the user of JBuilder must make is what Look and Feel (L&F) will be used with JBuilder. Generally, L&Fs do not affect the workings of JBuilder; they're simply skins that can enhance appearance. Some developers with special needs (such as limited sight) use different L&Fs because of the way they display the JBuilder interface. The only common one across all versions is Metal, Look and Feel designed by Sun as part of the Java Foundations Classes (JFC) that is shipped with the standard JDK. The other L&Fs are as follows:

- Windows for the Microsoft Windows operating system
- Aqua for the Apple Macintosh systems

These are not included in any other operating system installs of JBuilder. If JBuilder was loaded onto a Linux box, the only two L&Fs would be CDE/Motif and Metal because each operating system has an exclusive L&F for the underlying operating system. CDE/Motif is included in the current versions of JBuilder for Windows, Solaris, and Linux because that L&F was completed early on and has always been included with the JDK on these systems. If Sun decided to remove it from the Windows distribution, then it would be available on only the Solaris and Linux operating systems. Usually the major difference between L&Fs is the appearance of the windowing technique being used. A windowing technique is the look of the widgets being used (buttons and listboxes and the window interface itself), which usually resemble the underlying operating system's paint mechanisms. Each L&F can have distinct characteristics that may hinder their use; one such characteristic can be found in the CDE/Motif L&F. Overall, that particular L&F seems to be rather sluggish, and the mouse movement is definitely different than in the other L&Fs, making it seem very "clunky" when using it. Most developers avoid CDE/Motif unless it is the L&F the developer is most comfortable with.

An example of that "clunky" feeling is found when working with the Main menu. Instead of scrolling across menus with each one becoming active as the pointer goes over it, CDE/Motif makes the user click on each menu item to actually select it. Metal seems to be the most reliable of all the L&Fs currently available, and it is available on all operating systems supporting a JDK. Each subsequent release of the JDK has seen major improvements in available L&Fs, such as the one found in JDK 1.4 for Windows, which is being touted as a major advance in the emulation of Windows.

A feature that finally made it into JBuilder is the ability to adjust the fonts in all of the other panes; however, it is not as completely user-definable as the Content pane. The reason for not making it completely definable is that it is believed that once the font has been changed to affect the major informational elements of the AppBrowser they will not be moved. Borland has given developers the ability to add or subtract a point size from the default font being used. This setting affects all menus, tabs, Tree views, and other displays, but it does offer a solution to the problem. It also can be used by the visually impaired to enhance the effectiveness of the interface, especially the Structure/Component panes and menus. Most likely, this setting will have to be manipulated until the developer finds the look that he or she is seeking.

### CUSTOMIZING LOOK AND FEELS

**When Look and Feel (L&F) was first introduced with the Swing libraries from Sun, it was thought that companies would develop unique L&Fs. Currently only two major companies have specialized support for L&F: Sun and Apple. Apple's L&F is by far the most detailed on the market.**

**Other companies and individuals have created free L&Fs that can be used with JBuilder, which can be found on the Borland Developer Network (http://bdn.borland.com). Usually copying a file or two into the jbuilder/lib/ext directory is all it takes to get these L&Fs installed. Custom L&Fs address common complaints about how the tabs are shown, and they clean up and enhance the interface display.**

**The JBuilder IDE in Figure 2.4 is a free L&F that mimics the Aqua Look and Feel from Apple. It is not as complete as the Aqua L&F, but it handles most things very well, such as the way tabs are painted on the screen, making it very easy to see what tab is active. This may not be as easy to notice on other L&Fs, plus it gives a nice new look to the standard AppBrowser.**

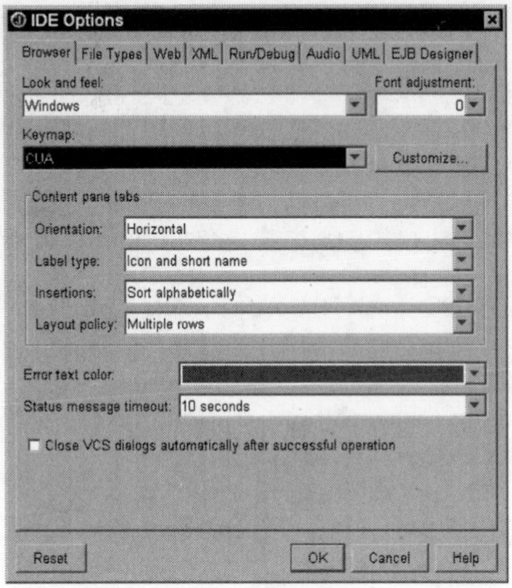

**Figure 2.3** Browser panel.

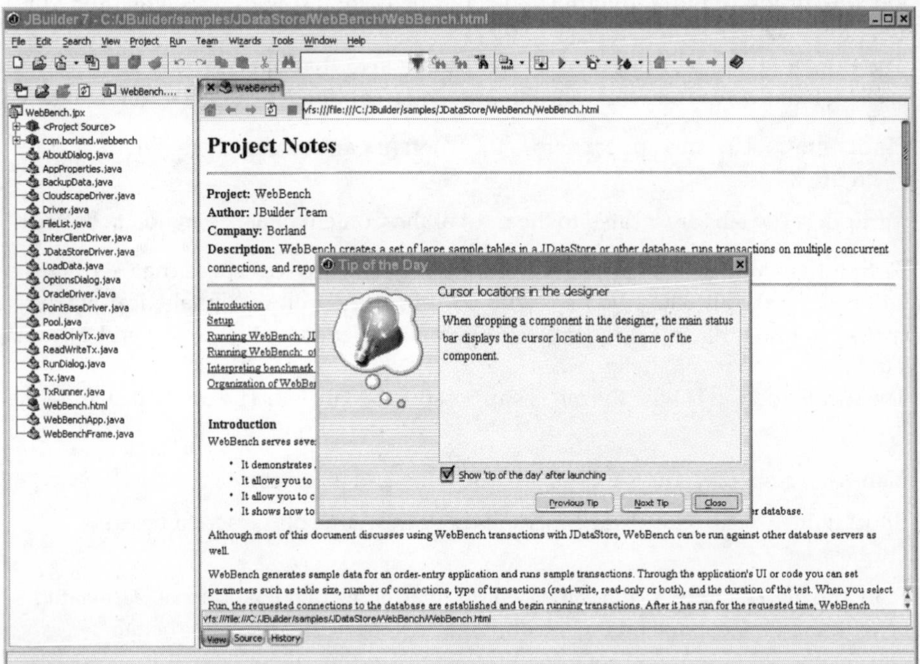


**Figure 2.4** Custom Look and Feel.

The AppBrowser/editor supports keymaps, which emulate the key bindings found in other popular editors and IDEs. Changing a keymap does not replace the underlying editor; it merely defines a set of key combinations found with the particular editor and IDE. Currently Brief, Common User Access (CUA), Emacs, Macintosh, Macintosh Code Warrior, and Visual Studio key bindings are supported. These key bindings satisfy most developers with a standard set of features supported within the editor; however, some developers miss some of the advanced features that may be found in a particular editor.

The Emacs editor is one example of a keymap. Currently, the AppBrowser supports about 90 percent of the overall keymappings — including the fire-ring process — but it does not support the buffering system found inside the Emacs editor. The buffering system inside Emacs includes a different paradigm for working with other files, which could become very confusing for people using the standard AppBrowser interface.

You can customize the keymappings of any feature defined by the keymap. When using the editor, when an option is changed it will become bold to represent a changed keymapping. The keymapping editor can also have a key combination assigned to it, to bring it up at the touch of a few keys. One thing that will become apparent is that the AppBrowser supports a lot of standard functions, and usually the editor or IDE that the AppBrowser is trying to emulate is a very small subset of the overall functions included in the AppBrowser editor. Be sure to check the complete list of functions before discarding JBuilder; the function could be there but with no keymapping or a different keymapping altogether.

The Content pane tabs (Figure 2.3) are the one area that has the most effect on the overall look of the AppBrowser. The tab orientation options include the following:

**Horizontal.** The tabs appear across the Content pane screen, as shown in Figure 2.1.

**Vertical.** The tabs are located to the right of the Content pane, going top to bottom.

Setting the value to Horizontal will most likely take up less space than setting the value to Vertical, but using Vertical with sorting turned on to alphabetical makes it very easy to find a file in a large project. Again, it depends on the project and comfort level of the person using the interface.

The second option is how the tab is supposed to be labeled. The options include the following:

**Name.** This represents the complete filename and extension.

**Short name.** The Short Name includes only the name of the actual file in question.

**Icon and short name.** This is the default. It adheres to the Node icon associated with the Project pane on the tab and attaches the actual name to the tab.

**Icon only.** Icon only means that the developer understands all the icons used by the AppBrowser because that would be the only hint that would be given; the tab would contain only the icon, nothing else.

The third option available to the Content pane tabs is the insertions option, where new tabs will be inserted on to the Content pane. Choices include the following:

- Sort alphabetically
- Sort display order
- Insert at beginning
- Insert to left of tab for active node
- Insert to right of tab for active node
- Insert at end

Most of these options are self-explanatory, but the others may need some additional information to make them useful. The Insert to right... or Insert to left... basically states that whatever tab (file) is currently active, the next tab to be added will be added in the defined direction next to the active tab, either right or left. The Sort display order corresponds directly with the Project pane; this means the files will be in the order of the project layout.

The fourth and final option is the Layout policy; this represents how the AppBrowser should handle a number of tabs that occupy more than one row. The options available to the developer are Multiple rows or Single row with scroll control. If you choose Multiple rows, keep in mind that each tab row takes up a significant amount of that screen space. However, using the Single row option can become a problem, depending on how the sorting of the tabs is done. If an excessively large number of files are open, the developer may lose track of which are open and where they are located in the list. If this ever occurs, simply double-click on the file again in the Project pane to bring the current focus to that file.

The last three options on the first page of the IDE Options dialog deal with reporting information back to the developer:

**Error text color.** As the Message pane displays information about contextual changes and errors that may be occurring within the tools found inside JBuilder, the messages will be displayed in this color. Most developers like the RED color because it normally represents a problem; however, in some cases this color may need to be changed to either the developer's likes or because of accessibility reasons, like the possibility of being color-blind or having other sight-related problems.

**Status message timeout.** This deals with the text sent to the Status bar; if additional informational text were being sent to the Status bar, this would control the length of time it is displayed before clearing the line. This option can be set to Never, which would mean the line would not be cleared until the next message was displayed.

**VCS integration.** This allows the AppBrowser to close any dialogs from the VCS integration upon successful completion of an operation. The default behavior is to press the OK button to continue with the VCS dialog when an operation is completed.

For the most part, the AppBrowser wizards interfaces all follow the same multi-tabbed interface and have four process buttons located at the bottom of the dialog. First is the Reset button, which returns all of the items back to the values in place when the dialog was opened. Once the OK button is pressed, the Reset function will initialize a new list of default values — in other words, it won't remember any prior setting after the OK button is pressed. The rest of the buttons either accept the changes when the OK button is pressed or decline the changes the Cancel button is pressed. Press the Help button to activate the AppBrowser's context-sensitive help system and explain the features of any wizard or dialog. Chapter 6, "Using the JBuilder Help System," covers all the major issues associated with the integrated help system.

## File Types

The File Types panel is broken into two areas:

**File types.** Cannot be changed or deleted from JBuilder, and they can be added only through the OpenTools API.

**File Extensions.** These are the extensions associated with the file types.

In Figure 2.5, each file type has an associated icon. This is the icon that will be used inside the Project pane to represent a file. These icons are extremely important, as icons are defined as the moniker for the tabs for the Content pane.

A question that usually arises is why does the AppBrowser need to support multiple file extensions for the same file. In Figure 2.5, the Archive file is selected on the top portion of the Dialog pane, and the associated extensions are listed on the bottom. One thing Java has been rather good at is using different file extensions to represent different functionality for the language, but all the types share a common underlying structure. The rar, war, zip, jar, and ear files are all basic files that implement the LZW compression algorithm but are used for different purposes within the Java language. An example of where additional file extensions may be added include .bat/.cmd files in the Text File type.

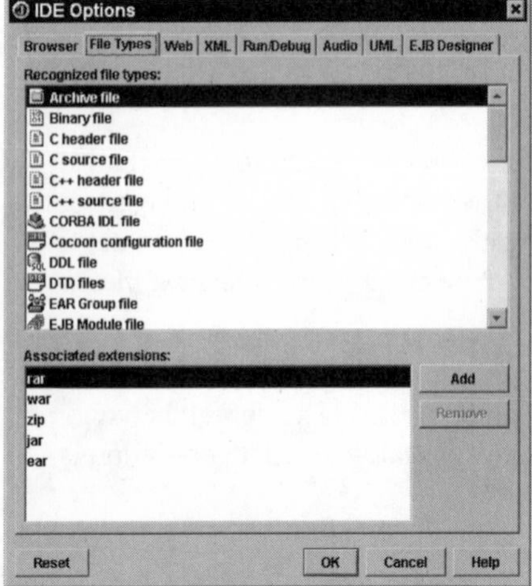


**Figure 2.5** File Types panel.

## Web Panel

The Web panel is responsible for setting how the AppBrowser will deal with Internet browser-based interactions (see Figure 2.6). This dialog should not be confused with the Browser panel. The Browser panel is associated only with the AppBrowser, not the actual Internet browser.

The most important option on this page is the Copy Web Run/Debug/Optimize launch URL to clipboard. This ensures that the developer will have the actual URL for starting the Web-based interaction. Much the same way that the Message pane shows the command line on the first line, which can be copied to start a program, this option makes sure the operating systems clipboard has the proper URL for pasting into the developer's favorite browser.

The next set of options pertains to the fact that the developer might want to use something other than JBuilder's built-in Web view pane. Generally, it is preferred that Web-based applications be tested on all possible browsers before being deployed. These options give you full control over how that should be accomplished:

- The first option, Launch separate process and use Web View, will cover both options in a single click. The name is a little misleading because JBuilder does not kick off a separate Internet browser, as might be thought by the title. It will use the integrated Web view panel inside the AppBrowser and also allow an Internet browser in a separate process to be viewed. Thus allowing both views to be verified, keep in mind that the additional process will add a little bit of time to the overall process, but for quality assurance it is worth it.
- The next option, Use the Web View on running process if possible, allows the AppBrowser to save a little time and memory by recycling the current Web view process. The underlying Web server must be running for this option to actually work; if the Web server (Tomcat or Borland Enterprise Server) is not running, a new process will be started from scratch.

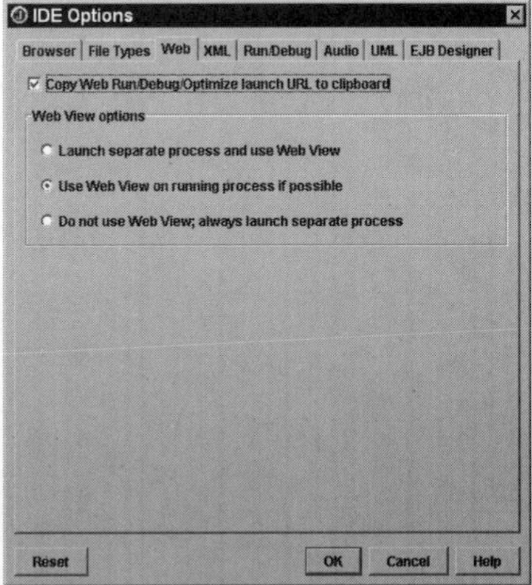


**Figure 2.6** Web panel.

- The final option is Do not use Web View; this will always start the default Web server and wait for an Internet browser to access it for that machine. This does save system resources, however; it can be a little more costly on the back-end time because the AppBrowser is starting a Web server and waiting.

Because the Web view process is compliant up to a certain level with the Web specifications, the default (external) browser may be more advanced, and can show and act differently.

## XML Panel

The XML panel determines how the AppBrowser will interact with XML documents. First we want to enable the Browser view; this allows an XML file to be viewed inside the Web view. This is similar to viewing XML in Microsoft Internet Explorer. This is not the default; however, when it is selected, you will see another tab added under the Content pane for general viewing of XML documents.

Next, Apply default stylesheet is used to display XML using a Tree view layout. It is possible to associate a different stylesheet with an XML file, which will be shown later in the chapter. The final option is Ignore DTD. This will allow the AppBrowser to display the XML file without the DTD being read without being validated.

The Transform trace option allows output to be generated during the stylesheet transformations. In Figure 2.7, the trace options can be set for Generation, Elements, Templates, and Selections. These can also be turned on in the Transform view.

The following example will show how the XML integration works inside the AppBrowser. First either open an existing project or create a new one with the defaults (see Chapter 4). You can use the default project that JBuilder ships with for this example because the output will not be saved. To use the default project in the AppBrowser, follow these steps:

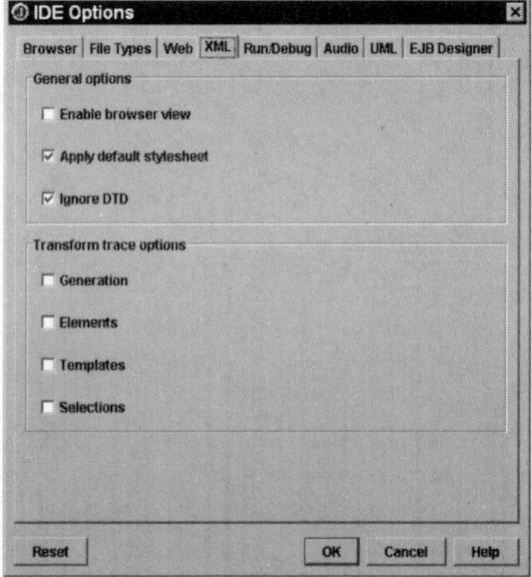


**Figure 2.7** XML panel.

1. Click the Help | Welcome project (sample) menu item from the Help menu. Once that has been selected JBuilder will load the project that is loaded when JBuilder is first installed onto a machine.
2. Set the XML options on the IDE Options dialog; pressing the Tools | IDE Options menu item and selecting the XML tab panel can accomplish this. Then select the Enable browser view option and press the OK button to continue.
3. Load an XML-based file, using the File | Open File... menu item, and load the file category.xml from the /jbuilder/extras/BorlandXML/example/b2b/products/classes/xsl directory. Once this occurs, the XML file will be loaded into the AppBrowser; notice that a few new tabs are present under the Content pane:
   - View tab, enabled by setting the IDE Options dialog, and it will display the XML as if it were being viewed inside the Microsoft Internet Explorer browser.
   - Transform view, which uses the integrated XSLT processor to transform the documents inside the AppBrowser. Notice that when the Transform view tab is selected, it reports an error because the default stylesheet is unable to display the current XML. The AppBrowser's Content pane using the Transform view can use any stylesheet to show the contents.

Notice in Figure 2.8 that the URL line at the top of the Transform view panel has a set of hot buttons. The first allows you to use the default stylesheet. The second button refreshes the display. The third button is used to set the trace options. Once the trace options have been set, a refresh should be performed to update the display. Keep in mind that if no errors occur, the Message pane will remain blank. The final button is the Add stylesheet; this allows the developer to assign a stylesheet (XSL extension) to the XML file. Press the Add stylesheet button to display the dialog in Figure 2.9.

Press the Add... button to display a standard FileChooser dialog. It should be located in the same directory in which the category.xml file was found. Then select the category_html.xsl file, and press the OK button to continue. The file will be listed in the list box inside the Configure node stylesheets; it is possible to load multiple XSL files for one XML file. Once the selection has been made, press the OK button to continue.

The XML source is now being displayed in the proper format as the category_html.xsl prescribes. In Figure 2.10, a new tab was added when a proper XSL was used, which is the Transform View Source tab. This tab can be pressed and then modified like any other file inside the AppBrowser. Also notice that the URL line at the top of the Transform view is a drop-down choice control. This becomes a handy feature if, in the prior step of loading a valid stylesheet, more than one was loaded. Simply use the drop-down choice control to pick the stylesheet to be used for the transform process. When you are ready to close a project, it is not necessary to save the files before continuing.

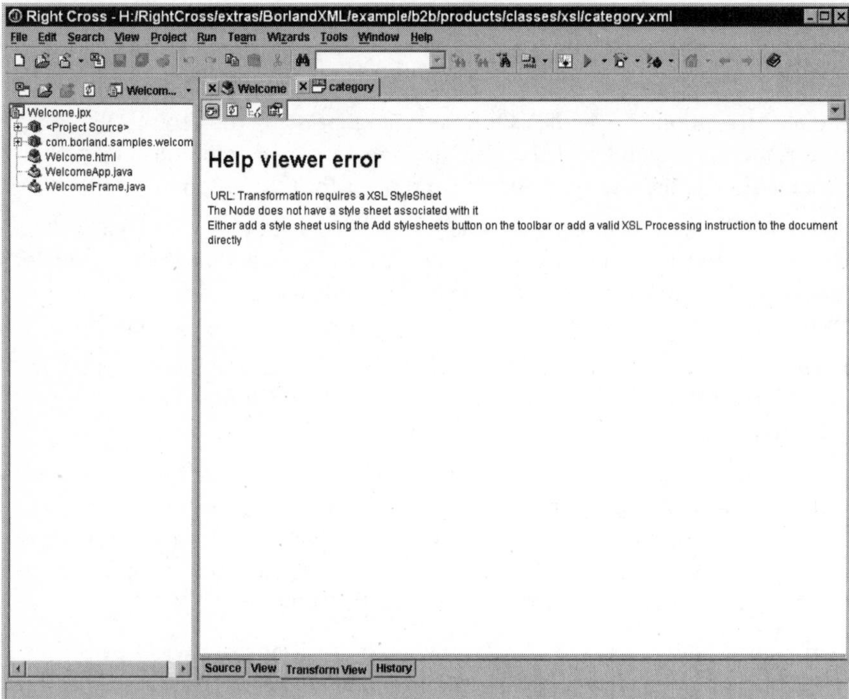


**Figure 2.8** AppBrowser Content pane, Transform view.

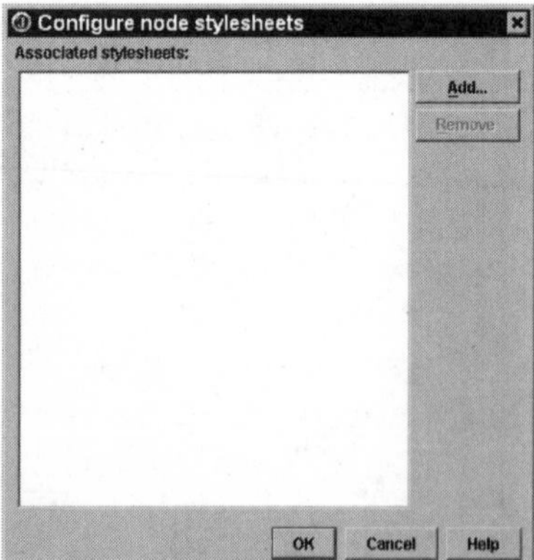


**Figure 2.9** Configure node stylesheet.

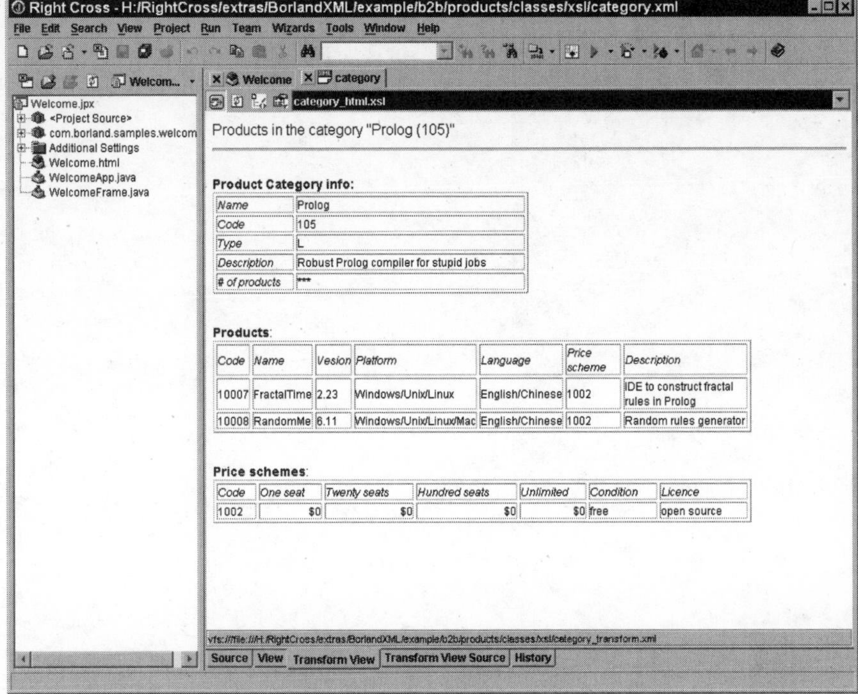


**Figure 2.10** Transform view with valid stylesheet.

## Run/Debug Panel

The next tab located on the Tools | IDE Options... menu item is the Run/Debug panel (see Figure 2.11). This panel is used by the AppBrowser to set the callback time associated with each option. Generally, these options do not change very often. Each of these options can be set differently, depending on what the machine running JBuilder is doing. Keep in mind that if the intervals are set really short, the CPU for the machine will be seriously taxed to meet the requirements. If a lot of additional processes are always occurring on the development machine, like system testing and other CPU-intensive operations, then setting these intervals to be larger will give a better performance feel.

The Runtime update intervals, which includes the Console output, is set to 100 milliseconds (ms), and the Debugger update intervals include the Console output set at 100 ms and the Process state set at 150 ms. If you notice really sluggish performance during the debugging phase and the application(s) that are being debugged include a lot of CPU interaction, you can lengthen both of these options for better performance.

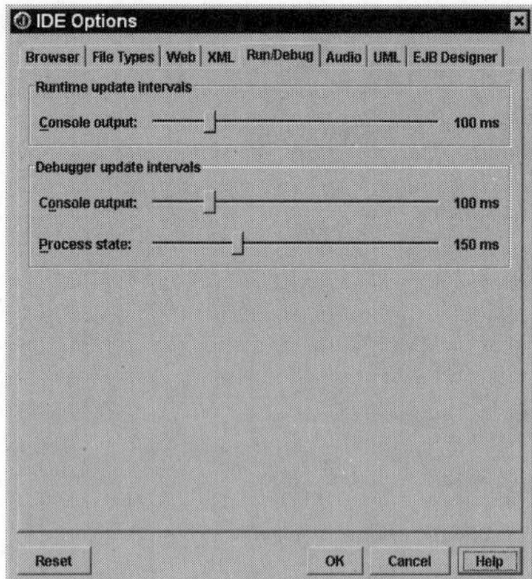


**Figure 2.11** Run/Debug (defaults).

## Audio Panel

Audio feedback was added to help developers hear progress with the development process. It was also added to help visually impaired developers be more productive with the use of audio feedback.

The Audio panel (see Figure 2.12) includes two real options:

- Enable the Audio feedback in the first place
- Actual volume for the playback

The next section of the dialog is the Theme option. Currently JBuilder ships with only one theme, but it is possible to create additional themes. See the Borland Developers Network (http://bdn.borland.com) for additional themes created by the JBuilder community, which can be downloaded and installed.

Adding themes to audio is a simple process:

1. Make sure all recordings are done in 16-bit .wav file format. The length of the recording is not an issue, but keep in mind that a long recording will have to play each time the event occurs, which can cause a slowdown in the development process.
2. The filenames must correspond exactly to the following names: build_errors.wav, build_successful.wav, build_warnings.wav, exception.wav, find_failed.wav, find_in_path.wav, process_stopped.wav, and stopped_at_breakpoint.wav.
3. Once 16-bit recordings for each of the preceding files have been created, create a new archive — compressed or uncompressed, it does not matter — with the extension of .audiopak.

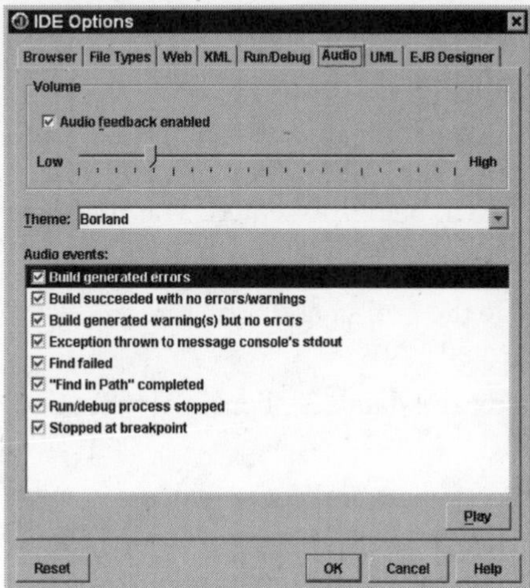


**Figure 2.12** Audio panel.

4. Place this archive into the /jbuilder/lib/audio directory.
5. Restart JBuilder, and the new theme should be displayed when the drop-down choice control is activated. The new theme and events should now have your defined custom sounds.
6. Choose what audio event should have sounds associated with it. These options can be selected or deselected manually.

A suggested project might include creating a new extension in the File Type panel with an .audiopak extension; this will allow JBuilder to recognize the file inside the AppBrowser. Then create a new project with the previously listed files recorded in 16-bit .wav format; then create an archive with the name of the theme and an extension of the .audiopak, build the archive, and deploy it.

**NOTE Some common Linux JDKs have a problem playing sound that causes JBuilder to crash. If you experience this, just disable audio feedback.**

The last two tabs on the IDE Options dialog are these:

- UML panel
- EJB designer panel

These features are covered in greater depth in Chapter 12, "UML Visualization," and Chapter 20, "Developing EJB 2.x." The configuration of the features will not be covered in those chapters. These two panels pertain only to the display of the information, not the information itself, so explanations of the interface will happen in this section. To learn how to modify the information being displayed by the interfaces, go to the appropriate chapter for further details.

## UML Panel

The UML panel is responsible for the appearance of the UML visualization tools included in JBuilder. This tool appears in the Content pane area and can be activated by pressing the UML tab located under the Content pane (see Figure 2.13). This dialog allows for the customization of the look of the UML being presented. The first four options are as follows:

**Use visibility icons.** This uses the icons inside the Project and Structure panes to show the developer what a diagram represents.

**Sort alphabetically.** This displays the methods and data members in alphabetical order.

**Group by visibility.** This groups like classes members and data members together.

**Display properties separately.** This replaces data members with a getter and setter at the bottom of the object diagram representing the Java program. For more information on setter and getter, refer to Chapter 8, "Modifying Classes."

The final section of the UML panel allows you to customize each element of the diagram by selecting the Screen element and then setting the associated color — that is all there is to it. You can revert to the default settings at any time by pressing the Reset all to default option after customization.

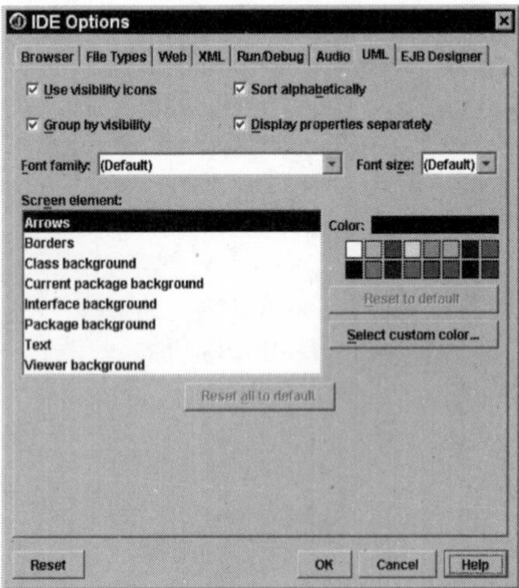


**Figure 2.13** UML panel.

## EJB Designer

The EJB Designer is responsible for the display of the screen elements (see Figure 2.14). The only option that is included on this panel that has any bearing on the code is the first one: Always regenerate interfaces. Because the EJB Designer is a two-way tool, which means that changes in the code will be noticed in the designer and that the changes in the designer will change the code. The EJB Designer can always regenerate the interfaces if new methods are added in the code; this can remove a couple steps in the development process. Be aware that any customizations that have been completed on the underlying Home and Remote interfaces will be *lost* if this option is turned on!

The rest of the options follow the last dialog and pertain to the font use and the colors associated with each screen element. After the font has been chosen, pick a screen element in the list box and select its color. Press the Reset all to default button at any time to return the display to the preset JBuilder defaults. Press the OK button to accept the changes. Not all panels have to be viewed or updated to accept changes.

## Generic Setup for IDE Options

Table 2.2 shows the properties and their values for the IDE Options dialog and can be used as a quick hit sheet. These properties cause the AppBrowser to take on a slightly different look; it includes different coloring and shading, font sizes for the Main menu, Project and Structure pane changes, and resized dialogs.

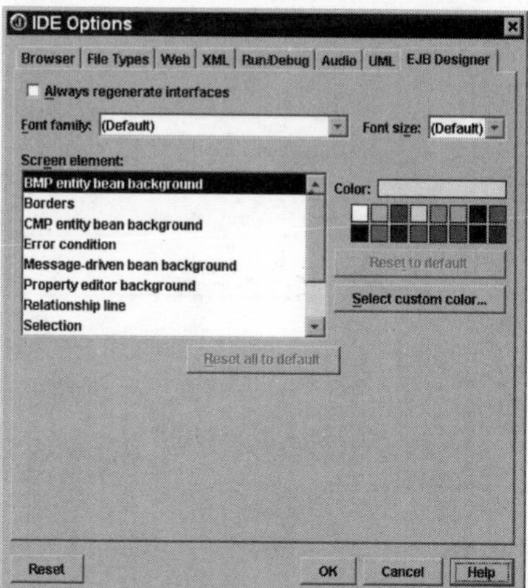


**Figure 2.14** EJB Designer.

**Table 2.2** Generic Settings for IDE Options Dialog

| TAB | PROPERTY | VALUE |
|---|---|---|
| Browser | Look and Feel | Metal |
| Browser | Font adjustment | +2 |
| Browser | Keymapping | CUA |
| Browser | Orientation | Horizontal |
| Browser | Label type | Icon and short name |
| Browser | Insertions | Insert at end |
| Browser | Layout policy | Multiple rows |
| Browser | Error text color | RED (same as default) |
| Browser | Status message timeout | 10 seconds (same as default) |
| Browser | Close CVS dialogs | Checked |
| File Types | No changes | |
| Web | Copy Web Run/Debug/Optimize launch URL to clipboard | Checked |
| Web | Launch separate process and use Web View | Selected |
| XML | Enable browser view | Checked |
| Run/Debug | No changes | |
| Audio | Audio feedback enabled | Deselected |
| UML | No changes | |
| EJB Designer | No changes | |

# Configuring the AppBrowser with Editor Options

Up to this point, the AppBrowser configuration focused on the actual look and the way it will interact with the developer. Now it is time to switch gears and focus on how the editor will interact with the developer. There are two major ways to get to the Editor Options... dialog:

- Press the Tools | Editor Options... menu item.
- Use the Context menu either by right-mouse clicking in the Content pane or by pressing the Shift-F10 key combination inside the Content pane and selecting the Editor Options... menu item.

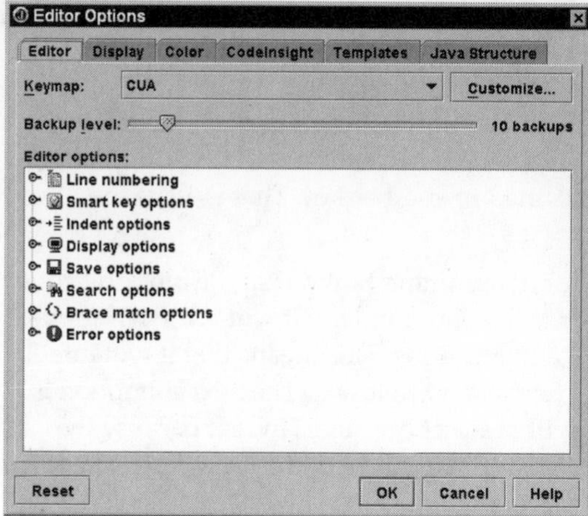


**Figure 2.15** Editor panel.

## Editor Panel

The Editor panel (see Figure 2.15) is responsible for setting a major portion of the options available to the developer. The first option available to the developer is the Keymap, which is the same option that is available on the IDE Options covered in the previous section. The next option is the Backup level; this represents the total number of backups for each file. The top number is 90, and if the number is exceeded that is defined by the slider bar, the number will start from 0 and increment toward the higher number. This option becomes very important for the use of the History tab (see Chapter 9, "Integrated Team Development") and the feature that was added to JBuilder to allow the developer to Revert to a prior save point. To activate the Revert feature, press the File | Revert menu item.

These options are located inside the Tree view control and are made up of various editor guidelines that cover the following:

**Line numbering.** You can turn the line numbering option on and off to display numbers inside the Content pane, next to the gutter. Currently the only reason not to have them enabled is because of limited screen/editing space.

**Smart key options.** Smart key options are responsible for moving the cursor to various locations on the current line. Each one of the three suboptions, Smart Home, Smart End, and Smart Tab, moves the cursor either to the first noncharacter position or to the beginning of the actual line when it comes to the Smart Home option. The Smart End option will move to the last noncharacter position or to the actual end of the line if the noncharacter position is passed. The Smart Tab is responsible for aligning the line under the past line if one exists. This option has a huge dependency on the formatting features that are now part of the formatting code functions, which are covered in Chapter 4. Be aware that the Tab key has become more of a format key then an actual tab; this was one of the major changes when code formatting was added to JBuilder. Changing these options can have a direct effect on the formatting settings and make the formatting function quirky. Remember that the developer using the custom keymapping facilities found inside the AppBrowser can define certain key functionality, so if the Tab key is supposed to be a Tab key in the real sense, by adding spaces to a line, these mappings can be redefined to another key. That is what the keymap functionality is all about.

**Indent options.** This is responsible for determining how to handle blocking code inside the editor. The first suboption is the Smart indent; it will try to indent the current line in the appropriate level and locations. This means that it will intelligently try to understand the indent format and follow it. The next suboption is the Block indent, which if selected will deselect the Smart indent because the Block indent is an alternative to the Smart indent. Using the Enter key on a new line after the "{", the block-indent will occur, or if the prior line is indented it will try to follow the pattern. The main difference between the two is that one tries to follow the pattern and the other uses the Enter key to establish the pattern. The last option is the Smart paste, which will format the lines to the proper aspect of the previous line's formatting. As stated previously, most of these options can be set in a more generic form by using the Formatting features of JBuilder (see Chapter 4).

**Display options.** The Display option really has only one purpose. If the developer wants to see a blinking cursor at the current location, then this option is checked. If not, then the developer will see a solid caret at the current cursor location.

**Save options.** The Save options have three suboptions, which do not have anything to do with the actual process of saving the file. The options address the format of the file being saved:

- Strip trailing white space removes blank characters at the end of the line during the save operation.
- Change leading tabs to spaces is responsible for changing the "\t" character to spaces.
- Change leading spaces to tabs converts spaces to "\t" characters.

**Search options.** The first Search option is if the search dialog should be displayed when a search operation fails. By default the option is checked. The other option is Search word at cursor, which can start a search operation on the word that the cursor is over at the time of the search.

**Brace match options.** The Brace match options further customize the editor. The *generate closing brace* is the first suboption, and it does exactly what the name implies. If you start a line with a "{" brace and hit return, the corresponding closing brace "}" will be added. Remember, the indentation and formatting will follow the established rules from the previous options and in the formatting area of the project. The next two options, *Enable brace match highlight* and *Highlight opposing brace*, dictate only how the editor will highlight curly braces.

The first will always highlight both braces; you must be inside the brace to get the highlighting on the starting brace, and you must be outside the closing brace. The second option will highlight only the opposing brace following the rules just stated; if both options are selected, then the highlight opposing option will take precedence. When discussing braces, the editor extends the highlighting beyond the standard "{ }"; it also supports the "( )" and the "[ ]" pairs as well. The final option is the Ignore the neighboring braces; this stops the highlighting on empties, which means {}, (), or [] will be ignored when it comes to the highlighting rules.

**Error options.** The final set of options relates to how errors in the code will be displayed and handled. This has always been one of JBuilder's trademarks — the ability to tell when a syntax error has occurred. The first time Borland showed this feature at the JavaOne conference in 1999, it was the first all-Java JBuilder code named Primetime, and it was a huge hit. This feature is constantly upgraded in hopes of eliminating the need to do the compile/run/debug loop that most developers go through each and every day. One of the first advances was the ability to underline unknown errors; much like what Microsoft Word did with word processing. Whenever an error is found, it will be underlined with a red squiggly, thus giving the developer a visual queue of where the code is wrong. In combination with the underlining feature, the second option can give spot information on the error at hand and now supports the ability to start the context-sensitive help to explain the error in its entirety.

As with the debugger, you can utilize the tooltip functionality to point to the error and give it an integrated button in the form of a magnifying glass that can be clicked to start the help system. Each option is turned on by default. The last option, Show in gutter, places an icon in the gutter, much as a Breakpoint icon is red with a white exclamation mark in the middle and gives another visual clue that an error is occurring on that line.

## Display Panel

The Display panel is responsible for setting the font and size that will be used inside the editor. The first set of options on the Display panel (see Figure 2.16) deals with the right margin settings; the first is the Visible right margin option. If this option is checked, then a thin line will be displayed inside the editor denoting the right margin setting in the next option. The right margin is where developers are told they are at the end of the line; this number can be as high as 1024 characters and as few as 0.

The next set of options deals specifically with the font for the editor. When the Display panel is accessed for the first time, the AppBrowser scans monospaced font sets available on the machine. Once this scan is completed, the Font family drop-down choice control will be populated. Selecting the font and size is really a developer choice, but the Sample area does try to let the developer know exactly how the font and size chosen will represent in the editor.

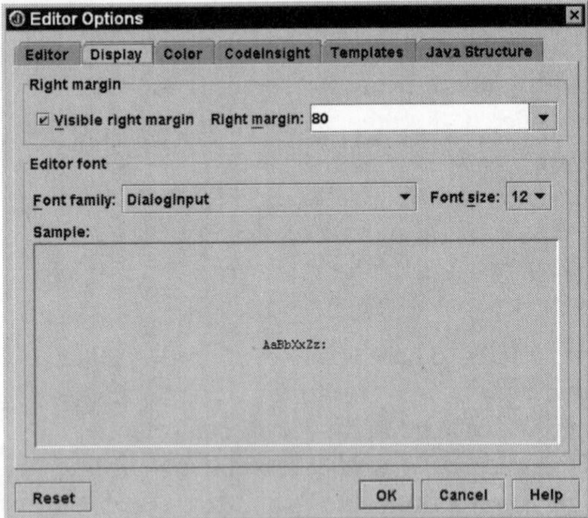


**Figure 2.16** Display panel.

## Color Panel

The Color panel, like all the color dialogs, allows for complete customization of the look of the editor (see Figure 2.17). The first option available on the Color panel is the Editor color scheme, and JBuilder ships four different sets of options:

- Default, or the white background
- Classic, a medium blue background reminiscent of the old WordStar days of Microsoft DOS
- Twilight, which uses a black background
- Ocean, based on a light cyan green background

As with fonts and sizes, it is difficult to predict what any one developer will want as a color environment for coding. This is why the AppBrowser has so many customization features for the editor. The whole bottom half of the panel is dedicated to the customization of the colors used in the editor. This also allows tweaking of any of the default sets shipped with the product. These options also work with the other options covered in the section on highlighting curly braces and such; most any screen element can be customized.

## CodeInsight Panel

The CodeInsight panel of the Editor Options dialog (see Figure 2.18) is responsible for configuring how the AppBrowser will handle three Insight technologies found in JBuilder:

**ClassInsight.** Pressing the hot-key combination inside a method ClassInsight (Ctrl-Alt-H–CUA) will display all the classes accessible in the classpath. This list can then be scrolled until the proper object is found; when the object is selected, it will be inserted in the editor.

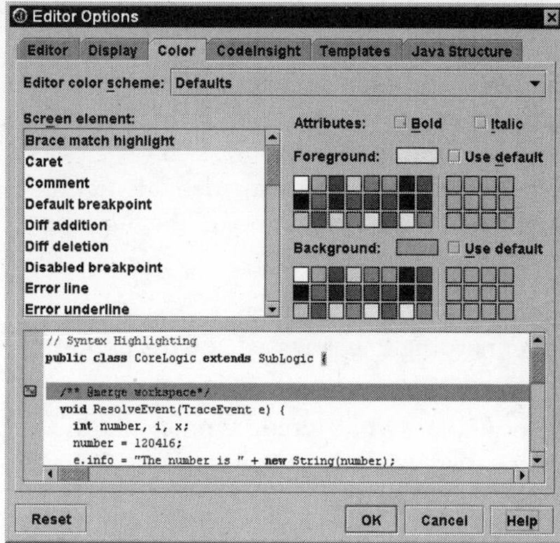


**Figure 2.17** Color panel.

**MemberInsight.** MemberInsight (Ctrl-space–CUA) continues the process by showing all the valid methods and data members for that class; again, once the object is selected, it will be added to the editor.

**ParameterInsight.** ParameterInsight (Ctrl-Shift-space–CUA) works the same as ClassInsight and MemberInsight, but it shows the list of valid parameters for the class and methods. A full example showing how to use the Insight technologies can be found in Chapter 13.

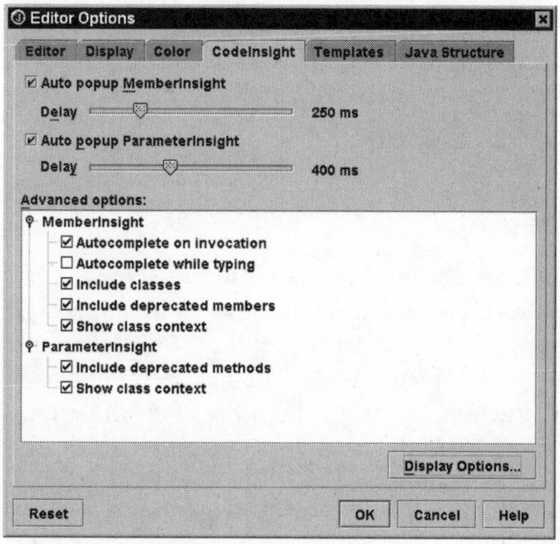

**Figure 2.18** CodeInsight panel.

The first set of options enables the Insight technologies and specifies what the delay for the popups should be. By default, the Insight technology is enabled. Setting the Delay is developer preference. Most experienced developers do not want the popups to appear quickly because they feel the popups are in the way. Other developers choose to set the delay to "as quick as possible" and use the Insight technologies as a spell-macro-format function. If the developer is using a less-than-adequate machine, these options can be turned off to speed up the overall performance of the machine.

Advanced options for MemberInsight include the following:

**Autocomplete on invocation.** Autocomplete on invocation inserts the text as soon as a match is found with no Enter needing to be pressed and the popup display never being shown.

**Autocomplete while typing.** The Autocomplete while typing is much like the invocation except, as the popup is being displayed, if a match is found, the text will be inserted and the popup will automatically disappear.

**Include classes.** The Include classes will allow classes to be included in the MemberInsight popup.

**Include deprecated members.** The Include deprecated members option will show the methods that have been deprecated with a line through them; remember the JavaDoc associated with the Java API set's deprecation marker.

**Show class context.** The Show class context puts the classes at the top of the list.

The ParameterInsight advanced options, Include deprecated methods and Show class context, work as described earlier. The CodeInsight panel also includes a button for customizing the Display Options. When pressed, it generates a two-panel dialog, one for MemberInsight and one for ParameterInsight, and both panels display the options available for customizing their display inside the AppBrowser.

The Show entry types as an icon will attach the icons used in the Structure pane for additional visual queues inside the MemberInsight popup; the only reason to deselect this option would be for a limited performance increase. The rest of the options deal with the display properties and are the same on each subpanel and are fairly self-explanatory.

## Template Panel

The Template panel is responsible for putting static text into the editor (see Figure 2.19). The static text can be anything the developer desires: comments, Java code, snippets of code, and so on. The AppBrowser comes with a large list of standard templates, and the developers are free to add any number of custom ones. The key to templates is making sure that the code being used by the template is a valid piece of information.

Adding a template is a simple procedure. Press the Add... button, and a quick dialog will display a dialog that will ask for a Name and Description of the template. Pressing the OK button will give you a blank Code area. When naming a template, remember that the names are case sensitive. When using templates inside the editor by pressing the Ctrl-J (CUA–Keymap), a context dialog will be displayed showing all the possible matches to what is being typed. As the developer types more of the template name, the list will become shorter until a match is found. Once a match is found, the template will be activated, and the text for the template will be inserted into the editor. Because all the standard templates are lowercase, adding a template called "mike" would appear after the main template. If "Mike" were used as the name, it would show at the top of the list.

When designing templates, you should not only ensure that the code or text being inserted is correct but also consider where the next input should start because templates allow for setting the cursor position. The pipe " | " character can be used inside a template to place the cursor after the text has been inserted. You should use only one " | " per template; any others will be ignored.

One of the interesting concepts to come from templates is the notion of super templates. These are small templates used together to create a single template. Chaining templates together in this manner results in a customized piece of code that follows a standard format.

An important feature is currently missing from the templates; this feature would allow templates defined in other versions of JBuilder to be used in the current version very easily. The templates, though, are just standard text and can be found in the JBuilder.Home directory in the User.properties files. All templates will use the following format: *editor.template;templates.1=Mike,Temp,//whatever*. Templates can be copied from the file and placed into the new versions of the User.properties file.

## Java Structure Panel

The Java Structure panel defines how the Structure pane will display the Java code hierarchy (see Figure 2.20). When working with really large files, the Parse delay option can be set higher to eliminate slowdowns in the editor. This option tells the AppBrowser how long it should wait before scanning the code and making sure the Structure pane is in sync with the code.

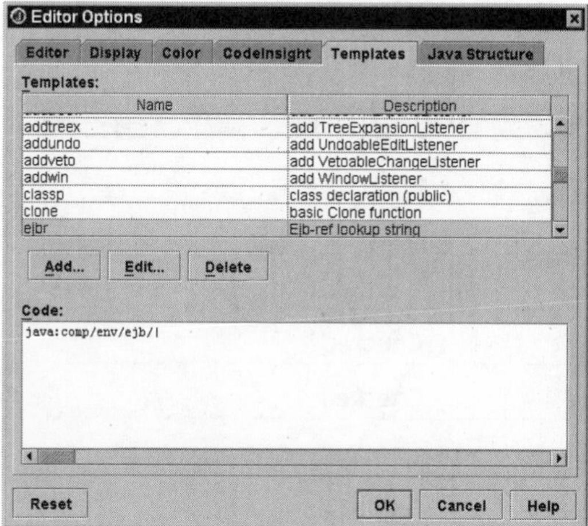


**Figure 2.19** Template panel.

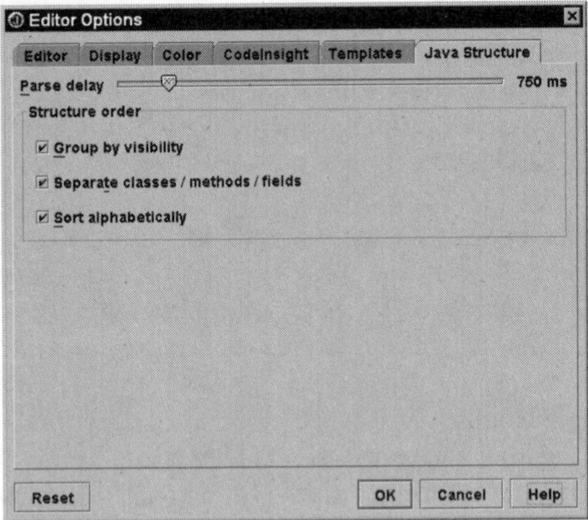


**Figure 2.20** Java Structure panel.

The Structure order is responsible for how the Java elements will be viewed; when the Group by visibility option is checked, it will make sure that public, and then protected, then private is the order of visibility.

Using the Structure order options Separate classes/methods/fields option will sort the elements into the proper order.

As with the Tools Options dialog, when you are working with the Editor Options, you do not need to visit all the panels. Once a customization has occurred, pressing the OK button will accept that customization, and you can continue your work in the editor.

## Generic Setup for Editor Options

Table 2.3 shows the properties and their values for the Editor Options dialog and can be used as a quick hit sheet. The properties cause the AppBrowser's editor to act a little differently, and things like keymapping, fonts, and indenting will be changed.

**Table 2.3** Generic Settings for Editor Options... Dialog

| PAGE | PROPERTY | VALUE |
|---|---|---|
| Editor | Keymap | CUA |
| Editor | Backups | 20 |
| Editor | Smart home | Checked |
| Editor | Smart end | Checked |
| Editor | Smart tab | Checked |
| Editor | Search word at cursor | Checked |
| Display | Courier New | |
| Display | Font size | 20 |

## Content Tabs

A number of tabs are found in the AppBrowser, especially with the Content pane. These tabs are usually viewed in the context of the file being worked with — in this chapter; working with XML has altered which tabs are available. The same is true of the following standard JBuilder tabs:

- Graphics
- UML (covered in Chapter 12)
- EJB (covered in Chapter 20)
- Source
- Design (covered in Chapter 8)
- Bean (covered in Chapter 8)
- Doc
- History (covered in Chapter 9)

### Graphics

One of the newer features available in the AppBrowser is the Image viewer. It allows images to be viewed and scaled, their background color set, and their files saved in a Portable Network Graphic (PNG) format. Using the default sample project shipped with JBuilder, load the splash.gif graphics from that project's images file.

Once a graphic file has been added to the project, double-clicking on the file node inside the Project pane will set the file into focus in the Content pane. Notice that in Figure 2.21 the slider bar is used as the scaling mechanism and that it can be reset to the original 100 percent if the desired changes do not work. If the file is saved as a PNG file format, all coding changes need to be made to the underlying code, and the new graphic will have to be added and the old graphic removed from the project, and all references updated with the new extension.

### Source

The Source tab is the main lifeline to the developer as it is the interface with the editor. A great many pages in this chapter have been dedicated to the editor and how to configure it. One great feature of how JBuilder is constructed is that each pane area inside the AppBrowser is a self-contained application. This means that features can be added for a specific pane that have nothing to do with the AppBrowser interface, but everything to do with the information the pane in question is manipulating. The Editor pane has had significant upgrades over its history.

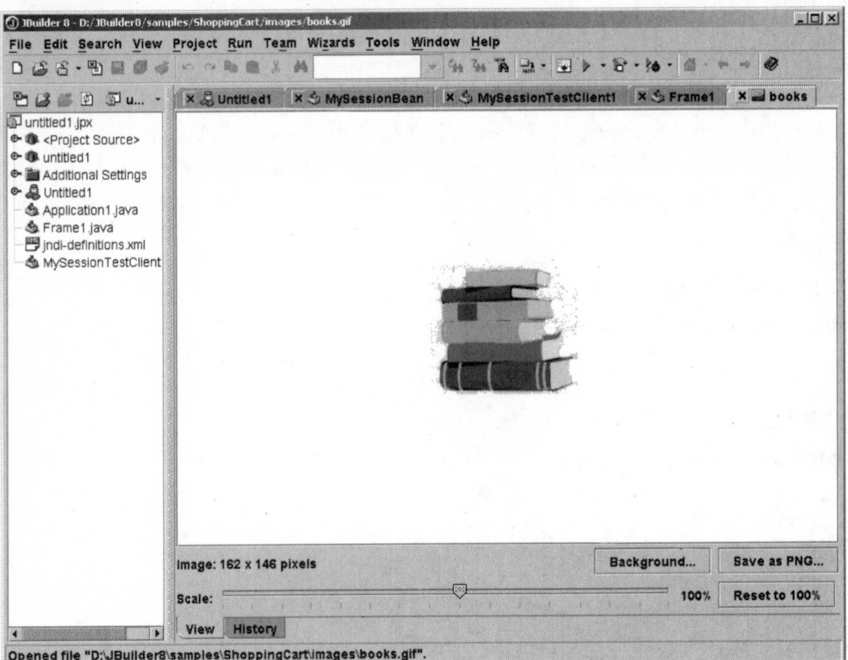


**Figure 2.21** Image viewer.

Using Figure 2.1 as a reference, a new button-enabled Source status bar has been added. Notice that the filename is displayed above the Source tab and that the keyboard setting is being displayed with Insert turned on. Another section can be present if the character encoding is different than the default; this option cannot be changed from this location as it is for informational purposes only. The next section is the line number and column associated with the cursor position inside the editor. Right beside the number is a drop-down arrow that will display a Context menu that includes going to a particular line number and also giving a quick way to set the Show line numbers option in the editor. If the Go to line option is chosen, a quick dialog will be displayed with an Edit dialog box to put the number in; once OK is pressed, the cursor will be moved to that location.

The next section is a fast way to set the keymapping being used inside the editor. In Figure 2.1 the keymapping is set to CUA; by hitting the drop-down arrow, the developer can select the preferred keymapping available to the AppBrowser.

The final section is the new Zoom feature, which allows the ability to make the font size larger by zooming in on the text and to make the font size smaller by zooming out on the text. It also has an option to reset back to normal. Most of these features are great, especially when several people are using JBuilder to solve a problem. The ability to set the keymapping and font size makes a great addition to the Source pane. The zoom feature is used on a file-by-file basis and is not shared among all files open.

## Doc

Originally, the Doc tab allowed you to open a Java source file and view its associated JavaDoc documentation. This was fairly limited, as the JavaDoc had to be in the classpath to be displayed.

Now the AppBrowser has an on-the-fly JavaDoc compiler that will scan the Java source and generate the associated JavaDoc if none can be found. A quick example of how the Doc tab works follows (see Figure 2.22):

1. Open the WelcomeApp.java file located inside the default Sample project that ships with JBuilder. The project can be reopened at anytime by pressing the Help | Welcome project (sample) menu item.
2. Once the WelcomeApp.Java is in focus, place the cursor on the JFrame declaration located on the class definition line.
3. Right-mouse click or press Shift-F10 to active the Context menu and select the Find definition menu item. This will bring the source code of the JFrame into the AppBrowser.

**NOTE That this did not add the class to the project; it is only being viewed.**

4. Click the Doc tab below the Content pane, and the associated JavaDoc will be displayed for the JFrame.java class.

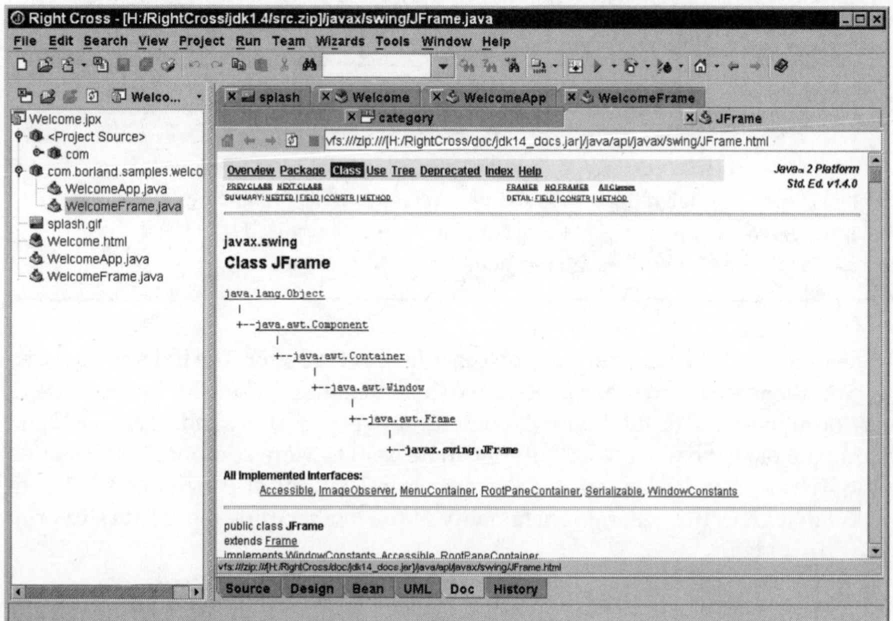


**Figure 2.22** Doc tab.

## GETTING THE MOST OUT OF A RESOURCE-STARVED SYSTEM

**One of the common questions that arises from the development community is this: If I don't have the latest equipment and a ton of memory, can and will JBuilder perform? For more information on the memory and Garbage Collection algorithm settings, review Chapter 1, "Installing JBuilder." The settings you choose can have a real effect on performance. Table 2.4 shows the settings you should use for resource-starved hardware.**

**Table 2.4** Settings for the Resource-Starved AppBrowser

| DIALOG | PAGE | PROPERTY | VALUE |
|---|---|---|---|
| IDE Options | Browser | Look and Feel | Metal |
| IDE Options | Browser | Orientation | Horizontal |
| IDE Options | Browser | Label Type | Icon |
| IDE Options | Browser | Insertions | Insert at end |
| IDE Options | Browser | Layout Policy | Single row |
| IDE Options | Browser | Close CVS dialogs | Unchecked |
| IDE Options | Audio | Audio feedback enabled | Unselected |
| Editor Options | Editor | All options | Turn them off |
| Editor Options | CodeInsight | All options | Turn them off |
| Editor Options | Java Structure | Parse delay | 5000 |
| Editor Options | Java Structure | All options | Turn them off |

**Also the Project and Structure/Component panes can be hidden. Setting all these options did make a small difference in the performance running JBuilder on a Pentium 3, with 128 megabytes of memory. The functionality that was sacrificed for the sake of a few seconds here and there was felt not to be worth the trade-off.**

The Doc viewer works the same as any other Internet browser. The links can be used throughout the interface to move around the documentation. The URL line includes a toolbar for going back to the home document, moving forward and backward, and refreshing the page; finally, the URL itself can be used to view additional information from the Web as a standard integrated Web browser. The pane also includes a full Context menu that gives the general functionality of the toolbar, plus the abilities to print and zoom in and out.

## Using Multiple AppBrowsers

Multiple AppBrowsers are especially handy when working with multiple projects (see Chapter 4). Simply click the Window | New AppBrowser menu item to create a new AppBrowser.

Recall that a change made in one AppBrowser is made in all AppBrowsers, so if you're working on a large project, creating new AppBrowsers can be a real resource depleter. Multiple AppBrowsers can save a lot of power this way.

# Summary

AppBrowser customization continues to evolve as new features and functions are added to JBuilder. The two major interfaces that allow insight into all of the settings and options for the AppBrowser are really the IDE Options... and the Editor Options... dialogs.

Using good system management and working with some of the settings available to you for the AppBrowser, it is possible to get a great programming interface, no matter what kind of a machine you are dealing with.

CHAPTER

3

# Controlling Java Configurations

There seem always to be two truths to Java: The Java platform is always changing, and the APIs keep expanding and getting larger, which makes it a real headache to keep track of every single classpath. Since the inception of Java these truths have been self-evident with more than 30 releases of the Java Development Kit (JDK) alone. That number includes major patches and does not include the number of companies that have had to create special versions of a particular JDK for their projects. Thinking back to the beginning, getting that first poster that outlined the API list of Java 1.0 and 1.1 was great — and the list fit on a 2- x 2-foot poster. Today, not including J2ME or J2EE, the latest poster for the base Java language that was readable was around 4 x 5 feet; yes, some current posters are much smaller, but most people need a magnifying glass to read them. JBuilder recognized the issues from the beginning and took steps to make it as easy as possible to manage this ever-changing world of Java.

This chapter focuses on the tools provided by JBuilder to work in this type of chaotic environment. Dealing with multiple JDKs and working with an ever-growing list of APIs and archive files, this chapter outlines the tools provided by JBuilder to help eliminate some of the development headaches.

## Overview of Java Development Kits

JBuilder has always been considered a premiere development environment, not because it was easy to use or bundled some great products, but because it was built to be dynamic like the Java language. One of the constants about Java was that it was going to be a language that evolved over time. The base JDK 1.0 was hardly adequate for doing the simplest tasks in an applet. The language, though, was transforming at a very rapid rate, and new features were always in the works. This led the JBuilder development team to design an environment that could adapt to the changes in the language and exploding API sets. One of the first features to be touted by JBuilder was its ability to switch JDKs.

The capabilities to switch JDKs included with JBuilder have grown over the life of JBuilder, but still people are confused by exactly what JDK switching is and how it works. JBuilder is hosted as an all-Java program on a JDK; this JDK may or may not be the one that is currently shipping and publicly available from Sun. The reasons for having a specific JDK to ship on are rather obvious — you need to have as stable a JVM as possible, and in many cases that JVM may show problems that need to be fixed to ensure that the development environment is stable and can handle the job it is being asked to do. This meant that the JBuilder product has shipped over it lifespan on Borland-specific builds of the JDK that included fixing errors, bugs, and nuances that could cause the IDE to fail or not work as expected. This part of the JDK deals only with the running of the JBuilder IDE.

When it comes to general compiling of Java programs, JBuilder uses its own compiler and dependency checker. When compiling Java programs, this is one of the main reasons why JBuilder has always been considered one of the fastest Java compilers on the market. The dependency checker eliminates files from the compile list so that JBuilder does not waste time and resources compiling unneeded files; the compiler was optimized to work with the dependency checker to ensure the fastest compile possible. The optimized compiler was based on the JDK that was used to run the IDE.

Until recently, the use of the JBuilder default compiler and dependency checker was mandatory, thus not allowing developers to point to the Java compiler of their choice. In recent builds, JBuilder has started to allow different compilers to be used to build projects. More information on the JBuilder build system can be found in Chapter 10, "Using Build Systems," and Chapter 4, "Project Properties and Configurations." This feature came about from customer requests asking to point the compilation process to a different compiler because of the use of specialized JDKs for areas of AppServer, Web servers, and even other specialized JDKs. Using alternative JDKs to compile a project can have a direct effect on the time needed to compile. Borland certifies only its compiler.

Still, although the JDK switching has not occurred, the actual concept of switching comes in three areas. The first area is the APIs that are exposed to the JBuilder environment with regard to using the Insight technologies. The second concept involves the running of the program once it has been compiled. The third concept is actually setting the project to use the specific JDK for the compilation process. In essence, the first two concepts were the definition of JDK switching from Borland. Now JDK switching includes the concept of using a different Java compiler that has been defined in the JBuilder environment.

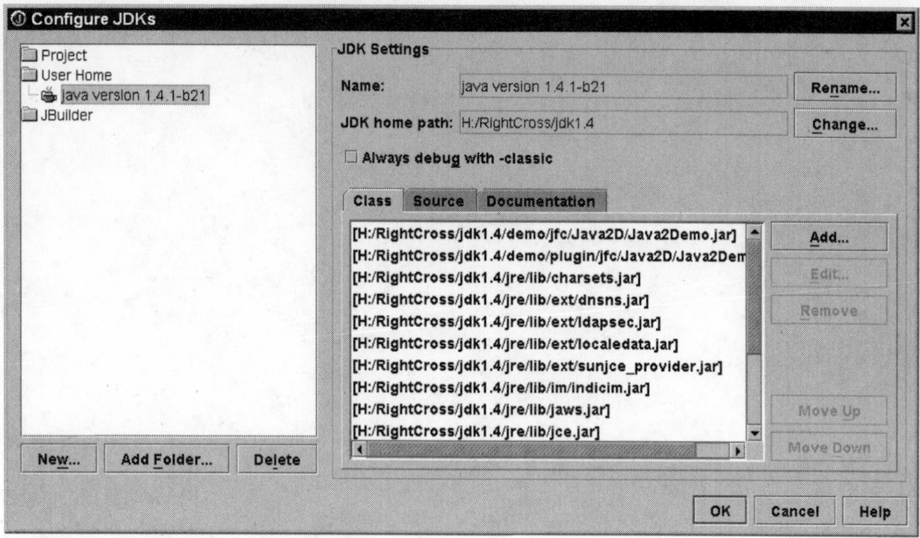


**Figure 3.1** Configure JDKs dialog.

## JDK Definitions

The first step is to add another JDK to the JBuilder environment by clicking the Tools | Configure JDKs... menu item. The dialog box that appears can be seen in Figure 3.1.

The Configure JDKs dialog is divided into a few areas. The JDK list on the left-hand side lists the loaded JDKs in a sorted format. This format is broken into four main areas:

- The Project, which assigns a JDK to the project level, meaning that it will be available in only a certain project and all files associated with the JDK definition will be kept in the project.
- The User Home, which is where all the default properties are held. This location can be different depending on the operating system being used. See Chapter 1, "Installing JBuilder," for configuration details.
- The JBuilder, which stores all the JDK definitions in the /jbuilder/lib directory.
- User-defined, which allows the developer to define a location of his or her choice for holding the JDK properties file.

The JDK properties file is an XML-based file that lists all the needed attributes of a shipping JDK. In Figure 3.1, the JDK version is 1.4.1-b21 and is being held in the Home directory. The source of the file is shown in Source 3.1.

```
java version 1.4.1-b21.library
<?xml version="1.0" encoding="UTF-8"?>
<library>
  <!--JBuilder JDK Definition File-->
  <fullname>java version 1.4.1-b21</fullname>
  <homepath>../../jdk1.4</homepath>
  <debug/>
  <class>
    <path>[../../jdk1.4/demo/jfc/Java2D/Java2Demo.jar]</path>
    <path>[../../jdk1.4/demo/plugin/jfc/Java2D/Java2Demo.jar]</path>
    <path>[../../jdk1.4/jre/lib/charsets.jar]</path>
    <path>[../../jdk1.4/jre/lib/ext/dnsns.jar]</path>
    <path>[../../jdk1.4/jre/lib/ext/ldapsec.jar]</path>
    <path>[../../jdk1.4/jre/lib/ext/localedata.jar]</path>
    <path>[../../jdk1.4/jre/lib/ext/sunjce_provider.jar]</path>
    <path>[../../jdk1.4/jre/lib/im/indicim.jar]</path>
    <path>[../../jdk1.4/jre/lib/jaws.jar]</path>
    <path>[../../jdk1.4/jre/lib/jce.jar]</path>
    <path>[../../jdk1.4/jre/lib/jsse.jar]</path>
    <path>[../../jdk1.4/jre/lib/rt.jar]</path>
    <path>[../../jdk1.4/jre/lib/sunrsasign.jar]</path>
    <path>[../../jdk1.4/lib/dt.jar]</path>
    <path>[../../jdk1.4/lib/htmlconverter.jar]</path>
    <path>[../../jdk1.4/lib/tools.jar]</path>
  </class>
  <source>
    <path>../../jdk1.4/demo/applets/Animator</path>
    <path>../../jdk1.4/demo/applets/ArcTest</path>
    <path>../../jdk1.4/demo/applets/BarChart</path>
    <path>../../jdk1.4/demo/applets/Blink</path>
    <path>../../jdk1.4/demo/applets/CardTest</path>
    <path>../../jdk1.4/demo/applets/Clock</path>
    <path>../../jdk1.4/demo/applets/DitherTest</path>
    <path>../../jdk1.4/demo/applets/DrawTest</path>
    <path>../../jdk1.4/demo/applets/Fractal</path>
    <path>../../jdk1.4/demo/applets/GraphicsTest</path>
    <path>../../jdk1.4/demo/applets/GraphLayout</path>
    <path>../../jdk1.4/demo/applets/ImageMap</path>
    <path>../../jdk1.4/demo/applets/JumpingBox</path>
    <path>../../jdk1.4/demo/applets/MoleculeViewer</path>
    <path>../../jdk1.4/demo/applets/NervousText</path>
    <path>../../jdk1.4/demo/applets/SimpleGraph</path>
    <path>../../jdk1.4/demo/applets/SortDemo</path>
    <path>../../jdk1.4/demo/applets/SpreadSheet</path>
    <path>../../jdk1.4/demo/applets/SymbolTest</path>
    <path>../../jdk1.4/demo/applets/TicTacToe</path>
    <path>../../jdk1.4/demo/applets/WireFrame</path>
```

**Source 3.1** JDK properties file (XML format)

```
    <path>[../../jdk1.4/demo/jfc/FileChooserDemo/FileChooserDemo. ⮐
jar]/src</path>
    <path>../../jdk1.4/demo/jfc/FileChooserDemo/src</path>
    <path>../../jdk1.4/demo/jfc/Font2DTest/src</path>
    <path>../../jdk1.4/demo/jfc/Java2D/src</path>
    <path>[../../jdk1.4/demo/jfc/Metalworks/Metalworks.jar]/src</path>
    <path>../../jdk1.4/demo/jfc/Metalworks/src</path>
    <path>[../../jdk1.4/demo/jfc/Notepad/Notepad.jar]/src</path>
    <path>../../jdk1.4/demo/jfc/Notepad/src</path>
    <path>[../../jdk1.4/demo/jfc/SampleTree/SampleTree.jar]/src</path>
    <path>../../jdk1.4/demo/jfc/SampleTree/src</path>
    <path>../../jdk1.4/demo/jfc/Stylepad/src</path>
    <path>[../../jdk1.4/demo/jfc/Stylepad/Stylepad.jar]/src</path>
    <path>../../jdk1.4/demo/jfc/SwingApplet/src</path>
    <path>[../../jdk1.4/demo/jfc/SwingApplet/SwingApplet.jar]/src</path>
    <path>../../jdk1.4/demo/jfc/SwingSet2/src</path>
    <path>[../../jdk1.4/demo/jfc/SwingSet2/SwingSet2.jar]/src</path>
    <path>../../jdk1.4/demo/jfc/TableExample/src</path>
    <path>[../../jdk1.4/demo/jfc/TableExample/TableExample. ⮐
jar]/src</path>
    <path>[../../jdk1.4/demo/jpda/examples.jar]</path>
    <path>../../jdk1.4/demo/plugin/applets/Animator</path>
    <path>../../jdk1.4/demo/plugin/applets/ArcTest</path>
    <path>../../jdk1.4/demo/plugin/applets/BarChart</path>
    <path>../../jdk1.4/demo/plugin/applets/Blink</path>
    <path>../../jdk1.4/demo/plugin/applets/CardTest</path>
    <path>../../jdk1.4/demo/plugin/applets/Clock</path>
    <path>../../jdk1.4/demo/plugin/applets/DitherTest</path>
    <path>../../jdk1.4/demo/plugin/applets/DrawTest</path>
    <path>../../jdk1.4/demo/plugin/applets/Fractal</path>
    <path>../../jdk1.4/demo/plugin/applets/GraphicsTest</path>
    <path>../../jdk1.4/demo/plugin/applets/GraphLayout</path>
    <path>../../jdk1.4/demo/plugin/applets/ImageMap</path>
    <path>../../jdk1.4/demo/plugin/applets/JumpingBox</path>
    <path>../../jdk1.4/demo/plugin/applets/MoleculeViewer</path>
    <path>../../jdk1.4/demo/plugin/applets/NervousText</path>
    <path>../../jdk1.4/demo/plugin/applets/SimpleGraph</path>
    <path>../../jdk1.4/demo/plugin/applets/SortDemo</path>
    <path>../../jdk1.4/demo/plugin/applets/SpreadSheet</path>
    <path>../../jdk1.4/demo/plugin/applets/SymbolTest</path>
    <path>../../jdk1.4/demo/plugin/applets/TicTacToe</path>
    <path>../../jdk1.4/demo/plugin/applets/WireFrame</path>
    <path>[../../jdk1.4/demo/plugin/jfc/FileChooserDemo/ ⮐
FileChooserDemo.jar]/src</path>
    <path>../../jdk1.4/demo/plugin/jfc/FileChooserDemo/src</path>
    <path>../../jdk1.4/demo/plugin/jfc/Font2DTest/src</path>
    <path>../../jdk1.4/demo/plugin/jfc/Java2D/src</path>
```

**Source 3.1** *(continued)*

```
    <path>[../../jdk1.4/demo/plugin/jfc/Metalworks/Metalworks.
jar]/src</path>
    <path>../../jdk1.4/demo/plugin/jfc/Metalworks/src</path>
    <path>[../../jdk1.4/demo/plugin/jfc/Notepad/Notepad.jar]/src</path>
    <path>../../jdk1.4/demo/plugin/jfc/Notepad/src</path>
    <path>[../../jdk1.4/demo/plugin/jfc/SampleTree/SampleTree
.jar]/src</path>
    <path>../../jdk1.4/demo/plugin/jfc/SampleTree/src</path>
    <path>../../jdk1.4/demo/plugin/jfc/Stylepad/src</path>
    <path>[../../jdk1.4/demo/plugin/jfc/Stylepad/Stylepad
.jar]/src</path>
    <path>../../jdk1.4/demo/plugin/jfc/SwingApplet/src</path>
    <path>[../../jdk1.4/demo/plugin/jfc/SwingApplet/SwingApplet
.jar]/src</path>
    <path>../../jdk1.4/demo/plugin/jfc/SwingSet2/src</path>
    <path>[../../jdk1.4/demo/plugin/jfc/SwingSet2/SwingSet2
.jar]/src</path>
    <path>../../jdk1.4/demo/plugin/jfc/TableExample/src</path>
    <path>[../../jdk1.4/demo/plugin/jfc/TableExample/TableExample
.jar]/src</path>
    <path>[../../jdk1.4/src.zip]</path>
  </source>
  <documentation>
    <path>[../../doc/jdk13_docs.jar]/java/api</path>
  </documentation>
</library>
```

**Source 3.1** *(continued)*

The XML file in Source 3.1 is located on the machine's Home directory with a name of java version 1.4.1-b21.library. The filename is exactly the same as the name in the JDK settings, except it has an extension of library at the end. After further examination of the code in Source 3.1, the layout is really simple and is broken into three parts:

**Class.** Class is responsible for listing the locations of the needed Jar files of the JDK.

**Source.** Source lists the location of the available source files included with the JDK; in this example, most of them are our example programs.

**Documentation.** This is the documentation location included with the JDK. This file will be found in whatever location you determine when defining a new JDK — Project, Home, JBuilder, or user-defined. The JDK settings are located on the right side of the Configure JDK dialog. These represent the attributes found in the JDK properties file. Changing these values will change the underlying JDK properties file.

## Adding a JDK

Adding a JDK to JBuilder begins with the developer determining if the standard locations are fine or if a new user-defined location is needed. A user-defined folder would enable sharing among team members and possibly keep the project more organized, but it may not be a wise choice for large projects. Multiple projects are usually created when working on a really large development effort, and some settings may end up lost or forgotten.

Once you've made this decision, press the New... button to open a New JDK dialog (see Figure 3.2). The wizard dialog is simple:

1. Point to a base JDK using the ... button.
2. Press the OK button on the enhanced FileChooser (Figure 3.5) dialog.

The wizard will do the rest. You can customize the name of the JDK; in this instance, the jbuilder7 name was added as a visual reminder. The final step is to point to the location where the JDK properties file will be located; in this case, Project was chosen because of the limited overall impact of this getting confused with other projects on the system.

Click the OK button to add all settings automatically. Unless the developer needs to add Jar files, Source files, or documentation, the process should now be complete.

## Configuring a JDK

The last option on the Configure JDKs dialog is the JDK home path. You should always debug with the –classic option. This option does not pertain to JDK 1.4.x and higher — only the Java 2 version up to JDK 1.3.0, as used in the example. Java and JBuilder use a special VM called Hotspot, which can drastically improve performance across the board. When using the Hotspot VM, however, certain debug information was lost or not available (such as synchronization and thread information). The –classic option made the JVM run in a normal mode not utilizing the aggressive optimization of the Hotspot VM, thus allowing the information in a debug session to be as accurate as possible.

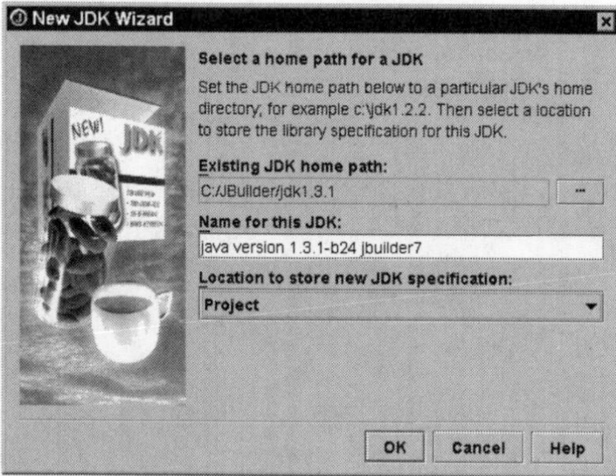


**Figure 3.2** New JDK Wizard.

Normally, the wizard will check to see if a classic JVM is present during the JDK definition phase. If it is, it must be a version earlier than JDK 1.3.1; if it determines that a problem may exist, it will set the flag automatically. This can be turned on as a default and then overridden using the VM parameters in the project properties with parameters native, hotspot, green, or server.

## JDK Switching

The process that needs to occur after understanding how a JDK is defined is how to add a new JDK to JBuilder. The last issue with JDKs is using the switching features found in JBuilder and determining what JDKs the environment supports. JBuilder can support any JDK in a base-switching mode. What is base-switching mode? Before Java 2 (which was Java 1 with the releases of 1.1.0 through 1.1.8), the JDK did not include a standard debugger. The old JDKs relied on "sniffing" programs to get the debugging information from the JVM. Beginning with Java 2 version 1.2, JBuilder supports Java Platform Debugger Architecture (JPDA) and has standardized on the information being exposed to the debugger. See Chapter 6, "Using the JBuilder Help Sytem," for more information on debugging. This means that switching to a JDK prior to Java 2 version 1.2 will not have debugging support, which really limits the power of JDK switching. Compiling and running on an earlier JDK should work fine; however, the no-debug features found in JBuilder will not be available. Switching to versions of the JDK based on Java 2 and beyond 1.2 should work fine and give a complete JBuilder user experience.

# Configuring Libraries

JBuilder has always addressed classpaths management. The concept behind the classpath is simple. Like the path used on any operating system, a classpath simply points to Java archives or directories containing the classes. Problems can arise when there is an explosion of archives and when locations and archives are dependent on other archives. In this situation, managing the list can be a huge task.

JBuilder stepped up to the plate with the concept of libraries. Libraries are collections of archives, classes, documentation, and source code saved with a .library extension. JBuilder uses the libraries to build the classpaths needed to develop programs inside the JBuilder environment, and it uses them again to build the classpath to compile, run, and debug projects.

The interface for working with libraries is very similar to the interface for defining new JDKs. Click the Tools|Configure Libraries... menu item to start the dialog (Figure 3.3). On the left-hand side is the library list, broken into four subcategories:

- Project
- User Home
- JBuilder
- User-defined

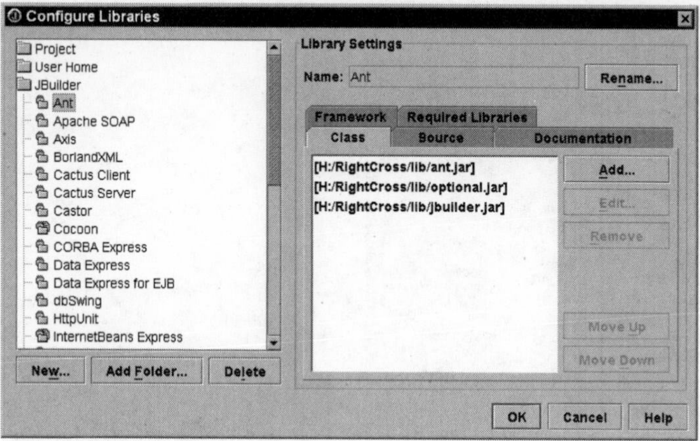


**Figure 3.3** Configure Libraries dialog.

The category selected dictates where the files with the .library extension will be located, and the definitions for the categories are the same as with the JDK categories described earlier this chapter. The .library file looks very similar to the JDK properties files outlined in Source 3.1.

The Library Settings on the right-hand side of the dialog — the Name and associated Class, Source, Documentation, Framework, and Required Libraries tabs — outline the library file's contents. The controls to the right of the tab interface allow the developer to add, edit, and remove files from the list. The lower part of the control gives the ability to move file order up or down the list. This becomes extremely important as certain classes or archives need to be loaded first and others loaded last. This gives complete control over the order in which the classpath will be constructed. Unlike the add JDK process, this wizard has no way of figuring out any additional information about the files that may be associated with them. In other words, it is necessary to point to the Source and Documentation tabs manually.

The next tab, Required Libraries, is responsible for setting up the dependencies between libraries. The list box interface uses a three-color coding system to tell the developer the status of the dependency. If the name in the list box is *black,* then it is a valid library. If the library is *gray,* it needs to be updated; this occurs when using a version of JBuilder that does not support or include that library. This may mean that the version of JBuilder needs to be upgraded to the next edition for that particular feature. If the library is *red,* then the current library is not valid and should either be removed or pointed to a proper version of that library.

The Framework tab is associated with Web development and tag libraries. This is covered in Chapter 15, "Server and Service Configuration."

The first decision that needs to be made is where is the library file going to be located. The location is critical for many reasons, especially the exposure to the JBuilder environment. If a library file is placed in the project setting, it will have exposure only to the Classes and Archives from within that particular project. Using JBuilder or the Home will give increased exposure to all new projects added. Using the user-defined option can be a great way of organizing and sharing libraries.

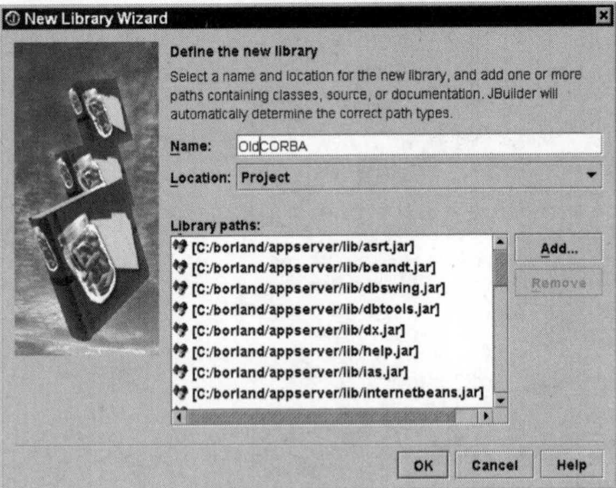


**Figure 3.4** New Library Wizard.

Only a few clicks are needed to add a library to the JBuilder environment. Press the New... button to display the New Library Wizard dialog (see Figure 3.4). Once the dialog has been displayed, the name and location must be filled out. For this example, we used the name OldCORBA and Project for the location. Using Project will again lower the exposure to other projects because it is defining a set of archives that are from an older version of VisiBroker. Pressing the Add... button will display an enhanced version of the standard FileChooser.

This FileChooser on the left-hand side includes three favorites:

- JBuilder.Home
- Project
- Samples

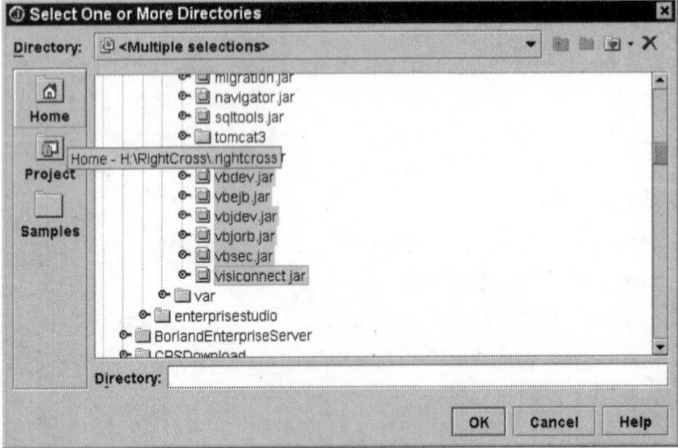


**Figure 3.5** Enhanced FileChooser.

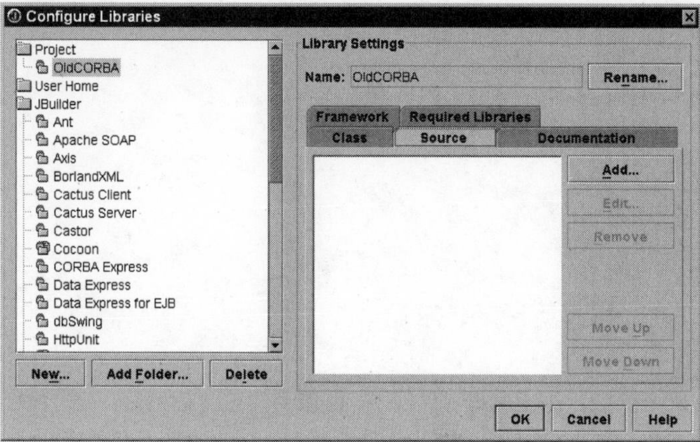


**Figure 3.6** Updated Configure Libraries dialog.

Pressing one of the icons automatically changes the focus of the file list to that directory. Because none of the three directories has the old CORBA archives, we use the standard FileChooser features to navigate to the location and choose files. Once you've selected files for the archive, press the OK button to continue.

The new display will show that OldCORBA is not a library and point to the selected .jar files from the prior step. The Source tab in Figure 3.6 is blank; this is true for the Documentation, Framework, and Required Libraries tabs. If Source or the other additional information is available, simply use the Add... button and add the required files. The Class list can hold other files besides .jar files; it can hold standard Java classes, EARs, RARs, WARs, Zips, and any other valid archive that Java might support in the future.

Once the information is complete, press the OK button to finish the task and write the OldCORBA.library file in the project's main directory. This library is used by the project to point to the archives listed in the Classes list box. Each class or archive listed in the list box can have its order changed at any time by using the Move Up and Move Down buttons located next to the tab interface. For more information on using libraries, see Chapter 4.

# Summary

This chapter covers the key areas pertaining to Java Development Kits; it explains how to define, add, and configure them to use them inside the environment. It also covers the vast world of exploding Java classes and archives and shows how to manage these files using libraries, which, in turn, makes using the environment simple when working with projects of all sizes. JBuilder continues to enhance its capabilities in these areas as it has added the ability to point to custom compilers, dependency, and support for frameworks.

CHAPTER

4

# Project Properties and Configurations

You can create a simple project inside JBuilder without a lot of special knowledge or skill. It basically involves following a simple wizard through a couple of steps, and then the process is complete. The files generated and the properties for each of the files to be included in the JBuilder project are basically obscured from the developer. In most cases, ignorance is bliss — for simple projects most developers do not need any more information than what is presented. If a team of developers is defining large, complex packages and they build scripts, then the project properties and their understanding can be worth their weight in gold.

This chapter takes you through the basic steps to create a project, explains how files associated with a project (called nodes) are used in projects, and covers the advanced features of JBuilder project properties management.

## Creating a Simple Project in JBuilder

Creating a project in JBuilder begins by clicking the File | New Project... menu item. The Object Gallery could be used at this time also; that is covered in Chapter 7, "Creating Classes."

The Project wizard, where the basic information will be defined, appears first (see Figure 4.1). The first option is to name the project; this will be the name associated with the project from this point forward. This is usually only a single name, or the name could use the standard Java naming guidelines. Off to the right, notice the Type option; it is responsible for defining how the actual project file will be defined internally. Two options are available:

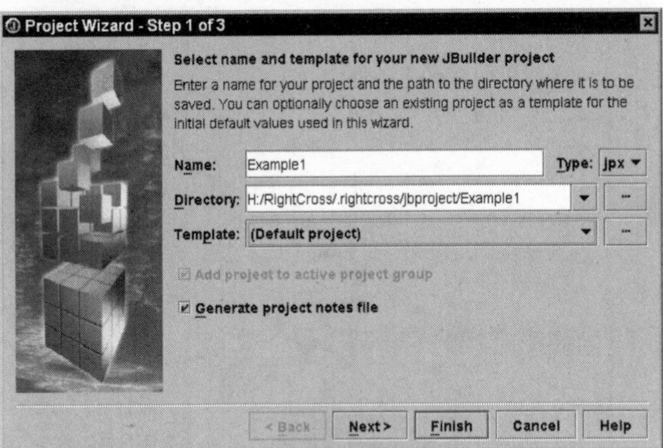


**Figure 4.1** Step 1 of 3 for Create New Project.

- JPX, which is an XML file and the standard for JBuilder projects
- JPR, which represents the OLD property file format of project files and is based on standard value/key entries

Unless the developer has something against XML, or if he or she is going to use the project being created with a really old version of JBuilder, using the JPX format is recommended. The second option is the Directory, which is where the .jpx or .jpr will be located. The Directory has nothing to do with the package layout of the files, and it represents only the top directory for the project. The third option is the Template; this comes with a standard drop-down choice control and gives the developer the opportunities to use another project's properties as a base for this project. This feature is extremely nice when you are working with a series of projects that are special but are not used enough to make them the default project properties.

The next option will be available only if a Project group is present; this is covered later in the chapter. The last option is the Generate project notes file option, which should be checked if the developer wants to have HTML files included with the project that can be used for notes or to explain the project's purpose. The first is Next; which will take the wizard to the next step in the process of creating a project. The Finish key will accept the defaults for all the other project wizard's screens. The Cancel button is available; this button does exactly what one would expect — it stops the project creation and returns to the AppBrowser. The other two buttons are really not options; the Back button is disabled because, of course, this is Step 1 of 3, and the Help button can be pressed at any time to get context-sensitive help on the Project wizard.

Press the Next button to move to Step 2. This panel gives the developer the ability to set the JDK and the default locations for the files in the project. Notice in Figure 4.2 that the current file locations are based on the user.home environment variable; learn more about how and when to use it in Chapter 1. The first option allows you to choose a different JDK if desired; this could include JDK 1.2.1, JDK 1.3.1, or any other JDK defined.

JDK switching is covered in Chapter 3, "Controlling Java Configurations." The Output path, Backup path, and Working directory are where files will be placed throughout the development cycle. The Output path will hold the compiled classes generated by the compiler; the Backup path will hold a copy of the last saved version of the files. This works in accordance with the number of backups set in the Editor options. The Working directory is the base directory where JBuilder will start a project when it is run inside the environment.

The tabbed interface below these settings controls what is included with a project and what is not. The first tab is the Source tab; notice in Figure 4.2 that it has two button controls, for the default locations of Source and Test. By the way, these can be the same, but in most cases developers like to keep them separated for organizational reasons. Files that are generated from the wizards on the Test tab located in the Object Gallery (covered in Chapter 7) will be generated in the Test Source directory. It is also possible to have multiple Source and Test directories included with a project; if the developer includes more than one directory, it will cause JBuilder to create multiple source roots for the project. This is not a problem, just something that the developer needs to understand; this topic is covered in the section on multiple source roots later in this chapter. The second tab is the Documentation tab, which is responsible for where the HTML files and files generated by JavaDoc will be located for the project; it also allows for pointing to additional locations of documentation to be included with the project. The final tab, Required Libraries, works as it did in Chapter 3, and it allows you to add defined libraries to the project. This will make those APIs available to the project by adding the libraries to the classpath, which then can be exposed through the Insight technologies included with JBuilder. On this tab, there is an additional button called Add Project... that will allow pointing to a project and adding the libraries defined in that project to the current project.

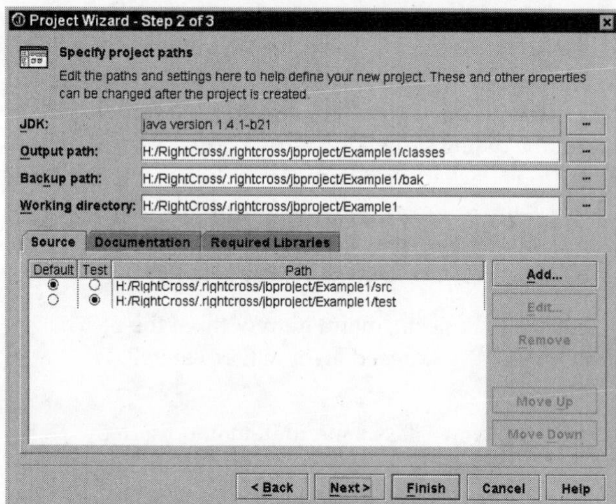


**Figure 4.2** Step 2 of 3 for Create New Project.

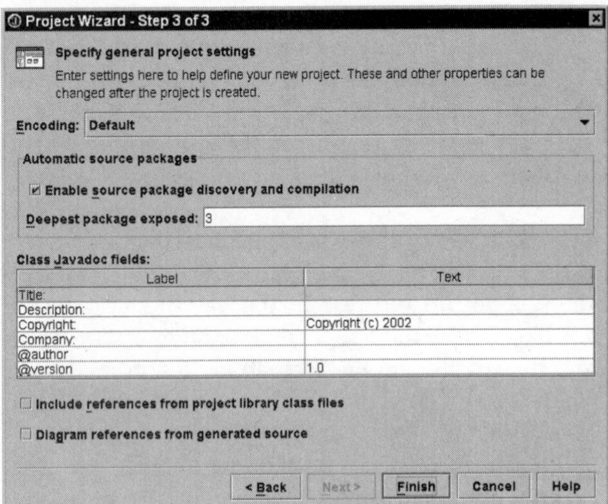


**Figure 4.3** Step 3 of 3 for Create New Project.

The options available at the bottom of the wizard are the same as in the last step except that the Back button is now enabled. If the Back button is pressed, the wizard will take the user back to Step 1. Pressing the Next button will take the wizard to the third and final step of creating a simple project.

The first option is to define the character encoding to be used with this project (see Figure 4.3). This gives JBuilder the ability to work with other character sets besides ASCII text and to specify the character set accordingly. The default encoding is whatever the operating systems default encoder is set to.

The Automatic source packages option has multiple effects on the projects being defined. When this option turns on, the default is to show all packages that appear from the Source directory or the directories defined in the prior step. It will compile all the .java files located in those packages automatically and will copy them to the defined Output directory defined. Keep in mind, though, that the last option is how deep the discovery should search; in the dialog shown in Figure 4.3, it is set to 3, meaning that if you have an exceptionally long package list, it might not be seen by the auto-discovery feature. Developers may want to lower the number of files listed in the Project pane, thus making it easier to manage normal use of this feature.

An example at this point may be needed to bring these concepts to light:

1. First, create a new project File | New Project... menu item with all the default settings. This will mean that the exposed level will be set to 3, as in Figure 4.3.

2. Next add a class to the project File | New Class... menu item and fill in the package option with the following package layer: com.wiley.borland.mastering .jbuilder. Change the class name option to jbunit, and press the OK button. Now, that package level should represent five layers; however, currently the project is set to three layers, so is there a problem? No, a package layer is

considered valid only if an actual buildable Java file is located in that package. In this example it is only at level 1, as can be seen by looking at the second package under the <Project Source> entry that shows the com.wiley.borland.mastering.jbuilder as the package line and jbunit.Java under it.

3. Now click on the mastering entry under the <Project Source> entry, and then click the File | New Class... menu item, select the com.wiley.borland.mastering package, change the class name option to mastunit, and press the OK button. Again, because a buildable Java file was added, the project layer exposed is 2. Looking at the package under the <Project Source> entry, notice that the com.wiley.borland.mastering is not the package level and under it is now the jbuilder and jbunit.
4. Now do the same thing for the borland package as explained in the prior step, change the new file to borunit, and Press the OK button. This time the third layer should be defined and the second package entry should show com.wiley.borland with the other package underneath it, just like the prior examples.
5. The next attempt will change a few things. Click on the wiley package as in the prior steps, add a New Class for that package called wileyunit, and press the OK button. This should have added another package-level entry with com.wiley, which breaks the threshold set and starts a new display. Later in this chapter, a discussion of filtering will show how to extend this capability even further.

Class JavaDoc fields options are the base fields to be included if the Generate Header options is selected when creating a new class for a project. The fields that are included are basically set; the developer can, however, set up a different set of tags and key by double-clicking in the table and modifying it. Following is an example of the output from creating a new class using a modified JavaDoc field for title.

```
/**
 * <p>My Title: </p>
 * <p>Description: </p>
 * <p>Copyright: Copyright (c) 2002</p>
 * <p>Company: </p>
 * @author not attributable
 * @version 1.0
 */
```

The Include references from Project library class files option will allow the AppBrowser to scan for references inside the libraries defined, which will be used by the refactoring tools. By default, this option is not checked; however, if the developer is new to the project or to the libraries, this option should be turned on or checked. This will then ensure that if a reference is being searched, it will show in the AppBrowser during a Find Reference process procedure. The last option is the Diagram references from generated source option; this simply allows references in the UML visualization to be defined inside the generated code of the project when the UML features are being used. For full details on the features included with JBuilder Enterprise on UML, check out Chapter 12, "UML Visualization." The following AppBrowser will be produced by pressing the Finished key; notice that in the top left-hand side is the Project pane, which includes the sample project just created.

The Project pane that will include the Example1.html file is highlighted in the Project pane. When it was double-clicked inside the AppBrowser, it became the active file in the Content pane. The Untitled1.java was also created in this project. If two or more files are selected, use either the Shift-click or the Ctrl-click method to open everything at once. After all the files are selected, right-mouse click on the files to display the Context menu and select the Open menu item. Whichever file is selected last will be the focus file when the open task is complete. Finally, the <Project Source> entry tells the developer that Automatic source packages option is turned on; if that entry does not exist, then the option is turned off.

## Multiple Source Roots

In the prior section, the concept of Source Roots was raised; this is where JBuilder looks when trying to find files for a project. These Source Roots are then part of the compile chain and will be displayed inside the actual project.

In Figure 4.4, notice that the /src directory was added for the untitled4 project. This will cause the files from untitled4 to be included in the project.

Now in Figure 4.5, notice that an additional package has been added to the Project pane, which is untitled4, and all the files included are now part of the project. This now has an effect on where the files are to be located when adding new files. Now, using this example, add a new Class by pressing the File | New Class... menu item to start the New Class wizard.

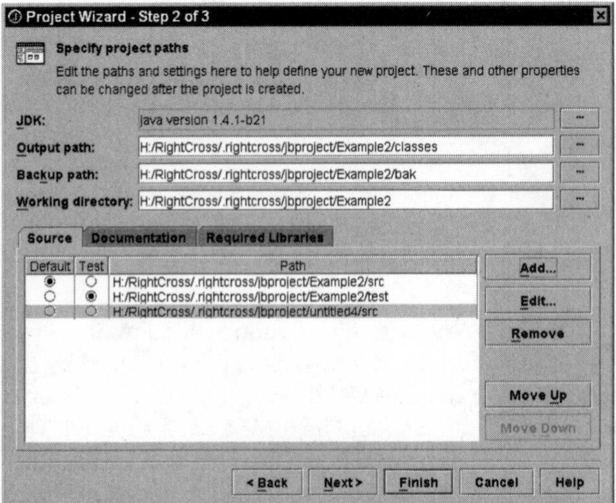


**Figure 4.4** Step 2 of 3 New Project wizard, added Source Root.

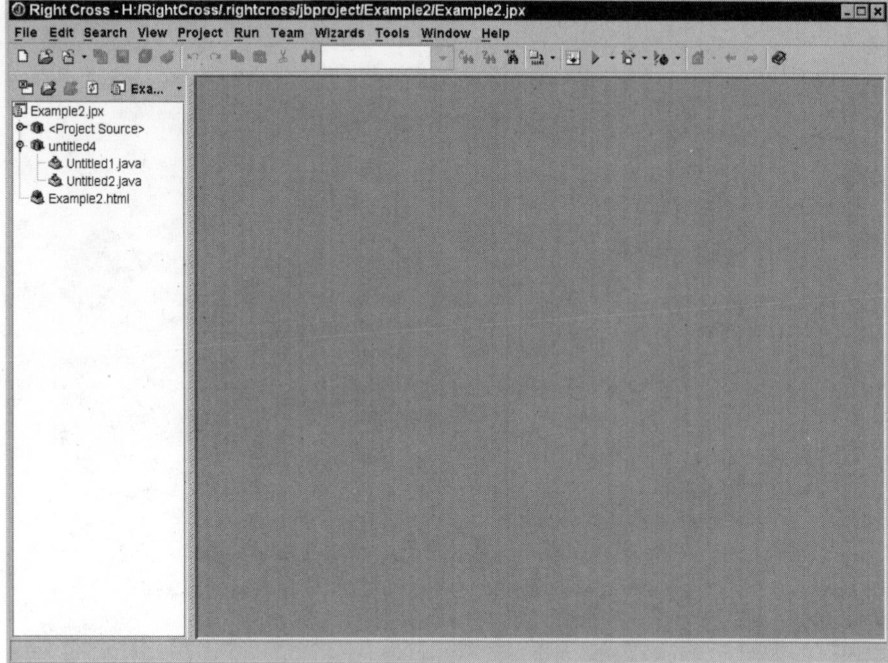


**Figure 4.5** The New Source Root for the Example 2 project.

Where the file will be added depends on the location of the selected file located inside the Project pane. Looking at Figure 4.6, notice that the selected package is untitled4, then notice that the new Class wizard screen, located inside the AppBrowser, is displaying on the Package line both untitled4 and example2 for where the new class should be located. If the selected package were anything other than the untitled4 package, then only the example2 package would be displayed as a choice. This means that when multiple Source Roots are included in a project, the developer needs to be aware of exactly where the files will be placed or additional rework could be required.

## Project Groups

One of the newer features of JBuilder is the ability to support multiple projects from within a single project file called project groups. Most of the functionality can be accomplished using multiple AppBrowsers and the multiple projects' support found in the existing JBuilder AppBrowser. That approach, though, causes projects to be handled in a certain sequence and build order. Having the ability to create a project group, each project can still live independent of the group, but when a project is included in a group, it is handled together, which means tasks can be assigned to the group, such as build, clean, compile, and other functions that can be defined using the build system. Another great use for this functionality is having a project that includes a project for server-side processing and having the other client-side projects included in one large group. This gives the ability to run all the projects without having to change from project to project.

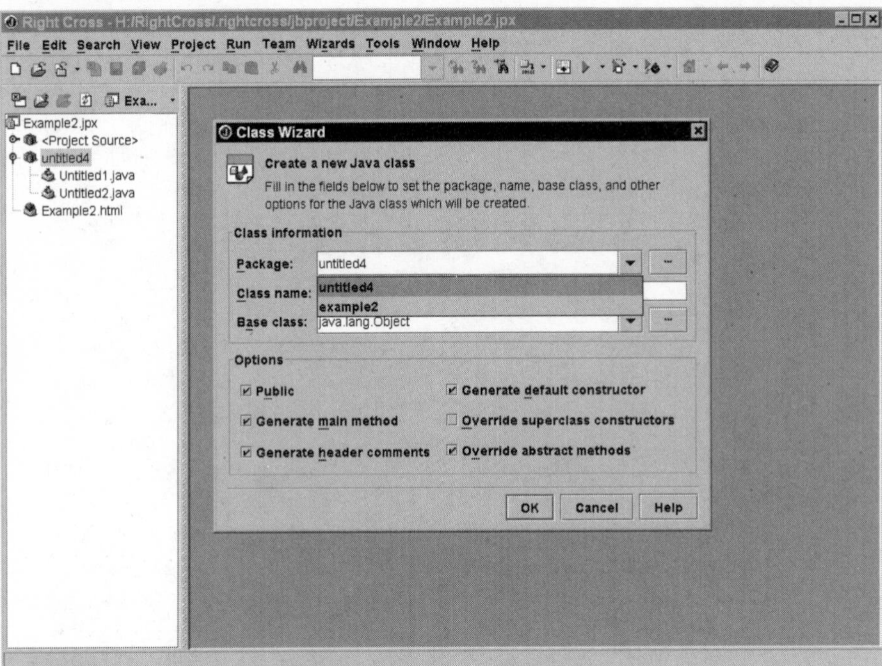


**Figure 4.6** Adding a new Class with multiple Source Roots.

To create a Project group, the developer must use the Object Gallery at this time; for full details on how to use all the features of the Object Gallery, check out Chapter 7. Click the File | New... to start the Object Gallery, then click on the Project tab, followed by the Project group icon, and finally click the OK button. This will start the Project Group wizard (see Figure 4.7).

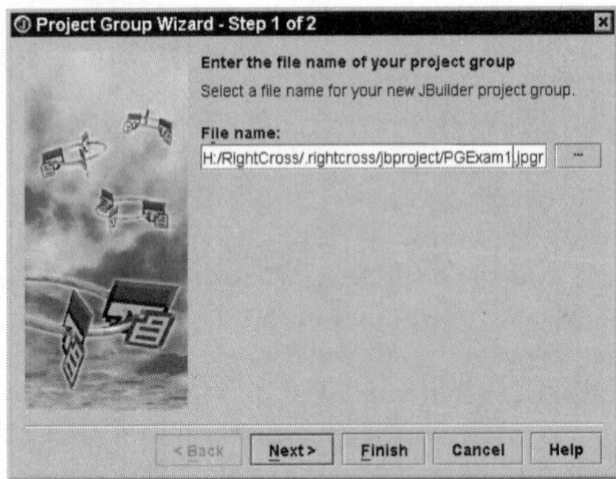


**Figure 4.7** Project Group Wizard, Step 1.

The Project Group wizard is very simple; the first page is where the Project Group file will be held. Notice in Figure 4.7 that a new file type has been added for JBuilder to understand. The .jpgr file stands for JBuilder Project GRoup. Once this location has been defined, click the Next button to continue. At this point, your options are the Finish, Cancel, and Help buttons. *Finish* will create a basic empty Project group file that will allow for adding projects later. The *Cancel* button can be pressed any time throughout the wizard and can stop the creation of the Project group. *Help* can be used to get context-sensitive help at any time.

The second step in the wizard allows for adding projects to the group, which can be done by clicking the Add... button (see Figure 4.8). The Add Recursively... button will start at the top of the project location and scan all the lower directories for .jpx or .jpr files to be added to the group. Once the files have been added, click the Finish button to continue.

Notice in Figure 4.9 that the PGExam1.jpgr is at the top of the Project pane; then notice that both example1 and untitled3 are included in the project. The example1 project is in bold to represent the active project. To switch projects, either double-click on the other .jpr/.jpx file (in this case, it would be the untitled3) or use the drop-down choice control on the top line of the Project pane. This will show the available individual projects under the PGExam1.jpgr line in bold. Click the item indented under the top group, and it will become the active project. When the active project is changed, the bold highlighting will change as a visual queue to the developer.

Now that a project group has been defined, we can add projects or change the projects associated with the group. This can be done in two ways. The fastest way to add a project to an existing group is to right-mouse click on the PGExam1.jpgr and click the Add Project... menu item. This will bring up the FileChooser dialog and allow the developer to add another project file. The second method allows you to add one or more projects. It begins in the same manner, by right-mouse clicking on the PGExam1.jpgr file. Now, however, click the Properties menu item. It can also be accomplished by clicking the Project | Project Group properties... menu item. This will spawn a new Project Group dialog.

The first page of the project properties looks very much like Figure 4.8 and works the same way. The second page is the Menu Items page, and it is responsible for managing the tasks that will be available to the context-sensitive menu items and the toolbar options. This is covered in more detail in Chapter 10, "Using Build Systems." The interface is rather simple; just use the Add... button to add tasks, which will be shown in a Selection List dialog. Click the OK button when you are finished to set the group properties. Keep in mind that each project that is included in the group has its own project properties. This means that all the advanced features (covered later in this chapter) can be modified for each project, but if a single project in the group is modified, it will be modified outside of the group.

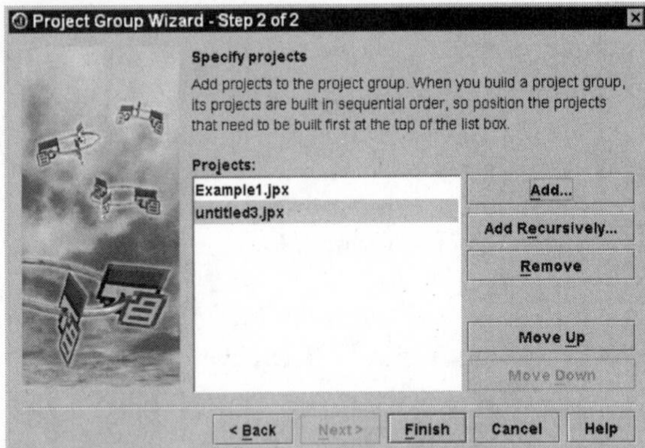


**Figure 4.8** Project Group Wizard, Step 2.

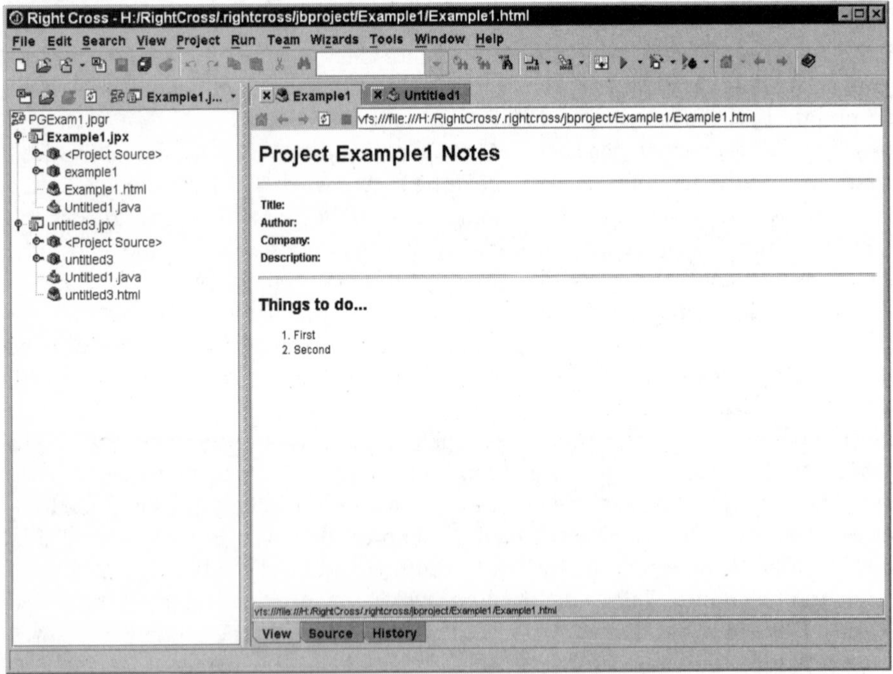


**Figure 4.9** An active Project group.

## Using Nodes

Files located inside the Project pane are referred to as *nodes*. Nodes can be many types; ironically a node can be a file node, but it also can be an archive node or a project node or even a folder node. Each one of these nodes is associated with the File Types found in the IDE Options dialog and can have special properties associated with each type.

Figure 4.9 shows multiple File Types (nodes) included in the project: .java nodes, an HTML node, and project nodes. Each of these nodes has a distinct property set associated with it. To work with each of the node's properties, simply right-mouse click on the node and select the Properties menu item to activate the accompanying dialog.

Each file type has special attributes that can be set to tell the build system how it should handle each node. For instance, the HTML node has the Resource panel that allows the developer to set the copy attribute, if this file should be copied to the output directory or if it is not supposed to be copied. It also allows for setting the attribute project wide. The node properties of the Java file can set RMI or JNI settings; if either of these two options is modified, the next build cycle will start the associated compilers to handle the task. The Java file also has the Resource panel included with its properties and works the same way as described previously. The final example of an Archive node's properties shows that it has four panels to modify or customize to the developers liking and each of the settings. This has a direct effect on how the compiler works with the associated files for the archive. For more information on the archive project, check out Chapter 10.

The key concept to keep in mind is that every node that appears in the Project pane can have additional properties that can affect the way that node is handled throughout its development process. Learning and understanding these properties is a small investment in the overall development time, and in the end doing so can save a lot of headaches.

## Advanced Project Properties Features

Now that we have a basic understanding of how to create projects and project groups, we can look at how the properties included with a project can change a project's behavior over its development process. The interface to interact with these properties is handled through a wizard-based process. The Project Properties dialog can be accessed via many different paths; the first is the Project | Project Properties... menu item. The second way of accessing it is from the Project pane; right-mouse click on the project.jpr/jpx file, and select the Properties menu item. This will display the last tab visited; if the Paths pane is not active, click the Paths tab.

### Paths Panel

The interface for the Paths panel should look very similar to the interface displayed in Figure 4.2 (used as a reference) during the creating of a project. This is where you change the JDK if desired and define multiple Source Roots for the project.

## General Panel

This panel, like the Paths panel, should be the same interface that was explained in Figure 4.3 (used as a reference). It also works the same way as what was explained in that section. The key areas to look for in the panel are the automatic source packages and the nuances that are associated with working with that option.

## Run Panel

This panel, shown in Figure 4.10, is responsible for listing the available Runtime configurations. These configurations allow you to set different switches pertaining to building and running a Java program inside a project. The Run panel has six options in the form of buttons to control these configurations. The New... button will spawn a dialog that will allow for adding a configuration. The Copy... button will make a copy of the selected configuration in the list box. The Edit... button will allow any of the parameters on the selected configuration to be changed. The Remove... button will do exactly that: remove the selected configuration. The last two buttons control the order of the configuration in the list box. This order relates to the order on the Run / Debug / Optimize toolbar button drop-downs; also on the toolbar drop-down list is an option for bringing up this dialog. The other way to show this interface is to use the Run | Configurations... menu item.

These configurations become extremely important when working with projects that contain AppServer-specific code, Java applications, and Web server-specific code or have specific switches or debug parameters that must be set to execute a program properly. When adding a new configuration using the Add... button, the first option is the name associated with the configuration. The second option is the build target, which can be selected from the drop-down list (covered in Chapter 10). The next area of the dialog is the Tab panels that include the following:

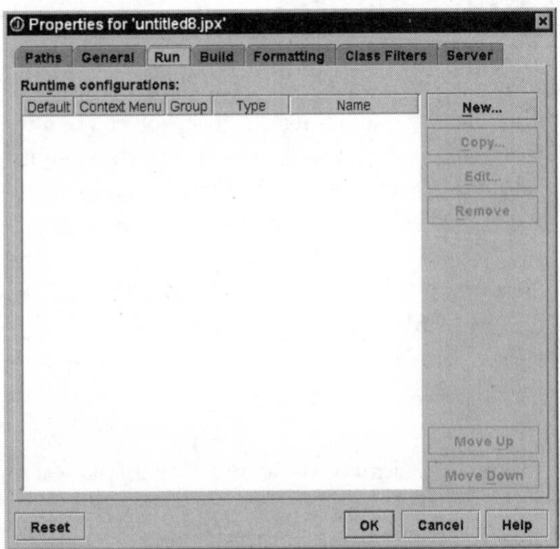


**Figure 4.10** Run panel, Project Properties.

**Run.** This tab sets the parameters for the type of Java file to be executed. This will be explained further in the Type option discussion.

**Debug.** This tab allows for the advanced debug configuration to be set; it is also where remote debugging can be turned on and its parameters set. Debugging is covered in Chapter 5, "Debugging with JBuilder."

**Optimize.** This tab allows parameters needed for the OptimizeIT product to be set. The OptimizeIT product is outside the scope of this book.

The real horsepower comes from the Run tab; notice in Figure 4.11 that the Type option has a number of choices:

**Application.** When this option is selected, the rest of the panel will show options pertaining to that type of Java program. In the case of Application, it will allow VM parameters and Application parameters to be set.

**Applet.** When this option is selected, the rest of the panel will show the options pertaining to Applet programs. The Applet options include the main class to be executed, the HTML associated with the class, VM parameters that might be needed, display properties, and finally the Applet parameters.

**Server.** When this option is selected, the rest of the panel will show the options pertaining to the Web or Application Server associated with that configuration. This basically gives the same interface as in Figure 4.18 later in this chapter. The options are covered completely in Chapter 15, "Server and Service Configuration."

**Test.** When this option is selected, the rest of the panel will show the options pertaining to the Testing integration based on JUnit. The options available include the class to test, packages where the test classes can be found, an area of VM parameters, and finally the type of Test Runner to be used.

**OpenTools.** When this option is selected, the rest of the panel will show the options pertaining to working with the OpenTools interface. The options include the new tools output path, the tools .jar file location, VM and JBuilder parameters for running the tool, and the options for where it should be located and if it should overwrite what is in JBuilder loaded classes.

Once the Type and options associated with that type are selected, pressing the OK button to continue will write the configuration. From that point forward, it will be available to the JBuilder interface.

## Build Panel

The Build panel (see Figure 4.12) is responsible for setting up how the AppBrowser will handle the build process. Many options are available from this interface, which directly affects how the JBuilder compiler will handle the underlying build process. Almost all aspects of the build process can be exposed or modified through this interface. The Build panel is covered in Chapter 10. For more information on the interface, proceed to that chapter.

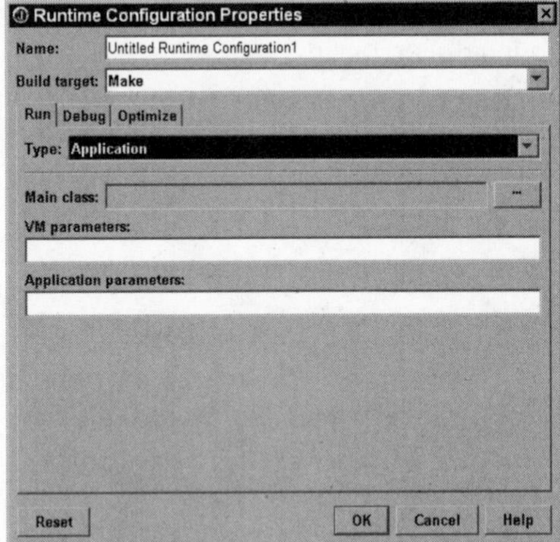


**Figure 4.11** Runtime Configuration Properties dialog.

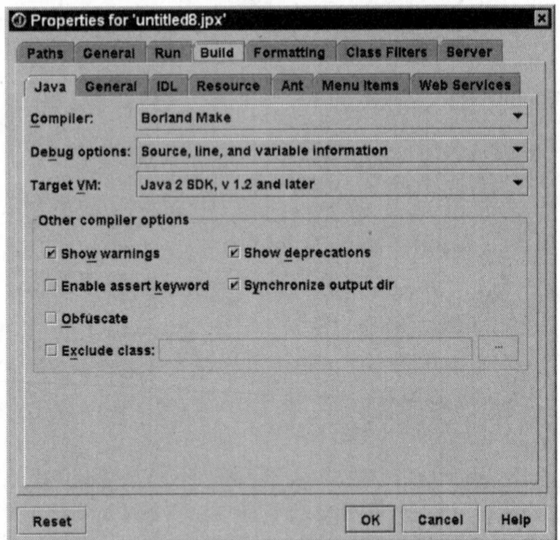


**Figure 4.12** Build panel, Project Properties.

## Formatting Panel

One of the most requested JBuilder features is Java beautification. This allows the developer to set a few properties and run a wizard to generate reformatted code. Not until the extreme programming movement did JBuilder address this issue. The first attempt at simple formatting came in the form of common event handling; this feature has been part of the AppBrowser since JBuilder 2's introduction for supporting anonymous adaptors, which is still available today on the Generated tab. JBuilder is making huge strides in the area of formatting, almost to the point that there may be too many options. Point in case: Currently there are 54 checkbox options and 2 radio button options; this represents a factorial of 54 options that could be multiplied by 2. The number of total formatting options currently available to the JBuilder developer is 2.308436973392413e + 71, which is the base number generated from the 54 factorial. Needless to say, the AppBrowser now supports Java beautifications in a major way.

JBuilder tried to add many features that were requested over the years and actually came up with a nice interface to test the formatting before accepting the changes, thus eliminating a lot of guesswork. This interface will be put to the test as the developer tries different options for different kinds of code. In Figure 4.13, the formatting options available to the developer are listed on the tabs, which include Basic, Blocks, Spaces, Blank Lines, Wrapping, Generated, and Imports. Using the advanced AppBrowser interface, the developer can play what-if games until he or she is satisfied with the results in the preview window. It is also recommended that the dialog be expanded to accommodate the full lines so that all changes can be noticed or viewed.

The first tab, Basic, is tasked with the most basic of settings; these pertain to general indentation rules. Keep in mind that these work in accordance with the Tools | Editor Options... dialog. How it preserves end-of-line characters and tabs and how the tabs and spaces are formatted can be overridden by the project properties. The second tab is Blocks; it is responsible for how the code will be arranged when logical blocks of code are defined, such as classes, try...catch, ifs, and many others. The third tab is the Spaces tab; it is responsible for how and when a space or spacing is to affect the code, and with 14 specific options available, most developers should be satisfied. The fourth tab is the Blank Lines tab; it is responsible for where to put the blank lines, but it also gives the flexibility to set the number of lines for each of the seven options in the Tab pane. The fifth tab is the Wrapping options, which gives seven options, two of which can have specific columns to determine where the wrapping functions should start; it also gives the ability to match the existing code. The sixth tab is the Generated tab; it has the same interface and functionality as mentioned previously, and it outlines how to work with events.

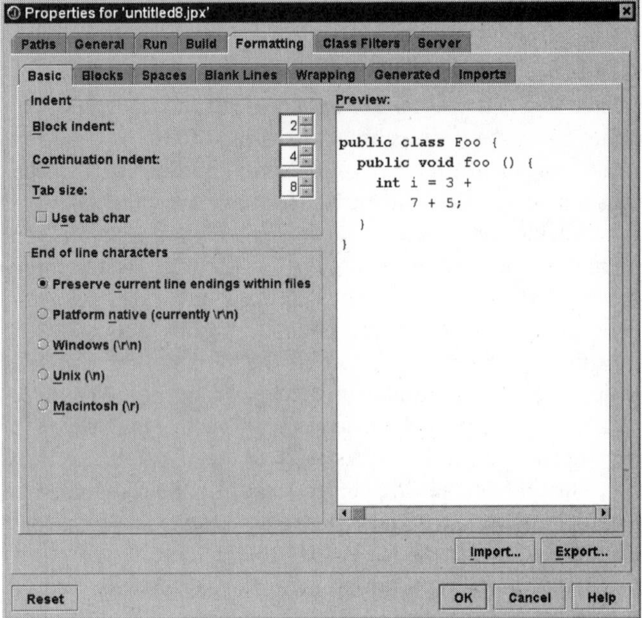


**Figure 4.13** Formatting panel – Basic, Project Properties.

## *Generated Tab*

Besides handling how the AppBrowser will generate event code, two other major options are available on the screen (shown in Figure 4.14). The first is Visibility of instance variables; this will set the access level — private, package, protected, and public. This means that when an instance variable gets added to the code using one of the two-way tool designers like the GUI, it will be added using that visibility. The last option deals with using the Beans.instantiate method. Look at the following two pieces of code:

```
JButton jButton2; //Instance variable
jButton2 = (JButton) Beans.instantiate(getClass().getClassLoader(),
JButton.class.getName()); //actual creation of bean
jButton2.setText("jButton2"); //setting property
```

This code uses the Beans.instantiate option, so it will create jButton2 using the current class loader and loading a serialized instance of the bean. This option is normally used when an exact copy of a bean is to be created; using a previously serialized version of the bean does this. It is recommended that Beans.instantiate should be used only when the preceding is necessary because of the overhead associated with instantiating a serialized bean.

```
JButton jButton2 = new JButton(); //Instance variable and creation
JButton2.setText("jButton1"); //setting property
```

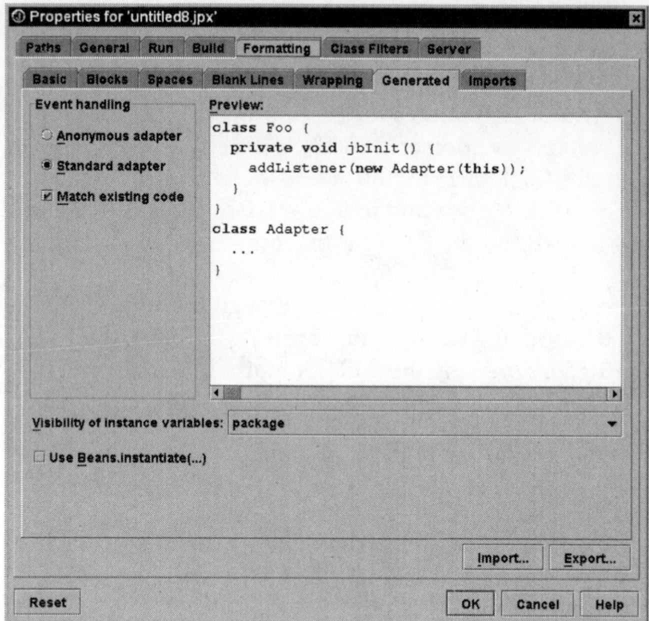


**Figure 4.14** Generated panel – Events, Visibility, and Beans.

This second code example is the standard code that JBuilder would generate. It is much simpler to read, and the creation of the object occurs when the class gets loaded, not when it gets initialized.

## *Imports Tab*

The final tab is the Imports tab, which has two subpanels: Thresholds and Sort Order. The first panel lets the developer set the threshold of the import statements. Keep in mind that the threshold is the same one that was defined in the previous section on automatic source packages in this chapter. This means that a valid Java class must be in the package before it represents a level. Looking at the standard interface if the option is set to 1, notice that the import for java.math.* is changed to java.math. BigInteger. This happened because the threshold was exceeded, and thus a fully qualified import was generated. The developer can also set it so that all of the imports are fully qualified by simply checking the Always import classes option. The second panel is the Sort Order, which allows the developer to define the sequence of the imports. If the developer likes javax package to come before java package, this is where he or she sets these options.

Now that the formatting options are set, how do you use them? Formatting settings can be used on a package, Java file, block of code, and even just a simple line of code. To format a package in a project, simply select the project in the Project pane and right-mouse click (this will display the Context menu and then select the Format Package menu item). For a Java file, clicking the Edit | Format All menu item will do the trick; if you want to format a block of code or a single line, select the line and press the Tab key.

There is some controversy over the Tab key functionality because the AppBrowser uses the Tab key as a format key instead of a simple Tab key and the F2 key is now the Tab key. Many developers are not happy with this keyboard configuration issue. This is easily fixed by using the keymapping features in the AppBrowser (see Section 2, "JBuilder as a Rapid Application Development Tool"). First click the File | IDE Options... menu item, then click the Customize button beside the keymap option. Then scroll to the indent section where Format-code and indent are defined, and switch the two options. Now the Tab key is a tab and the F2 key is the format; either way, the job still gets done.

Another formatting quirk to keep in mind is that even though the Imports tab is located on the Formatting tab, this option is not activated by using the tab (default) formatting key. It is actually activated by pressing the Edit | Optimize Imports menu item or by pressing the Ctrl-I (CUA keymap). If the developer highlights the imports and presses the Tab key, nothing will happen.

## Class Filter

The next tab on the Project Properties dialog is the Class Filters tab, which is responsible for limiting the classes displayed during certain operations. In Figure 4.15, the Class Filters panel is a very simple interface. It focuses on two major areas: first, where to filter, and second, what to filter. The "where" filter is divided into three distinct locations:

- Find classes dialog, which is responsible for limiting the classes shown in the Select Package/Class dialog. This dialog has the same interface as the Class Filters dialog explained in Chapter 8, "Modifying Classes."
- The second filter option, the Unit test stack trace, which is responsible for limiting the classes displayed when using the built-in unit testing facilities.This option has already been defined.
- The third location,the UML diagram, which is responsible for limiting the classes displayed by the UML visualization. This ability can be extremely important and a real time-saver, especially on very large projects or projects that make use of particular classes throughout a project. An example of this may be the Swing classes if a lot of GUI code is present. The "what" is just a list of classes that should be filtered. It should be noted that the class filters are for all the files located in a project.

Open the Welcome project that ships with JBuilder by clicking the Help | Welcome project (Sample) menu item. Then right-mouse click the Welcome.jpx located in the Project pane, and select the Properties... menu item. Click the Class Filter tab; it should show the Find Classes dialog on the drop-down list box. Click the Add... button to display the Select Package/Class dialog, and select the java.lang package, as displayed in Figure 4.16.

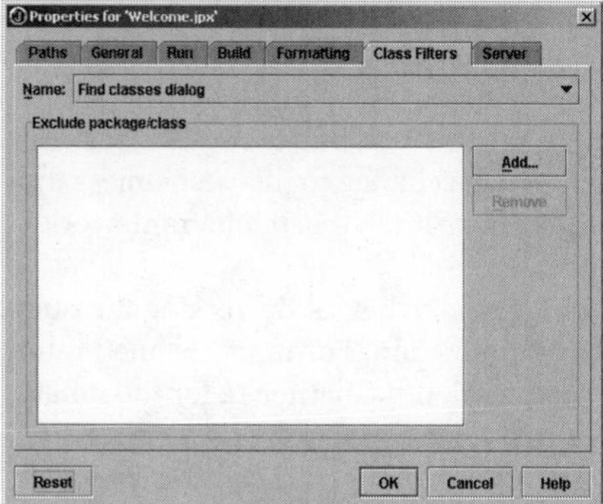


**Figure 4.15** Class Filters panel, Project Properties.

Click the OK button to return to the Class Filters panel with the java.lang added to the list. Press the OK button on the dialog, which will return the focus back to the project; double-click on the WelcomeFrame.java file located inside the Project pane, then hit the Ctrl- - (minus) key combination. This will display the Find Classes dialog, so in the Edit box start typing in the java.lang.String line. Notice that when the input character gets to the "l", the display goes blank because the filtering is on all of the lang package, thus eliminating it from the list. If the java.lang package needs to be viewed, click the Browse tab at the top of the dialog and drill down into the java.lang package; all the classes will be displayed.

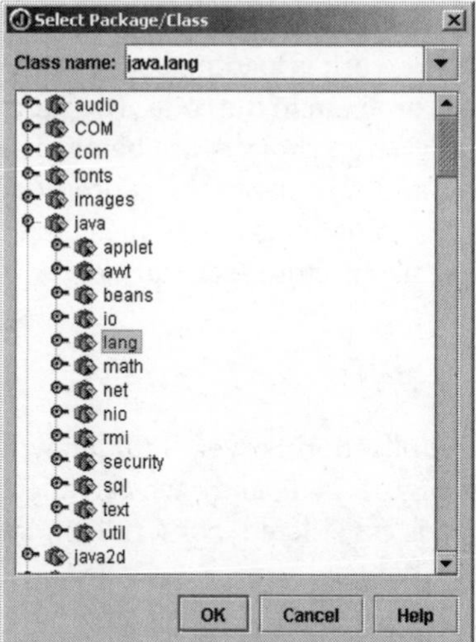


**Figure 4.16** Select Package/Class dialog.

The Unit testing stack trace option found on the drop-down list in the Class Filters tab has already been defined, and if the unit testing is being used inside JBuilder, then this functionality has already been used. The developer can simply add or remove classes from this dialog using the same technique as described previously and see what the changes might be. Most developers will not make a change to this area unless they are focusing on the JUnit framework or they believe that the JUnit framework is responsible for errors in the testing environment.

The UML diagram item from the drop-down is responsible for decreasing the number of classes displayed while using the UML Visualization. For more detailed information on the UML Visualization and its options, check out Chapter 12 for full details. Using the same project as described previously, rebuild the project by clicking the Project | Rebuild Project "Welcome.jpx" menu item. Then double-click on the WelcomeFrame.java file located inside the Project pane, and then select the UML tab under the Content pane. Notice that all the java definitions are displayed in the diagram-making note of the javax.swing packages. Now, go into the Project Properties dialog, this time using the Project | Project Properties... menu item that takes the developer to the same location as using the Context menu. Click on the Class Filters tab, select the UML dialog item from the drop-down list box, and press the Add... button. Using the same technique, you can then select the javax.swing package. Click the OK button to finish the dialog, and then press the OK button on the Project Properties dialog. To see the changes, the developer can rebuild the project following the same steps, then click the UML tab again to see the changes.

In Figure 4.17, the javax.swing packages are no longer displayed, which is a huge time-saver. Using the filter processes reduces the amount of time to display available classes, as it eliminates classes that may be considered redundant. Something like the java.lang package may be considered by some developers as too basic, with no need to display it. Using the filtering on the stack traces when unit testing can really save time by not having to review all the things that the JUnit framework is loading and unloading, when generally it has nothing to do with the actual problem in the code. The same can be said for the UML filter; sometimes when really large projects are being displayed, seeing all the packages can be overwhelming and take away the conceptual effect of what the diagram is trying to convey. Simply eliminating some of the classes being displayed may help the developer grasp the overall structure more quickly.

## Server Panel

The Server panel is responsible for defining what Application Server JBuilder will work with. There are many options on this panel (see Figure 4.18), and each can affect how and what JBuilder generates as far as server code is considered. For a full explanation of the options and features of this dialog, go to Chapter 15.

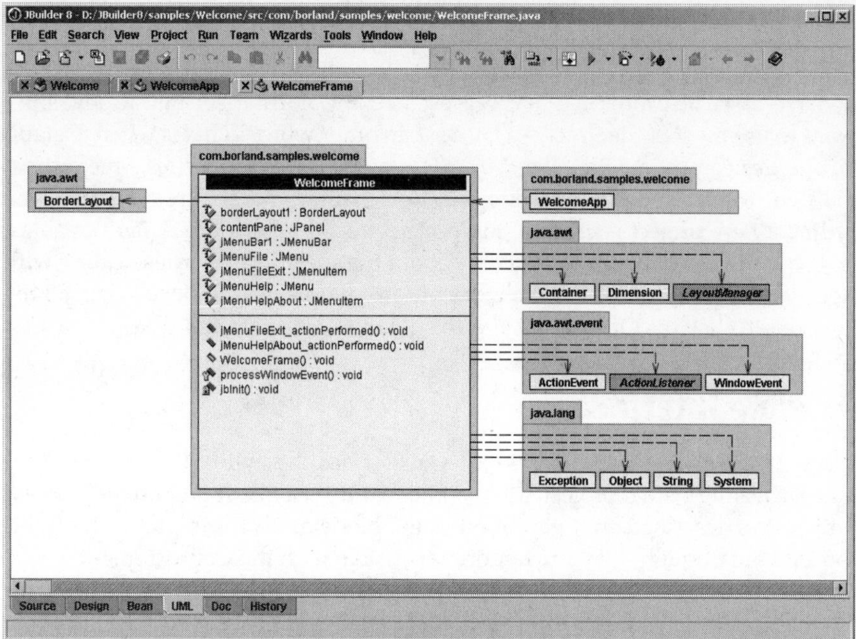


**Figure 4.17** UML Visualization with filtered javax.swing package.

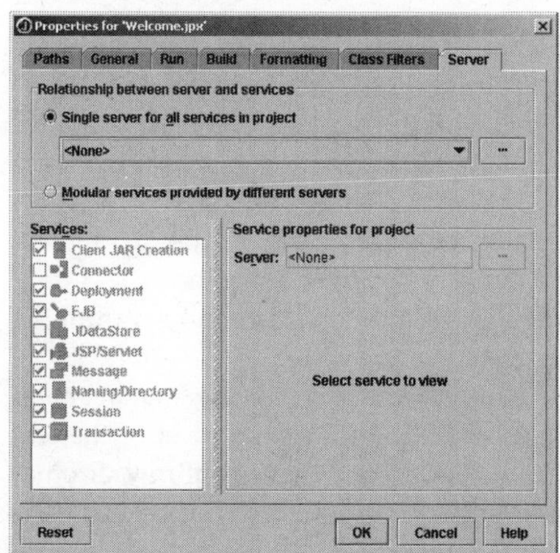


**Figure 4.18** Server panel, Project Properties.

## Default Project Properties

With all of the project properties that can be set, it would be nice if JBuilder gave the option to save a set of properties that represented the normal set that a developer would want to use most of the time — a base set, in other words. That is where Default Project Properties comes in. Click the Project | Default Project Properties... menu item to use the same interface defined throughout this chapter and set up a default. That way, anytime a new project is created, the project would inherit the default settings. Then the developer has to be concerned only about the specific properties dealing with that project, which really simplifies the work of setting up a new project. When all the properties are set, click the OK button, and the default will be saved.

## Project Pane Interface

The Project pane itself is a very diverse interface; it has the ability to accomplish all kinds of tasks dealing with a project. Most of the features can be found on the Context menu, which was described as it pertained to the Node and Project properties interface. Keep in mind, though, that much more is possible with the Context menu.

Another great feature of the Project pane is the quick search. This helps you find files quickly in the Project pane. Click anywhere inside the Project pane, and then start typing a word of a file located inside the project; the focus will automatically change as more of the word is typed.

## Context Menu

One of the interesting things about the Context menu is that its features and capabilities are dictated by the "context," location, or the selection of the items inside a Project pane. Most of the time the Context pane will deal with the general features of a project like adding files and packages, removing files and packages, opening files in a new AppBrowser, and closing a project. It can also deal with Build or Run subsystems. If a .java node is selected, most likely it can be built, compiled, cleaned, run, debugged, and tested. Most files can be deleted, renamed, or even removed from the project definition. When the file is deleted, it is gone; when it is removed, it is removed from the project file list.

Additional features — like exposing Web Services or source code management (SCM) — may be made available through the Context menu. Again, most of the features located on the Context menu are available elsewhere in the AppBrowser environment; it is mostly a convenience to the developer to organize and categorize the features in one location.

## Project Pane Toolbar

Above the Project pane is a toolbar, and the icons on it are responsible for closing a project, adding files or packages, removing files or packages, refreshing the Project pane's display, and choosing the project interface.

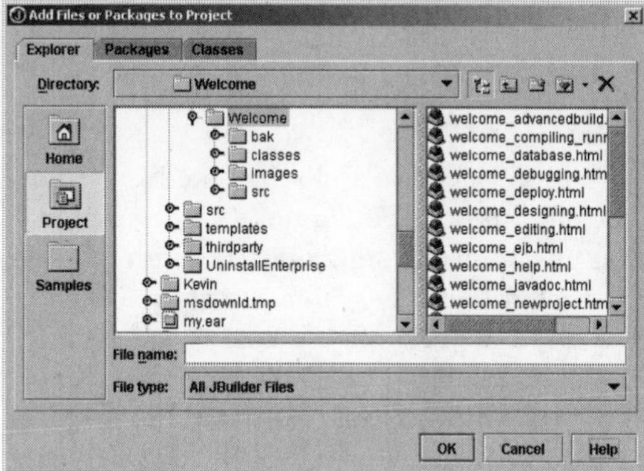


**Figure 4.19** Add Files or Packages to project.

Often developers want to add files or packages to a project. One of the quickest ways to do this is to click the Add files/packages icon (second from the left) on the Project pane toolbar (see Figure 4.19).

The interface is divided into three tabs:

**Explorer tab.** Allows for general hunt functions pertaining to a specific file.

**Packages tab.** Looks like the Browser interface on the Class Filters interface.

**Classes tab.** Add specific classes.

Once the file, package, or class has been found, select it, and hit the OK button to continue. The interface also has a Favorites section along the left-hand side; you can add to this list by right-mouse clicking inside it and selecting the Add Favorite menu option. Whatever file, package, or class is selected will be added to the area, which can be managed by using the Manage Favorites menu item by right-mouse clicking inside the area. This makes it very convenient to go to a particular location for files.

For removing files, select a file and hit the Remove from Project icon (third from the left). A confirmation dialog will be displayed to confirm a removal. Once the process has been approved, the file will be removed from the project file list. If the developer wants to delete or permanently erase a file from the file system, use the Delete operation found on either the Context menu or the File menu.

The Refresh icon (fourth from the left) will update the Project pane. This button is extremely important when using the Automatic Source packages options covered at the beginning of this chapter.

## Advanced Features

The Project pane includes advanced features to make JBuilder project management a breeze: organization folders, specialized pointer directories, and build filters, just to name a few of the features that can save time.

The first advanced feature is the Folders option, available on the Context menu inside a project. Folders are meant to help organize code visually inside a project, even though they have nothing to do with the files or their locations. They can be nested for better organization.

To create a folder, right-mouse click in the Project pane and select the New Folder menu item, name the Folder, and press the OK button; a Folder node will be added to the Project pane. Next, select the Folder; at this point a nesting operation can be done, or files and packages can be added. If a nested folder is wanted, simply add New Folder, name it, and press the OK button. If files and packages are to be added, click the Add files/packages menu item, select the files to be added to the Folder, and press OK. Notice that when a file is moved to a folder, it is removed from the general project files and placed inside the folder — hence, the organization features. This used to be a large feature inside JBuilder, but because the package handling has been improved so much over the years, this feature is not as important. It is used a lot of times on very large projects where certain developers may be responsible for specific packages or files and folders can be organized to reflect work responsibilities.

The Directories view option is a newer feature that allows JBuilder to point to a directory that may contain specific files important to a particular project. As a developer, you always have a set of files with code developed over the years that you are particularly proud of and use all the time. Some developers create a directory where they keep these files; now, with the Directories view feature, simply create a New Directory view menu item from the Context menu, and choose the directory to be added to the project. When the OK button is hit, the directory will be listed; open it, and all the files located in that directory can be seen by simply double-clicking on a file and copying or reviewing its contents.

One of the newer features to be added to JBuilder is the concept of build filters. These options are available on all packages located in the Project pane. Currently four options are available. The first is the Exclude packages and subpackages option, which will completely remove all the files from the build process. The opposite is the Include packages and subpackages option, which will add all the buildable files back into the build process. The other two options, Exclude package and Include package, are part of the interactions with the Automatic source package. Click on a package, and the developer can either Exclude it from the build package or Include it in the build package.

Note that all files are marked as build enabled by default. If the Automatic source package is being used, this can be managed in a generic sense; these additional menu options give finite control over the process.

## Summary

This chapter has covered a lot of material pertaining specifically to projects in JBuilder. As JBuilder continues to evolve and mature, the project properties will most likely evolve with it. This growth will most likely be seen in the areas of project groups, build tasks, increased ANT integration, VCS control, and server support, just to name a few. As the Java platform and underlying language continue to evolve, so will the properties needed to support them. An example of this pertains to server properties for AppServer, which were not even on the radar when JBuilder 4 was being created. Yet, by JBuilder 6, they started to be added, and they have been increasing with each release of JBuilder ever since. The end result of having an extensible tool like JBuilder is that it can morph right along with the technology because it is made up of the same technology.

CHAPTER

5

# Debugging with JBuilder

Early Java developers relied on C++ sniffer programs that would interrogate the JVM and report back the results through some type of proprietary brokering technique. With the introduction of JDK 1.2.2 that all changed — the base Java language finally included the needed architecture and hooks to enable a whole new world of debugging.

Java Platform Debugger Architecture (JDPA) (see Figure 5.1) allows for all Java programs based on JDK 1.2.2 or higher to be debugged. The architecture is made up of three different parts, each part representing a logical separation between the need for information and how to return that information to an interface that can relate back to a human interface. The first of the three parts is JDI (Java Debug Interface), which is the actual programming interface used by JBuilder and other debugging tools. The JDWP (Java Debug Wire Protocol), like any wire protocol, defines the structure of the messages being passed between the program being debugged and the human interface being used to interpret the results. Then finally, you have the JVMDI (Java Virtual Machine Debug Interface), which defines a native interface to the Java virtual machine. These three pieces fit together to give a comprehensive solution to debugging that includes single-process, multiprocess, and, of course, remote debugging.

JBuilder employs the tools and interfaces supplied by the Java platform to ensure that the debugging interface is exposed in the most productive way possible. The JBuilder product has extensive visualization and information presentation during the debugging process, and we believe that one of the best parts about the debugger is that it is natural. This is important because to use any tool effectively you must feel that it is a natural extension of the task at hand. This task may be debugging a very simple single-process program or the most complex multitier program that calls JSPs, EJBs, CORBA servers, and even JNI processes, all in one consistent logical presentation.

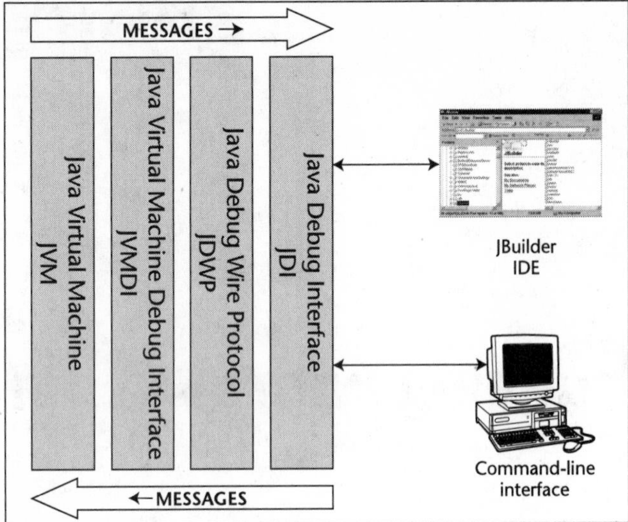


**Figure 5.1** JPDA architecture.

What can you expect to understand after reading and using the examples in this chapter? Well, first are the basics of using the debugger — including start, pause, and break and how the interface relates this information back to you. This is followed by discussions of control, watches, inspections, properties, and even cut/copy/paste operations and multiprocess sessions in a debug session. We conclude our discussion with advanced topics like threading, deadlocks, and remote debugging. This chapter will also make use of a single project with many different examples to highlight JBuilder's debugging capabilities.

## Debugging Basics

One of the first things you need to understand about the JBuilder debugger is its interface. JBuilder adds more insight into the program with the debug window. This window is located during debugging in the Message pane location, and the pane is divided into logical parts depending on the function or operation you are trying to complete.

The first program to get started with the debugger will be SimpleDebug; it will show the very basics. Create a new Project using the File | New Projects menu item, and call the project TheDebugger. Then add a new class using the File | New Class menu item, and make the package state com.wiley.mastering.jbuilder.debugexamples and the class name equal SimpleDebug. Remember to click the Generate Main method and then click the OK button to finish. For an example of the New Class dialog, see Figure 5.11 later in this chapter.

```
package com.wiley.mastering.jbuilder.debugexamples;

/**
```

```
 * <p>Title: Debug Examples</p>
 * <p>Description: This will be used for the Debugging Chapter</p>
 * <p>Copyright: Copyright (c) 2002</p>
 * <p>Company: </p>
 * @author Michael J. Rozlog
 * @version 1.0
 */

public class SimpleDebug {

  public SimpleDebug() {
  }

  public static void main(String[] args) {
    SimpleDebug simpleDebug = new SimpleDebug();
    System.out.println("Welcome to JBuilder Debugging!");
  }

}
```

Once the OK button was pressed, JBuilder should have generated a skeleton program to add the two lines inside the main method, as shown in the preceding code. Once the program is completed, save and rebuild the project.

It is now time to review the build properties for the project; this can be accomplished by right-mouse clicking on the The Debugger.jpx file in the Project pane. Then select the Build tab, as shown in Figure 5.2.

You should note a few things in Figure 5.2. First, the compiler being used is responsible for compiling each file located in the project. Moreover, if this value is changed midstream throughout the project, then certain files could be missed or recompiled without the developer's knowledge. Please review Chapter 10, "Using Build Systems," for full details on the idiosyncrasies of this option. If files are missed during the compile process, either no or old debug information may be present during the debug process. The second option is the most important as it pertains to the debug process; the Debug options include four options:

- Source, line, and variable information
- Source and line information only
- Source information only
- None

Source, line, and variable information is the most complete debugging option. It can be set, and the information will be held inside the .class file. Source and line information gives only limited exposure to what is happening inside a class. Giving any information to the debugger is the Source only, and it will include just basic information about the code itself. The None option is just that; it does not generate any additional information in the .class file.

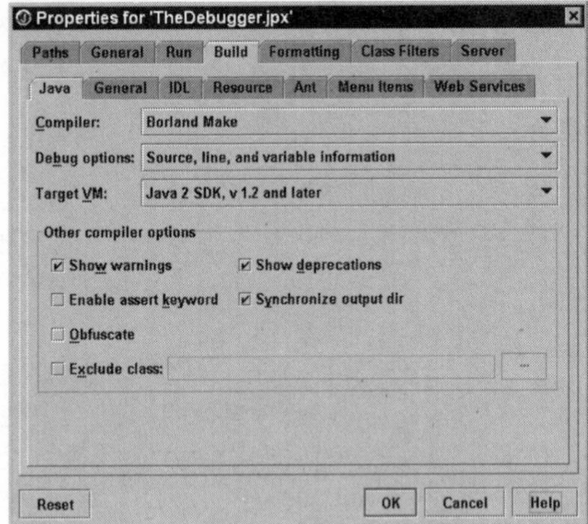


**Figure 5.2** Project Properties, Build/Java for debugging.

Notice in Figure 5.3 that almost everything about the class is found in the file. In Figure 5.3 the empty boxes represent special characters that normally would not be displayed. The sixth line of the display is where things start to get interesting — that line defines all of the tables used for the debugging information and finishes with the name of the source file.

In Figure 5.4, no extra code is included — not even the "this" object is loaded into the file. Also, notice the size of the file compared to the SimpleDebug.class with ALL debug information included. This is a very small class, and it could make a significant difference if the class was exceptionally large.

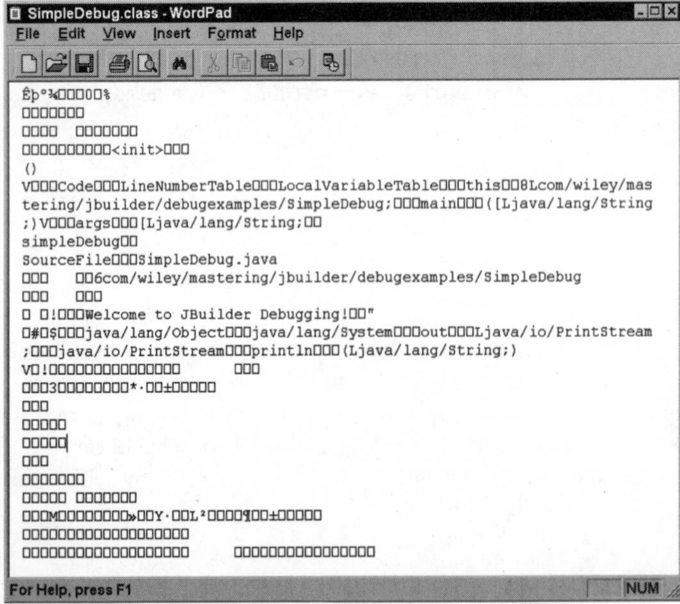


**Figure 5.3** SimpleDebug.class with full debug Information.

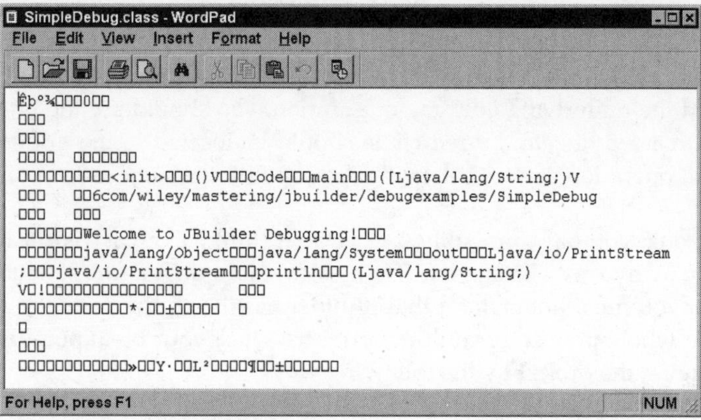

**Figure 5.4** SimpleDebug.class with no debug Information.

**TIP** **For the fastest execution and smallest .class files, compile the final pass with Debug options set to None.**

For certain features it makes a difference what Target VM is used. If any advanced features like the Smart Swap feature were going to be used, they would have to be set to Java 2 SDK, 1.4 or later. The final option to be aware of on this page is the Obfuscate, which will "cloud" the information in the .class file by renaming variables and methods (name mangling) to make it harder to be decompiled.

**NOTE** **Using JBuilder's Obfuscate is no guarantee that individuals will not be able to decompile the code that has been obfuscated. For better protection, use a commercial Obfuscator.**

The developer should understand that setting the debug options lower than the source, line, and variable can significantly reduce the ability to see what is going on during a debug session (more on this a little later in the chapter). It is also a reminder that, if either the Debug options or Obfuscator is adjusted, a Save All and a Rebuild must occur before any changes in the .class files will occur.

# Line Breakpoints

Now it is time to set a simple line breakpoint in the program. This can be accomplished in a number of ways:

- Place the cursor on the line where the breakpoint should be set, then click the F5 key.
- Right-mouse click on the line, and select the Toggle breakpoint menu item.
- Click once in the light gray area called the gutter along the left margin of the Content pane.

Keep in mind that other types of breakpoints exist in JBuilder; they are covered throughout the chapter. Set a breakpoint on the System.out.println ("Welcome to JBuilder Debugging!") line. Try all the ways listed previously to toggle the breakpoint. If you have not changed the underlying editor configuration, you should see the line become highlighted with a red hue, and a red circle should be located in the gutter. Simply repeating the set operation can toggle off the breakpoint; the same is true for turning it back on again.

By this point in the book, you have probably noticed that JBuilder can accomplish the same task or tasks in many ways. This is true for how to start a debugging session in JBuilder as well. First you must understand that JBuilder has the ability to debug a single file in a project, a whole project, or multiple projects. Once your breakpoint is set, you can start debugging the project by the following ways:

- Right-mouse click on the SimpleDebug.Java file in the Project pane, and select the Debug using defaults menu item.
- Define a Runtime configuration for debugging; remember to define the main class. For more information on creating a Runtime configuration, review Chapter 4, "Project Properties and Configurations."

Once a Runtime configuration has been defined, the following ways are possible to start a debug session:

- Click the Debug icon on the Main toolbar, or use the drop-down listbox to select the appropriate configuration.
- Click the Run | Debug Project menu item on the Main menu.
- Hold down and press the Shift-F9 keys to activate the debugger on the default debug configuration.

All these techniques will actually start a debugging session. You will notice that the Message pane area that is at the bottom of the screen is replaced with the look shown in Figure 5.5.

The debugging window is a very dynamic interface. The window helps to represent the concept of debug sessions and Debug views. The debug session, which the interface supports as a tab at the bottom of the pane, is shown in Figure 5.5. The concept of a session also extends itself to support multiprocess and distributed debugging in one consistent interface just with multiple tabs. Notice the options included on the Java command line of the debug session:

**-Xdebug.** Enables debugging support in the VM; it is a required parameter.

**-Xnoagent.** Disables support for the oldjdb communications; it is required on Classic VM.

**-Djava.compiler=None.** Disables the JIT compiler; it is a required parameter on Classic VM.

**-Xrunjdwp:transport=dt_socket,address=Yoda:4619,susupend=y.** Loads debug libraries, form of communication and address; it is a required parameter.

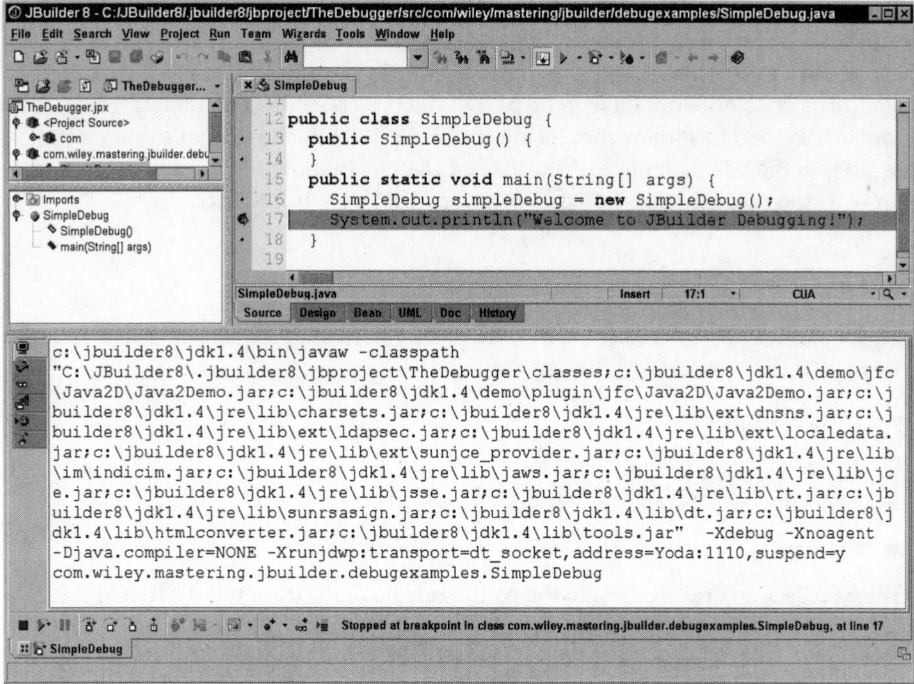


**Figure 5.5** Debugging session.

# Debug Toolbar

The toolbar icons in Figure 5.6 give you the power to take control of the debug session and are divided into five distinct groups.

## *Main Group*

Three buttons control the debugger:

- Stop debug session
- Resume debug session
- Pause debug session

The first group includes the red box that allows you to stop the execution and reset the program. The green arrow allows you to start another session or to continue a paused session. Because we mentioned a paused session, you can press the double vertical lines to do just that — pause the execution of a program. The following are the hot-keys associated with the main group:

**F9.** Allows the developer to start or resume a debug session.

**Ctrl-F12.** Allows the developer to stop or reset the program during a debug session.

These hot-keys will be used often when debugging large and complex threading programs. If a program seems to hang or if a breakpoint cannot be determined by pressing the Pause button or if the Pause button is pressed, the current executing is loaded. The class does not have to be part of the project and is most likely going to be a class that is located somewhere inside the classpath, which is usually some obscure class deep in the Java language. If the loaded class is unknown, clicking the Reset program will stop the debug session and return control back to JBuilder.

## Control Group

This group of four buttons controls how the debugger will move throughout the debug process:

- Toggle Smart Step
- Step Over
- Step Into
- Step Out

The next section of icons, called the control group, goes from the right in Figure 5.6. It includes the execution stepping tasks. The Toggle Smart Step is essential on large projects because it allows you to control what classes you are going to step into or skip during the debug process. This is covered in depth later in the chapter. The next icon is the Step Over task; it is the most common debug task because it simply executes the line it is on. Keep in mind that it does not matter if the line is calling a method or is just an assignment statement; the Step Over task will do just that — it will not trace into a method. The next icon is the Step Into task, which does allow you to Step Into a method. The hot-keys for the methods of the group are as follows:

**F8.** Allows a Step Over operation to occur.

**F7.** Allows a Step Into operation to occur.

Then finally is the Step Out icon, which allows you to revert to the calling method from which you step into. This is really handy, especially when you step into a method that is going to iterate 5 million times, walk through the iteration once, see the information you came to see, and then press the Step Out icon, and you are back to the method that called it.

## Code Modification Group

This group of two buttons is responsible for controlling modification to the code during a debug session:

- Smart Swap
- Set Execution Point

### Code Type Group

This one button allows for the defining of the source code to be viewed when debugging a mixed-language environment like Java and JSPs:

- Smart Source

Both the Code Modification and Code Type groups are covered in the next section of the chapter. These items all have to do with the ability for JDK 1.4.1 and above to modify code while in the debugging process without having to start, recompile, and re-debug; more on this follows later in this chapter.

### Information Group

This group of three buttons is about setting stops in the code, reviewing information, and going to the current active thread location.

- Add Breakpoints
- Add Watch
- Show Current Frame

The Information group is the final set of icons in the Debug session toolbar shown in Figure 5.6. Going from the right, it includes the Add Breakpoint icon, which has a drop-down button, and it allows you to set all the available breakpoints. The next icon is the Add Watch task, which allows you to name your watch and give it a complete description. This helps when you have a lot of watches, and with some of the coding standards today, you may need a description to figure out where you are. The last icon represents the Show Current Frame option; it simply means to take the developer to the currently running thread of execution, which is the current frame.

**TIP** **The fastest way to see all of the program variables and threads is to press the Show Current Frame icon.**

## Debug Views

The second concept presents Debug views; this is where the debugging window changes, depending on the view enabled by the right-side vertical icons, as defined in Figure 5.7.

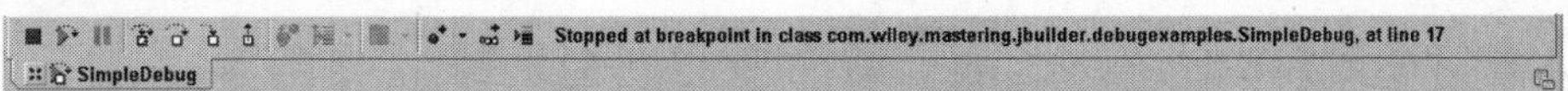


**Figure 5.6** Debug toolbar.

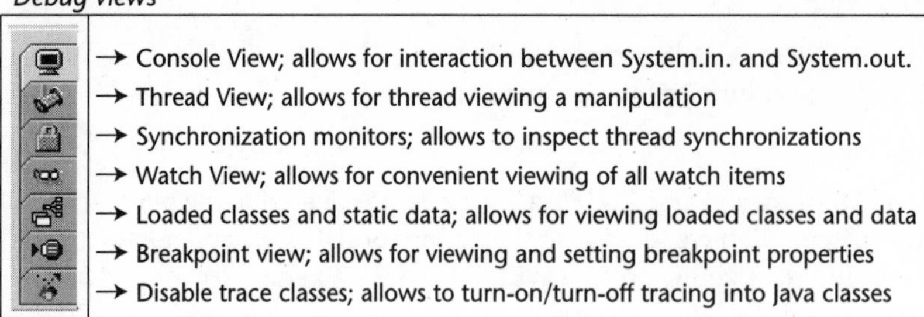

Debug views
→ Console View; allows for interaction between System.in. and System.out.
→ Thread View; allows for thread viewing a manipulation
→ Synchronization monitors; allows to inspect thread synchronizations
→ Watch View; allows for convenient viewing of all watch items
→ Loaded classes and static data; allows for viewing loaded classes and data
→ Breakpoint view; allows for viewing and setting breakpoint properties
→ Disable trace classes; allows to turn-on/turn-off tracing into Java classes


**Figure 5.7** Debug views.

The Debug views give in-depth information during a debugging session. In Figure 5.7, each icon represents a view that you can activate at any time by clicking on it. When the developer is running the first debug session, he or she will not notice the gold/yellow lock. The program is being debugged with the Hotspot compiler, and it does not provide the synchronization information back to the JDI. This is explained in detail later in this chapter.

During the first debugging session of the SimpleDebug.java program, there is not much to show because the program does not really do anything. It would be good to note that in Figure 5.8 the debugger starts in the Console view and prints out the Java command line.

**TIP** **The Java command line found in the Message pane or the Debug pane can be used on a command line or inside a command script.**

## Loaded Classes and Static Data View

This is one of the Debug views available; it shows all the classes that have been loaded in the current frame. Clicking on the Debug view tab for Loaded classes will show all the packages that have been loaded, and a tree expander is beside each package. This lets the developer drill down into each package to see exactly what classes have been loaded. Using this SimpleDebug program, you will notice that one available package is the com; it can be drilled into our class, and then our class can be expanded, which shows Object, thus giving an object hierarchy. It is also possible to set watches and copy values in this interface. If a data item is of interest, simply right-mouse click to display the Context menu for the options available on the particular objects.

## Current Frame

Now click on the Show Current Frame icon on the Debug toolbar. This will change the current view to show all available threads, but, more importantly, it will show the main thread and all object values for the current scope. Figure 5.8 shows exactly what is happening with the program.

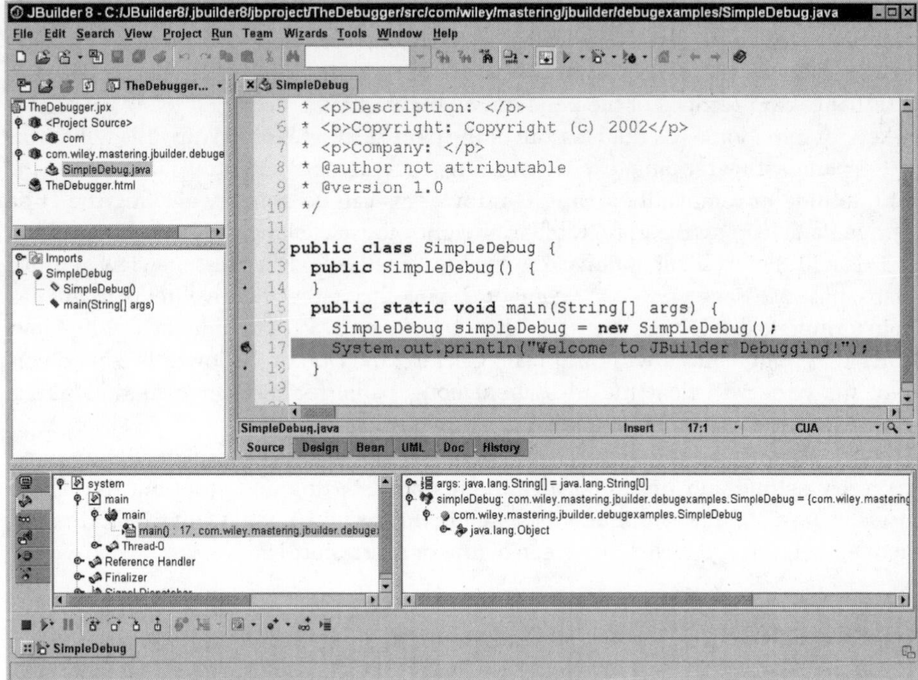


**Figure 5.8** Current frame.

If you review the program SimpleDebug.java, you will notice that it extends java. langObject (inherently defined by default), it has a static void main(String args) line, it creates itself, and finally it prints out a single line to the console.

If you look at the view provided by the thread icon, you will notice that it has a main thread, which is seen on the left. On the right, we notice that we have two items located inside the view: One item represents the args variable, which is a string array, and the other is the SimpleDebug object. If you click on the tree expander in view, it will disappear because it has no arguments. If you click the table extender on the SimpleDebug object, it will show you the actual class inside it, which has a tree expander. If you extend it, this will show you java.lang.Object, which is the base for all objects. Even with this simple program you can get a lot of information about how it is constructed and what is going on inside it.

The next thing to do is to continue execution of the program. This can be done by clicking the green arrow or by pressing the F9 key. Again, either way will cause the program to execute to the end — we have not set any other breakpoints, and the program needs no interaction from us, so it just finishes up. You will also notice that all of the Debug views disappear except for the Console view, which is displayed at the top of the Debug view. You will notice that because it completed, the System.out line has been executed and "Welcome to JBuilder!" is displayed.

**NOTE The Console view tab icon changes as messages are written to the console. Green means that messages have been written to the console, red means that errors/exceptions have been written to the console, and Black means that nothing is being written to the console.**

Inside the Debug or Message panes, a few options can be set. The first is Clear All, which will remove all text located inside the view. The Copy All option will copy everything inside the pane and put its contents onto the system clipboard (keep in mind that certain sections of the pane can be highlighted and copied using the Ctrl-C hot-key combination). The final feature of the pane is to set Word Wrap; this will reformat the pane with wrapping text. Other things to remember about the tabs include the ability to hide or remove the debug window. This can be done by clicking the Hide Message Pane icon on the Main toolbar or right-mouse clicking on the Debug session tab. This will show a set of options: remove Message view, clear Message view, remove all tabs, hide Message view, copy content. If you click either remove items it will ask you to terminate the debug process. In this case, we only want to hide the Debug view, so click that option and it will disappear. Clicking the icon in the lower left-hand corner of the pane will float the Message/Debug pane; for more information please review Chapter 2, "Customizing the App/Browser."

Congratulations! Your first successful debug session is now complete. Before moving on, try setting and unsetting breakpoints and starting and stopping the debug process using all of the techniques discussed in this section. If you want to start the session over, you can again click the green arrow or press Shift-F9.

## Understanding DebugShow

The next example should give you more confidence when it comes to understanding the interface that is included with JBuilder for debugging. After completing this example, developers should feel very comfortable about the debug interface. The program DebugShow was developed to show most of the basic features of the JBuilder debugger. This program was originally written with the first cut of Primetime, and it was used at JavaOne™ in 1999.

Using the TheDebugger project defined in the last example, a new class needs to be added. Clicking the File|New Class menu item can do this. In the New Class dialog, the package name should read:

package com.wiley.mastering.jbuilder.debugexamples

The Class name should be DebugShow, and the Generate main method option should have been set and that the base class is still Java.lang.Object. When this is completed, click the OK button. The wizard will generate the skeleton program in Source 5.1.

```
package com.wiley.mastering.jbuilder.debugexamples;

/**
 * <p>Title: Debug Examples</p>
 * <p>Description: This will be used for the Debugging Chapter</p>
 * <p>Copyright: Copyright (c) 2002</p>
 * <p>Company: </p>
 * @author Michael J. Rozlog
```

**Source 5.1** DebugShow.java.

```
 * @version 1.0
 */

import java.awt.*;

public class DebugShow {
  private String aName;
  private String aLastName;
  public int starter = 1;
  protected boolean maybe = false;
  public transient static int nonKeeper = 0;
  public volatile int reallybad = 0;
  public String[] array = new String[10];
  java.util.Vector vector = new java.util.Vector(10);

  public DebugShow() {
  }

  public static void main(String[] args) {
    int i;
    DebugShow debugShow1 = new DebugShow();
    for (i = 0;i < 10; i++){
     debugShow1.array[i] = "Mike " + i;
    }
    for (i = 0; i < 10; i++){
     debugShow1.vector.add(debugShow1.array);
    }
    debugShow1.setAName("Michael");

    System.out.println(debugShow1.getAName());
    debugShow1.setALastName("Rozlog");
    System.out.println(debugShow1.getALastName());
    debugShow1.starter = 1;
    debugShow1.maybe = true;
    System.out.println(debugShow1.toString());
    System.out.println("Thomas");
    try {
     System.out.println("Please hit return, to Exit program");
     System.in.read();
    } catch (Exception e){
     System.err.println(e.toString());
    }
    System.out.println("Program Finished");
    System.exit(0);
  }

  public void setAName(String newAName) {
    aName = newAName;
```

**Source 5.1** *(continued)*

```
    nonKeeper++;
    System.out.println("Nonkeeper is " + nonKeeper);

  }

  public String getAName() {
    return aName;
  }

  public void setALastName(String newALastName) {
    aLastName = newALastName;
  }

  public String getALastName() {
    return aLastName;
  }
}
```

**Source 5.1** *(continued)*

Using the code defined in Source 5.1, modify the skeleton program that was generated to look like it for the following example. Once these modifications have been completed, take a look at the code, and notice that the instance variable section at the top of the code defines a couple of different types of variables and objects. Some of these objects are static or transient, an array and a vector have been defined, and a couple of properties have been created. For more information on properties, review Chapter 8, "Modifying Classes." The first time through this program, set the breakpoint on the first statement of the main method (line 27 if line numbers are being used), which is represented by the following statement:

```
int i;
```

Right-mouse click on the DebugShow.java file located in the Project pane and proceed with the debug. Notice that the program does not stop and that in the Debug pane the program is asking Press Return to Exit the program. Looking at the Debug pane, notice that the line that had the breakpoint set is now green and that the red circle in the gutter area has an "x" through it. Line breakpoints can be set only on executing lines of code, meaning the comments and declarations will not stop the debugger— because the line above is a declaration, it is marked as an invalid line. The debugger uses this visual queue: Each valid line that could have a breakpoint set has a blue dot in the gray gutter on the left-hand side of the Content pane. Clicking once in the Debug pane and pressing the Return key will cause the program to print the final message and return control to the editor.

The second time through the program, set a line breakpoint on the next line:

```
DebugShow debugShow1 = new DebugShow();
```

Restart the debugger on the DebugShow.java file; this time the debugger will stop. Then click the Show Current Frame icon on the Debug pane toolbar. Notice in the Data view (the left side) at this time that the only thing defined is the args variable found inside the main method. Stepping over the line using the F8 key will cause the current frame to change. The execution point should be on the next line, and DebugShow1 should be under the args Data view. Expanding the table expander will show all the fields defined during the creation of the DebugShow1 object. At this time, reset the execution of the program by hitting the Ctrl-F12 key combination.

This time restart the debugger on the DebugShow.Java file, instead of stepping over the object creation, Step Into the statement. This can be accomplished by pressing the F7 key; the first time the key is pressed, notice that the execution of the program goes to the default constructor. Also notice that the Data view is now showing only 'this'; when the 'this' is expanded, it represents the items available to the 'this' object when programming. It is also important to realize that even though the debugger is displaying all the instance variables, they are not yet assigned. The debug info included in the .class file has the variable table included. Hitting F7 again will move the execution point to the first int called starter, and hitting the F7 again will assign the int associated with starter to a number 1. Hitting the F7 key again will set the maybe variable to 'false,' and this will be displayed in the Data view. Now, right-mouse click in the Data view on the maybe variable, and select the Change value menu item (see Figure 5.9).

When the Change Value dialog is displayed, it gives a good amount of information. First, it gives the type of expression being viewed; in this case it is of type Boolean. It also gives its current value, which is currently set to 'false'. Change the value to 'true' without the single quotes. When changing the value, the print inside the edit area will not be bold, but once the value is a valid type such as 'true', the font will become bold. The Change Value dialog works with almost any type; however, it follows the same rules as the type defines. Once complete, press the OK button to continue. An example of this would be a variable that was represented by type char, whose value would have to include the single quotes around it like 'C'. If the variable was of type String, it would need double quotes surrounding it, like "Hello World".

**WARNING** **Trying to change a value inside the Change Value dialog can be very frustrating if you forget to use the Java language code rules for values. For example, string values must be in double quotes " ", and characters must be in single-quotes ' '. If a value is entered into the dialog that does not adhere to the proper syntax, JBuilder will not accept the value.**

The value for the maybe variable should not be changed to 'true' and the execution point is now setting on the reallybad variable. It appears that the line above reallybad was skipped, or so it seems — it was created when the object was created because it is a static variable, and statics are the first to be created when an object is created. This can be viewed by expanding the item under the 'this' object for DebugShow; notice that nonKeeper is on the same level as the java.lang.Object item. Pressing the F7 key three more times will finish the assignment statements and return the execution point to the closing bracket of the default constructor.

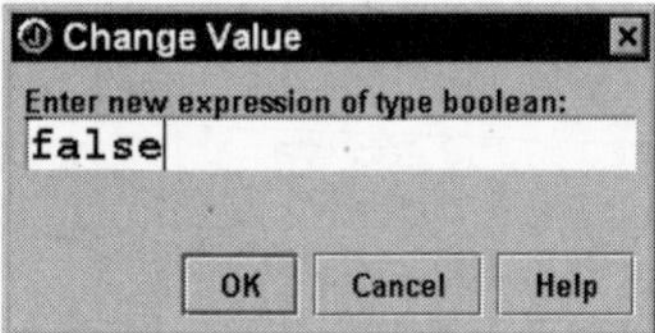


**Figure 5.9** Change Value dialog.

Figure 5.10 shows all the things that have been discussed; it also shows the execution point as the closing bracket of the default constructor. Anytime during a debugging session the execution point becomes unknown, using the Run | Show Execution Point menu item will do the trick. A blinking cursor should be in the first column of the line where the program is stopped. Hitting the F7 key again will then return the execution point to where this whole exercise started on the DebugShow creation line. F7 must be pressed again to move to the next statement because the debugger has stepped through the underlying methods. After following these steps, the result is the same as the second time debugging the program with the execution ready to start the for-loop (more on that follows later in the chapter). Pressing Ctrl-F12 will reset the program to be debugged again.

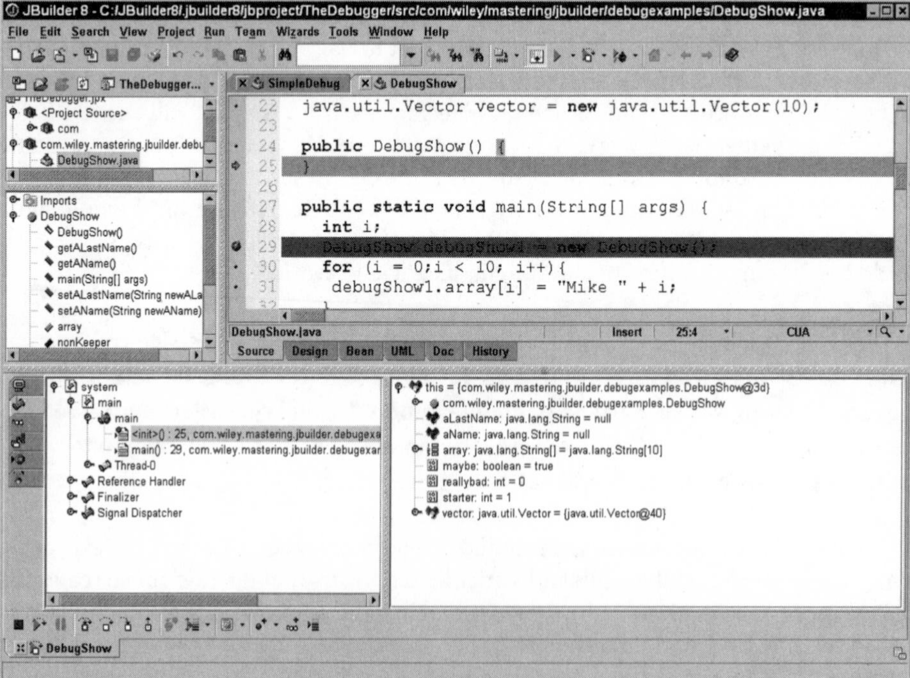


**Figure 5.10** Debugging using the Step Into method.

It is possible for the debugger to either eliminate or add classes to debug into; this can be accomplished by clicking the Run | View Classes with Tracing Disabled menu item or the Classes with Tracing disabled tab.

In Figure 5.11 the java.* line is selected, and the option to Step into Class/Package has been enabled. Once this is complete, restart the debugging process as before on the DebugShow.Java file. This time, pressing F7 twice will load an additional file Object; this example shows a greater depth than the prior example of how objects are created and the steps that need to be performed to get work done. Hitting F7 again will exit from the Object class and put the execution point back to the int starter line; press the F8 key until the execution point is located on the Vector line.

```
java.util.Vector vector = new java.util.Vector(10);
```

The next couple steps will outline the process of creating a simple Vector with an initial size of 10. These steps will highlight just how many things have to occur to complete this process. Hit the F7 key the first time, and notice that the ClassLoader class is loaded. Hit the F8 key to step over the current line; this will take the execution to the security method for the objects being created. Then hit the Step Out icon on the debug session toolbar, which is the seventh icon from the left. This can also be accomplished by clicking the Run | Stop Out menu item. This will return the execution point back to the DebugShow's Vector line. At this time, the Smart Step option should be turned on to eliminate extra stepping in classes that most likely does not need to occur. The additional stepping that can be eliminated includes Constructors and Symbolic methods, and the Smart Step will remain on until it is clicked again or the debug session is completed. The only way to turn the Smart Stepping on or off is to click the fourth icon from the left on the Debug session toolbar, then hold the mouse pointer over the icon to display its current status. Now hit F7 again; this time the Vector class is finally loaded, and at this point the developer can either continue stepping through the code or again press the Step Out icon to return to the Vector line in DebugShow. The Step Out icon allows the developer to finish the execution of the current process and return the execution point back to the calling process. Hitting F7 once more will actually step past the Vector creation line, and the execution point should now be at the end of the default constructor. Hitting the Ctrl-F12 key combination will reset the program to be debugged again.

The first thing to reset is the Class/Package Trace settings. Using the same technique described previously, deselect the Step into Class/Package on the java.* line, as shown in Figure 5.11. This will eliminate going into objects like ClassLoader, Object, and Vector, have a lot of step in the debugging process, and allow for the focus to be on the code created by the developer.

Leaving the breakpoint in the same location as the previous examples, start the debugging process on the DebugShow.java file. Once the execution has been stopped on the DebugShow line, set the cursor to the second start of the second for-loop, then click the Run | Run to Cursor menu item. This will continue the execution past the first for-loop process. Now press the View Current Frame icon on the Debug session toolbar. Because the first for-loop focused on filling the array, look at the array in the Data view portion of the debug window.

**Figure 5.11** Classes with Tracing Disabled dialog.

Expand the array; it will show values of "Mike 0" through "Mike 9", each with its own expansion icon. In the Data view, all data items can have their values changed. Using the same technique as before, right-mouse click on the "Mike 3" array item, and select the Change Value menu item. This will display a dialog like the one shown in Figure 5.9. Following the rules for a String, make it look like "Mike 99" and then press the OK button to continue. The value will now be set to the changed value. The next process to highlight is the ability to copy and paste inside an array or vector. Select the "Mike 0" array item, then right-mouse click and select the Copy menu item. Then click on the "Mike 9" array item, and again right-mouse click and click the Paste menu item. This operation should have copied the value so that both the first and the last array locations show "Mike 0" for values.

**WARNING Remember to be very careful when using the Cut, Copy, and Paste features; changing values and locations can be very problematic.**

It is also possible at this time to Create Array Component Watch simply by selecting one of the array items and right-mouse clicking the item and selecting that menu item. When creating watches of any type, JBuilder will always ask for a name in a popup dialog.

A meaningful name to use for this type of watch would be something like Array X, with X as the value selected to watch. Once a watch has been named and OK has been pressed, it will be added to the watch list. This list can be viewed anytime by changing the Debug view by clicking the appropriate tab along the left side of the screen. Refer to Figure 5.7 for details on what each tab represents. For this example, the tab with the Glasses icon should be chosen. From the Watch view, any listed watches can be changed following the same procedures as outlined here. Returning to the Data view is as easy as clicking the Show Current Frame icon again.

## Advanced Breakpoints

One of the really nice features of breakpoints is the ability to set them on properties. Looking at Figure 5.10, notice that two variables are listed, aLastName and aName, and both have black icons beside them, which represent properties. Setting a breakpoint on the aName property is very simple. Select the item in the Data view, then right-mouse click and select the Create field watch menu item. Now the JBuilder debugger gives finer control over the breakpoint than just setting it on the property. Change to the Breakpoint view by clicking the Breakpoint tab along the left-hand side of the Debug pane; this will show a list of all set breakpoints. Use Figure 5.7 for a reference on tab functionality.

Once in the Breakpoint view, the property breakpoint can be selected. Then right-mouse clicking on the item will display the Context menu. Notice that in Figure 5.12 the ability to set the Break on Read or Break on Write option is available. For this example, remove the check beside the Break on Read because the program should stop when the properties setter is being called. For more information on properties, review Chapter 8.

At this point, setting additional breakpoints of different types can be accomplished. First, notice in Figure 5.12 that two additional breakpoints have been defined. The first is always defined, which is to stop on all uncaught exceptions; the second one is the breakpoint that was set at the beginning of the examples showing DebugShow. The next breakpoint to define is the Method breakpoint; this can be accomplished by clicking the Add Breakpoint icon on the Debug session toolbar. It is the eleventh icon from the left and has a drop-down selection associated with it. Select the Add Method Breakpoint menu item.

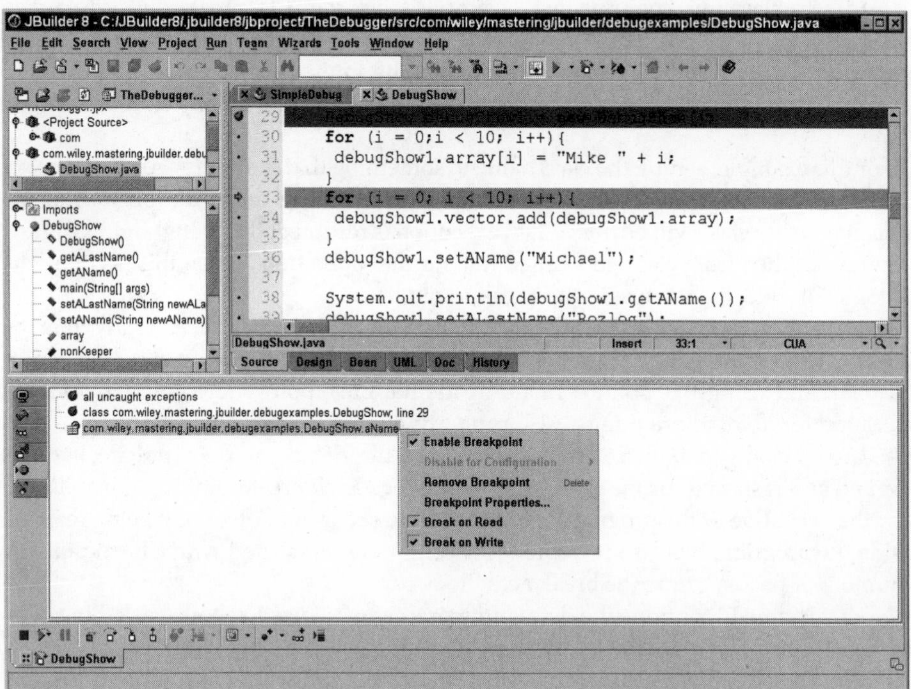


**Figure 5.12** Breakpoint viewer.

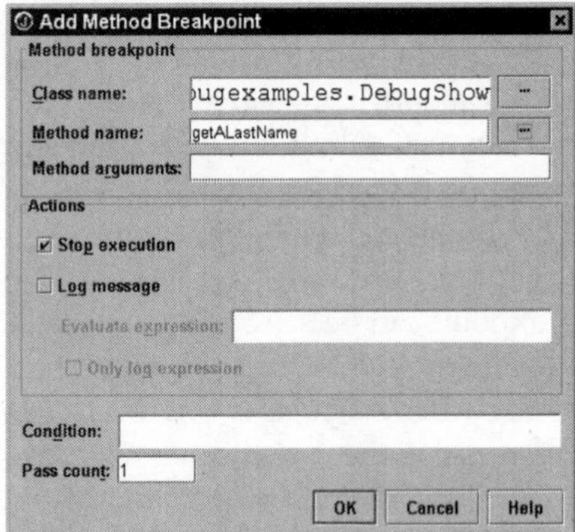


**Figure 5.13** Add Method Breakpoint dialog.

In Figure 5.13, the dialog needs some information to be completed. The first piece of needed information is the Class name, which in this case should be the DebugShow class, which can be found using the ... button and the class finder interface. Once the class has been defined, clicking the ... button on the Method name will display all available methods for that class. If any arguments are needed for the method, they must be defined or JBuilder will ignore the entry. Once these have been completed, clicking the OK button to continue will return you to the Breakpoint view.

Adding a class breakpoint is just as simple. Click the Add Breakpoint icon again, and click the Add Class Breakpoint menu item, using Figure 5.13 for reference. The only difference between breakpoint dialogs is the limited information they need to break on. For method, it needs class, method, and parameters; for object, it needs class name.

For this example, setting the class name to something that normally would not be set will highlight the power of this type of breakpoint. Using the ... button to find the java.lang.String class will be fine; when execution is resumed, it will highlight just how many times the String class gets called in a normal operation. When this is complete, click the OK button to return to the Breakpoint view.

Pay attention to a couple things about the Breakpoint view interface. At any time the developer has complete control over the breakpoints defined, they can be deleted or disabled, and using the Context menu inside the Breakpoint view will allow global operation for doing those things. Also property, class, and method breakpoint properties can be changed midstream, meaning that the debugger does not need to be stopped and restarted for the changes to take effect. Each breakpoint has the ability to stop the execution of the program or just to log the occurrence of a point being reached inside the program. It is also possible to set conditions associated with a breakpoint or a number of passes before the break actually occurs.

Now it is time to continue the debugging process we started a while back. First click the Show Current Frame icon to return to the Data view, then click the Resume icon on the Debug session toolbar, the second icon from the left. The first thing that should be apparent is that the String class gets loaded and is hit right away; using the Resume button many times will return you to the String class. As stated previously, normally that would be a bad example of setting a breakpoint on a class. Click on the Breakpoint view tab, then select the Class breakpoint and right-mouse click and remove the breakpoint. Then return to the View Current Frame tab and press the Resume icon. Each time one of the breakpoint values is achieved, the program will stop execution; at that time you can use the data, breakpoint, and classes with Tracing Disabled views to interact with the program. Try to set property breakpoints on the readers, writers, or both. Also, try setting counts inside the breakpoints properties, working with the cut, copy, and paste features with different types of objects to see how the debugger acts. All these things are possible using DebugShow as a test bed for debugging.

# Intermediate Debugging

Learning and understanding the JBuilder debugger can be difficult at first. There are so many places to get and interact with information that some developers feel that too much information is given at the same time. The DebugShow program is a great starter program; many things could be added to the program to test different aspects of the debugger. The preceding examples should have given you an overview of the debugger's interface and the information that is being returned from JVM to the developer. Now the focus can change from the "what" to the "how," focusing on debug session modifications and multiprocess debugging.

## Modifying Code in a Debug Session

The next area to cover is a new feature available in Java that lets the developer change the code while in a debug session. JBuilder has exposed its functionality by adding Smart Swap, Set Execution Point, and Smart Source toolbar icons and menu items. These features are available only on JDK 1.4.1 and higher because of the additional information being stored in the class files that are generated by the compiler.

This example will use the DebugShow from the prior section; however, the type of Target VM needs to be changed in the project properties. Right-mouse click on the TheDebugger.jpx node inside the Project pane and click the Project Properties menu item to display its dialog. Click on the Build tab. Change the Target VM to the Java 2 SDK v 1.4 and later option, then click the OK button to continue. Next, save the project; then perform a Clean operation by again right-mouse clicking on the TheDebugger.jpx node and selecting Clean. This will remove all generated classes from prior builds and then rebuild the project.

Remove all breakpoints by using the Run | View Breakpoints menu item, then right-mouse click inside the dialog and click the Remove All menu item. Only the exception breakpoint should be left. Click the Close button to return to the AppBrowser. Now, set a breakpoint on the `aLastName = newALastName;` line inside the setALastName method, and then start the debugger on the DebugShow.java file. Once the breakpoint is hit, add the following code under the assignment statement:

```
nonKeeper++;
System.out.println("A Last name Nonkeeper is " + nonKeeper);
```

Changing any of the files associated with a debug session, the Smart Swap option activates Set Execution Point. If no changes have been made to the debug properties associated with a Runtime configuration, clicking the Smart Swap icon, eighth from the left on the Debug session toolbar, will compile and update the modified classes in the session. Once this has been completed, most likely the execution point will need to be reset. Clicking on the ninth icon from the left on the Debug session toolbar will display a list of possible execution points. For this example set it to line associated by calling the setALastName method.

Notice in the Data view that the stack becomes invalid; this will be true until the first step is taken after the compile is completed. During this time, using the fly over evaluation or the Evaluate/Modify will return unknown results. Use the F8 key to sStep oOver the `System.out.println(debugShow1.getALastName());` method to update the stack with the appropriate information. Now, use the Evaluate/Modify dialog (see Figure 5.14) to change the value of the method just completed. Either right-mouse click on the variable in the Code view and click the Evaluate/Modify menu item, or use the Run | Evaluate/Modify menu item and type in the needed information.

Using Figure 5.14 as a guide, add the expression debugShow1.setALastName("geoff"), then click the Evaluate button. This will call that method midstream, and the results will be void because the method does not return a value. These evaluations and modification are not done inside a sandbox — these are live changes. This means that the variable nonKeeper has been incremented by 1 and that the output is sent to the console; this work can be checked in the Console view. One really great feature of the Evaluate/Modify dialog is that CodeInsight is fully implemented in the edit box, which means that pressing the Ctrl-H key combination will display the available objects just as with the editor operations. Now change the edit box to read debugShow1.nonKeeper, and hit the Evaluate button again. This will return some value. Now, in the New Value edit box, make it read 99, and hit the Modify button; the Result pane will reflect the changes. It is now possible to use the drop-down choice control and reselect the debugShow1.setALastName("geoff") method and hit the Evaluate button. The console will be updated with another "geoff" and the value of 100.

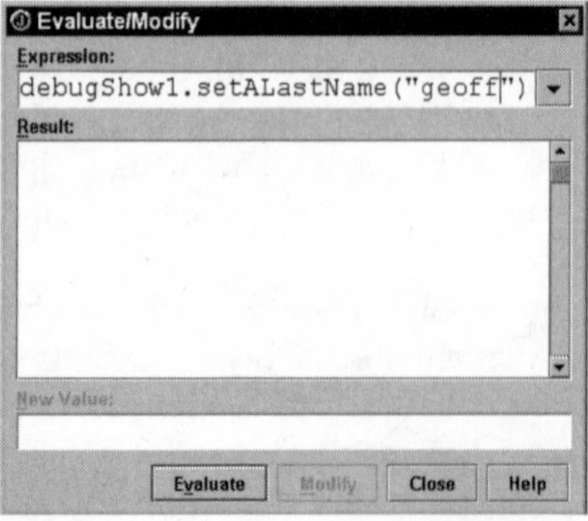


**Figure 5.14** Evaluate/Modify dialog.

## Multiprocess Debugging

From the beginning, JBuilder has had a strong multiprocess debugging solution. In the later versions of JBuilder, Borland and the JDK have made several changes to enhance the ability to debug these types of programs. The following programs will define a server and client based on socket communications to highlight the abilities of JBuilder. The server program is called Dserver; it is responsible for returning information to a client. Both of the programs have additional println() methods to give extra information back to the developer. This ensures that the developer understands which process is responsible for which output.

Using the TheDebugger project used in all the examples in this chapter, add two new classes to the project following the steps in the previous examples. The first class should be located in the same package as all the other programs and should have the name DServer.

```
package com.wiley.mastering.jbuilder.debugexamples;

import java.io.*;
import java.net.*;
import java.util.*;
import java.text.DateFormat;

/**
 * <p>Title: </p>
 * <p>Description: </p>
 * <p>Copyright: Copyright (c) 2002</p>
 * <p>Company: </p>
 * @author not attributable
 * @version 1.0
 */

public class DServer {

  ServerSocket serverSocket = null;
  Socket socket = null;
  InputStreamReader inputStreamReader = null;
  BufferedReader bufferedReader = null;
  OutputStreamWriter outputStreamWriter = null;
  BufferedWriter bufferedWriter = null;

  public DServer() {
  }

  public static void main(String[] args) {
    DServer DServer1 = new DServer();
```

**Source 5.2** DServer code. *(continued)*

```
    System.out.println("Getting Connection");
    DServer1.getConnection();
    System.out.println("Connection established");
    System.out.println("Reading Request");
    DServer1.getRequest();
    DServer1.doClose();
    System.out.println("ServerSocket Closed.");

  }

  public void getConnection(){
    try {
      serverSocket = new ServerSocket(10001);
      socket = serverSocket.accept();
    } catch (IOException ex) {
      ex.printStackTrace();
    }
  }

  public void getRequest(){
    String closeString = "";
    try {
      inputStreamReader = new
InputStreamReader(socket.getInputStream());
      bufferedReader = new BufferedReader(inputStreamReader);

      outputStreamWriter = new
OutputStreamWriter(socket.getOutputStream());
      bufferedWriter = new BufferedWriter(outputStreamWriter);

      while (!closeString.equals("Close")) {
        closeString = bufferedReader.readLine();
        Date checkdate = new Date();
        Calendar calendar = new GregorianCalendar();
        calendar.setTime(checkdate);
        //Ctrl-alt-space to bring up class insight
        DateFormat dateFormat =
DateFormat.getDateTimeInstance(DateFormat.FULL, DateFormat.SHORT);

        if (closeString.equals("Date")) {
          bufferedWriter.write(dateFormat.format(checkdate));
          System.out.println("Date was sent");
        }

        if (closeString.equals("Time")) {
          bufferedWriter.write("Current Time: " +
calendar.get(Calendar.HOUR) +
                            ":" + calendar.get(Calendar.MINUTE) + " " +
```

**Source 5.2** *(continued)*

```
                              calendar.get(Calendar.AM_PM));
          System.out.println("Time was sent");
        }

        bufferedWriter.newLine();
        bufferedWriter.flush();
      }
    } catch (IOException ex) {
      ex.printStackTrace();
    }
  }

  public void doClose(){
    try {
      socket.close();
    } catch (IOException ex) {
      ex.printStackTrace();
    }
  }
}
```

**Source 5.2** *(continued)*

The client program, called DClient, is responsible for making the connection to the socket on the server and then requesting information from the server. The second class to be added should also have the same package and have the class name DClient.

```
package com.wiley.mastering.jbuilder.debugexamples;

import java.io.*;
import java.net.*;
import java.text.*;

/**
 * <p>Title: </p>
 * <p>Description: </p>
 * <p>Copyright: Copyright (c) 2002</p>
 * <p>Company: </p>
 * @author not attributable
 * @version 1.0
 */

public class DClient {
  InetAddress inetAddress = null;
  Socket socket = null;
  InputStreamReader inputStreamReader = null;
  BufferedReader bufferedReader = null;
```

**Source 5.3** DClient code. *(continued)*

```
  OutputStreamWriter outputStreamWriter = null;
  BufferedWriter bufferedWriter = null;

  public DClient() {
  }

  public static void main(String[] args) {
    DClient DClient1 = new DClient();
    System.out.println("Get Connection");
    DClient1.getClientConnection();
    DClient1.serverInteraction();
    DClient1.doClose();
    System.out.println("Client socket is closed");
  }

  public void getClientConnection(){
    try {
      inetAddress = InetAddress.getByName("127.0.0.1");
      socket = new Socket(inetAddress, 10001);
    } catch (IOException ex) {
      ex.printStackTrace();
    }

  }

  public void serverInteraction(){
    String commandString = "";
    try {
      inputStreamReader = new
InputStreamReader(socket.getInputStream());
      bufferedReader = new BufferedReader(inputStreamReader);

      outputStreamWriter = new
OutputStreamWriter(socket.getOutputStream());
      bufferedWriter = new BufferedWriter(outputStreamWriter);

      BufferedReader screenReader = new BufferedReader(new
InputStreamReader(System.in));

      System.out.println("Input: Date, Time, end as commands");
      while (!commandString.equals("end")) {
        commandString = screenReader.readLine();
        System.out.println("command accepted");
        bufferedWriter.write(commandString);
        bufferedWriter.newLine();
        bufferedWriter.flush();
        System.out.println(bufferedReader.readLine());
      }
      bufferedWriter.write("Close");
```

**Source 5.3** *(continued)*

```
            bufferedWriter.newLine();
            bufferedWriter.flush();
        } catch (IOException ex) {
            ex.printStackTrace();
        }


    }

    public void doClose(){
        try {
            socket.close();
        } catch (IOException ex) {
            ex.printStackTrace();
        }
    }
}
```

**Source 5.3** *(continued)*

The older style of multiprocess debugging had the developer setting breakpoints in both the client and the server. This could become troublesome, especially if remote debugging was being used. This example, though, is on the same machine. Remote debugging is discussed in the section on advanced debugging later in this chapter. For this example, both the client and the server are located on the same machine.

In the DServer program, set a breakpoint in two places, the first `System.out.println("Date was sent");` line located inside the getRequest method and the second breakpoint in the doClose method on the `socket.close();` line.

In the DClient program, set a breakpoint in two places as well, the first on the line `bufferedWriter.flush();` inside the serverInteraction method and the second breakpoint in the doClose method on the `socket.close();` line.

Now start the debugger on the DServer node, using the technique discussed in the previous examples. The console window should display Getting connection. Then start the debugger on the DClient node the same way; it should display a command list. Click inside the Debug pane, type Date, and press the Return key. The console should update with a response stating that the command was accepted, and the debugger should stop the execution on the flush() line. Hitting the Resume icon on the Debug session toolbar should change the focus to DServer. The execution at this point should have stopped again and should be waiting for the next debug process. Because this is his or her first time into the DServer program, a developer may need quick information on what the data values are, so the debugger makes it incredibly easy to check variables by just using the keyboard and mouse over the code.

When a program is in suspend mode, moving the cursor over objects, variables, and expressions can return valuable information to the developer. In Figure 5.15, the mouse pointer was placed over the closeString in the if-statement; after a second the value will be displayed in the tool tip area. This value will remain on screen until the mouse is moved. The second feature is the ExpressionInsight technology; Ctrl-right-mouse clicking on an Object or Variable can activate the Context Data view. This view works exactly like the Data view inside the Debug/Message pane; the only difference is that it shows the item only in context. The Context view will disappear as soon as a mouse-click occurs outside the Context view.

From this point, when the Resume key is hit on the DServer program, the debug context does not change back to the DClient because DClient is waiting for a command to be entered. If the DServer continued executing and went to the DClient and hit a breakpoint, then the context would have been changed. On the DClient program, notice that the Date has been returned to the program and placed on the Systeml.out stream. Click inside the Debug/Message pane, and type the "end" command. Hitting Return again will take the execution to the flush method. Hit the Resume key again, and the execution will now go to the DClient's doClose method because no breakpoint was hit on the DServer. Hitting the Resume key will end the DClient program; however, the DServer program does not. The control was sent back to the client for execution, putting the DServer into a pseudo-suspend mode. Clicking on the DServer tab in the debug session and looking at the Stop and Resume icons on the Debug toolbar will not give any indication of whether the program is paused or running. The only visible indication the developer has is to look at the other Debug toolbar icons and notice whether they are still active. At this point, hitting the Resume toolbar icon will finish the program.

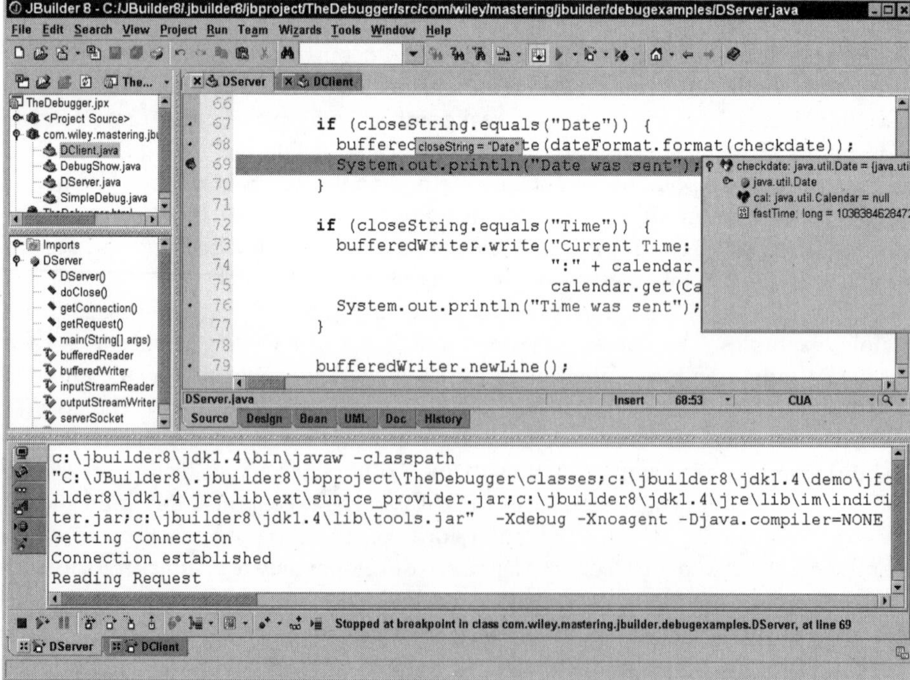


**Figure 5.15** Tooltip and ExpressionInsight.

The newer multiprocess debugging method uses cross-process breakpoints; these are discussed in the next section. Using the older style of multiprocess debugging has a few areas that can put a snag into the process; however, it gives the greatest amount of control over when and where a program should break. The cross-process breakpoints allow only for breaking on a method of a specific class, not a specific line or line number.

# Advanced Debugging

In the prior examples, different aspects of debugging have been covered. Today most developers feel that programs dealing with threads and distributed processes are advanced areas of debugging. The first program is going to deal with a deadlock situation that occurs when two threads are blocking each other and will show how the debugger's synchronization monitor can deal with it. The second set of examples will explore remote debugging using JBuilder.

Using the same project that has been used throughout the chapter, add a New Class to the project in the same package as used before and call it DeadLock. This program does a classic blocking code routine; it will become a deadlock situation with thread 1 and thread 2 blocking each other.

```
package com.wiley.mastering.jbuilder.debugexamples;

/**
 * <p>Title: Debug Examples</p>
 * <p>Description: This will be used for the Debugging Chapter</p>
 * <p>Copyright: Copyright (c) 2002</p>
 * <p>Company: </p>
 * @author Michael J. Rozlog
 * @version 1.0
 */

public class DeadLock {
  public static void main(String args[]) {
    final String one = "One";
    final String two = "Two";
    final String three = "Three";
    synchronized (three) {
      synchronized (one) {
        new Thread() {
          public void run() {
            synchronized(two) {
              synchronized(one) {
                System.out.println("Got one!");
              }
```

```
                }
              }
            }.start();
            try {
              Thread.sleep(500);
            }
            catch (Exception ex) {
            }
            synchronized (two) {
              System.out.println("Got two!");
            }
          }
        }
      }
    }
```

Trying to debug this program using JDK 1.4.x and above will be challenging because the default debugger included with that JDK uses the HotSpot JIT compiler. The synchronization information is lost when using the JIT compiler. Normally you would be able to set a switch that would put the Java VM back into interpreted mode; however, in the current JVM edition from Sun, it does not include this feature. This means that, for this example, the target JDK is going to have to be switched from JDK 1.4.1 to JDK 1.3.1.

You must have JDK 1.2.x or 1.3.x to see the synchronization monitors. For information on how to load a new JDK, review Chapter 3, "Controlling Java Configurations." Once a compatible JDK has been configured, continue with the example. The changes needed are easy to make; right-mouse click on the TheDebugger.jpx, click on the Properties menu item, click on the Paths tab, select JDK 1.2 or JDK 1.3, and then click on the Build tab. Here change the Target VM to Java 2 SDK v 1.2 or later, then hit the OK button to continue. It is a good practice that anytime the JDK is switched, debug information level is changed, obfuscation settings are changed, or any operation that would change the byte-code to save all on the source files. Then a Clean operation should also occur to remove all generated and compiled code. Finally rebuild the project after these steps. Make sure that the classic switch is set on the Runtime configuration or the option is selected in the JDK configuration. Both subjects are covered in their entirety in Chapters 3 and 4.

Start the debugger on the DeadLock node. When the program starts, notice that nothing happens because a thread deadlock has already occurred. Hit the Pause icon on the Debug session toolbar to stop the program so that the developer can see what is going on.

In Figure 5.16, clicking on the Thread Synchronization monitor that is the Lock View tab shows two threads that are blocked. Red denotes that, at this point, the developer understands that he or she has a deadlock situation and can go back to the code and make the appropriate changes to rectify the problem.

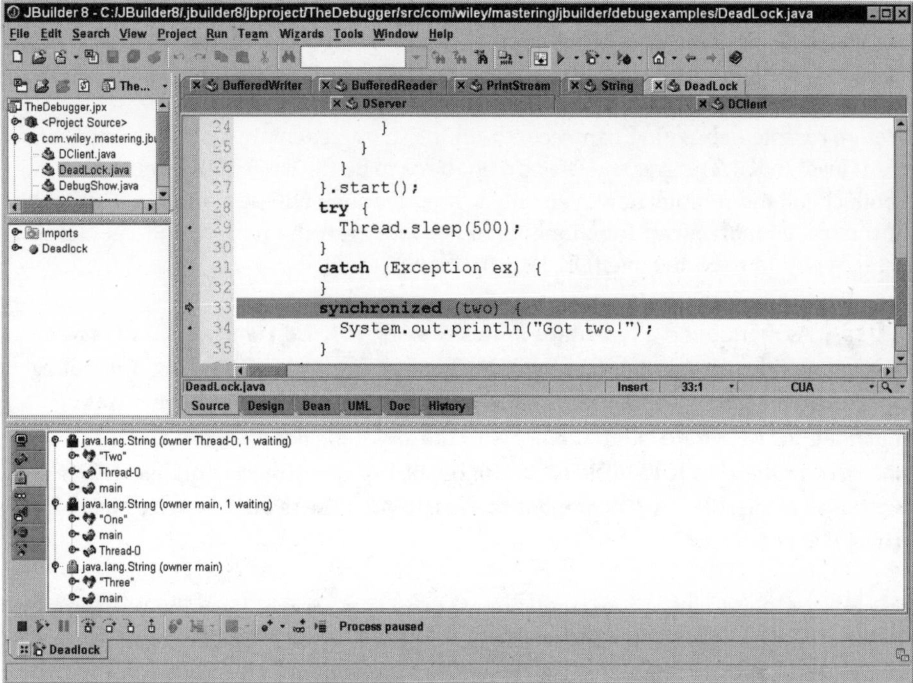


**Figure 5.16** Thread Synchronization monitor.

# Remote Debugging

Remote debugging is not much different from regular debugging. The debugging interface used in Java uses JPDA and communicates using either socket or shared memory, so the only real difference is the fact that one process is on another machine. Basically all features available in the regular local debugger are available to you in a remote debugging situation, including JDK 1.4.1's ability to do Smart Swapping.

The one option that might cause confusion is the `-Xrunjdwp:` option. It has a number of options that can be set depending on the desired effect. The most confusing option is the `dt_shmem`, which is available only on the Windows operating system. This transport uses the shared memory primitives to communicate from the VM to the debugger; this can be used only when both the debug application and the VM are on the same machine.

**WARNING** **Remote Smart Swap inside the EJB container would have to be supported by the container. Depending on how the class is replaced in the JVM, the registered class loader that is responsible for loading the class may or may not be aware that the class it loaded has been swapped out. The deployed .jar file will most likely not be affected at all because this is strictly an IDE-to-JVM communication channel, which means that the JVM knows about only the classes loaded, not the compiled class in the EJB archive. Certain application server providers could offer an enhanced communication layer to handle this.**

Remote debugging offers a few choices on just how the debugging should occur. They include launching and debugging on a remote machine, debugging an existing process on a remote machine, and debugging local code in a separate process. The additional breakpoint option is the cross-process breakpoint.

Before remote debugging can occur, both the debug client and debug remote must have at least JDK 1.2 or greater. They do not have to be the same JDK version numbers on both client and remote; however, only shared features will be available. This means that if remote Smart Swap functionality is needed, both the remote and client debug machines would need to have JDK 1.4.1 or above.

**NOTE As mentioned a few times in this chapter, JDK 1.4.1 and above change a few capabilities and switch requirements when it comes to debugging. The debug switches Xnoagent and –Djava.compiler=NONE are obsolete. –Xnoagent was intended for backward compatibility with the sun.tools.debug agent and was included in the classic VM JDK 1.2 through JDK 1.4. The –Djava.compiler=NONE was used to disable the JIT compiler on classic VMs. These switches are needed if using JDKs under 1.4.**

No matter how you use remote debugging, make sure that both the server classes and the client debugger source files are the same. Inconsistencies between .class files and their sources can have unpredictable results when debugging remotely.

Concentrating on only the client debugger, it must have the source files loaded into a project. The project then needs to have a Runtime configuration created for handling the debugging request, no matter if the debug style is to launch a process or to attach to an existing process. For more information on creating Runtime configurations, review Chapter 4. Loading the TheDebugger.jpx example project from this chapter will give us all the files we need. As stated earlier in the chapter, remote debugging is not much different from local debugging; for these examples, if you do not have two machines to work with, they can be done on a single machine.

In TheDebugger project, look at the project properties by right-mouse clicking on TheDebugger.jpx and selecting the Properties menu item. Then click on the Paths tab to make sure the JDK is set to 1.4.x or greater. Then click on the Build tab and verify that the Target VM is set accordingly; these two settings normally should match. Now click on the Run tab, and click the New button to display the Runtime Configuration Properties dialog (see Figure 5.17). Then click on the internal Debug tab.

The first setting that you want to concentrate on is the Build target; this should be set to None because the actual .class code in a normal remote debugging situation is on a remote machine and there is no need to waste a compile execution. The next set of options deals with the Smart Swap and Smart Step setting covered in the *Modifying Code in a Debug Session* section of this chapter. The final area to concentrate on is the Remote settings area of the dialog. Again, no matter which type of remote debugging will occur, the first setting is the most important. Enable remote debugging should be selected. The rest of the options will be covered, depending on the type of debugging attempted, and we will refer back to this dialog.

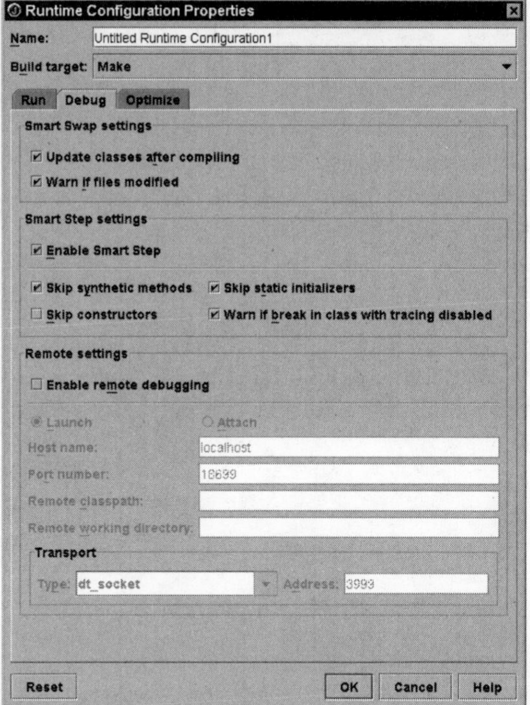


**Figure 5.17** Runtime Configuration Properties dialog.

## *Launching*

JBuilder ships additional software to make launching and debugging remote processes very easy. The software is located in the /jbuilder/remote directory; it includes three files: DebugServer, DebugServer.bat, and DebugServer.jar. The DebugServer and DebugServer.bat are essentially the same scripting files; the one without an extension is for Unix, and the one with the .bat extension is for Windows. When the program DebugServer script is run, it will produce a window (see Figure 5.18) with a menu for exiting and looking at the About window. It is recommended that this entire directory be placed on the remote debugging machine. Only the script and the .jar file are needed, but this approach keeps the files together and organized. The files can be run from any directory including the one that holds the .class files. The DebugServer(.bat) script takes four parameters:

**Debugserver.jar_dir.** This is the location of the debugserver.jar file on the remote machine.

**Jdk_home_dir.** This is the location of the JDK that will be used on the remote machine.

**-port.** This is an optional parameter, which defaults to 18699. The port range can be from 1024 to 65535. Make sure to remember the number because the debug client will need to use it.

**-timeout.** This is the number of milliseconds to wait while trying to connect to the remote computer. The default value is 60000 milliseconds.

Making the assumption that the complete /remote directory and its contents were copied to the remote machine and leaving the default parameters, the command line should look something like this on the remote machine:

```
DebugServer c:/remote c:/jbuilder/jdk1.4
```

The drive letter may need to be changed for your machine requirements, and the actual JDK does not need to be the one included with Jbuilder. It can be the standard downloaded JDK from Sun. Entering this command will display the DebugServer window (see Figure 5.18).

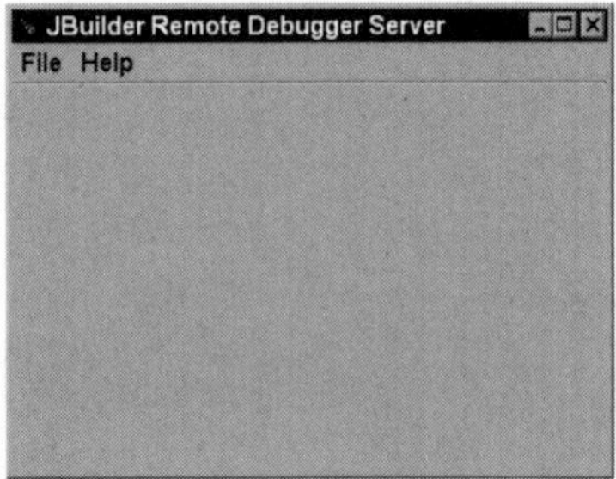


**Figure 5.18** JBuilder Remote Debug Server window.

With the debug server running on the remote machine, it is time to create a directory on the remote machine called myclasses. Then copy the TheDebugger class files to the remote directory on the remote machine called c:/myclasses. Once the class files are copied, the directory structure should look like the following: /myclasses/com/wiley /mastering/jbuilder/debugexamples. This is where the five example files should be located.

On the client debug machine running JBuilder, start the TheDebugger project in JBuilder and display that project's properties. Then click on the Run tab, and hit the Add button to create a new Runtime configuration. When the Runtime Configuration properties dialog is displayed, name the configuration Launch and set the Build target to None. Now, focusing on the Remote settings, make sure to check the Enable remote debugging setting and then follow these settings for this example:

**Launch.** This will instruct JBuilder to launch a new debug process on the remote machine. If the process is running on the remote machine, JBuilder will create a new one by default. If you wanted to attach to that running process, proceed to the next section on Attaching.

**Host name.** This is the actual IP address or network name of the remote machine. For the examples in this book, the address for the remote machine will be 192.168.1.140.

**Port number.** This is the port used when running the DebugServer script; because the default was used, it is 18699.

**Remote classpath.** This is the path where the .class files are located on the remote machine. The remote classpath applies only to this debug session, so this will not affect any other classpaths set on the machine. For this example, this should be set to c:/myclasses.

**Remote working directory.** This is the working directory on the remote machine. Remember that this option is not recognized on JDK 1.2 and will throw error messages to the command window of the DebugServer on the remote machine. For this example, this should be set to c:/myclasses.

**Transport.** This can be dt_socket or dt_shmem. Usually it will be dt_socket; the only time to use dt_shmem is when doing remote debugging on a local process on a Windows-only machine. Even then, this option is not required. For this example, this should be set to dt_socket.

**Address.** This is the port associated with the socket for the transport. When launching a process, this option will not be available.

Once the parameters have been set on the Debug tab of the new Runtime configuration, press the OK button to continue. Then press the OK button on the Project Properties dialog to continue. Because JBuilder has the project loaded, set a breakpoint inside the DebugShow.java program, then right-mouse click on the DebugShow and select the Debug with Launch configuration. If you can see the router that connects the machines, you will notice a flurry of activity establishing the connection. Other than that little flurry of activity, no visible changes to the JBuilder debugger are noticeable. The remote machine's output will be captured inside JBuilder, so no evidence of a debug session occurring will be visible on the remote machine.

After working with the debugger, you will notice no changes in how it works; however, because JBuilder does not report or log any activity on the remote machine. People seem to feel that the debugging process is not remote. To test this after working with the remote debugger, change the Runtime configuration properties to the wrong machine name or change the IP address; it should return an exception reporting a timeout. This will, at least, establish that a connection was being made to the machine.

Finally, if you want to try this technique with the DServer and DClient, make sure to change the IP address on the DClient.java to the remote machine's IP address for proper communication. For this example using the machine listed, it would look like this:

```
inetAddress = InetAddress.getByName("192.168.1.140");
```

After the proper address is added, kick off the debugger or run the DClient program — it does not matter which you do. Make sure that the breakpoints are set on the DServer in JBuilder so that it will stop. Once this is complete, the DebugServer program on the remote machine can be stopped, and that will end the communication between the two computers.

JBuilder makes it very easy to launch a process that needs to be debugged; just set a couple of properties and use the debugger as normal — that is it. In the next section, the discussion turns to attaching to an already running process.

## Attaching

Now that you understand the launch process, you'll see that attaching is not much different. It comes down to making sure that the remote machine's code is started properly with the right parameters. For this example, we will be using TheDebugger.jpx for the source of the example. Remember that the .class and source need to be at the same level to eliminate unknown debugging errors.

The fastest way to establish the proper startup script is to use the JBuilder launch features. Run JBuilder, bring up the TheDebugger.jpx, select the DebugShow.java program, and run it with no special Runtime configurations. The console window will display the command used to start the DebugShow program; simply copy it from the console window and place it in a script/.bat file on the remote machine. The command should look something like the following:

```
c:\jbuilder8\jdk1.4\bin\javaw -classpath
"C:\JBuilder8\.jbuilder8\jbproject\TheDebugger\classes;c:\jbuilder8\jdk1
.4\demo\jfc\Java2D\Java2Demo.jar;c:\jbuilder8\jdk1.4\demo\plugin\jfc\Jav
a2D\Java2Demo.jar;c:\jbuilder8\jdk1.4\jre\lib\charsets.jar;c:\jbuilder8\
jdk1.4\jre\lib\ext\dnsns.jar;c:\jbuilder8\jdk1.4\jre\lib\ext\ldapsec.jar
;c:\jbuilder8\jdk1.4\jre\lib\ext\localedata.jar;c:\jbuilder8\jdk1.4\jre\
lib\ext\sunjce_provider.jar;c:\jbuilder8\jdk1.4\jre\lib\im\indicim.jar;c
:\jbuilder8\jdk1.4\jre\lib\jaws.jar;c:\jbuilder8\jdk1.4\jre\lib\jce.jar;
c:\jbuilder8\jdk1.4\jre\lib\jsse.jar;c:\jbuilder8\jdk1.4\jre\lib\rt.jar;
c:\jbuilder8\jdk1.4\jre\lib\sunrsasign.jar;c:\jbuilder8\jdk1.4\lib\dt.ja
r;c:\jbuilder8\jdk1.4\lib\htmlconverter.jar;c:\jbuilder8\jdk1.4\lib\tool
s.jar"  com.wiley.mastering.jbuilder.debugexamples.DebugShow
```

As stated previously, copy this into a script/.bat file on the remote machine. For this example, because you already copied the classes directory from the client debug machine and placed them in the myclasses directory on the remote machine, this is where to locate the script/.bat file. It should be called debug1.bat (Windows).

Once the preceding line is copied into a file, some small modifications are needed to give it the ability to debug. The first change is to remove the "w" from the javaw command; then add the following parameters between the Java and the –classpath option:

**Classpath.** Don't forget to add the directory in which the .classes are located to your classpath.

**-Xdebug.** This enables debugging in the JVM. This option is required.

**-Xnoagent.** This is used with classic VMs JDK 1.2 through JDK 1.3. It allowed backward compatibility between JPDA and the old Sun debugger. These options are ignored on JDK 1.4 and above.

**-Djava.compiler=NONE.** This is used with classic VMs JDK 1.2 through JDK 1.3.

It told the classic VM to disable the JIT compiler in the VM. This option is ignored on JDK 1.4 and above.

**-xrunjdwp:transport=dt_socket,server=y,address=3999,suspend=y.** This should look very similar to the options exposed in the JBuilder Debug tab. The same rules apply, and each of the subitems should be separated with a comma. The suboptions are as follows:

- **dt_socket or dt_shmem.** These options represent the message transport used by the VM and the debugger. This option is required. The only time to use dt_shmem is on a local process on a Windows machine.
- **server.** This is an optional parameter; if it is set to 'y', it will listen for the debugger application to attach. If it is set to 'y' and no address is attached, it will display the port it is listening to so that it can be used by the debugger client application.
- **address.** This suboption applies to the server. If the server = y, then listen for a connection at this address. If the server = n, then attempt to attach to the debugger application at this address.
- **suspend.** This option allows the process to be stopped when the debug process is started. Setting the suspend = n will allow the application to continue to run; if no breakpoints are present, the program will execute to the end. If set to server = y, the process will stop and wait for the debugger application to attach.

With the options added to the script/.bat file, it should look like the following:

```
c:\jbuilder8\jdk1.4\bin\java -Xdebug -Xnoagent -Djava.compiler=NONE
-xrunjdwp:transport=dt_socket,server=y,address=3999,suspend=y -classpath
c:\myclasses;"C:\JBuilder8\.jbuilder8\jbproject\TheDebugger\classes;c:\j
builder8\jdk1.4\demo\jfc\Java2D\Java2Demo.jar;c:\jbuilder8\jdk1.4\demo\p
lugin\jfc\Java2D\Java2Demo.jar;c:\jbuilder8\jdk1.4\jre\lib\charsets.jar;
c:\jbuilder8\jdk1.4\jre\lib\ext\dnsns.jar;c:\jbuilder8\jdk1.4\jre\lib\ex
t\ldapsec.jar;c:\jbuilder8\jdk1.4\jre\lib\ext\localedata.jar;c:\jbuilder
8\jdk1.4\jre\lib\ext\sunjce_provider.jar;c:\jbuilder8\jdk1.4\jre\lib\im\
indicim.jar;c:\jbuilder8\jdk1.4\jre\lib\jaws.jar;c:\jbuilder8\jdk1.4\jre
\lib\jce.jar;c:\jbuilder8\jdk1.4\jre\lib\jsse.jar;c:\jbuilder8\jjk1.4\jr
e\lib\rt.jar;c:\jbuilder8\jdk1.4\jre\lib\sunrsasign.jar;c:\jbuilder8\jdk
1.4\lib\dt.jar;c:\jbuilder8\jdk1.4\lib\htmlconverter.jar;c:\jbuilder8\jd
k1.4\lib\tools.jar"

com.wiley.mastering.jbuilder.debugexamples.DebugShow
```

The bold areas are the changes to the command. Save the script/.bat file, and because the suspend option is set to 'y', this script/.bat file can be executed on the remote machine. When executed, the whole command will be displayed, and the program will wait for the JBuilder debugger to make contact.

Now in JBuilder, bring up the project properties for the TheDebugger project, and click the Run tab. Then click the New button to create a new Runtime configuration.

When the Runtime Configuration Properties dialog is displayed, click the Debug tab, then change the name to Attach and set the Build Target to None. Next check the Enable remote debugging option, and notice that most of the options become grayed out because they are not used in this type of remote debugging. The options left should have the following values:

**Host name.** This is the network name or IP address of the remote machine. For this example, it is 192.168.1.140.

**Type.** This is the type of communications being used; for this example, it should be set to dt_socket. This should always match the script/.bat file transport.

**Address.** This is the address that the communication will use. For this example, it should be set at 3999. This should always match the script/.bat file address.

Press the OK button when the changes are complete, then press the OK button again to close the project properties. Because the remote machine is still waiting for the debugger to contact, make the node that is being debugged active in JBuilder. Then press the Run | Step Over or the Run | Step Into menu item. This will display a Choose Runtime Configuration dialog (see Figure 5.19). Then select the Attach item inside the listbox, and press the OK button to continue.

This will place the cursor at the top of the node; from here breakpoints can be set and executed. Notice that the Debug Windows tab has a partial host and address displayed on it, showing that a connection is made. This time all System.out streams will be displayed on the remote machine and not in the client debugger console. The debugger works the same as it would if it were a local node being debugged. The remote machine's command window should not be closed until the client debugger has detached from the machine. If a Ctrl-Break key combination is executed on the remote machine, it could have undesired results like throwing exceptions and killing Windows. The best way to detach is to hit the Stop button on the Debug toolbar.

**TIP When using JDK 1.2 and 1.3, always use the Java.exe from the \bin directory because this will allow the debug library to be loaded. Do not use the one located inside the \jre\bin.**

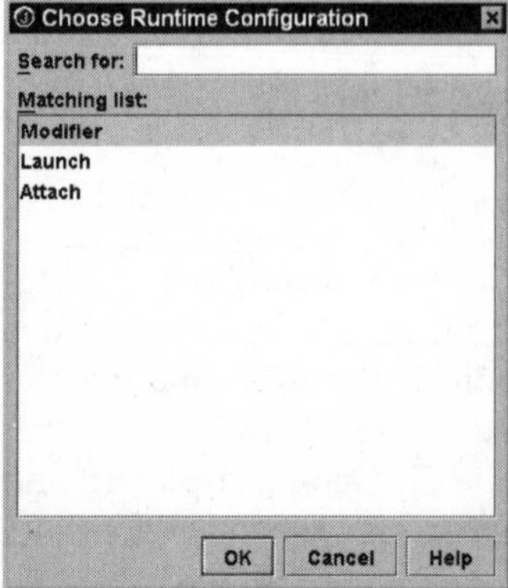


**Figure 5.19** Choose Runtime Configuration dialog.

The ability to attach to an existing, executing application works the same when doing client/server remote debugging. Change the debug(.bat) script file on the remote machine so that the class being called is the DServer instead of the DebugShow, then follow the same steps as previously outlined to start the remote session. Then in JBuilder, using the Attach debug configuration, right-mouse click on the DServer and start the debug process. You will notice on the remote machine that it will be waiting for a connection. From here breakpoints can be set and the DClient process can be run or debugged locally until completion.

The final feature to discuss when it comes to remote debugging is the cross-process breakpoint option. Starting the server as described previously and then setting a breakpoint in the DClient program, start the DClient in debug mode. When the breakpoint is hit in the DClient, click the Run | Add Breakpoint | Add Cross-process breakpoint menu item. The Cross-Process Breakpoint dialog looks similar to the normal Add Method Breakpoint dialog (see Figure 5.13) and works the same way. Find the class; in this case, it would be com.wiley.mastering.jbuilder.debugexamples.Dserver. Press the OK button, then select the method to break on; when the (...) button is pressed, choose the method. If any parameters are needed, they will be filled in. Then hit the OK button. Now, go to the DServer program and set the breakpoint at the same location. When that breakpoint gets hit, make sure to do a Step Into to proceed; if the Step Over is used, it will skip the method breakpoint.

As you can see, the difference between attaching to a debug session or launching a debug session is minimal, and the results are the same. Launching a process is very convenient if access to a machine is limited; attaching is nice because you can attach, detach, and then reattach to the same debug session, making it very flexible. The best part is that there is nothing else to learn when it comes to remote debugging.

## Summary

Understanding the basic debugging interface, getting a debug test bed to try new things safely, and understanding how to work with multiple processes, threads, and remote debugging should give confidence to the developer when he or she faces the daunting task of answering the questions: Why doesn't it work on my machine, and why did it not work today?

As you can see, the debugging capability found in JBuilder is rather extensive. Because the JBuilder team tries always to adhere to the open standards of Java, further advances may come slowly. This includes the ability to hot-fix during a debugging session, which would allow the developer to change code during a debug session without restarting the session from scratch to see the code changes. Although this could have been accomplished long ago, the JBuilder team decided to wait until it became a standard of the debugging architecture. The first production version in the JDK has features missing, such as the ability to add method or inner classes. As soon as the JVM supports those features, JBuilder will implement them.

CHAPTER

6

# Using the JBuilder Help System

The JBuilder help system is rich with features and capabilities that make looking for the answer as easy as possible without having to leave the environment. This chapter covers the finer details and features available in the help system; it focuses on how to use the interface and get the results you are looking for using the search features; it also discusses the concepts behind tip-of-the-day and advanced features hidden in the properties files. Most developers have used a help system before in an integrated development environment, so the expectation of what the system should be able to do is well defined. In the beginning, the JBuilder help program needed a little help; it did not cover a lot of areas, it was spotty, and it would cause JBuilder to disappear without notice. Times have changed and so has the JBuilder help program. It now supports a fairly complete reference to what is JBuilder and how to use JBuilder, and it provides much better context-sensitive help.

The first thing to make clear before we start is the use of the words "tabs" and "panes." Tabs happen on both sides of the explorer interface; make sure to use the inserted figures to see exactly what is being talked about as a guide. It can get confusing when both major areas have the same capabilities.

## Getting Started

The JBuilder help interface can be started by clicking the Help | Help Topics menu item. This will start the help system with a standard Explorer-style interface. The base help system, shown in Figure 6.1, has a simple "Explorer" interface, with the topic window broken into two areas: the toolbar and the interface used to display a Tree view of book sets. Book sets are based on the concept that a book defines each area of help and that each book is broken into chapters. The chapters are broken into topics, and each topic is assigned a topic id. This is what the help system used to find a specific topic in the book set. The toolbar has the basic Home, Back, and Forward options, which work like a basic Internet browser interface. The Home button will always return to the introduction of the JBuilder help system.

The navigation system is based on an index of topics viewed. Each time a topic is viewed, the topic id gets placed into a list, which then allows the developer to move either forward or backward in that list. The Back button is responsible for moving the current index to the previous topic id if one exists; likewise, the Forward button advances the current topic id one, again if the item is available in the list. The next two toolbar buttons are the Print and Find in Page functions, which are used in the context of the current help topic. The Print function will print the complete topic; at this time, the range cannot be set or limited. Another thing to keep in mind is that the print setting from the main JBuilder program does not extend to the help system.

**TIP** **PDF versions of the documentation are available on the product CD. Using a PDF viewer will give a finer set of controls when printing the documentation.**

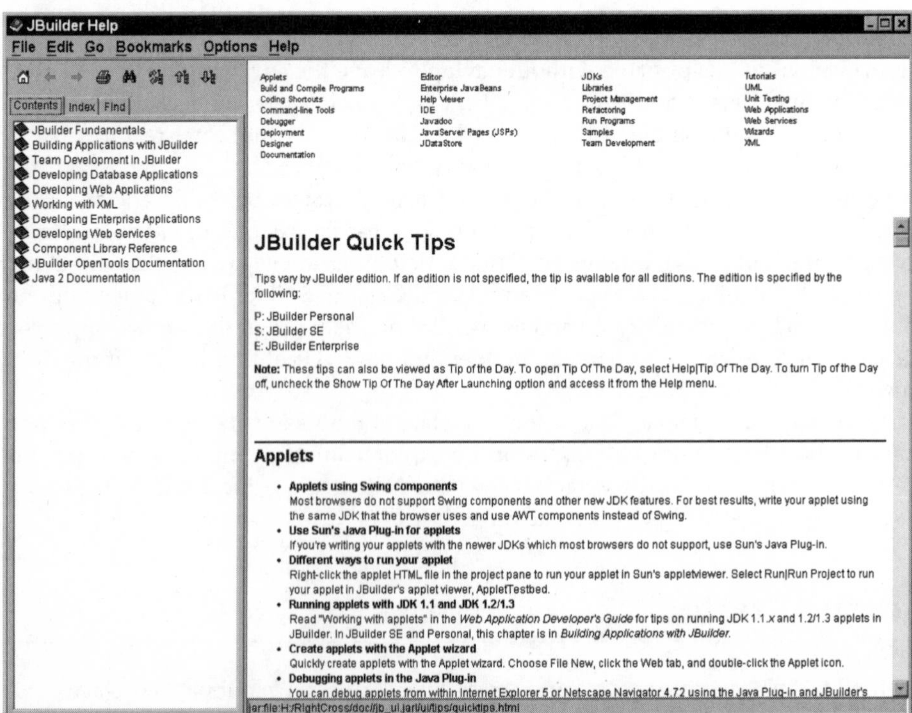


**Figure 6.1** Base-level help.

The Find on Page tool will display a simple dialog that will allow simple text or a phrase to be entered. When the Find Next button is pressed, it will try to find that exact text or phrase in the current topic. If the text is found, it will move the focus to that first occurrence. This dialog will remain active until the Done button has been pressed. A nice feature that the Find on Page function has is the ability to move from topic to topic and still keep active the same search by pressing the F3 function key. The Find on Page dialog also retains a list of text or phrases searched for in that session; the search list is cleared when JBuilder is restarted.

The next three toolbar buttons are used to synchronize the table of contents, to move to the Previous topic, or to move to the Next topic located inside a book set. This may seem confusing because the Home, Back, and Forward buttons were explained, but remember that those buttons are based on the visited topic index list. These next three buttons are focused on the book sets and the location inside them. The Synchronize button will do one of two things; it will either move the current focus in the book set to the current chapter of the topic being displayed, or it will move the focus to the next available book or chapter that has topics associated with it. This depends on where the focus is located in the book set. This will all happen in the book set display on the right-hand side of the explorer interface. The Previous topic button will then move the book set focus to either the prior chapter or the first chapter in an earlier book. The same can be said for the Next topic button; it will move the focus forward to the next chapter or book set.

This explanation may sound confusing, but following the upcoming example will highlight the use the buttons to locate almost any book, chapter, or topic and will help clear up the concepts:

1. Open JBuilder help by selecting the Help | Help Topics menu item.
2. Under Contents window, double-click on JBuilder Fundamentals book. (It should be the book on top.)
3. Start randomly clicking on chapters and topics; this should be done four or five times.
4. Click the Back button once; it should take you back to the prior topic that was clicked on.
5. Click the Back button again, and it should take you back to its prior topic.
6. Click the Forward button; it should take you to the topic just viewed.
7. Click the Forward button again, and it should take you to the location where you were before you clicked the first back button.
8. Notice that only the topic changes; the book set, chapters, and topics remain at the same focus level.
9. Click the Home button; this will move the focus topic to Introducing JBuilder.
10. Click the Synchronize topics button; this will move the book set focus to the JBuilder Fundamentals book and then to the Introduction chapter.
11. Click the Next topic button; this will move the book focus and the topic focus to the JBuilder documentation set chapter.
12. Click the Next topic button again and it will move the book focus and chapter focus to the Additional Resources chapter.

13. Pressing the Previous topic will move the book focus back one chapter to the JBuilder documentation set.
14. Click on the Using the AppBrowser chapter (Chapter 4) a few times below the current focus on the right-hand side.
15. Click the Synchronize topics button; it will fully expand that chapter and all the items below it.

## Index Pane

The Index pane allows keyword searches. Once the Index tab has been clicked, enter the name of the topic to be searched, and the focus will move as each character is being typed. The input box also has the paste feature enabled, which will allow the pasted word to be searched. If no word is present, start deleting characters until a match is found. The general idea behind the Index pane is to find the top-level topics and that the sublevel topics that are displayed are related to the top-level topic. This can be frustrating when doing a search on a specific topic that may be considered a sublevel topic. As stated previously, the sublevel topics are included in the top-level topic, but typing in a sublevel topic will not always return the top-level topic in the search. If a topic has multiple listings, hitting the Enter key on the topic will split the Index pane and break the topics into subtopics.

The next example shows how to limit search items using the Index pane.

1. Open the JBuilder's help system by clicking the Help | Help Topics menu item.
2. Click the Index tab.
3. Type "J2SE" in the edit box and hit Return; notice that two subtopics are returned in the lower split pane.
4. Click on either of the subtopics to display the topic.
5. Clear the edit box, type in "ORB class", and hit Return. Two subtopics are returned. The ORB class has a number of sublevel topics. If you try to type in the exact sublevel topic name in the edit box, the topics will not be found. If you use the mouse to navigate to a sublevel topic, the location of the topic display is not changed. This is there only to give additional information to the searcher.

## Find Pane

The Find tab located next to the Index tab gives the most functionality when trying to find specific topics. First, the edit boxes found on the Find tab act just like the edit box found on the Index tab. As words are starting to be typed in, the topic index will start to try to match the word or phrase. When the Enter key is pressed on the edit box, a topic list will be returned. This list can have a very large number of returns, especially if a generic term is used, such as the word "Java."

The Find pane does include Boolean search capabilities; these include both (AND) and (OR). By using the "+" key for (AND) and the "," for the (OR) operator, topic searches can be limited to some degree. White space does not have any effect on the overall search, so typing in a line like "Java,CORBA" or "Java, CORBA" is functionally the same, and the results have no differences. When the topic is selected in the found topics pane, when it is displayed, the topic will show all the search words in a highlighted format.

Following is an advanced search example showing how to limit the number of returned hits. It focuses on using the Boolean search capabilities built in to the environment. Open the JBuilder's help system and click the Help | Help Topics menu item.

1. Click the Find tab.
2. Type "Java" in the edit box, and hit Return; the search will return 4648 topics.
3. Clear the edit box and type "Jakarta" in the edit box. Hitting Return will return 7 topics.
4. Adding a "," and the word "Java" will return 4648 topics because this is the OR operator and because Java is found that many times.
5. Changing the "," to a "+", which is the AND operator, will return 7 topics because each of the 7 topics that are Jakarta-specific also include the keyword Java.

## Content Pane

As stated previously, the Content pane is responsible for displaying book sets. These book sets consist of a set of HTML pages, images, and other resources needed to display the help contents; these are packaged into a standard .jar file. These book sets are located in the /jbuilder/doc directory and can be unjarred using the standard jar tool included with the JDK. Once a doc .jar file is unjarred it can then be viewed in a standard HTML browser.

**NOTE None of the advanced JBuilder help system tools will be available once the doc files have been unjarred and are displayed in an HTML browser.**

In the Content pane, double-clicking on a book will open it; this will then display all the chapters found inside. By clicking on the Table Expansion icon, this will list a series of topics included in the chapter. Using the Content pane, the developer searching for information needs to know not only the book in which the information may be located, but also what the exact topic is named. One feature that is available to the Content pane is the type-in feature; this feature allows the developer to start typing in the name of the topic to search, and it is based on the first character typed. This is the same feature that is found in the AppBrowser Project, Structure, and Component panes covered in Chapter 5, "Debugging with JBuilder." This feature, though, is limited in the help system; it will search only on the open books, chapters, or topics. It does not expand them or try to drill down to the contents below the open area.

Matching capabilities are also limited; if the focus is located on an item that has the same name as an item that is open, the focus will not change until three characters have been typed. Then the focus will go to the third character typed, which is the first character in the new search. If a character is typed and the focus changes, the next character typed is the first character in a new search. If multiple words with the same starting character are in the list, use the first character of the word again and again to move through the list of words starting with that character. This feature is intended only to make it easier to navigate book sets without a mouse, and it is very limited from that perspective. The character buffer is also rather limited; if the help system is trying to display a topic, any characters typed into the buffer will be lost until the topic has been displayed and the help system starts accepting keystrokes again. For more advanced topic search, use the Index or Find tabs, which are explained later in the chapter.

### Context-Sensitive Help

Context-sensitive help is supported in some designers, Project panes, Structure panes, Component panes, Object Inspectors, and Editors. Press the F1 key to activate the context help system. By default it is a simple modal dialog, which can cause problems when trying to do tutorials and keep things alive. The JBuilder help system can be run in a separate VM. Starting the JBuilder help system can be done by pressing the Help | Help Topics menu item; once the help system is started, press the Options | More menu item, and the VM parameter can be set in the More dialog.

If the Use simple dialog for context sensitive display option is unchecked, the modal dialog will not be displayed, and all topics will be forced to the standard help system. The help system needs to be closed, and JBuilder needs to be restarted before the option will take effect.

### Using the Doc Tab

The Doc tab is found on the Content pane. For more information on the AppBrowser, review Chapter 2, "Customizing the AppBrowser." The Doc tab displays the associated JavaDoc for Java class files. It also shows the JavaDoc for files that do not include documentation with a JavaDoc parser to parse the code on the fly.

## Tip of the Day

The tip-of-the-day (TOD) feature is normally displayed during the startup process for JBuilder. This can be stopped, if desired, just by deselecting the Show after launching option on the TOD dialog. TOD can also be displayed at any time by pressing the Help | Tip of the Day menu item. In Figure 6.2, it is possible to read all of the tips by using the Next Tip button or the Previous Tip button.

It is possible to add topics to the tip-of-the-day (TOD) feature. The TOD texts are found in the /jbuilder/doc/jb_ui.jar file. This is a simple .jar (Java Archive) file; it can be manipulated by using the standard jar tools that are included with the Java JDK. Also, most of the ZIP utilities can read .jar files types, which gives advanced tools for manipulating a .jar's contents. The following steps outline how to add new tips to JBuilder.

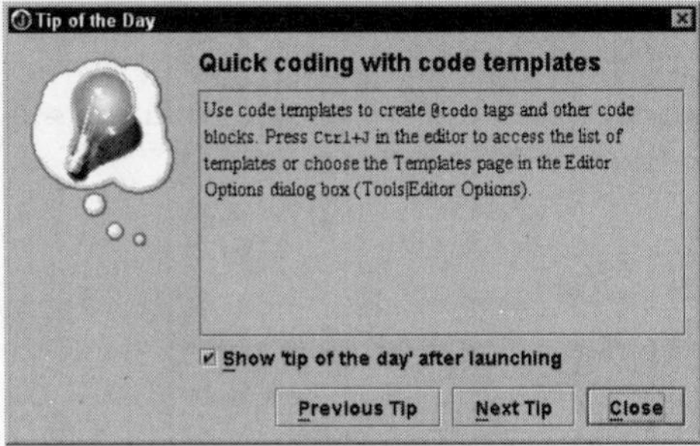


**Figure 6.2** Tip of the Day dialog.

To add custom tips of the day, follow these steps:

1. Close JBuilder.
2. Create a directory structure /ui/tips.
3. Create a text file called NewAdd.txt.
4. The first line should read: Custom Tooltip.
5. The second line should read: This is a new tip added to the JBuilder Tip of the Day feature.
6. Save the file.
7. Make a copy of the jb_ui.jar file found in the /jbuilder/docs directory for safe keeping.
8. Add the NewAdd.txt file with the complete path name included. The jar command should look like the following: jar uf \jbuilder\doc\jb_ui.jar ui.

   The preceding command will add all the files located inside the un/tips directory, plus it will add the directories to the archive file.

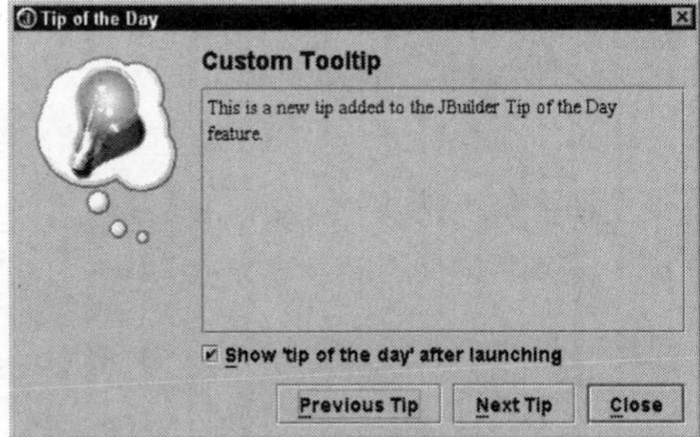


**Figure 6.3** Custom tip of the day.

If multiple tips are defined for a specific feature, add a number to the file naming. Examples of this would be file1.txt, file2.txt, and so on. Once the new tips have been added to the jb_ui.jar file, it can then be distributed to other users of JBuilder, thus giving a common way to share hints and tips that are self-discovered.

# Advanced Help Features

The JBuilder help system has advanced features that may not make it into the normal material or daily use but that can be helpful if you know about them. Some of these include file viewing, display options, bookmarks, and copy buffers.

The JBuilder help system can also be used as a simple file viewer. The viewer has the ability to work with JSP, ASP, XML, XSL, and DTD, and it is fully JavaScript enabled. To view one of these types of files, simply click the File | Open menu item inside the JBuilder Help system. This can be used when trying to look at a file very quickly without changing the focus from the help system.

Another advanced feature is the ability to change the font in the help viewer; this feature is called zooming. Three types of zoom are possible: Out, In, and Normal. Out can be accomplished by pressing the Options | Zoom Out menu item or by pressing the Ctrl-D key combination, which will increase the font size. The In operation can be accomplished by clicking the Options | Zoom In menu item or by pressing Ctrl-U, which will decrease the font. The final option is to set the font back to Normal; this can be done by clicking the Options | Normal menu item only.

## Bookmarks

The JBuilder help system also has the ability to set bookmarks. Once a topic of interest is found, the fastest way to always find that piece of information is to set a bookmark. The default number of bookmarks that JBuilder can display is 25. It is possible, though, to increase this number by modifying the help.properties file located in the jbuilder.home or user.home directory. For more information on jbuilder.home and user.home files, review Chapter 4, "Project Properties and Configurations." With the maxMenuBookmarks=25 property, changing the value of the number changes the number of items that can be displayed on the Bookmarks menu.

**TIP Always exit JBuilder when working with JBuilder property files. JBuilder may overwrite or rewrite property files on exit. This means that changes most likely will not be saved.**

To control bookmarks inside the JBuilder help system, a bookmark first needs to be added. Once the first bookmark is present, the help system will allow full manipulation of bookmarks. In Figure 6.4, the bookmark editor allows you to organize current bookmarks as well as remove one or remove all. This dialog will also give the ability to go to the actual bookmark from this interface. If the number of bookmarks is large, this dialog is the best way of navigating to a particular bookmark.

## Fonts

Besides setting the maxMenuBookmarks property inside the help.properties file, it is also possible to set the fonts. The property DefaultFont.1=Western European\:dialog-plain-14 will set the help display font to dialog, with a setting of plain and a font size of 14. Now when the help system starts, this font will be the default. Use the Options|Font menu item to initially set the property; it then can be manipulated through that dialog or through the property file. The new font will be used not only in the help system, but also in the Doc viewer located in the Content pane in the AppBrowser.

## Copy Buffers

The help system has many hidden features, one of which is the ability to copy text and place it on the system's clipboard, which can be used later in other programs. The copy feature can be activated by selecting the area that is to be copied and pressing the Ctrl-C key combination. This can be done anywhere inside the interface, including the book view, Content pane, and status bar. In Figure 6.1, notice the Status Bar, which states something like: "jar:file:...". This area will contain whatever is being displayed in the Content pane. This is especially important when viewing HTML content that would be better interacted with in a standard Internet browser. Simply highlight the area intended to be copied, and use the Ctrl-C combination to paste the contents into a favorite browser and continue surfing.

The menu system found in JBuilder's help system mimics the base functionality covered in this chapter. It is always recommended that if a menu item is present for configuration that it be used instead of working with the underlying Help.properties file. If a menu item is not present for a particular setting, manipulating the property file is completely acceptable.

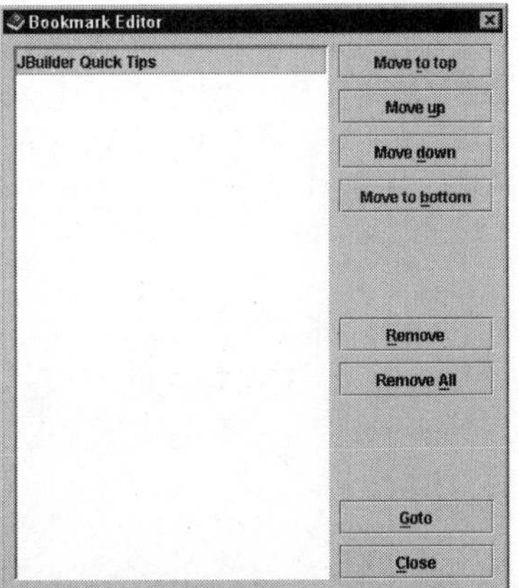


**Figure 6.4** Bookmark Editor dialog.

## Summary

The help system found in JBuilder is really an integral part of the total development package. It has become a reliable tool that can be expanded and customized to meet the developer's needs. The content has continued to be updated and made available throughout the JBuilder environment. In the areas of context-sensitive help, JavaDoc, and standard help files, it truly is only a click away.

PART

Two

# JBuilder as a Rapid Application Development Tool

Understanding the basics of the JBuilder IDE is great, but what really starts to add productivity is using the development tools to their full extent. JBuilder has always been focused on getting the tools in the hands of developers and letting them decide how best to utilize them. Taking pages from the early Delphi days and the tools it provided to its developers that made them productive, JBuilder tried and succeeded in enhancing the developer interaction by making tedious tasks simple.

Many things developers now expect from an IDE were once considered to be revolutionary, including the following:

- Wizards, which could generate code or provide a framework as a good starting point.
- GUI designers, which allow drag-and-drop functionality of completely assembled components to be connected together to make a graphic interface. The concept of GUI designers has been extended over the years by adding drag-and-drop component development to database, distributed applications, and Web services.
- Two-way tools, which allow developers to make changes in code and have them reflected in a GUI designer and, likewise, make changes in a GUI designer and have the underlying code be changed and kept synchronized.

JBuilder continues to add developer support to make the development cycle as short as possible. This effort falls under the umbrella of Rapid Application Development (RAD). JBuilder has taken the concept of two-way tools beyond the humble beginnings of supporting only GUI development; it now supports a two-way approach for working with databases and especially EJBs. New integrated wizards that allow for interaction throughout the application lifecycle have shortened Java projects considerably, especially when BeansExpress can be used. Today, new tools, such as refactoring, are being added with unit testing and UML visualization to make developers as productive as possible.

Part Two shows you how to use all the built-in tools included in the JBuilder IDE and helps you understand the best way to use them:

**Creating Classes.** Chapter 7 covers the basic wizards included with JBuilder and exposed through the Object Gallery. These wizards are focused on all points in the development process, from creating a simple framework to generating test clients, unit tests, and even creating and working with deployment features.

**Modifying Classes.** Chapter 8 covers the basics of creating Java classes that use all the tools available in JBuilder to make the effort as painless as possible.

CHAPTER

7

# Creating Classes

Now it is time to start using JBuilder to get some work done programming Java. Up to this point, we've focused on defining the JBuilder user interface and the base tools for getting work done. Those included JBuilder, its configuration, projects and their layouts, understanding debugging, and understanding the help system. By now you should have a fairly good understanding of that part of JBuilder. Now you are going to explore how JBuilder can shorten the Java development cycle by exposing the Java language through this great tool. The JBuilder programming environment has a plethora of shortcuts, tools, and wizards to help make you more productive. JBuilder makes it convenient by placing a majority of wizards in one place, the Object Gallery, which contains most of the common tasks in creating a Java programming environment. Understanding how to use the Object Gallery can save time throughout the Java development lifecycle, especially when starting new development projects.

This chapter focuses on using and understanding what the Object Gallery is and what it can do for you. The Object Gallery tabs cover the organized wizards that JBuilder includes; give special attention to classes, applications, frameworks, and applets; and point you to the chapter that covers those wizards.

# Overview of the Object Gallery

The Object Gallery has a unique interface, found by using the File | New menu item from the main menu in JBuilder or pressing Ctrl-N on the keyboard. Figure 7.1 shows an object gallery.

The window that appears has a tabbed interface. The tabs are used to organize the wizards into logical tasks that the developer will interact with. All of the Object Gallery wizards are based on the open interface that JBuilder is built on, called OpenTools. Using OpenTools means that users of JBuilder can add custom wizards to the Object Gallery at any time. Most of the wizards that are found in the Object Gallery are based on a multiple-step process in which the developer selects options and presses a Finish button, and JBuilder produces the output from the selection criteria.

**NOTE Wizards are not designed from a two-way tool perspective; they are usually single-pass processes that will generate code. A two-way tool allows the developer to make changes to either the code or the graphic representation and have all changes be kept in sync with each programming interface. Borland is known for letting developers use the two-way tool paradigm for developing programs; it actually holds the patent for the process. In early GUI development environments, this allowed the developer to make a change in the GUI designer while maintaining the underlying code. This technique is still one of the unique features of the JBuilder IDE.**

On occasion, wizards become more than just simple code generators. This was the case with JBuilder's EJB wizards. Since JBuilder 3.5, the EJB wizard was a single-sheet interface that allowed programmers to select either SessionBean or EntityBean and press Finish. The resulting code was basic and did nothing to help the developer generate good EJBs.

The EJB wizard became more intelligent and faster, but the output was still very static. If you needed to make a change in the underlying code, you had to generate the code again, which usually resulted in a loss of code. With JBuilder 6 and the J2EE 1.3 specification, JBuilder introduced a brand new way of using the base wizards in a two-way tool manner. This allows J2EE developers to graphically design the business back end using a point-and-click method and to change to code or the model at any time while keeping everything synchronized. For more information on the EJB development, please refer to Parts Five and Six of the book.

Even though most of the wizards in the Object Gallery generate static code, they are still very valuable to the developer. They can save a lot of time and help establish standards that eliminate common coding mistakes that otherwise add to a project's life span. Some wizards have extra intelligence to make sure that the developer using them is in the proper place. For example, the Object Gallery wizard checks to see if a project is open, and if a project was not found, the Application wizard would call the New Project wizard first. This ensures that a project is created before any code can be defined in the JBuilder environment.

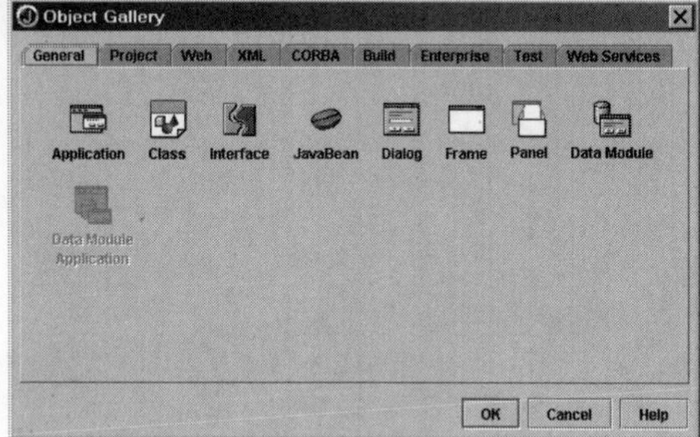


**Figure 7.1** Base Object Gallery.

# Object Gallery Tabs

Currently the Object Gallery is divided into nine tabs in JBuilder Enterprise: General, Project, Web, XML, CORBA, Build, Enterprise, Test, and Web Services. As stated earlier, each tab defines a process that a developer may want to use in a development lifecycle. The Object Gallery tabs are shown in Figure 7.1.

The Object Gallery will most likely be the first place that developers notice a distinction between JBuilder editions:

- JBuilder Personal is Borland's free IDE, which can be downloaded from the Borland Web site. The Personal edition includes only the General tab, with Application and Class wizards included.
- The SE includes the rest except for the Enterprise, Test, and Web Services tabs.
- JBuilder Enterprise includes all nine tabs listed.
- JBuilder MobileSet includes all of the additional wizards for doing J2ME. JBuilder MobileSet is outside the scope of this book.

## General Tab

Until now in this book, all examples have been created using the File | New Class menu item. The same outcome could have been achieved using the Object Gallery's General Tab and selecting the Class wizard. The Class wizard is one of the most basic of all wizards inside JBuilder.

Generic information is defined in the single-page dialog. The wizard allows the setting of the basic information needed when developing a new class in Java (see Figure 7.2). The Class wizard needs three basic inputs for the class. They include things like Package location, Class name, and Base class that the new class will extend. The next set of options, selectable by checkboxes, is the class's characteristics. The options include Public, Generate a main method, Generate header comments, Generate default constructor, Override superclass constructors, and Override abstract methods. The basic output from this wizard with the options of Public, Generate header comments, and Generate default constructor would look like the following:

```
package unknown;

/**
 * <p>Title: NewClass</p>
 * <p>Description: Example new class</p>
 * <p>Copyright: Copyright (c) 2002</p>
 * <p>Company: </p>
 * @author Michael Rozlog
 * @version 1.0
 */

public class NewClass {
  public NewClass() {
  }

}
```

**Source 7.1** Generated new class.

Not much output was produced from the wizard; however, the work that JBuilder has completed should not go unrecognized. The wizard allowed for the definition of the package, class Name, and base class plus a set of options. This information — coupled with the information defined in the project properties — produces this simple class file in the proper directory location following the information from the package and the Projects properties (refer to Chapter 4, "Project Properties and Configurations"). Try to imagine creating a new class by hand with a package name of com.borland.util.display.memmanager.opensource.unknown.NewClass. This would be a nightmare!

Understanding this simple wizard that creates a new class is important when learning JBuilder. It is used as the base wizard for many of the other wizards included in JBuilder. JBuilder works the same way: Something that looks incredibly simple may be used throughout the environment many times over in many unexpected ways, so this base knowledge is always important.

The next wizard found in all editions of JBuilder is the Application wizard. This is a multistep wizard that defines a complete GUI application. The wizard is one of the quickest ways to have success with JBuilder the first time out. The code that is generated will produce a running application that includes the About box.

The first step of the Application wizard is easy; it requires only three options to be completed. They include the Package, Class name, and Generate header comments. The framework used in this wizard first sets up an application class it will be responsible for, called a GUI frame. The class name in Step 1 of the wizard represents the application name; that is why the default name is Application1.

The second step of the Application wizard is for defining the GUI frame class. Figure 7.3 shows the options available in this step. The options include class name, title of the frame, and a set of additional features to add to the application.

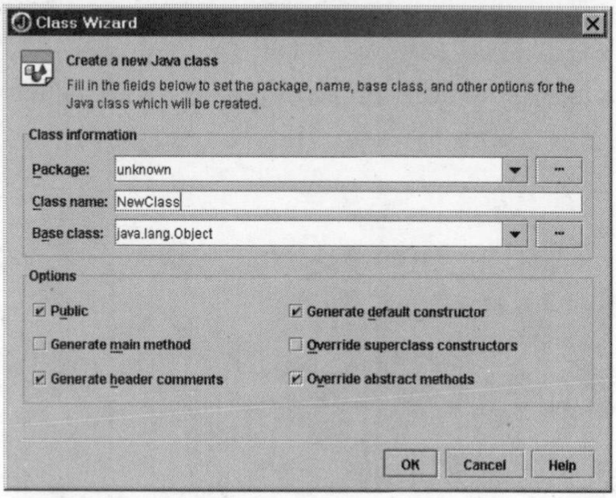

**Figure 7.2** New Class wizard.

The final step of the wizard was new starting with JBuilder 7. The Application wizard was modified to work in the Runtime configuration process and to select a base Runtime configuration from other projects of the same type. For more information on Runtime configurations, refer to Chapter 4.

The steps to follow to produce a Java application using JBuilder are these:

1. Create a new project.
2. Open the Object Gallery, select the Application Wizard, and press OK to continue.
3. Leave defaults for values in the Application Wizard Step 1 of 3, and click the Next button.
4. Leave defaults and select all available options for the Application Wizard Step 2 of 3, and click the Next button.
5. Leave the defaults, and click the Finish button.

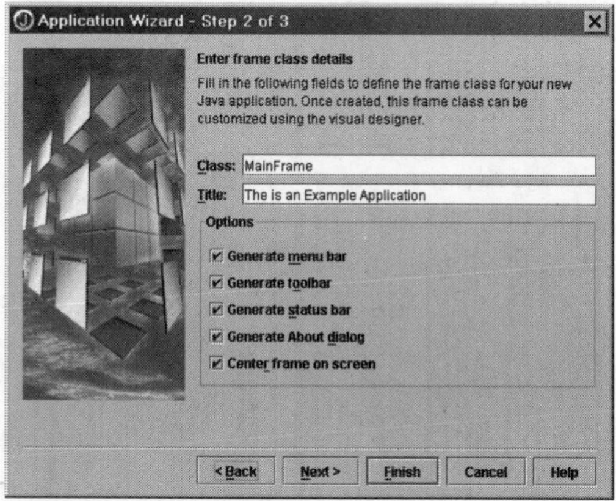


**Figure 7.3** Application wizard Step 2 of 3.

When the Finish button is clicked, JBuilder will generate a complete application following the preceding descriptions and should produce two files. The first file produced is the application class; it has a name Application1.Java, and the code looks like the following:

```
package unknown;

import javax.swing.UIManager;
import java.awt.*;

/**
 * <p>Title: Application1</p>
 * <p>Description: An Example Application</p>
 * <p>Copyright: Copyright (c) 2002</p>
 * <p>Company: </p>
 * @author Michael Rozlog
 * @version 1.0
 */

public class Application1 {
  private boolean packFrame = false;

  //Construct the application
  public Application1() {
    MainFrame frame = new MainFrame();
    //Validate frames that have preset sizes
    //Pack frames that have useful preferred size info, e.g. from their
layout
    if (packFrame) {
      frame.pack();
    }
    else {
      frame.validate();
    }
    //Center the window
    Dimension screenSize = Toolkit.getDefaultToolkit().getScreenSize();
    Dimension frameSize = frame.getSize();
    if (frameSize.height > screenSize.height) {
      frameSize.height = screenSize.height;
    }
    if (frameSize.width > screenSize.width) {
      frameSize.width = screenSize.width;
    }
    frame.setLocation((screenSize.width - frameSize.width) / 2,
(screenSize.height - frameSize.height) / 2);
    frame.setVisible(true);
```

**Source 7.2** Application 1

```
  }
  //Main method
  public static void main(String[] args) {
    try {

UIManager.setLookAndFeel(UIManager.getSystemLookAndFeelClassName());
    }
    catch(Exception e) {
      e.printStackTrace();
    }
    new Application1();
  }
}
```

**Source 7.2** *(continued)*

This code shows that Application1.java is the main class. A visual clue to this fact is apparent in the Structure pane, where the icon to the left of the Application1() method has a yellow center surrounded by a border, and as per the UML specification, that icon represents a main class. JBuilder is always trying to reinforce standards throughout the interface, and this is just one example. This means that the class can be executed by either right-mouse clicking on the node in the Project pane and choosing Run or by pressing the Run toolbar item. Clicking the Run icon on the toolbar will work only if the Application1 class is defined as the default Runtime configuration. Refer to Chapter 4 for more information on Runtime configurations. The code also includes the standard technique for centering a window on a screen in Java and sets the Look and Feel for the Java program. The generated code uses the default system properties for this program.

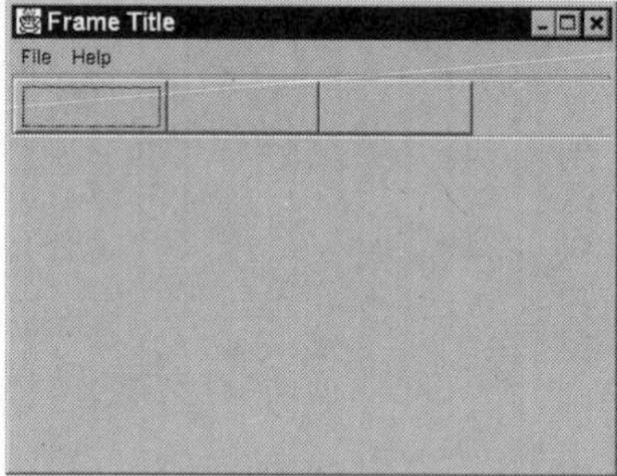


**Figure 7.4** Running the generated application.

The Frame class that was generated and defined on the second page of the wizard with all options chosen generated the following code:

```
package unknown;

import java.awt.*;
import java.awt.event.*;
import javax.swing.*;

/**
 * <p>Title: MainFrame</p>
 * <p>Description: Example Frame class</p>
 * <p>Copyright: Copyright (c) 2002</p>
 * <p>Company: </p>
 * @author Michael Rozlog
 * @version 1.0
 */

public class MainFrame extends JFrame {
  private JPanel contentPane;
  private JMenuBar jMenuBar1 = new JMenuBar();
  private JMenu jMenuFile = new JMenu();
  private JMenuItem jMenuFileExit = new JMenuItem();
  private JMenu jMenuHelp = new JMenu();
  private JMenuItem jMenuHelpAbout = new JMenuItem();
  private JToolBar jToolBar = new JToolBar();
  private JButton jButton1 = new JButton();
  private JButton jButton2 = new JButton();
  private JButton jButton3 = new JButton();
  private ImageIcon image1;
  private ImageIcon image2;
  private ImageIcon image3;
  private JLabel statusBar = new JLabel();
  private BorderLayout borderLayout1 = new BorderLayout();

  //Construct the frame
  public MainFrame() {
    enableEvents(AWTEvent.WINDOW_EVENT_MASK);
    try {
      jbInit();
    }
    catch(Exception e) {
      e.printStackTrace();
    }
  }
  //Component initialization
  private void jbInit() throws Exception  {
    image1 = new
ImageIcon(unknown.MainFrame.class.getResource("openFile.gif"));
    image2 = new
ImageIcon(unknown.MainFrame.class.getResource("closeFile.gif"));
```

**Source 7.3** Generated Frame1.java.

```
    image3 = new
ImageIcon(unknown.MainFrame.class.getResource("help.gif"));

//setIconImage(Toolkit.getDefaultToolkit().createImage(MainFrame.class.g
etResource("[Your Icon]")));
    contentPane = (JPanel) this.getContentPane();
    contentPane.setLayout(borderLayout1);
    this.setSize(new Dimension(400, 300));
    this.setTitle("The is an Example Application");
    statusBar.setText(" ");
    jMenuFile.setText("File");
    jMenuFileExit.setText("Exit");
    jMenuFileExit.addActionListener(new ActionListener()  {
      public void actionPerformed(ActionEvent e) {
        jMenuFileExit_actionPerformed(e);
      }
    });
    jMenuHelp.setText("Help");
    jMenuHelpAbout.setText("About");
    jMenuHelpAbout.addActionListener(new ActionListener()  {
      public void actionPerformed(ActionEvent e) {
        jMenuHelpAbout_actionPerformed(e);
      }
    });
    jButton1.setIcon(image1);
    jButton1.setToolTipText("Open File");
    jButton2.setIcon(image2);
    jButton2.setToolTipText("Close File");
    jButton3.setIcon(image3);
    jButton3.setToolTipText("Help");
    jToolBar.add(jButton1);
    jToolBar.add(jButton2);
    jToolBar.add(jButton3);
    jMenuFile.add(jMenuFileExit);
    jMenuHelp.add(jMenuHelpAbout);
    jMenuBar1.add(jMenuFile);
    jMenuBar1.add(jMenuHelp);
    this.setJMenuBar(jMenuBar1);
    contentPane.add(jToolBar, BorderLayout.NORTH);
    contentPane.add(statusBar, BorderLayout.SOUTH);
  }
  //File | Exit action performed
  public void jMenuFileExit_actionPerformed(ActionEvent e) {
    System.exit(0);
  }
  //Help | About action performed
  public void jMenuHelpAbout_actionPerformed(ActionEvent e) {
    MainFrame_AboutBox dlg = new MainFrame_AboutBox(this);
```

**Source 7.3** *(continued)*

```
    Dimension dlgSize = dlg.getPreferredSize();
    Dimension frmSize = getSize();
    Point loc = getLocation();
    dlg.setLocation((frmSize.width - dlgSize.width) / 2 + loc.x,
(frmSize.height - dlgSize.height) / 2 + loc.y);
    dlg.setModal(true);
    dlg.pack();
    dlg.show();
  }
  //Overridden so we can exit when window is closed
  protected void processWindowEvent(WindowEvent e) {
    super.processWindowEvent(e);
    if (e.getID() == WindowEvent.WINDOW_CLOSING) {
      jMenuFileExit_actionPerformed(null);
    }
  }
}
```

**Source 7.3** *(continued)*

This code generates a complete example (see Figure 7.5). After the instance declarations, you will see that the constructor for the class includes a try block that includes a method call to jbInit(). This private method is the key to all GUI applications in JBuilder. The GUI designer found inside JBuilder specifically hunts for this method when defining the GUI screen.

Seeing the jbInit() method in a class also tells you that a developer has used the GUI designer inside JBuilder. If you click the Design tab under the Content pane, it will change to a GUI designer.

**NO PROPRIETARY CODE GENERATED**

**JBuilder does not use any proprietary markers or nonstandard Java when developing with components or generating code. Other Java IDEs use special tags or compiler markers that could not be moved or modified because the IDE needed to keep track of them to keep the views synchronized. JBuilder, on the other hand, uses a standard method to place all of the GUI code; that way when you change a piece of code in that method, the designer knows to update. Vice versa, when the GUI changes, it will update the code as well. This inconsistency between IDEs is due to a limitation in the JavaBean specification, which does not require GUI code to be located in a certain place or initialization area. This means technically that you could spread your GUI code throughout your class and the Java compiler has to assemble everything. This makes it incredibly hard for IDEs to handle; thus there are different ways to solve the problem.**

Reviewing the code located in the jbInit() method shows all the components that are part of the GUI interface. Clicking the Design tab under the Content pane will give you a sneak peak at the GUI designer found in JBuilder (more on this in Chapter 8, "Modifying Classes"). In Figure 7.5, notice that the Structure pane has been changed to a component tree. An Object inspector has been added to the right side of the screen that allows for changing the properties and events of JavaBean components. Remember that all changes made in this view are made in the code at the same time; this is what gives JBuilder its two-way tool ability.

This simple example has a few coding tricks to make note of. It shows how to use icons in a GUI application and menus and how to work with dialogs, which are nice to know when designing GUI applications. This first application generated by JBuilder had no additional code provided by the developer to make it work. This application could be used by any developer to get a project to the prototype stage very quickly, and it shows that generated code can be good, useful code.

The Interface wizard works exactly like the Class wizard. It is a single-page wizard that allows the setting of the package, interface name, and base interface. Once the criteria have been selected and the Finish button is clicked, JBuilder will produce a standard interface file. This wizard is found only in the SE and Enterprise editions.

The JavaBean wizard is covered in detail in Chapter 13, "Building the Database with JDataStore." This wizard is also available only in the SE and Enterprise editions.

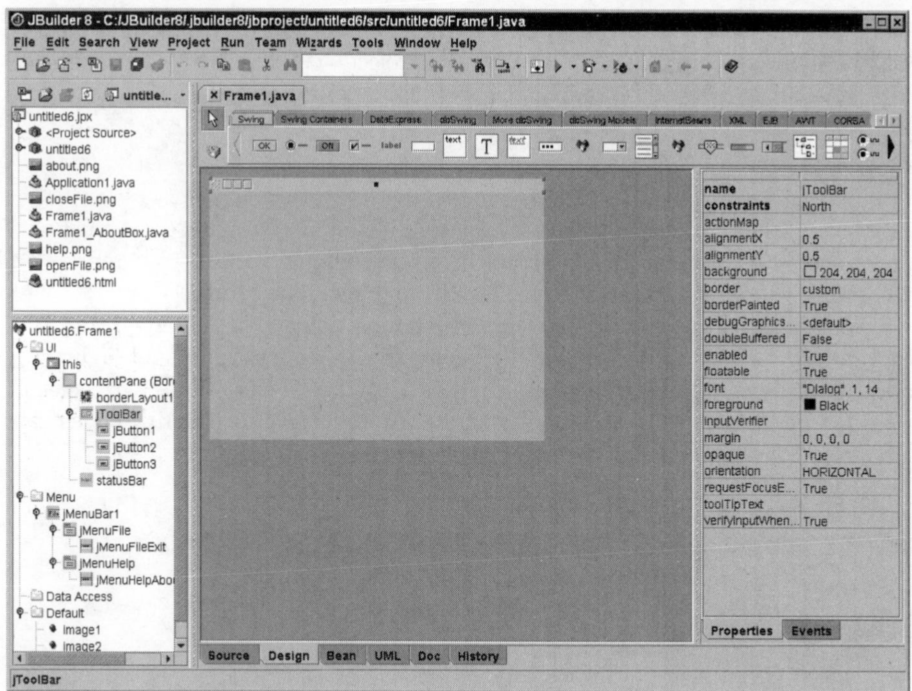


**Figure 7.5** The GUI designer.

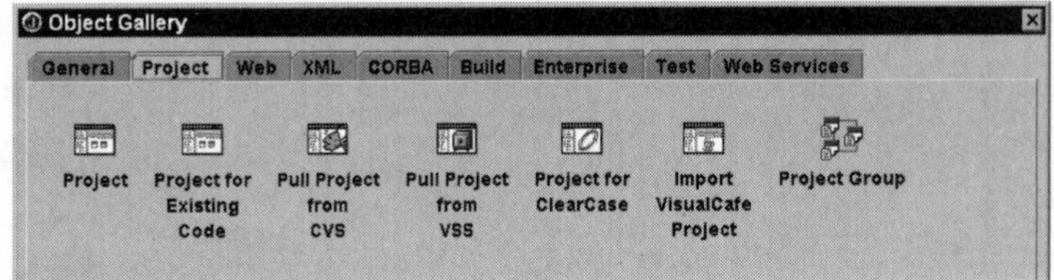


**Figure 7.6** Project tab.

The Dialog, Frame, and Panel wizards are all single-page wizards that allow for creating simple classes of those types. The Dialog wizard will produce a standard dialog with a panel included; the GUI designer is used to customize the dialog. Source 7.3 gives an example of the proper way to call a dialog and the method public void jMenuHelpAbout_actionPerformed(ActionEvent e). The Frame and Panel wizards generate standard empty frames and panels that the GUI designers can manipulate and customize.

The final two wizards on this tab, Data Module and Data Module Application, are covered in Chapter 13 and Chapter 14, "DataExpress and DBSwing Applications." These two are found only in the Enterprise Edition of JBuilder.

## Project Tab

The Project tab (see Figure 7.6) includes all the necessary wizards for setting up projects to use from within JBuilder. The complete Project wizard and its associated properties were covered in their entirety in Chapter 4.

## Web Tab

The Web tab (see Figure 7.7) is found in all JBuilder editions; however, the Applet wizard is the only one enabled in all editions. The remaining wizards are covered in Part Five, "Web Development with Servlets, JavaServer Pages, and Struts."

The one wizard that will not be covered beyond this point is the Applet wizard. This is a multipage wizard for creating and running applets. In Figure 7.8 and Figure 7.9, notice that only two pages of the Applet wizard are displayed — these two pages in particular are the pages that produce the output from the wizard. The first page deals with the standard information JBuilder needs to create a class file.

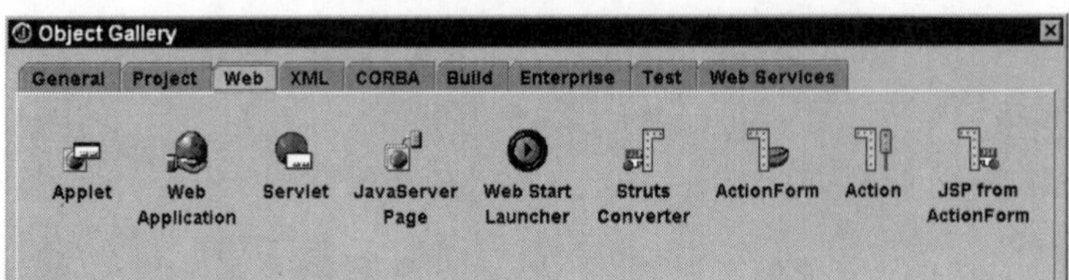


**Figure 7.7** Web tab.

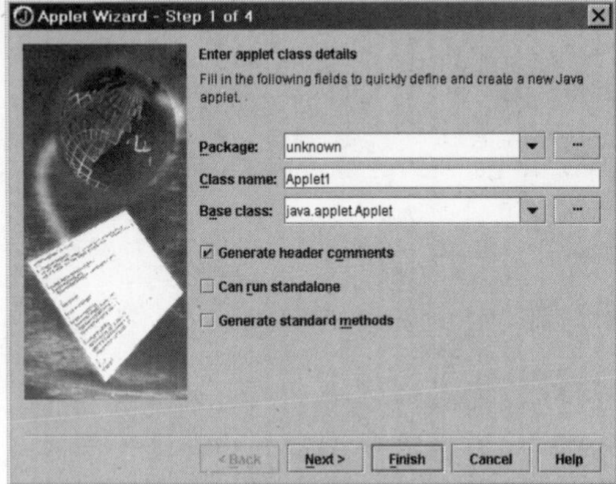


**Figure 7.8** Applet wizard, Step 1 of 4.

The second page allows for parameters to be defined for the HTM file that will be generated, and the final page (Figure 7.9) is used for setting up a Runtime configuration, as covered previously. When the Finish button is clicked, the output includes two files, one of which is a base-level HTML page that includes the <applet> tag. The other is the applet class based on the java.applet.Applet or javax.swing.JApplet.

Just with the information exposed here, the first area of contention is exposed. This is a classic dilemma of supporting the older Applet base class or the new JApplet class. The first thing to remember is that if you are going to use the JApplet class, most likely you will need to have the latest Java/JDK plug-in installed on the executing machine. This also means that at deployment time, if the executing computer does not have the JDK plug-in, the applet will not run. The user of that system will have to download the appropriate files from Sun before they can proceed. This is only one issue when it comes to dealing with applets; there are many more. There are just too many problems with applets to list in this text; many books, articles, and Web sites have been developed over the years to outline all the issues and give suggestions about how to get around the major ones.

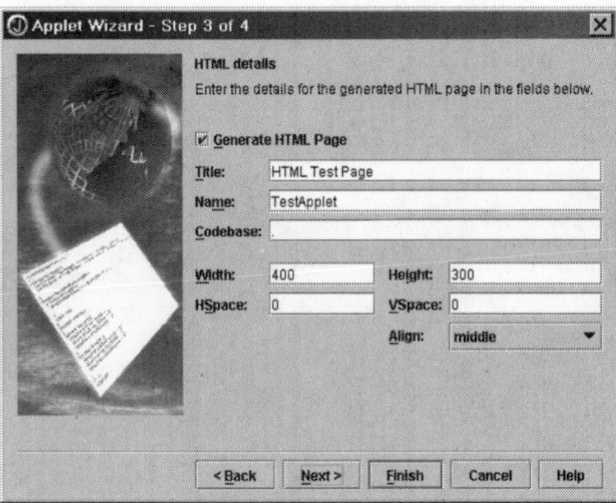


**Figure 7.9** Applet wizard, Step 3 of 4.

In this case, we recommend reading the JBuilder documentation ("Working with Applets"). It covers most of the basic information and has additional pointers from various people who have put in major time and effort trying to get applets to work in their environment.

We have included the output from the wizard here to highlight some of the interesting programming techniques found in the source:

```
package untitled7;

import java.awt.*;
import java.awt.event.*;
import java.applet.*;
import javax.swing.*;

/**
 * <p>Title: </p>
 * <p>Description: </p>
 * <p>Copyright: Copyright (c) 2002</p>
 * <p>Company: Borland Software</p>
 * @author Michael Rozlog
 * @version 1.0
 */

public class Applet1 extends JApplet {
  private boolean isStandalone = false;
  //Get a parameter value
  public String getParameter(String key, String def) {
    return isStandalone ? System.getProperty(key, def) :
      (getParameter(key) != null ? getParameter(key) : def);
  }

  //Construct the applet
  public Applet1() {
  }
  //Initialize the applet
  public void init() {
    try {
      jbInit();
    }
    catch(Exception e) {
      e.printStackTrace();
    }
  }
  //Component initialization
  private void jbInit() throws Exception {
    this.setSize(new Dimension(400,300));
  }
  //Get Applet information
  public String getAppletInfo() {
    return "Applet Information";
```

**Source 7.4** Generated Applet1 code.

```
    }
    //Get parameter info
    public String[][] getParameterInfo() {
      return null;
    }

    //static initializer for setting look & feel
    static {
      try {
  //UIManager.setLookAndFeel(UIManager.getSystemLookAndFeelClassName());

  //UIManager.setLookAndFeel(UIManager.getCrossPlatformLookAndFeelClassNam
  e());
      }
      catch(Exception e) {
      }
    }
  }
```

**Source 7.4** *(continued)*

The only real difference between the java.applet.Applet and the javax.swing.JApplet is a static initializer used for setting the swing Look and Feel. The other interesting area of code is the use of the Ternary (set of three) operator or conditional Boolean operator as defined by Sun, found in the public String getParameter(String key, String def method.

A Ternary operator is one that will produce a value. It is set up as follows:

boolean-expression ? value-0 : value-1

If the boolean-expression is true, then value-0 will be set; if the boolean-expression is false, then value-1 will be set. The question may be raised as to why use a Ternary expression. The answer is fewer keystrokes than if-else block, and the execution should be faster. A word of caution, though, when using a lot of Ternary operators: They can become very difficult to read after a while. This is a perfect example of saving space but making the code more complicated than it really needs to be. It uses a nested Ternary expression, and the value-1 is another Ternary operator, which again will produce either a value-0 or a value-1, which again will satisfy the return value for the calling Ternary expression.

## XML Tab

The XML tab (Figure 7.10) is found only in the JBuilder Enterprise edition.

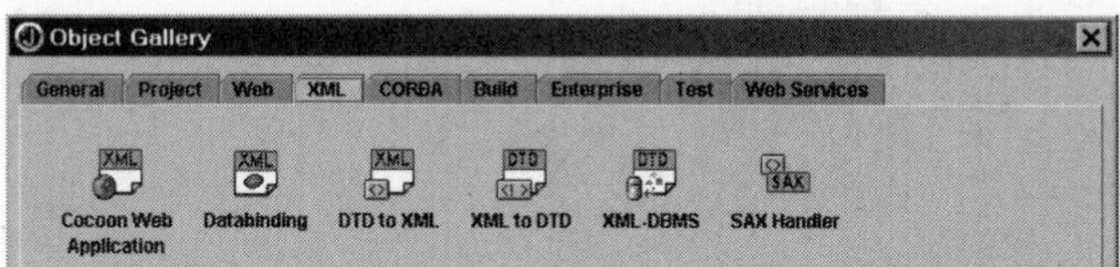


**Figure 7.10** XML tab in the Enterprise edition only.

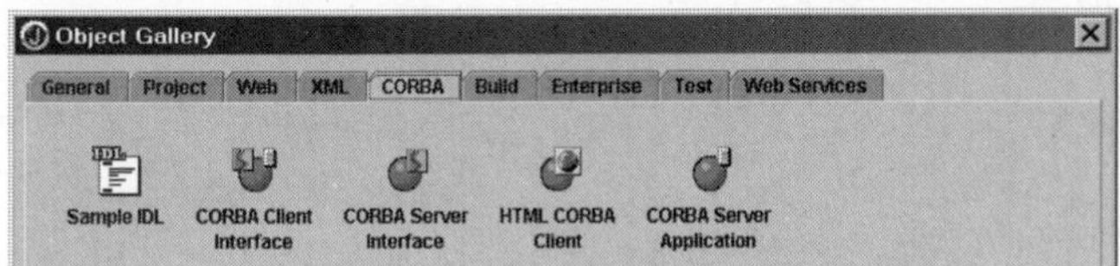


**Figure 7.11** CORBA tab in the Enterprise edition only.

## CORBA Tab

The CORBA tab (see Figure 7.11) is found only in the JBuilder Enterprise edition and is covered in Chapter 22, "CORBA Development with JBuilder."

## Build Tab

The Build tab (see Figure 7.12) is found only in the JBuilder SE and Enterprise editions and is covered in Chapter 10, "Using Build Systems."

## Enterprise Tab

The Enterprise tab (see Figure 7.13) is included only in the Enterprise edition and is covered in Part Six, "Enterprise Development with Enterprise JavaBeans."

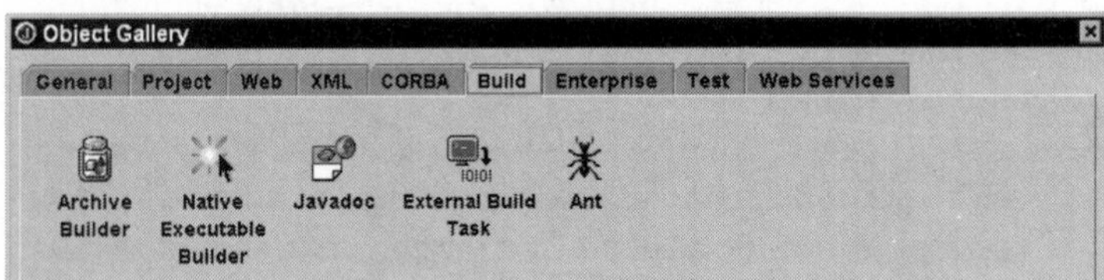


**Figure 7.12** Build tab in the SE and Enterprise editions only.

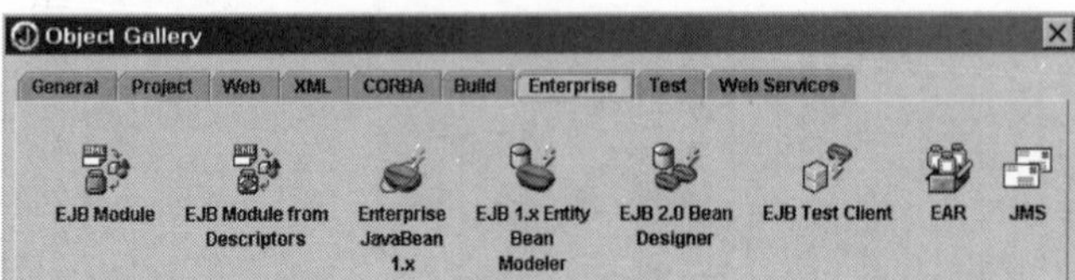


**Figure 7.13** Enterprise tab in the Enterprise edition only.

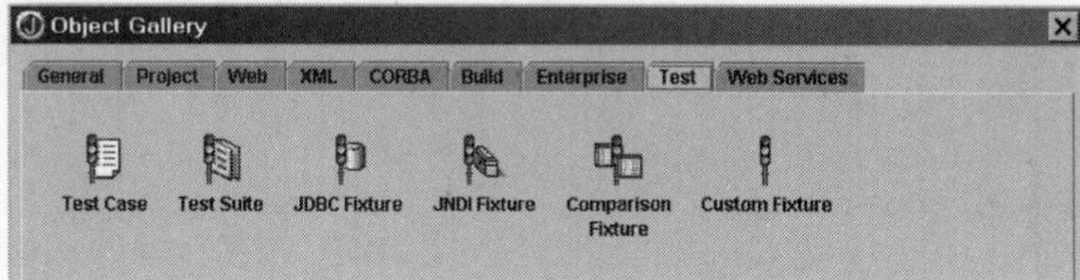


**Figure 7.14** Test tab in the Enterprise edition only.

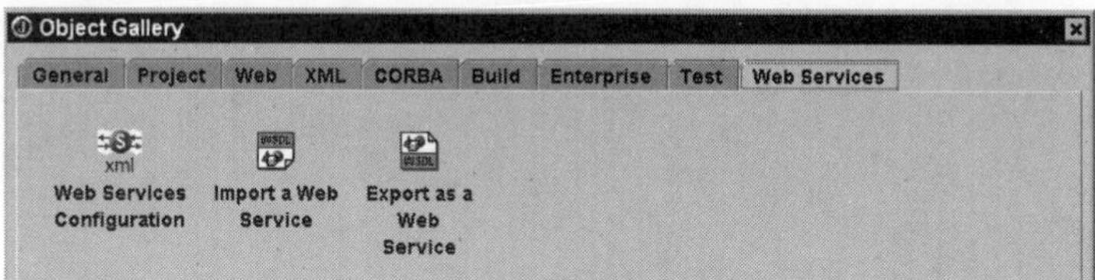


**Figure 7.15** Web Services tab in the Enterprise edition only.

## Test Tab

The Test tab (see Figure 7.14) is included only in the Enterprise edition and is covered in Chapter 11, "Unit Testing with JUnit."

## Web Services Tab

The Web Services tab (see Figure 7.15) is found only in the JBuilder Enterprise edition and is covered in Chapter 23, "Web Services Development with JBuilder."

# Summary

The Object Gallery is full of useful wizards that eliminate a lot of tedious tasks and, we hope, lower the amount of simple errors in setting up projects. Most of the wizards defined are very simple in nature, but they open the door to the power of JBuilder.

CHAPTER

# 8

# Modifying Classes

Understanding the complete JBuilder environment can be a daunting task. Learning about all the shortcuts, wizards, editor options, and plug-ins can be time-consuming; then add the number of new features added to JBuilder with each new release and a very fast release schedule, and you have a lot of time needed to master the tool. This chapter relieves the pain of using an ever-expanding tool by exposing all the panes, tools, wizards, and shortcuts available to the JBuilder developer.

One of the first features that JBuilder brought to the Java development community was its ability to develop JavaBeans to the 1.1 specification. One of the interesting historical items is that JBuilder was actually redesigned to take advantage of that specification and that the prior internal version was killed. The example that is used throughout this chapter covers creating a couple of JavaBeans; the first is a basic business bean, and the second adds a GUI to expose the underlying functionality of the first bean. JavaBeans can be either GUI based or non–GUI based; the important part is that each JavaBean component can be manipulated during the construction phase in a Java IDE that supports JavaBeans. This chapter focuses on creating a set of beans and exposing their functionality through the JBuilder IDE. The example goes over a major portion of the JBuilder environment and shows how to manage all its capabilities.

## Creating the First JavaBean

The first step is to create a new JBuilder project and name it: basebean. For this example, the basebean will be the non-GUI business logic bean. This can be accomplished by either clicking the File | New Project menu item or by bringing up the Object gallery and selecting the Project tab and either double-clicking the Project icon or just selecting the Project icon and then clicking the OK button.

The next step is to create a JavaBean by clicking the File | New menu item, selecting the JavaBean icon, and clicking the OK button. This will display a single-page dialog (see Figure 8.1) that will help define the JavaBean.

Notice that the package was defined by name in the project definition phase (for reference, projects creation was covered in Chapter 4, "Project Properties and Configurations"). This is the first opportunity to change this, or you can change it later using JBuilder's refactoring features. The next option is to name the class (for this example, name it MyBaseBean), followed by choosing what base class will be used for this JavaBean; this should be java.lang.Object. Keep in mind that the base class must not be final; an example of this would be trying to extend a class like java.lang.String. JBuilder will warn the developer of such mistakes and not allow them to continue.

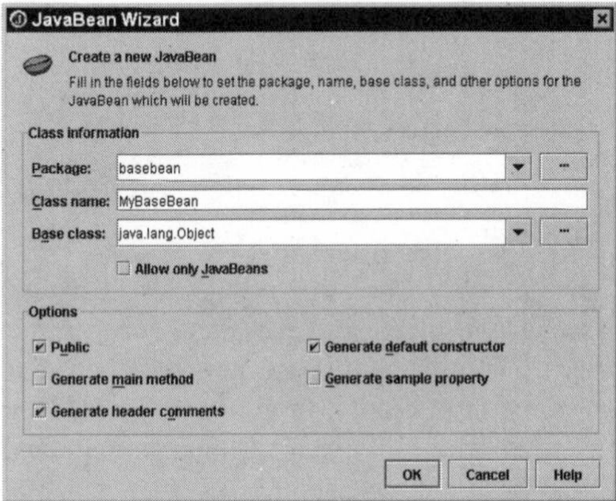


**Figure 8.1** JavaBean wizard.

## WHERE DID JAVABEANS COME FROM?

**JavaBeans are developed using a standard framework for creating components that Sun released with its JDK 1.1. These components are everywhere in the Java platform; GUI components, JFC (Swing), and JSP all are making use of them. The original intent was to have these components developed by a specialized group of developers who would release these components to the Java community to be used by the standard developer. This followed the successful pattern started with the ActiveX community for Microsoft. One of the main requirements for JavaBeans stated that most of the functionality would be exposed through Java IDEs. A JavaBean is rather simple to construct, and no "extra" knowledge is needed to create them. This has been a huge advantage for Java because this makes the technology available to everybody, not just a select group of gurus, as in the Microsoft ActiveX community. One of the nice features about JBuilder is that it will step through the process of creating JavaBeans and has additional tools to determine whether a class is really a JavaBean.**

The wizard remembers the last six beans used as the base class. The most commonly used ones include the java.lang.Object and javax.swing.Panel. You can also search the entire library collection of objects that could be used as the base class for a JavaBean by using the (...) button; the class filter will be display.

When the class filter is displayed, it will show the Object as highlighted because this was the object selected in the JavaBean wizard. This tool has a lot of intelligence included, and it will become the developer's favorite tool as he or she learns its features. If the developer needs to find a class like BoxLayout but does not know where the package is located, select the Search tab, and in the Search for: edit box start typing the word "box", without the quotes, and the class filter will display all classes with the same name in the listbox. The Class filter tool will search all the defined libraries (see Chapter 2, "Customizing the AppBrowser") in the project and return a list of matching classes to the search criteria.

**TIP The class filter can be displayed anytime in the editor by pressing the Control-minus key combination for fast file viewing.**

For the example, erase the "box" and replace it with "object", then select the java.lang.Object from the list and click the OK button to continue. The next option on the JavaBean wizard is a checkbox for "Allow only JavaBeans," which will tell JBuilder to warn the developer if he or she tries to add any classes to the class that do not adhere to the JavaBean specification. This option can be left blank for our example.

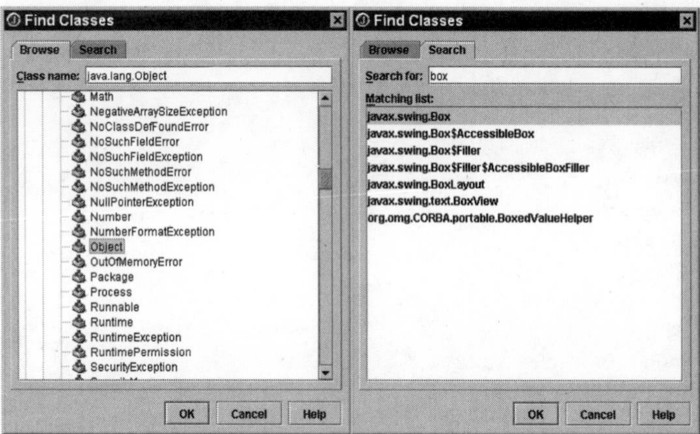


**Figure 8.2** Find Classes.

The next block of options adds characteristics to the class that will be generated. Notice the options selected for the developer. The Public, Generate default constructor, and Generate header comments options are checked, and the first two are required for JavaBeans. The last option adds the JavaDoc header to the file. The Generate main method and Generate sample property are not needed for this example so leave them blank. You may recall that, in Chapter 7, "Creating Classes," when the new Class wizard was discussed, it shared some of the same options. Click the OK button to continue. The output from the code generator may seem a little light, but it does adhere to all of the JavaBean specifications:

```
package basebean;

/**
 * <p>Title: MyBaseBean</p>
 * <p>Description: A generic business bean</p>
 * <p>Copyright: Copyright (c) 2002</p>
 * <p>Company: Borland</p>
 * @author Michael Rozlog
 * @version 1.0
 */

public class MyBaseBean {

  public MyBaseBean() {
  }
}
```

A JavaBean requires a public class with a public constructor, which the generated class definitely has. It supports the concept of properties, methods, and events. Properties represent attributes of the JavaBean that has accessor methods for *getting* and *setting* the values. Standard Java methods are used to manipulate the JavaBean component and work with the accessor methods. Finally, the events are a way for JavaBeans to send and receive notification to one another. Notice that none of the characteristics of a JavaBean is outside the Java programming language, which makes understanding JavaBeans a logical extension to understanding how to work with Java.

```
package example;

/**
 * <p>Title: </p>
 * <p>Description: </p>
 * <p>Copyright: Copyright (c) 2002</p>
 * <p>Company: Borland</p>
 * @author Michael Rozlog
 * @version 1.0
 */

public class MyBaseBean {
  private String sample = "Sample";

  public MyBaseBean() {
  }
  public String getSample() {
    return sample;
  }
  public void setSample(String sample) {
    this.sample = sample;
  }
}
```

If in the last example the Generate sample property option had been checked, then an instance variable and two methods would have been added. The first would have been a getter, and the second would have been a setter, which would make the instance variable a property by the JavaBean specification.

How can you tell if the Java class created is a JavaBean? JBuilder SE and Enterprise offer a tool called BeanInsight that allows you to check any class for JavaBean characteristics. This can be helpful when you are trying to understand why a class behaves a certain way when you think it should work another. A quick example explains one of the questions people always ask about: Why does JBuilder include BoxLayout2 instead of using the standard javax.swing.BoxLayout class? The answer is that BoxLayout is not a JavaBean. Using BeanInsight will show exactly where javax.swing.BoxLayout is lacking. Click the Tools | BeanInsight menu item to start the tool.

By using the (...) button in the tool, the class filter (see Figure 8.3) will be displayed. Using the Search tab in the interface and then typing boxlayout, then selecting the javax.swing.BoxLayout and clicking OK will add that class to the BeanInsight tool; then click the Examine Bean button. The output from the examination can be found in Figure 8.4; as you can see, it reports that javax.swing.BoxLayout is not a JavaBean. To understand why it is not a bean, click the View Details button.

Notice that javax.swing.BoxLayout is not a JavaBean because of the lack of a parameterless default constructor. All information for the bean can be reviewed through this interface; additional information on the BeanInfo, Properties, Events Sets, Property Editors, Customizer, and Attributes can be obtained on the tabs. This would be the reason for JBuilder to include its own class for doing box layout called BoxLayout2; its only purpose is to inherit the original javax.swing.BoxLayout and add a parameterless constructor in the new class, thus allowing it to be used in the JBuilder IDE correctly.

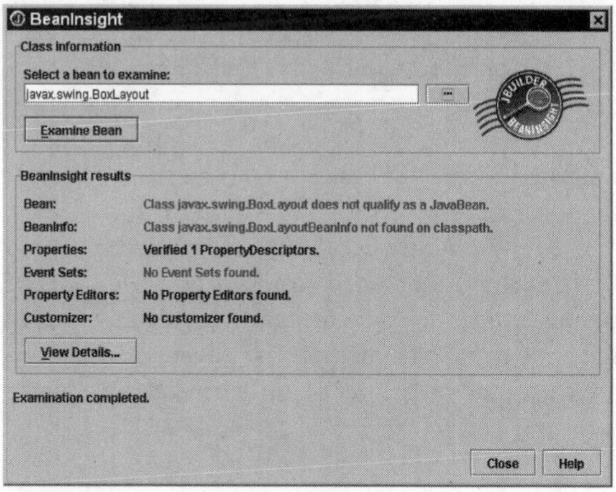

**Figure 8.3** BeanInsight interface.

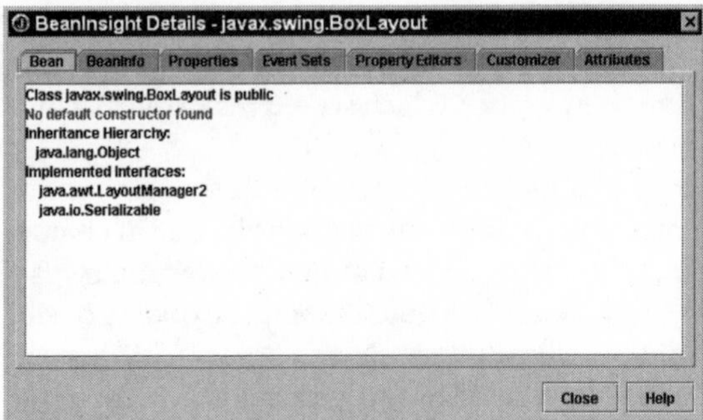


**Figure 8.4** BeanInsight Details dialog.

## Adding Properties

The JavaBean specification has been reviewed, and some JBuilder tools have been exposed. Now it is time to define the rest of the JavaBeans that will be covered in this example. Adding properties is easy in the JBuilder environment. This example uses BeansExpress (see Figure 8.5) to help define and simplify the JavaBean building process. BeansExpress was one of the first specialized designers added to JBuilder 1.0. It made creating and manipulating JavaBeans very simple and very accessible, and it cuts the amount of typing the developer has to do to create JavaBeans. Clicking on the Bean tab under the Content pane will start the BeansExpress designer.

BeansExpress can be used with any Java class. This helps when you want to add properties or an event to a class. Almost any class can be a JavaBean if it follows the simple rules, public class, and public parameterless constructor and uses the JavaBean design patterns of properties, methods, and events. Interestingly enough, BeansExpress was developed using those concepts for the interface and follows that same pattern.

In Figure 8.5, the General tab for BeansExpress is always selected when first started. The first decision that needs to be made is whether the JavaBean will support persistence. Java serialization comes free with Java and is the fastest and easiest way to support persistence; it ensures the "write once, run anywhere" paradigm. In some cases, however, this persistence mechanism has far too many limitations to be reliable. There are also various other methods of persistence from other file formats that use some of the newer APIs found in the JDK for persistence to XML as examples. This example does not use serialization, so nothing needs to be done on the first page. Again, if you wanted to use it, just click the checkbox, and the readObject() and writeObject() methods would be added to the JavaBean.

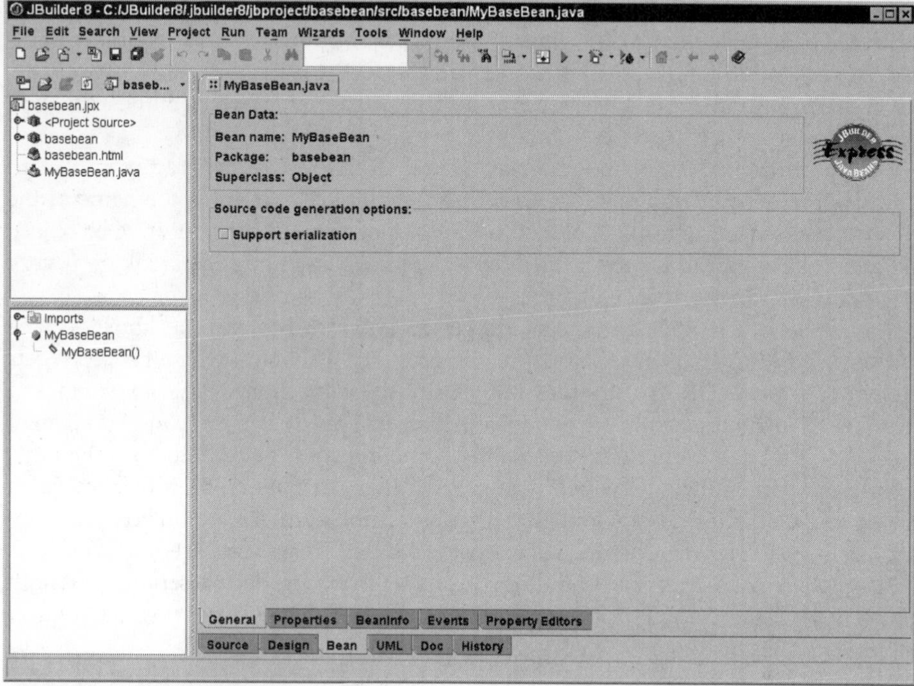


**Figure 8.5** BeansExpress interface.

MyBaseBean will have three properties associated with it. Table 8.1 outlines the types of attributes the bean includes.

**Table 8.1.** MyBaseBean Properties

| NAME | TYPE | GETTER | SETTER | BINDING | EVENT |
|---|---|---|---|---|---|
| aName | String | Yes | Yes | None | NameChange |
| aZip | String | Yes | Yes | Bound | None |
| aAmount | int | Constrained | None | | |
| aText | String | Yes | Yes | None | None |
| aValue | int | Yes | No | None | None |

Clicking on the Properties tab will move the designer to the next step. The main Properties page is defined by the class in focus. Two buttons are located on the page: Add Property and Remove Property. The Add Property button will produce an interface (see Figure 8.6); this interface has additional advanced capabilities that are explained later in the chapter.

The top portion of the New Properties dialog (Figure 8.6) is where the important information for the attribute will be captured. The first data point is the name of the property; the second data point refers to the type of data, either primitive or object. Using the (...) will produce the class filter tool (shown in Figure 8.2), making it very easy to find the class that is being included.

The next set of checkboxes refers to add getters and setters; these checkboxes can be selected to add the accessor methods for the property. The main way a property gets exposed to a Java IDE like JBuilder is by using introspection of the JavaBean and returning all attributes that have getters and setters. This does not mean that all attributes of a class need both methods; actually, sometimes it is better to have only a getter for a particular attribute, which would make that attribute read-only. Likewise, if only a setter method is present for that particular attribute, then it would be write-only. Later in the chapter, other methods of exposing properties are discussed.

The final area of discussion is binding; this refers to the property's sending out notification in the form of events that its value has changed. You have three possible settings for binding:

**None.** This means that no events are fired when a value is changed.

**Bound.** This refers to a generic event being fired, the PropertyChangeListener. This allows general objects to listen for that change event and act accordingly.

**Constrained.** This shares the same characteristics of a bound property, but it also has the ability to be vetoed. This means that other objects can reject the change in value and make the component revert to another value.

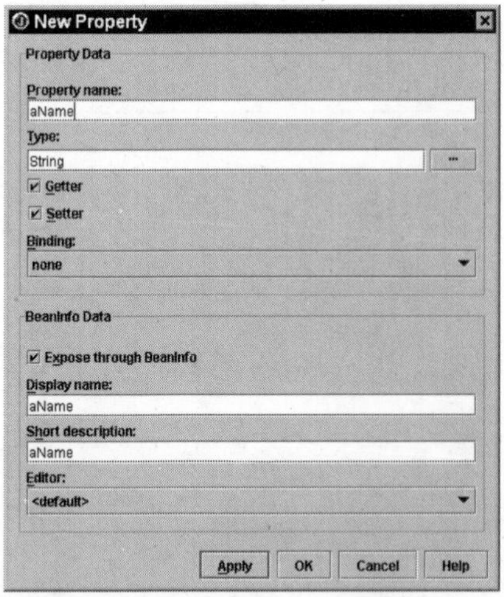

**Figure 8.6** New Property dialog.

The New Property dialog is very simple to use because the first attribute to make into a property will be aName. Type that name into the Property name field. The type of aName is a String, and as it states in the MyBaseBean property table, it has both a getter and a setter. Because everything has been filled in, you can just press Return, and the dialog is ready for the next attribute. Each time you add an attribute to the dialog box in the Structure pane, a private variable for the attribute is added and a getter and setter method for that attribute is added. This produces a JavaBean property, as defined in the JavaBean specification:

```
private String aName;

public String getAName() {
  return aName;
}

public void setAName(String aName) {
  this.aName = aName;
}
```

The aZip property has the same default except that it is a bound property. Click the drop-down listbox and select the bound item. Because a change was made with the mouse or the focus is away from the name field, clicking the Apply button is necessary to add the attribute. The code generator did more than just add the private attribute and its accesssor methods, it also added a PropertyChangeSupport object and the Add and Remove PropertyChangeListener methods:

```
    private String aZip;
    transient private PropertyChangeSupport propertyChangeListeners =
new
                                          PropertyChangeSupport(this);

  public void setAZip(String aZip) {
    String  oldAZip = this.aZip;
    this.aZip = aZip;
    propertyChangeListeners.firePropertyChange("aZip", oldAZip, aZip);
  }

  public String getAZip() {
    return aZip;
  }

  public synchronized void
        removePropertyChangeListener(PropertyChangeListener l) {
          propertyChangeListeners.removePropertyChangeListener(l);
  }

  public synchronized void
        addPropertyChangeListener(PropertyChangeListener l) {
          propertyChangeListeners.addPropertyChangeListener(l);
  }
```

The first noticeable point of the code is that the PropertyChangeSupport object is marked as transient. This is done so that if the class had defined to be persisted with Serialization, this object would not get serialized. The other interesting part about the code is that both the add and remove methods are synchronized to ensure that the object references do not get lost with multiple referencing hitting them. The last point to be made about the code added is the actual setAZip() method. Notice the statement for saving the old value. Then the next expression changes the value, and, because this property is bound, it sends a generic message stating that it has been changed by sending the name of the property and its old and new values.

The next property in the MyBaseBean property table is the aAmount; it is of type int, and it is a constrained property. The binding listbox needs to be set to constrained. Click the Apply button to add the attribute. Like the aZip property, because aAmount is constrained, extra code is generated to support the veto ability of the property:

```
    private int aAmount;
    transient private VetoableChangeSupport vetoableChangeListeners =
new
                                                  VetoableChangeSupport(this);

  public void setAAmount(int aAmount) throws
                                             java.beans.PropertyVetoException {
    int  oldAAmount = this.aAmount;
    vetoableChangeListeners.fireVetoableChange
            ("aAmount", new Integer(oldAAmount), new Integer(aAmount));
    this.aAmount = aAmount;
    propertyChangeListeners.firePropertyChange
            ("aAmount", new Integer(oldAAmount), new Integer(aAmount));
  }

  public int getAAmount() {
    return aAmount;
  }

  public synchronized void
         removeVetoableChangeListener(VetoableChangeListener l) {
           vetoableChangeListeners.removeVetoableChangeListener(l);
  }

  public synchronized void
         addVetoableChangeListener(VetoableChangeListener l) {
           vetoableChangeListeners.addVetoableChangeListener(l);
  }
```

Like the aZip bound property, the aAmount attribute uses the same code setup. The VetoChangeSupport is marked as transient for the same reasons, and the add and remove methods are both synchronized the same way. The interesting area is located in the actual setAAmount() method. First the method throws a PropertyVetoException, and then the old value is kept. The method fires the VetoableChange event, which includes the name of the property and the old and new values for the change. This allows any object that is listening for the event to accept or veto the change. Once that method has completed, the new value is set and the actual fire PropertyChange method is called to notify all listing objects that the object has changed.

Both the PropertyChangeSupport and the VetoChangeSupport objects are generic in nature, allowing each object to be used with multiple objects. When a VetoableChange event occurs, the listening program throws the PropertyVetoException, which is then caught by the method. A property can be vetoed, and the logic for setting another value has to be accepted. The coding structure allows for only two passes; that is why it is important to add the logic for reverting to the prior value.

The final two attributes, aValue and aText, have no special meaning at this time. They can be added by following the MyBaseBean table and setting the appropriate options; the aText property is discussed later in the chapter. The aValue property is just an example of a read-only property; it also has a special purpose, which is discussed later in the chapter. Once these two attributes have been added, click the OK button to continue. It is always wise to save your work periodically, so it is also not a bad idea to save the project at this time.

## Adding Events

Using BeansExpress to add the attributes to MyBaseBean saved a lot of typing and added a lot of functionality with a few checkboxes. Events are just as easy to add. One of the properties that we added was aName. This property had nothing special associated with it, but whenever the name is changed, it would be nice to fire an event that states that the name has been changed. Events in the JavaBeans specification are broken down into two basic objects and one interface. The first object is the Event source, which is responsible for firing the event. The second type of object is called the event object; these objects get fired from the event source. Then the event listeners — the interface portion of the event chain — handle the event through its implementation. Event listeners have to register with the event sources through the event objects, which allow for the completed circle of communication.

Using the BeansExpress interface, click on the Events tab to display a list of generic events that can either be fired or listened for by the bean (see Figure 8.7). The events that are listed are from the Abstract Windows Toolkit (AWT) event model and the Swing event model. None of the events currently has anything to do with the aName property. You now have two options. The first option is the Import event set, which, once imported, will be added to the available event list and then its options can be checked to be either fired or listened for from the class. The other option is to create a custom event, which will give the ability to define a new type of event set. Click the Add new event button to display the dialog, as shown in Figure 8.7.

The first option is to name the new event set; this should be changed to NameChange. The new event object and listener will be added with the new name. The next is the actual events that will be included in the event set. For this example, you will fire only one event — the nameChanged event. Others could be added by simply clicking the Add new event button. For every event added, a fire method will be created for that event; this gives the developer the option to create a whole set of events under one common event type. Once this has been completed, clicking the OK button will return to the events page.

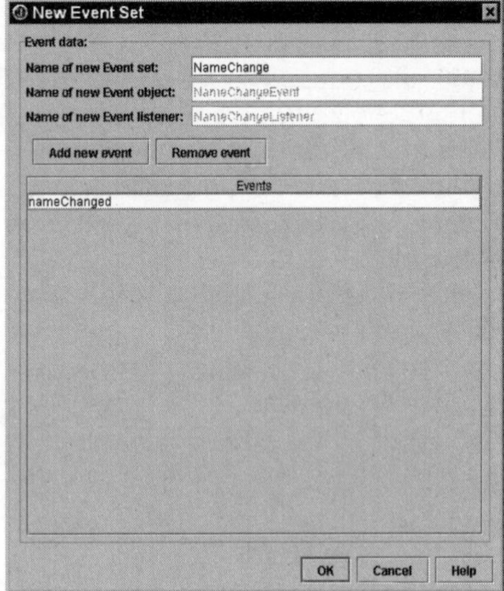


**Figure 8.7** New Event Set dialog.

Two new files have been added to the Project pane, the NameChangeEvent and the NameChangeListener. Notice also that the event list shows the new NameChange events for both firing and listening. Click the NameChange under the fire list; a fireNameChange method will be added to the Structure pane for MyBaseBean.

```
  transient private Vector nameChangeListeners;

 public synchronized void removeNameChangeListener(NameChangeListener l)
{
    if (nameChangeListeners != null && nameChangeListeners.contains(l))
{
      Vector v = (Vector) nameChangeListeners.clone();
      v.removeElement(l);
      nameChangeListeners = v;
    }
  }

public synchronized void addNameChangeListener(NameChangeListener l) {
    Vector v = nameChangeListeners == null ? new Vector(2) : (Vector)

nameChangeListeners.clone();
    if (!v.contains(l)) {
      v.addElement(l);
      nameChangeListeners = v;
    }
  }
```

```
protected void fireNameChanged(NameChangeEvent e) {
    if (nameChangeListeners != null) {
      Vector listeners = nameChangeListeners;
      int count = listeners.size();
      for (int i = 0; i < count; i++) {
        ((NameChangeListener) listeners.elementAt(i)).nameChanged(e);
      }
    }
  }
```

Again, the vector that holds the NameChangeListeners objects is marked as transient because the state should not be kept between instantiations and the add and remove method are still synchronized. The interesting part of the code comes with the fireNameChange(NameChangeEvent e) method, which is responsible for notifying each resisted listener that the value has changed. Notice in Figure 8.8 that the new NameChange event has been added to the list of possible events to either fire or listen for. Saving a rebuilding at this stage is always recommended, although the time to recreate the project to this point would be insignificant.

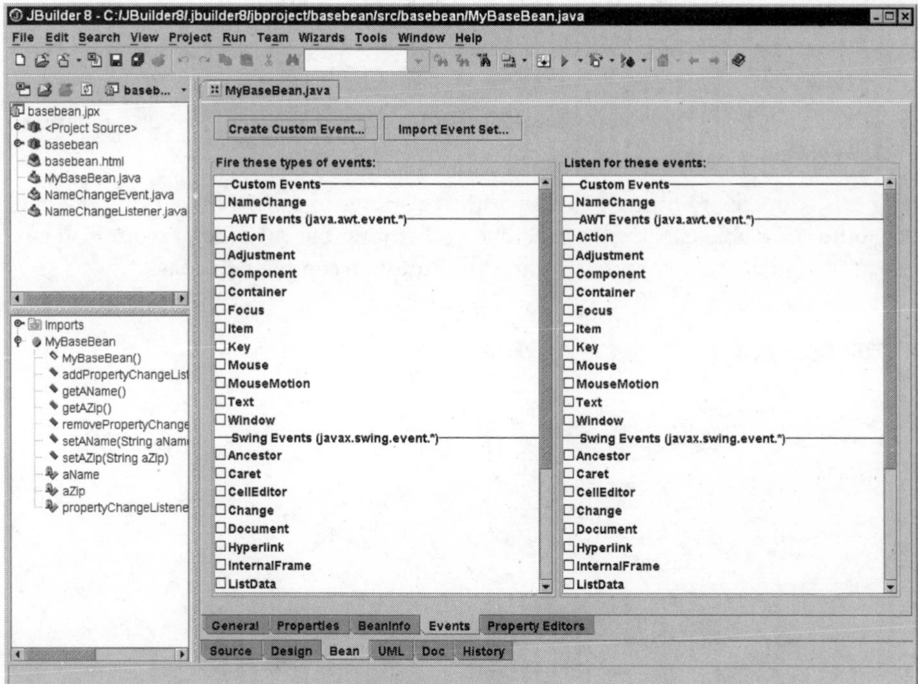


**Figure 8.8** JBuilder and Events panel.

## Adding Property Editors

Often, properties can have defined values or can be represented by other objects that have a full set of attributes associated with them. The JavaBean specification outlines property editors, which are specialized classes that the Java IDEs can use to help set properties. Some of the common property editors that most people have been exposed to while using a Java IDE like JBuilder include border, color, and font properties. Each is packaged with specialized editors from Sun. The BeansExpress interface gives a very easy way to add customized property editors to your JavaBean. The property aZip could have a set of Zip codes returned, making it very easy for the developer to choose the proper Zip code, thereby eliminating typing and bad information.

To add a property editor in BeansExpress, simply click the Property Editor tab. This will display all the registered property editors for this project. As with the Events tab, two options are available, Create Custom Editor or Import Property Editor. Click the Create Custom Editor option to show the dialog (see Figure 8.9).

The first task is to name the new Property Editor ZipList. The second task is to select the type of editor it will become. The choices include the following:

- String List, a set of string values that get selected
- String tag list, a value pair with both values being type String
- Integer tag list, which includes a display String, int value, and Java initialization string
- Custom Editor Component, which includes the name of the class and whether the editor will paint itself

For this editor, use a String List and add five strings to the list by clicking the Add Entry button. Double-clicking on each line and editing the value can accomplish customization of the String values. Click the OK button to complete this task.

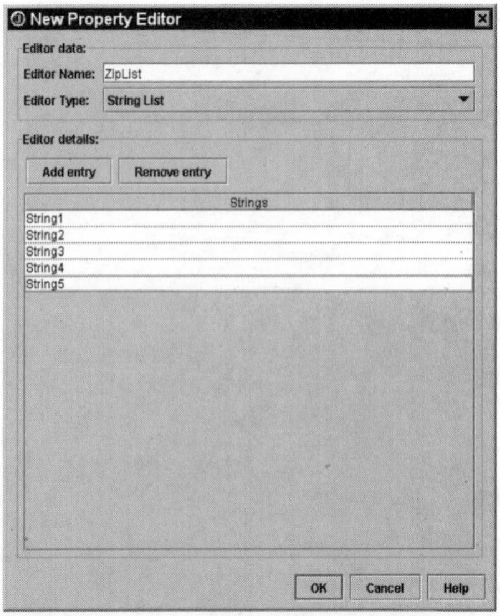

**Figure 8.9** New Property Editor dialog.

## Adding a BeanInfo Class

JavaBeans use introspection and reflection to obtain information about JavaBean classes and whether the specification design patterns were adhered to when creating a JavaBean. This technique works well. Additional properties and resources need to be added to the JavaBean, though. A JavaBean is meant to be used in the Java IDE, and the BeanInfo class was created to hold resources like images to be used on a component pallet, attributes for overriding exposure of properties, and the ability to assign property editors to a particular property. All these things need to be included with a JavaBean and are held in the BeanInfo class. Click the BeanInfo tab in the BeansExpress interface to start the designer (see Figure 8.10).

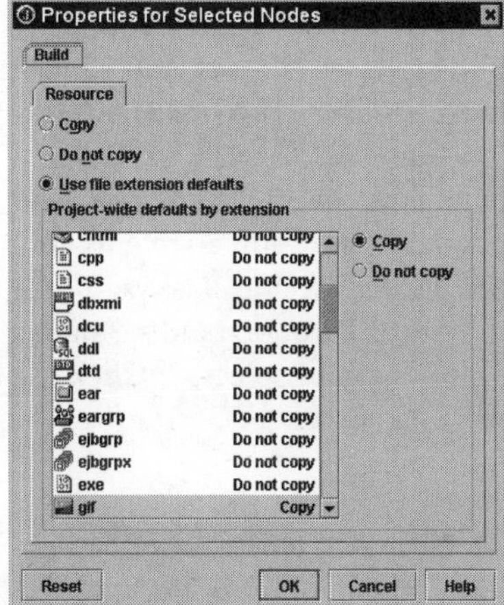


**Figure 8.10** BeanInfo interface.

The following steps need to be taken:

1. Add icons.
2. Set property editors.
3. Limit exposure of properties.

The first thing to take care of is to add icons to the project source to be added to the interface. Starting with JBuilder 8 and JDK 1.4.x, the drag-and-drop has finally been enabled so that it is now possible to drag a file from a file explorer and drop it into the JBuilder editor. Currently this adds it only for viewing purposes; it does not add it to the project. This can be done using the Add file to project button at the top of the Project pane. The most successful way to handle this task is to copy the images to your source directory first, then add them to the project using the Add file button. Use any 16 x 16 and 32 x 32 icons that are available. If no icons are associated with the BeanInfo class, JBuilder will assign a generic icon; however, JBuilder will also throw an exception explaining that a resource is missing in the GUI designer. This exception will not cause the component not to work; it is more for information purposes. Once the files have been added to your project, right-mouse click on the files and verify the properties for this node type (see Figure 8.11), and it should be set to copy.

Setting the property to copy will make sure that the images are copied into the output directory and can be built in a proper fashion during that process. For more information on the build process, refer to Chapter 10, "Using Build Systems." Once this is complete, click the OK button to continue.

Once the images have been copied and the properties set, it is time to associate them with the BeanInfo. Clicking in the (...) beside the icon edit box will allow you to assign the images. You can use color images for both color and mono icons.

Next, the property editor needs to be set for the aZip property. This can be done by double-clicking in the editor cell on the aZip row and adding the ZipList name; make sure to press Return to save the value.

The last attribute that needs to be set in the BeanInfo class is to turn off exposure of the aText property. There are times when properties are part of the class; however, they are not to be exposed to the Java IDEs. This gives the developer the ultimate control over the exposure level. To un-expose the property, simply deselect the aText and AText properties.

Once the resources, assignments, and exposures have been set, the final task is to generate the BeanInfo. Before the button is clicked, another option is available to you, to Expose superclass BeanInfo. If a lot of properties from the underlying class would be useful to the developer, and if they will not interfere with the understanding of the component, this option can be selected. For our object, leave it unselected. Click the Generate BeanInfo button, and the JBuilder code generators will create the BeanInfo class.

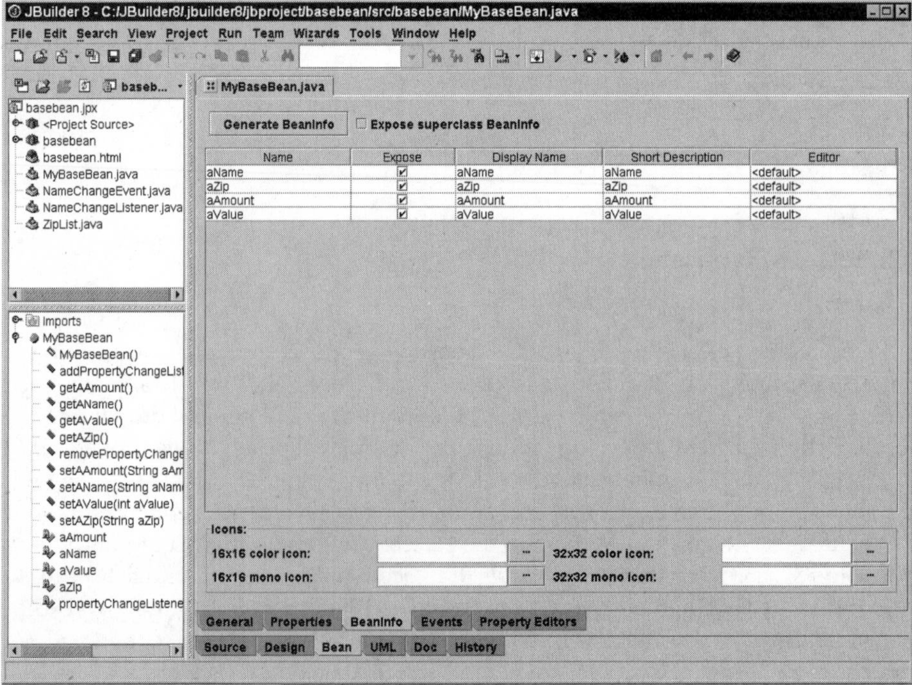


**Figure 8.11** Properites for Selected Nodes dialog.

The lower half of the Add Properties dialog in Figure 8.6 exposes a single location for setting BeanInfo data. This lower part of the dialog can be used to set exposure levels, define new labels for properties, and point the property to the custom property editor. This can save time and help the developer expose these options early in the development process.

**WARNING Sometimes BeansExpress can be too smart for its own good. Sometimes when the BeanInfo or properties need to be changed, JBuilder will not allow changes to occur, no matter how the developer tries to fix the problem. If this occurs, simply exit JBuilder and go to the source directory and delete the {bean name}.jpx and {bean name}.jpx~ files and restart JBuilder. These files are used by BeansExpress so that it remembers where it was if you come back to a session at a later time.**

Now is a good time to save and rebuild the code. This should take only a few names and button clicks, as BeansExpress should have generated everything up to this point.

## Adding Custom Code

A few lines of custom code are needed to make the JavaBean complete. The first task is to add a fireNameChange event when the name gets changed. Because the NameChange event is a custom event set, the extra line needs to be added to the source code. Click the source tab, and then click on the setName(String aName) method to take the focus to that method. Add a line after the aName value is set. Then using ClassInsight (Ctrl-H), start typing in the word fire, select the fireChangeName method, and press Return. This will put the cursor inside the first open parentheses; notice that ParameterInsight tells the developer that the method is expecting NameChangeEvent. Because a NameChangeEvent is not lying around, create a new NameChangeEvent (again, when the ParameterInsight appears, it will ask for a source). Because the object is changing the name in this bean, use the this keyword and finish the line. It should appear like this:

```
fireNameChanged(new NameChangeEvent(this));
```

You should also check to see whether the base level object methods should be overridden. These methods include toString(), hashcode(), equals(), and sometimes clone(). Good coding practices state that whenever you create a new object, these three methods should be overridden. In general practice, most new objects can be made without overriding these methods without a problem. For insight into the problem, press the Ctrl-minus key combination; this will start the Class filter. Click on the Search tab and enter the object in the edit box, then select the java.lang.Object and click OK to continue. This will load the java.lang.Object source into JBuilder. Click the Doc tab, and review the Hashcode() and Equals() methods documentation on the subject. Various articles have been written on the subject of just how to write the best methods for hashcode() and equals(), which is outside the scope of this book.

## Java's Way of Solving the Problem

Currently it depends on the situation you are trying to solve; however, looking at the JDK for answers can be a great place to start. One object that always has to follow the rules set in the Java documentation would be the java.lang.String class. Keep in mind that the String class is marked as final, but the equals() and hashcode() methods give some great examples.

This code actually counts the value of the string to make sure another string matches it:

```
public boolean equals(Object anObject) {
       if (this == anObject) {
           return true;
       }
       if (anObject instanceof String) {
           String anotherString = (String)anObject;
           int n = count;
           if (n == anotherString.count) {
                  char v1[] = value;
                  char v2[] = anotherString.value;
                  int i = offset;
                  int j = anotherString.offset;
                  while (n-- != 0) {
                      if (v1[i++] != v2[j++])
                              return false;
       }
       return true;
           }
       }
       return false;
}
```

The hashcode method creates value of the string:

```
public int hashCode() {
       int h = hash;
       if (h == 0) {
           int off = offset;
           char val[] = value;
           int len = count;

         for (int i = 0; i < len; i++) {
             h = 31*h + val[off++];
         }
         hash = h;
     }
     return h;
}
```

Both examples ensure that each object will adhere to the stated rules for overriding these methods when creating a new object.

This example uses simple techniques to get around the technical issues associated with creating a new object in Java. Because the JavaBean will not be used often and most likely will not be searched in large hashtables, these techniques will not cause major problems. If, however, the object would be used in those types of systems that have huge hashtables, then the methods might have to be rewritten to maintain the speed of the search.

JBuilder wizards can be used to override these methods. Make sure the current class in focus inside JBuilder is the MyBaseBean, then click the Wizards | Override Methods menu item; this will display the object's methods that can be overridden.

Notice that the inherited classes show only the java.lang.Object because MyBaseBean extends only objects. If other objects were present, they would be presented in a separate tree node. You can also select the class from the drop-down listbox located inside the dialog; keep in mind that it is read only and cannot be modified. Select the equals(Object), hashCode(), and toString() methods by holding down the Shift key while using the mouse to select. Click the OK button, and you will notice that three new methods were added to the Structure pane. The To Do tree-node icon located in the Structure pane should also be added. If expanded, the tree should show all three new methods.

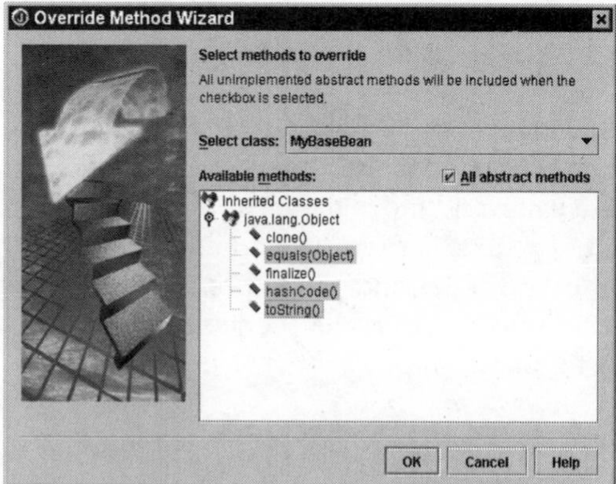


**Figure 8.12** Override Method Wizard dialog.

## Setting To-Do's Inside Code

Any time you want to leave a note, message, or reminder about a piece of code, you can leave a simple to-do JavaDoc tag. This can be done almost anywhere in the code by typing todo and pressing Crtl-J. The JavaDoc to-do tag will be placed at the cursor position; then type the message or task that needs to be completed, and it is done. The to-do will be added to the To-Do tree-node; selecting the to-do in the Structure pane will automatically put the focus on the line of the to-do.

## Overriding the equals() Method

Clicking on the top to-do from the list will put the focus at the equals() method. It should show a return method like this:

```
return super.equals(parm1);
```

This method should not be used because our method's super class is Object, which means the methods will return false if they do not have the same memory addresses in the JVM. A better implementation of the method would be:

```
return this.getClass().equals(parm1.getClass())
```

This method will, at least, compare the two classes on the same level. Once this code has been added, you can remove the to-do line above the method.

## Overriding the toString() Method

You cannot count on the toString() method being overridden automatically, so this should be done in all newly created classes. Most of the time, garbage is returned with the toString() method because the base java.lang.Object will use the following method to return a string value:

```
return getClass().getName() + "@" + Integer.toHexString(hashCode());
```

Notice that this code returns the class's name and its hashcode in Hex, which is useful. For MyBaseBean, its toString() method will support full toString characteristics. Click on the first to-do line in the Structure pane, and move the focus to the toString() method. Because this class is very limited, it will be easy to support all values; however, if this class was large and had a lot of attributes and properties, a dip into the reflection and introspection APIs might be in order to make the job more generic. Using the following code will do the trick for our example:

```
String text1 = this.getAName() + ", ";
String text2 = this.getAZip() + ", ";
String text3 = String.valueOf(this.getAAmount()) + ", ";
String text4 = String.valueOf(this.getAValue()) + ", ";
String text5 = this.getAText()+". ";
return getClass().getName() + ": " + text1 + text2 + text3+ text4 +
                                       text5;
```

When this method is called, it will return a string value that might represent something useful. Remove the to-do line above the return to finish the method.

## Overriding the hashCode() Method

The final override is of the hashCode() method. Click the last to-do line in the Structure pane to begin this process. One of the main reasons for adding the aValue property was to use it as the hashCode for the object. Once the hashCode has been set for the object, it should not be changed. One of the simplest ways to solve the hashCode rules, as stated previously, is to return the same number; some people use zero (0), and others use another standard number like 7777. In most cases, this will not cause a problem because the object is made in limited quantities, thus eliminating the possibility of performance problems or lost hashCode keys. Keep in mind, though, that a true hashCode should be equally distributed across the integer's number range, as is the case with the code above used in the java.lang.String class. For this example, we will use the following code:

```
this.aValue = 7777;
return aValue;
```

Once this is complete, remove the to-do tag and do a Save all to the project. Finally, MyBaseBean is complete; it has all the base elements of a standard JavaBean. MyBaseBean has exposed attributes that have been made into properties, both read-write and read-only, plus we added a property that has the getter and setter but is not exposed through the use of the BeanInfo class. This bean has exposed a generic property editor that surfaces a string list for the Zip codes. The JavaBean also exposes a few standard events, which include the standard bound and constrained properties. It also implements a custom event set for when the name is changed.

It is time to rebuild the code and make sure that it does not have any errors or base typing problems. About 10 lines of custom code should be added; everything else was generated by either the BeansExpress designer or JBuilder itself. JBuilder scans for syntax errors before compiling and notifies the developer of problems. This allows the developer to make the simple changes without compiling the code, which lowers the overall time spent getting code ready to test. Normally, a test unit would be created at this time to run some very basic tests on the bean to ensure that all of the code created was correct. See Chapter 11, "Unit Testing with JUnit," for more information on adding this later in the project lifecycle.

Another process that would most likely be done is an archive build process. Chapter 10 gives the details of this process — again, this can be done at a later time. Once the rebuild has been successfully completed by clicking the Project | Rebuild MyBaseBean.java menu item or by clicking the drop-down build task button on the toolbar, it is time to move to the next part of the example, which is adding a visual interface to the MyBaseBean.

## Building a Visual JavaBean

Now that we have created the first bean, it is time to create a visual JavaBean that will expose MyBaseBean's functionality so that it can be used in an application. After creating a new project called visualbean, the next step is to create a new JavaBean. This can be accomplished by clicking the File | New menu item that will display the Object Gallery. Select the JavaBean icon, and press the OK button to continue. This will generate the New JavaBean dialog (see Figure 8.1 for reference), which we used in the first part of the example.

This time name the JavaBean MyVisualBean, and make sure that its base class is javax.swing.JPanel. This can be accomplished by clicking the drop-down listbox on the base class or by using the (...) button to start the Class Filter dialog and typing in JPanel (see Figure 8.2 for eference).

Next, check the Allow only JavaBeans checkbox to ensure that only JavaBeans are added to the class. This way, attempts to add non-JavaBean classes will result in a warning. Again, because the desired output from this is a JavaBean, leave the Public, Generate default constructor, and Generate header comments with checks. The Generate main method and Generate sample property do not need to be selected because this bean is not meant to run stand-alone. It will not need a main method, and the BeansExpress designer can be used to create new properties if needed. Press the OK button to continue.

Differences between this class and the first one created include the default constructor, a jbInit() method, which is covered in detail in Chapter 7. Also, this class extends from JPanel, which is found in the javax.swing package. Notice also that imports have been added to handle these concepts.

## Using the GUI Designer

To activate JBuilder's GUI designer, click the Design tab under the Content pane. While the designer is being activated, you will see a message stating that it is loading. Lazy-loading — the concept of not loading tools until they are needed — is another advanced feature of JBuilder. As a result, JBuilder loads faster and has a smaller memory footprint to manage.

Once the GUI designer has been loaded (see Figure 8.13), the interface completely changes from the coding interface. The only thing that has stayed in place is the Project pane; the Structure pane and coding Content pane have all been replaced. The Structure pane has been replaced with a component tree, and the coding Content pane has been replaced with a component palette, a design space, and an Object Inspector.

The component palette contains more than 100 predeveloped JavaBeans that are both visual and nonvisual. These JavaBean components come from many sources, including Sun's JFC (Java Foundation Classes and AWT) and Borland (DataExpress, DBSwing, InternetBeans, XML, EJB, and CORBA) components. The component palette is completely configurable, as is demonstrated later in this section.

The Object Inspector allows quick changing of property values and firing events from the interface. It uses the reflection and introspection APIs to display all the JavaBean properties and events, as well as the BeanInfo class (if it is present). The designer works with the component tree, component palette, and the Object Inspector.

When creating a JavaBean that extends a JPanel, the developer will be presented with a standard panel that has a layout manager of BorderLayout. This does not mean that BorderLayout is the default layout manager for JPanel; it just means that JBuilder normally sets the base visual component to BorderLayout, if possible. The completed interface can be seen in Figure 8.14.

The first component added to the GUI designer is another JPanel. This can be placed a number of ways. First, click the Swing Containers tab on the component palette, and then click the JPanel icon, which is the first icon on the particular tab. This may not be obvious the first time using the components; place the mouse pointer over the icon images, and the fly-by help will display the full class name in a few seconds. Once the JPanel has been selected, it can be placed either onto the designer where a visual representation of the panel is shown or on the component tree under the "this" image. If the JPanel is dropped onto the visual representation inside the designer, make sure it is dropped (clicked) in the approximate area of where the panel is supposed to be located. Because this panel is supposed to be located in the South constraint of the BorderLayout,

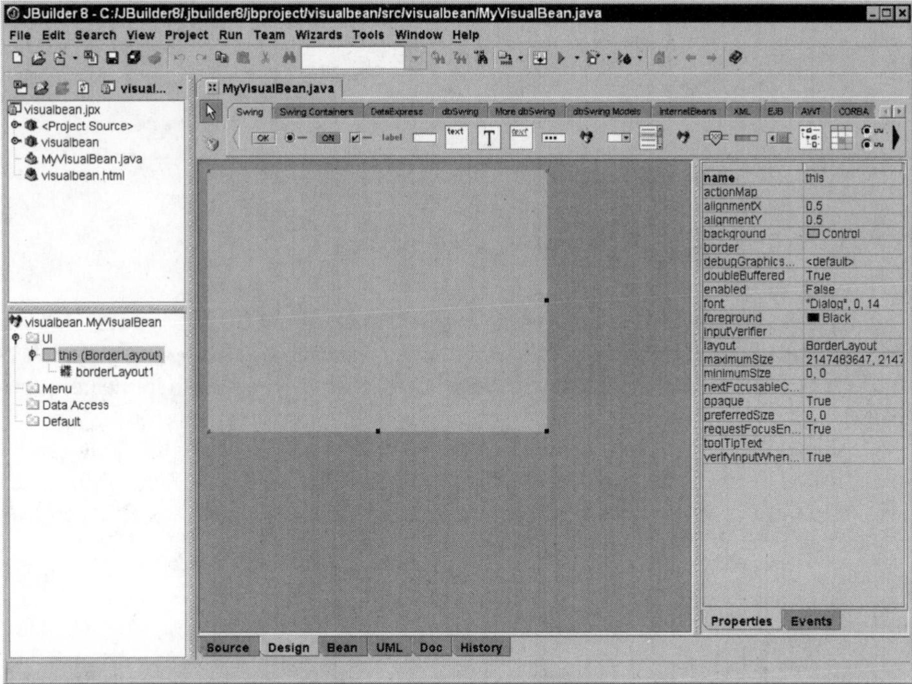


**Figure 8.13** JBuilder's GUI designer.

it should be dropped (clicked) near the bottom of the visual representation of the panel. If the panel is dropped (clicked) in the proper location, the Object Inspector constraints for the dropped panel should show South. If the panel was dropped (clicked) inside the component tree, it most likely will have the constraint of North. This can be changed by clicking on the constraints property in the Object Inspector and selecting South. Once this has been done, the visual representation of the panel will be moved to the lower part of the panel.

Now that the panel is in the proper location, it needs to have its Border property set. This can be set by using the drop-down list and selecting the RaisedBevel property. The layout manager then needs to be set for this component, as shown in Figure 8.15.

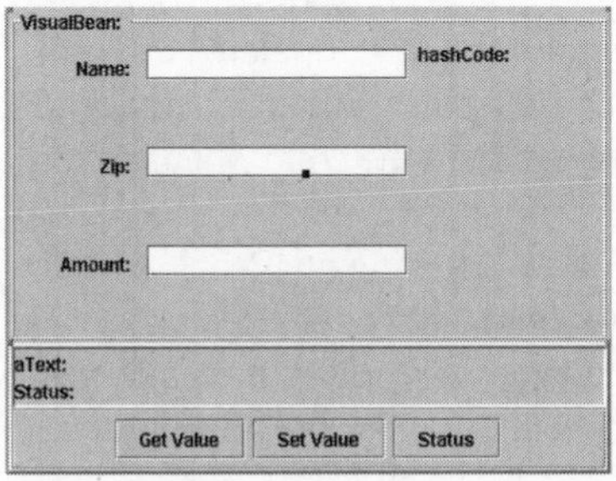

**Figure 8.14** GUI interface for MyVisualBean.

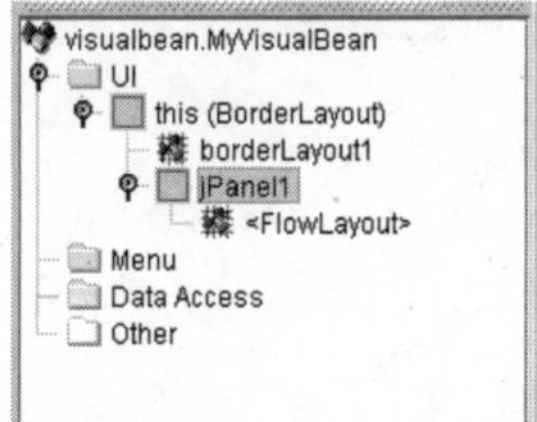


**Figure 8.15** Default layout manager.

In Figure 8.15, the expanded tree-node for the jPanel1 shows FlowLayout inside < > symbols. This represents the default layout manager for this JavaBean. The default layout does not allow you to change layout properties. This will be shown in the next couple of steps.

This jPanel1 needs to have a different layout manger — GridLayout. This can be accomplished by changing the layout property for the jPanel1 component. Once it has been set to GridLayout, you'll notice that the image under jPanel1 has changed (see Figure 8.16).

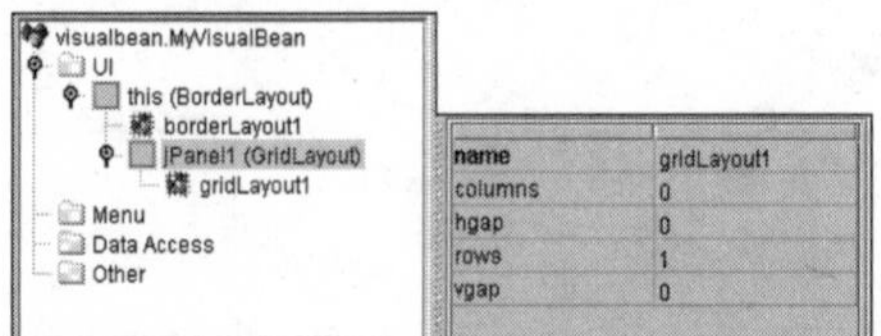


**Figure 8.16** Standard layout and properties.

Again, notice that no < > are present, which means that it is either a true instance variable or the layout manager for this component has changed. Figure 8.16 also shows that one gridLayout property is set for the jPanel1. It can be selected, and its properties can be set in the Object Inspector. Currently, the rows property is set to 1, but this needs to be changed to 2. When changing a value inside the Object Inspector, it is a best practice to press Return after making a change; this ensures that the new value has been accepted. The reason behind this is that properties can be constrained like aAmount in MyBaseBean and that a value change can be vetoed.

Once the jPanel1's gridLayout manager row's property has been set to 2, it is time to add the next two components. Click the JPanel again on the component palette, then click on the jPanel1 located inside the component tree. This will place a jPanel2 under the jPanel1 component. Next, click on the JPanel component again on the component palette, and click on the jPanel1 component located inside the component tree. This should add another panel under jPanel1, which is represented by jPanel3. Clicking on jPanel3 to make sure it is selected, click the border property for that component. Using the drop-down list, select the LoweredBevel, and then change its layout manager to gridLayout. Once gridLayout has been selected, expand the jPanel3 tree control and set its rows property to 2 and press Return.

After that has been set, add labels to the jPanel3. Select the Swing tab on the component palette, then the JLabel component (the fifth component from the right). Then click on the jPanel3 inside the component tree to drop the JLabel, then repeat the process again so that two JLabels are on top of one another. Figure 8.14 gives an example of how the layout should look. Once the labels have been placed inside the jPanel3, it is time to label each one of them. This can be done by selecting each label and setting its text property to "aText:" for the top and "Status:" for the bottom label.

**NOTE The order of the component can be changed with the drag-and-drop features inside the designer or by changing the order of the code located in the jbInit() method. If drag-and-drop is used, make sure to hold down the mouse when selecting the component and then drag it to the desired location inside the container. Do not go outside to the parent container; the component will be placed there if the mouse is released. If the code order is changed, it will be reflected in the tab order because the tab order is set by the creation order.**

jLabel1 should be set to "aText:" and jLabel2 should be set to "Status:" for this example. The next step is to add three JButtons to jPanel2. Again, following the same steps described previously, click the JButton icon on the component palette, and click on the jPanel2 located inside the component tree. This should be done three times. Then, using the drag-and-drop technique discussed previously, put the jButtons in order of 1,2,3. Again, another way of completing the task would be to drop the jButtons in order on the actual jPanel2 visual representation. Once the jButtons are in order, change the text properties to show "Get Value" for jButton1, "Set Value" for jButton2, and "Status" for jButton3. Using the component tree is useful when a lot of nested containers are used. This gives absolute control to the developer, thus allowing the properties to be changed after the components have been dropped. The last thing that needs to be set on jPanel2 is its border property, which should be set to etched from the drop-down list.

The next step in developing a GUI for MyBaseBean — the top portion of the layout — is the most important. Click the Swing Containers tab, select a JPanel from the component palette, and then click in the center of the visual representation. It should set the new panels constraints to Center.

## Creating a Border Component

Setting the border for jPanel4 is a different process than the process we used to before; we will create a custom border. Click the (...) on the border property for jPanel4. This will display a custom property editor for creating borders (Figure 8.17).

This custom property editor is broken into five major parts. The first part is how the objects are going to be created. If an instance of a border exists in the class, it can be reused for another component, or an instance variable can be created for the border that will be created when the interface is finished, or everything can be done with static instances. The second part of the property editor is focused on type and location. The third major part is focused on the border style and the options associated with the style. The fourth part is focused on labeling and using inner borders. The final part is focused on previewing the properties selected in the editor, which allows you to play "what-ifs" for the components.

A JPanel4 border begins with the creation of an instance variable. You then use the Etched type, with no changes to the insets. The Bevel Style and Options will be the default, and the Title property should be set to "VisualBean:". Once all the properties for the border have been set, click on the preview area to see the example of the border to be created. You can change the properties of the border until it looks the way you want it to, rather than manipulate code to get it right. When you are satisfied, click the OK button to continue.

Once the custom border has been added, it is time to set the layout manager for jPanel4. Set jPanel4's layout manager to XYLayout; this will allow absolute positioning using x/y coordinates from the top left position. The XYLayout is a custom layout manager provided by JBuilder to help developers control the placement of components inside a component container. This can also be done using the Null layout provided by Sun's JFC libraries, but the XYLayout manager is portable across multiple systems, which means it will show more true positioning on Solaris, Linux, and Mac than what Null will.

**WARNING GUI interfaces should *never* be deployed with either the XYLayout or the Null layout managers. These are for designing only and will most likely give unwanted results when deployed. These managers have no concepts of expanding or contracting the components as the window's properties change, as is found in other layout managers.**

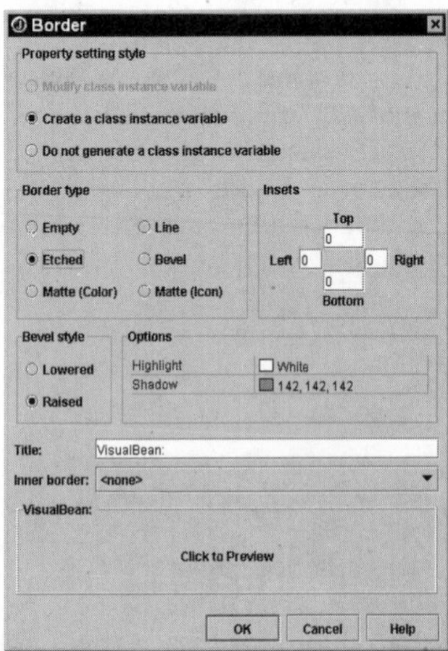


**Figure 8.17** Custom property editor for creating borders.

## Maximizing the Designer

The first step in making the most of the designer is to drop a JLabel on jPanel4. Click the JLabel on the Swing tab located on the component palette. Once the component has been dropped, use the mouse to click and hold on the jLabel3, then press the Ctrl key and drag the mouse. Notice that another copy of the JLabel has been created. This procedure can be used with multiple components by using the Shift key to select multiple components and on the last component holding down the mouse key and pressing Ctrl and dragging every component selected. You should have two JLabels on the jPanel4. For multiple components, hold the Shift key and then select the component from the palette — in this case, a JLabel. Notice that the component on the palette will have a different outline. Then just click inside the jPanel4 three more times, and notice that two more jLabels have been added. This should be a total of five JLabels added to the jPanel4.

Next, add three JTextFields to the jPanel4; this again can be done as discussed in the prior examples. The next operation is the placement of the items like the representation found in Figure 8.18. This can be done using the simple drag-and-drop; however, because JBuilder is using either XYLayout or Null layout managers, JBuilder has added a few extra abilities to the designer.

You can use the multiselect options inside the designer. Ways to do this include using the Shift key and mouse clicking on each component, or holding down the Shift key and clicking the desired components in the component tree, or using the lasso command, which can be accomplished by holding down the Shift key and dragging the mouse around the desired components. Each technique has it advantages; your choice depends on the layout and what you are trying to accomplish.

Once you have a component or multiple components selected, you can use the fine adjustment feature by pressing the Ctrl-Arrow key combination. This will move the component(s) in the direction of the arrow key by one pixel. If the Ctrl-Shift–Arrow key combination is pressed, the component(s) will be moved eight pixels in the direction of the Arrow key pushed.

You can use the right-mouse click menu or Context menu (see Figure 8.18) to do general placement procedures such as left, center, right, top, or bottom, or to make the components the same size. Keep in mind that when it comes to size, the first component picked will be the standard for all other components. The Context menu can be displayed anytime and anywhere now by using the Shift-F10 key combination.

It is now time to change jLabel3's text property to read "Name:", jLabel4 to read "Zip:", and jLabel5 to read "Amount:". Drag jLabel3 to the desired location from the top, then drag jLabel5 to the desired location along the bottom. Using the adjustments capabilities discussed previously, hold down the Shift key and select jLabel4 and jLabel3 again. Display the Context menu by either right-mouse clicking or pressing the Shift-F10 key combination and choosing the Align Right menu item. This will make the three jLabels align to the ":" characters. Deselect the jLabels by clicking on any object except one of them; you will notice that the gray nubs will disappear. Then select jLabel3, jLabel4, and jLabel5 in that order and use the Context menu to select Even Space Vertical. This will put equal space between the components.

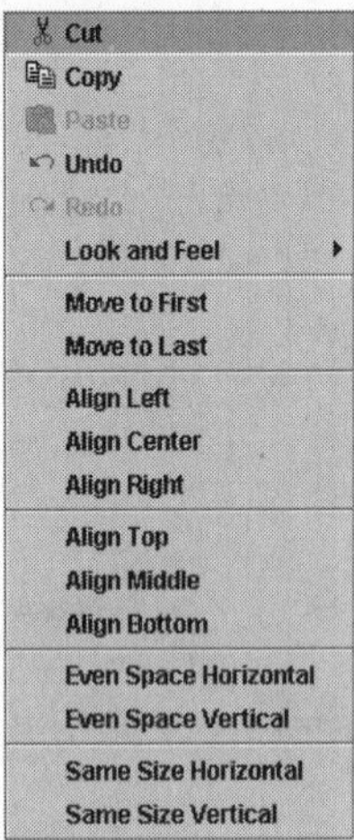


**Figure 8.18** Context menu.

Next move jTextField1 to the desired location from the "Name:" label and create a desired size for that component. It should be larger than the default size. Hold the Shift key, select the jTextField2 and jTextField3 components, and then use the Context menu (right-mouse) to select the Align Left menu item. Display the context menu again, and select Same Size Horizontal. This should produce three JTextFields that are aligned to the left and are of the same size.

Next, click on the "Name:" label, hold down the Shift key, and select the jTextField1 component. Then display the Context menu and select Align Bottom. Select the "Zip:" label, and select the jTextField2 by again holding down the Shift key; then display the Context menu and Align Bottom. Follow the same procedure for the "Amount:" and jTextField3 components, and set its alignment to bottom.

Deselect the components by clicking another component; then multiselect the JTextFields and remove the string from the text property inside the object inspector. Double-clicking on the right side of the text property and hitting the Delete key then Return can accomplish this. When selecting multiple components, the Object Inspector will show all common properties that are shared between them. If one value is changed when in multiselect mode, all of the components will be changed. The interface should resemble the one in Figure 8.14.

The last two JLabels can be dragged to the top right-hand corner. Change jLabel6's text property to read hashCode and jLabel7's to be a "-". Use the fine adjustments and the Context menu to set the alignment.

## Drag and Drop; Copy, Cut, and Paste

The GUI designer in JBuilder has many of the features found in an editor. It is possible to copy, cut, and paste components. This feature is also available from the component tree, and it allows components to be copied and cut from the designer and pasted in the component tree. This is handy if you are moving components from one GUI container to another. The same can be done with drag-and-drop, but in this case the functionality is relative to the area that started the operation. If a drag operation is started in the component tree, then it has to be dropped in the component tree. The same is true for the visual representation. Another cool feature is that if you make a mistake, the undo/redo features are enabled in the designer.

## Changing XYLayout to GridbagLayout for Deployment

A feature that most developers are not aware of is the fact that JBuilder can switch between one layout manager and another and back again. This is incredibly important when it comes to using XYLayout or null layout managers. In the preceding example, so far jPanel4's layout manager has been either XYLayout or null, but these two layout managers should not be used in production. They will not scale or display information on multiple platforms consistently. jpanel4 should be set to GridbagLayout for deployment; to do this, select the jPanel4 inside the component tree and set its layout manager to GridbagLayout. You should not see any major changes in the layout; if you look at the source, you will notice that all the GUI objects located inside the jbInit() method now have full constraints added to them. Going back to the designer, everything again should look the same.

This GUI is now ready to ship, but what if you need to make a change to jPanel4 in the future? Simply go to its layout manager and set it to XYLayout or null and make the changes; then when the changes are complete, set the layout back to GridbagLayout — no fuss or headaches in using that method. GridbagLayout is considered to be a very challenging layout manger, and it has a lot of options that can be set. JBuilder exposes all of the features in two ways: When the layout is set to GridbagLayout, the context-sensitive menu that can be viewed by right-mouse clicking on any component inside that controls the container will show that the options are Show Grid, Constraints, Remove Padding, Fill Horizontal, Fill Vertical, Remove Fill, and finally Weight Horizontal, Weight Vertical, and Remove Weights. All these options can be used on individual controls; the menu item to take note of is the Constraints item, which will display all the control's constraints in a nice logical dialog (see Figure 8.19).

This dialog will stay displayed on top until the OK or Cancel button is pressed. This allows the developer to click on other controls in the GUI designer and set their constraints without having to restart the dialog on every control. The last item to discuss is the GUI designer itself; when a control is selected, that control will have a set of multicolored nubs that go around its perimeter. The blue nubs manipulate the fill for the particular grid in which the control resides, and the black nubs manipulate the control's actual size. The combination of both the Context menu and Constraints dialog give most GUI developers the control they need to make even the slightest of modifications to the control. Switching layout managers has fewer issues to worry about. Change the layout back to XYLayout or null, and change the GUI to meet the requirements, then reset the layout back to GridbagLayout. No need to worry about fills, size, or multiple constraints; just make it look right and change the layout manager to the shipping GridBagLayout.

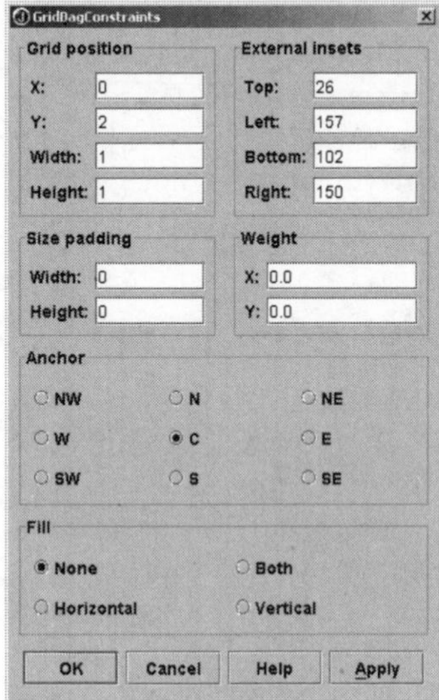


**Figure 8.19** GridBagConstraints dialog.

## Adding a Nonvisual Bean to the Palette

Now that the GUI has been created, it is time to save all and wire the visual to the nonvisual bean. The first step in hooking these two beans together is getting the first bean onto the component palette so that it can be dragged from the component tree. Right-mouse click on the component palette, and click the Properties menu item to customize the menu, or you can choose the Tools | Configure Palette (see Figure 8.20) from the main menu. The Palette Properties dialog allows complete configuration of the component palette. You can do the following:

- Change the tab order
- Change the components on each tab
- Add tabs and components to a tab

On the Pages tab, select Other item. You will see a blank component palette if no components have been added that particular page.

Next, select the Add Components tab (see Figure 8.20). This allows you to set the properties to add components to the Other tab. The first thing that needs to be selected is the library where MyBaseBean is located. Because this has not been created, click the Select Libraries button (see Figure 8.20).

Click the New button to display a new library dialog (see Figure 8.21). Chapter 2 covers all the properties associated with creating libraries.

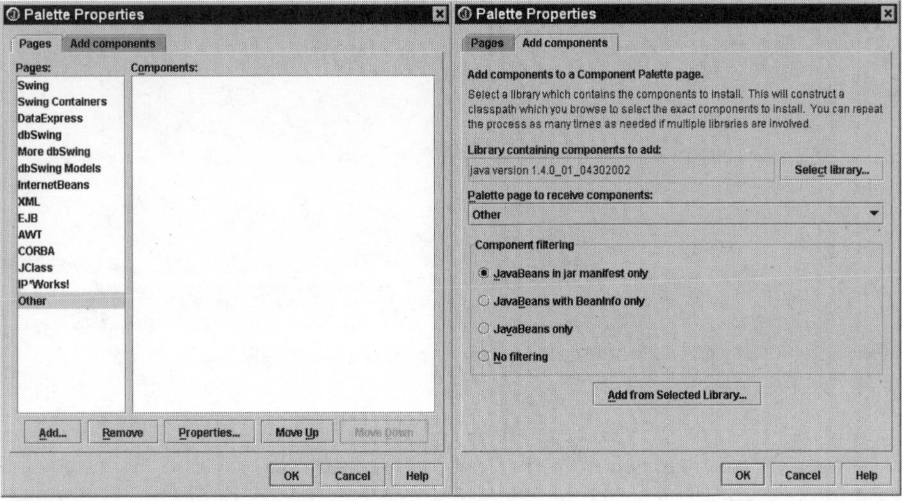


**Figure 8.20** Palette Properties dialog.

For this example, name the library OurBeans, and set the location to be JBuilder. This will give all JBuilder projects the ability to find these beans when JBuilder is started. Click the Add button to display the Select one or more directories dialog (see Figure 8.22). This should be set to the classes directory for basebean. Click the OK button on the dialog to return to the New Library dialog; click the OK button again to return to the Select a different Library dialog. Click the OK button to continue setting up the new components on the palette. The series of OK button clicks has returned the focus back to the Palette Properties dialog; now select the JavaBeans Only radio button, then click the Add from Selected Library button.

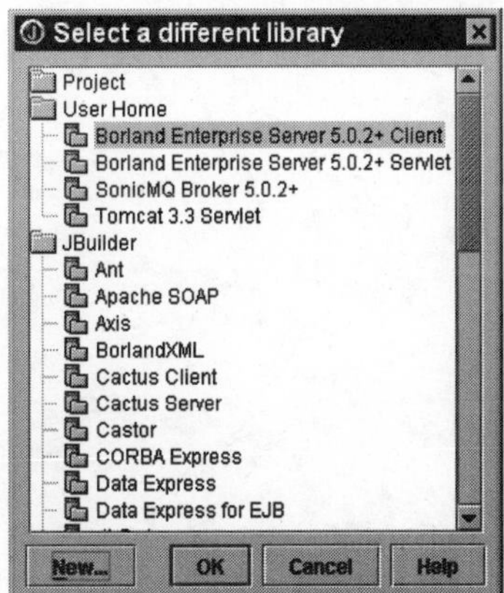


**Figure 8.21** Selecting a library.

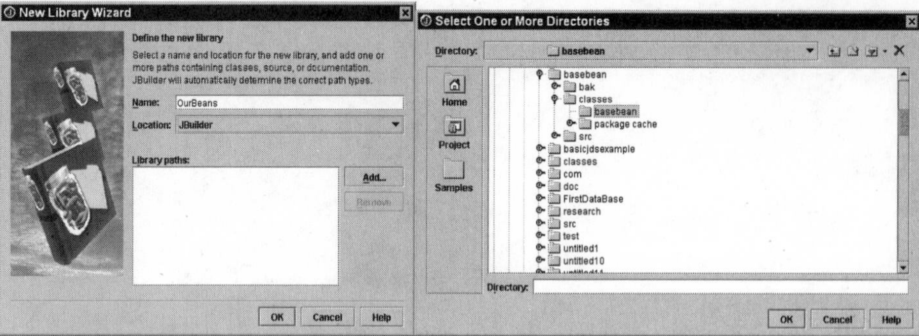


**Figure 8.22** Creating a new library.

The dialog in Figure 8.23 will be displayed; it allows for the selection of the beans to add. Because the bean created in the first part of the example was found in basebean, expand the tree-node and select the MyBaseBean. Click the OK button to continue. A Results dialog will be displayed, stating that the bean was added to the Other page of the component palette. Press its OK button to continue, and then press the OK button on the Palette Properties dialog to finish the process.

**Figure 8.23** Select the bean to add.

## Adding the Component to the Visual Component

Now that the component has been added to the component palette, it is as easy as clicking the component and clicking inside the component tree. Once the component has been added to the tree, notice that the Object Inspector shows all the exposed properties and has all the property editors loaded (see Figure 8.24); it also has all the exposed events for the class.

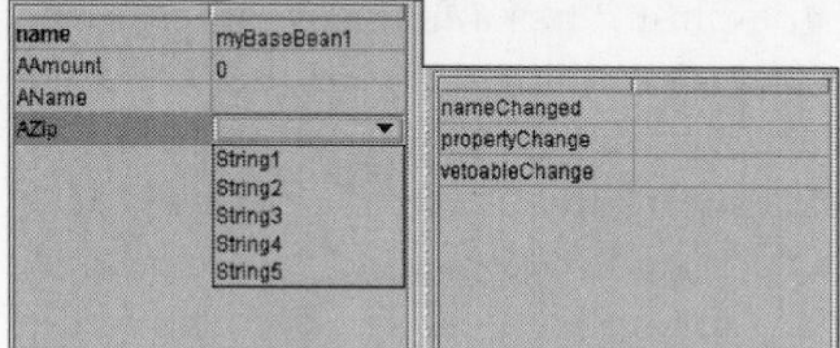


**Figure 8.24** All things working properties and events.

Once the properties for the bean can be set, set the AAmount property to 100. Then set the AName property to your name, and set the AZip property to String 5. Next it is time to add the events to the visual designer. Click the Event tab located under the Object Inspector, then double-click on the nameChanged empty area to the right of the label. This will generate the appropriate method. Add the following code:

```
jLabel2.setText("Status:  Name has been changed!");
```

Go back to the designer by clicking the Design tab under the coding Content page. Select the myBaseBean1 from the component tree, and click Events tab again under the Object Inspector, this time double-clicking on the propertyChange area to generate the event and add the following code:

```
jLabel2.setText("Status:  " + e.getPropertyName() +
                ": value changed from " +
                e.getOldValue() + " to " + e.getNewValue() + ".");
```

This code is rather simple because the property change object includes the name of the object changing and the old and new values, and this method returns that information. Remember that because multiple objects can use the property change object, the code to report the action needs to work this way.

Again, go back to the designer, click the myBaseBean1, double-click the vetoableChange event, and add the following code:

```
        jLabel1.setText("Status:  " + e.getPropertyName() +
                        " value not changed " +
                        e.getNewValue() + " > 300");
    }
```

This code reports whether a veto has occurred with an Amount property. Now is a great time to save all on this project.

The buttons now need to be implemented; double-click on the Get Value button. This should generate an event method, and the following code should be added:

```
jTextField1.setText(myBaseBean1.getAName());
jTextField2.setText(myBaseBean1.getAZip());
jTextField3.setText(String.valueOf(myBaseBean1.getAAmount()));
jLabel1.setText(myBaseBean1.getAText());
jLabel7.setText(String.valueOf(myBaseBean1.getAValue()));
```

This looks fairly normal as far as a method goes, but it has a few extra lines and it may need to be called in other places later. JBuilder offers a great refactoring ability to generate a method from this block of code. Refactoring can be completed by selecting all the lines shown, then bringing up the Context menu either by right-mouse clicking or pressing Shift-F10, then selecting the Extract Method (Ctrl-Shift-e) menu item. A quick dialog will be displayed showing the lines that are supposed to be included in the method; it also asks for a name for the new method, which should be getValue. This results in another quick status dialog stating that refactoring is occurring, and then the new code should be generated.

The next button to implement is the Set Value button. Double-click on the button, generate the event, and add the following code:

```
myBaseBean1.setAName(jTextField1.getText());
myBaseBean1.setAZip(jTextField2.getText());
```

These two lines work great, then you add the next line:

```
    myBaseBean1.setAAmount(new
Integer(jTextField3.getText()).intValue());
```

Suddenly, JBuilder throws a fit about the preceding line. In the designer, swiggly lines appear under the setAAmount. If you place your cursor on the lines, it will report an unreported exception (see Figure 8.25).

Click the "?" mark located inside the blue box to activate the JBuilder help system. This is going to give only the technical reason for why it is reporting the problem, not the solution. Because it states an unreported exception, JBuilder has a refactoring tool for Surround with Try/Catch (Ctrl-Shift-c). Select the line, right-mouse click, and execute the Surround with Try/Catch operation. That has appeared to solve the problem; notice the code generated by the operation:

```
try {
  myBaseBean1.setAAmount(new
                        Integer(jTextField3.getText()).intValue());
}
catch (NumberFormatException ex) {
}
catch (PropertyVetoException ex) {
}
```

Then add the rest of the code:

```
myBaseBean1.setAText("Hello from the bean");
```

## Vetoing an Event

JBuilder does a considerable amount of work to make sure that it can test for a veto property change on aAmount. The current code would not stop any value from being set because the underlying base MyBaseBean does not listen for a VetoChange event, nor does MyVisualBean. The following will show how to add the support needed for a veto event.

```
void jButton2_actionPerformed(ActionEvent e) {
  myBaseBean1.setAName(jTextField1.getText());
  myBaseBea   Unreported exception: java.beans.PropertyVetoException; must be caught or declared to be thrown
  myBaseBean1.setAAmount(new Integer(jTextField3.getText()
}
```

**Figure 8.25** Advanced code checking.

## Implementing Interfaces

JBuilder allows any interface to be added to a class, and all the interface's methods will be added to that class. Because the example in this chapter uses VetoChangeSupport, it needs to implement the VetoableChangeListener. This can be done by clicking the Wizards | Implement Interface menu item and selecting the java.beans.VetoableChangeListener, then clicking OK to continue (see Figure 8.26).

The VetoableChange method will now be added to the class. It is also reported in the to-do section of the Structure pane. The code that should be added to the method should look like the following:

```
int aValue = new Integer(evt.getNewValue().toString()).intValue();
if ((aValue) > 300) {
  throw new PropertyVetoException("Value must be less then 300", evt);
}
```

This code takes the passed-in object evt and gets a value for the property. It then checks to see whether that is a valid property;. If it is, everything continues as normal; if not, a PropertyVetoException is thrown with a description and the object itself.

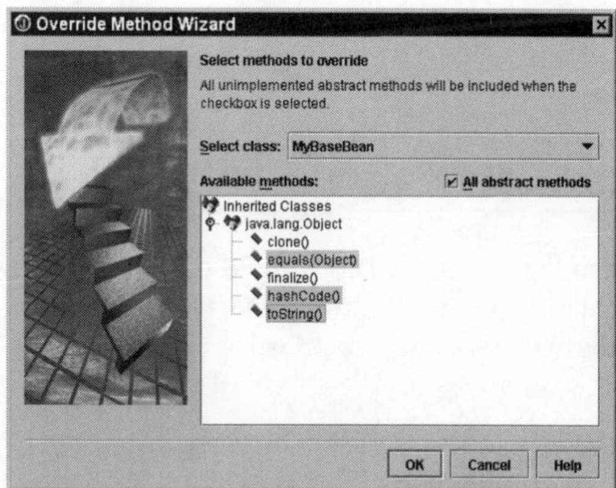


**Figure 8.26** Override Method wizard.

Next, you need to change the Try/Catch block that was added when the exception was not being reported in the prior section. Replace the Try/Catch block with the following code:

```
     try {
       int temp = new Integer(jTextField3.getText()).intValue();
       vetoableChange(new PropertyChangeEvent(myBaseBean1, "aAmount",
                new Integer(myBaseBean1.getAAmount()), new
Integer(temp)));
       myBaseBean1.setAAmount(temp);
     }
     catch (PropertyVetoException ex) {
       jTextField3.setText(String.valueOf(myBaseBean1.getAAmount()));
       ex.printStackTrace();
     }
```

The first thing the Try/Catch attempts to complete is getting the new value from the jTextField3. It then calls the vetoableChange method to create a new PropertyChangeEvent with the actual bean and new and old amounts. It then tries to set the value to new value, but if the value is not within the allowed range, an exception will be thrown in the VetoableChange method and will be propagated back to the calling method, thus resulting in a Catch situation. When the catch is implemented, it sets the value back to the original value and prints the exception to standard out.

Finally, double-click the Status button and generate the event. The following code should be added:

```
     System.out.println(myBaseBean1.toString());
```

This will allow the developer to return a completed value for the object at any time and not interfere with the interface because the code will be sent to the standard out.

It is now time to save this project and do a rebuild. Type Project | Rebuild MyVisualBean.java, or click the Build task icon on the main tool bar. Once a clean rebuild is generated, the final step of the example can be started. Keep in mind that a few steps were not taken in Part 2 of the example. No BeanInfo class or archive was generated to hold all the classes. These two things can be done later. Also, a unit test was not generated for this class. This can be generated after the example is complete. See Part Four of the book to review how to apply the Application Lifecycle Management (ALM) to this example.

## Building an Application

The final part to this example is to create an application that can hold our new visual JavaBean. This can be accomplished by creating a new JBuilder project and naming it theapplication. You can use the Object Gallery to generate a standard application. Click on File | New, select the Application icon, click the OK button, and then click the Finish button on the Application wizard to accept the defaults. This will generate a standard JBuilder application. Next click the Design tab under the code Context pane to go to the GUI designer.

We now need to add a component to the palette. Adding the needed classes to the library created in the last example is the best way to accomplish this task. Click on the Tools | Configure Libraries menu item, and select ourbeans in the left-hand listbox. Notice that only the basebean package is included. Next, click the Add button. This will display a dialog for One or More Directories; review Figure 8.22 and add the classes directory of the visualbean package.

Once this has been selected, click the OK button to go back to the Configure Libraries dialog, then click the OK button to continue. Click the Tools | Configure Palette from the main menu to display its dialog for review (Figure 8.22), then click the Other page and the Add Components tab. Click the Select Library button, and choose the ourbeans item under the JBuilder tree-node. Press the OK button to continue.

Click the JavaBeans only radio button, and then press the Add from Selected Library button. Open the tree-node for visualbean, select the MyVisualBean, and click the OK button; a dialog will be displayed explaining that the bean has been added to the component palette. Press the OK button to return to the Add Components tab, then click the OK button to continue.

Click on the Other tab (on the component palette), and select the second icon that looks like a square, circle, and triangle. Click on the designer to display the full visual bean that we created in the last step.

Because the business logic was written for the basebean and the visualbean packages, no new code needs to be added. Save the project and run. You can test the interface, as shown in Figure 8.27. Again, this is the same interface that we created in the second part of this example.

You can try all of the business logic implemented by this series of JavaBeans. To test the interfaces, click the Get Value button and then start changing values. Try changing names, amounts, Zips, and get statuses.

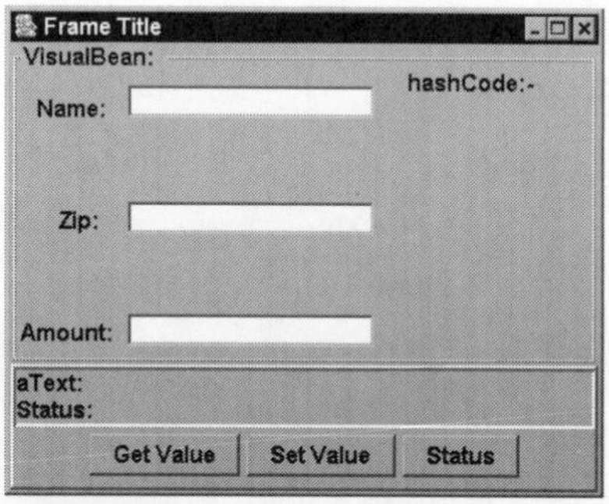

**Figure 8.27** Final application running.

## Summary

This example shows how to create a nonvisual bean and extend it with a visual representation. Once the business logic has been coded, adding the functionality is very simple. Using the JBuilder designers, like the BeansExpress interface and the GUI builder, can decrease the typing and time it takes to make classes.

PART

Three

# JBuilder and Application Lifecycle Management

Part Three focuses on the application lifecycle management aspects of JBuilder. When JBuilder first hit the streets, its vision was to be the best Java IDE plus the Borland heritage in developing RAD tools for almost 20 years. More than just a Java editor, compiler, and debugger wrapped into one interface, JBuilder starts its new life with deep integration of its developer-centric environment with enterprise software development lifecycle tools, which are team development, advanced build systems, unit testing, and UML visualization.

We will discuss the application lifecycle aspects in the following chapters:

**Integrated Team Development.** Chapter 9 covers JBuilder integration with team development and illustrates the uses of team development via JBuilder-CVS integration.

**Using Build Systems.** In Chapter 10, you will learn what the JBuilder build system is and how to best use it; second, the chapter will introduce the integration of JBuilder and Ant Builder.

**Unit Testing with JUnit.** JBuilder-JUnit integration is best for programmers doing unit test synchronously with their coding. Chapter 11 will guide you through the steps of creation and run unit tests for the Java component using the JUnit framework in the JBuilder.

**UML Visualization.** Chapter 12 shows that JBuilder uses UML structural diagrams to help developers visualize and traverse Java classes and packages.

CHAPTER

9

# Integrated Team Development

JBuilder is built on a team development concept, one that allows multiple developers working with the project in their JBuilder's workspace, synchronizing that project, and committing the project into a selected version control system. Integration with version control is essential for integrated software development. Version control utilities help multiple developers to work simultaneously and make changes to common resources without interfering with other developers' work. Developers can stay in sync with each other without leaving the JBuilder environment. JBuilder supports numerous market-leading version control tools, including the open source Concurrent Versions System (CVS), Borland TeamSource, Rational ClearCase, Microsoft Visual SourceSafe, and StartTeam through open-tool plug-ins. This chapter demonstrates how JBuilder supports integrated team development and how to best use it. We begin with a discussion of the tools available for team development and how to set up your project, followed by an example that uses Borland's CVS integration tool. CVS is used by millions of developers worldwide because of its flexible, extensible, and collaborative characteristics. And CVS is the selected version control tool that the JBuilder team uses.

## Team Development Tools

Team development is a client/server-based application that enables developers to archive and manage changes for software projects in a common central location. This location is usually called a *repository*. The server-side implementation for team development typically uses a distributed client/server approach to support thousands of concurrent accesses across organizations. The server repository process keeps track of all changes made to archived files; it also creates and maintains a historical database for the evolution of the software development lifecycle.

Meanwhile, client-side team development provides an interface for developers to perform version control tasks easily. For example, developers can obtain an older version of a particular file, view changes from the log file, and update the file as needed. There are also utilities for team development admin personnel to manage the changes to the contents of the repository. There are different tools supporting team development; we can name a few that JBuilder supports out of the box. They are Concurrent Versions System (CVS), Borland TeamSource, Rational ClearCase, Microsoft Visual SourceSafe, and StartTeam. In this session, we discuss team development in general as a version control system (VCS). In a later section, we take a look into how JBuilder integrates with Concurrent Versions System (CVS) in particular.

## Setting Up Your Project with a VCS

JBuilder provides two ways to connect a project to a VCS:

**Pulling a project from the VCS.** Select File | New | Projects, and choose Pull Project from a VCS; the steps are for creating a local workspace for a project that is located in the Version Control System. JBuilder will display a dialog with appropriate information depending on your VCS. When you select a project from the VCS, JBuilder will pull the entire project to your project space and automatically open the project file (.jpx) in JBuilder. If a JBuilder project file does not exist, JBuilder will create a new project file.

**Connecting the existing workspace to the VCS.** Open a JBuilder project, and select Team | Select Project VCS. Then choose your target VCS.

Note that a repository must be set up and configured before you can use JBuilder's VCS operations. When the repository is configured, JBuilder then enables the Team menu items for the VCS operations. Table 9.1 lists common version control commands and terminologies.

**Table 9.1** Version Control Commands

| FILE | FUNCTION |
|---|---|
| Update | Retrieve changes from the VCS repository and merge them to the open workspace with local changes. |
| Commit | Incorporate changes from the open workspace to the VCS repository. |
| Status | Show current status of the file in the VCS repository. |
| Add | Add new source files to the VCS repository. |

**Table 9.1** *(Continued)*

| FILE | FUNCTION |
|---|---|
| Remove | Delete source files from the VCS repository. |
| CVS watches | Order CVS to send notifications when there is action taken on a file. |
| Refresh | Refresh current status of the selected file. |
| Diff | Show the differences between two files. Usually, one file is the one that you are working on and the other file is the newest one in the VCS repository. |
| Checkout | Get a file in the VCS repository and make it available to the workspace. |
| Check-in | Save a file from the workspace into the VCS repository. |
| Revert | Update the workspace with the latest repository version of the file. |
| Repository | Store modules and revision records of source files. |
| Workspace | Serve as the local working area where files are changed, edited, and saved before being committed or updated to the VCS repository. |
| History | Show information on actions taken on the file. |
| Merge | Incorporate and combine changes from the VCS repository with changes in the workspace. If there is conflict, the changes will be preserved, flagged, and reconciled either by the user or automatically. |
| Version Label (or Tag) | Mark references to the entire project. |

## Manage Revisions of the Source Files

JBuilder provides two different approaches to compare files: File | Compare Files and the History view. This is how JBuilder can manage changes and revisions out of the box without using a VCS.

### *Compare|Files Dialog*

Using File | Compare Files, you can view two files side by side in the Source view or in the Diff view in the Compare Files dialog box. Using the Source view (see Figure 9.1), you can edit the source files in both sides by adding, cutting and pasting, and deleting texts.

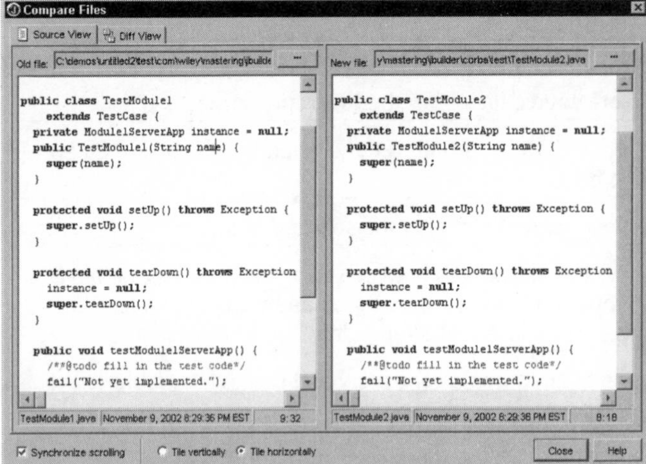


**Figure 9.1** Source view.

The Diff view highlights the different texts between the two files by merging the two files in one and shows the differences in color. In this view (see Figure 9.2), you can undo the selected changes.

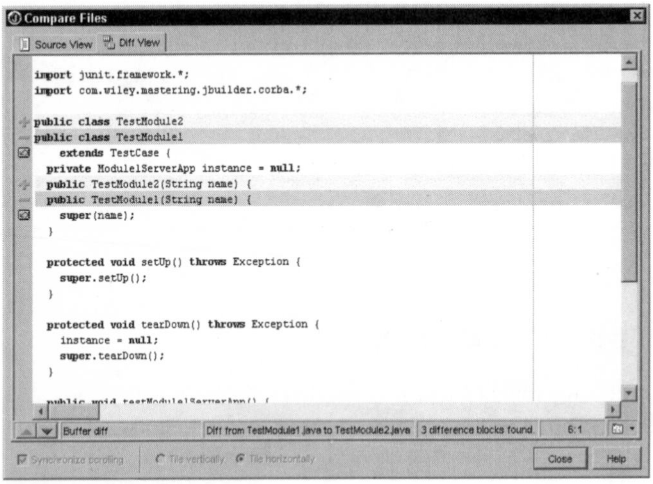

**Figure 9.2** Diff view.

## *History View*

The History pane displays historical changes for any file in the project. Also, the History pane provides diff, merge, and revert functions to any revision of the file. When the file is opened in the Content pane, the Content pane shows the History page with four tabs:

**Contents tab.** This page lists all accessible versions of the open file. You can sort the list by clicking on a heading of version type, revision number, label, date, or author, as shown in Figure 9.3. You can also access functions including refresh revision information, revert selected revision to previous revision, and synchronize scrolling for both sides of the Source view.

**Info tab.** Similar to the Content tab, this page shows the revision information of the open file with additional full-text view of labels and comments for any selected version. You can sort the list by clicking on a heading of version type, revision number, label, date, author, or comment. You can also choose Refresh Revision Info and Revert To Previous Revision here.

**Diff tab.** This page shows the differences between two selected versions of the open file (see Figure 9.4). Similar to the other two pages, you can sort the files shown in the revision lists by version type, revision number, or date. In addition to the Refresh Revision Info and Synchronize Scrolling, you can also enable "Undo selected changes" and the Smart Diff function. By default, each different block shows the diff deletion in red, indicated by the minus sign, and shows the diff addition in yellow, indicated by the plus sign.

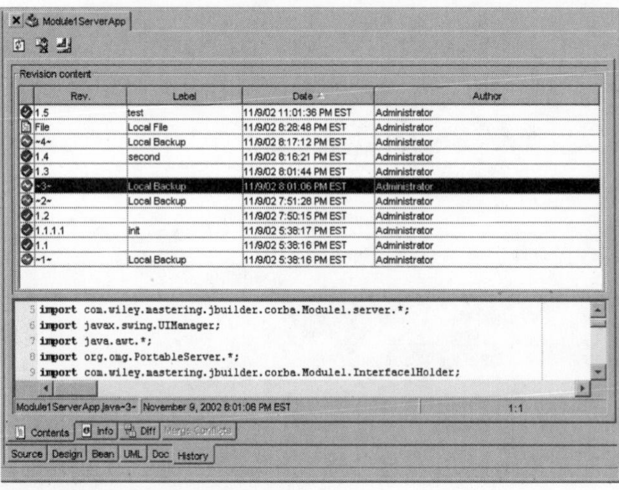


**Figure 9.3** Content Page view.

**TIP** **Smart Diff can help you filter out format-related changes in diff blocks where code format is changed, such as changes in the location and number of blank lines, the amount of indentation, or the use of spaces. When your cursor is in the Source view pane of the Diff page, press Shift-F10 to open a Context menu with options to enable or disable Smart Diff and navigate to previous and next diff blocks.**

**Merge Conflicts tab.** This page is active only when there are merge conflicts in the VCS. In the current release of JBuilder, the merge conflicts function is supported by integration to Concurrent Versioning System (CVS) or Visual SourceSafe (VSS) only. When there is a merge conflict in the VCS, the Merge Conflicts page shows the local workspace source with the repository source side by side. You can view and merge the conflicting blocks of codes, which are highlighted. In Figure 9.5, the Merge page shows the highlighted blocks of conflicting codes. By checking the radio button, you choose which block of code that you want to preserve either in the local workspace or in the repository.

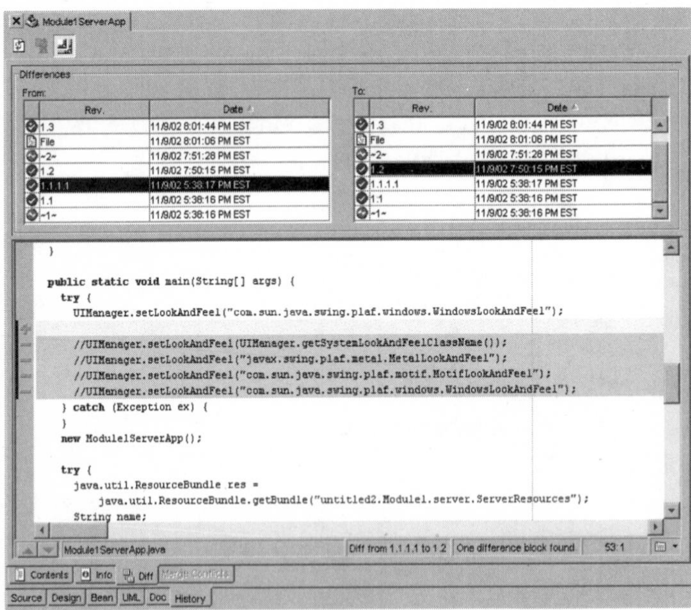


**Figure 9.4** Diff tab in History page.

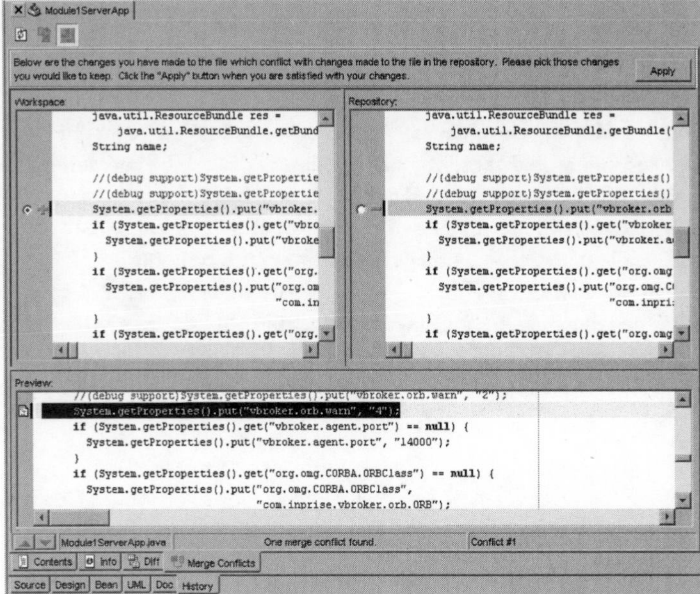


**Figure 9.5** Merge Conflict view.

The Preview pane displays a current snapshot of the file if the merges occur.

# CVS Integration

In this section, we explore JBuilder's integration to CVS. JBuilder automatically installs the latest version of CVS in <JBuilder Home Dir>/bin. You can verify the CVS installation by having your path include <JBuilder Home Dir>/bin and typing "cvs" at the command prompt. You should see the following CVS usage message:

```
C:/Borland/JBuilder8/bin/cvs
Usage: cvs [cvs-options] command [command-options-and-arguments]
  where cvs-options are -q, -n, etc.
    (specify --help-options for a list of options)
  where command is add, admin, etc.
    (specify --help-commands for a list of commands
     or --help-synonyms for a list of command synonyms)
  where command-options-and-arguments depend on the specific command
    (specify -H followed by a command name for command-specific help)
  Specify --help to receive this message

The Concurrent Versions System (CVS) is a tool for version control.
For CVS updates and additional information, see
    the CVS home page at http://www.cvshome.org/ or
    Pascal Molli's CVS site at http://www.loria.fr/~molli/cvs-index.html
```

**INSTALLING CVS**

**CVS is an open-source network-based version control system available on many platforms (www.cvshome.org). It manages historical changes of collections of files in its repository, stored as modules with any given names. After checkout, files can be modified and edited using JBuilder and committed back into the repository. Files can be compared against their revisions. Also, new files can be added or old files can be removed from the repository, or they can be merged with the committed changes of other CVS users. To install CVS from sources, download the cvs-1.11.tar.gz file from ftp://ftp.cvshome.org/pub/cvs-1.11/cvs-1.11.tar.gz. You can check to see whether there is a newer version of CVS at ftp.cvshome.org/pub. After downloading the file, unpack the tar file either using the command line or using your favorite ZIP tool. Here are some sample commands to build and install the new CVS.**

```
C:\utilities\tar -xzvf cvs-1.11.tar.gz
C:\utilities\cd cvs-1.11
C:\utilities\configure
C:\utilities\make
C:\utilities\make install
```

**Visit www.cvshome.org for more detailed installation instructions.**

## Creating CVS Repository

After selecting CVS as a version control system, you need to create a local CVS repository — unless you already have a CVS server set up. To create a new local CVS repository, select Team|Create Repository. Note that the local CVS repository is designed for a solo developer; it cannot be used by a multideveloper team.

The repository directory can be an empty directory, or you can enter a new one. Later, the repository can contain as many modules as you like.

## Configuring CVS Properties

In the Team menu, the CVS Properties dialog box is used to configure the CVS repository and CVS properties, shown in Figure 9.6. You will see CVSROOT many times as you use CVS. The CVSROOT environment variable contains a string format text indicating where the local/remote repository is located. Here are two samples of the CVSROOT path:

- Local CVS repository: CVSROOT=:local:C:\demos\cvs
- Remote CVS repository:
  CVSROOT=:pserver:anoncvs@cvs.apache.org:/home/cvspublic

The CVSROOT path indicates that the CVS client will connect to the remote CVS at cvs.apache.org under "anoncvs" user. Note that server and repository path information can be retrieved from your local CVS administrator.

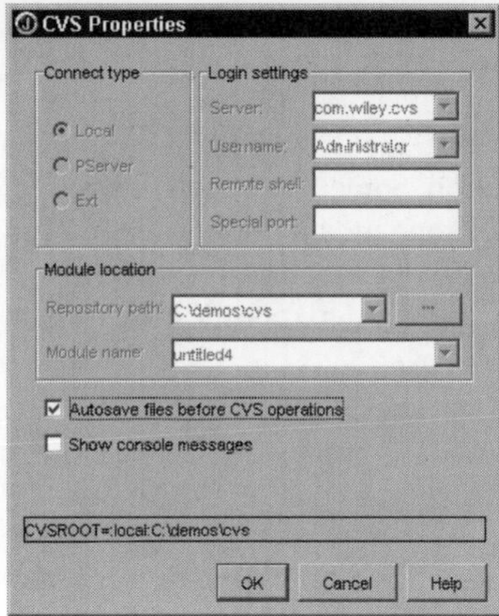


**Figure 9.6** CVS properties dialog.

## Checking Out a Project from CVS

The integration to CVS from JBuilder makes it easy to pull an existing project from CVS into JBuilder's workspace via a three-step wizard. Upon completion, your JBuilder project is configured for CVS operations with CVS commands from the Team menu and from the Context menu in the Project pane:

1. Point the target directory to a new directory or an empty one that will be used to hold your CVS module.
2. Select the CVS connection type and logon information to connect to the CVS server. You can choose from three different CVS connection types. Local connection indicates that you will connect to a local CVS repository, which can be local on your workstation or on a mapped location. PServer connection indicates that you will connect to a remote server with password-protection enabled. Most open-source projects allow developers to connect anonymously, or without passwords. For example, you can connect to apache.org and download many Apache open-source projects. Ext connection indicates that you will connect to a secure remote CVS server (SSH). If there is a port required for the CVS connection, you can specify the port in this step. The CVS pserver default port is typically set to 2401.

   Depending on what CVS connection you selected earlier, you need to provide appropriate log-on information to connect to the CVS server.
3. Enter a repository path. If the path is valid, you can use the drop-down list to view a list of available modules in the repository. Then select a module to check out to your JBuilder workspace. If there are different branches for the module, you can select the branch you want to work on. There are Scan buttons for the module name and branches. The Scan button will display the selected repository for a list of available modules or branches of the selected module.

There are two additional options in this final step. You can check the Autosave Files Before CVS Operations option to have your files saved before any part of CVS operation is performed. We recommend that you check this option, so that you will always have your files updated. In order to show all CVS operations in the JBuilder Message pane, you can check the Show Console Messages option. Sometime you will want to refresh your CVS command-line syntax and see what commands JBuilder calls against the CVS repository. This is a great learning tool if this is your first time using CVS.

Upon completing the steps, JBuilder will check out the selected module and make it available in your workspace.

## Placing a New Project into CVS

When you have existing projects in JBuilder and have not configured the project under any version control system, JBuilder provides a wizard to assist in placing projects into CVS. When the checking process is complete, the wizard will check the project again and make it available immediately in the JBuilder workspace:

1. Enter the CVS connection type with appropriate login information and module location. See Figure 9.7.
2. Enter descriptions for your new CVS module.
3. Include or exclude any project directories or files before checking the CVS repository. See Figure 9.8.

Click the Finish button. JBuilder will check in the selected items and check them out again to make them available in your workspace.

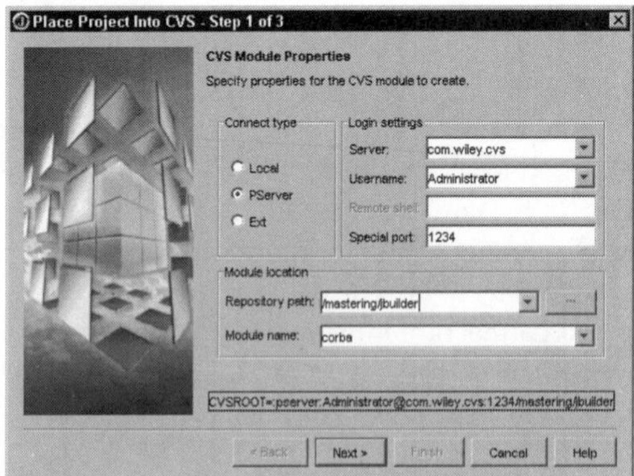


**Figure 9.7** Input CVS Module properties.

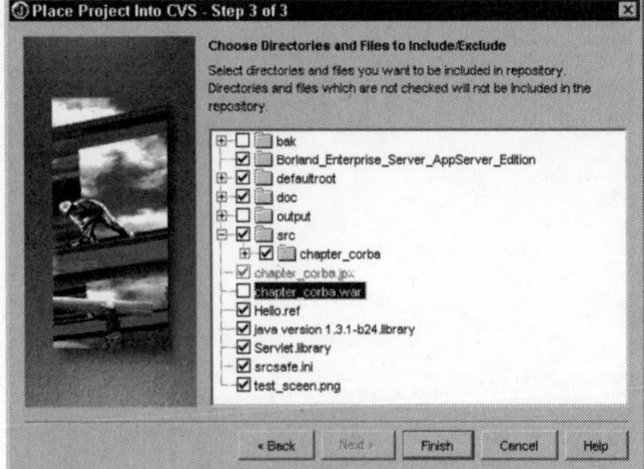


**Figure 9.8** Choose directories and files to place into CVS.

## CVS Project-Level Commands

You can access the project-level CVS command by right-mouse clicking on the project for a Context menu or via Team menu items:

**Update Project.** A CVS update command will be performed on the project. Your JBuilder workspace will be updated with changes that have been made to the repository.

**Status Browser.** This is a very informative GUI that shows the status of files in the version control. Within the Status browser, you can select a file and view the differences in many ways, using Workspace Source, Repository Source, Workspace Diff, Repository Diff, and Complete Diff.

**Commit Browser.** The Commit Browser command shows a drop-down list of actions that can be taken on each file. Within the Commit Browser, you can select a file and view the differences in many ways, using Workspace Source, Repository Source, Workspace Diff, Repository Diff, and Complete Diff.

**Add Version Label.** Labeling is recommended as one of the best practices when using CVS. When adding a new version label, JBuilder will apply the version label to the current version of every file that resides in the repository.

**Sync Project Settings.** This includes Pull Latest project from the CVS repository and Post current project to the CVS repository. When pulling the latest project, the workspace will reflect the current status of the repository. When posting the current project, the repository will reflect the current status of the project in the workspace.

Figure 9.9 shows typical project-level CVS commands.

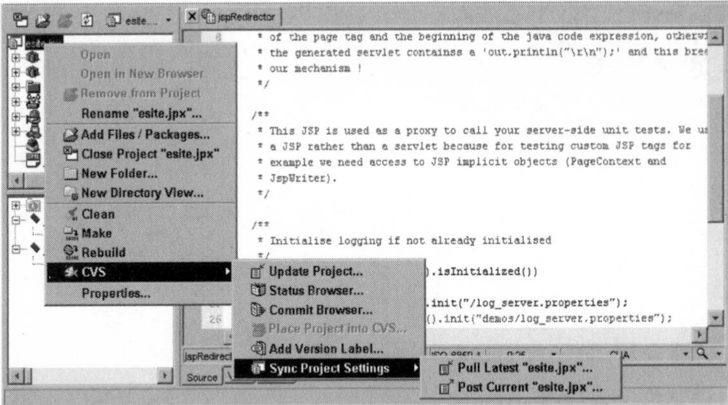


**Figure 9.9** CVS project-level commands.

# CVS File-Level Commands

CVS file-level commands are accessible from the Team menu or from the right-click operation on Project pane's Context menu. They include the following:

**Update.** After checking out a CVS project, part of our job is to modify files on CVS. Making the changes to your local workspace does not update the remote repository until you explicitly ask CVS to commit your changes. When you are sure that your modifications work properly and you are ready to commit your changes to the repository, you need first to update your files by activating the "Update" command on the files. This update command is equivalent to the actual CVS command line:

```
cvs update -d -l -P  filename
```

**Commit.** When selecting the Commit command, you will be prompted to enter a comment describing the new changes. JBuilder then checks whether the file has been updated. If the file has not been "CVS updated," the Commit operation will fail, and JBuilder will display an error message indicating that the CVS commit fails because the file had a conflict and has not been updated. This Commit command is equivalent to the actual CVS command line:

```
cvs commit -m
```

**Status.** This command shows the current status of the selected file and detects whether changes have been made in the local workspace or in the remote repository. If there is any conflict between the local copy and the remote copy, the command will prompt you with a conflict alert message.

**Add.** This command is used to add a new file to the CVS repository. If you do Status command on a new file, JBuilder will prompt you that the file is not in the CVS repository. "Add" is used to activate the CVS Add command on a selected file. You will be asked to enter a comment regarding the new file. Behind the scenes, JBuilder will issue a CVS Add and a CVS Commit command to permanently add the file to the repository.

**Remove.** This command involves a two-stage process. First it deletes the file from your local workspace, and you need to execute the CVS Remove command. The file will be permanently removed from both your local workspace and the CVS repository.

**Advance CVS.** JBuilder-CVS integration supports four file access notification commands: CVS watch, CVS remove watch, CVS edit, and CVS unedit. Using these CVS watch functions, you can be notified when changes have been made to files that you have set the watch on. After setting up CVS watch for a file, you can use Status Browser GUI to view the status.

Figure 9.10 shows file-level CVS commands.

## Resolving CVS Merge Conflicts

CVS and JBuilder integration issues an alert message when you update the file status and there is the possibility of merge conflict. It is recommended that you update the file before committing the changes. By doing so, you ask JBuilder to alert you if merge conflicts occur.

CVS will not allow you to commit the changes until all possible conflicts are resolved. Understand this CVS restriction; JBuilder provides a GUI for merge conflict resolution, as shown in Figure 9.5, so that you can scan the entire file for all conflicts. You can resolve the conflict manually or automatically by selecting a merge conflict block and applying updates to the file that is still in a local workspace. When you are confident about the changes, you can then commit your changes.

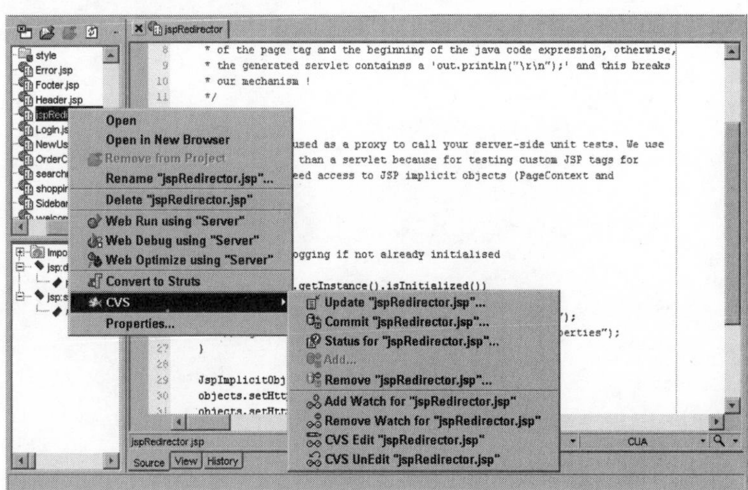


**Figure 9.10** CVS file-level commands.

## Summary

This chapter highlights the version control system integration in JBuilder and how it is necessary in a team development environment. VCS-JBuilder integration is helpful to assist you in your daily VCS operations. The benefit is that not only can each developer work independently of the others within JBuilder's environment, but the project can be synchronized across the team with all changes and historical activities recorded in the repository. The team development also plays a critical role in JBuilder's vision of an Application Lifecycle Management environment.

CHAPTER

10

# Using Build Systems

JBuilder has improved its build system over the years. Since version 7, the JBuilder build system has been based on Ant technology. Ant is an advanced Java-based build tool developed and maintained by the Jakarta Project (http://jakarta.apache.org/ant). Ant makes the JBuilder build system more flexible, and it is robust in building complex Java projects.

This chapter covers the basics of JBuilder build systems and the use of the JBuilder compiler, JBuilder archive builder, and JBuilder-Ant integration.

## Build System Basics

Developers have high expectations of what an integrated development environment should provide for its build utilities. We need a well-defined build process for projects of tens of thousands — sometimes hundreds of thousands — of code lines, with hundreds of components and libraries. The build systems should work across platforms and should be able to work with the existing build environment without forcing the existing environment to change.

JBuilder operates on similar build concepts as Ant: build tasks, build targets, and different build phases. The build systems are based on build components in JBuilder OpenTools API. *Build process* is actually more than just a terminology; it is a JBuilder OpenTool component named BuildProcess. The BuildProcess owns a whole build request, which can be used to schedule an orderly execution of a series of individual *build targets*. It is a multithreaded process that usually works as a background thread.

JBuilder uses a listener approach to monitor the build process states: initiation, progress, and completion. The BuildProcess then recursively updates its table with new registered Builders and its children. During the initiation phase, JBuilder instantiates its BuildProcess for a project.

The Build process is responsible for instantiating build tasks and build targets. Build target is a collection of one or many build tasks. Each build target can have dependencies with other build targets. For example, when building an Enterprise Archive (EAR) target, the EAR target itself should have a Web Archive (WAR) target. All dependencies will be built before executing the main target. Each build task belongs to a BuildTarget. Each BuildTarget can have more than one BuildTask. When the build is executed, its process runs in the background of JBuilder IDE.

There are six phases in the JBuilder build system:

**Clean.** .class files, JARs, WARs, EARs, and built output are removed.

**Pre-compile.** Any tasks that need to be done before compiling are completed. For example, Interface Definition Language (IDL) files need to be compiled into the Java stub/skeleton before building the whole project.

**Compile.** Java bytecode .class files are generated from source files.

**Post-compile.** Tasks, such as generating IIOP-compliant stubs and skeletons from Java interface classes, are completed after compiling.

**Package.** Files defined by BuildTarget are generated.

**Deploy.** Deployable archives are distributed to other places, such as an FTP or application server.

These six phases have no dependencies on each other, making JBuilder even more flexible. This allows each phase to be executed independently, and each phase can be configured with an external build task. JBuilder offers two default processes: Make and Rebuild. The Make process includes pre-compiling, compiling, post-compiling, packaging, and deployment; and the processes are executed sequentially. The Rebuild process includes cleaning and the Make process. Both processes are illustrated in Figure 10.1.

**TIP** **To rebuild portions of your project, select one or more packages or classes in the Project pane. Then right-mouse click and choose Make or Rebuild from the Context menu.**

**Figure 10.1** Make and Rebuild commands.

# Using the Compiler

JBuilder tools for building applications are more effective than using Java 2 SDK tools. JBuilder uses an advanced compiler called Borland Make for Java (bmj). The bmj supports all Java language compilation requirements. The bmj implements smart dependencies checking technique, which allows the compiling cycle to be faster and more efficient. The dependencies checker recognizes changes in source files so that the bmj will recompile only the necessary files. In Java, it is possible that one or more of the classes that the source produces depends on members in other classes that have changed. JBuilder is able to detect this situation to determine whether that change would not affect others. This capability is unique to JBuilder; it avoids recompiling files unnecessarily.

JBuilder also provides the option to change compilers. You can configure the JBuilder build system to use javac (Java2 SDK tool) as the main compiler. If you want to take advantage of JBuilder features, such as smart dependencies checking and refactoring, then you should use Borland Make for Java.

This session discusses compiler settings, project build settings, resource files and Ant libraries management, and Build menu configuration.

# Compiler Settings

JBuilder does not limit developers to working with one Java compiler. Compiler options for an open project can be configured on the Java tab of the Build page of Project Properties (Project | Project Properties), as shown in Figure 10.2. You can also right-mouse click the project file in the Project pane and choose Properties. Note that files in the project will be affected by the changes to the options. This also applies to files referenced by the project files.

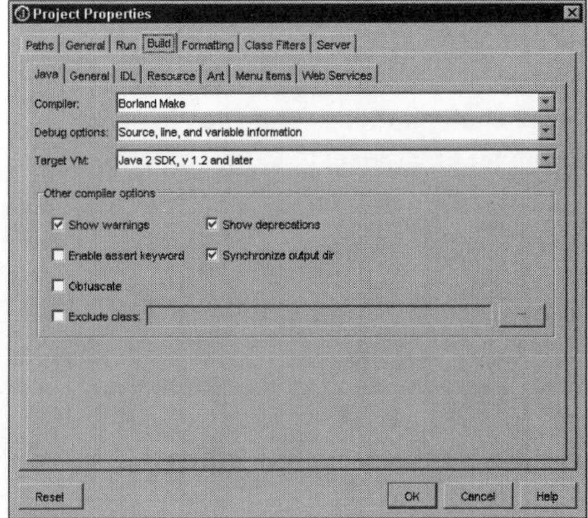


**Figure 10.2** Java compiler options.

JBuilder selects Borland Make as the default compiler. It provides settings for Synchronize output dir, Obfuscate, and Exclude class. If you select javac as the compiler for your project, these settings will not be enabled. When compiling with Borland Make (bmj), the project enables dependencies checking and refactoring features. If you want to use the host JDK compiler shipped with JBuilder, located in the <JBuilder Dir>/jdk1.4 directory, then select javac when compiling the project. If you want to use the compiler specified on the Project | Project Properties - Path tab, then select Project javac when compiling the project. Note that when you do not compile the project with bmj, JBuilder will not detect dependency changing on files until the project is rebuild.

**NOTE When you change any debug or obfuscation options on the Build page of the Project Properties dialog box, you must rebuild your project in order to have the changes take effect.**

Debug settings allow you to include or exclude variable information for debugging. If you select Source, Line, And Variable Information, the java .class files will be built with full debugging information, such as source name, line number, and local variable information. If you select Source And Line Information Only, the java .class files will be built with only source name and line number in its debug information. If you use JBuilder SE or JBuilder Enterprise, you can build your project with only source name in its debug information. In many cases, when we want to reduce the build size to the smallest size possible, then we need to select None to the debug information to include zero debug information.

You can use Target Virtual Machine (VM) to restrict the class files to work with a specific VM version. Choosing All Java SDKs generates Java .class files compatible with all VMs in JDK 1.1 and Java 2 JDKs. Otherwise, JBuilder will generate Java .class files, which work only for a selected VM. For example, if you select Java 2 SDK, v 1.4 and Later, the generated class files will work only on VMs in the Java 2 SDK, v 1.4 and later. They will not work on 1.1, 1.2, or 1.3 VMs.

**TIP When you select the target VM, you need to enter the following VM parameter on the Run page of the Runtime configurations dialog box in order for the Smart Swap debugger feature (JBuilder Enterprise) to work properly: Xverify:none.**

Select the Show Warnings option to display any compiler warning messages in the message pane. By default, the warning messages are displayed in yellow. The color code can be customized using JBuilder Editor.

Show Deprecations displays all deprecated classes, methods, properties, events, and variables when compiling the project. This option is very useful when we target existing applications to a new JDK. When this option is checked, we can see what specifically is deprecated.

If you select Borland Make as the compiler, Synchronize Output Dir will automatically be enabled in the Project Properties dialog. This option keeps the Output Dir in synchronization automatically with the current project by deleting class files on the output path so that we do not have their source files in the project.

To protect valuable source code from reverse engineering, you can use Obfuscate in Borland Make. We should obfuscate code to protect the intellectual property from hackers and dishonest competitors. Obfuscation reduces decompiling risk by replacing readable variable names with different names, altering symbols to make it hard to associate those variables with the source code.

You can also exclude Java source files from compiling. This can be done via checking the Exclude Class option. This option is checked, so the build also excludes the process of evaluating of the parameters passing to the static methods; the *bmj* could run faster.

## Common Build Settings

The common build settings are found in the General tab of the Build page of the Project Properties dialog, as shown in Figure 10.3. They include the following options:

- Automatically save project files before each compiling process.
- Automatically generate sources to a given output path.
- Automatically refresh the project before building.
- Automatically cancel the build process when error occurs.
- Always build before refactoring.
- Automatically check JSPs for errors at build time.

Select a SQL translator for the current project. When a SQLJ translator is selected, JBuilder automatically adds SQLJ files to the project. There are two supported SQLJ translators: Oracle translator for Oracle database and IBM translator for DB2 database. To set up a SQLJ translator, we open the Enterprise Setup dialog box (Tools | Enterprise Setup) and select an appropriate translator. More information on SQLJ can be found at www.sqlj.org.

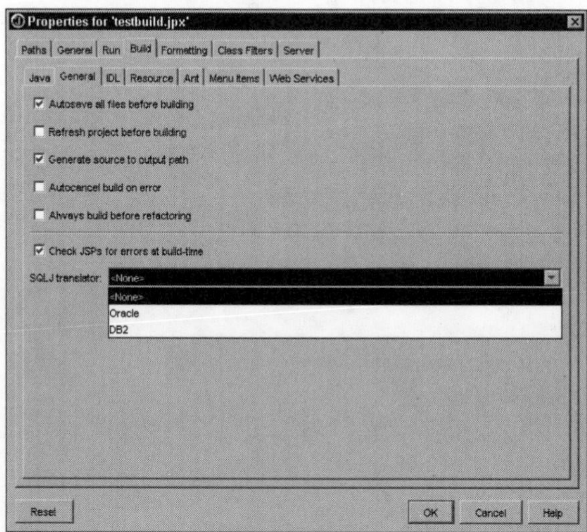


**Figure 10.3** General build settings.

## BORLAND BMJ AND BCJ COMMAND LINE TOOLS

JBuilder provides two utilities for the command-line compile option: bmj and bcj commands. When compiling with bmj, the project enables dependencies checking and generating a dependency file. bcj compiles only the specified Java source file without doing dependencies checking or being concerned about the dependency file. The two utilities are located in <JBuilder Dir>/bin directory. Here are the syntax and list of options for both.

bmj [OPTIONS] {source.java} {[-s] {source.java} | -p {package} | -c {class}}Valid options include the following:

```
-g                        Generate all debugging information
-g:none                   Generate no debugging information
-g:{lines,vars,source}    Generate only some debugging information
-verbose                  Output messages about what the compiler is doing
-quiet                    Generate no messages
-nowarn                   Generate no warning messages
-obfuscate                Obfuscate private symbols
-encoding <encoding>      Specify character encoding used by source files
-d <directory>            Specify the output directory
-deprecation              Output source locations where deprecated APIs are used
-classpath <path>         Specify where to find user class files
-bootclasspath <path>     Override location of bootstrap class files
-extdirs <dirs>           Override location of installed extensions
-sourcepath <path>        Specify where to find input source files
-target <release>         Generate class files for specific VM version
-exclude <classname>      Exclude use of class from compile
-source <release>         Accept source files for specific Java version
-rebuild                  Rebuild all class files
-nocompile                No compilation of class files
-nocheckstable            No checking of stable packages
-nomakestable             Compile only changed classes in a package
-sync                     Synchronize source and output directory
```

bcj [OPTIONS] [SOURCE FILES]Valid options include the following:

```
-g                        Generate all debugging information
-g:none                   Generate no debugging information
-g:{lines,vars,source}    Generate only some debugging information
-verbose                  Output messages about what the compiler is doing
-quiet                    Generate no messages
-nowarn                   Generate no warning messages
-obfuscate                Obfuscate private symbols
-encoding <encoding>      Specify character encoding used by source files
-d <directory>            Specify the output directory
```

```
-deprecation              Output source locations where deprecated APIs are used
-classpath <path>         Specify where to find user class files
-bootclasspath <path>     Override location of bootstrap class files
-extdirs <dirs>           Override location of installed extensions
-sourcepath <path>        Specify where to find input source files
-target <release>         Generate class files for specific VM version
-exclude <classname>      Exclude use of class from compile
-source <release>         Accept source files for specific Java version
```

## Managing Resource Files

JBuilder recognizes all defined resource types, and JBuilder can be configured to copy those files from the source path to the output path during its compilation. The resource information on files or by file extension can be configured on the Resource tab of the Build page of Project Properties (Project | Project Properties), as shown in Figure 10.4.

The tab displays a list of project scope default settings for file extension and their default deployment action. The action includes options for Copy or Do not copy option. When you select Copy, JBuilder copies the defined file types to the output path during its build process. When you select Do not copy, JBuilder will not copy the defined files to the output path during the build process, regardless of whether the file type is a common Java resource.

**TIP** **You can use the Default Project Properties dialog box (Project|Default Project Properties) to change default settings for all future projects.**

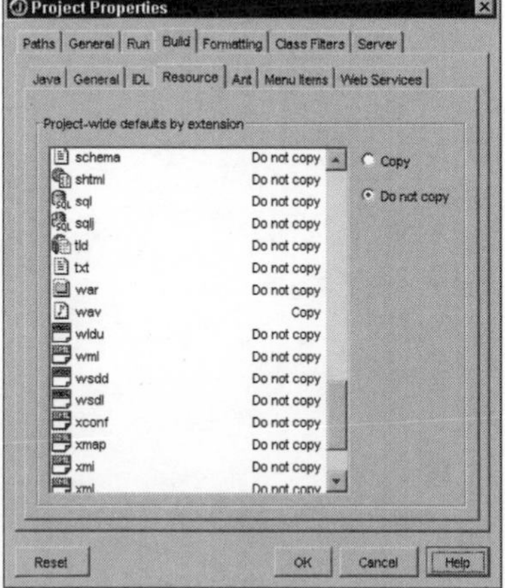


**Figure 10.4** Managing the Resource tab.

**JBUILDER COMMAND-LINE INTERFACE**

**JBuilder provides a command-line interface with arguments to help you build an entire JBuilder project from a Unix Shell console or DOS command console. Here is the argument list (F:\Borland\JBuilder8\bin>jbuilder -help):**

**build: Build JBuilder projects (not available in Personal)**
**help: Display help on command-line options**
**info: Display configuration information**
**license: Display the license manager**
**nosplash: Disable splash screen**
**verbose: Display OpenTools loading diagnostics**

**Example usage:**
**jbuilder -build wileyproject.jpx rebuild**

## Changing Ant Library

JBuilder integrates its build systems with the latest Ant version 1.5; however, you can add any Ant library or use a different version of Ant in the project. Changing Ant libraries can be configured on the Resource tab of the Ant page of Project Properties (Project | Project Properties), as shown in Figure 10.5.

JBuilder will use the new Ant libraries instead of the version shipped in the JBuilder lib directory.

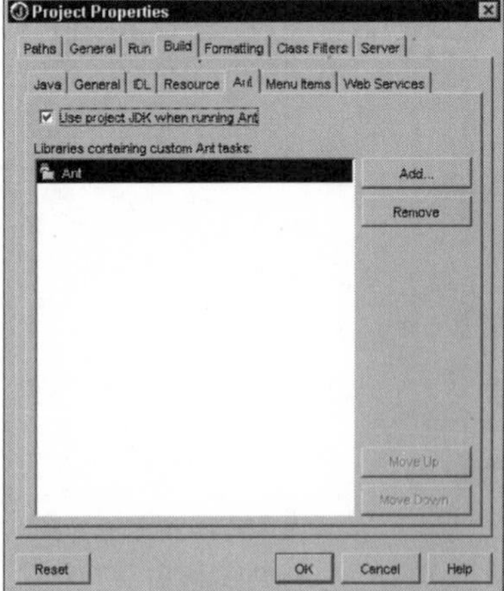


**Figure 10.5** Adding Ant libraries.

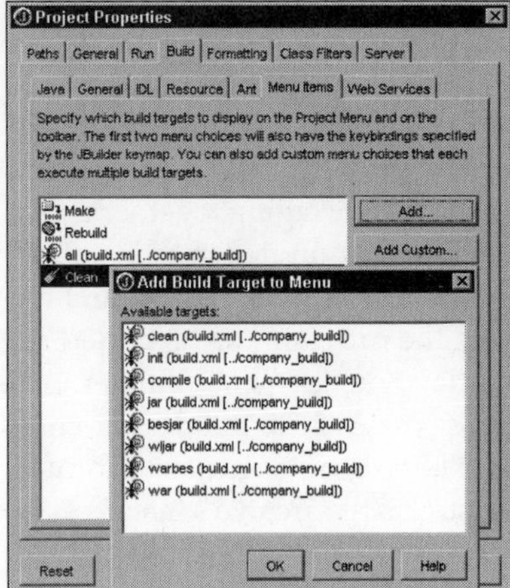


**Figure 10.6** Configure Build menu.

## Adding Items to Build Menu

Figure 10.1 showed two default items — Make and Rebuild — on the Build menu. You can add and customize target items on the Menu Items tab of the Build page of Project Properties (Project | Project Properties). See Figure 10.6 for an example.

The targets can be Clean, any Ant targets, or any external build tasks. You can move a target item up or down to make the item appear first on the Build drop-down menu. The default build item is listed first on the list. See Figure 10.7 for an example.

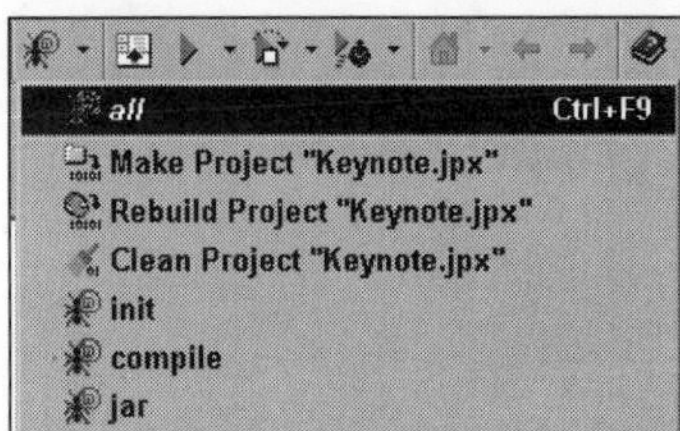


**Figure 10.7** Drop-down Build menu.

# Archive Builder

Java program deployment has gone far beyond applet deployment. Currently there are at least 10 different deployment formats for Java applications, including applets and advanced J2EE packets. A Java deployment process includes packaging together many Java .class files, html files, xml files, image files, and other files bundled in the application program. After packaging the file, the deployment process distributes the archive files onto a server computer or a client computer where the programs are executed.

Different formats require different steps to archive a Java deployment. JBuilder provides an Archive Builder to assist the deployment process. The Archive Builder automatically collects and bundles Java classes, resource files, and libraries into an archive format, such as .ZIP or .JAR files. At the same time, JBuilder constructs the archive's manifest.

Depending on what archive format you select, JBuilder's Archive Builder will lead you through the steps to create the archive. After compiling your project, you can either choose Wizards | Archive Builder to bring up the Wizard or do File | New | Build | Archive Builder, as shown in Figure 10.8.

First, the Archive Builder asks you to select an archive type (see Figure 10.8). Depending on what type you select in this step, the wizard will take you through a different number of steps and configuration parameters. Following are different archive types that the Archive Builder supports:

**Applet JAR.** An applet archive uses the compressed JAR that includes all required classes from imported libraries; therefore, the applet is not dependent on external files.

**Applet ZIP.** This archive is an alternative to the Applet JAR format. It supports older Web browsers that cannot host .JAR files.

**Application.** An application archive contains a main class file that contains the public static void main(String[] args) method. The archive is not compressed by default. Usually, the application archive type does not contain the supported libraries, which will be distributed along with the application installation.

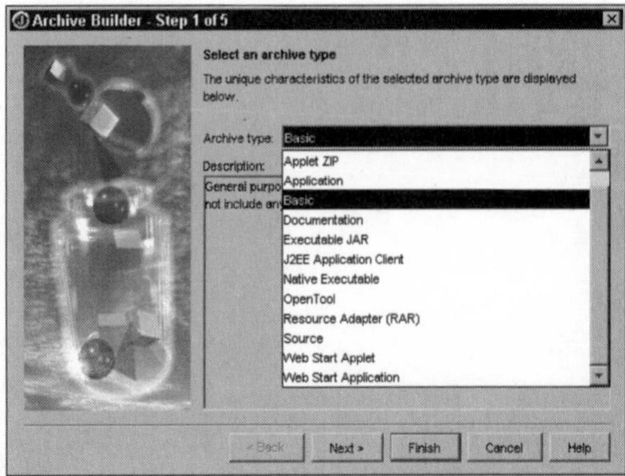


**Figure 10.8** Archive Builder wizard.

**Basic.** This archive type is almost the same as the Application archive; the only difference is that no main class is specified in the Basic archive.

**J2EE Application Client.** The J2EE Application Client archive uses the compressed JAR format, which includes the J2EE client deployment descriptors and class file. The deployment descriptor contains definitions of Enterprise JavaBeans (EJB) and any other external resources for the J2EE application.

**Native Executable.** The Native Executable archive type uses compressed JAR format. It also includes native executable wrappers for Windows, Linux, Solaris, and Mac OS X, as shown in Figure 10.9.

**OpenTool.** The OpenTool archive uses the .JAR format. To be compliant with the JBuilder OpenTools structure, you need to override the manifest file following JBuilder OpenTool template.

**Resource Adapter (RAR).** An RAR archive contains J2EE component implementations. In being compliant with the J2EE 1.3 specification, a JBuilder RAR archive includes the connector implementations. In the future, RAR will include other J2EE service implementations.

**Web Start Applet.** The Web Start Applet archive uses the JAR file format. Typically, it belongs to WebApp node, and it will be deployed to a Web application holder in a Web server. The Java Web Start now supports launching any Java applet or application from a hypertext link on a Web page, in any Web browser. Also, the Java Web Start includes automatic update features.

**Web Start Application.** Like the Web Start Applet archive, the Web Start Application archive uses the JAR file format and is deployable by Java Web Start technology.

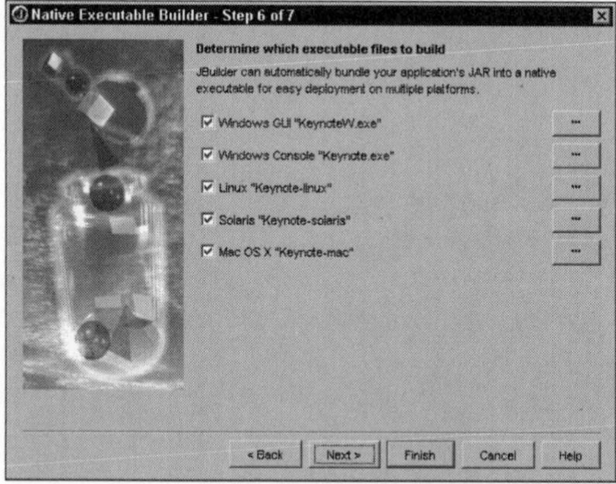


**Figure 10.9** Native Executable Builder.

# Using External Build Task

In a complex environment with multiple build processes for different types of applications, it is a nightmare for developers to manage and execute builds across applications and languages. JBuilder External Build Task (see Figure 10.10) allows us to configure and set the JBuilder build system to work with any external build processes and scripts that are already in place and working perfectly in the existing developing environment. To start the External Build Task wizard, choose File | New | Build page, and double-click the External Build Task icon.

In this step, it is important that you provide which phase the task is scheduled to execute in. Also, you should identify the targets that execute before and after the external build task for that given phase.

When you click on the Insert Macro button, JBuilder displays a macro list for the project (see Figure 10.11). You can select one or more items in combination to form an environment variable as you desire.

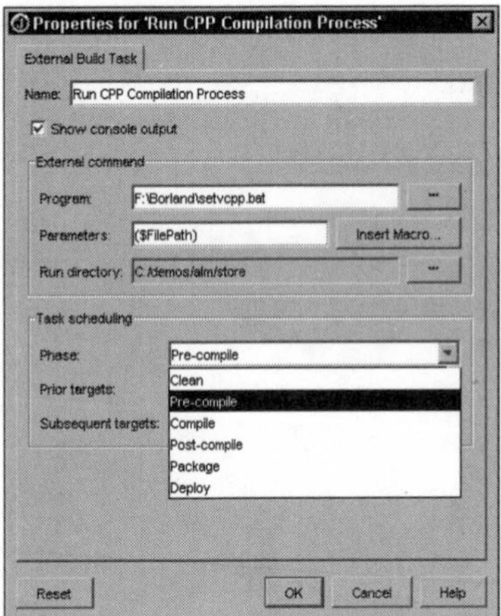


**Figure 10.10** External Build Task wizard.

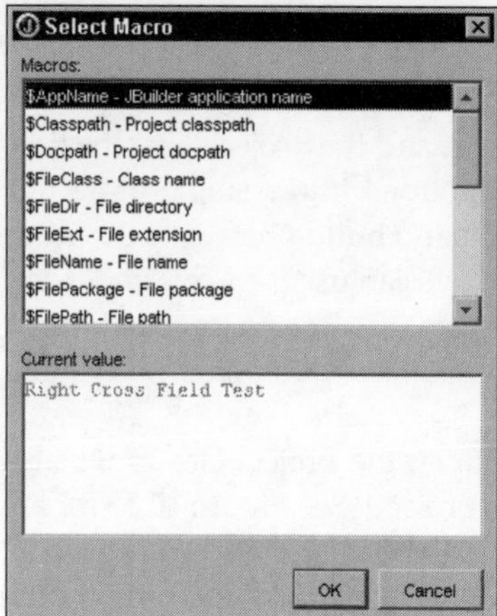


**Figure 10.11** Select macro(s) to define environment variables.

After you have the external task defined, you can click on the external task node and select Make to run the task. The JBuilder Message pane will display the Build tab information, which includes the Standard error output and Standard output texts, as shown in Figure 10.12.

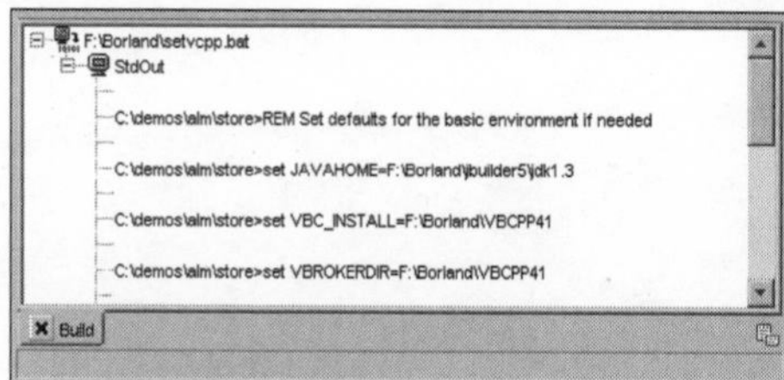


**Figure 10.12** StdOut message for External Build Task.

# Using Project Groups

Developers often work on many JBuilder projects at once, and the projects may be tied to each other. The idea of having all related projects grouped into a single project is very powerful. It helps not only during the development and build phase but also during packaging and deployment. For J2EE development, we can use the same codebase on multiple application servers. The Project Group information stores information in an XML-based project file. Subprojects within the group can be opened and built simultaneously.

After creating and configuring individual projects, open the Project Group wizard from the Project page of the Object Gallery (File | New | Project). See Figure 10.13 for an example.

Next, you need to add projects into the Project group. You can add one project at a time, or you can select the Add Recursively option to add all subdirectories and project files to the group. In this example (see Figure 10.14), the two projects (testbuild.jpx and testbuild2.jpx) will be added to the testbuild group.

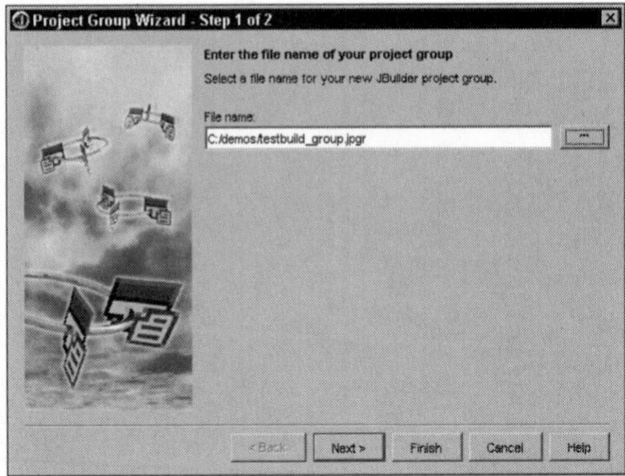


**Figure 10.13** Project Group wizard - Step 1.

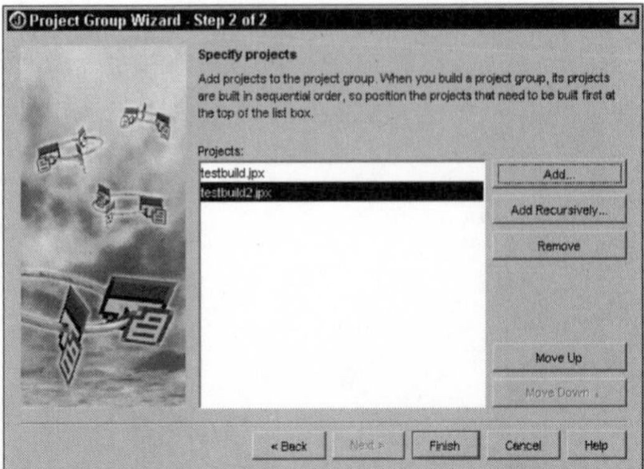


**Figure 10.14** Project Group wizard - Step 2.

You can move the subprojects up or down to set the order in which the subprojects will be built. This feature allows you to control the build order of all projects within the project group.

# Integrating the JBuilder Build System with Ant Build Files

Ant does not replace the IDE; it is a complement to the IDE. Borland JBuilder provides an integrated environment with Ant for building and automating complex Java projects. This section shows how JBuilder integration with Ant helps us be more effective with Ant Build Wizard and Ant configurations for the projects.

When you install JBuilder, it automatically sets up your environment to work with Ant. The latest version of Ant is installed in <JBuilder Dir>\extras\ant. If you want to run Ant as a command-line tool, you just need to set your PATH pointing to <JBuilder Dir>\extras\ant\bin. For example, set JAVA_HOME to <JBuilder Dir>/jdk1.4; set ANT_HOME to <JBuilder Dir>\extras\ant; set PATH including ${ANT_HOME}/bin.

## Ant Wizard

You can access the Ant wizard by doing File | New | Build | Ant or by Wizards | Ant. JBuilder will display the wizard dialog shown in Figure 10.15.

Select Add to browse and add existing Ant build.xml files to the project. You can also add existing Ant build.xml files by selecting Project | Add Files/Packages, navigating to the Ant build file, and adding to the current project.

By default, JBuilder recognizes and displays any Ant build.xml files in the Project pane. The build.xml is displayed with an Ant icon node with its relative path. This default setting helps us to identify different build.xml files in case we have multiple build.xml files in the project. Displaying the relative path can be disabled in the Ant Properties dialog. All build targets in the build.xml file are displayed as children of the build.xml node.

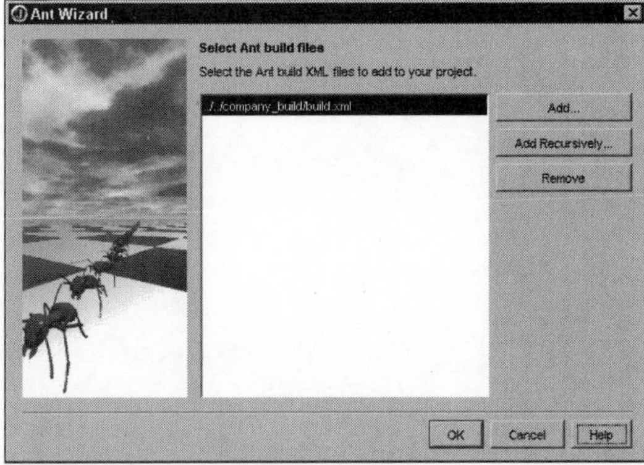


**Figure 10.15** Ant Wizard dialog.

**TIP** **JBuilder automatically recognizes any Ant build.xml file with the Ant icon node. You can set build files with other names as Ant build files in the Ant Properties dialog box. Right-mouse click the XML node, and choose Properties. Then choose the Ant tab, and check the Ant Build File option. See Figure 10.16 for an example.**

## Ant Build File Properties

To add Build File properties, right-mouse click the XML node and choose Properties. The Ant Properties dialog allows you to configure Ant settings, as shown in Figure 10.16.

When Ant build file is checked, the XML is defined as an Ant build file and JBuilder will apply all build properties to the XML file. If the build file is named build.xml, this option is grayed out. Show relative path is set by default to identify different build.xml files in case we have multiple build.xml files in the project. Log level sets details we want for message output. Four levels can be set — quiet, normal, verbose, or debug. Use log file is selected to send output messages to a log file instead of the JBuilder message pane. In addition, you can add, modify, or remove existing properties in the dialog. These property settings will override the equivalent settings in the build file.

Ant build file is considered a task in the JBuilder build system. This means that you can set Task Scheduling to determine the build phase in which the build file is executed. Also, you can select the other targets to be executed before and after the execution of the Ant build file.

If you want to automate your whole build system, you can check the Always run Ant when building project option. By doing this, JBuilder will run the Ant build process whenever it is building the project.

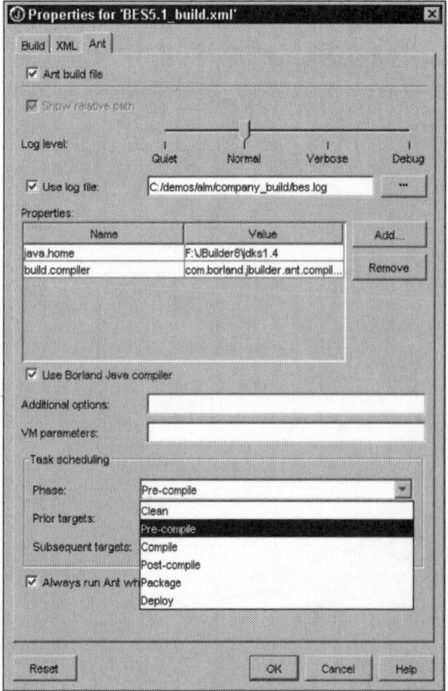


**Figure 10.16** Ant Build File properties.

**ANT COMMAND LINE USAGE**

Here are options for Ant command line tool.

```
ant [options] [target [target2 [target3] ...]]
Options:
  -help                  Print this message
  -projecthelp           Print project help information
  -version               Print the version information and exit
  -diagnostics           Print information that might be helpful to
                         diagnose or report problems
  -quiet, -q             Be extra quiet
  -verbose, -v           Be extra verbose
  -debug                 Print debugging information
  -emacs                 Produce logging information without adornments
  -logfile <file>        Use given file for log
    -l    <file>                 "
  -logger <classname>    Indicate the class that is to perform logging
  -listener <classname>  Add an instance of class as a project listener
  -buildfile <file>      Use given buildfile
    -file    <file>              "
    -f       <file>              "
  -D<property>=<value>   Use value for given property
  -propertyfile <name>   Load all properties from file with -D
                         properties taking precedence
  -inputhandler <class>  Specify the class that will handle input requests
  -find <file>           Search for buildfile toward the root of the
                         filesystem and use it
```

**TIP** **When running Ant as an external process from within JBuilder, you can set the heap size for the VM depending on the size of your project. For example, to set the maximum heap of the Java VM for Ant to 128MB, enter Xmx128m as VM parameters.**

By default, Borland Java Compiler is checked for the most optimized compilation. You can, however, uncheck the setting and configure JBuilder to use another java compiler, such as JDK javac.

## Ant Options

Following are additional Ant options for the Additional Options field of the Properties dialog box:

**help.** Prints this message.

**projecthelp.** Prints project help information.

**version.** Prints the version information and exits.

**emacs.** Produces logging information without adornments.

**-logger classname.** Indicates the class that is to perform logging.

**listener classname.** Adds an instance of class as a project listener.

**find file.** Searches for buildfile toward the root of the filesystem and uses the first one found.

These options allow you to maximize the usage of Ant in your build environment.

## Handling Compilation Errors with Ant

Building JBuilder projects is no different from running typical JBuilder build processes. Two types of error messages may occur: Error messages and Warning messages. Error messages show a problem that need to be fixed; for example, there is a syntax error. Warning messages show a suspicious problem that should be reviewed and fixed. And the warnings do not stop the compilation process.

JBuilder ErrorInSight indicates the true cause of the error when you click on the error # in the Message pane. JBuilder will locate the line of code containing the error when you double-click the error in the structure pane. The code line containing the error will be highlighted in the editor.

Examining a StdErr node displayed in the Message pane will give you error messages. In this example, StdErr shows one error:

```
        "CustomerBean.java":      [javac]
C:\demos\alm\company_build\src\keynote\ejb\CustomerBean.java:43: error
#200: ';' expected at line 43
          [javac]     this.entityContext = entityContext
          [javac]                          ^
```

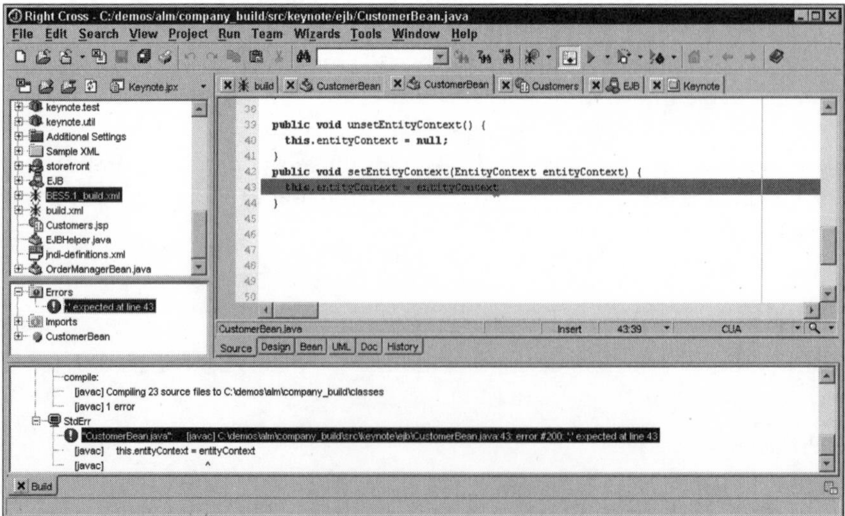


**Figure 10.17** Customer Bean. JAVA

## Summary

This chapter gives you a basic tour of the JBuilder build system and how to make it work efficiently in your developing environment. You have seen different build facilities, configuration, property settings, archive builder, and integration with Ant. The build system allows you to fully control and extend the build process in your development environment. The build system plays a critical role in JBuilder's vision of an Application Lifecycle Management environment.

CHAPTER

11

# Unit Testing with JUnit

Unit testing looks at code in small software components. Integration testing looks at larger components. The unit testing context fits well with the Extreme Programming methodology, which employs frequent builds and integration principles. The question facing programmers is this: How does the nature of unit testing affect our busy coding and deploying tasks? The Java community offers an excellent unit-level testing framework called JUnit, which is an open-source framework. Borland JBuilder built a tight integration with JUnit that enables programmers to unit test while they code.

This chapter gives you an overview of the JUnit architecture and focuses on how JBuilder integrates with JUnit to perform unit testing. This chapter also guides you through the steps of creating and running unit tests for the Java component using the JUnit framework in the JBuilder.

## JUnit Architecture

Thanks to the JUnit creators, Gamma and Kent Beck, the unit test framework was born in glory. The Java community quickly adapted to the framework by its features; JUnit TestCase and TestSuite firmly form a foundation that helps us write unit tests.

## TestCase

TestCase is the smallest unit in the JUnit framework; TestCase defines the state of initial values for a test context. This testing context is referred to as a test's fixture.

JUnit TestCase (shown in Figure 11.1) implements JUnit Test interface, which provides a public run() method to execute a test and collects its result into a TestResult instance. We can implement a TestCase by following these simple steps:

1. Implement a subclass of TestCase.
2. Define instance variables as the initial state of the test fixture.
3. Initialize the fixture state by overriding setUp() method, and clean up after a test by overriding the tearDown() method. TestRunner will execute the test case in the following order:
    1. TestRunner constructs one or more instances of the test case.
    2. Each test instance calls the setUp() method to configure the test environment, calls the testMethodXXX() method to do a test, and calls the tearDown() method to clean the fixture.

Here is an example:

```
public class TestSimpleCalculator extends TestCase {
  private  SimpleCalculator instance = null;
  long a, b, c;

  public TestSimpleCalculator(String name) {
    super (name);
  }

  protected void setUp() throws Exception {
    super.setUp();
    instance = new SimpleCalculator();
    a = 100;
    b = 10;
    c = 10;
}
// more codes
}
```

## TestSuite

TestSuite is composed of test objects that implement the JUnit Test interface. Usually, the components are test cases. We can run TestSuite as a batch processing to record a report

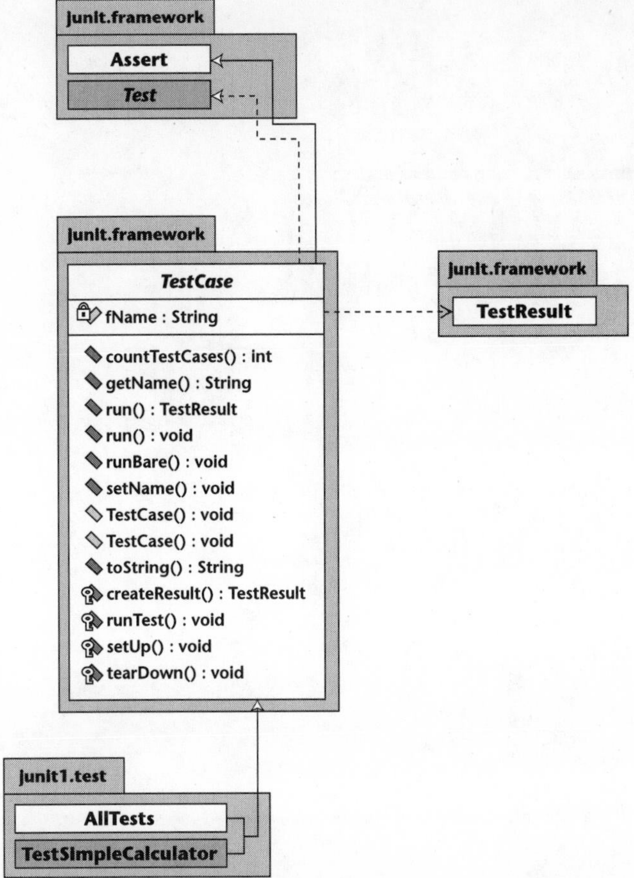


**Figure 11.1** UML view of JUnit TestCase.

of the success or failures of each test. By running the tests in an unattended batch process, we are rescued from running a hundred test cases one at a time. TestSuite is constructed by adding test objects to the suite via its addTest()or addTestSuites() methods. Also, we can construct a nested TestSuite depending on our test requirements. Here is an example of constructing a new TestSuite and adding tests to the suite:

```
TestSuite suite= new TestSuite();
 suite.addTestSuite(TestSimpleCalculator.class);
 suite.addTest(new TestSimpleCalculator("testSum"));
 suite.addTest(new TestSimpleCalculator("testSubtract"));
```

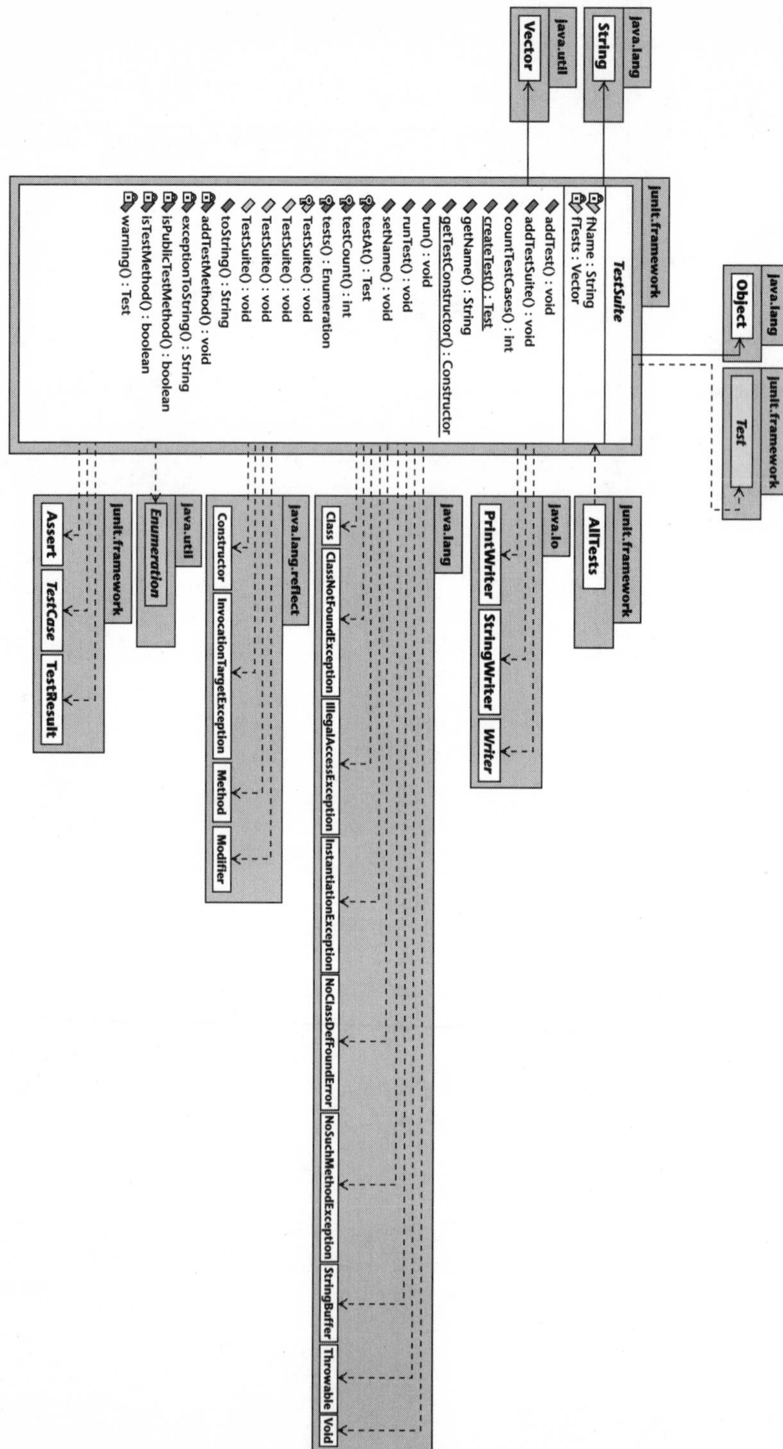


**Figure 11.2** UML view of JUnit TestSuite.

Table 11.1 summarizes TestSuite's methods.

**Table 11.1** TestSuite Methods

| RETURN TYPE | METHOD NAME |
|---|---|
| void | addTest(Test test)<br>Adds a test to the suite. |
| void | addTestSuite(java.lang.Class testClass)<br>Adds the tests from the given class to the suite. |
| int | countTestCases()<br>Counts the number of test cases that will be run by this test. |
| static Test | createTest(java.lang.Class theClass, java.lang.String name)<br>Creates new test based on a given test class. |
| java.lang.String | getName()<br>Returns the name of the suite. |
| static Constructor | getTestConstructor(java.lang.Class theClass)<br>Gets a constructor that takes a single String as its argument or a no arg constructor. |
| void | run(TestResult result)<br>Runs the tests and collects their result in a TestResult. |
| void | runTest(Test test, TestResult result) |
| void | setName(java.lang.String name)<br>Sets the name of the suite. |
| Test | testAt(int index)<br>Returns the test at the given index. |
| int | testCount()<br>Returns the number of tests in this suite. |
| java.util.Enumeration | tests()<br>Returns the tests as an enumeration. |
| java.lang.String | toString() |

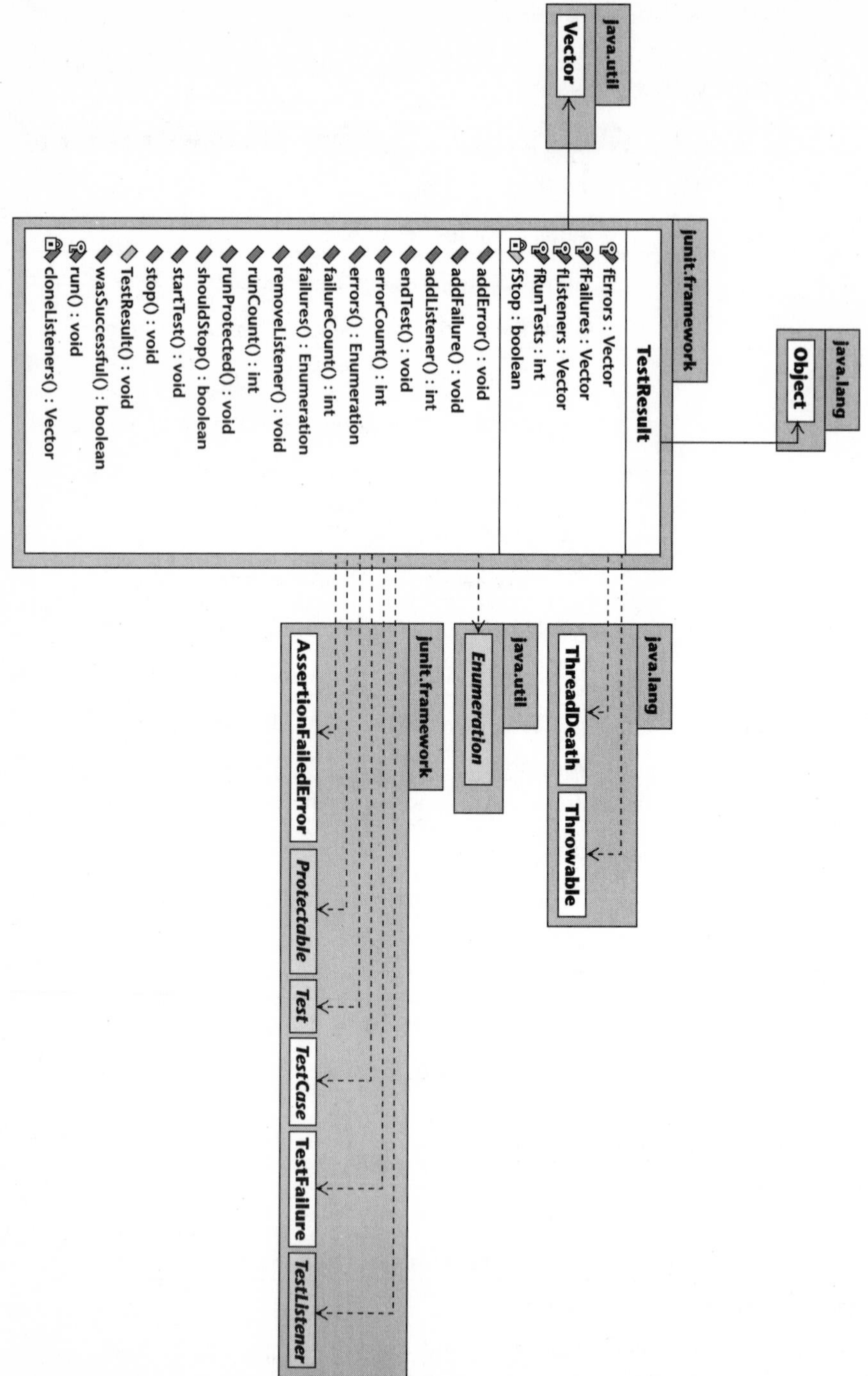


**Figure 11.3** UML view of TestResult class.

## JUnit Supporting Classes

There are two critical classes from the JUnit Framework: JUnit TestResult class and JUnit Assert class. TestResult gathers the results from running a test case in a collection. It is an excellent implementation of the Collecting Parameter pattern, which was introduced by Kent Beck in 1996. The JUnit framework, for the most part, handles the TestResult outputs behind the scenes; however, it is important to know about the TestResult class when you need to extend TestResult to meet your custom test result formats.

The JUnit test framework can distinguish between errors and failures. Errors are reported as unanticipated problems; for example, an ArrayIndexOutOfBoundsException occurs. On the other hand, a failure is predictable and checked for with assertions that are provided by the JUnit Assert class.

**TIP Asserts are statements that contain Boolean expressions showing the TRUE value to the developers' best knowledge. Assert statements are evaluated at runtime to catch errors if the expression results in false. By programming experiences, using assertions is one of the quickest and most effective ways to detect and correct bugs in the early coding phase. The assert process is turned off by default. To enable the Assert option in JBuilder, choose Project|Project Properties and click the Build tab.**

The Assert class contains a set of possible assert methods used to check expected values. When an assert fails, TestResult will record the information messages that the Assert class produces. Assert class has a few types of assert method: assertEquals(), assertFail(), assertTrue(), assertFalse(), assertSame(), assertNotSame(), assertNull(), assertNotNull(), and fail() methods. Each type contains a few static overloading methods to check on different given parameters. Table 11.2 shows all assert methods for JUnit Assert class.

There is a TestCase.assert() method, which is deprecated. We should not use the deprecated TestCase.assert() because it collides with the enforced keyword assert() in JDK 1.4.

**Table 11.2** Assert Methods

| METHOD NAME | DISCRIPTION |
|---|---|
| assertEquals(boolean expected, boolean actual) | Asserts that two Booleans are equal. |
| assertEquals(byte expected, byte actual) | Asserts that two bytes are equal. |
| assertEquals(char expected, char actual) | Asserts that two chars are equal. |
| assertEquals(double expected, double actual, double delta) | Asserts that two doubles are equal concerning a delta. |

*(continued)*

**Table 11.2** *(continued)*

| METHOD NAME | DISCRIPTION |
| --- | --- |
| assertEquals(float expected, float actual, float delta) | Asserts that two floats are equal concerning a delta. |
| assertEquals(int expected, int actual) | Asserts that two ints are equal. |
| assertEquals(long expected, long actual) | Asserts that two longs are equal. |
| assertEquals(java.lang.Object expected, java.lang.Object actual) | Asserts that two objects are equal. |
| assertEquals(short expected, short actual) | Asserts that two shorts are equal. |
| assertEquals(java.lang.String message, boolean expected, boolean actual) | Asserts that two Booleans are equal. |
| assertEquals(java.lang.String message, byte expected, byte actual) | Asserts that two bytes are equal. |
| assertEquals(java.lang.String message, char expected, char actual) | Asserts that two chars are equal. |
| assertEquals(java.lang.String message, double expected, double actual, double delta) | Asserts that two doubles are equal concerning a delta. |
| assertEquals(java.lang.String message, float expected, float actual, float delta) | Asserts that two floats are equal concerning a delta. |
| assertEquals(java.lang.String message, int expected, int actual) | Asserts that two ints are equal. |
| assertEquals(java.lang.String message, long expected, long actual) | Asserts that two longs are equal. |
| assertEquals(java.lang.String message, java.lang.Object expected, java.lang.Object actual) | Asserts that two objects are equal. |
| assertEquals(java.lang.String message, short expected, short actual) | Asserts that two shorts are equal. |
| assertEquals(java.lang.String expected, java.lang.String actual) | Asserts that two Strings are equal. |
| assertEquals(java.lang.String message, java.lang.String expected, java.lang.String actual) | Asserts that two Strings are equal. |
| assertFalse(boolean condition) | Asserts that a condition is false. |
| assertFalse(java.lang.String message, boolean condition) | Asserts that a condition is false. |

**Table 11.2** *(continued)*

| METHOD NAME | DISCRIPTION |
|---|---|
| assertNotNull(java.lang.Object object) | Asserts that an object is not null. |
| assertNotNull(java.lang.String message, java.lang.Object object) | Asserts that an object is not null. |
| assertNotSame(java.lang.Object expected, java.lang.Object actual) | Asserts that two objects refer to the same object. |
| assertNotSame(java.lang.String message, java.lang.Object expected, java.lang.Object actual) | Asserts that two objects refer to the same object. |
| assertNull(java.lang.Object object) | Asserts that an object is null. |
| assertNull(java.lang.String message, java.lang.Object object) | Asserts that an object is null. |
| assertSame(java.lang.Object expected, java.lang.Object actual) | Asserts that two objects refer to the same object. |
| assertSame(java.lang.String message, java.lang.Object expected, java.lang.Object actual) | Asserts that two objects refer to the same object. |
| assertTrue(boolean condition) | Asserts that a condition is true. |
| assertTrue(java.lang.String message, boolean condition) | Asserts that a condition is true. |

## Test Runners

JUnit offers two TestRunners: a text-based TestRuner and a GUI TestRunner implemented by using the standard Java Swing UI.

A text-based TestRunner outputs a number of test runs, test failures, and test errors. Typically, the text-based TestRunner is used to automate unattended test runs. Following is sample output from the text-based TestRunner:

```
Time: 0.02
There were 2 failures:
1) testGetAtt1(junitframework.TestJavaComponent2)junit.framework
.AssertionFailedError: Not yet implemented. at junitframework.
TestJavaComponent2. testGetAtt1(TestJavaComponent2.java:23)
2) testGetAtt2(junitframework.TestJavaComponent2)junit.framework.
AssertionFailedError: Not yet implemented. at junitframework.
TestJavaComponent2.testGetAtt2(TestJavaComponent2.java:28)
FAILURES!!!
Tests run: 2,  Failures: 2,  Errors: 0
```

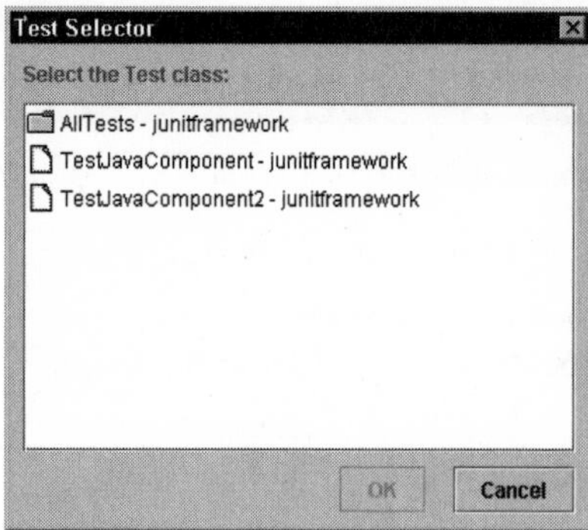


**Figure 11.4** Test Selector dialog.

The text-based TestRunner gives the quickest test results; however, for hundreds of tests, it really helps to have an informative graphical user interface. GUI TestRunner appears as a Java Swing-base application to configure how to execute the test and indicate the level of progress graphically.

The Swing UI TestRunner provides a Test Selector, shown in Figure 11.4, to select a test class to execute.

Each TestRunner can be configured two ways:

- The TestRunner can reload the testing class for each run. By doing this, we do not have to restart the TestRunner every time the codes are changed.
- TestRunner restarts after each run to load updated classes. To select a reload-configuration, as shown in Figure 11.5, Reload classes every run needs to be checked.

Upon completing the tests, the TestRunner provides a tally of the number of test runs, errors, and failures (see Figure 11.5).

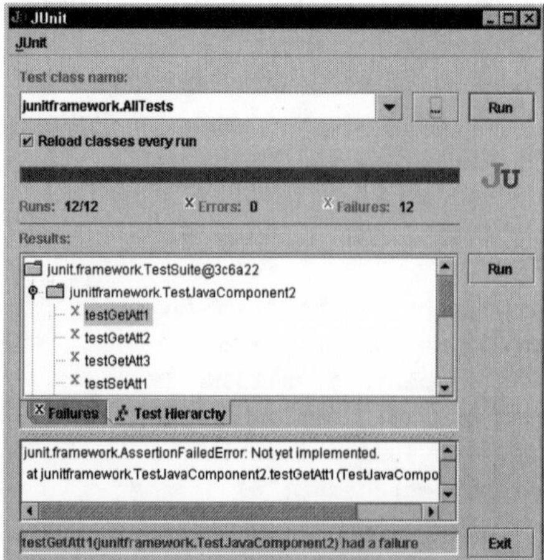


**Figure 11.5** JUnit Swing-based TestRunner.

Via the Test Hierarchy, we can select a TestSuite, a TestCase, or even a test method to execute; the test result will be displayed in the lower Message pane, and a text label will indicate whether the test has passed or failed after its execution.

The JUnit TestRunner is helpful, but it does bring up questions. How can it be used effectively with an IDE? How do we debug the test cases? How do we step into test method code? How can we quickly build a test framework for our components? How do we set up test fixtures? Borland JBuilder provides an IDE-level integration to JUnit framework; the integration helps developers rapidly set up their test environment for test cases and test suites. And, in addition to standard text-based TestRunner and GUI-based TestRunner, JBuilder innovates with JBuilder's TestRunner, enriched with IDE advantages using the Messageview to locate failures and errors more quickly.

# JUnit Integration with JBuilder

After we have the component coded, we can start building tests by clicking the File | New or by bringing up the Object Gallery and selecting the Test tab. JBuilder then displays the Test menu with all its wizards.

When the test class is created with the JUnit framework, JBuilder recognizes that test class and enables appropriate Runtime configurations such as Run Test and Debug Test. You can access these options from a Context menu by right-mouse clicking on the source filename in the Project pane.

JBuilder includes wizards for creating TestCases and TestSuites.

## Build a Test Case

When the Test Case wizard is run, JBuilder automatically generates a class that extends junit.framework.TestCase. At the same time, JBuilder creates an appropriate Runtime configuration and makes it available to the project Run Configuration. To help illustrate the Test Case construction, we use a very simple integer calculator example:

```
public class SimpleCalculator { // SimpleCalculator.java
  public SimpleCalculator(){
  }

  public long sum(long _1, long _2) {
     return _1 + _2 ;
  }

  public long multiply(long _1, long _2) {
     return _1 * _2 ;
  }

  public long subtract(long _1, long _2) {
   return _1 - _2 ;
  }

  public long divide(long _1, long _2) {
```

```
        return _1 / _2 ;
      }
    }
```

Creating a JUnit TestCase uses a four-step wizard, as outlined next.

## Step 1

First, choose a class to test, and choose one or more methods for building test methods (see Figure 11.6). In addition, the Available Methods tree displays the methods of all inherited classes of the selected class.

## Step 2

Next, we will provide class information for the new test case: package name, class name, and inheritance class (see Figure 11.7). By default, the wizard sets the inheritance class to junit.framework.TestCase. The test case can inherit from any parent class, which extends junit.framework.TestCase.

## Step 3

The third step is selecting predefined fixtures for the test case. Fixtures are constructed using the Fixture wizards. JBuilder supports JDBC fixture, JNDI fixture, Comparison fixture, and Customize fixture. The selected test fixtures are displayed in the fixture list. (See Figure 11.8.) You can add or remove any fixture item from the list by using the Add and Remove buttons. Also, you can move fixtures from the list up or down to change the order of the fixtures. The following code shows how fixtures are set up, constructed, and destructed in the setUp() and tearDown() method:

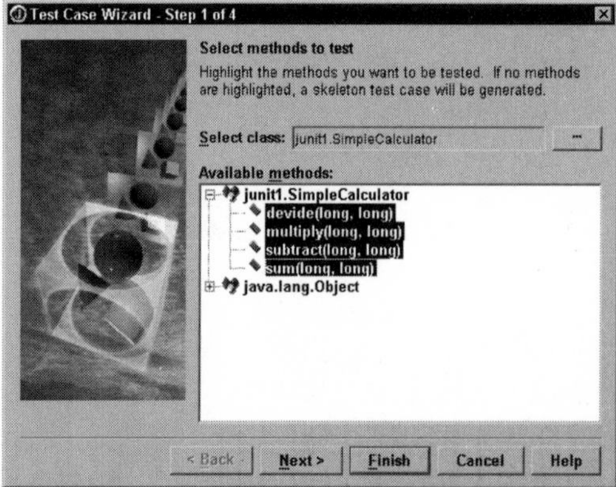


**Figure 11.6** Test Case wizard, Step 1.

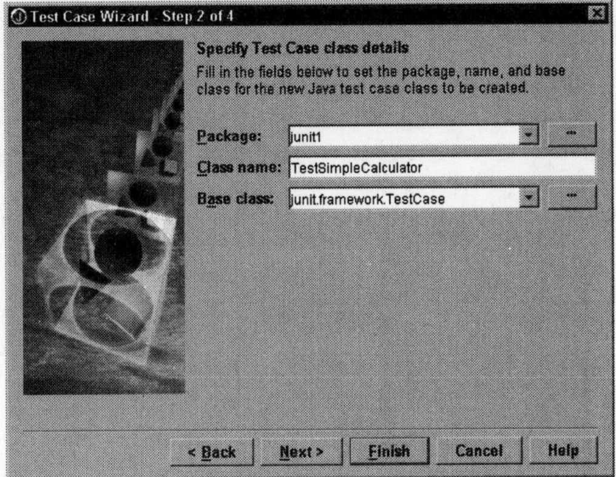


**Figure 11.7** Test Case wizard, Step 2.

```
protected void setUp() throws Exception {
  super.setUp();
  customFixture1 = new CustomFixture1(this);
  jdbcFixture11 = new junit1.JdbcFixture1(this);
  jdbcFixture12 = new JdbcFixture1(this);
  jndiFixture1 = new JndiFixture1(this);
  comparisonFixture1 = new ComparisonFixture1(this);

  customFixture1.setUp();
  jdbcFixture11.setUp();
  jdbcFixture12.setUp();
  jndiFixture1.setUp();
  comparisonFixture1.setUp();
}

protected void tearDown() throws Exception {
  instance = null;
  customFixture1.tearDown();
  jdbcFixture11.tearDown();
  jdbcFixture12.tearDown();
  jndiFixture1.tearDown();
  comparisonFixture1.tearDown();

  customFixture1 = null;
  jdbcFixture11 = null;
  jdbcFixture12 = null;
  jndiFixture1 = null;
  comparisonFixture1 = null;
  super.tearDown();
```

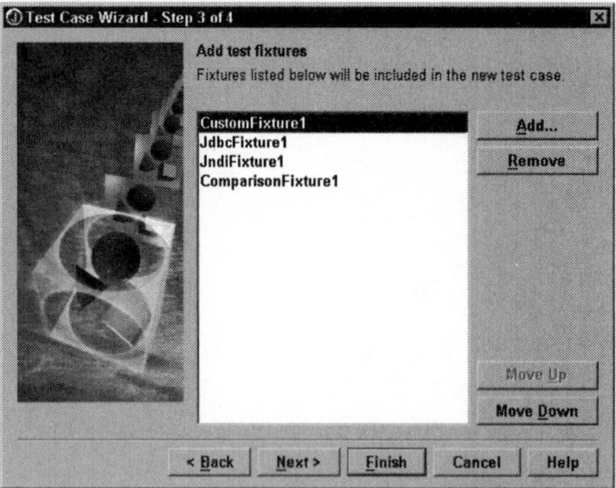


**Figure 11.8** Test Case wizard – Add test fixture.

When you click the Add button, JBuilder displays a Package Browser dialog box. You can search or browse to the fixture class that you want the test case to include.

## Step 4

The last step is to create a Runtime configuration for the new test case (Figure 11.9). If we check the Create a runtime configuration checkbox, the Test Case wizard will allow us to enter a name for the new runtime configuration. We also have the option of selecting a base configuration if we have any. The most important item in this step is to select a TestRunner for the TestCase. By default, it is set to JBuilder TestRunner; however, we can select JUnit Text-based or GUI-based TestRunner.

After finishing these four steps, JBuilder will generate a test case that extends junit.framework.TestCase. The generated code shows the test case skeletons, which are a placeholder for implementing real tests based on our test plan. Methods that still need to be completed are marked with @todo Javadoc comments. These comments are visible in the structure pane in the To-Do node of the tree. In this example, we complete the skeletons with the actual codes, as shown here:

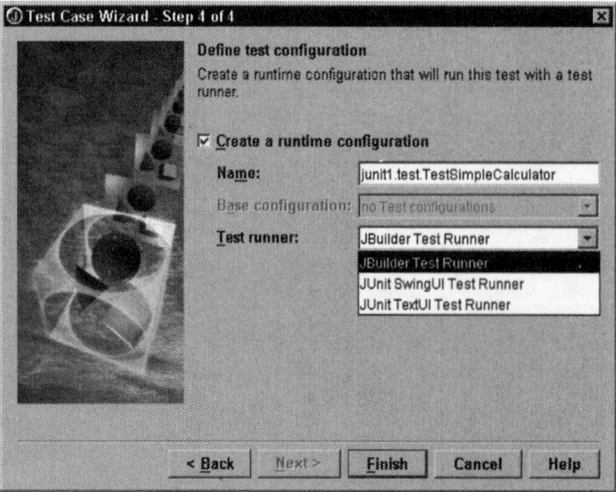


**Figure 11.9** TestCase wizard, Step 4.

```
// TestSimpleCalculator.java
package junit1.test;

import junit.framework.*;
import junit1.*;

public class TestSimpleCalculator extends TestCase {
  private  SimpleCalculator instance = null;
  long a, b, c;

  public TestSimpleCalculator(String name) {
    super (name);
  }

  protected void setUp() throws Exception {
    super.setUp();
    instance = new SimpleCalculator();
    a = 100;
    b = 10;
    c = 10;
  }

  protected void tearDown() throws Exception {
    instance = null;
    super.tearDown();
  }

  public void testDevide() {
    assertEquals(c, instance.divide(a, b));
  }

  public void testMultiply() {
    assertEquals(a, instance.multiply(b, c));
  }

  public void testSubtract() {
    long d = a - b;
    assertEquals(d, instance.subtract(a, b));
  }

  public void testSum() {
    long d = a + b;
    assertEquals(d, instance.sum(a, b));
  }
}
```

Running the test case using JBuilder TestRunner, we should see the results shown in Figure 11.10. The checkmark indicates that the test has passed. The cross sign indicates that the test has failed.

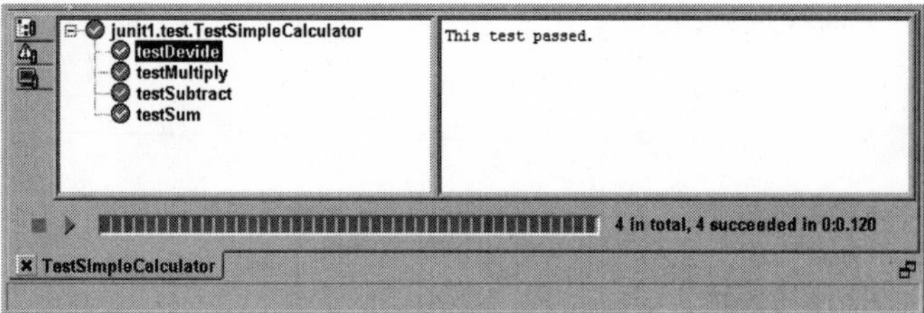


**Figure 11.10** JBTestRunner test hierarchy.

The JBTestRunner hierarchy shows that all four tests are passed. Let's modify one of the test methods to observe a failure case:

```
public void testDevide() {
  long d = 1;
    assertEquals(d, instance.devide(a, b));
  }
```

The JBTestRunner shows that there are four tests in total; three tests succeeded, and one test failed (see Figure 11.11). The purpose of this example is to observe a failure case. Our best unit test writing practice is that we always test for success. Errors or failures should be fixed at once when a test failure occurs.

The Test Failures message pane displays a JUnit assertion exception, which shows both the expected return value and the actual return value at the failed test method. If we click on the test method, JBuilder will take us directly to the test method where the error occurred. This is clearly an advantage of using JBuilder TestRunner instead of JUnit-based TestRunner. JBuilder TestRunner allows easy integration into its IDE.

## Build a TestSuite

TestSuite helps us run all tests as a single collection. The TestSuite layout (shown in Figure 11.2) contains one or many Test objects, which can be made up of individual test cases extending the JUnit Test class. Similar to creating the TestCase, the three-step wizard helps us create a TestSuite in an easy manner. To bring up the Test Suite wizard, select File | New from the menu to display the Object Gallery and then select Test Suite from the Test page (see Figure 11.12).

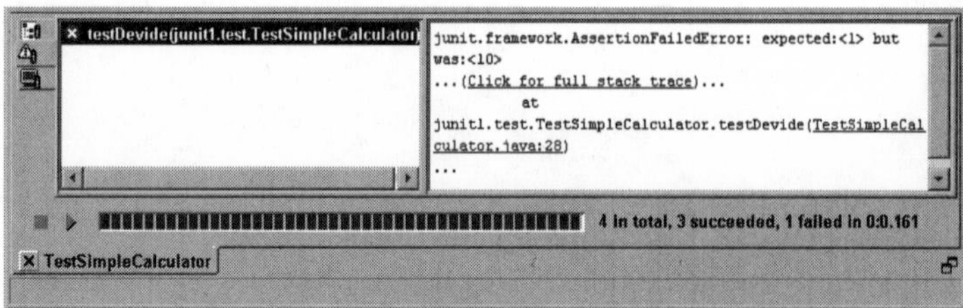


**Figure 11.11** JBuilder TestRunner test failures.

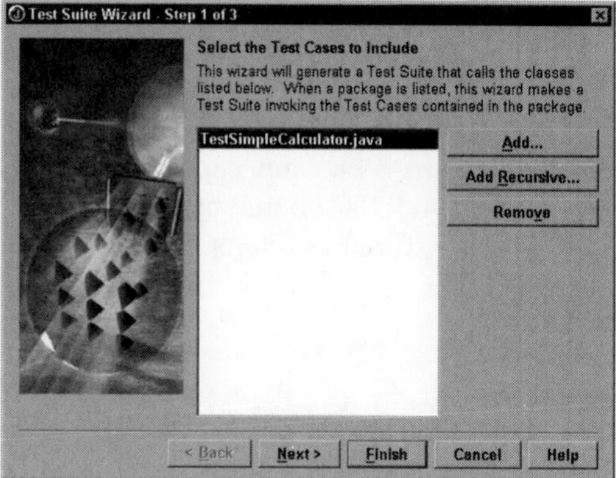


**Figure 11.12** TestSuite wizard, Step 1.

```
// AllTests.java
package junit1.test;

import junit.framework.*;

public class AllTests extends TestCase {

  public AllTests(String s) {
    super(s);
  }

  public static Test suite() {
    TestSuite suite = new TestSuite();
    suite.addTestSuite(junit1.test.TestSimpleCalculator.class);
    return suite;
  }
}
```

Similar to running a test case (Step 3), running a TestSuite will call a TestRunner. The TestRunner will automatically execute all the test cases specified in the suite. The result will be displayed accordingly in the TestRunner format.

After completing the three steps, JBuilder generates a TestSuite with all given test cases. To add more test cases to the suite, you would use the same format of addTestSuite() method for each test case. For example:

```
suite.addTestSuite(junit1.test.TestSimpleCalculator2.class);
```

## Using Test Fixtures

Test fixtures are defined as utility classes that are used to set up test contexts. Usually, we set up test fixtures to perform repeatedly in our test environment. JBuilder has wizards for creating common fixtures for JDBC, JNDI, and Comparisons.

## JDBC Fixture

To make it easier to write unit test cases involving JDBC connections, JBuilder provides JDBC Fixture as an extension to the JUnit Fixture paradigm. When the JDBC fixture is set up, the test case can use JDBC Fixture's methods to get a connection, run an SQL file, and set a URL. Table 11.3 summarizes the common JDBC Fixture methods.

Besides the common methods mentioned, JDBC Fixture has setters and getters for its private attributes, such as the following:

```
    private boolean verbose;
    private String schema;
    private String catalog;
    private boolean promptForPassword;
    private String password;
    private String username;
    private String driver;
private String url;
```

To create a new JDBC Fixture, open the Object Gallery, go to the Test tab, select the JDBC Fixture icon, and click the OK button. The two-step wizard will lead us through the creation of a JDBC Fixture (see Figure 11.13).

**Table 11.3** JDBC Fixture Methods

| RETURN TYPE | METHOD NAME |
|---|---|
| void | dumpResultSet(ResultSet rs, Writer writer) – Dumps the values in a result set to a Writer. |
| Connection | getConnection() – Returns a java.sql.Connection object defining the JDBC connection. |
| void | runSqlBuffer(StringBuffer buf, boolean abortOnFailure) – Runs an SQL statement contained in a StringBuffer. |
| void | runSqlFile(String s, boolean abortOnFailure) – Reads an SQL script from a file and runs it. Takes a String indicating the location of the file and a Boolean as parameters. |
| void | setUrl(String s) – Sets the URL property of the JDBC connection. Takes a String as a parameter. |
| void | setUsername(String s) – Sets the username for accessing the JDBC connection. Takes a String as a parameter. |
| void | setPassword(String s) – Sets the password for accessing the JDBC connection. Takes a String as a parameter. |

The Step 1 dialog asks for the generic information needed when developing a new class in Java such as Package, Name, and Base class. The dialog in Step 2 requests JDBC connection parameters. JBuilder supports JDBC drivers for many major databases on the market. The sample screen shows that we selected a com.borland.datastore .jdbc.DataStoreDriver accessing the following URL: http://jdbc:borland:dslocal:F :\Borland\JBuilder8\samples\JDataStore\datastores\employee.jds. Also, we need to have a user name and password to get authentication to access the database.

When completing the setup parameter, click Test Connection to check that you have been successful connecting to the database. A success message is displayed to the right of the Test Connection button. This step establishes a connection to a JDBC data source and configures connection parameters for the test classes.

Clicking the Choose Existing Connection button displays a Select Database dialog. In this dialog, JBuilder shows all the existing database connections we might have already previously defined. If we select an existing connection, JBuilder will automatically fill in all the fields on the page. The only field we need to complete is the Password field. The Extended properties allow us to define name/value pair properties for the connection. If you want to save the connection information for later use, just click on the Save Connection info button.

## *JNDI Fixture*

To help facilitate those unit test cases involving JNDI lookups, JBuilder provides JNDI Fixture, which extends the JUnit Fixture paradigm. To create a new JNDI Fixture, open the Object Gallery, go to the Test tab, select the JNDI Fixture icon, and click the OK button. The two-step wizard will lead us through the creation of a JNDI Fixture (see Figure 11.14).

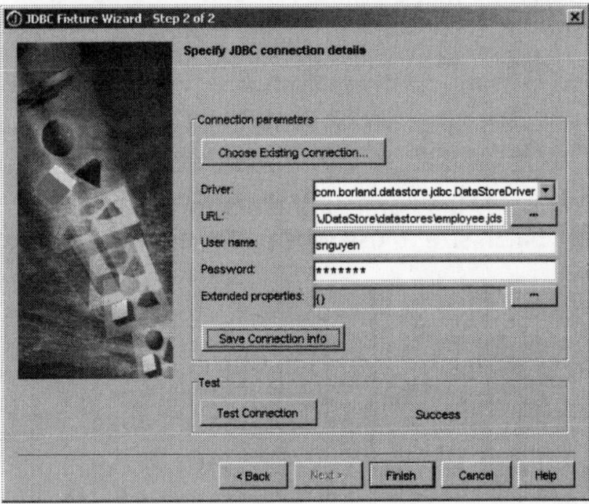


**Figure 11.13** JDBC fixture.

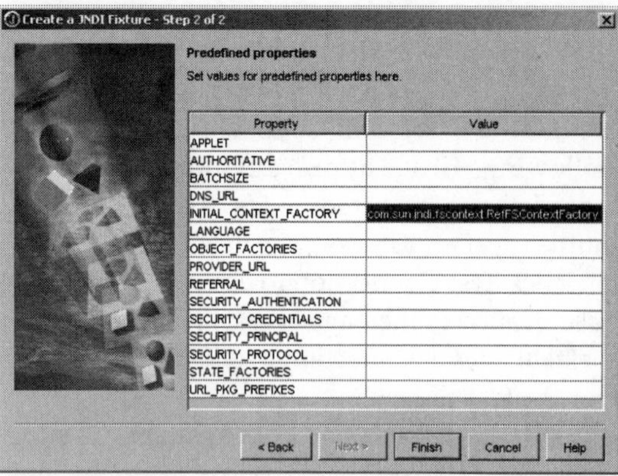


**Figure 11.14** Creating a JNDI fixture.

The JNDI Fixture wizard asks for 15 property name/value pairs to fill in required attributes in javax.naming.context. Those name/value pairs (listed in Table 11.4) will be used directly by the Fixture class; it will use the env.put() method to set the runtime environment for the test, for example:

```
env.put(Context.INITIAL_CONTEXT_FACTORY,
"com.sun.jndi.fscontext.RefFSContextFactory");
```

**Table 11.4** JNDI Key Attributes

| ATTRIBUTE | SUMMARY |
|---|---|
| static String | **APPLET**: Constant that holds the name of the environment property for specifying an applet for the initial context constructor to use when searching for other properties. |
| static String | **AUTHORITATIVE**: Constant that holds the name of the environment property for specifying the authoritativeness of the service requested. |
| static String | **BATCHSIZE**: Constant that holds the name of the environment property for specifying the batch size to use when returning data via the service's protocol. |
| static String | **DNS_URL**: Constant that holds the name of the environment property for specifying the DNS host and domain names to use for the JNDI URL context (for example, "dns://starswar/billing.com"). |
| static String | **INITIAL_CONTEXT_FACTORY:** Constant that holds the name of the environment property for specifying the initial context factory to use. |
| static String | **LANGUAGE**: Constant that holds the name of the environment property for specifying the preferred language to use with the service. |

**Table 11.4** *(continued)*

| ATTRIBUTE | SUMMARY |
|---|---|
| static String | **OBJECT_FACTORIES**: Constant that holds the name of the environment property for specifying the list of object factories to use. |
| static String | **PROVIDER_URL**: Constant that holds the name of the environment property for specifying configuration information for the service provider to use. |
| static String | **REFERRAL**: Constant that holds the name of the environment property for specifying how referrals encountered by the service provider are to be processed. |
| static String | **SECURITY_AUTHENTICATION:** Constant that holds the name of the environment property for specifying the security level to use. |
| static String | **SECURITY_CREDENTIALS**: Constant that holds the name of the environment property for specifying the credentials of the principal for authenticating the caller to the service. |
| static String | **SECURITY_PRINCIPAL**: Constant that holds the name of the environment property for specifying the identity of the principal for authenticating the caller to the service. |
| static String | **SECURITY_PROTOCOL**: Constant that holds the name of the environment property for specifying the security protocol to use. |
| static String | **STATE_FACTORIES**: Constant that holds the name of the environment property for specifying the list of state factories to use. |
| static String | **URL_PKG_PREFIXES:** Constant that holds the name of the environment property for specifying the list of package prefixes to use when loading in URL context factories. |

Similar to the JDBC Fixture getConnection() method, the JNDI Fixture getContext() method is also the most used method. The method returns a JNDI Context instance, which is created by the fixture constructor:

```
Context ctx;

public JndiFixture1(Object obj) {
  try {
    Hashtable env = new Hashtable();
    env.put(Context.INITIAL_CONTEXT_FACTORY,
"com.sun.jndi.fscontext.RefFSContextFactory");

    ctx = new InitialContext(env);
  }
  catch (Exception e) {
    System.err.println(e);
  }
}
```

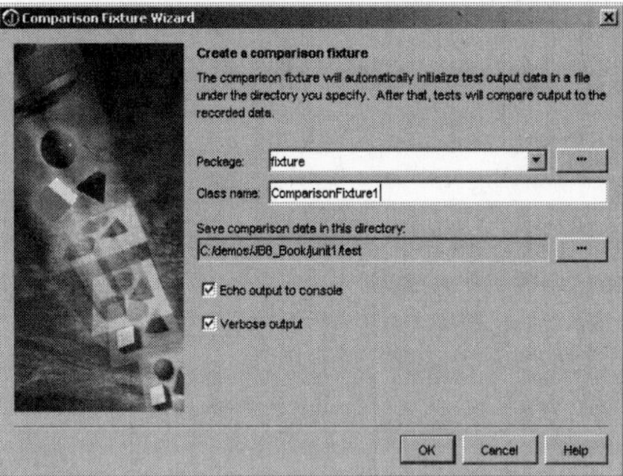


**Figure 11.15** Comparison Fixture wizard.

## *Comparison Fixture*

Comparison Fixture extends the JBuilder unit test component TestRecorder <com.borland.jbuilder.unittest.TestRecorder>, which takes advantage of the Java IO Writer class to record output results when executing a test. The output results will be used to compare to that of previous test outputs. To create a new Comparison Fixture, open the Object Gallery, go to the Test tab, select the Comparison Fixture icon, and click the OK button. The one-step wizard will lead us through the creation of a Comparison Fixture (see Figure 11.15).

In this example, we save comparison results in C:/demos/JB8_Book/junit1/test because the data will be used by the comparison fixture later. We check Echo output to console to echo the output results to the TestRunner console. Also, we have the Verbose output option checked to view more detailed information. Let's examine the comparison fixture's constructor:

```
  public ComparisonFixture1(Object obj) {
    super();
    super.setMode(UPDATE);
    super.setVerbose(true);
    super.setEcho(true);

    String fileName =
super.constructFilename("C:/demos/JB8_Book/junit1/test", obj);
    super.setOutputFile(fileName);
  }
```

super.setMode() method is called to set the output mode for the Comparison Fixture. TestRecorder class provides four public static constants that can be passed into the setMode() method:

```
static final int OFF = 0;     // Disable comparison fixture
static final int RECORD = 1;  // Records new output results, overwriting
existing data in the output file
```

```
static final int COMPARE = 2; // Compares new output result to the
existing output results
static final int UPDATE = 3;  // Compares and creates new output file,
and records new output results
```

**TIP** **If an existing output file contains incorrect data, set the output mode to RECORD after fixing the problem. Once you have recorded the desired output, set the mode back to UPDATE.**

The output file contains binary format data. Usually, the file has the same name as the test case. The test case is changing during the course of our development; therefore, we need to reinitialize the data file to have updated test results. In this case, we should use the RECORD option instead of the UPDATE option to avoid deleting the existing data file. Table 11.5 summarizes the most commonly used methods of the Test Recorder class.

Comparison Fixture extends the Java Writer class; therefore, it works effectively with the JDBC Fixture static dumpResultSet() method, which takes in an SQL result set and a Writer Object. For example:

```
    ResultSet rs = stmt.executeQuery("SELECT * FROM MYTESTTABLE");

jdbcFixture1.dumpResultSet(rs, comparisonFixture1);
```

This code snippet shows that we take the ResultSet return from executing the SQL query and use the JDBC Fixture's dumpResultSet() method to store the result set into the Comparison Fixture.

**Table 11.5** Test Recorder Common Methods

| RETURN TYPE | METHOD NAME |
|---|---|
| void | print(String s) – Prints a String that is passed to it as a parameter. |
| void | println(String s) – Prints a String that is passed to it as a parameter with a line break. |
| boolean | compareObject(Object) – Invokes the equals() method of an object to compare an object passed to it to an object that was previously recorded using recordObject(), and resets to the original mode when done comparing; returns TRUE if the object is successfully recorded. |
| boolean | recordObject(Object) – Records an object so that it can later be compared to another object using compareObject(); returns TRUE when it successfully records the data. |

### Custom Fixture

JUnit test fixtures set up test configurations and environments. We have seen JBuilder built-in JDBC, JNDI, and Comparison fixtures; in many cases, we want to set up custom fixtures to fit our test environment. The basic layout of a test fixture contains setUp() and tearDown() methods. The setUp() method is used to initialize the variables and construct other resources for the test to use. The tearDown() is used to release any permanent resources we have allocated during setUp():

```
public class CustomFixture1 {
// declare any test variable and resource

  public CustomFixture1(Object obj) {
    // additional pre-work can be done here when constructing the
CustomeFixture object
  }

  public void setUp() {
    // Initialize test variables
// Allocate resources
//
  }

public void tearDown() {
  // Close database connection
    // Release allocated resource
    // Clean up and reset variables
  }
}
```

## Unit Testing J2EE Applications

JBuilder's wizards for JUnit allow you to get away from the pains of writing test cases for standard Java components. Testing gets more complex when dealing with the server side of Java programming, writing distributed Internet applications with the J2EE framework. That EJB components are involved with local interface, remote interface, transactions, inter-EJB interactions, container services, and so on creates too many steps for most of us to set up an automatic test environment. Working to resolve these problems, Borland JBuilder engineers came up with the EJB Test Client wizard to assist us creating individual tests for each EJB component. EJB Test Client works with all J2EE applications supported by JBuilder. We can execute our routine unit test without leaving JBuilder to deploy or undeploy the Enterprise JavaBeans.

The EJB Test Client wizard provides three different types of unit test clients:

- An EJB test client application tests the EJB services of the bean.
- A JUnit test case enables the test with the JUnit framework.
- A Cactus JUnit test case simulates the client application to test the EJBs running on a remote server. This is covered in greater depth in Chapter 20.

# Summary

In this chapter, we reviewed how JBuilder integrates with the JUnit test process to build a solid code base. JBuilder combined its IDE and JUnit frameworks to make the entire testing process — from instantiating the class to be tested to calling its methods and checking the results — easier than ever for Java developers. The JBuilder wizards for JUnit testing with TestCase, TestSuite, and Test Fixtures help us do the unit tests in an easy manner and in an effective way.

CHAPTER

12

# UML Visualization

JBuilder is an evolving software application. By providing a sophisticated development environment with facilities for building Java applications across the J2SE, J2EE, and J2ME specifications, JBuilder becomes a technology itself. And JBuilder technology grows as Java developers demand better support for writing code. Because the Unified Modeling Language (UML) was adopted and has rapidly become an essential and common graphical language among software developers on software system design, JBuilder uses UML structural diagrams to help developers visualize and traverse Java classes and packages. With UML code visualization, we can do code review, code analysis, design problem detection, code refactoring, and communication on software design in the teamwork environment. This chapter focuses on how to use the UML visualization in parallel with the development process.

## BACKGROUND ON UML

**Supported by the object-oriented programming community since 1995, the Unified Modeling Language (UML) became a standard notation for modeling object-oriented software systems. In 1997, the Object Management Group (OMG) approved the UML specification and established a special task force behind the UML specification to define a graphical language for visualizing, specifying, constructing, and documenting the artifacts of distributed object systems. Currently, OMG has released and maintained the UML 1.4 specification (www.omg.org). In 2001, OMG task forces started working on UML 2.0 by announcing four RFPs: UML2.0 Superstructure, Object Constraint Language, and UML Diagram Interchange. The UML 2.0 works are continuing.**

## Visualize Your Codes

JBuilder is not designed to substitute or replace the UML design tools in the market; JBuilder mainly focuses on assisting developers with its innovated code visualization via UML diagrams. The two UML structural diagrams, package dependency diagrams and combined class diagrams, are used in JBuilder.

This package diagram shows how packages can be divided into modules with dependency relationships between packages. Typically, the package dependency diagram can be viewed as a high-level representation of a whole system or part of a subsystem of the big picture.

The key benefit of having a package dependency diagram is to view the logical modularization between packages visually. When the project is getting complex and large, during the design phase, the package diagram is very helpful in organizing and refactoring packages.

In JBuilder, the package diagram is intended to show all dependencies with the main package, as shown in Figure 12.1. After compiling or rebuilding the project, you can view the package dependency diagrams by opening the Package node in the Project pane, then selecting the UML tab in the Content pane; the package diagram will display.

A dashed line with an arrowhead represents Dependencies or Reverse Dependencies, which define dependency relationships between objects. The displayed packages with dependencies can be used for navigation from one package to another by double-clicking them in the diagram.

The class diagram shows the static structure of the object in the system. Every Java source file or class file can be visualized by its combined class diagram. When the file is opened in the Content pane, view the UML class diagram by selecting the UML tab at the bottom of the Content pane. The selected class will be displayed in the center of each diagram. JBuilder positions all association relationships on the left and all dependencies on the right of the class. Super classes or parent interfaces are placed on top of the class. And child classes or implementing classes are placed on the bottom.

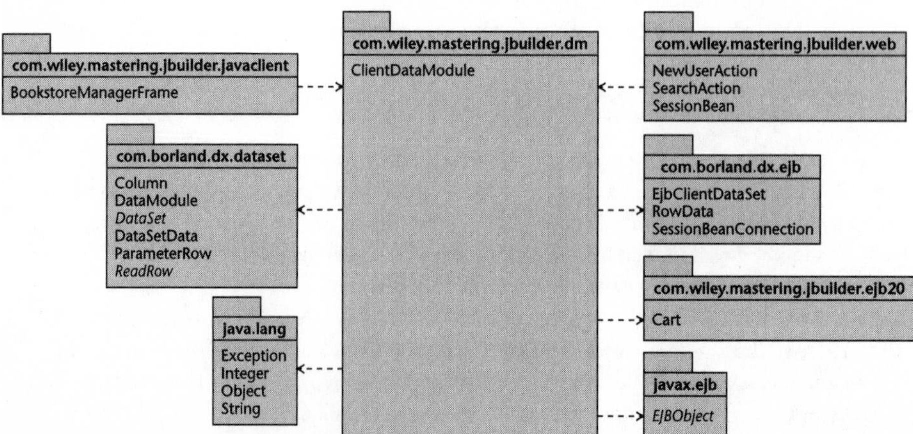


**Figure 12.1** Package dependency diagram.

Let's visualize the following code portion by using the UML class diagram (see Figure 12.2):

```
package com.wiley.mastering.jbuilder.ejb20;

import java.rmi.*;
import java.sql.*;
import java.util.*;
import javax.ejb.*;
import javax.sql.*;
import com.borland.dx.dataset.*;
import com.borland.dx.ejb.*;

public class CartBean implements SessionBean {
  private SessionContext sessionContext;
  private transient ServerDataModuleLocal serverDataModule;
  private String username;
  private String password;
  private Integer id;
  private transient User user;
  private transient UserHome userHome;
  private transient OrderHome orderHome;
  private transient OrderitemHome orderitemHome;
  private transient ShoppingCartHome shoppingCartHome;
  private transient javax.naming.Context context;

  public void ejbCreate() {
    ejbCreate(null, null);
  }
  public void ejbCreate(String username, String password) {
    this.username = username;
    this.password = password;
    lookup();
  }
  ff

  public void ejbActivate() throws RemoteException {
    lookup();
  }
  public void ejbPassivate() throws RemoteException {
  }
  public void setSessionContext(SessionContext sessionContext) throws
RemoteException {
    this.sessionContext = sessionContext;
  }
} // CartBean.java
```

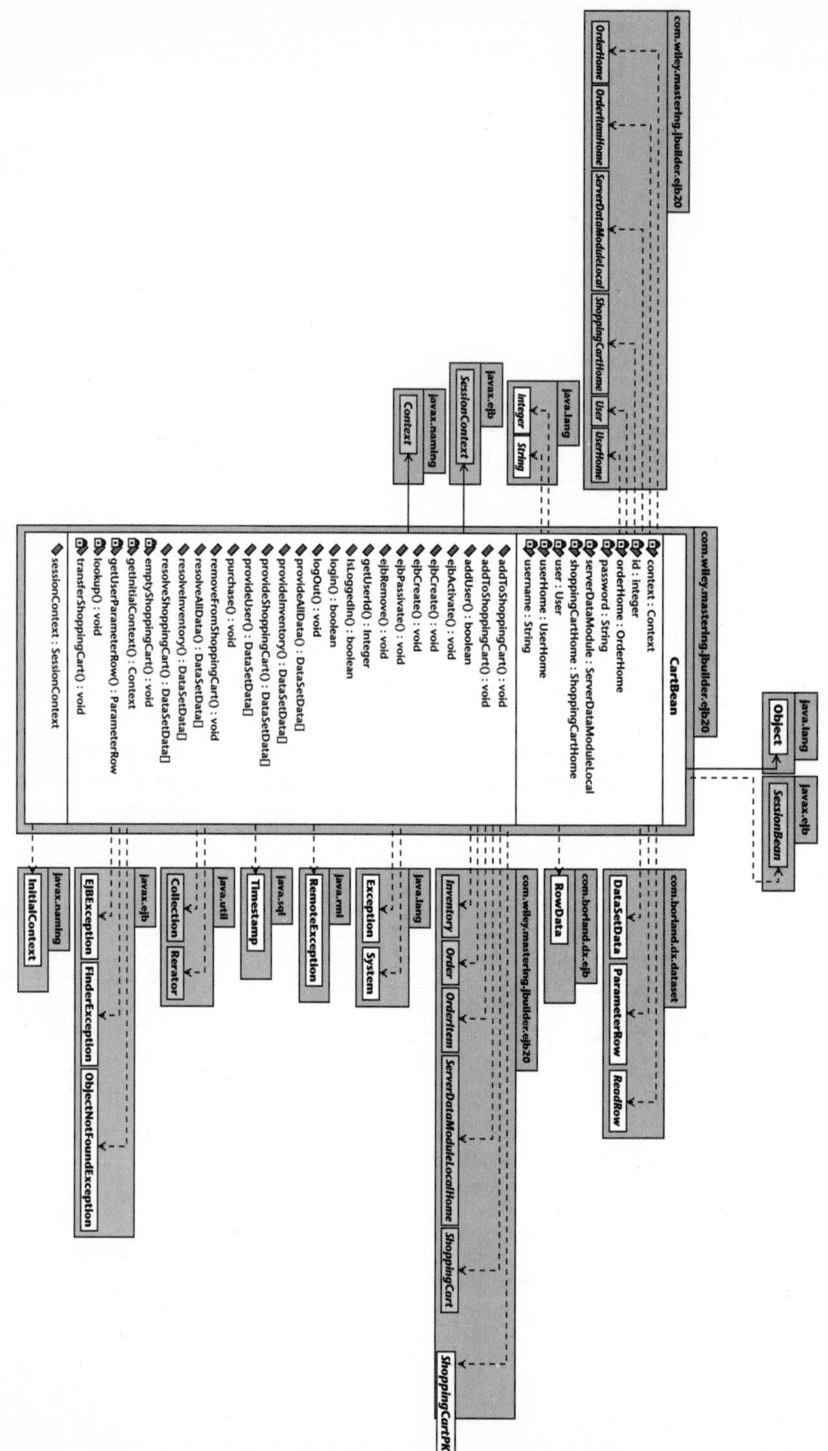


**Figure 12.2** Combined UML class diagram for CartBean.Java.

Classes that belong to a package are grouped into packages; for example, in Figure 12.2, DataSetData, ParameterRow, and ReadRow class are grouped into the com.borland .dx.dataset package. The class diagram in Figure 12.2 shows all associations and dependencies from the selected class to other classes. We can traverse from one class to other classes by double-clicking on the class we want to view. The UML diagrams can be saved as a PNG image by selecting Save Diagram from a Context menu; this is explained in the next section.

**NOTE PNG stands for Portable Network Graphics, which is a flexible and open format for storing bitmapped graphics images. PNG (pronounced as "ping") format provides a new and visually rich appearance compared to the GIF format. Also, PNG files are smaller than GIF files.**

As a typical UML class diagram, the Class view has four sections separated by horizontal lines. The first section displays the class name; the second section displays the attributes and their types; the third section displays the methods; the fourth section displays properties. In Figure 12.3, there is an option to set ON/OFF for the Properties display. By default, the option is ON. If it is turned OFF, properties will be displayed in the same sections with attributes and methods.

## Customize the UML Diagrams

Views of the UML diagrams can be customized via JBuilder IDE Options. Tools | IDE Options with the UML page allow us to set options for sorting, grouping of elements, determining font family and size, and setting the color of elements. The Tools | IDE Options | UML Page dialog is shown in Figure 12.3.

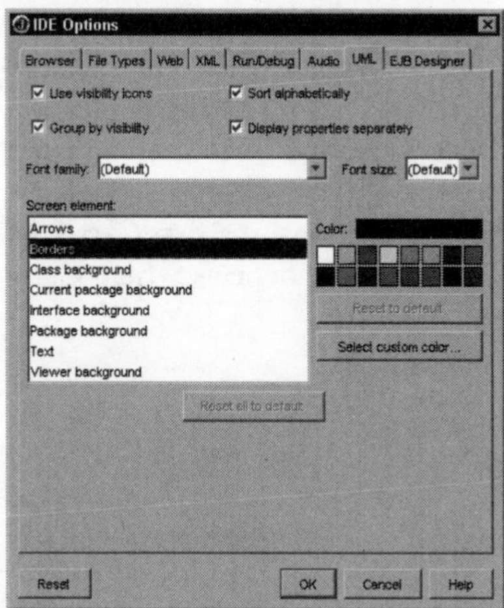


**Figure 12.3** UML browser options page.

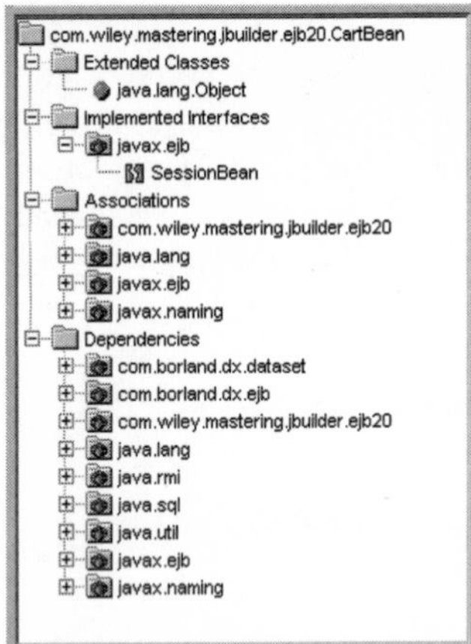


**Figure 12.4** Tree view of the UML diagram in the Structure pane.

There are complex classes that have many dependency classes and packages to fit in a UML class diagram. In order to simplify the UML view, you can exclude any classes or packages; usually, the system packages, such as java.io and java.lang, should be excluded for simplification. JBuilder Project | Properties dialog with the Class Filtering page provides classes and packages filtering for a UML diagram. When you add any classes and packages into the filtering list, the JBuilder UML view will filter out those classes or packages. JBuilder allows us to enable or disable the UL class filtering even if we exclude any classes or packages from the diagram.

### Structure View of UML Diagram

When the UML class diagram is displayed in the Content pane, the structure pane shows a Tree view of the UML diagram. This tree view includes Extended Classes, Implemented Interfaces, Associations, and Dependencies. The Structure pane can be easily used to traverse to other UML diagrams, as shown in Figure 12.4.

Extended Classes shows super-class classes whose attributes and methods are inherited from another class. Implemented Interfaces shows all interfaces that are implemented by the CartBean class. Associations shows relationships that CartBean class has that refer to other classes. Dependencies shows dependencies where CartBean class has references to other classes in the project.

## Context Menu for Refactoring

In addition to UML viewing and traversing functions, the UML browser provides a Context menu listing common commands during the coding process. Depending on what element in the UML pane we select, an appropriate Context menu for the selected element appears. Figure 12.5 shows a Context menu that appears when we right-mouse click and select a package.

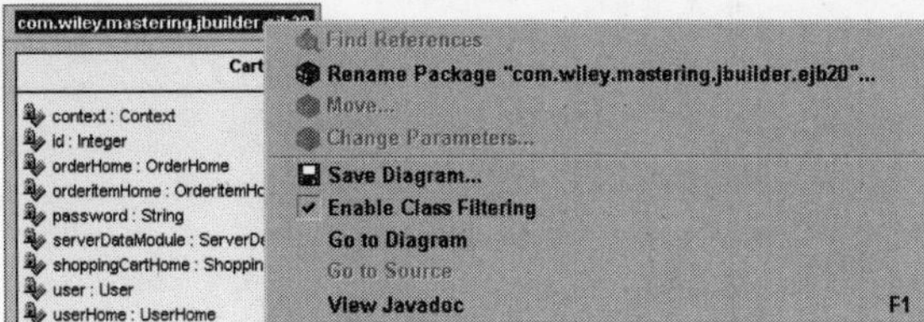


**Figure 12.5** Context menu on package element.

In this Context menu, we can access one of the refactoring features: Rename Package. This refactoring feature helps us rename a package and the whole subtree of the packages. When Rename refactoring a package, the package name and all import statements in other Java files are updated. Physically, the package, any subpackages, and all class source files are relocated to a new source directory on disk. If there exist any old files with the same name, those old files are deleted.

**NOTE The Rename refactoring not only gives a new name to a package, class, method, field, variable, or property but also makes sure that all references to that new name are changed accordingly across the project.**

Figure 12.6 shows a Context menu that appears when we right-mouse click and select a class in the UML browser.

The Context menu on class element enables these refactoring features:

- Find Reference is used to locate all references to a selected symbol. Found references will be displayed in the Search Results tab, as shown in Figure 12.7.
- Rename Class is used to change the class name to a new name, which will be reflected in the class declaration and in every instance of that class and every other reference to that class throughout the project.
- Move Class is used to move a selected class to a new package. Only the top-level public class is allowed to move. The required condition for this moving refactoring is that the new package does not already contain a source file with the new name. When the class is moved, JBuilder will update the package, import statements in the class source file, and all other referencing classes with the moved class.

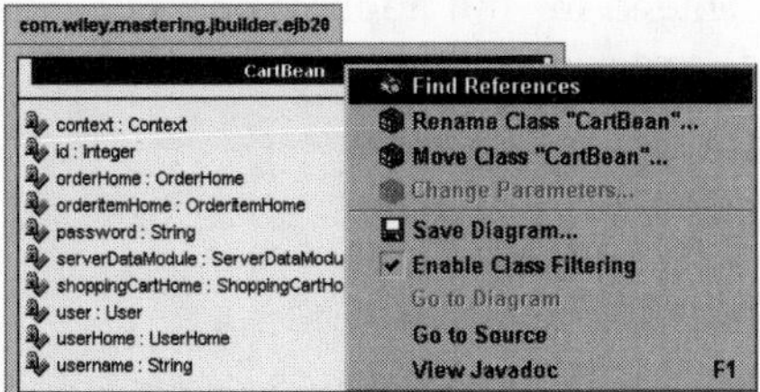


**Figure 12.6** Context menu on class element.

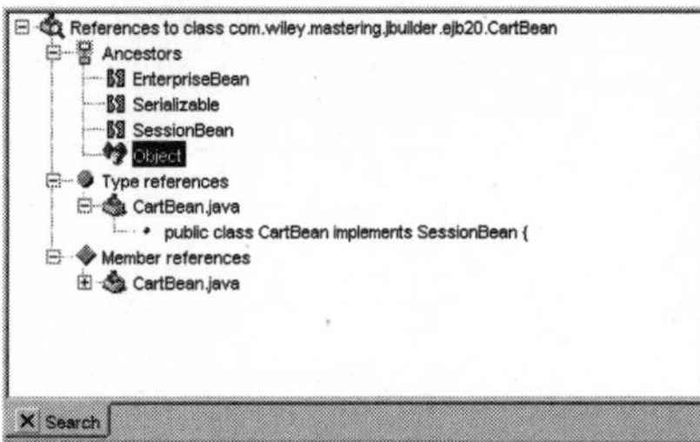


**Figure 12.7** Find Reference Results tab.

- Change Parameters is used to add, rename, delete, or rearrange a method's parameters. Using the UML diagram, right-mouse click on the method where the parameters are located. A dialog box will appear where you enter the new information for parameters. The dialog shows the class in which this method is located. Also, it shows current parameters of the method. To add or change the parameter, you need to enter a name for the parameter, a Java type of the parameter, and a default value for the parameter. Chapter 14, "DataExpress and DBSwing Applications," discusses refactoring in greater depth.
- Save Diagram is used to save the selected UML diagram as a PNG image format.
- Enable Class Filtering allows us to disable or enable the UML browser to display the excluded classes or packages.
- Go to Diagram is used to navigate and view the UML diagram of the selected object.
- Go To Source is used to view the source code in the editor quickly.
- View Javadoc will activate a Builder's help viewer to display the Java documentation, which is, in turn, generated from the Javadoc compiler.

# Summary

This chapter highlights the UML view in JBuilder visual designer. In the current release, this read-only UML view is designed to assist developers with code review, code analysis, design problem detection, code refactoring, and communication on software design. Although the UML view is not intended for full application design, it does give developers another helpful set of hands and eyes for the codes.

PART

Four

# Two-Tier Client/Server Development with JDBC

When JBuilder was first released, it had a very close tie to client/server programming. One of the lifelines for client/server is accessing a database. JBuilder introduced new tools and techniques to make two-tier development as easy as possible.

Back then, the only GUI framework was the Abstract Windows Toolkit (AWT). That GUI framework was so limited in what it could do that was not really ready for use in the real world. At the time, it was thought that companies would develop their own GUI frameworks to enhance the one provided by Sun. Borland was one of the first companies to introduce a standard-based GUI built on top of the AWT that enhanced or added the needed functionality. The new framework was called JavaBean component library or JBuilder component library (JBCL) and was architected by a Borland development engineer named Joe Nuxoll. The base of what JBuilder had to work with the JBCL was actually a great GUI framework; it extended the base components in every way and added some really great capabilities, especially the data-aware aspects of the components

About a year into the release of JBuilder, Sun announced a new GUI framework that would eliminate the shortcomings of the AWT and make a true interoperable GUI framework that was codenamed Swing. Swing garnered a lot of attention because it was being proposed by Sun, and the JBCL started to become one of those great attempts at moving something in the right direction and ending up with nothing. The JBCL later became the DBSwing libraries and was completely re-architected to be based on the Swing framework. Again, Borland did a great job with the implementation; however, the general Java community labeled the framework as proprietary. That was a real shame; the DBSwing libraries are still very useful today and have a lot of nice features that are still on the side of cutting-edge. One thing to keep in mind about DBSwing is that it is a completely open and standard library. It is based on the Swing architecture and makes use of data-aware models. This means that if you want to use the standard Java Foundation Classes (JFC, a.k.a. Swing), you can. This can save considerable time and energy trying to recreate the functionality that is already packaged with JBuilder.

At the same time that the JBCL was being created, Borland was working on a new framework for JDBC. The DataExpress framework was born and extended the base functionality supported by the 1.0 JDBC drivers of the time. DataExpress added key features like cursors, providers/resolvers used in briefcase model computing, and the ability to persist subsets of data. DataExpress continued to evolve from a lightweight database API into a complete object/relational database called JDataStore. More information and history on the evolution of how JBuilder supports JDBC are included in this part of the book.

Part Four focuses on understanding how to use JDataStore and the tools in JBuilder to create client/server-based applications:

**Building the Database with JDataStore.** Chapter 13 covers the product from beginning to end. It shows how to use the graphic tools included with JBuilder and how to do the same tasks using regular programming techniques.

**DataExpress and DBSwing Applications.** Chapter 14 brings attention to the frameworks included in JBuilder that can help developers build great client/server applications without a lot of fuss. The tools included with JBuilder can literally generate a complete application with no coding that will allow for manipulation of generic data sources, JDBC or not.

Once the developer has completed this part of the book, he or she should feel confident about the use of JDataStore and know how to use the database frameworks included with JBuilder to create client/server applications.

CHAPTER

13

# Building the Database with JDataStore

The JDataStore (JDS) product that is included with JBuilder is a great all-Java object-relational database. Its functionality is limited only to the users of the product; it can be extended in ways that can help fit any problem.

This database includes advanced enterprise features found on the most expensive databases available today, including the following:

- GUI tooling that enhances the productivity of the product
- Strong encryption
- XA (eXtended Architecture)-supported transactions that allow for two-phase commits
- Two type 4 JDBC drivers, one for local access and the other for remote
- Very small footprint, both physical (hard drive space) and memory
- Ability to run on any JDK 1.2 or above

There are many ways to take advantage of JDS's flexibility. This chapter shows how to create and use JDatastore; it includes understanding JDataStore Explorer functions and features from a GUI perspective and then covers how to accomplish the same results programmatically. This chapter highlights creating JDataStores, adding tables, setting up access rights, and working with encryption features. Each section focuses on using the GUI to establish the concepts of working with the product and during the programming parts. JBuilder wizards and components are used wherever possible.

## Database Design for JDataStore

The data structure for the JDataStore is shown in Figure 13.1. It includes three tables, CATALOG, CATEGORIES, RESPONSE, all with a common reference called CATALOG_ID, which is a foreign key in CATEGORIES and RESPONSE tables. In JDS this will not be the case, as it does not currently support foreign keys. This may be seen as a limitation of JDS, but some of the newer frameworks — like J2EE — require a flat data structure of the database. JDS can make the implementation easier than traditional implementations by enabling optimizations on reads and integrity checking. This structure will be used in the example in Chapter 14, " DataExpress and DBSwing Applications."

The ID field for all three tables is the primary key; it will also be defined as an AutoIncrement field. AutoIncrement fields have special advantages and handling in JDS. This is for fields of either integer or long data types and will have the following criteria: Only one AutoIncrement field will be defined per table, they will always be unique, they will never be NULL, and values that have been deleted from the database will not be reused. Defining the ID fields as primary keys will ultimately save space. JDS does not need that integer column or index associated with it because the AutoIncrement field is the same as the internal row, which is the default table manager JDS uses to control tables.

**NOTE** **If you change an integer or long data type to an AutoIncrement field, set the *column.setAutoIncrement(true);* before opening the database. If you set a column to AutoIncrement after the database has been opened, then you will have to call a Restructure method, for example, *StorageDataSet.restructure();*.**

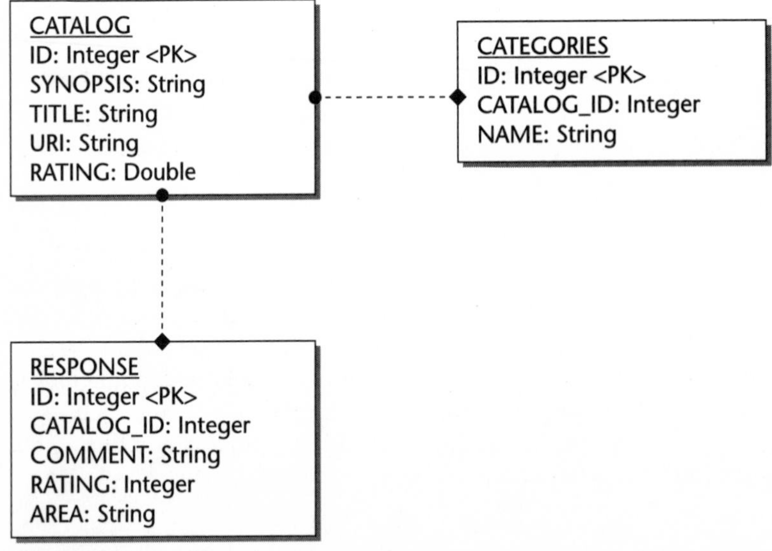


**Figure 13.1** Database layout.

Laying out the types of fields that will be included in the tables is the next task; a fair amount of attention was given to the ID fields of the tables because of its special data type. The rest of the fields will be defined next, and any special information will be noted:

- The SYNOPSIS field will be of data type String and will be responsible for holding a short description of the report a customer may choose to read.
- The TITLE field will be of data type String and represent the name of the reports that a customer may choose to read.
- The URI (Uniform Resource Identifier) field will be of data type String and will represent the location that will contain the document.
- The RATING field will be of data type Double because of the possibility that it may not be properly represented by a whole number.
- The CATALOG_ID field of the CATEGORIES table will make it possible to execute a query quickly to find all reports that are part of that category. The data type will be Integer for this field to match the ID field in the CATALOG table.
- The NAME field will be of data type String and represent the category.
- The CATALOG_ID field of the RESPONSE table will make it possible to execute a query quickly to find all responses dealing with a specific report. It will have a side benefit; if it does not exist, then it will represent feedback not related to a specific report. The data type will be Integer for this field to match the ID field in the CATALOG table.
- The COMMENT field will be of data type String and represent the actual response from the feedback mechanism.
- The RATING field will be of data type Integer and be one way a customer can give instant feedback.
- The AREA field will be of data type String and will be used for possible future search criteria.

**NOTE The Uniform Resource Identifier (URI) is sometimes confused with the more common Uniform Resource Locator (URL) that has been popularized by the Internet browsers on the market today. URL is a specific type of URI. Read more about it at www.w3.org/Addressing.**

## Launching JDataStore Explorer

An all-purpose GUI called JDataStore Explorer has been developed for doing general tasks with JDS, such as creating tables, packing tables, importing information into the tables, setting security, and performing many other database-related tasks. There are several ways to start JDataStore Explorer:

- Using the command line: /jbuilder/bin/jdsexplorer.
- Setting the proper classpath and calling its main class, com.borland.dbtools.dsx.DataStoreExplorer, found in the dbtools.jar file in the /jbuilder/lib directory. For more information on the .jar files needed for proper execution from the command line, review the jdsExplore.config file located in the /jbuilder/bin directory.
- If you are using a graphic environment like Windows, KDE, or Aqua from Apple, JDataStore Explorer, launching from the item in the JBuilder group.

Starting JDataStore Explorer from the JBuilder group will load a common explorer-style interface. The Main menu holds all the functions available from the interface; the toolbar allows for limited functions to be done, including new JDataStore, Open JDataStore, General SQL, and Verifying a JDataStore. The rest of the interface includes a Hierarchal view of JDataStores on the left and a Context view in the Content pane, then finishing the interface with a Status Bar.

# Creating a New Database

Creating a new JDataStore database is very simple. For this example you will place all the databases into a single directory structure. Using JDataStore, start by selecting the File | New menu item, which will display the New JDataStore dialog (see Figure 13.2), or you can click the Database icon on the toolbar.

We want to create a database that is called xyzanalyst.jds, so your edit box in the dialog should be /masteringjbuilder/databases/xyzanalyst.jds. If you need to create a special directory, or if you do not like to type, then you can press the ellipsis button that displays the standard Java JFC file manager. This dialog allows you to browse the file system and gives you general file/directory handling capabilities. JDS is based on a single file storage mechanism and usually updates the format with every release. This normally is not a problem because JDS is completely backward compatible, so you can take advantage of the new tools that may be introduced in JDS without being required to use an older, less feature-rich version of the product. It also supports legacy database versions that may be in production. Examples include Inprise AppServer 4.1x, which used version 3.51, and the Borland AppServer 4.5x, which used version 4. Be sure to select the 6.0 file version for the database being created.

When JDS creates a new database, it uses the block size to determine how data will be written to the database. Four is the default block size. If a block size is too small, a performance hit will be incurred when your data is constantly causing the database to allocate more space. If you choose a block size that is too large, you will incur a database with a large amount of wasted spaces. This property is used only when the database is created; after creation, attempts to modify it will be ignored. It can be read from the database for helping to optimize the buffering when coping functions are being executed:

```
byte[] buffer = new byte[ 4 * store.getDataStore().getBlockSize() * 1024 ];
```

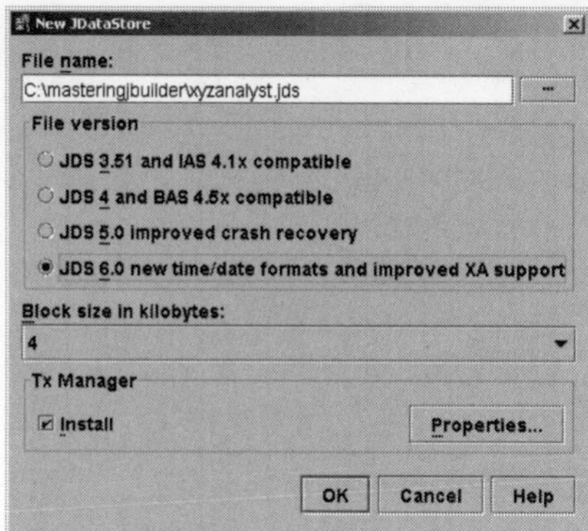


**Figure 13.2** New JDataStore GUI.

This results in a reference to the DataStore called store with the getDataStore() method. Once that is obtained, you can retrieve the block size that was set when the database was created. This number is returned in kilobytes and is multiplied by 1024, and then an arbitrary number is multiplied against the prior number. For this example it is 4; this will then set the buffer size for reading from the database. This is not an exact equation, and some tweaking may be required to find the proper number to fit your data. JDataStore ships a program called WebBench located in the /jbuilder/samples/jdatastore/webbench directory. This JBuilder project will allow testing of different blocking and buffering schemes to see which one performs the best. This program also allows benchmarks to occur between different JDBC drivers.

One of the major enterprise features of JDS is the fact that it fully supports 'xa'/two-phase commits. The XA protocol is a specification developed by IBM for a standard way of handling multiple transactions, usually with different data sources inside one transaction. This is often very important in large distributed systems that may need to write to different data sources. The transactions are handled by a transaction manager (TX Manager) that manages the transaction to a recoverable cache, ensuring that each individual transaction can be written to its data source called an xa resource. All xa resources are required to register with the transaction manager, which controls the process, if they want to participate in the transaction. Once all the transactions have been written, the TX Manager performs a prepare commit operation that asks each xa resource whether the write to recoverable storage was successful. Each xa resource then votes, either commit or rollback. All xa resources participating in that particular transaction must vote commit; if this occurs, the TX Manager performs a commit operation. Once a commit operation is executed, it is up to each database to ensure that the transaction completes. If any xa resource votes rollback, all the resources are told by the TX Manager to roll back, thus removing them from the temporary storage area and making it appear that nothing happened. This process is logged for many reasons; the most important is recovery purposes. Normally, two-phase commits are architected out of the database because of the inherent overhead associated with this process.

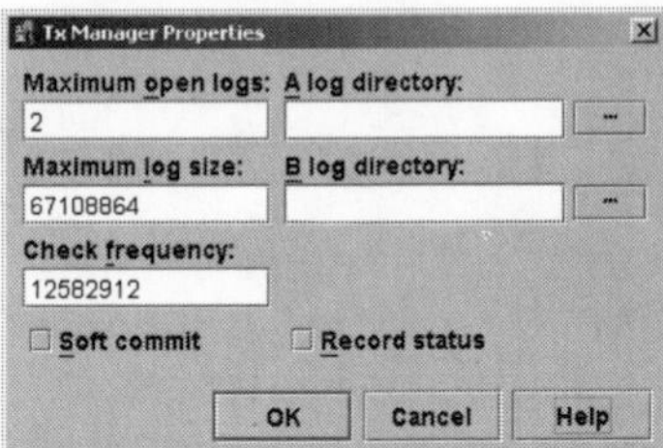


**Figure 13.3** Tx Manager Properties dialog.

Clicking the Properties button inside the New JDataStore dialog (see Figure 13.3) will display the TX Manager properties for this database. They include Maximum open logs; higher numbers can produce better performance, but the overhead may be increased at the same time. The Maximum log size, if exceeded, will cause an incremental log to be created, whose default size is 64 Megabytes. The Check frequency option is the frequency in which checkpoints are made. The smaller the number, the better crash recovery, but the logs will grow faster. The smaller the number, the crash recovery process is slowed, but the logs will grow at a much slower pace. The default is 2 Megabytes, and this option needs to be tested for best results. The soft commit relates to the type of commit guarantee that is needed, turning soft commits on supports only application crash recovery and is very fast, but it does not support O/S or hardware failures. Turning soft commits off will guard against all types of failures, but performance may suffer. The A and B log directories are the location to which the developer wants to write the log files. The Record status controls the level to which messages are written to the A log, which can affect performance. When the properties have been set, click the OK button to continue.

The last process that we have to handle is clicking the OK button to continue. The screen will pause momentarily and return with a pie chart revealing the current size and block allocations.

## Creating a New Database Programmatically

This section shows how to create the exact same table, this time programmatically. Start JBuilder, and create a new project with a package name of basicjdsexample. Then create a new class called JDSExample.java with a main method; review Chapter 7, "Creating Classes," and Chapter 4, "Project Properties and Configurations." Once the new class has been created, click the Design tab under the Content pane to take JBuilder into the GUI designer. Then click on the DataExpress tab on the component palette. A review of the environment is located in Chapter 8, "Modifying Classes." The screen should resemble the one in Figure 13.4.

Click the DataStore component on the DataExpress component palette, and click anywhere in the Content pane or Structure pane. You will notice under the Data Access folder in the Structure pane that a dataStore1 Java Bean has been added. Next click the TX Manager component in the same fashion, and you will also see it appear in the

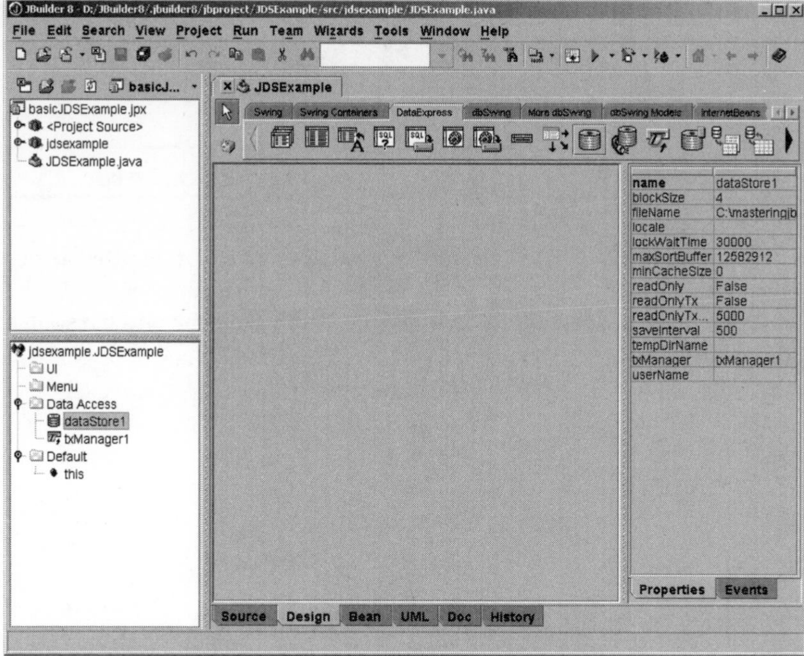


**Figure 13.4** JBuilder in Designer mode with DataExpress.

Structure pane as txManager1. Using the Java Bean property editor, we can set the parameters for each component. Table 13.1 outlines the TxManager Properties, and Table 13.2 lists DataStore Properties that should be set in the object inspector. This can be done by selecting TxManager1 in the component tree, setting its properties, and then doing the same to the DataStore.

**NOTE The attributes that we are setting on the components with the Java Bean editor reflect the same ones we set using the JDataStore Explorer. By adding the components in the designer, JBuilder will automatically add the proper libraries for supporting JDataStore.**

**Table 13.1** Tx Manager Properties

| ATTRIBUTE | VALUE | NOTES |
|---|---|---|
| aLogDir | /enterprisejava/databases/ | This is where the transaction log will be stored. |
| bLogDir | /enterprisejava/ | This is where the backup of the transaction log will be stored. |

**Table 13.2** DataStore Properties

| ATTRIBUTE | VALUE | NOTES |
|---|---|---|
| fileName | /enterprisejava/databases /xyzanalyst.jds | |
| txManager | txManager1 | Select from the choice box. |

In a production system, the DataStore and Tx Manager would have the names changed. This can lead to confusion in example text, so for these examples we use the default names. When the properties have been set, click the Source tab and the source code should look as follows:

```
package basicjdsexample;

import com.borland.datastore.*;

/**
 * <p>Title: Basic JDS Example</p>
 * <p>Description: </p>
 * <p>Copyright: Copyright (c) 2002</p>
 * <p>Company: </p>
 * @author Michael J. Rozlog
 * @version 1.0
 */

/**
 * Notice that the DataStore and TxManager have been
 * created as instance variables from the interaction from
 * the JBuilder IDE.
 *
 */
public class JDSExample {
  DataStore dataStore1 = new DataStore();
  TxManager txManager1 = new TxManager();

  /**
   * When the class is first created the constructure
   * will call the private jbInit() method that JBuilder's
   * designer creates for a logical separation of GUI code
   * and standard code.
   */
  public JDSExample() {
    try {
      jbInit();
    }
    catch(Exception e) {
      e.printStackTrace();
    }
  }
```

```
  /**
   * The static void main method will first create
   * the actual JDSExample1 object. Once that is created
   * then we will check to see if the JDataStore file
   * has been created; if it has then we will open the
   * database; if not then we will create the database with
   * the defined parameters.
   * @param args could be used for arguments on the command line
   */
  public static void main(String[] args) {
    JDSExample JDSExample1 = new JDSExample();

    try {
      //General best practice is to open a database with a user name
      //and password. Even though we have not defined one at this
      //point.
      JDSExample1.dataStore1.setUserName("");
      JDSExample1.dataStore1.setPassword("");

      if ( !new java.io.File(
            JDSExample1.dataStore1.getFileName() ).exists() ) {
        JDSExample1.dataStore1.create();
        System.out.println("JDataStore created");
      } else {
        JDSExample1.dataStore1.open();
        System.out.println("JDataStore opened");
      }

      JDSExample1.dataStore1.close();
      System.out.println("JDataStore closed");
    } catch ( com.borland.dx.dataset.DataSetException dse ) {
        dse.printStackTrace();

    }
  }

  /**
   * This method is used for setting the components that have
   * been added from the JBuilder IDE and initializing them.
   *
   * Notice the filename and the setting of the txManager1 attribute
   * @throws Exception
   */
  private void jbInit() throws Exception {
    dataStore1.setFileName(
      "C:\\EnterpriseJava\\databases\\xyzanalyst.jds");
    dataStore1.setTxManager(txManager1);
    txManager1.setALogDir("C:\\EnterpriseJava\\databases");
    txManager1.setBLogDir("C:\\EnterpriseJava");
  }
}
```

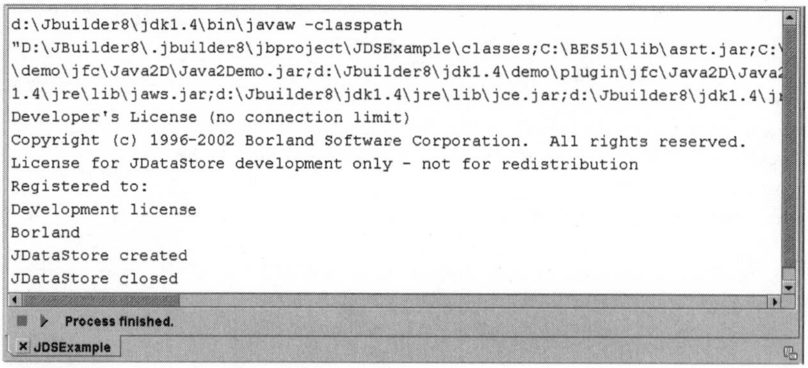

```
d:\Jbuilder8\jdk1.4\bin\javaw -classpath
"D:\JBuilder8\.jbuilder8\jbproject\JDSExample\classes;C:\BES51\lib\asrt.jar;C:\
\demo\jfc\Java2D\Java2Demo.jar;d:\Jbuilder8\jdk1.4\demo\plugin\jfc\Java2D\Java2
1.4\jre\lib\jaws.jar;d:\Jbuilder8\jdk1.4\jre\lib\jce.jar;d:\Jbuilder8\jdk1.4\j
Developer's License (no connection limit)
Copyright (c) 1996-2002 Borland Software Corporation.  All rights reserved.
License for JDataStore development only - not for redistribution
Registered to:
Development license
Borland
JDataStore created
JDataStore closed
Process finished.
JDSExample
```

**Figure 13.5** First run of JDSExample.

The boldface code needs to be added to the program before running it. This program will expand as each process is completed. Once the code has been added, press File | Save All and then press Run | Run Project, or you could right-mouse click on the JDSExample.java file node located in the Project pane.

**TIP The first time you run the project, you may have to define the application main class for JBuilder. For this example, it would be JDSExample. A review of runtime configurations can be found in Chapter 4.**

When you run the project (see Figure 13.5), you should see the Message pane display the Java command line and then System.out messages.

The JDataStore was created and then closed. If you run the project again, the Message pane will report that the JDataStore was opened and then closed. The program has done the same steps that were completed in the prior section on Creating a new JDataStore using JDataStore Explorer.

# Adding Tables to the Database

The next task is to create the tables that will be used in the example. To create a table in the JDataStore Explorer, restart the JDataStore Explorer if it is not running and use the Tools | Create Table menu item to start the designer (see Figure 13.6).

In this example, the Table name edit box should be filled with CATALOG for the name; the Table locale should be set to en_US for the Unicode type. Because JDS fully supports Unicode, which is a 16-bit character encoding, JDataStore is completely internationalized and will fully support the world's major languages. The resolvable option, when checked, can add overhead to a database. It is primarily used when a database is going to be used in a briefcase model, which allows disconnected or offline editing of the databases. The process works by doing a query into a local data store, disconnecting from the data source, pointing the program to use the local data store, doing normal operations on the database, and then reconnecting to the database and resolving all the changes located inside the local data store back to the real database. Selecting the option means that additional meta data must be kept to ensure data integrity when applying changes back to the database at a later time. For this example, please check the option. The Uppercase table and column names option for SQL compliance can be checked.

The next part of the screen is the navigational control; it will be used for controlling the fields that will be created in this table. If you have ever used a database navigation control (prior, next, add, and delete operations), this interface uses the same metaphor.

**NOTE The navigational control will insert field information in reverse order. This is why the *Up* and *Down* buttons have been added; so that order can be manipulated after the vital information about the table has been captured.**

To review, the Catalog table will include three data fields and one primary key field; this can be found in Figure 13.1. The primary key field will be designated as an integer type; the data fields will all be represented as String values.

Using the navigational control, we can add fields to the Catalog table. Press the + button to add a row to the grid display. The following are the definitions of the attributes associated with the definition of a column that resides in the table:

**Column Name**. The column name or identifier that will be part of a row of data located in the table. The character limit for the column name is 132 bytes.

**Data Type**. The Data Type field is represented by a drop-down box, which will allow you to select the proper data type. The current valid field types are all represented by proper Java object types. The reason for displaying only Java object types is that the underlying architecture has the field extending the java.lang.object type. This gives users of the database incredible flexibility. A field can be represented by InputStream or be of type Object. This does not affect the overall speed of JDS. JDS is designed to manage large data types efficiently. This means that if a field is larger than 64 bytes, JDS will automatically store that field internally as a BLOB type — reducing the overhead when querying or manipulating the database.

JDS can technically store any type of data that can be manipulated with Java. For instance, you could store whole files or graphics inside JDS. JDS also has the ability to represent a complete file system. This means that in certain embedded cases you may want to use JDS as the complete file system and the database for the entire application, thus reducing the overall footprint of the files on a machine.

**Precision**. This can be viewed at the maximum for that field. An example is a data type of String with the precision set to 30, meaning a max of 30 characters would be allowed in that field.

**Scale**. In most applications, if you do not set the scale item, the number will include too many numbers.

**Required**. This is equivalent to setting the column not NULL.

**AutoIncrement.** This allows a number value to be incremented by a standard unit. An example would be setting a data type to integer and using the AutoIncrement feature to add 1 every time a new row is inserted.

**Default.** This value can represent the initial value of a field. It can also be set using a database FUNCTION like CURRENT_DATE.

**Fixed Precision.** This value relates true if a fixed number of decimals is being held for the field or false if not.

**Max Inline.** This allows a value for Strings and InputStreams to override the 64-byte max size. As stated in the data type definition, if you have a data type that exceeds 64 bytes, it will be saved as a BLOB; this value will allow for a larger rule to be followed. Keep in mind that setting this value can limit the size of the row or the amount of columns in a table.

**Java Class.** When using the data type of a Java object, this will represent the object's class.

**Hidden.** This is used internally by the JDS; it is not recommend for developers' use.

**Local.** This will set the field to the proper double-byte character set.

The next column in this highlighted row is now ready for input. Click on the empty Column Name field, and type ID for the name. The data type for the ID column should be type INT; once the selection has been made, the rest of the row will be activated. Double-click on the AutoIncrement option so that a check mark is present. This will allow the key ID field, which represents our primary key, to be incremented without program or user intervention.

The next four columns (SYNOPSIS, TITLE, URI, RATING) use the same method as described, except that they will be of type STRING. Click the + button; again you will notice that a new line is inserted above the line added. Then fill in the needed values from the previous layout; no additional field attributes are needed for the fields. The final field is the RATING field, and a Double data type will represent it.

Once this step is completed, you will notice that the field order is not organized with the ID field at the top. Select the row by clicking on it, and use the UP and DOWN buttons on the navigational line to create the proper order.

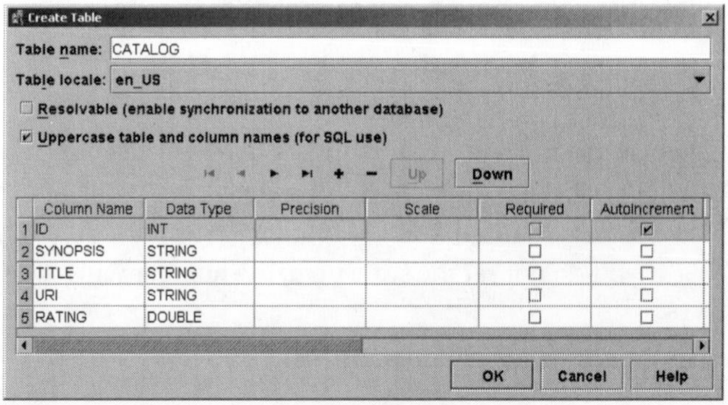

**Figure 13.6** Create Table dialog after using the Up and Down buttons.

**NOTE As a general rule, try to make all the necessary changes in the Create Table dialog before clicking the OK button. Once the table has been created, any changes that may need to occur will cause the database to have to be restructured. This restructuring process could cause data loss in some extreme cases.**

The Create Table dialog should appear (see Figure 13.6). Click the OK button to create the table. The screen will automatically return to the JDataStore Explorer window when it is finished.

In the Catalog table, you will notice that it has three additional tables under it. Looking at Figure 13.7, you will notice that we set the table to Resolvable; as stated in the prior text this allows extra meta data to be kept on the table for making offline edits. We have a single table for each type of modification: Deleted Rows, Added Rows, and Updated Rows. This process works by keeping the SQL statement that was used to produce the dataset; then, as changes to that dataset occur, they will be logged into the appropriate table. When it is time to write the changes back to the master database or the database comes on line again, these changes will be resolved back to that database. The process will call the same SQL and then try to make the necessary changes to the online database in the same order that they were made to the offline dataset.

The Catalog table is considered the major table because it will have the most interaction with the applications connecting to it. Some support tables, though, are necessary to add functionality that will be needed throughout the application's lifecycle:

- The Categories table is responsible for handling the growing number of categories for the reports being generated. In the future, customers will be able to sort or view limited Category views to help lower the search criteria.
- The Response table monitors each catalog entry and helps handle the responses or feedback about the Web site.

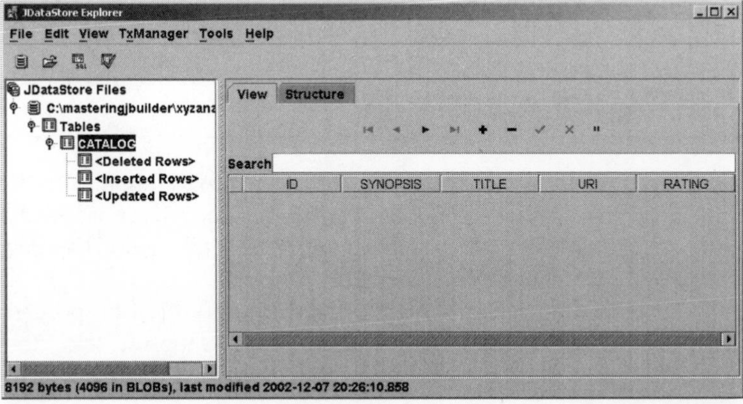


**Figure 13.7** Showing the meta data tables located under the Catalog table.

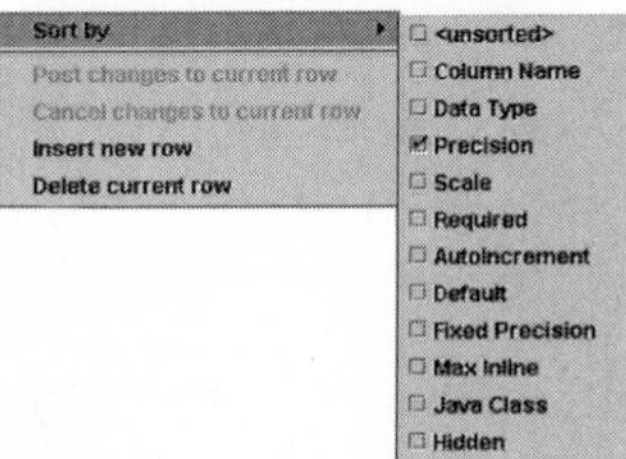


**Figure 13.8** Context menu inside the table designer.

We follow the same instructions to add these tables. Use the Tools | Create Table menu item to start the Create Table dialog. Start with the Categories table, and this time deselect the Resolvable checkbox and remember to select the en_US for the locale. This will be the same for the Response table as well. Another useful shortcut is right-mouse clicking in the Create Table dialog to view the Context menu (see Figure 13.8). This allows you to Add, Delete, Post, and Cancel Row changes and set the table's sort attribute.

The final JDataStore Explorer should resemble Figure 13.7, except it now has both the CATEGORIES and RESPONSE tables under the CATALOG table. Notice that both the Categories and the Response tables do not have the additional meta data tables under them; this is because we did not select the resolvable feature on each of these tables. The resolvable feature can be turned on later without interfering with the overall layout of the table, or you can set it programmatically at a later time.

The Structure tab in the Content pane of the JDataStore Explorer GUI was also clicked. This is where you can make structural changes to the table. For instance, if you wanted to change the Table locale, you could select a different Unicode character set or you could turn on Resolvable. Each of these changes should not affect the underlying table except that when changing from one locale to another, certain characters may not be supported. If you change the order or add or delete fields, data most likely will become an issue. It would be better to create a new table and then create a quick conversion program for moving the data from the old table to the new.

## Adding Tables Programmatically

This section picks up from where we created the database programmatically. In JBuilder, use the File | Open Project and load basicjdsexample project, if it is not already loaded. If you have not developed that project to this point, review the section *Creating a New Database Programmatically* earlier in this chapter.

The first step is to add the DataExpress library to the JBuilder project properties. Either right-mouse click on the basicjdsexample.jpx in the Project pane and select the Project Properties menu item, or click the Project | Project Properties menu item to reach the same location.

Next, click on the inner tab set with the label Required Libraries tab on the Path panel. Add the DataExpress from the list; it will be added to the libraries that are supported by the project. Click the OK button to continue. For more information on library use and configuration, refer to Chapter 2, "Customizing the AppBrowser."

Now that we have added the proper libraries to support table creation, we need to add an import statement to make the objects available to the project:

```
import com.borland.dx.dataset.*;
```

Once this is added to the imports in the Source tab, click the Designer tab again so that we can drop three TableDataSets (second icon on the DataExpress tab) under the Data Access tree item in the component tree in the design mode. Name each TableDataSet table1, table2, and table3, respectively. Then click the Source tab and add three methods, all returning *void*, called createTable1(), createTable2(), and createTable3(). Once the methods have been added, we will add the code needed to create columns and their attributes, just as in the prior steps of creating tables. Source 13.1 is the completed version with all methods completed.

```
package basicjdsexample;

import com.borland.datastore.*;
import com.borland.dx.dataset.*;

/**
 * <p>Title: Basic JDS Example</p>
 * <p>Description: </p>
 * <p>Copyright: Copyright (c) 2002</p>
 * <p>Company: </p>
 * @author Michael J. Rozlog
 * @version 1.0
 */

/**
 * Notice that the DataStore and TxManager have been
 * created as instance variables from the interaction from
 * the JBuilder IDE.
 *
 */
public class JDSExample {
  DataStore dataStore1 = new DataStore();
  TxManager txManager1 = new TxManager();
  TableDataSet table1 = new TableDataSet();
  TableDataSet table2 = new TableDataSet();
  TableDataSet table3 = new TableDataSet();


  /**
   * When the class is first created the constructure
   * will call the private jbInit() method that JBuilder's
   * designer creates for a logical separation of GUI code
   * and standard code.
   */
```

**Source 13.1** Add table code to database. *(continued)*

```
public JDSExample() {
  try {
    jbInit();
  }
  catch(Exception e) {
    e.printStackTrace();
  }
}

/**
 * The static void main method will first create
 * the actual JDSExample1 object. Once that is created
 * then we will check to see if the JDataStore file
 * has been created; if it has then we will open the
 * database; if not then we will create the database with
 * the defined parameters.
 * @param args could be used for arguments on the command line
 */
public static void main(String[] args) {
  JDSExample JDSExample1 = new JDSExample();

  try {
    //General best practice is to open a database with a user name
    //and password. Even though we have not defined one at this
    //point.
    JDSExample1.dataStore1.setUserName("");
    JDSExample1.dataStore1.setPassword("");

    if ( !new java.io.File(
         JDSExample1.dataStore1.getFileName() ).exists() ) {
      JDSExample1.dataStore1.create();
      System.out.println("JDataStore created");
    } else {
      JDSExample1.dataStore1.open();
      System.out.println("JDataStore opened");
      JDSExample1.createTable1();
      JDSExample1.createTable2();
      JDSExample1.createTable3();
    }

    //Generally use close for restructuring the database
    JDSExample1.dataStore1.close();

    //Use shutdown for removing the cache and closing all streams
    JDSExample1.dataStore1.shutdown();

    System.out.println("JDataStore closed");
  } catch ( com.borland.dx.dataset.DataSetException dse ) {
    dse.printStackTrace();
```

**Source 13.1** *(continued)*

```
    }
  }

  /**
   *  Method used for creating table 1 finishes with a restructure
   *  because the table already exists.
   */
  private void createTable1(){
    try {
      table1.setStoreName("Catalog");
      table1.setStore(dataStore1);
      table1.open();
      if ( table1.getColumns().length == 0 ) {
        table1.close();
        table1.addColumn( "ID"          , Variant.INT );
        table1.addColumn( "SYNOPSIS"   , Variant.STRING );
        table1.addColumn( "URI"         , Variant.STRING );
        table1.addColumn( "TITLE"       , Variant.STRING );
        table1.addColumn( "RATING"      , Variant.DOUBLE );

        //Setting the ID column to have AutoIncrement turn on
        table1.getColumn("ID").setAutoIncrement(true);

        table1.open();

        //Good practice anytime you create a table
        table1.restructure();

        System.out.println("table 1 - created");
      }
    }
    catch (com.borland.dx.dataset.DataSetException dse) {
      dse.printStackTrace();
    }
    finally {
      try {
        table1.close();
        System.out.println("Table 1 - closed");
      }
      catch (com.borland.dx.dataset.DataSetException dse) {
        dse.printStackTrace();
      }
    }
  }

  /**
   *  Method used for creating table 2 finishes with a restructure
   *  because the table already exists.
   */
```

**Source 13.1** *(continued)*

```
private void createTable2(){
  try {
    table2.setStoreName("Categories");
    table2.setStore(dataStore1);
    table2.open();
    if ( table2.getColumns().length == 0 ) {
      table2.close();
      table2.addColumn( "ID"         , Variant.INT );
      table2.addColumn( "CATALOG_ID" , Variant.INT );
      table2.addColumn( "NAME"       , Variant.STRING );

      //Setting the ID column to have AutoIncrement turn on
      table2.getColumn("ID").setAutoIncrement(true);

      //This will turn off briefcase model, which does not
      //create the meta table information
      table2.setResolvable(false);

      table2.open();

      //Good practice anytime you create a table
      table2.restructure();

      System.out.println("table 2 - created");
     }
  }
  catch (com.borland.dx.dataset.DataSetException dse) {
    dse.printStackTrace();
  }
  finally {
    try {
      table2.close();
      System.out.println("Table 2 - closed");
    }
    catch (com.borland.dx.dataset.DataSetException dse) {
      dse.printStackTrace();
    }
 }
}

/**
 *  Method used for creating table 3 finishes with a restructure
 *  because the table already exists.
 */
private void createTable3(){
  try {
    table3.setStoreName("Response");
```

**Source 13.1** *(continued)*

```
      table3.setStore(dataStore1);
      table3.open();
      if ( table3.getColumns().length == 0 ) {
        table3.close();
        table3.addColumn( "ID"          , Variant.INT );
        table3.addColumn( "CATALOG_ID" , Variant.STRING );
        table3.addColumn( "COMMENT"    , Variant.STRING );
        table3.addColumn( "RATING"     , Variant.INT );
        table3.addColumn( "AREA"       , Variant.STRING );

        //Setting the ID column to have AutoIncrement turn on
        table3.getColumn("ID").setAutoIncrement(true);

        //This will turn off briefcase model, which does not
        //create the meta table information
        table3.setResolvable(false);

        table3.open();

        //Good practice anytime you create a table
        table3.restructure();

        System.out.println("table 3 - created");
      }
    }
    catch (com.borland.dx.dataset.DataSetException dse) {
      dse.printStackTrace();
    }
    finally {
      try {
        table3.close();
        System.out.println("Table 3 - closed");
      }
      catch (com.borland.dx.dataset.DataSetException dse) {
        dse.printStackTrace();
      }
    }
  }

  /**
   * This method is used for setting the components that have
   * been added from the JBuilder IDE and initializing them.
   *
   * Notice the filename and the setting of the txManager1 attribute
   * @throws Exception
   */
  private void jbInit() throws Exception {
```

**Source 13.1** *(continued)*

```
      dataStore1.setFileName
        ("C:\\EnterpriseJava\\databases\\xyzanalyst2.jds");
      dataStore1.setTxManager(txManager1);
      txManager1.setALogDir("C:\\EnterpriseJava\\databases");
      txManager1.setBLogDir("C:\\EnterpriseJava");
    }
  }
```

**Source 13.1** *(continued)*

Source 13.1 JDSExample.java now has the ability to create three tables just like the tables created using JDataStore Explorer. The three methods for creating the tables and adding the columns are essentially the same; the only difference is the table name, number of columns, and their data types:

```
private void createTable1(){
    try {
      table1.setStoreName("Catalog");
      table1.setStore(dataStore1);
      table1.open();
      if ( table1.getColumns().length == 0 ) {
        table1.close();
        table1.addColumn( "ID"          , Variant.INT );
        table1.addColumn( "SYSNOPSIS"   , Variant.STRING );
        table1.addColumn( "URI"         , Variant.STRING );
        table1.addColumn( "RATING"      , Variant.DOUBLE );

        //Setting the ID column to have AutoIncrement turn on
        table1.getColumn("ID").setAutoIncrement(true);

        table1.open();

        //Good practice anytime you create a table
        table3.restructure();

        System.out.println("table 1 - created");
      }
    }
    catch (com.borland.dx.dataset.DataSetException dse) {
      dse.printStackTrace();
    }
    finally {
      try {
        table1.close();
        System.out.println("Table 1 - closed");
      }
      catch (com.borland.dx.dataset.DataSetException dse) {
```

```
                dse.printStackTrace();
            }
        }
    }
```

The boldface code is the main workhorse of the method. The rest is exception handling. Because of the way this program was constructed for this book, certain design issues are present. The architecture of the program is to allow for multiple executions to highlight the different behaviors and the code that is being executed. After setting the storename (table name) and the store name (database name), the table is opened. This will automatically create the table at that time; the table columns and attributes could have been defined before the open, and a restructure would not have to occur. Because this program will be run multiple times, checking to see whether columns have been added is a nice way to ensure that it is the first time through the code. After adding the columns, then you can retrieve the columns and set advanced attributes like AutoIncrement. When the table is open, the new columns will be written and a restructure is processed; when the process is complete, the table is closed.

**WARNING Restructuring should occur anytime a table attribute is changed, especially if column data types have changed. This can cause data type coercions; more information can be found in the JDataStore Developer's Guide: Persisting data to a JDataStore.**

Also, notice the following line located in the main method:

```
//Generally use close for restructuring the database
JDSExample1.dataStore1.close();

//Use shutdown to remove the cache and close all streams
JDSExample1.dataStore1.shutdown();
```

General practice dictates that you use the close() method when you plan on restructuring the underlying database. This method also returns a Boolean so that you can check to see whether a database is closed; this also works equally well with a table located inside the database. Use the shutdown() method when you are done with the database; this method will release all existing resources tied to the database, including its file cache.

Before running the program, make sure that all databases are closed, then remove the database from the /enterprisejava/databases/ directory. This will ensure a complete show of the code in the program.

The first time you run the program, the Message pane will simply display the Java command line and two output lines. One is JDataStore created, and the other is JDataStore closed. The second time you run it, you will notice the following display in the Message pane:

JDataStore opened

table 1 - created

table 1 - closed

table 2 - created

table 2 - closed

table 3 - created

table 3 - closed

JDataStore closed

Notice how the JDataStore was opened, and then each table was created and closed before the JDataStore was finally closed. The final time you run it, you will notice that the JDataStore is opened, each table will be closed, and then the JDataStore will be closed.

## Adding Access Control to the Database

After creating the tables, we now need to add some security to the database. In the next chapter, we will discuss how to encrypt the database, but for this phase of the project we want to limit the people who can get into the database and make changes to it. JDS has a built-in User Administration feature that will allow for custom database rights to be assigned to each user. Each user must have a unique user name and password. The password is encrypted using the same algorithm used in the encryption process for the complete database. Each database will have an administrator that will have an administrator password. The administrator should have all database attribute rights assigned to him or her for long-term data integrity.

**NOTE Once the administrator has been defined and a password set, it cannot be removed. Also, if the password for the administrator is lost or forgotten, Borland has no way of getting it back or resetting it. *Please* do not forget or lose it.**

The Tools | Administer Users menu displays the dialog, which has three fields that need to be filled in. The Administrator user name is sysdba, and the password is masterkey, which needs to be typed twice. Both name and password are case sensitive. When this is complete, press the Enter key to continue. When the dialog is removed, JDataStore will display an Administer Users dialog, which will show the user as sysdba with all rights checked. Click the OK button to continue. Close the database, then reopen the database; notice that the user name should be sysdba and the dialog should be waiting for the password. Type masterkey, and click the OK button.

**NOTE The administrator will always have all rights. Any new users added to the table will require setting their attributes.**

Expanding the database in the Tree view on the left side will reveal that the database is now writing an additional stream called SYS, which contains a users table (see Figure 13.9). This is where all information will be kept on all users added.

As you can see, JDS has multiple authorization attributes, which are used to manage the access and rights of each user who has access to the database. If you do not set up an administrator and password for the database in JDS, then technically no user name or password is required. If you are accessing the database programmatically, then you will at least have to set blank strings for the attributes; the JDSExample.java–Example 1 project shows the best practice.

The authorization rights are outlined next. They can be mixed and matched; however, only a few combinations make sense. The ability to assign new rights is the responsibility of the users with administrator rights only:

**Administrator**. This allows you to add, remove, and change the rights of users and gives you the ability to encrypt the database. Startup rights are given by default to the administrator, but they can be removed. The ability to WRITE, CREATE, DROP, and RENAME cannot be removed from the administrator. The administrator rights can be assigned to multiple users of the database.

**Startup**. This allows you to open a database that is shut down. Keep in mind that a user password is required to add startup rights to a user.

**Write**. Write to a file or table inside a JDS.

**Create**. Create a new file or table inside a JDS.

**Drop**. Remove a file or table from JDS.

**Rename**. Rename a file or table in JDS.

Now that we have added the administrator to the database, we are complete with this part of the requirements. Your final look at the JDataStore Explorer should resemble Figure 13.9.

**NOTE Whenever access control is added to a database in JDS, it will cause the database to be restructured. Because the underlying table structure is not tampered with, this operation is completely safe. Always make sure that you have a backup before doing major restructuring to any database.**

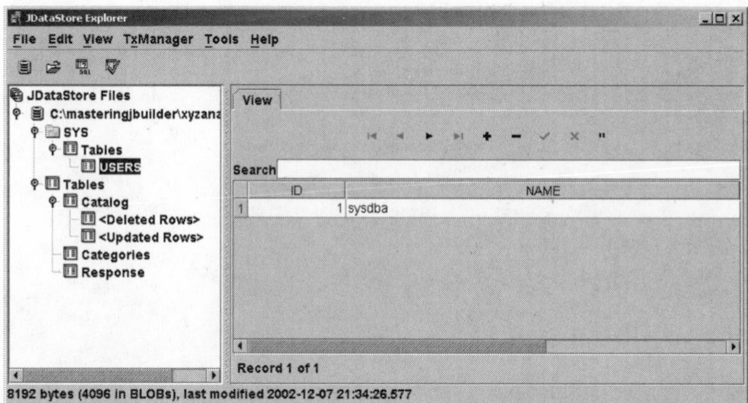


**Figure 13.9** Completed creation of the tables and access control in JDataStore Explorer.

# Adding Access Control to the Database Programmatically

Using the same JDSExample.java program, it is time to modify it again so that we can see how to add access control as we did using the JDataStore Explorer. We need to add another component to the program, so click the Design tab, click the DataExpress tab, and add the DataSetConnection component to the Data Access in the component tree. Then click the Source tab, and add another method that returns void, called addAccessControl(). The complete program is shown in Source 13.2; add only the lines that are in bold if you have the rest written.

```
package basicjdsexample;

import com.borland.datastore.*;
import com.borland.dx.dataset.*;

/**
 * <p>Title: Basic JDS Example</p>
 * <p>Description: </p>
 * <p>Copyright: Copyright (c) 2002</p>
 * <p>Company: </p>
 * @author Michael J. Rozlog
 * @version 1.0
 */

/**
 * Notice that the DataStore and TxManager have been
 * created as instance variables from the interaction from
 * the JBuilder IDE.
 *
 */
public class JDSExample {
  DataStore dataStore1 = new DataStore();
  TxManager txManager1 = new TxManager();
  TableDataSet table1 = new TableDataSet();
  TableDataSet table2 = new TableDataSet();
  TableDataSet table3 = new TableDataSet();
  DataStoreConnection dataStoreConnection1 = new DataStoreConnection();


  /**
   * When the class is first created the constructure
   * will call the private jbInit() method that JBuilder's
   * designer creates for a logical separation of GUI code
   * and standard code.
   */
```

**Source 13.2** Access control added programmatically. *(continued)*

```
public JDSExample() {
  try {
    jbInit();
  }
  catch(Exception e) {
    e.printStackTrace();
  }
}

/**
 * The static void main method will first create
 * the actual JDSExample1 object. Once that is created
 * then we will check to see if the JDataStore file
 * has been created, if it has then we will open the
 * database, if not then we will create the database with
 * the defined parameters.
 * @param args could be used for arguments on the command line
 */
public static void main(String[] args) {
  JDSExample JDSExample1 = new JDSExample();

  try {
    //General best practice is to open a database with a user name
    //and password. Even though we have not defined one at this
    //point.
    JDSExample1.dataStore1.setUserName("");
    JDSExample1.dataStore1.setPassword("");

    if ( !new java.io.File(
          JDSExample1.dataStore1.getFileName() ).exists() ) {
      JDSExample1.dataStore1.create();
      System.out.println("JDataStore created");
    } else {
      JDSExample1.dataStore1.open();
      System.out.println("JDataStore opened");
      JDSExample1.createTable1();
      JDSExample1.createTable2();
      JDSExample1.createTable3();
      JDSExample1.addAccessControl();
    }

    //Generally use close for restructuring the database
    JDSExample1.dataStore1.close();

    //Use shutdown for removing the cache and closing all streams
    JDSExample1.dataStore1.shutdown();

    System.out.println("JDataStore closed");
```

**Source 13.2** *(continued)*

```
    } catch ( com.borland.dx.dataset.DataSetException dse ) {
      dse.printStackTrace();
    }
  }

  /**
   *  Method used for creating table 1 finishes with a restructure
   *  because the table already exists.
   */
  private void createTable1(){
   try {
     table1.setStoreName("Catalog");
     table1.setStore(dataStore1);
     table1.open();
     if ( table1.getColumns().length == 0 ) {
       table1.close();
       table1.addColumn( "ID"          , Variant.INT );
       table1.addColumn( "SYSNOPSIS"   , Variant.STRING );
       table1.addColumn( "URI"         , Variant.STRING );
       table1.addColumn( "RATING"      , Variant.DOUBLE );

       //Setting the ID column to have AutoIncrement turn on
       table1.getColumn("ID").setAutoIncrement(true);
       table1.open();

       //Good practice anytime you create a table
       table3.restructure();

       System.out.println("table 1 - created");
     }
   }
   catch (com.borland.dx.dataset.DataSetException dse) {
     dse.printStackTrace();
   }
   finally {
     try {
       table1.close();
       System.out.println("Table 1 - closed");
     }
     catch (com.borland.dx.dataset.DataSetException dse) {
       dse.printStackTrace();
     }
   }
  }

  /**
   *  Method used for creating table 2 finishes with a restructure
   *  because the table already exists.
```

**Source 13.2** *(continued)*

```
 */
private void createTable2(){
  try {
    table2.setStoreName("Categories");
    table2.setStore(dataStore1);
    table2.open();
    if ( table2.getColumns().length == 0 ) {
      table2.close();
      table2.addColumn( "ID"          , Variant.INT );
      table2.addColumn( "CATALOG_ID" , Variant.INT );
      table2.addColumn( "NAME"        , Variant.STRING );

      //Setting the ID column to have AutoIncrement turn on
      table2.getColumn("ID").setAutoIncrement(true);

      //This will turn off briefcase model, which does not
      //create the meta table information
      table2.setResolvable(false);

      table2.open();

      //Good practice anytime you create a table
      table2.restructure();

      System.out.println("table 2 - created");
     }
  }
  catch (com.borland.dx.dataset.DataSetException dse) {
    dse.printStackTrace();
  }
  finally {
    try {
      table2.close();
      System.out.println("Table 2 - closed");
    }
    catch (com.borland.dx.dataset.DataSetException dse) {
      dse.printStackTrace();
    }
 }
}

/**
 *  Method used for creating table 3 finishes with a restructure
 *  because the table already exists.
 */
private void createTable3(){
  try {
```

**Source 13.2** *(continued)*

```
    table3.setStoreName("Response");
    table3.setStore(dataStore1);
    table3.open();
    if ( table3.getColumns().length == 0 ) {
      table3.close();
      table3.addColumn( "ID"          , Variant.INT );
      table3.addColumn( "CATALOG_ID" , Variant.STRING );
      table3.addColumn( "COMMENT"     , Variant.STRING );
      table3.addColumn( "RATING"      , Variant.INT );
      table3.addColumn( "AREA"        , Variant.STRING );

      //Setting the ID column to have AutoIncrement turn on
      table3.getColumn("ID").setAutoIncrement(true);

      //This will turn off briefcase model, which does not
      //create the meta table information
      table3.setResolvable(false);

      table3.open();

      //Good practice anytime you create a table
      table3.restructure();

      System.out.println("table 3 - created");
     }
  }
  catch (com.borland.dx.dataset.DataSetException dse) {
    dse.printStackTrace();
  }
  finally {
    try {
      table3.close();
      System.out.println("Table 3 - closed");
    }
    catch (com.borland.dx.dataset.DataSetException dse) {
      dse.printStackTrace();
    }
 }
}

/**
 * Used to add access control to the database
 * the first level of security. Close the table
 * re-open the table with a user name, this is
 * because the database is transactional and
 * anytime the users are going to change it needs
 * to be logged. Create a DataStoreConnection that
```

**Source 13.2** *(continued)*

```
     * will write a user file stream, set the user name
     * open the connection and add user.
     */
    private void addAccessControl(){
      try {
       dataStore1.close();
       dataStore1.setUserName("none");
       dataStore1.open();
       dataStoreConnection1.setUserName("none");
       dataStoreConnection1.setFileName(dataStore1.getFileName());
       dataStoreConnection1.open();
       dataStoreConnection1.addUser("sysdba","sysdba","masterkey",
           DataStoreRights.FULL_RIGHTS);
       System.out.println("User added, with full rights");
      }
      catch (com.borland.dx.dataset.DataSetException dse) {
        dse.printStackTrace();
      }
      finally {
        dataStoreConnection1.close();
      }

    }

    /**
     * This method is used for setting the components that have
     * been added from the JBuilder IDE and initializing them.
     *
     * Notice the filename and the setting of the txManager1 attribute
     * @throws Exception
     */
    private void jbInit() throws Exception {
      dataStore1.setFileName
        ("C:\\EnterpriseJava\\databases\\xyzanalyst2.jds");
      dataStore1.setTxManager(txManager1);
      txManager1.setALogDir("C:\\EnterpriseJava\\databases");
      txManager1.setBLogDir("C:\\EnterpriseJava");
    }
  }
```

**Source 13.2** *(continued)*

The first time the program is run, it will display an additional line in the Message pane stating the following:

```
User added, with full rights
```

The second time the program is run, the Message pane will report the following:

```
See com.borland.datastore.DataStoreException error code:  BASE+51


com.borland.datastore.DataStoreException: You do not have STARTUP rights
for this JDataStore

           at com.borland.datastore.DataStoreException.b(Unknown Source)
...
```

The reason for this is that the code has the user name and password as empty strings. Change the code to reflect the sysdba and password as masterkey. This will get the code to run again until it gets to the addAccessControl() method; once the username is set to "none" and the open() is attempted, the user is not known. To fix the problem, wrap the statements inside the addAccessControl() method with the following if statement:

```
    if (!dataStore1.getUserName().equals("sysdba")) {
                                       current lines In the method...
}
```

The access control method completes the same steps as JDataStore. Because the database has transactions enabled, close the database. Now, reopen the database with a user name because a user name has not been used before, and use the user name of none. Once the user name has been set, open the database. JDataStore has three default file streams that it uses for various tasks, listed in Table 13.3.

The CONNECTIONS stream is a table, and its columns are used for holding the valid JDBC connections to the database. The QUERIES stream is a table, and its columns are used to hold valid queries that can be run against tables in the database. The USERS stream is a table, and its columns are used by JDataStore to store users, passwords, and rights for each user. As an extra security measure, RIGHTS and ID fields are encrypted into the PASSWORD field. If the RIGHTS are tampered with by an intruder, the tampering will have no effect on the security of the system.

**Table 13.3** Default JDataStore File Streams

| NAME | FUNCTION |
|---|---|
| /SYS/CONNECTIONS/ | Defines the table and column names for the /SYS/CONNECTIONS system table. |
| /SYS/QUERIES/ | Defines the table and column names for the /SYS/QUERIES system table. |
| /SYS/USERS/ | Defines the table and column names for the /SYS/USERS system table. |

Because everything was done programmatically, there has been no process to ensure that a correct database has been setup. This can be accomplished by running JDataStore Explorer and opening the database. Figure 13.9 shows the screen you should see after running the program for the final time.

## Adding Encryption

Once the access rights have been added to the JDataStore, it can be encrypted; this will change the contents of the file. This can be done by going to the JDataStore Explorer and using the Tools | Encrypt JDataStore menu item. This process will copy the existing database for backup purposes and then encrypt the new one. Once the operation is complete, there is no going back; you must use the backup database to return.

**WARNING Borland has no good password or back door to this process. Once a JDataStore is encrypted and password protected, it cannot be opened or reverse engineered back to the original format.**

JDataStore uses the TwoFish block cypher, which is state-of-the-art encryption technology that has never been beat. People trying to stop people from breaking into a secure JDataStore should understand that the JDataStore file is not password protected; this would allow people to view its contents in encrypted form. All passwords are encrypted using the same cipher as the database, and it uses a pseudo-random number generator as the initialized encryption process.

**WARNING The remote JDBC driver that is shipped with JDataStore uses socket communication and does not include a secure channel. The local JDBC driver is in process, so the communication is secure.**

# Summary

This chapter highlights JDataStore, an all-Java object-relational database, by showing how to create databases, tables, and access rights in a GUI and programmatically. It also covers encryption that is included with JDataStore. JDataStore is incredibly versatile, and many of its features are not discussed in this chapter, such as programming streams, user-defined Functions (UDFs), and remote access.

CHAPTER

14

# DataExpress and DBSwing Applications

Companies are always trying to reduce the cost associated with a project or system lifecycle. One way to ensure that developers and teams are as productive as possible is by abstracting major design problems into known ideas or processes. Creating objects that abstract the complex into real-world items is one the main principles of object-oriented programming (OOP).

Extending these objects to handle different circumstances and packaging them together create libraries. The libraries can be used in a framework that removes a lot of the tedious work that most developers have to endure. This is where DataExpress and DBSwing come into the picture. DataExpess is a general JDBC enhancement class library, and DBSwing is a component library that is based on Swing that understands the DataExpress components. These combined frameworks can remove significant complexity when developing database-specific applications. Each one of these frameworks can run independently of the other; however, they work best when used together.

This chapter covers the wizards that are included with JBuilder to create standard two-tier database applications. The concept of Data Module is introduced and used throughout the chapter; this allows a lot of functionally to be created with very little code.

DataExpress architecutre and DataExpress technologies go back to the beginning of Java and JBuilder. At that time, the concept of going beyond the applet world with a small graphic doing cartwheels was not on most people's radar. The JDBC 1.0 specification was being kicked around, but one of its main objectives was matching Open DataBase Connectivity (ODBC) by Microsoft. These broad initiatives led to companies writing specific drivers for their databases. At the time, it was conceived that with four different driver types, every database would have an implementation that would be native to get the best performance or would wrap the existing drivers to communicate with the database. Again, a primary concern was to get communication established. The first cut of the JDBC spec was limited in functionality because of the other issues being addressed. Remembering back, the only operations available were select, insert, delete, and update. There was more, of course, but the functionality behind it was so limited that is was almost unusable. Borland had a vast amount of brainpower to put behind the effort of making working with databases as easy as possible. The heritage of Paradox, dBase, and InterBase as in-house databases and its integration with the award-winning Delphi, the best IDE for developing Windows-based applications, had given Borland a real lead in this area. A team led by Steve Shaughnessy developed a framework in JBuilder that simplifies the complexities found in raw JDBC, which can slow the development process.

The DataExpress architecture can be broken into three main concepts. The first concept, "Providing," allows you to retrieve a subset of information from any underlying data source, which is then placed into a dataset. Once the data is held in a dataset, it can be freely navigated and edited; this is called the "Manipulation" concept. The dataset is completely separate from the database, thus eliminating database communication while working with the data. The last concept, "Resolving," occurs after all the changes to the dataset are complete. Resolving saves the changes made to the dataset back to the data source from which the data came. DataExpress offers sophisticated built-in reconciliation technology that helps eliminate data conflicts.

The DataExpress approach is well suited for partitioned applications because the Providing and Resolving stages (called the deferred update model or briefcase model) are done in separate processes with an arbitrary amount of time for editing.

DataExpress's dataset can be broken down into a class hierarchy that allows for the entire functionality found in the DataExpress components. The first layer is an abstract object that represents data in a two-dimensional array. It gives the ability to sort the array and make relationships of a master-detail nature, plus it introduces the concept of rows to the data. The second object to make up the hierarchy is the StorageDataSet; also abstract in nature, it adds some key functionality, such as the concepts of table names from a database, maximum rows retrieved from the data source, and marking the information as read-only. The following objects are the ones commonly exposed in the JBuilder GUI environment:

**DataStore.** It adds the ability to save the dataset's contents into a high-performance all-Java file system.

**QueryDataSet.** The QueryDataSet allows you to use industry-standard SQL statements to retrieve data from the data source.

**ProcedureDataSet.** The ProcedureDataSet allows you to call prepared or stored procedures inside the database.

**TableDataSets.** The TableDataSet gives you the ability to connect to an arbitrary file and manipulate its contents.

These objects all share common methods because of the inheritance found in the DataExpress hierarchy. The JDataStore product was initially conceived from the underlying research of DataExpress.

## Evolution of DBSwing Architecture

While one Borland team was working on getting the underlying framework together for getting data back to a developer, another team was working on a GUI framework to help work with the new DataExpess technology. The first incarnation was called JBuilder Component Library or JavaBean Component Library (JBCL). This GUI framework far exceeded the current technology offered by Sun at the time, which was the Abstract Windows Toolkit or Awful Windows Toolkit (AWT).

The first few versions of AWT were not based solely on the JavaBean component architecture and were therefore rather limited to the underlying GUI widget system on which Java was running. The major problem with this approach was that not all GUI widgets were available on each operating system, which caused Sun to limit the number of supported widgets to the lowest common denominator. The architecture — called a peer system because the underlying widgets relied on the operating system for rendering AWT — is still used today as the initial window in JFC. Most were unable to develop real applications, though, and it competed with technologies that had complete native development products — Delphi, C++Builder, Visual Basic (P-code interpreted), and Visual C++.

The JBCL offered a new component framework that was based on JavaBeans, but it would be available on all platforms that supported a compliant Java VM, and it was completely data-aware to the DataExpress libraries. At the same time, JavaSoft was working on a whole new concept for using widgets in Java. This Swing project promised to deliver true platform independence and definable look and feels; it would be completely object-oriented and would not be reliant on any special underlying hardware or software. After the Swing libraries were released to the general public under the name Java Component Framework (JFC), adoption became rather quick. This caused Borland to rethink the current direction toward the new Swing libraries.

JBuilder 2 introduced a new data-aware framework designed on top of the Swing libraries, called DBSwing. DBSwing has gone through many changes over a couple of releases and has settled down into a reliable, easy-to-use data-aware framework that can fully support native Swing applications as well as it does DBSwing applications. It is one of the fastest ways to get data integrated into an application.

## Wizard Building Applications

In Chapter 13, "Building the Database with JDataStore," JDataStore was used to create a new database with three tables. The data design was not complex, and the techniques discussed were more important than just a simple database. That simple database, though, needs to get data into it so that the business can get to the Web. JDataStore Explorer does fully support inserting data into the tables, but it is rather limited in how it can do that. In this section, we use JBuilder's wizards to build applications, using the JBuilder GUI designer and components, discuss how to do it programmatically, and cover how to use Swing with DataExpress.

## Using Data Modules to Generate Applications

The first step is to create a new project in JBuilder by clicking the File | New Project menu item. The project name will be FirstDataBase, and the Directory will be /mastering jbuilder/jbproject/firstdatabase/. Make sure to turn on Project notes, and then click the Next button to continue with the wizard or the Finish button to complete. For additional information on setting up a project in JBuilder, refer to Chapter 4, "Project Properties and Configurations."

Now that the project has been created, click the File | New menu item. This will display the Object Gallery; this dialog is used several times in this chapter, but for this example we focus on the Application, DataModule, and the DataModule Application icons on the New tab. For more information on the Object Gallery, please refer to Chapter 7, "Creating Classes."

The first application will talk to the database that was created in Chapter 13. It will allow for interaction with each table. No relationships between the tables will exist in this application.

### *Creating a Data Module*

Select the Data Module icon on the New tab in the Object Gallery. and then click the OK button. This will display a new Data Module dialog (see Figure 14.1), which allows for the defining of the Data Module. This includes the Package where the Data Module will be located and the name of the Data Module for this project. Two additional items are options when creating a Data Module. The first is Invoke Data Modeler, which will allow queries to be graphically created; the second option is Generate headers. Both of these options are to be selected. The Package should be com.wiley.mastering.jbuilder .firstdatabase, and the Class name should be DMBasic.

A Data Module is a specialized interface for holding your data access components and their logic. It even extends to the concept of business-logic. It makes a very nice separation of function, which allows the program to have a more modular setup.

**NOTE** **A Data Module must be compiled before it can be referenced in a project.**

When you click the OK button, the Data Module wizard will start the Data Modeler. The Data Modeler is a nice GUI interface where you can define your data interactions and set up all the needed SQL for each table. You can also add data sources or JDBC connections to use with the wizard. This wizard can be reentered from within a project by right-mouse clicking on the Data Module node in the Project pane and selecting the Activate the Data Modeler menu item.

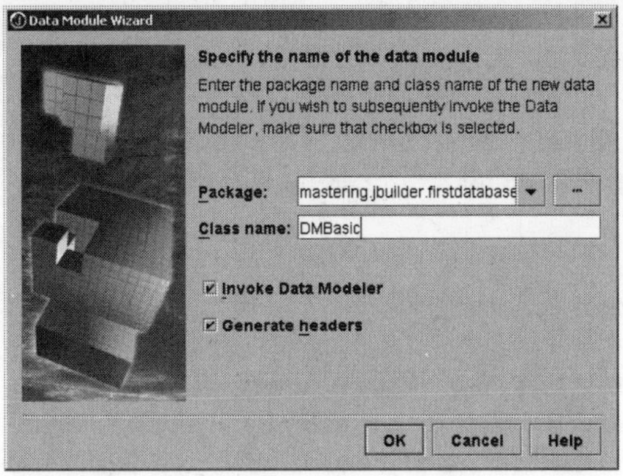

**Figure 14.1** Data Module wizard.

## *Data Modeler*

The Data Modeler (see Figure 14.2) is divided into a two major areas:

- The Queries, where the queries will be defined.
- The Current query, which is a tab interface for defining and creating SQL statements in a point-and-click manner.

Once a query is defined, a representation will be located in the Queries pane. The current example requires that three queries be created.

The first step in the process is to open the database connection. There should be one already defined by the last chapter; if not, select the Database menu item and select the Add connection URI. This will bring up a new dialog that will allow for the selection of the JDBC driver located on your machine. After the selection from the choice control, the location of the database is needed. After that has been completed, then click the OK button to continue. Once you have clicked the OK button, the JDBC connection will be added to available columns in the first pane, where it displays the JDBC connection strings. Select that string or the string that represents the databases from the last projects; it should be the one that is located in the /masteringjbuilder/ directory. If security is turned on, then a popup will appear for the user name and password for that database. The database that was defined in the prior chapter had the user name of sysdba and a password of masterkey.

**NOTE** **The user name and password are both lowercase because the database is case sensitive.**

This will expand the Tree view for that connection; notice that, once the connection has been started, it will expand to show the Table icon under the connection string. Open the Table icon and notice that it lists all the tables that were defined in the prior project. Select the Catalog table; notice that the second pane with the Definition will be updated to show the properties of that table. A Data tab is located next to the Definition tab; clicking on the Data tab will automatically show the data in that table.

**NOTE If you have a really large database, clicking the Data tab could take a rather long time to execute because it tries to load the complete table.**

Now click the Copy All button on the right-hand side of the dialog. You will notice that all the table columns are in the Selected columns area and that the Queries section has been updated to show Catalog.

Click the SQL+ button on the toolbar, and you will see a new item added to the Queries section called <new query>. Select the Categories table under the JDBC connection string. Click the Copy All button, and notice that the same things occur: The Queries pane changes, and the columns are listed under the Selected columns. Repeat this operation one more time with the Response table. After that is complete, you should see three queries in the Queries pane: Catalog, Categories, and Response tables.

Select the File | Save menu item to call the template that generates the code defined during the selection of the tables. Next, select the File | Exit menu item, and notice that the JBuilder Project pane has a new package located in it that includes one file called DMBasic.java file. Save the project by clicking the Save All icon, or select the File | Save All menu item and then rebuild the project.

## *Generate an Application*

Now that a Data Module has been created, creating a DBSwing application is only a matter of a couple clicks of the mouse. Select the File | New menu item, click the Data Module Application icon, and click OK to continue. This will display a Data Module Application wizard, and the only thing that you need to create an application is to click on the choice control for Data Module, select DMBasic, and click the OK button to continue.

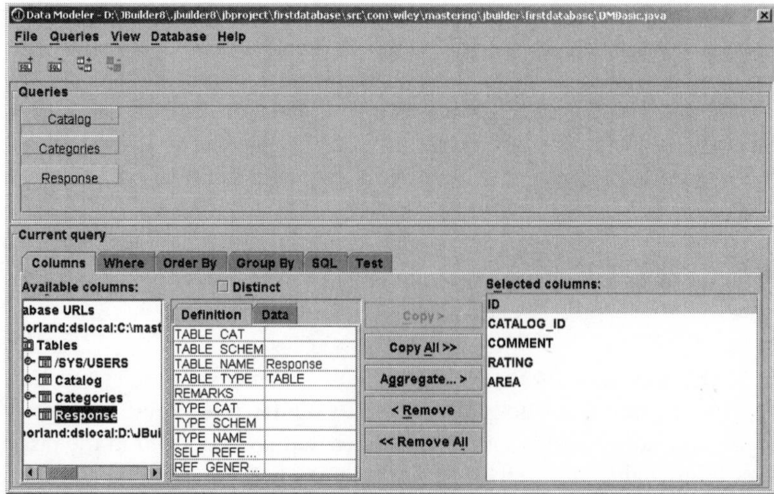


**Figure 14.2** New Data Modeler.

**TIP** **If you do not see the Data Module for the project in the choice control or want to use a Data Module that has already been defined in another, click the (...) button to the right of the choice control. This will start a Class Browser interface. Select the class from the package that holds it, and then click the OK button to continue.**

When the code is being generated for the DBSwing application, a quick dialog may be displayed showing the progress of the generation. It will disappear, and the Project pane has changed. In your package, the DMBasic becomes a package itself and has children located underneath the two-tier package. This is where all of the DBSwing files have been generated. Notice that outside the package there are now two additional files; one is a .html, which represents all of the files that were generated. The other is the runner application that calls all of the code that was generated.

The first code to review is the actual Data Module code (see Source 14.1). This will show all the QueryDataSets, which are the components that wrap the JDBC Select statement. The code is also responsible for making the connections to the database.

```
/**
 * <p>Title: </p>
 * <p>Description: </p>
 * <p>Copyright: Copyright (c) 2002</p>
 * <p>Company: </p>
 * @author not attributable
 * @version 1.0
 */
package com.wiley.mastering.jbuilder.firstdatabase;

import java.awt.*;
import java.awt.event.*;
import com.borland.dx.dataset.*;
import com.borland.dx.sql.dataset.*;

public class DMBasic implements DataModule {
  private static DMBasic myDM;
  Database database1 = new Database();
  QueryDataSet catalog = new QueryDataSet();
  QueryDataSet categories = new QueryDataSet();
  QueryDataSet response = new QueryDataSet();
  public static DMBasic getDataModule() {
    if (myDM == null) {
      myDM = new DMBasic();
    }
    return myDM;
  }

  public DMBasic() {
```

**Source 14.1** DMBasic.java. *(continued)*

```
    try {
      jbInit();
    }
    catch(Exception e) {
      e.printStackTrace();
    }
  }
  private void jbInit() throws Exception {
    response.setQuery(new
com.borland.dx.sql.dataset.QueryDescriptor(database1, "SELECT
\"Response\".ID,\"Response\".CATALOG_ID,\"Response\".COMMENT,\"Response\
".RATING,\"Response\".AREA " +
      "FROM \"Response\"", null, true, Load.ALL));
    categories.setQuery(new
com.borland.dx.sql.dataset.QueryDescriptor(database1, "SELECT
\"Categories\".ID,\"Categories\".CATALOG_ID,\"Categories\".NAME " +
      "FROM \"Categories\"", null, true, Load.ALL));
    catalog.setQuery(new
com.borland.dx.sql.dataset.QueryDescriptor(database1, "SELECT
\"Catalog\".ID,\"Catalog\".SYSNOPSIS,\"Catalog\".URI,\"Catalog\".TITLE,\
"Catalog\".RATING " +
      "FROM \"Catalog\"", null, true, Load.ALL));
    database1.setConnection(new
com.borland.dx.sql.dataset.ConnectionDescriptor("jdbc:borland:dslocal:C:
\\masteringjbuilder\\xyzanalyst.jds", "sysdba", "masterkey", false,
"com.borland.datastore.jdbc.DataStoreDriver"));
  }
  public Database getDatabase1() {
    return database1;
  }
  public QueryDataSet getCatalog() {
    return catalog;
  }
  public QueryDataSet getCategories() {
    return categories;
  }
  public QueryDataSet getResponse() {
    return response;
  }
}
```

**Source 14.1** *(continued)*

When we used the Data Modeler, we defined three queries. Notice the number of instance variables using QueryDataSet; there should be three. Also notice that a Database object is created, which holds all the information needed to connect to a database — it is just a simple wrapper for a JDBC connection string. Inside the jbInit() method is where the values for database1 and queryDataSet (1,2,3) are set. For most developers, this code does not need to be explained. It is also possible to click the

Design tab in JBuilder and look at each component's property using the GUI designer. Remember that any changes made in the designer will be made to the code and that any code changes will be made in the designer.

To understand what the Data Module Application builder did, you first might want to look inside the /jbuilder/templates directory. There you will find a number of code templates that JBuilder uses to generate code for Data Modules and CORBA. These templates can be modified; however, that topic is outside the scope of the book. JBuilder reads the Data Module and then generates the appropriate application from its contents using the templates in that diretory. The resulting application looks something like this:

```
DMBasic->Generates->DMBasicTwoTier.java->which calls the framework ->
           ClientFrame.java -> which calls the generated UI beans for ->

CatalogUIbean -> CategoriesUIBean -> ResponseUIBean
```

Plus, some of the other classes are also loaded, such as the about box and client resource classes. Looking at only one of the generated UI beans for Catalog, the code resembles Source 14.2.

```
/**
 * Copyright (c) 2002
 * Template File
 *   ColumnarUIBean.java.template
 * DataModule Object
 *   DMBasic.Catalog
 * Generation Date
 *   Sunday, December 8, 2002 12:47:22 AM EST
 * DataModule Source File
 *
D:/JBuilder8/.jbuilder8/jbproject/firstdatabase/src/com/wiley/mastering/
jbuilder/firstdatabase/DMBasic.java
 * Abstract
 *   Implements a columnar user interface for a particular DataSet.
 * @version 1.0
 */

package com.wiley.mastering.jbuilder.firstdatabase._DMBasic.twotier;

import java.awt.*;

import com.borland.dx.dataset.*;

public class CatalogUIBean
    extends javax.swing.JPanel {
  StorageDataSet dataSet;
  com.wiley.mastering.jbuilder.firstdatabase.DMBasic module;
```

**Source 14.2** CatalogUIBean.java. *(continued)*

```
  FlowLayout flowLayout1 = new FlowLayout();
  GridBagLayout gridBagLayout1 = new GridBagLayout();
  GridLayout gridLayout1 = new GridLayout(1, 2, 3, 0);
  javax.swing.JPanel panelID = new javax.swing.JPanel();
  com.borland.dbswing.JdbLabel labelID = new
com.borland.dbswing.JdbLabel();
  com.borland.dbswing.JdbTextField fieldID = new com.borland.dbswing.
      JdbTextField();
  javax.swing.JPanel panelSYSNOPSIS = new javax.swing.JPanel();
  com.borland.dbswing.JdbLabel labelSYSNOPSIS = new com.borland.dbswing.
      JdbLabel();
  com.borland.dbswing.JdbTextField fieldSYSNOPSIS = new
com.borland.dbswing.
      JdbTextField();
  javax.swing.JPanel panelURI = new javax.swing.JPanel();
  com.borland.dbswing.JdbLabel labelURI = new
com.borland.dbswing.JdbLabel();
  com.borland.dbswing.JdbTextField fieldURI = new com.borland.dbswing.
      JdbTextField();
  javax.swing.JPanel panelTITLE = new javax.swing.JPanel();
  com.borland.dbswing.JdbLabel labelTITLE = new
com.borland.dbswing.JdbLabel();
  com.borland.dbswing.JdbTextField fieldTITLE = new com.borland.dbswing.
      JdbTextField();
  javax.swing.JPanel panelRATING = new javax.swing.JPanel();
  com.borland.dbswing.JdbLabel labelRATING = new
com.borland.dbswing.JdbLabel();
  com.borland.dbswing.JdbTextField fieldRATING = new
com.borland.dbswing.
      JdbTextField();
  com.borland.dbswing.JdbNavToolBar navigatorControl1 = new
com.borland.dbswing.
      JdbNavToolBar();
  com.borland.dbswing.JdbStatusLabel statusBar1 = new
com.borland.dbswing.
      JdbStatusLabel();

  public CatalogUIBean() {
  }

  public void
setModule(com.wiley.mastering.jbuilder.firstdatabase.DMBasic
                        module) {
    this.module = module;
    try {
      jbInit();
    }
    catch (Exception e) {
```

**Source 14.2** *(continued)*

```
      e.printStackTrace();
    }
  }

  private void jbInit() throws Exception {
    dataSet = module.getCatalog();
    this.setLayout(gridBagLayout1);
    navigatorControl1.setDataSet(dataSet);
    navigatorControl1.setLayout(new GridLayout(1, 11));
    this.add(navigatorControl1,
             new java.awt.GridBagConstraints(1, 1, 2, 1, 1.0, 1.0,

java.awt.GridBagConstraints.NORTH,

java.awt.GridBagConstraints.
                                              HORIZONTAL,
                                              new Insets(3, 0, 3, 0), 0,
0));

    labelID.setText("Id");
    fieldID.setColumnName("ID");
    fieldID.setDataSet(dataSet);

    panelID.setLayout(gridLayout1);
    labelID.setHorizontalAlignment(javax.swing.SwingConstants.RIGHT);
    panelID.add(labelID);
    panelID.add(fieldID);
    this.add(panelID,
             new java.awt.GridBagConstraints(1, 2, 2, 1, 1.0, 1.0,

java.awt.GridBagConstraints.NORTH,

java.awt.GridBagConstraints.
                                              HORIZONTAL,
                                              new Insets(3, 0, 3, 3), 0,
0));

    labelSYSNOPSIS.setText("Sysnopsis");
    fieldSYSNOPSIS.setColumnName("SYSNOPSIS");
    fieldSYSNOPSIS.setDataSet(dataSet);

    panelSYSNOPSIS.setLayout(gridLayout1);

labelSYSNOPSIS.setHorizontalAlignment(javax.swing.SwingConstants.RIGHT);
    panelSYSNOPSIS.add(labelSYSNOPSIS);
    panelSYSNOPSIS.add(fieldSYSNOPSIS);
    this.add(panelSYSNOPSIS,
             new java.awt.GridBagConstraints(1, 3, 2, 1, 1.0, 1.0,
```

**Source 14.2** *(continued)*

```
                                                  java.awt.GridBagConstraints
.NORTH,

java.awt.GridBagConstraints.
                                                  HORIZONTAL,
                                                  new Insets(3, 0, 3, 3), 0,
0));

    labelURI.setText("Uri");
    fieldURI.setColumnName("URI");
    fieldURI.setDataSet(dataSet);

    panelURI.setLayout(gridLayout1);
    labelURI.setHorizontalAlignment(javax.swing.SwingConstants.RIGHT);
    panelURI.add(labelURI);
    panelURI.add(fieldURI);
    this.add(panelURI,
            new java.awt.GridBagConstraints(1, 4, 2, 1, 1.0, 1.0,

java.awt.GridBagConstraints.NORTH,

java.awt.GridBagConstraints.
                                                  HORIZONTAL,
                                                  new Insets(3, 0, 3, 3), 0,
0));

    labelTITLE.setText("Title");
    fieldTITLE.setColumnName("TITLE");
    fieldTITLE.setDataSet(dataSet);

    panelTITLE.setLayout(gridLayout1);
    labelTITLE.setHorizontalAlignment(javax.swing.SwingConstants.RIGHT);
    panelTITLE.add(labelTITLE);
    panelTITLE.add(fieldTITLE);
    this.add(panelTITLE,
            new java.awt.GridBagConstraints(1, 5, 2, 1, 1.0, 1.0,

java.awt.GridBagConstraints.NORTH,

java.awt.GridBagConstraints.
                                                  HORIZONTAL,
                                                  new Insets(3, 0, 3, 3), 0,
0));

    labelRATING.setText("Rating");
    fieldRATING.setColumnName("RATING");
    fieldRATING.setDataSet(dataSet);

    panelRATING.setLayout(gridLayout1);
```

**Source 14.2** *(continued)*

```
    labelRATING.setHorizontalAlignment(javax.swing.SwingConstants
.RIGHT);
    panelRATING.add(labelRATING);
    panelRATING.add(fieldRATING);
    this.add(panelRATING,
             new java.awt.GridBagConstraints(1, 6, 2, 1, 1.0, 1.0,

java.awt.GridBagConstraints.NORTH,

java.awt.GridBagConstraints.
                                                 HORIZONTAL,
                                                 new Insets(3, 0, 3, 3), 0,
0));

    statusBar1.setDataSet(dataSet);
    this.add(statusBar1,
             new java.awt.GridBagConstraints(1, 7, 2, 1, 0.0, 0.0,

java.awt.GridBagConstraints.SOUTH,

java.awt.GridBagConstraints.
                                                 HORIZONTAL, new Insets(3,
0, 3, 0),
                                                 0, 0));
   }
}
```

**Source 14.2** *(continued)*

This is the basic panel for the Catalog that was used in the application. The best part about this is that it is a complete JavaBean. For more information on how to work and create JavaBeans, review Chapter 8, "Modifying Classes." This means that this bean could be put onto the component pallet and used again in another program if desired. The code is really not that interesting; it has a lot of formatting for where the components are located because of the use of GridBagLayout layout manager. Notice that the Data Module reference gets passed into the class and is used to display the data. These connections are called datasources.

This program is completely extensible; using the GUI designer, additional fields or components could be added in a drag-and-drop environment.

Execute the code, and see what kind of program was generated for all the hard work so far. Right-mouse click on the DMBasicTwoTierApp.java, and select the Run menu item. This will start the application (see Figure 14.3).

The application generated has a tab interface. Each tab represents one of the tables located inside the database. The ability to remove tabs and display the help area is available; these can be added at a later time.

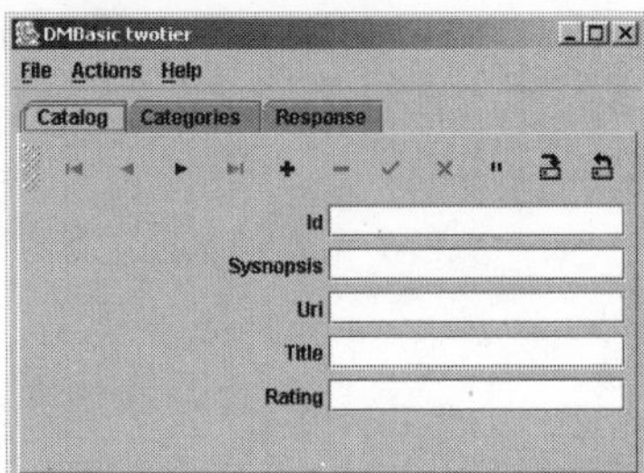


**Figure 14.3** Application 1, running.

If you have not added any data to the database, this would be an excellent time to do so. Starting with the Categories might help, but remember that you have to have a category available to add to the catalog entry. Make sure to add a few; this way the next example will show how those relationships can be exploited using the templates in JBuilder.

## Master-Detail Relationships

DataExpress is designed to handle the master-detail relationship in a database. The current data structure has a perfect master-detail relationship between the Categories and Catalog tables, and Borland created an Application wizard smart enough to handle it.

For this example, continue with the existing one that we just completed. Select the File | New menu item, and activate the Object Gallery. Then click the Data Module icon, and click the OK button to continue. The New Data Module dialog will be displayed, so make this Data Module's name DMMasterDetail and leave all options selected. This time when the Data Modeler wizard appears, the JDBC definition should already be defined. If this is still the same session, click on that JDBC connection string; it will show the tables. Expand the tables to show the children under the Table icon.

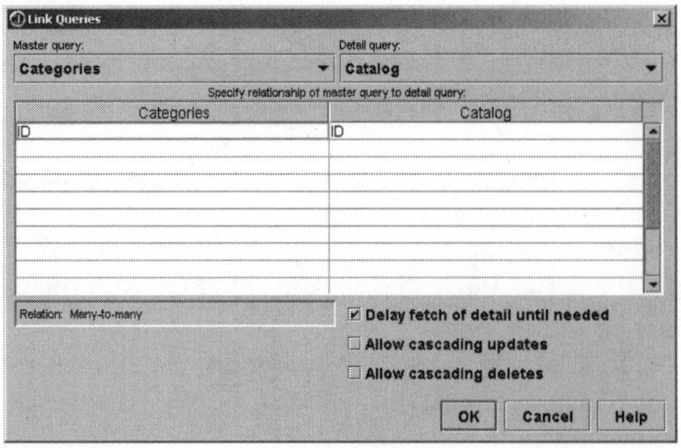

**Figure 14.4** Link Queries dialog.

**NOTE** **If you need to add another session, add the user name and password to access the tables.**

Select the Catalog table, and then click the Copy All button; this will add the query to the Queries pane. Then click the SQL+ button on the toolbar, select the Categories table, and click the Copy All button; the Categories will then be added to the Queries pane. The Queries pane allows for relationships to be drawn between one or more tables. Click and hold the left-mouse button to draw a line between the Categories table and the Catalog table to establish a relationship between the two tables; always draw the line from the master table to the detail table. This would mean the Categories table would be considered the master table and the detail table would be the Catalog table. The result will be a Link queries dialog, as shown in Figure 14.4.

Once the Link Queries dialog has been displayed, the interface allows for customizing the relationship between the tables and keys. For the Categories table, leave the ID as the main key. For the Catalog table, click the Choice box and select the CATEGORIES_ID for the link key. Other options are available on the screen — the ability to allow for both cascading updates and deletes. Cascading updates will allow changes to the master table to be processed through the detail table. This will have to be set if you were using multiple master-detail relationships throughout an application; this would occur when a detail record is a master record for another relationship. The same can be said about the cascading deletes because when you delete the master record, the detail children will be deleted in the same operation.

Once these keys are defined, click the OK button to continue, and a line will be drawn between the two tables (see Figure 14.5). Notice that the order of the tables has changed. Select the File | Save menu item to save and generate the Data Module and the relationship code that was just defined, then select the File | Exit menu item to continue.

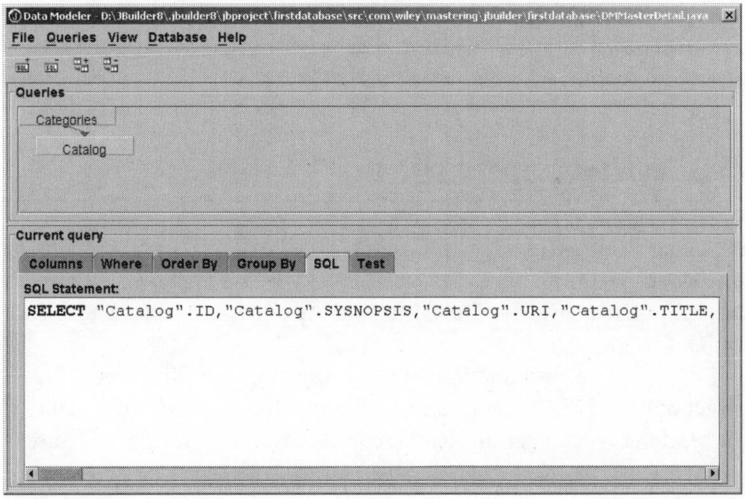

**Figure 14.5** Data Modeler.

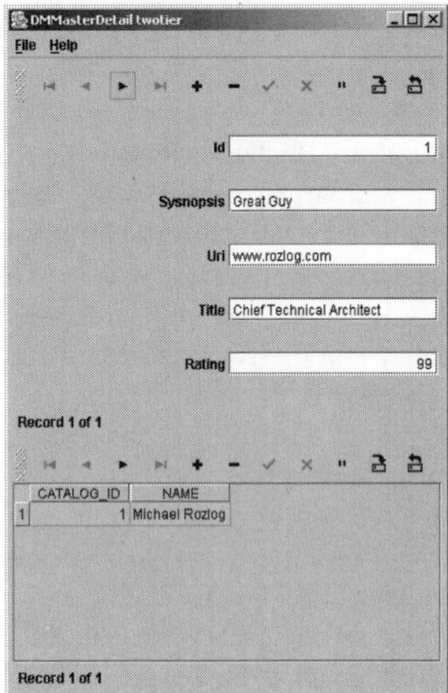


**Figure 14.6** Master-Detail application.

Back in the application, save the current project and recompile it. The next step is to generate the application for the new master detail Data Module that was created with the Data Modeler. Select the File | New menu item, click the Data Module Application icon, and click the OK button to continue. Again, the Data Module Application dialog will be displayed. Select the DMMasterDetail from the choice box; if you do not see it, click the (...) icon and select the Data Module from the current package. Once this has been selected, then click the OK button. Again, the Progress dialog could display briefly and then clear. After the generation is complete, save the project and recompile it.

It is now time to run the new application. Right-mouse click on the DMMaster DetailTwoTierApp.java file in the Project pane, and select the Run menu item. Figure 14.6 shows what should be displayed when the application runs.

# Creating a DBSwing application

The final example to show in this chapter is creating a standard DBSwing application using the GUI wizards and designers included with JBuilder. You will notice that it is not much more difficult than using the Data Module Application wizard to create something very similar.

Create a new project called seconddatabaseapp, by selecting the File | New Project menu item. Then select the File | New menu item, and select the Data Module, name it MyDM, use the Data Modeler and Generate Header comments, then click the OK button to continue. Now open the defined database in the Data Modeler; you may be asked for user name and password (sysdba and masterkey). If you started this chapter at the example, please review the beginning steps of the first example. Click the Catalog button, click the Copy All>> button, then click the SQL+ icon. Select the Categories table, and click the Copy All>> button. Then draw a line between Catalog and Categories; this will produce the Link dialog. Click the OK button to continue. Finally select the File | Save all menu item, and then select the File | Exit menu item.

The next step is to create an application; this can be done by selecting the File | New menu tiem, clicking the Application icon, and clicking the OK button. For this example, click the Finish key to generate the code. Once the application is generated, click the Design tab to start the GUI designer.

Select the Wizards | Use DataModule menu item (see Figure 14.7); this is responsible for establishing the reference to the Data Module in the Frame class. It should already have MyDM for the Data Module and have a definition of MyDM1 for the field declaration. The last option is for how the Data Module should be created:

- Create new instance of DataModule. This means that if multiple applications are hitting the Data Module, a new unique instance of the Data Module will be created.
- Share (static) instance of DataModule. This will share the connection between instances of the applications hitting it. This conserves resources and database connections.
- Caller sets instance with setModule. This gives ultimate control over access and creation to the developer.

Leave the Share selected, and click the OK button to continue.

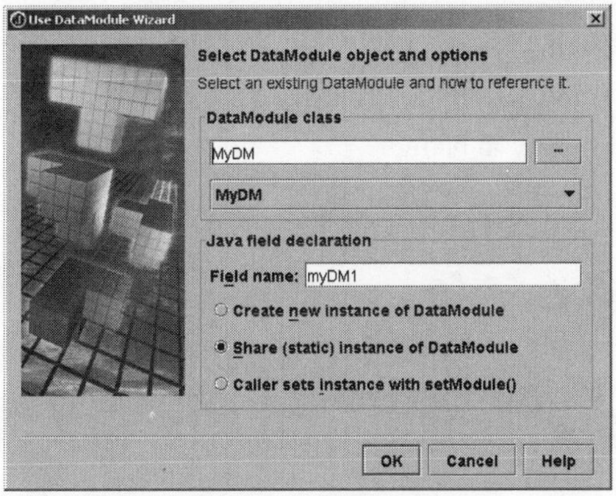

**Figure 14.7** Use Data Module wizard.

Under the Data Access in the component tree, you should notice a new item called myDM1, which is the reference to the Data Module we just created.

Now it is time to create the GUI interface for our application:

1. Click the dbSwing tab in the designer. Select the jdbNavToolbar, and drop it on the top of the frame; its constraints properties should read North.
2. Select the jdbStatusLabel, and drop it on the bottom of the frame; its constraints properties should read South.
3. Click the Swing containers, select a Jpanel, and drop it in the center of the GUI. Its constraints should be set to Center.
4. jPanel1 layout property should be set to grid.
5. Expand the jPanel1 in the component tree, and select its layout manager (set to grid), then set the rows to 2.
6. Then drop two JPanels off the Swing containers tab under the jPanel1 in the component tree.
7. Click on jPanel2, and set its border property to Etched.
8. Click on jPanel3, and set its border property to line.
9. Next select the jPanel2 panel, and set its layout manager to null.
10. Drop two JDBTextFields onto jPanel2.
11. Set jPanel3 layout manager to BorderLayout.
12. Drop JTableScrollPane into the center of jPanel3.
13. Drop a JDBTable inside the JTableScrollPane.
14. Now select jDBTextFields using the multiselect feature, using the Shift-click operation.
15. Set the dataSet property MyDM Categories.
16. Set jDBTextField1 columnName property to ID.
17. Set jDBTextField2 columnName property to Name.
18. Click the jDBTable, and set its dataSet property to MyDM Catalog.

**NOTE This example is being done to show how easy it is to create a GUI master-detail application without using the Data Module Application wizard. The process is about getting it done with the fewest steps for this example. The code generated was already explained.**

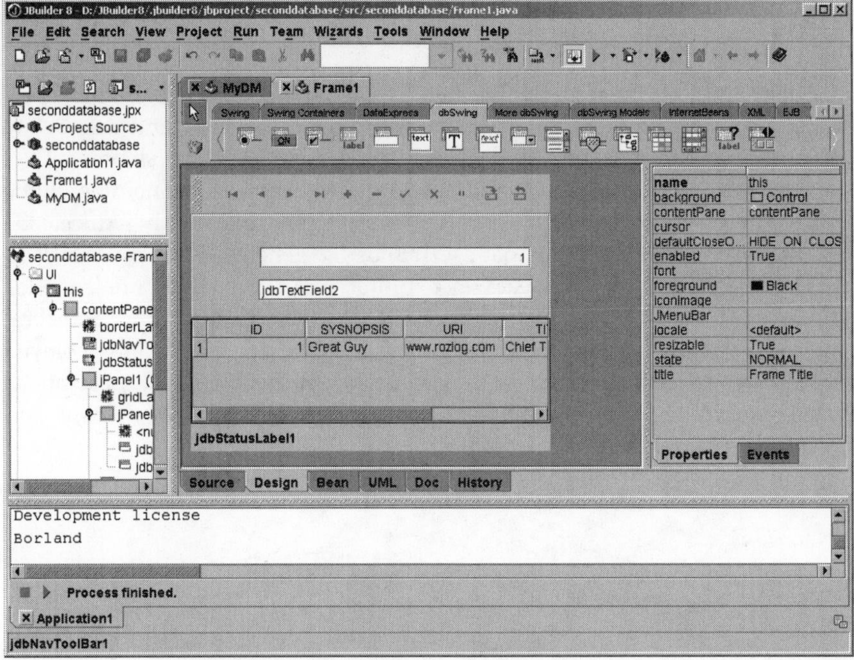


**Figure 14.8** GUI layout in the Designer.

Once these steps are followed, select File | Save All and the Rebuild the project option; then finally run it (see Figure 14.9). It should have the same functionality as the master-detail in the last example. Again, no programming is needed. One highlight is that the jdbNavToolbar and jdbStatusLabel are context aware, meaning that we did not set their dataset properties, which means that every dataset has focus at the time of the operation that has control over that control.

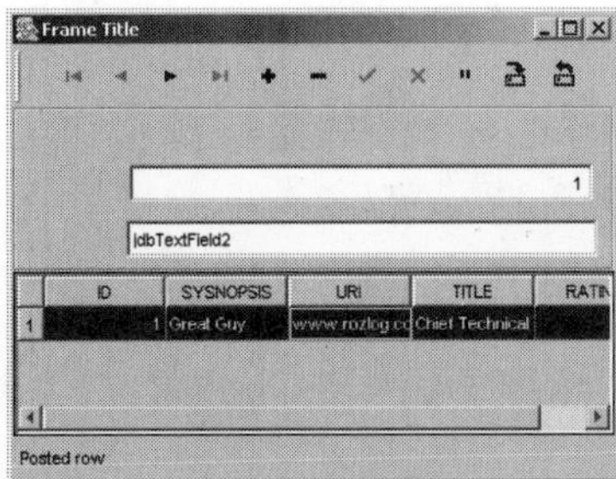


**Figure 14.9** Programmed master-detail application.

## Summary

This chapter highlights just how easy it is when a robust framework is available. JDBC programming is greatly simplified by using the DataExpress libraries, and data-aware GUI development is a snap when using the DBSwing libraries. Understanding Data Modules and how they are an abstraction of a centralized container for holding all the database access in one location eliminates confusion and can significantly reduce code complexity. Then using the built-in template technology to generate a full two-tier database application with no coding is a great way to prototype an application's data model. Generating the exact application, but doing so using JBuilder's GUI designer and components to produce a fully functioning application that can be run, tested, and deployed and again with no code, can really increase the developers' productivity and get solutions to the market in a breeze. When combined with programming logic, DataExpress and DBSwing can be a great combination.

PART

Five

# Web Development with Servlets, Java Server Pages, and Struts

J2SE (Standard Edition) is intended for client-side development and can be used to develop traditional two-tier client/server-based applications. While Sun continues to expand the number of technologies included in the Standard Edition, borrowing technology from the Enterprise Edition (J2EE), it also keeps expanding the technologies that make up J2EE.

While J2EE development does not officially have a major and a minor component, unofficially the Java development community has separated Web development from the rest of J2EE. This separation is at least supported by the fact that two distinctly different containers manage J2EE components. The Web container manages servlets and is responsible for compiling JavaServer Pages into servlet source code as well as providing the infrastructure that supports the model view controller framework know as Struts. The EJB container manages Enterprise JavaBeans and provides the infrastructure that supports Session, Entity, and Message Driven Beans. Part Five focuses on the development of technologies that are deployed in the Web container. While the components that are deployed in these two containers are very different, the various services of J2EE are available to both worlds.

This part is broken into four chapters:

**Server and Service Configuration.** JBuilder itself does not provide the technologies that are compliant with the various specifications that make up J2EE. To develop solutions within J2EE, an application server will need to be configured. Chapter 15 goes over the setup and configuration principles common to all servers.

**Web Enablement with Servlets.** Developing servlets that will be packaged in a given Web application's Web archive is the focus of Chapter 16. In addition, basic edits to the Deployment Descriptor specific to servlets are also discussed.

**Moving from Basic Servlets to JavaServer Pages.** Expanding on the servlet technology, Chapter 17 explains how JavaServer Pages allow developers to separate presentation from Java code by using tags within HTML. Developers can also create their own tags by developing Tag Libraries.

**Chapter 18, Developing with Struts.** Taking full advantage of the servlet, JavaServer Page, and Tag Library capabilities outlined in the previous chapters, Chapter 18 covers the Struts Framework, which provides a model view controller architecture for developing dynamic Web applications.

CHAPTER

15

# Server and Service Configuration

Within complex distributed frameworks like J2EE, developers create several components according to certain business requirements. How these components are developed and the target application server that is chosen usually determine the bounds to the capability limits that these components can achieve. Each application server has its own set of services and environment settings, plus its own particular way of developing the components that are to run in these environments. These application servers are typically responsible for making various services available to the components that they host. These services include Naming and Directory Services, Stateful Session Services, Transaction Services, and even the different Containers in which the components will run. Although it is true that all J2EE application servers are compliant with a version of the J2EE specification, this specification is open for interpretation in many areas.

Learning the varying complexities of this development process for each application server takes time. JBuilder helps simplify this complexity into a few basic concepts. For Java development, most of this complexity centers on the management of paths, parameters, and tools. For instance, there are the various versions of the Java Development Kit (JDK), external compilers, third-party libraries as well as the class, source, and document locations for each project. Dealing with third-party development platforms adds yet another layer to the mix. Similar to the manner in which JBuilder deals with third-party libraries and versions of the JDK, JBuilder allows the developer to configure the various paths, parameters, and tools of the target J2EE application server.

This chapter will start out with setting the global properties that affect the way that JBuilder works with various servers. We will also look at other enterprise configurations that affect other tools that JBuilder uses in the development of applications for these servers, and we will continue with the more specific settings that affect individual projects. Within a given project, there can be several project nodes, referred to as Web applications and EJB modules, that further refine how JBuilder will build and how the Web and EJB containers should manage the various components to be developed. And we will look at how the final products, the Web, EJB, and Enterprise Archives, are deployed and run in the target server's Web and EJB containers. These concepts are organized as follows within this chapter:

**Configure Your Server.** JBuilder can develop J2EE solutions for a variety of servers. Each server has its own particular environment, and the OpenTool that JBuilder uses to communicate to the Server during development needs to be configured properly.

**Enterprise Setup.** In addition to configuring JBuilder to work with a particular server, there are additional enterprise settings that can affect the development environment equally across all application servers. This includes which CORBA ORB and RDBMS implementations are chosen.

**Selecting Server Options.** Once JBuilder is configured properly for all of the target servers and additional enterprise resources that are needed, the individual project will need to know which server it is to work with and which additional enterprise tools will be used. The capabilities of each server are defined as services. Within a single project, only one server can provide the capabilities of an individual service. Multiple servers can be used, but only one can be assigned to each service.

**Building Server Components.** Within a project, developers will build Web components and EJB components. Collections of Web components are defined within a Web application, and collections of EJB components are defined within EJB modules. Each JBuilder project can work with multiple EJB modules as well as multiple Web applications.

**Deploying the Finished Product.** After development has reached a point where it is ready to be tested or deployed to a target, the Web and EJB archives are deployed to the target server's container. Additionally, Enterprise Archives can be built that contain both Web and EJB archives. These Enterprise Archives can also be deployed to the target server. Runtime configurations are used to define exactly how JBuilder is to deploy each of these archives to the server's container. These runtime configurations can also define what services are to be made available.

## Configuring Your Server

Most servers have basic configuration information in common. Each server may also have some proprietary or custom information that may also need to be configured. It is important to note that if you have a mapped drive to install an application server on a machine, the install that you configure within JBuilder must be for the same operating system. Just because you can map a drive to a directory on a Solaris machine does not mean that JBuilder running on a Windows machine will be able to use this installation.

Often, the tools that JBuilder evokes to call various compilers, verifiers, and even the launching process of the server are native applications and not pure Java applications.

For this reason, we recommend using a local install rather than a remote install on a server. You may also notice performance issues if the libraries that you build against are somewhere across the network on another machine.

## Configuring Borland Enterprise Server, AppServer Edition

Before a server can be used, it must first be enabled and properly configured. From JBuilder's Tools menu, select Configure Servers. You will see a list of application servers that JBuilder supports. Additional servers are supported by third parties. If your application server vendor has manufactured an OpenTool for development within JBuilder, you will need to download and install that OpenTool in order to see your server on the list of servers. The JBuilder OpenTool API is an open specification for how to develop extensions to the JBuilder IDE. To configure an application server, select the application server that you have installed and set the Home Directory to the root directory to which you installed the application server. In Figure 15.1, notice that an Enable server checkbox is checked. If you do not enable the server, you will not be able to edit the configuration.

### *Configure General Server Settings*

Each server will have similar settings. For the most part, each server performs and behaves the same from a developer's point of view. There are server-specific APIs that JBuilder must interact with. Each server has a plug-in associated with it that uses the following settings to interact with the tools and programs specific to each server.

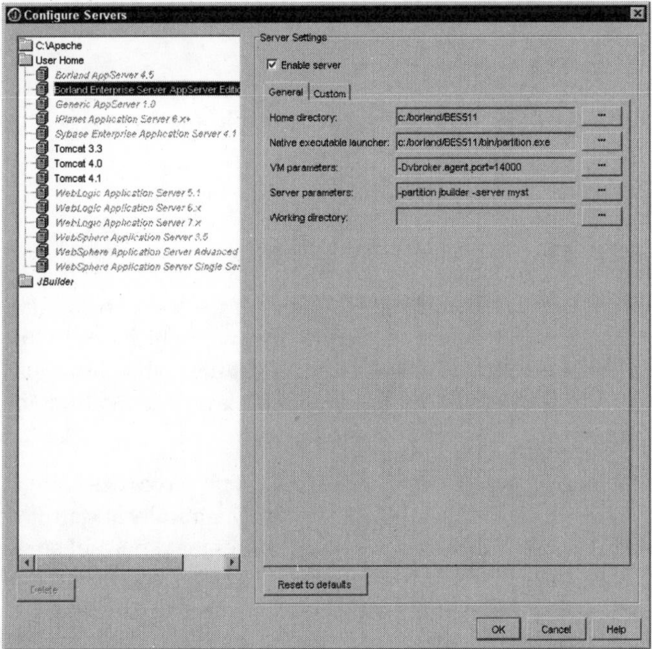


**Figure 15.1** Borland Enterprise Server General settings.

**Home Directory.** Set to the root directory where the application server has been installed. Usually it is enough to set the Home Directory setting. The Home Directory is used to set the default for most of the other settings. Most of the OpenTools developed for each server are aware of the default relative location of the various classes, directories, executables, and jar files.

**Native Executable Launcher.** If this option is available, your target application server will begin the process. If this process is not automatically initiated, it does not necessarily mean that your application server is not Java-based. Often vendors wrap the native java.exe entry point in their own code to control the use of various system parameters. In such cases, the defined native executable will be executed by the Runtime configuration.

**Main Class.** Because the Borland Enterprise Server uses a Native Executable Launcher to start, the Main class setting is not accessible. Other servers may have a Main class that defines how the server is started. This class launches the application server from the Runtime configurations.

**VM Parameters.** This setting passes information to the Java Virtual Machine that will be used to run the application server. When starting a Java process, there are two types of parameters than can be passed in; VM Parameters pass information into the Java Virtual Machine. These parameters include and are not limited to control of the memory allocation, instructions on which just-in-time compiler or Hotspot compiler to use, and debug information.

**Server Parameters.** This passes information used by the application server. Similar to VM Parameters, Server Parameters are information that is passed to the server. When writing Java programs, this would be the String array that is passed into the main() method that defines the entry point into the application's process. Server parameters vary depending on the target application server that has been selected.

**Working Directory.** Not all application servers need this parameter set. Often it will default to the project's Working Directory or to the application server's Home Directory.

## Library Settings for Servers

Some servers also define Library Settings from the General tab of the server configuration screen (see Figure 15.1). The Borland Enterprise Server does not, which is why the following is not displayed. The following additional Library Settings, when available, will be added to the project's settings when the application server is configured from the Server tab of the Project Settings.

**Class.** This includes the location of any classes that the application server needs to operate. Some application servers build their lists of classes dynamically at startup. Therefore you may need to include only a minimal set of classes that know where to load all additional classes, such as a bootstrap class as utilized by Tomcat 4.0. Therefore you will want to consult the documentation on the application server you are configuring prior to setting up the classes. Some application servers add classes to their respective classpaths dynamically.

**Source.** This includes the location of any source files that the debugger can walk through while you are debugging and that OptimizeIt can access while optimizing your code.

**Documentation.** This includes the location of any JavaDoc associated with the classes and source files that JBuilder will display when selecting the Doc tab.

**Required Libraries.** If you have already configured a set of libraries that you wish to include in the operation of the application server, you can add those libraries here — for instance, utility classes that were either purchased from a third party or built in house. These Required Libraries will be added to the classpath when the application server is run, debugged, or optimized.
Just because the application you are building requires additional classes and packages does not mean that the application server is also dependent on these classes and packages. There are other mechanisms to add classes to a server's classpath without having to modify the required libraries of the server. You can modify the Runtime configuration to add required libraries of the project to the classpath of the server, and you can also add required libraries of the project to any resource files or archives that are to be created and deployed. This particular Required Libraries setting should be reserved to define any required classes that the server needs to operate normally.

## *Configure Custom Server Settings*

Each server can also have more specialized settings. These settings are configured on the Custom tab of the Configure Servers dialog. The most common of the custom settings for each server is the ability to specify a specific version of the JDK on which the server depends. JBuilder itself is hosted on a particular JDK, and this JDK should not be swapped out for a newer version. The same holds true for application servers. By making the target JDK specific for an application server, each time the project properties change its server configuration, the target JDK configuration will also change. In addition to setting the target JDK for a server, other settings include adding access to various server tools to the Tools menu as well as configuring logon id and passwords that are required by some application servers in order to use their console and even deploy packaged modules into their environment.

## *Reset to Defaults*

If you have edited several of the properties and nothing is working the way it should, you can change them all back to their default values. This includes their default setting for the installation directory. Only the currently selected server's setting will be affected. After reviewing the installation directory setting, check the remaining defaulted parameters, and click the OK button. You may have to exit JBuilder and restart because JBuilder must add certain libraries to its own classpath in order to complete the configuration.

# Enterprise Setup

Application servers are not the only enterprise tools that JBuilder needs to interact with. IDL compilers, JDBC drivers, and SQLJ executables are also necessary when developing applications for deployment into a given server's environment. These tools may be used in conjunction with an application server, or they may be utilized on their own. On the Tools menu there is an item titled Enterprise Setup. This is where additional tools are configured. Some of these configurations require JBuilder to restart in order for certain libraries to be added to JBuilder's classpath.

## Configuring CORBA

The Object Management Group (OMG) defines the standard for the Common Request Broker Architecture (CORBA). CORBA is a technology for creating, distributing, and managing processes across network, operating system, and development language boundaries. There are several implementations of what is called an Object Request Broker (ORB) and the necessary tools required to build both clients and servers within this architecture. JBuilder Enterprise comes with a developer's license of Borland Enterprise Server AppServer Edition that includes all of the tools and technologies necessary for developing CORBA-based solutions in Java. If you have already configured the Borland Enterprise Server (BES) as a server, then you will notice that the required CORBA settings for VisiBroker (the CORBA ORB implementation that comes with BES) have already been configured (see Figure 15.2).

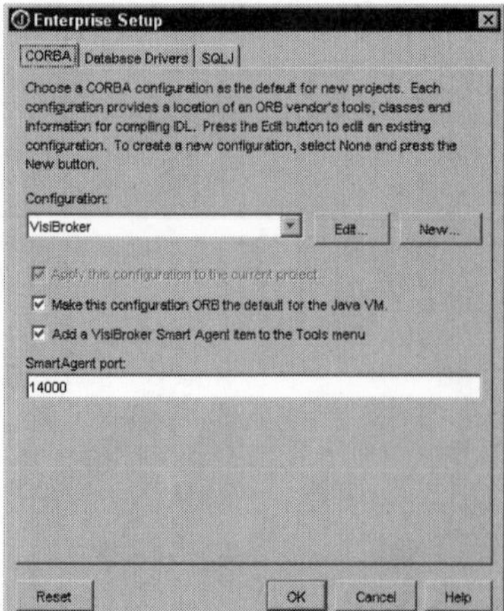


**Figure 15.2** Enterprise Setup dialog for CORBA.

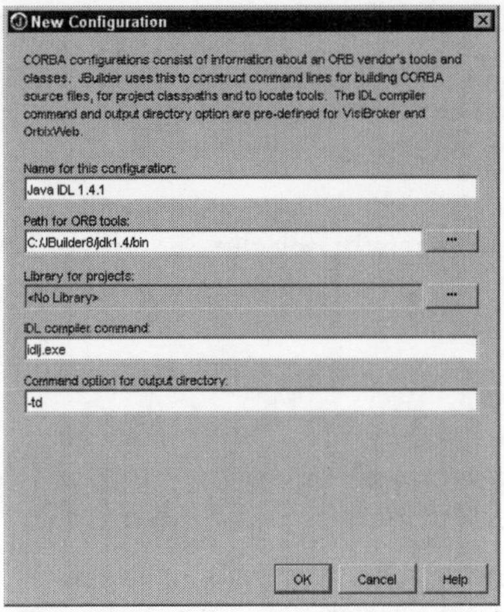

**Figure 15.3** Java IDL configuration.

## *Setting Up Java IDL as CORBA Compiler*

Chances are that the version of the target JDK you have set up as the default JDK for your projects within JBuilder already has an implementation of an ORB. This implementation is commonly referred to as Java IDL. JBuilder by default is not configured to use this ORB. You can, however, create a CORBA configuration for Java IDL. From the Enterprise Settings on the Tools menu, select the CORBA tab and click on *New*. Here you will see the setting necessary for JBuilder to evoke an external IDL compiler (see Figure 15.3). Consult the tools documentation that comes with the Java Developers Kit you are working with to verify the proper parameters for using the IDL-to-Java Compiler. For Java IDL, the settings are these:

**Name for this configuration.** Any name will do. It may be wise to include a version number in the name in case you have multiple Java Development Kits installed and configured on the same machine. For this example "Java IDL 1.4.1" was used as the name for this configuration.

**Path for ORB tools.** This is where the directory containing the IDL Compiler Command is located. JBuilder will look in this directory for the executable and any of its necessary native libraries. For Java IDL, this would be the bin directory located just under the JAVA_HOME location for the Java Developers Kit installation.

**Library for projects.** Unlike the path that indicates the location of the native libraries and executables, this library was configured containing all of the Java packages and classes that are part of the implementation of the ORB that is to be configured. For Java IDL, no additional library is necessary to configure. The VisiBroker configuration uses the Borland Enterprise Server Library, which is automatically configured when configuring the server.

**IDL compiler command.** JBuilder does assume that the IDL compiler is a native executable. This configuration option need be only the full name of the executable. For JavaIDL this would be specified as idlj.exe.

**Command option for output directory.** When JBuilder builds the project, the location of the output directory will need to be passed in as a parameter so that the generated output can be directed to the location of JBuilder's project output. For Java IDL, this parameter is specified in the JDK tools documentation. This is specified as "-td".

Once these parameters are set, they can be accessed again by selecting Edit from the CORBA tab of the Enterprise Setup dialog. There are four additional settings for each IDL compiler that is configured:

**Apply configuration to the current project.** On the Project Properties page, you can select which IDL complier is utilized during the build process. If a new IDL compiler configuration is configured while an existing project is open, this option will change the settings within the currently open project to use this new IDL compiler.

**Make configuration's ORB the default for the Java VM.** Although the Java IDL compiler ORB that comes with the Java Developers Kit does not need to be named specifically for the Java Virtual Machine, other ORBs do. By selecting this option, a file titled orb.properties will be created in the JAVA_HOME's lib directory. This properties file contains the information necessary to select a particular ORB as the default ORB for a running instance of the Virtual Machine. Following is an example of the file that would be utilized for configuring VisiBroker as the default ORB:

```
# Make VisiBroker for Java the default ORB
org.omg.CORBA.ORBClass=com.inprise.vbroker.orb.ORB
org.omg.CORBA.ORBSingletonClass=com.inprise.vbroker.orb.ORB
```

**Add a VisiBroker SmartAgent item to the Tools menu.** This configuration is obviously VisiBroker-specific. This process — called the Smart Agent or OSAgent — is executable when running acts as a sort of naming agent, similar in effect to a naming service.

**Smart Agent port.** Also specific to VisiBroker is the port that the Smart Agent will use.

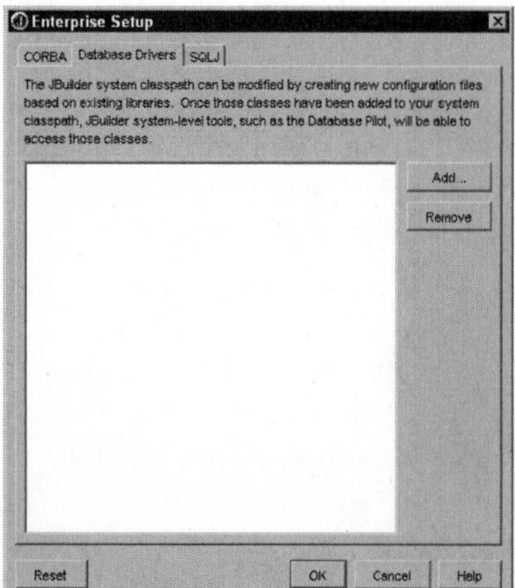


**Figure 15.4** JDBC database driver configuration.

## Configuring Database Drivers

Certain database productivity tools that JBuilder utilizes during the development process require that the Java database connectivity drivers be configured (see Figure 15.4). This is so that JBuilder can add the necessary libraries to its own classpath to make these drivers accessible. Prior to adding a database driver to JBuilder's Enterprise Setup, you must first configure a library for this driver. It is therefore beneficial to keep all database drivers configured as their own separate library, and add these libraries to other libraries only when necessary. Configuring a new library that points to the location of a JDBC driver will allow a project to compile, run debug, and optimize using the JDBC driver, but if that library is not configured as a database driver on the Enterprise Setup tool, the JDBC driver will not be added to JBuilder's classpath. It is important to add the JDBC driver to JBuilder's classpath so that JBuilder can use the JDBC driver during development. This includes the ability to design DBSwing applications using live data to populate DataExpress components, the use of database tools such as the Database Pilot, and the ability to create a DataSource in the EJB 2.0 Designer, which is used, in turn, to create Container Managed Persistence Entity Beans.

### *Setting Up the InterClient JDBC Driver*

The following steps can be used to install any JDBC driver, but for our example we will use InterBase InterClient JDBC Driver. InterBase is a SQL92-compliant relational database management system (RDBMS) manufactured by Borland. InterBase uses a Type-3 JDBC driver, which means that there is actually an intermediary server (referred to as the InterClient Server) that listens for JDBC connections and brokers such calls on to the actual InterBase Database Server.

The first step is to ensure that a library has already been configured and that only the JDBC driver is included in this library. As noted previously, libraries themselves can specify other libraries as dependents. Therefore, if you feel that you need to include a given JDBC driver with a collection of other classes and packages, just make the JDBC drive library a dependent library of the other. If a library has not been created for the InterClient JDBC packages and classes, create one using the Tools menu's Configure Libraries option to create a new library and add the directory jar full of classes to the libraries classpath (see Figure 15.5).

Next, enter the Enterprise Setup's Database Driver tab, and click on Add. Scroll through the list of libraries, and select the library that contains the classpath information for the InterClient JDBC Driver. Click OK.

Once JBuilder accepts this configuration, a file will be added to JBuilder's lib/ext directory using the name of the Library. A list of such files will be displayed on the Database Drivers tab of the Enterprise Setup. The file contains the addpath information that JBuilder will use at startup time. It is therefore sometimes necessary to restart JBuilder for these changes to take effect. Following is the typical content for such a file:

```
addpath C://Borland/InterBase/InterClient/interclient.jar
```

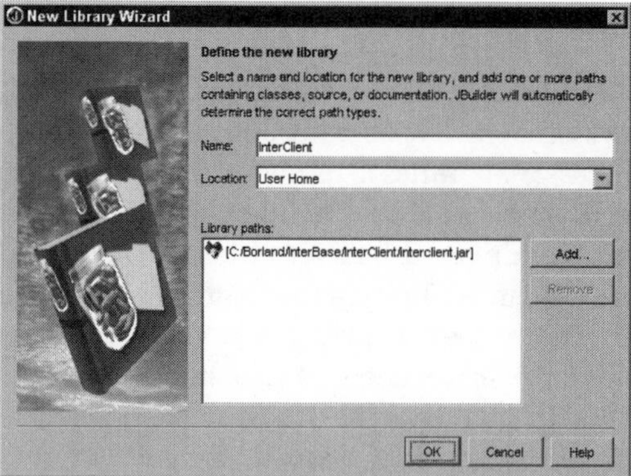


**Figure 15.5** Create the InterClient library.

JBuilder is able to add only one version of each JDBC drive to its classpath. You could establish several libraries in JBuilder for each JDBC driver—possibly including the version number in the name of the library—and then go into the Enterprise Setup for Database Drivers and add each to JBuilder's classpath. JBuilder would still append each configuration to JBuilder's classpath, and the classloader will load the class from the location it finds first. If you are curious about the order of JBuilder's resulting classpath from all of the additions that have been made, select the Info tab on the About JBuilder menu item located on the Help menu (see Figure 15.6). Double-click on the java.class.path item in the list to see its value. Check here to resolve any classpath conflicts that you may encounter.

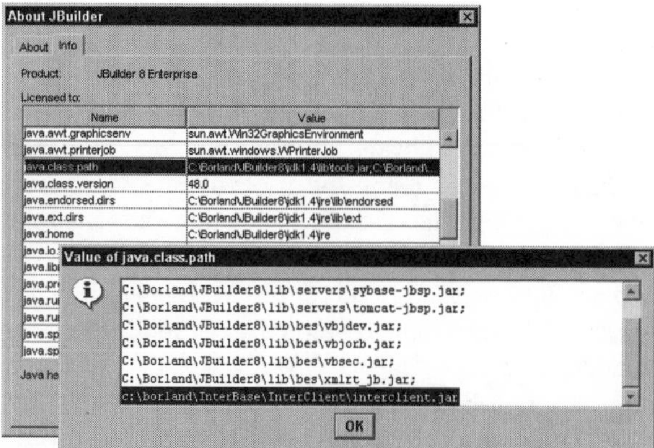


**Figure 15.6** JBuilder's classpath.

## Configuring SQLJ

Other programming languages like C have been able to take advantage of extensions to SQL. SQLJ is the term used to refer to the SQL extensions for Java. This allows developers to embed SQL statements into Java methods. JBuilder can be configured to call the SQLJ translator for any .SQLJ files in the project. Both Oracle and DB2 SQLJ are configurable from Enterprise Setup. The configuration is very similar to the CORBA configuration. You must instruct JBuilder about the location of the external executable and inform JBuilder of any additional parameters that must be passed into said executable. When properly configured, JBuilder will process the .sqlj files included in a given project and generate the necessary .java files. These .java files will appear as nodes to the .sqlj file. Once the .java files have been created, JBuilder will compile the .java files. To configure JBuilder to use an SQLJ translator during the build of a project, go to the SQLJ tab of the Enterprise Setup dialog (see Figure 15.7) to edit the following:

**SQLJ executable.** Browse to and select the SQLJ executable that evokes the SQLJ translator. You may have to download this tool separately, depending on which vendor's SQLJ translator you are planning to use.

**Additional options.** Include any additional parameters that you wish to pass into the SQLJ executable.

**Libraries.** If the SQLJ executable requires additional classes or packages, you can instruct JBuilder to use the classes and packages specified in any one of the libraries that have already been defined. If the classes and packages you require do not have libraries defined, you will have to configure them. You can also select the order in which the libraries will be passed.

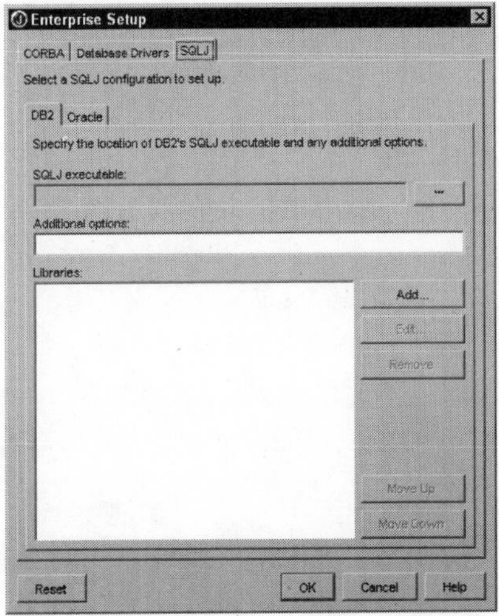


**Figure 15.7** SQLJ translator settings.

## Selecting a Server's Services

Typically, each project will work with just one server configured for the entire project, but there are times when more than one server configuration is necessary for a given project. Services add the ability to select multiple servers for a single project. Because you cannot select multiple servers for a single service within a project, services break down the capabilities of each server. This selection of which server will be utilized for a given service is specific to a project and therefore configurable on the Project Properties' Server tab.

Beyond the basic configuration of the parameters and paths of the server, each service can also be configured within a project. JBuilder controls the application server through a combination of servers and services. Just because an application server is configurable as a server does not necessarily mean that all services that the application server poses will be available. The service that JBuilder requires will depend on the capabilities of both the application server and the OpenTool developed to support that application server. Not every application server will have every service available.

Once you're in JBuilder, you can configure the project to use one application server and the services available to that particular application server, or you can assign a different server for each service. Services can also be turned on and off for a given project by deselecting the checkbox to the left of the service. You can set the following services in the default project properties:

**Client JAR creation.** Client Java Archive (JAR) files can be created from a deployable Enterprise JavaBean JAR file and then used in the development of an EJB client.

**Connector.** This will instruct the application server to turn on support for J2EE connectors when the application server is started.

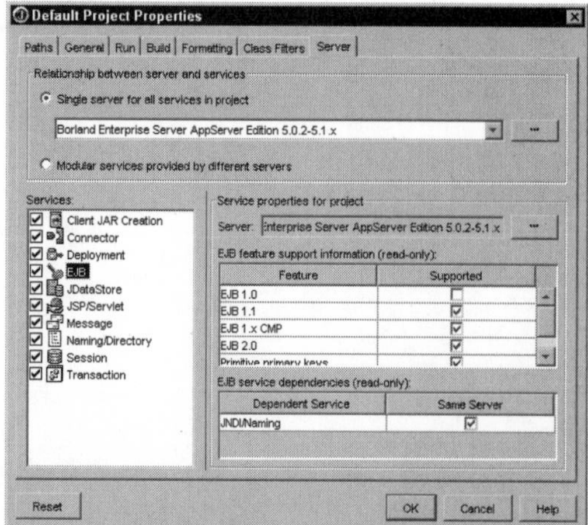


**Figure 15.8** Default Project Properties dialog.

**Deployment.** JBuilder build tasks can be evoked prior to deployment. This can be turned on and off to ensure that unnecessary builds are not performed or that the most recent changes are reflected in the build that is to be deployed. It is up to the individual developer to determine which setting best fits his or her development style.

**EJB.** The EJB container can be configured to support various versions of the specification (see Figure 15.8). If the EJB container for a particular application server supports only EJB 1.1, it will be reflected in this read-only property. This affects the availability of the EJB 2.0 designer. The EJB 2.0 designer will not be accessible to a project that has selected an application server that does not support the EJB 2.0 specification. Some EJB containers will also be dependent on other services. These dependent services will also be listed here in this read-only property:

**JDataStore.** This is primarily used by Borland Enterprise Server, so you can configure which port the JDataStore Server listens to.

**JSP/Servlet.** The Web container that is to be utilized can be configured to support various versions of the specification (see Figure 15.9). If the Web container for a particular application server supports only JSP 1.1, it will be reflected here in this read-only property.

**Naming Directory.** This instructs the application server to turn on support for the Naming and Directory Service when the application server is started.

**Session.** This tells the application server to turn on support for the Stateful Session Service at startup.

**Transaction.** This turns on support for the Transaction Manager when the application server is started.

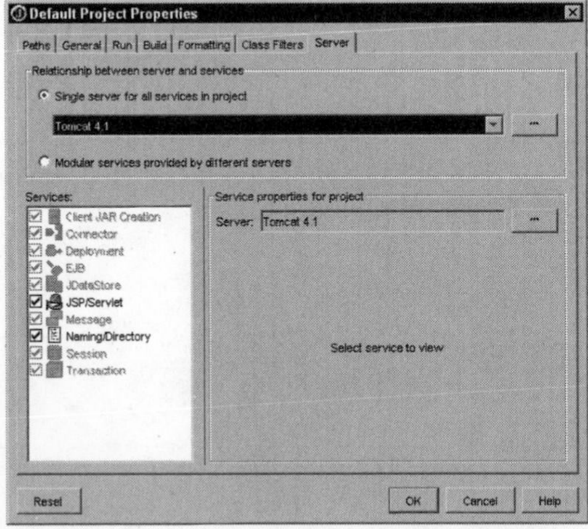


**Figure 15.9** Default Project Properties dialog.

JBuilder does not provide the necessary integration between application servers if a mix is chosen. You may, in fact, be able to instruct JBuilder that you intend to use Borland Enterprise Server as your JSP and Servlet Engine, iPlanet as your Naming Services, WebLogic as your EJB container, and even WebSphere for your deployment. It is up to you to ensure that each application server environment is configured properly to work in such a configuration. JBuilder does not have the context smarts to actually resolve any conflicts that you may have introduced in the configuration; it would simply evoke the appropriate compilers and launching executables as you have configured them. You will see errors and exceptions in the Message view.

The project properties do *not* allow the developer to assign a particular service to an application server that does not have such a service available. Tomcat 4.0, for instance, cannot be configured to be the project's EJB container.

To configure the default server that will be used by all future projects you create, edit the Default Project Properties Server tab.

## Configuring the CORBA IDL Compiler

Each project can use a different IDL compiler, but you cannot configure multiple IDL compilers within the same project (see Figure 15.10). For instance, if you use VisiBroker as the IDL compiler for the server and Java IDL as the compiler for the client, you would need to set up two separate projects. You can point both projects at the same directory structure, but you will need two .jpx files.

To configure the IDL compiler that is to be used by JBuilder projects, select Default Project Properties from the Project menu, and choose the IDL tab from the Build tab. Here you can choose which IDL compiler to use as well as specify the behavior of the IDL compiler.

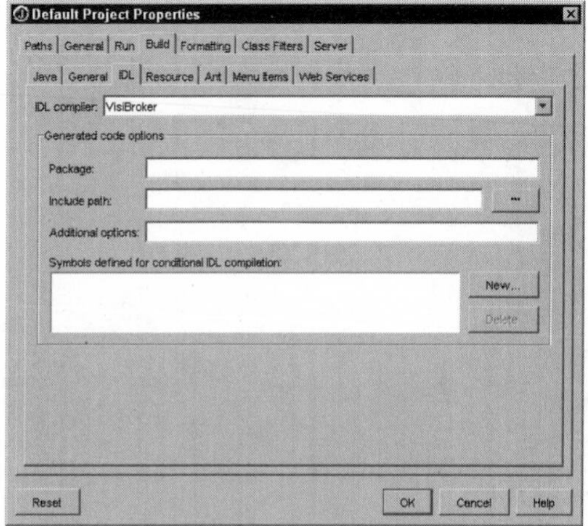


**Figure 15.10** Default Project Properties dialog.

## Building Server Components

Some servers need to have various tools evoked during JBuilder's build process. These tools can be configured from the project properties. JBuilder projects not only have to know how to interact with a given server when building, running, debugging, and optimizing; JBuilder projects also need to manage the various components that developers want to work with. These components range from servlets to Java Server Pages to Enterprise JavaBeans. Within a project, there are various project nodes that JBuilder uses to manage these components. The two main classifications of nodes that JBuilder manages for a server are called Web applications and EJB modules. Web applications manage servlets and Java Server Pages in addition to the developed classes, required libraries, and deployable content that are to be part of the Web archive that the Web application also manages. EJB modules manage Enterprise JavaBeans in addition to the developed classes and required libraries that are to be part of the Java archive that the EJB Module also manages. Both Web applications and EJB modules manage a deployment descriptor that contains the configuration information specific to the servlets, Java Server Pages, and Enterprise JavaBeans that they manage.

### Web Applications

The basis for all Web development in JBuilder begins with the Web application. The Web application is a managed node within a JBuilder project that contains all of the content for a particular Web site. As per the J2EE specification, this also includes all of the necessary information and content necessary to create a compliant Web archive (WAR). All Web-based components that are to be part of the WAR must be added to a Web application somehow. This includes the all-important Deployment Descriptor for Web applications. The Deployment Descriptor is an XML file (web.xml) that contains the information that the Web container needs to manage the deployed content of a Web application. A Deployment Descriptor Editor exists to help edit and manage the elements of the Deployment Descriptor. Each server that JBuilder supports can have additional configuration information specific to that particular server. When working with Web applications, the necessary vendor-specific deployment descriptor information will also be added to the WAR. The dependent libraries of the project will also become the dependent libraries of the Web application. Configuring the dependencies of the Web application will also allow developers to decide which libraries will be deployed as part of the WAR and which libraries will not be deployed. A decision to include these required libraries in the generated WAR file will place them in the WEB-INF/lib directory of the WAR file.

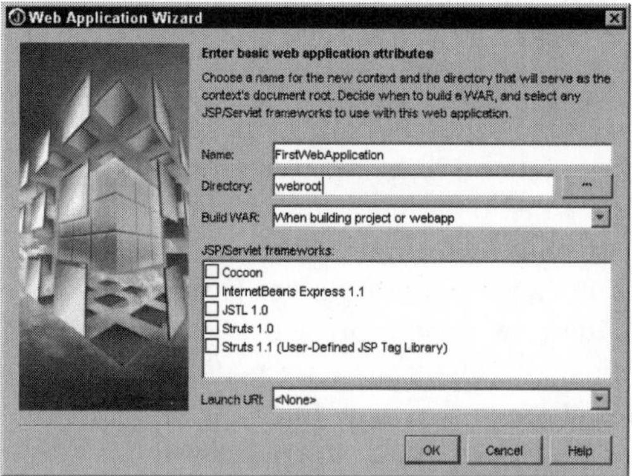


**Figure 15.11** Web Application wizard.

If a Web application has not been created, JBuilder will create a default Web application and add all new Web-based content to this default Web application. A single project can manage several Web applications. Creating a new Web application to be added to an existing project requires some basic information. All of these settings can, of course, be modified after the Web application has been created, by right-clicking on the Web application node in the Project pane and modifying the Web application's properties. To create a new Web application, open the Object Gallery, and click on the Web Application wizard (see Figure 15.11) on the Web tab to enter the following information:

**Name.** The name of the Web application will affect the URL of all of the content within the Web application. This is not just the name of the managed node in the JBuilder project; it is the deployed name relative to the Web server's root that will be utilized by the Web container. The name of the Web application also has an effect on the URL used to access the contents of the Web application. For instance, if the name of the Web application is "FirstWebApplication," then the root URL for this Web application would be http://localhost:8080/FirstWebApplication. If you rename the Web application, you will change the URL as well.

**Directory.** The directory selected will be the root directory of the Web application. This will be the location that is used for all of the Web application content. If you already have a directory of HTML documents and image files, you can point the Web application's directory to this directory. When creating a Web archive (WAR), the contents of this directory will be added to the root directory of the WAR file. If you do decide to add static content to this directory, or perhaps an images directory, you may notice that the files and directories that you have created do not immediately show up under the Root Directory folder node of the Web application. When this happens, just click on the Refresh toolbar button just above the Project pane, and the contents should display.

**Build WAR.** Web archives (WARs), as defined by the J2EE specification, are self-contained Web sites. The Web application determines what will and what will not be included in the WAR. Depending on the amount of content, building a

WAR could take considerable time. For this reason, you can configure exactly how often a Web application's WAR file is to be generated: when building either the project or Web app, when building the project only, when building the Web app only, or never.

**JSP/Servlet Frameworks.** There are several different frameworks that a given Web application can decide to implement. You can select these when the Web application is created, or you can add them later by modifying the Web application's properties:

**Cocoon.** Part of the Apache XML Project, Cocoon is a servlet-based framework for distributing XML documents formatted with XSL stylesheets. This framework allows for the separation of content, style, and business logic.

**InternetBeans Express 1.1.** Borland's DataExpress technology is an extension of the JDBC technology that implements provider and resolver capabilities for distribution of DataSets. DBSwing is a collection of DataSet-aware visual components for designing rich client/server-based Swing applications. InternetBeans Express is also a collection of DataSet-aware visual components, for designing rich Web-based HTML applications.

**JSTL 1.0.** The JavaServer Pages Standard Tag Library (JSTL) is a collection of Tag Libraries that have been accepted as an industry-standard set of Tag Libraries. Apache's Jakarta Project manages an implementation of JSTL.

**Struts.** Based on servlet and JavaServer Pages technology, Struts is a model, view, controller-based framework for developing Web-based systems using Java.

**Launch URI.** This will be used as the default URI that is requested if you right-click on the Web application node in the Project pane and select Run, Debug, or Optimize.

## Web Application Properties

To access a Web application's properties, right-click on the Web application in the Project pane and select Properties (see Figure 15.12). The Web application's properties contain instructions for JBuilder's build system on how to create and manage the content of the Web archive (WAR). Each Web application can manage one and only one WAR. The properties of the Web aAplication can also affect the contents of the WAR's Deployment Descriptor (web.xml). There are five tabs located on the Web applications Properties dialog: WebApp, Directories, Classes, Dependencies, and Manifest:

**WebApp.** The first tab should look very similar to the Web Application wizard. On the WebApp tab you can modify the name and location of the WAR that is to be created as well as name of the Web application itself. You will also notice the listing of frameworks that can be selected. You can also choose the frequency of how often the WAR file will be built. If you like to compile the classes of your project frequently, but you do not want to rebuild the WAR file each time, you can set the build option to never.

**Directories**. There are two types of directories, directories of project content to exclude and directories of Web content to include. The first list of exclude directories can be expanded to list any directory that the archive should explicitly not include the content of when building the WAR file. The WAR file will automatically create a WEB-INF directory. This WEB-INF directory is where the Deployment Descriptor is stored. Only the Web container has access to files in the WEB-INF directory. You can choose to include additional content from the WEB-INF directory other than just the Deployment Descriptor (web.xml). You can also create additional directories under the WEB-INF directory. Placing resources, HTML documents, and even JavaServer Pages in the WEB-INF directory hides this content from external access. Only servlets and JavaServer Pages can request content from the WEB-INF directory by using the forward and include functionality. If you do wish to include such content in the generated WAR, be sure to select "Include regular content in WEB-INF and subdirectories."

**Classes**. The output directory of the project is where candidate classes are chosen to include in the classes directory of the WAR. These classes will actually be stored in the WEB-INF/classes directory. You can choose to include all of the classes and resources or to include only the specified list of classes and resources. If you choose to include only the specified classes, JBuilder can check to make sure that all dependent classes are included as well. You can add individual classes or entire packages of classes to the specified classes and resources list.

**Dependencies**. Each project also has a list of required libraries. These required libraries can be added to the WEB-INF/lib directory of the WAR. You can choose to always include the dependent libraries or to never include the dependent libraries on an individual basis. To control the size of the WAR file, you may consider including the classes that are actually used. This is not the only way to add classes to the classpath of the Web container. You can also modify the classpath of the Web container by modifying the dependent libraries for the server's configuration from the Tools menu, or you can elect to make the project's output path available to the Web container from the server settings of the Runtime configuration properties for the server you have selected.

**Manifest**. All archives can elect to include a Manifest file listing the contents of the archive. You can choose to maintain the manifest file yourself, or you can have JBuilder generate one for you each time the Web archive is built.

**Deployment**. Not all servers support the ability to deploy Web archives from JBuilder to a target server running somewhere on the attached network. If the server that has been selected does support the ability to deploy Web archives, then the particular settings that enable JBuilder to deploy are configured on the Deployment tab of the Web Archives Properties dialog. JBuilder does not actually know how to deploy per se; what JBuilder actually does is access the target server's deployment tool and pass in the necessary project-related information including the location and name of the Web archive that is to be deployed.

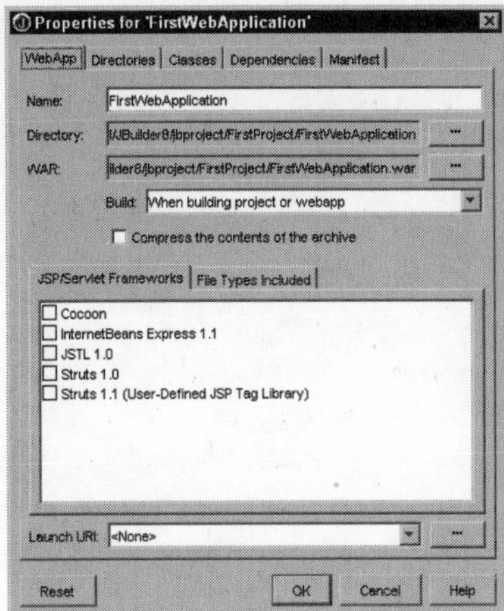


**Figure 15.12** Web application properties.

# EJB Modules

Before you create a new EJB module (see Figure 15.13), you may want to check to be sure that the server that you selected in the Server tab of the Project Properties dialog is capable of supporting EJB development. A project must first have an EJB module if you plan on developing EJBs. There are two types of EJB modules to choose from: EJB 1.1-compliant modules and EJB 2.0-compliant modules. EJB modules contain the build information that JBuilder uses to create the EJB Java Archive, including the Deployment Descriptor file. When working with EJB modules, the vendor-specific deployment descriptor will be added to the META-INF directory. Each application server has its own compiler for the generated stubs and skeletons, as well as a verifier that is used to ensure that the information in the Deployment Descriptor is correct. You can configure the Web module to evoke or not to evoke these utilities from within the given Web Modules properties. It is also possible to configure the server-specific deployment configuration for each EJB module.

**Name**. Unlike the name of the Web application, the name has no effect on the running status or name of the EJBs. The name is used only to distinguish one EJB module in a given project from another.

**Format**. Originally, JBuilder would save project and EJB modules in a binary file format. JBuilder has since changed to using an XML file format for the project and EJB modules it creates and manages. You can still elect to create a binary file by selecting binary instead of XML. It is recommended that you use XML.

**Version**. Here you will choose between a 1.1- or a 2.0-compliant EJB module. If you choose 1.1, then you will use the EJB wizards located on the Enterprise tab of the Object Gallery to create your EJBs. If you choose 2.0, you will use the EJB Designer to create your EJBs.

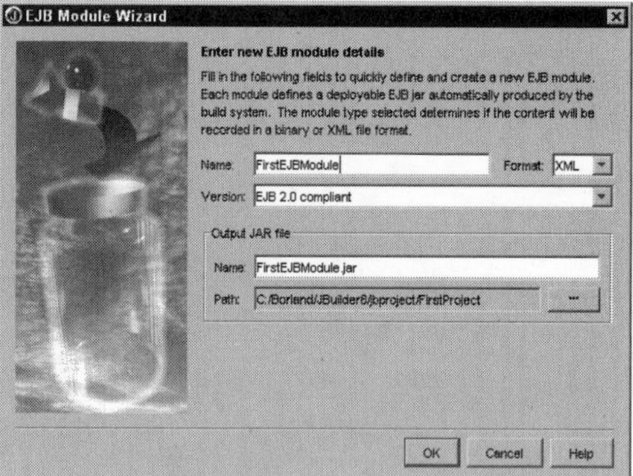


**Figure 15.13** EJB Module wizard.

**Output JAR file Name.** The main task of the EJB module is to create and manage the contents of the EJB Archive that will be deployed to a target application server. The name of the EJB module is not important; just make sure that it is not the same name used by another EJB module or Java Archive already being managed by the project.

**Output JAR file Path.** You can specify the location to which JBuilder will generate the completed EJB archive. Some developers like to specify the location that the target application server will use to deploy the EJB Archive from.

## EJB Modules from Existing Deployment Descriptors

If you already have developed a collection of EJBs and would like to continue development with JBuilder, you can create a project and add a new EJB module to that project using the existing Deployment Descriptor files that you have already created. This wizard (see Figure 15.14) does make the assumption that the Deployment Descriptor file ejb-jar.xml is located in a directory named META-INF and that this directory is located in the source directory. Set the following when using this wizard:

**Directory.** Set to the directory where the ejb-jar.xml file is located. The wizard will proceed to look for Deployment Descriptor files and will try to identify the parent directory as the root directory that the source code is located within.

**Identified EJB Descriptors.** A list of Deployment Descriptors that the wizard has located will be displayed.

**Identified Root Source.** Once the root source is identified, you will have the option of adding this directory to the list of source paths on the Project Properties Paths tab.

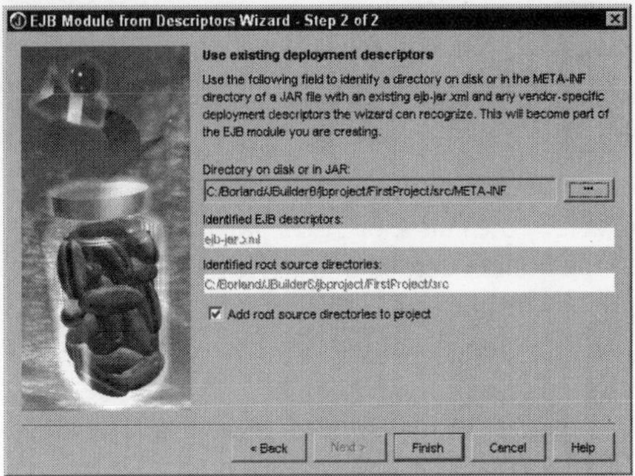


**Figure 15.14** Using existing deployment descriptors.

## EJB Module Properties

To access the properties of an EJB module, right-mouse click on the EJB module in the Project pane and select Properties (see Figure 15.15). For the most part, the properties are very much the same for all servers that are capable of managing EJBs. For that matter, there are considerable similarities with the properties of the Web application as well. The major difference between the Web application and the EJB module's properties actually has more to do with the layout of the Web and EJB archive file structures. When you open the EJB Modules properties, you will notice the following tabs:

**Build.** EJB modules not only help JBuilder projects manage EJB components, EJB modules also are responsible for managing the instructions that JBuilder's build system will use in the creation of the EJB archive. This includes basic information such as the name and location of the archive to be generated as well as the content that is to be added to the archive as well. The Build tab of the EJB module's Properties lists the Deployment Descriptor files that are to be copied into the META-INF directory of the EJB archive when it is created. The actual Deployment Descriptor files are embedded in the .ejbgrpx file. If you have an existing Deployment Descriptor file that you wish to use, you can simply add that file to the descriptors already in the module. This action will replace the descriptor files that are already embedded in the .ejbgrpx file. You can have JBuilder make a copy of these files each time the EJB archive is built by specifying a directory to which the descriptor files should be copied. Certain servers will also have their own tab on the EJB module's Build tab to specify how the stub files are to be created and what parameters are to be passed into the compiler that generates the stub files.

**Content.** Almost exactly the same as the Web application's Properties classes tab, the Content tab of the EJB module's Properties determines which classes are to be included in the EJB archive that is generated. EJB archives more closely resemble Java Archives in that the root of the archive is also the root of the classpath for the archive. Web archives have two separate classpaths located under the WEB-INF directory located in the classes and lib subdirectories. EJB archives have only one classpath, and that is the root of the archive itself; that is why EJB archives contain individual classes.

**Dependencies.** When a Required Library listed on the Dependencies tab of the EJB module's Properties dialog is selected, the classes in that particular library will be copied into the EJB archive. This means that each individual class will be copied, not the .jar file associated with the library, as is the case with Web applications. Web applications will copy all .jar files into the Web archive's WEB-INF/lib directory, but no such directory exists in the EJB archive. Therefore JBuilder will copy the individual classes into the EJB archive when Include all is choosen.

**Manifest.** All archives can elect to include a Manifest file listing the contents of the archive. You can choose to maintain the Manifest file yourself, or you can have JBuilder generate one for you each time the EJB archive is built.

**Deployment.** Not all servers support the ability to deploy EJB archives from JBuilder to a target server running somewhere on the attached network. If the server that has been selected does support the ability to deploy EJB archives, then the particular settings that enable JBuilder to deploy are configured on the Deployment tab of the EJB module's Properties. JBuilder does not actually know how to deploy per se; what JBuilder actually does is access the target server's deployment tool and pass in the necessary project-related information including the location and name of the EJB archive that is to be deployed.

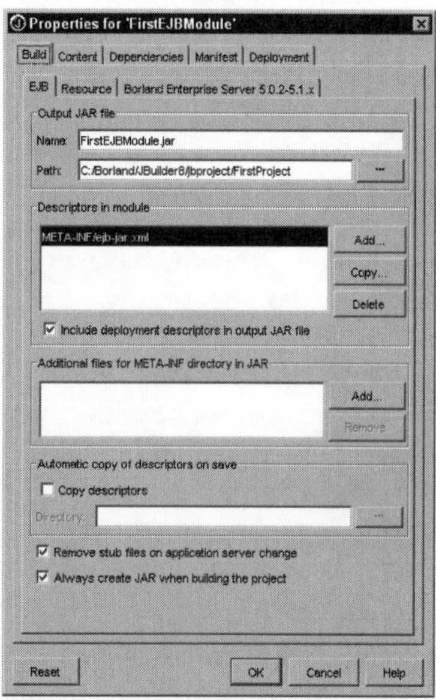


**Figure 15.15** EJB module properties.

## Enterprise Archives

Web as well as EJB archives can all be contained within one Enterprise Archive (EAR) file. If a project has multiple EJB modules and multiple Web applications, a single Enterprise Archive can be created that will combine all of the files in one easily deployable archive. Like Web applications and EJB modules, it is also possible to configure the server-specific deployment configuration for each Enterprise Archive. To create a new Enterprise Archive, select the EAR wizard from the Object Gallery's Enterprise tab. The wizard will walk you through a series of steps asking which existing modules and resources already managed by the project are to be included in the Enterprise Archive. These settings are accessible after the wizard has completed by accessing the Enterprise Archive's properties (see Figure 15.16) in the same manner that the Web application and the EJB module's properties are accessed. When you open the Enterprise Archives properties, you will notice the following tabs:

**Build.** This specifies the name and location of the Enterprise Archive that is to be generated as well as the name of the Enterprise Archive node in the Project pane. The Enterprise Archive also has a Deployment Descriptor file application.xml that defines the modules that are contained within the archive and specifies what type they are.

**EJBs.** This specifies the EJB archive files that are to be included. The first tab will list all of the EJB modules in the project. Because each EJB module can manage only one EJB archive, selecting a module is the same as selecting the archive that the module manages. You can also include any external EJB archives that are not associated with the current project.

**Connectors.** Resource Adapter Archives (RARs) can also be added to the Enterprise Archive. Resource adapters are components that comply with J2EE's Connector specification. The J2EE Connector architecture defines the manner in which the components of a J2EE system, namely EJBs, can communicate with other non–J2EE-based systems that may already exist.

**AppClients.** Similar in concept to Web Start clients, application clients are deployable client application archives. Application clients are archives that contain client applications that run in their own Java virtual machines and start with their own main() methods. Application client archives also have their own Deployment Descriptor files typically named application-client.xml. These Deployment Descriptors are similar to the Deployment Descriptors of Web archives and EJB archives in that they contain information that the application container will use to provide access to external components, most likely EJBs running inside EJB containers. A server can deploy these application client archives, but exactly how they are required to deploy such archives is not clear. The technology that exists that is most closely related to such a task is the Web Start technology. Web Start is a way to deploy Java Archives containing applications over the Web.

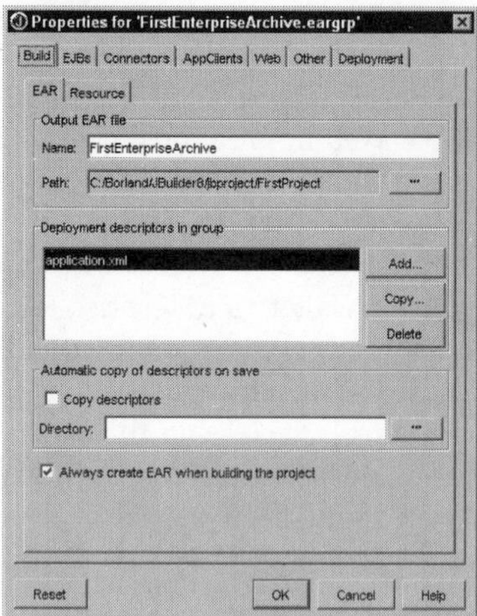


**Figure 15.16** Enterprise Archive properties.

**Web.** Web applications that are part of the project will display, and you can choose which Web application's Web archives are to be included in the Enterprise Archive. You can also select Web archives that are not part of the project and add them to the Enterprise Archive as well.

**Other.** Just about any additional file can be added to the Enterprise Archive including other Java Archives and even native libraries and documentation.

**Deployment.** Not all servers support the ability to deploy Enterprise Archives from JBuilder to a target server running somewhere on the attached network. If the server that has been selected does support the ability to deploy Enterprise Archives, then the particular settings that enable JBuilder to deploy are configured on the Deployment tab of the Enterprise Archive Properties dialog. JBuilder does not actually know how to deploy per se; what JBuilder actually does is access the target server's deployment tool and pass in the necessary project-related information including the location and name of the Enterprise Archive that is to be deployed.

# Deploying the Finished Product

Once JBuilder is configured properly for the server you are developing with the project and is set up to utilize the services that the server provides properly, and you have added several Web applications, EJB modules, and Enterprise Archives to your project, it is time to develop the various J2EE components. The following chapters outline how to develop these components. Once you have finished a particular stage of development, you will undoubtedly want to run or deploy your work into the target server's environment for testing. There is a specific type of Runtime configuration that exists that was specifically designed to select and configure the use of the target server as well as the services that the target server has to offer.

## Runtime Configurations for Servers

The part of JBuilder's Project Properties dialog that is responsible for managing the launch commands for each server is located on the Run tab. You can either open the Project Properties and select the Run tab, or you can directly access the Runtime configurations from the Run menu's configurations (see Figure 15.17). The type of Runtime configuration this chapter is going to focus on is "Server."

### *Controlling the Server*

The settings that are used to control how the server is started come from the Project Properties Server tab, which in turn comes from the server configuration. This three-layer approach narrows the options and configurations until you get to the specific Runtime configuration used to launch the server. The following three categories exist that are specific to the server:

**Command Line.** JBuilder uses Runtime configurations to control the way in which new processes are launched. The VM and server parameters come from the server configuration. You can also elect to make the project's output path and Required Libraries classpaths part of the classpath of the command line that is used to launch the server. This is an all-or-none configuration. Either all Required Libraries are to be added to the server's classpath, or none are added.

**Libraries.** The project's Required Libraries can alternatively be deployed to the container that the Web, EJB, or Enterprise Archives are also being deployed to. Choosing between making all Required Libraries part of the server's classpath and deploying individual Required Libraries will most definitely have an impact on how the server will locate and load a Library's classes. In most servers, the container has its own classloader; in some cases, each deployed archive has its own dedicated classloader assigned to it. So, depending on the server, how and where you deploy dependent libraries will have an effect on the container's ability to locate and find the classes it needs. The third option is, of course, to include the Required Library in the archive that is being deployed. This is typically configured on the Dependencies tab of each archive's properties.

**Archives.** Each project can manage several archives. Each archive can be a different type, or they can all be of the same type. You can choose which archive to deploy. Multiple Runtime configurations can be created, each one deploying a separate archive to a different container.

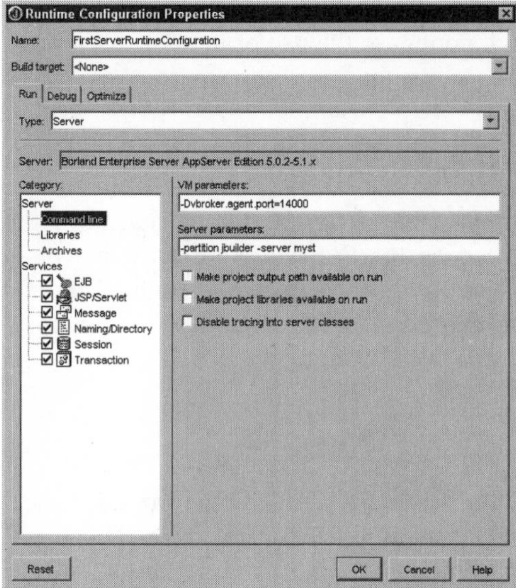


**Figure 15.17** Runtime Configuration Properties dialog.

### *Selecting the Services*

In the server configuration and in the Project Properties dialog, you were configuring the availability of the various services of a given server. In the Runtime configuration for a server, you are actually instructing the server on exactly which services to start and which services not to start. JBuilder will pass in the necessary options to the server to control which service is started depending on which available services are checked.

## Deploy Options

For certain servers, there will be an additional menu that is available when you right-mouse click on the various enterprise nodes in the Project pane. This option is titled "Deploy Options." It is assumed that, by accessing these deploy options, the target server as defined in the deployment settings of the Web application's, EJB module's, or Enterprise Archive's properties is already running. If the archive has not been deployed yet, you can select to deploy the archive. Otherwise, you can either redeploy the archive or undeploy the archive. If you are not exactly sure which archives have been deployed, you can choose to list the deployed archives.

## Enterprise Deployment

Once the application has been developed, tested, and optimized, it is time to deploy the finished product. From the Tools menu, select Enterprise Deployment to start the server-specific deployment tool. The server selected determines which deployment tool to evoke. If the tool supports it, the generated Web application WAR files, EJB module JAR files, and Enterprise Archive EAR files will be passed in to the deployment tool.

## Summary

In this chapter we saw how JBuilder manages the components of J2EE applications at three different layers: from the server-end enterprise configuration, to a project's properties and the definition of Web Applications and EJB Archives managed by a project, to the specific Runtime configurations that control how the J2EE server is to execute the application. In the forthcoming chapters, we will focus on how to develop these components.

CHAPTER

16

# Web Enablement with Servlets

Delivering dynamic content over the Web to avoid the pains of software distribution is a driving force behind developers' use of Java technologies like servlets to develop Web-based systems. The Internet Engineering Task Force (IETF) manages while the World Wide Web Consortium (W3C) formally recognizes the Hyper Text Transfer Protocol (HTTP) as the standard for Web-based communications. Sun Microsystems helped form the Java Community Process (JCP) that develops and revises Java technology specifications, reference implementations, and technology compatibility kits. Java Specification Request (JSR) 154, Java Servlet 2.4 Specification, and its predecessors define the objectification of Hyper Text Transfer Protocol (HTTP) in Java. The Apache Software Foundation manages the Jakarta Project, which develops and maintains Apache Tomcat. Apache Tomcat is the official reference implementation for the Java Servlet and Java Server Pages technologies. JBuilder ships with two versions of Apache Tomcat; version 3.3.1 supports the Servlet 2.2 and the JSP 1.1 APIs, and version 4.0.4 supports Servlet 2.3 and JSP 1.2 APIs.

This chapter covers the following topics:

**Objectifying client requests and server responses.** Taking the raw set of characters that make up an incoming HTTP request, the servlet specification defines how to transform this request into a Java object. Once the request is in object form, servlet programmers can develop business and data access logic to create dynamic content on the Web. There are three basic types of servlets to choose from. The most common is the Standard Servlet.

**Creating a new Standard Servlet.** Servlets are the backbone of dynamic Web delivered-content in Java. This section will go over the steps necessary to create servlets in JBuilder and add them to a Web application. In addition, various Deployment Descriptor settings will also be covered.

**Creating a Filter Servlet.** Filter Servlets are used to perform specific tasks for well-defined URL request patterns. This section walks through the steps of creating a Filter Servlet that helps explain the subtle differences between Standard and Filter Servlets.

**Using DataSources.** Accessing a database is key to dynamic content development with servlets. This section outlines the steps necessary to add a DataSource to the Deployment Descriptor and bind that DataSource to Tomcat's naming service. Three different techniques for adding a JDBC driver to the Web container's classpath are also discussed.

## Objectifying Client Requests and Server Responses

The Hyper Text Transfer Protocol (HTTP), or RFC 2616, defines the structure of data and its meta data for stateless communication between a client (or requestor) and a server (or responder). Each message that a client (or Web browser) sends to a server (or Web server) is called a *request*. This request is primarily composed of a message header and a message body. The message header specifies the Uniform Resource Identifier (URI), request method type, and version. Using the TCP Monitor located on the Tools menu (see Figure 16.1), you can review the request and response from any Web browser to any Web server.

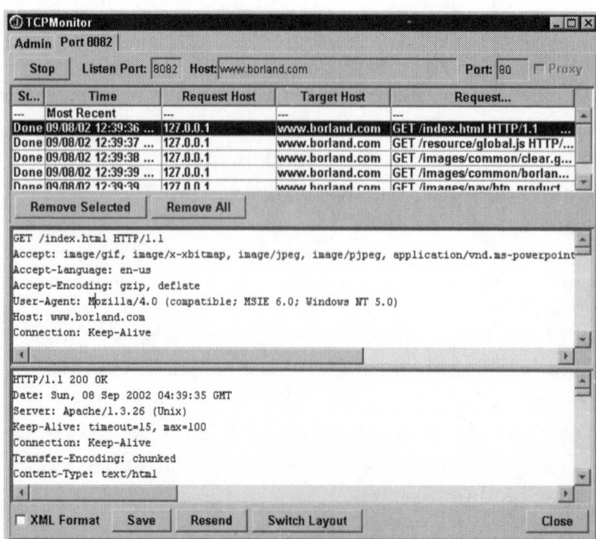


**Figure 16.1** Monitoring HTTP requests.

Launch the TCP Monitor and stop listening to port 8082. Set the host to the name of any Web server (for this example, we use www.borland.com), set the port to the default HTTP port 80, and start listening to port 8082 once again. The TCP Monitor will actually act as a proxy to www.borland.com. Any request for localhost:8082 will actually proxy to www.borland.com. Use any Web browser and browse to http://localhost:8082/index.html. In this example, a typical Web browser may send the following HTTP request to a Web server:

```
GET /index.html HTTP/1.1
Accept: image/gif, image/x-xbitmap, image/jpeg, image/pjpeg,
application/vnd.ms-powerpoint, application/vnd.ms-excel,
application/msword, */*
Accept-Language: en-us
Accept-Encoding: gzip, deflate
User-Agent: Mozilla/4.0 (compatible; MSIE 6.0; Windows NT 5.0)
Host: www.borland.com
Connection: Keep-Alive
```

A browser may, in fact, display http://www.borland.com/index.html as the Web address or Uniform Resource Locator (URL), but the browser actually used "www" as the host name, borland.com as the domain, and the default HTTP port 80 to connect to the Web server and send the formatted HTTP request. The URI in this example would be /index.html, the request method is GET, and the version is HTTP:/1.1. Once the Web server receives this GET request method from the Web browser, it will determine whether the URI is valid and respond to the Web browser by sending the following HTTP response header:

```
HTTP/1.1 200 OK
Date: Sat, 07 Sep 2002 18:26:26 GMT
Server: Apache/1.3.26 (Unix)
Keep-Alive: timeout=15, max=100
Connection: Keep-Alive
Transfer-Encoding: chunked
Content-Type: text/html
```

An HTTP response is also made up of a message header and a message body. The message header contains the version, a status message, and content type. In this example, the version is HTTP/1.1, the status is 200 OK, and the content type is text/html. Following this response header would be the message body content, or more specifically, the HTML page titled index.html. Writing a basic Web server is as simple as listening to a TCP/IP port and parsing through streams of characters, according to the HTTP specification.

The Java Servlet API primarily defines the object-oriented form of the HTTP protocol in the Java language. This technology provides the necessary framework to allow developers to extend the static capabilities of Web servers and provide dynamic content to its clients. A Java-enabled, dynamic Web server will typically have a *Servlet Engine*, also called the Servlet's container or a Web container (the terminology is defined in the J2EE spec and can be used to describe a process that understands HTTP and hosts servlets or JSP). This container is responsible for handling all network activity as well as creating the object-oriented equivalent of an HTTP Request and Response objects. The container is also responsible for managing the lifecycle of the servlet.

When an HTTP request comes into a Web server, a servlet — specifically an extension of javax.servlet.http.HttpServlet — decides what to do with the request, and something needs to prepare an HTTP response to send back to the client or Web browser. The HttpServlet contains all of the information contained in the HTTP request and is responsible for creating all of the information and content of the HTTP response. When the Web container creates an instance of an HttpServlet, the Web container has already created an instance of an HttpServletRequest object with all of the information that the client has sent to the server as well as an empty HttpServletResponse object that will be populated and sent back to the client.

Some Web servers are responsible for providing access to HTML documents and other information that never change. This content that does not change is referred to as static content. With static-based Web servers, the rule of thumb is if the Web page or image exists, send a copy back to the client. Each request that comes in can produce one and only one response each and every time. On the other hand, developers also want to be able to provide dynamic content. In this case, each request that comes to a Web server can produce from one to many different responses. With dynamic base Web servers, developers typically write code or business logic that determines what to do with the information in an incoming request and how to construct the appropriate response. This is the responsibility of the servlet. A Standard Servlet is an extension of HttpServlet that implements one of the doGet(), doPost(), doPut(), or doDelete() request methods. It is not a Listener or a Filter.

## Creating a New Standard Servlet

Before you start creating servlets, you must first have created a project and added a Web application to that project. If you do not add a Web application to the project, a default Web application will be created for you. To create a new Standard Servlet in JBuilder, open the Object Gallery, go to the Web tab, select the Servlet wizard, and click the OK button. A Standard Servlet is the most common type of servlet, and it implements at least one of the following HTTP request methods: GET, POST, PUT, or DELETE. In addition to Standard Servlets, there are also Filter and Listener Servlets. The first step (see Figure 16.2) of the Servlet wizard is the same for all three types of servlets. Once you select a Standard, Filter, or Listener Servlet, the number of subsequent steps will change. Standard Servlets can have a total of five steps, whereas Filter and Listener Servlets have only three steps. The first step is as follows:

**Package and class name.** Servlets are Java classes and can exist in any package. It used to be that the package and class name also affected the URI of the servlet itself, but this is no longer the case. You can create a servlet with any class name and place it within any package while accessing it from a completely independent URI. The Web container is responsible for managing the relationship between a servlet's URI and its class name. This information is configured in the Deployment Descriptor or web.xml file located in the WEB-INF directory of the Web archive and is set when you enter the WebApp details while creating the servlet.

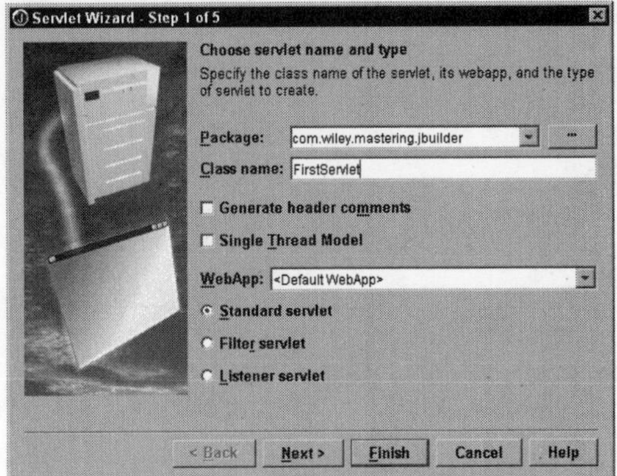


**Figure 16.2** Choose servlet name and type.

**Generate header comments.** Not to be confused with the HTTP header, selecting this option will utilize the project properties for title, description, company, author, and version. You can edit these values on the General tab of the Project Properties using the following code. Selecting this option will produce the following header comments in the generated source code:

```
/**
 * <p>Title: </p>
 * <p>Description: </p>
 * <p>Copyright: Copyright (c) 2002</p>
 * <p>Company: </p>
 * @author unascribed
 * @version 1.0
 */
```

**Single Thread Model.** If selected, the generated servlet class will implement the javax.servlet.SingleThreadModel interface. This interface has no methods, but it ensures that only one thread will ever access a servlet's service method at the same time. This will guarantee that each servlet will handle only one request at a time. Selecting this option will generate the necessary implementation of the SingleThreadModel interface as follows:

```
public class FirstServlet extends HttpServlet implements
SingleThreadModel {
```

**WebApp.** A Web application is a managed node of a JBuilder project that manages the content of a Web site and generates a Web archive. If no Web application exists, a default Web application will be generated. If a JBuilder project has multiple Web applications, you can select to which Web application this new servlet was to be added. Each Web application also manages the Deployment Descriptor for the Web archive. The Deployment Descriptor contains information about the content of a Web archive. The Deployment Descriptor also has information about the Web archive that the Web container needs to control the behavior and access to the various contents within a Web archive.

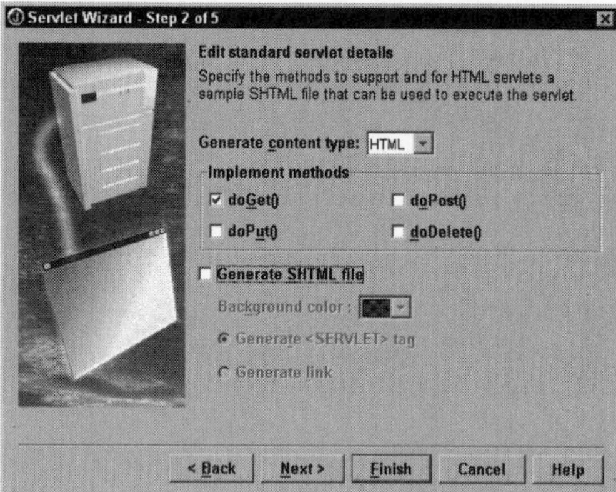


**Figure 16.3** Edit standard servlet details.

## Content Types and Response Message Body

A servlet's response will be in HTTP format and will contain content. The format of this content can come in almost any form. As shown in Figure 16.3, there are standard media types in which the body of a response will be formatted. Clients need to know what type of media they are receiving inside a given server's response message body. The content type of the response message header tells the requesting client what type of media is being delivered.

Each media type can also be further classified by subtype. For instance, a servlet may send text data to a client browser, and this text data may be HTML. Therefore, the content-type would be text/html. For the servlet class being generated, a private static final String variable named CONTENT_TYPE will be created as a data member of the servlet, and it will be set to the value specified here. There are four values to choose from — HTML, XHTML, WML, and XML — when selecting which type of content to generate. For the XML values, an additional static final String variable named DOC_TYPE will be created as a data member of the servlet. This DOC_TYPE element will be used to specify what kind of HTML is being used in the message body. Depending on which option you select, the following declarations will be generated:

```
//HTML set as Generate Content Type
private static final String CONTENT_TYPE = "text/html";

//XHTML set as Generate Content Type
private static final String CONTENT_TYPE = "text/html";
private static final String DOC_TYPE = "<!DOCTYPE html PUBLIC \"-
//W3C//DTD XHTML 1.0 Strict//EN\"\n
\"http://www.w3.org/TR/xhtml1/DTD/xhtml1-strict.dtd\">";

//WML set as Generate Content Type
private static final String CONTENT_TYPE = "text/vnd.wap.wml";
```

```
private static final String DOC_TYPE = "<!DOCTYPE wml PUBLIC \"-
//WAPFORUM//DTD WML 1.2//EN\"\n
\"http://www.wapforum.org/DTD/wml12.dtd\">";

//XML set as Generate Content Type
private static final String CONTENT_TYPE = "text/xml";
/**@todo set DTD*/
private static final String DOC_TYPE = null;
```

This CONTENT_TYPE will be used to set the Response object's content type attribute in the implemented response method's message body. You set the content type in the response object as follows:

```
response.setContentType(CONTENT_TYPE);
```

Because the message body of an HTTP response is always character-based, using java.io.PrintWriter makes sense. The PrintWriter is an attribute of the response attribute of the servlet:

```
out.println("<?xml version=\"1.0\"?>");

out.println(DOC_TYPE);
```

It is also possible to stream binary data back to a requesting client by getting the ServletResponse.getOutputStream() and writing to it. If you are creating a servlet for this purpose, you will have to generate the preceding code and delete it after the wizard is finished.

## Request Methods of a Servlet

Here is where you decide which request methods of the HttpServlet to override. HTTP has a limited set of request methods: GET, POST, DELETE, PUT, HEAD, OPTIONS, and TRACE. Each of these methods can evoke a completely different behavior for a given URI. The URI and the request method determine which servlet is created and which method of the servlet is evoked. The URI typically determines which servlet is created, and the request method determines which method of the servlet is evoked.

HTTP GET is implemented in an HttpServlet's doGet() method. The purpose of this method is to retrieve whatever information is associated with the request URI. This is one of the two most common request methods utilized by Web servers. Some refer to the following information at the end of the address or URL as a query string:

```
http://localhost:8080/<webapp-name>/<servlet-
name>?name1=value1&name2=value2&name3=value3
```

Typically this information at the end of the URL is formatted as a series of name-equals-value pairings separated by ampersands. The first pair is usually separated from the URL's absolute path by a question mark.

HTTP POST is implemented in a HttpServlet's doPost() method. The second of the two most commonly used request methods, the POST method is typically used within an HTML's form as shown here:

```
<form method=POST action="http://localhost:8080/<webapp-name>/<servlet-
name>">
<input TYPE="text"     NAME="name1"   VALUE="value1">
<input TYPE="hidden"   NAME="name2"   VALUE="value2">
<input TYPE="password" NAME="name3"   VALUE="value3">
<input TYPE="submit"   NAME="request">
</form>
```

This is the proposed method to use when sending data to the server for processing. When using HTML forms, the Web browser will send the data as part of the HTTP message body, not as part of the query string at the end of the URL.

HTTP DELETE is implemented in an HttpServlet's doDelete() method, and HTTP PUT is implemented in a HttpServlet's doPut() method. PUT is generally a request to store the message body at the location specified by the URI. DELETE is generally a request to delete any content located at the location specified by the URI. Think of these two methods as a means to use an HTTP server as a sort of FTP server, putting and deleting content. A popular extension of these HTTP request methods is WebDAV, used for developing Web-based version control systems.

HTTP HEAD is implemented in an HttpServlet's doHead() method. HEAD should be treated the same way that GET is treated, except HEAD will not return any content; only the headers are to be returned. The default behavior implemented in the HttpServlet's doHead() method is compliant with the HTTP RFC 2616, and therefore it is not necessary to override.

HTTP OPTIONS is implemented in an HttpServlet's doOptions() method. OPTIONS should respond with usage information about the URI. This may include a listing of implemented request methods and expected data. The default behavior implemented in the HttpServlet's doOptions() method is compliant with the HTTP RFC 2616, and therefore it is not necessary to override.

HTTP TRACE is implemented in an HttpServlet's doTrace() method. The content type of the message header of a response to a TRACE request method will be message/http, and the message body of the response to a TRACE request method will be an exact copy of the HTTP request that was sent to the server. The default behavior implemented in the HttpServlet's doTrace() method is compliant with the HTTP RFC 2616, and therefore it is not necessary to override. The HttpServlet's doTrace() method would send the following as a response:

```
HTTP/1.1 200 OK
Content-Type: message/http
Content-Length: 334
Date: Mon, 09 Sep 2002 01:06:23 GMT
Server: Apache Tomcat/4.0.3 (HTTP/1.1 Connector)


** client: data from 127.0.0.1:8080 (334 bytes)
TRACE /firstservlet HTTP/1.1
```

```
accept: image/gif, image/x-xbitmap, image/jpeg, image/pjpeg,
application/vnd.ms-powerpoint, application/vnd.ms-excel,
application/msword, */*
accept-language: en-us
accept-encoding: gzip, deflate
user-agent: Mozilla/4.0 (compatible; MSIE 6.0; Windows NT 5.0)
host: localhost
connection: Keep-Alive
```

## SHTML and Server-Side Includes

Similar to the <jsp:include> tag used in Java Server Pages, servlet developers can use SHTML to replace <servlet> tags within a given HTML document with the body of the response from a servlet. This technology is also referred to as server-side includes because you are technically instructing the Web server to replace the <servlet> tag with dynamic content. Depending on which request methods are selected, the options will be different. If the doGet() method is selected and the option to generate a <Servlet> tag is selected, all requests for *.SHTML are handled by the com.borland.jbuilder.webserverglue.shtml.ShtmlLoaderEcho servlet, and the webserverglue.jar file is added to the WAR files WEB-INF/lib directory. The Deployment Descriptor for the Web application is also modified so that all requests for documents ending in .shtml will be mapped to the ShtmlLoaderEcho servlet as follows:

```
<servlet>
  <servlet-name>servlet-shtml</servlet-name>
  <servlet-
class>com.borland.jbuilder.webserverglue.shtml.ShtmlLoaderEcho</servlet-
class>
</servlet>
<servlet-mapping>
  <servlet-name>servlet-shtml</servlet-name>
  <url-pattern>*.shtml</url-pattern>
</servlet-mapping>
```

Only selecting the doGet() method along with the <servlet> tag will produce the desired result of inserting dynamic content within an HTML document. Unlike using <applet> tags, which will execute Java code within the browser, this technique does not allow the developer to execute a servlet's Java code within a Web browser. The resulting HTML code includes the following:

```
<servlet
  codebase=""
  code="com.wiley.mastering.jbuilder.FirstServlet.class"
>
<param name="name1" value="value1" />
<param name="name2" value="value2" />
<param name="name3" value="value3" />
</servlet>
```

Selecting the doPost() method removes the option of generating a <Servlet> tag. Instead, the SHTML page generated will include a <form> tag that will not evoke the servlet until the Submit button is clicked. This will evoke the implemented doPost() method:

```
<form action="/firstservlet" method="post">
<p>param  <input type="text" name="name1" value="value1"></p>
<p>param  <input type="text" name="name2" value="value2"></p>
<p>param  <input type="text" name="name3" value="value3"></p>
<p>press Submit to post to servlet ThirdServlet</p>
<p><input type="submit" name="Submit" value="Submit">
<input type="reset" value="Reset"></p>
</form>
```

If you opt to select Generate link instead, the outcome is not quite the same. The resulting HTML page will contain a <a href> tag, which will not evoke the servlet until the link is clicked. This will evoke the implemented doGet() method:

```
<a href="/firstservlet">Click here to call Servlet: FirstServlet</a>
```

## URL Mapping

Rather than specify the servlet's fully qualified class name in the URI, the Web container maintains a list of names for the servlets in each Web archive. The Deployment Descriptor contains the mapping between the servlet class and the URL mapping. Each servlet will be managed by a particular name (see Figure 16.4), and each servlet's name will map to a specified URL. This value can be modified in the Web application's Deployment Descriptor's properties for servlets as follows:

```
<servlet>
  <servlet-name>firstservlet</servlet-name>
  <servlet-class>com.wiley.mastering.jbuilder.FirstServlet</servlet-
class>
</servlet>
<servlet-mapping>
  <servlet-name>firstservlet</servlet-name>
  <url-pattern>/firstservlet</url-pattern>
</servlet-mapping>
```

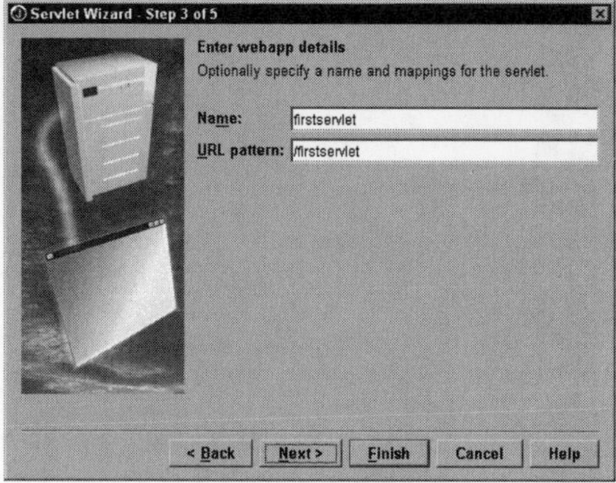


**Figure 16.4** Enter webapp details.

# Accessing a Request's Incoming Parameters

As noted in the GET and POST request methods, data can be sent from the client to the server. This data is part of the Request object's attributes and is accessible using the getParameter(), getParameterNames(), getParameterValues(), and getParameterMap() methods. If you already know that certain data will be sent to the servlet for processing, you can specify the name and data type of that information here (see Figure 16.5). The name entered is to be used in the <FORM> element (such as an input tag, not the form tag itself) of the HTML file or in the GET query string. JBuilder will use this value when generating the <SERVLET> tag of the SHTML file. JBuilder does not generate a sample HTML file with <FORM> tags for servlets:

```
<servlet
  codebase=""
  code="com.wiley.mastering.jbuilder.FirstServlet.class"
>
<param name="name1" value="value1" />
</servlet>
```

This setting will be used as the pass-in value for accessing the information using the request object's getParameter() method. If the value is not set, a default value can be assigned using the following code:

```
//some comment
String variable1 = request.getParameter("name1");
if (variable1 == null) {
  variable1 = "value1";
}
```

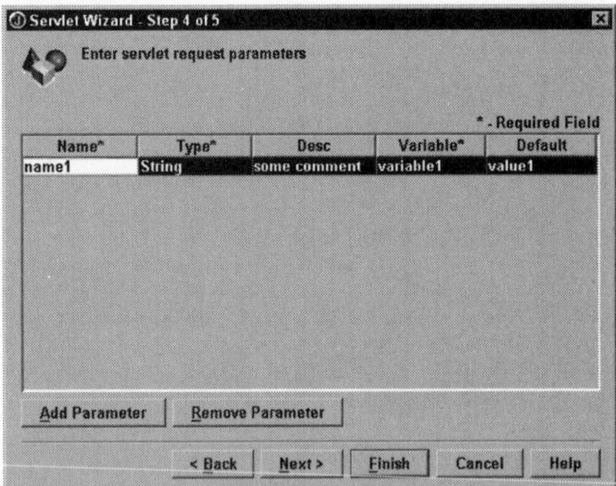


**Figure 16.5** Enter servlet request parameters.

Runtime configurations are used to set up and run, debug, and optimize the Java applications created in JBuilder. The Standard Servlet wizard can automatically create a Runtime configuration for the Standard Servlet being created (see Figure 16.6). When this option is selected, a server will be selected as the run type, and the server will be set to the server that was selected for the project.

## Modifying a Standard Servlet's Deployment Descriptor Properties

The Standard Servlet wizard makes all of the initial entries into the Deployment Descriptor that are necessary for a given servlet. Additional modifications can be made using the Deployment Descriptor editor for servlets (see Figure 16.7).

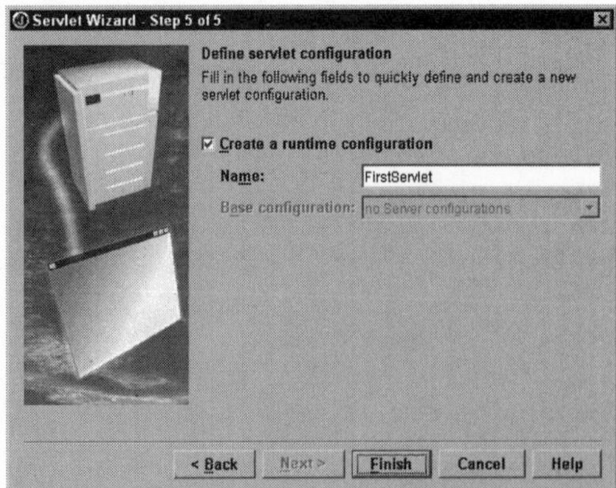


**Figure 16.6** Define servlet configuration.

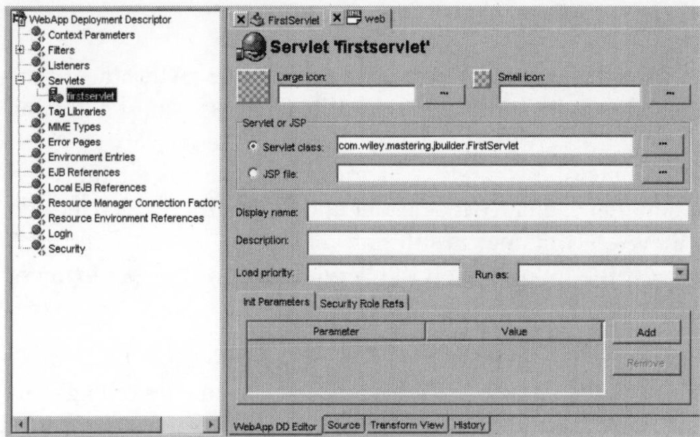


**Figure 16.7** Deployment Descriptor servlet configuration.

To access the Deployment Descriptor editor, double-click on the Web application's web.xml file located under the Deployment Descriptors node in the Project pane. In the Content pane you should notice servlets with a plus sign to the left. Under Servlets, there should be an entry for each Standard Servlet that was added to this Web application using the Servlet wizard. If you click on the Servlets node in the Content pane, you will see a listing of all URL mappings of servlets for the Web application. You can change the URL mapping on this window, but to change the servlet name you must right-mouse click on the Servlet name in the Content pane and choose Rename. You can edit the following on the Servlet view of the Deployment Descriptor:

**Large icon, small icon, display name, and description.** Administration tools and deployment tools can best utilize these self-explanatory fields, much as how JBuilder utilizes similar fields on the Designers Palette for JavaBeans.

**Servlet class.** This is the fully qualified class name of the servlet. This is the servlet class that the Web container will create when the predefined URL pattern is requested. Each named servlet in the Deployment Descriptor has a predefined URL pattern.

**JSP file.** A Web container can maintain a URL mapping for either a servlet or a JSP. If this node were created for a JSP page, the name of the JSP page would be entered here.

**Load priority.** If a positive integer value is set, the Web container should create and initialize the servlet at startup rather than when a servlet is first accessed. The startup order will be determined by the value entered. Servlets with lower values will load first. If two servlets have the exact same value, it is at the Web Container's discretion which servlet is loaded first.

**Run as.** When using security roles, a given servlet can run with the authorities of a given role.

## The Servlet Lifecycle

The Web container manages the lifecycle of the servlet. It first creates an instance of the Servlet class and then calls that servlet's init() method. Whenever a request matching the mapped URL for the servlet is received by the Web container, the servlet's service() method is called. The service() method is rarely overridden because it is the inherited HttpServlet's implementation that evaluates the header and determines which request method to evoke. When the Web container is shutting down, the servlet's destroy() method is called. You can edit the following on the Servlet view of the Deployment Descriptor:

**Init parameters.** A parameter list can be created when the servlet is initialized. This list of keys and associated values can be accessed at runtime by calling this.getInitParameter(), passing in the string name as a key to retrieve the specified value. Although these parameters can be accessed at any time, it is customary to use them in the init() method of the servlet.

**Security role refs.** If the code in the servlet is already utilizing a role that is not the same name as the role defined in the Deployment Descriptor, this grid can be used to maintain a mapping of servlet role names to Descriptor role names.

## Project Properties and Required Libraries

Depending on which server has been selected in the Project Properties dialog prior to using the Servlet wizard, there will be an addition to your project's Required Libraries.

By right-mouse clicking on the Standard Servlet in the Project pane, you can access properties specific to servlets. The Web Run properties will enable right-mouse click access to the Web Run, Web Debug, and Web Optimize functions from the Project pane. This setting should be automatically set for all servlets that were created using the Servlet wizard.

# Creating a Filter Servlet

Filtering allows the developer to review and even change the contents of the Request object coming in, as well as the Response object before it goes back out. Filters do not typically handle an incoming request and directly respond as a Standard Servlet does. A Filter Servlet is a type of servlet that implements the javax.servlet.Filter() interface that requires an implementation of a doFilter() method. For registered filters within the Web application's Deployment Descriptor, the Web container will call the Filter Servlet's doFilter() method rather than a Standard Servlet's service() method. Similar to the inherited implementation of the HttpServlet's service() method, Filter Servlets have access to the Request and Response objects. The generated doFilter() method will look like this:

```
public void doFilter(ServletRequest request, ServletResponse response,
FilterChain filterChain) {
  try {
    filterChain.doFilter(request, response);
  }
  catch(ServletException sx) {
```

```
      filterConfig.getServletContext().log(sx.getMessage());
    }
    catch(IOException iox) {
      filterConfig.getServletContext().log(iox.getMessage());
    }
  }
```

To create a new Filter Servlet in JBuilder, open the Object Gallery, go to the Web tab, select the Servlet icon, and click the OK button (see Figure 16.8). The Filter Servlet wizard is similar to the Standard Servlet wizard. Because Filter Servlets do not process requests like Standard Servlets, not all the information necessary in the Standard Servlet is required.

The main difference between the Standard and Filter Servlet lies in both how the URL mapping is defined, as well as how it is used. The URL mapping for Standard Servlets is defined on the Enter webapp details page, whereas Filter Servlets use the URL pattern that the Web container defines for all incoming requests that fit a certain pattern. Filter Servlets were not designed to be the only servlet evoked for an incoming request. They were designed to filter through incoming requests, perform some small task, and hand processing over to a Standard Servlet or Java Server Page for final processing. You can also create a Filter Servlet that handles all incoming requests for a particular named servlet already in the Web application.

Like Standard Servlets, rather than specify the Filter Servlet's fully qualified class name in the URI, the Web container maintains a list of names for the servlets in each Web archive. The Deployment Descriptor defines this list. Each servlet will be managed by a particular name, and each servlet's name will map to a specified URL. This name value can be modified in the Web application's Deployment Descriptor's properties for servlets. Each Filter Servlet can be registered to filter all requests to a URL pattern or to filter all requests to a specific servlet:

```
<filter>
  <filter-name>firstfilterservlet</filter-name>
  <filter-class>com.wiley.mastering.jbuilder.firstfilterservlet</filter-
class>
</filter>
```

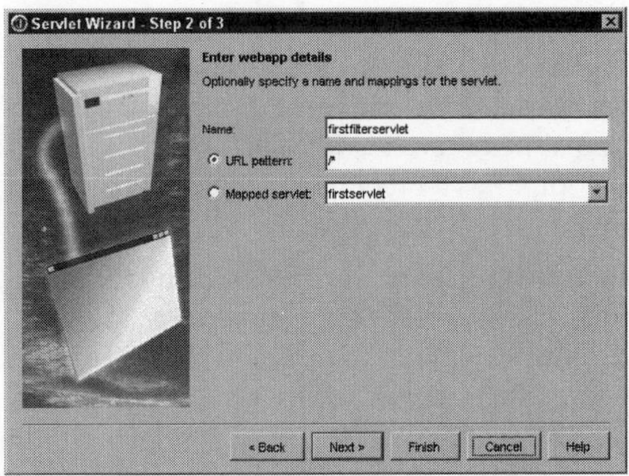


**Figure 16.8** Enter webapp details.

Filter Servlets that are to be registered to filter all requests to any URL pattern are specified here. For all requests that match this particular URL pattern, the Web container will evoke the registered Filter Servlet's doFilter() method:

```
<filter-mapping>
  <filter-name>firstfilterservlet</filter-name>
  <url-pattern>/*</url-pattern>
</filter-mapping>
```

Rather than specify a particular URL pattern, a Filter Servlet can be registered to filter all requests to a specific servlet. The servlet's name is used rather than its class. The Web container will first notice that the incoming URI is for the named servlet and then realize that a Filter Servlet has been registered to filter all requests. Rather than evoke the named servlet's service() method, the Filter Servlet's doFilter() method will be evoked:

```
<filter-mapping>
  <filter-name>firstfilterservlet</filter-name>
  <servlet-name>firstservlet</servlet-name>
</filter-mapping>
```

## Filter Servlet's Deployment Descriptor Properties

Like the Standard Servlet, there are settings in the Deployment Descriptor for Filter Servlets that are similar to those of the Standard Servlet. On the filter mappings, you can right-mouse click on the Filters node in the WebApp Deployment Descriptor to either add or remove a filter. You add filters in the same manner as you add servlets. When you add a new filter, you will be prompted for a name. Once it is added, you can move filters up and down in the list. The order does make a difference; it is the order in which the filters will be applied.

Double-clicking on a filter name in the Content pane will open the individual Filter Servlet's properties (see Figure 16.9) for editing the following information:

**Large icon, small icon, display name, and description.** Administration tools and deployment tools can best utilize these self-explanatory fields, similar to how JBuilder utilizes similar fields on the Designers Palette for JavaBeans.

**Filter class.** Like the Standard Servlet, this is the fully qualified class name of the Filter Servlet. This is the Filter Servlet class that the Web container will create when the predefined URL pattern or mapped servlet is requested. Each named Filter Servlet in the Deployment Descriptor has a predefined URL pattern or mapped servlet.

**Init parameters.** A parameter list can be created when the servlet is initialized. This list of keys and associated values can be accessed at runtime by calling this.getInitParameter(), passing in the string name as a key to retrieve the specified value. Although these parameters can be accessed at any time, it is customary to use them in the init() method of the servlet.

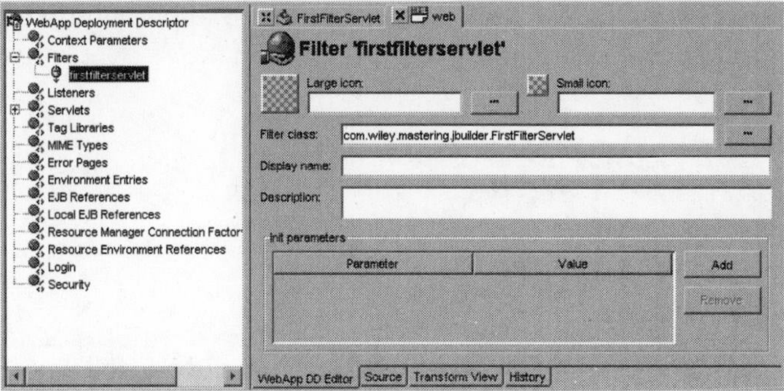


**Figure 16.9** Filter servlet Deployment Descriptor.

# Using DataSources

DataSources are part of the Java standard extensions of the Java Database Connectivity (JDBC) technology. It is recommended that developers work with DataSources provided by the Web container rather than establish a JDBC Connection by itself. Typically DataSources are bound to some sort of name server and accessed via the Java Naming and Directory Interface (JNDI). An initial context to the JNDI service is established, and the DataSource is located using the standard lookup() method as follows:

```
javax.naming.Context initCtx = new javax.naming.InitialContext();
javax.naming.Context envCtx =
(javax.naming.Context)initCtx.lookup("java:comp/env");
javax.sql.DataSource ds =
javax.sql.DataSource)envCtx.lookup("jdbc/EmployeeDB");
java.sql.Connection conn = ds.getConnection();
```

# Deployment Descriptor

The string name that is used in the lookup() method, "jdbc/EmployeeDB", must be defined in the Deployment Descriptor so that the Web container knows about the resource that the components it is responsible for managing will ask for. All the resources that any component within the Web container will need should be defined within the Deployment Descriptor, not just DataSources.

## *Resource Manager Connection Factory References*

Each Web application node in the Project pane has a Deployment Descriptors folder; double-click on the web.xml file under this folder to bring up the Deployment Descriptor editor. In the Content pane, locate the Resource Manager Connection Factory References (see Figure 16.10); this is where you will add the necessary information about the DataSource that you want to use from within your Web application. The XML that is added to the Deployment Descriptor will be as follows:

```
<resource-ref>
  <res-ref-name>jdbc/EmployeeDB</res-ref-name>
  <res-type>javax.sql.DataSource</res-type>
  <res-auth>Container</res-auth>
  <res-sharing-scope>Shareable</res-sharing-scope>
</resource-ref>
```

You can enter this information using the deployment descriptor editor as follows:

**Resource name.** This is the name that will be used as the JNDI lookup() sting. In the preceding example code, this would be jdbc/EmployeeDB.

**Type.** Set the type to javax.sql.DataSource, and you should see that the resource name is automatically modified to begin with a jdbc/. You will still need to modify the resource name to match the name used in the JNDI lookup() code.

**Authentication.** This sets the authentication to either application if you wish to perform the resource sign-on programmatically or sets it to container if the sign-on is to be based on the supplied mapping information.

**Sharing scope.** The resource factory can either be shareable or unshareable.

**Description.** A description can be added to help distinguish similar resources.

## Binding the DataSource to the Server's Naming Service

Each application server will handle the binding of DataSources to the naming service a little differently. Some application servers will expect that all DataSources be defined globally as part of the server's configuration; others will allow for DataSource definitions to be deployed to a running container.

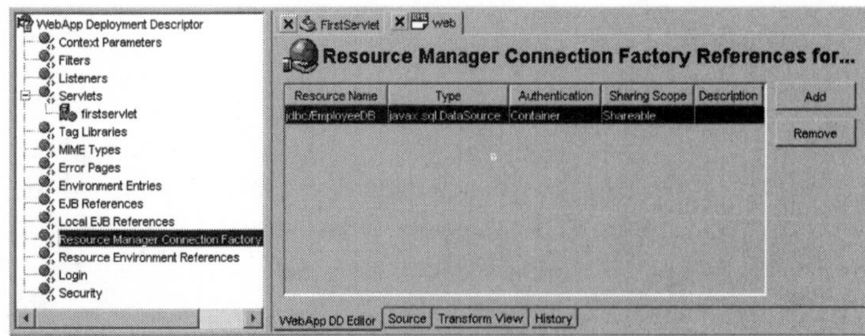


**Figure 16.10** Resource Manager Connection Factory References.

## *Tomcat DataSource Binding*

When JBuilder runs an instance of the Tomcat 4.0 Web container, a new directory titled ./Tomcat will be created in the working directory of the project (by default, this will be located in the root directory of the project). There will be a temporary directory created called names ./conf. This directory will exist only when Tomcat is actually running. If you look in this directly while Tomcat is running, you will notice a file named server8080.xml. This is the server.xml file that is used. The goal is to modify this generated temporary file in order to add the necessary elements to create the DataSource that the Deployment Descriptor has defined and that the Servlet code intends to access. Examining the contents of this file, you will see the following:

```
<!--This file, generated by JBuilder, may be deleted and regenerated at
any time.-->
```

When you exit or shut down the running instance of Tomcat that created this file, the file will be deleted. To prevent this from happening, you will need to delete the comment that claims that the file is generated and may be deleted. You can also create a server8080.xml file in the ./Tomcat/conf directory without running the server, and JBuilder will use this file as well. If you do, it will most likely look something like this:

```
<?xml version="1.0" encoding="UTF-8"?>
<Server debug="0" port="8081" shutdown="SHUTDOWN">
  <Service name="Tomcat-Standalone">
    <Connector acceptCount="10"
className="org.apache.catalina.connector.http.HttpConnector"
connectionTimeout="60000" debug="0" maxProcessors="75" minProcessors="5"
port="8080"/>
    <Engine debug="0" defaultHost="localhost" name="Standalone">
      <Host
appBase="C:\Borland\JBuilder8\jbproject\FirstProject\Tomcat\webapps"
debug="0" name="localhost" unpackWARs="true">
        <Context debug="0"
docBase="C:\Borland\JBuilder8\jbproject\FirstProject\webapp"
path="/webapp" reloadable="true"
workDir="C:\Borland\JBuilder8\jbproject\FirstProject\Tomcat\work\webapp"
>
          <Resource name="jdbc/EmployeeDB" auth="Container"
type="javax.sql.DataSource"/>
          <ResourceParams name="jdbc/EmployeeDB">

<parameter><name>factory</name><value>org.apache.commons.dbcp.BasicDataS
ourceFactory</value></parameter>

<parameter><name>username</name><value>sample</value></parameter>

<parameter><name>password</name><value>sample</value></parameter>

<parameter><name>driverClassName</name><value>com.borland.datastore.jdbc
```

```
.DataStoreDriver</value></parameter>

<parameter><name>url</name><value>jdbc:borland:dsremote://localhost//Bor
land/JBuilder8/samples/JDataStore/datastores/employee.jds</value></param
eter>
          </ResourceParams>
        </Context>
      </Host>
    </Engine>
  </Service>
</Server>
```

The edits that you make to this server8080.xml file will be global to all Web applications that are defined within the project. For Tomcat 4.1, a more modular approach was adopted. Each Web application has its own server configuration file located in the ./Tomcat/webapps directory. This file is also generated automatically and will have the same comment as the server8080.xml file. You can edit just this file to make the resource available to only one Web application, rather than all Web applications. The file you create will look like this:

```
<?xml version="1.0" encoding="UTF-8"?>
<Context debug="0"
docBase="C:\Borland\JBuilder8\jbproject\FirstProject\webapp"
path="/webapp" reloadable="true"
workDir="C:\Borland\JBuilder8\jbproject\FirstProject\Tomcat\work\webapp"
>
  <Resource name="jdbc/EmployeeDB" auth="Container"
type="javax.sql.DataSource"/>
  <ResourceParams name="jdbc/EmployeeDB">

<parameter><name>factory</name><value>org.apache.commons.dbcp.BasicDataS
ourceFactory</value></parameter>
    <parameter><name>username</name><value>sample</value></parameter>
    <parameter><name>password</name><value>sample</value></parameter>

<parameter><name>driverClassName</name><value>com.borland.datastore.jdbc
.DataStoreDriver</value></parameter>

<parameter><name>url</name><value>jdbc:borland:dsremote://localhost//Bor
land/JBuilder8/samples/JDataStore/datastores/employee.jds</value></param
eter>
  </ResourceParams>
</Context>
```

In both examples, the Jakarta Commons Database Connection Pool (DBCP) was used. You will have to download and configure a library for the DBCP, which is dependent on the Collections and Pool Jakarta subprojects. All three libraries will need to be added to the Web container's classpath in the same manner as the JDBC driver is added to the Web container's classpath.

## Adding the JDBC Driver to the Web Container's Classpath

It is important first to ensure that a library has been created for the JDBC driver that you want to use. You will also want to configure the enterprise settings located on the Tools menu to add the JDBC driver to JBuilder's classpath. This will ensure that JBuilder can use the JDBC driver as well. If the JDBC drive is not defined as within one of the Required Libraries of the project, JBuilder will not be able to add the JDBC driver to the server's classpath. Each option to add the JDBC driver to the server's classpath will actually modify the classpath in very different ways. Depending on which technique you employ, a different class loader may actually have access to the JDBC driver. You may have to experiment with each technique if you experience problems accessing and using the JDBC driver from within the Web application that you are deploying.

### *Deploying the Driver in the WEB-INF/lib Directory*

Required Libraries can be added to the Web archive's WEB-INF/lib directory by modifying the dependencies of the Web application's properteis (see Figure 16.11) The WEB-INF/lib directory is the most portable solution. It is also the most limited solution. If multiple Web applications are deployed to the Web container, and all Web applications will need to use the same JDBC driver, then each will need its own copy of the JDBC driver in its own WEB-INF/lib directory. Web applications do not share the resources located in their respective WEB-INF directories. When the WAR file is created, the JDBC driver will be added. Depending on how many dependent libraries are included in the Web application's WAR file, the build process may take a while. You may want to configure the Web application's properties not to build the WAR file each time the project is built. You may want to take exclusively manual control of when the WAR file is actually constructed by setting the WAR's build property to never.

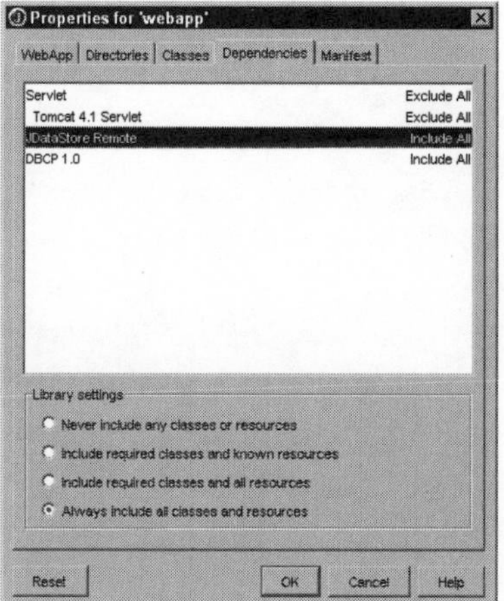


**Figure 16.11** Deploy libraries.

## Making All Required Libraries of the Project Available on Run

The Runtime configuration can be set up to modify the classpath used to launch the process that starts the server (see Figure 16.12). You can choose to make the output path part of the server's classpath, and you can also choose to make all the Required Libraries of the project part of the server's classpath. You cannot pick and choose which dependent library you want to add to the server's classpath; it is all or none. You could notice the modified classpath used in the Message view the next time you run the server.

## Deploy JAR Files to Web Container

The Runtime configuration can also be set up to deploy various Required Libraries of the project to the Libraries directory of the server (see Figure 16.13). Select the Libraries node located under the server in the Runtime configuration that you use to launch the server. If you are creating a new Runtime configuration, make sure that your run type is set to server. You should see a listing of the Required Libraries of the project in the list. Check the dependent libraries that you wish to deploy. These libraries will be deployed each time you run this configuration.

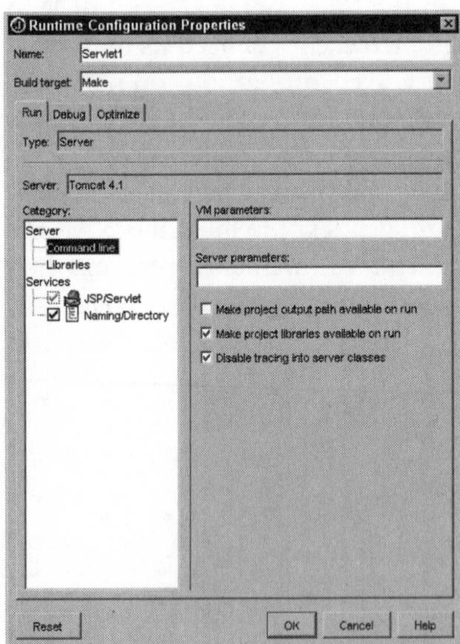


**Figure 16.12** Run Libraries.

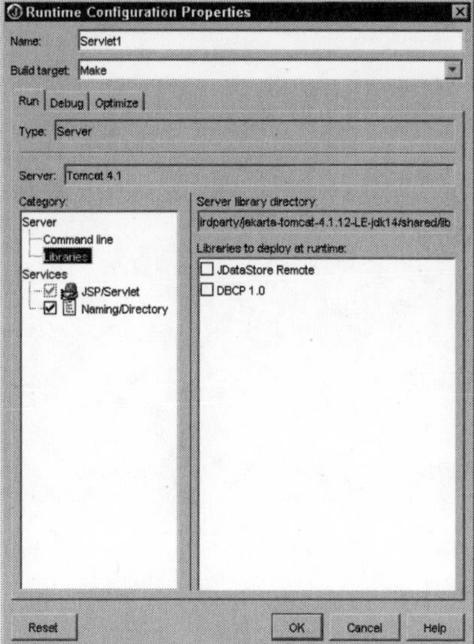


**Figure 16.13** Deploy Libraries.

# Summary

This chapter helped explain the core of dynamic, Web-based development in Java — namely servlets. From a basic understanding on how browsers and servers communicate to how that communication layer was objectified into Java classes, the servlet specification was explained through the eyes of the tools and wizards of JBuilder. The creation of Standard and Filter Servlets and the associated Deployment Descriptor editors were discussed. When it comes to dynamic content, relational databases are typically utilized to provide the data on which the dynamic content is based. Using DataSources to establish connections to databases using a JDBC driver is a key skill to master for all servlet developers. Leveraging three different techniques to modify the Web container's classpath is a critical component of getting DataSources to work the way they should.

CHAPTER

# 17

# Moving from Basic Servlets to Java Server Pages

A typical servlet contains Java source code wrapped around blocks of HTML text. Servlet developers work with the java.io.PrintWriter object to generate both the primarily static as well as the dynamic portions of an HTML document. Web developers quickly realize that the majority of characters that make up a single HTML document remain the same each time the same URL is requested and that this primarily static HTML content is the most volatile when it comes to the initial design of a Web site. Unlike a servlet, a Java Server Page (JSP) is a file containing HTML or XML text with tagged blocks of Java source code. The Web container will turn the JSP inside out to create a servlet.

Once a JSP is converted into a servlet, it follows the same lifecycle within the Web container as a regular servlet. As far as the JVM is concerned, it is just another Java class. Similar to how the Web container handles an incoming request for a servlet, the Web container also handles incoming requests for Java Server Pages. The main difference is that the Web container must first compile the Java Server Page into Java source code and then compile the Java source code into Java class files. It is the manner in which the JSP compiler turns the scripted mixture of HTML, XML, and Java into the classes necessary to complete the task at hand. There are structured commands that evoke a series of standard actions that instruct the JSP compiler to generate specific blocks of Java code.

These structured commands, or tags, must follow the same syntactical format constraints that XML documents follow. Developers can also create their own collections, or libraries, of tags to instruct the JSP compiler to work with predefined interfaces of specialized Java classes called Tag Libraries. A standard set of these Tag Libraries called the Java Server Pages Standard Tag Library (JSTL) has been developed and can now be considered part of the specification:

**Java Server Pages Tags.** Using Apache Software Foundation's reference implementation for the JSP specification, this chapter opens with a discussion of the basic concepts of what a JSP is and what it is capable of. Emphasis is placed on understanding the relationship between JSPs and servlets and the realization that they are very similar.

**Creating a Java Server Page.** Using the wizards, the steps involved with creating a Java Server Page are outlined.

**Tag Libraries.** Controlling access to your JavaBean in a manner that allows Java Server Page developers to focus more on the HTML than the Java code, Tag Libraries provide a mechanism for creating custom tags. Creating a custom tag library and adding it to a Web application will become a common practice for many Java Server Page developers.

# JSP Tags

A tag is an instruction that is passed from the developer or designer to the compiler or rendering engine. In the case of an HTML document created by a user interface designer, tags are used to instruct the Web browser how to operate or, more simply, how to display images and text. For the Java Server Page developer, tags are used to instruct the Java source code generator how to construct the resulting servlet's source code. The most basic of tags utilized by the Java Server Page developer simply instructs the code generator to insert the following Java source code. More complex tags can be used to perform a set of standard operations. Developers can also create their own Tag Libraries and even use existing Tag Libraries developed by other developers.

Converting a Java Server Page into Java source code sounds easy. Just create a single servlet with an implementation of a doGet() method, and stream the entire content into one massive out.println() parameter. Actually, it is converted into a class that is an implementation of the javax.servlet.jsp.HttpJspBase interface, an extension of the servlet interface, and the method being evoked is actually the _jspService() method.

For the most basic of Java Server Pages, it is almost this easy, but there is, of course, much more to it than just one big println() method call. In fact, you can embed Java source code anywhere in the content of the Java Server Page using reserved tags that the Web containers compiler understands. To begin, the most basic and common tags for developing Java Server Pages are the open parenthesis followed by a percent sign. Because this code will actually be within the scope of the HttpJspBase's _ jspService () method, certain references to familiar classes are made available to the Java Server Page developer. Besides the HttpServletRequest and the HttpServletResponse objects that are used throughout basic servlet programming, two other implicit objects are available to the Java Server Page developer: the PageContext and the JspWriter.

## Working with the JspWriter

The JspWriter is similar to the PrintWriter used in servlet programming. The local handle to this object is defined as "out". Java Server Page developers have access to this object's handle and can use it just as in servlet Programming, as demonstrated in the following scriptlet:

```
<HTML>
<!-- This is a comment. -->
<%
out.println("Hello World");
%>
</HTML>
```

There is also a variation of this tag that will pass the String results of a command directly to the JspWriter without having to use the println() method called the expression tag:

```
<HTML>
<%=
%>
<HTML>
```

## Standard Actions of a Java Server Page

Beyond just adding blocks of Java code to an HTML or XML document for the JSP compiler to invert, there are also structured commands that instruct the JSP compiler to generate specific blocks of Java code. The original premise here is to allow nonprogrammers to have a little bit of control of the classess within the Web container without having to learn Java. These standard actions are also useful to the trained Java programmer. The range of actions varies from creating instances of simple Java Beans and accessing their properties, to passing control to other Java Server Pages and servlets. The tags that make up the collection of standard actions are identified by the jsp prefix.

# Creating a Java Server Page

Unlike servlets, Java Server Pages do not actually have to contain *any* Java code. You could actually take an existing HTML document and change its file extension to .jsp, and you would have a Java Server Page. The Java Server Page wizard in JBuilder generates HTML code and adds a few tags specific to Java Server Pages, based on the options selected. The wizard will also make any necessary edits to the Web application's Deployment Descriptor and create a Runtime configuration if desired. To create a new Java Server Page in JBuilder, open the Object Gallery, go to the Web tab, select the Java Server Page icon, and click the OK button.

## Declare JSP and Components

The first step (see Figure 17.1) in the wizard allows the developer to choose with which Web application this Java Server Page is to be associated, the file name, and which additional components to create. Selecting additional components will add steps to the process of creating a Java Server Page. Define which Web Application is to be used as follows:

**Web App.** Like servlets, Java Server Pages are added to Web applications. The major difference is that where a servlet's Java source code is added to the Project's source path, the Java Server Page is added to a given Web application's root directory. If a Web application does not exist, a default Web application will be created automatically and added to the project. If the JBuilder project has several Web applications, you can select which Web application this Java Server Page will be part of. Where servlets are placed in the project's source directory, Java Server Pages are placed in what is defined as the root directory of the Web application.

**Name.** This will be the file name of the generated Java Server Page that will be placed in the root directory of the Web application. It is not necessary to add the .jsp file extension. In fact, the period is an illegal character for this edit box, and you will not be able to proceed to the next step of the wizard if you try to enter this file extension.

**Generate sample bean.** It is good practice to keep the amount of Java Source Code in the Java Server Page to a minimum. Java Server Pages can easily access the attributes and methods of other classes. To make accessing these classes easier, the Standard Action tag <jsp:useBean> is utilized to create a reference to the class. The wizard can also create a new class just for this use. Selecting Generate sample bean will add the necessary <jsp:useBean> Standard Action tag as well as generate the Java source code for a new Java Bean that will also be added to the project. The details will be added in an upcoming step. Selecting Generate sample bean will either enable or disable access to the additional step. You do not have to Generate sample bean in order to access additional classes from a Java Server Page; an upcoming step, Enter additional beans, will also allow you to select existing JavaBeans.

**Generate error page.** If an exception occurs during the processing of a Java Server Page, you can designate a specific Java Server Page to handle the exception. The following will be included in the generated Java Server Page:

```
<%@ page errorPage="FirstJavaServerPage_error.jsp" %>
```

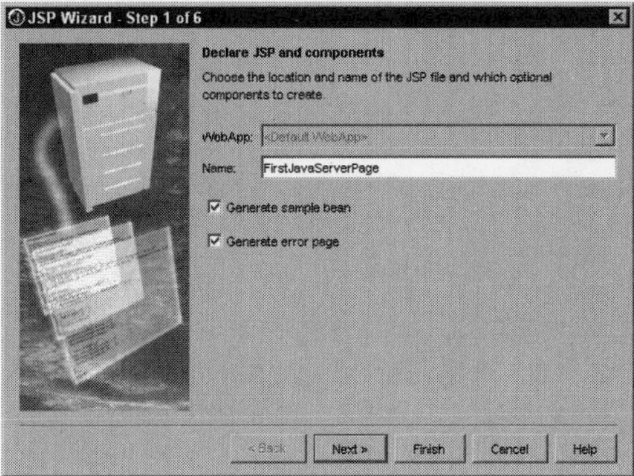


**Figure 17.1** Declare JSP and components.

## Edit JSP File Details

The second step (see Figure 17.2) controls the generation of the initial HTML code used in the Java Server Page as follows:.

**Background.** The default is that no background color is set for the JSP, but you can select the background color of the HTML of the generated Java Server Page.

```
<body bgcolor="#ffffc0">
```

**Generate submit form.** A self-serving form tag will be implemented in the resulting HTML that is generated for the Java Server Page. A single input value will be inserted into the HTML <FORM> as well as a Submit button.

```
<form method="post">
<br>Enter new value   :  <input name="sample"><br>
<br><br>
<input type="submit" name="Submit" value="Submit">
<input type="reset" value="Reset">
<br>
Value of Bean property is :<jsp:getProperty name="
firstJavaServerPageBeanId" property="sample" />
</form>
```

**Tag Libraries.** Tag Libraries are collections of classes that are referred to as Tag Handlers. This is similar to simply using Java Beans from within a Java Server Page with one major exception; Tag Libraries can be utilized without writing any Java code in the Java Server Page. The Tag Libraries that are available on this step are all third-party Tag Libraries. In order to use Tag Libraries in a Java Server Page, a Tag Library Directive is defined somewhere in the Java Server Page. Selecting individual Tag Libraries in this step will generate the necessary Tag Library Directive code in the Java Server Page being generated. The following is an example of the Tag Library Directive for the JSTL core library:

```
<%@ taglib uri="http://java.sun.com/jstl/c" prefix="c" %>
```

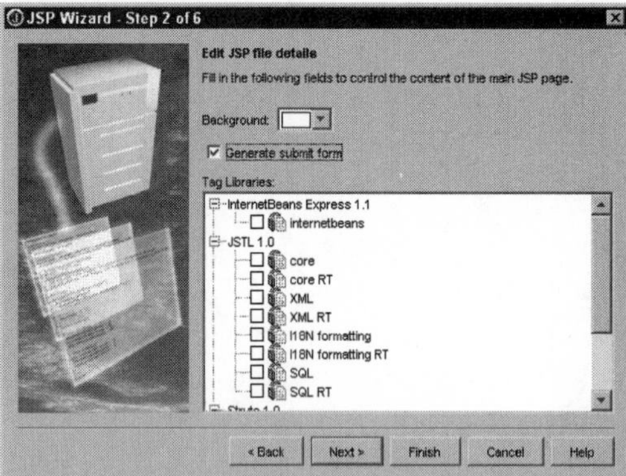


**Figure 17.2** Edit JSP file details.

## Edit Sample Bean Details

This step is accessible only if the Generate sample bean option is selected in the first step of the wizard. This page is a watered-down version of the new Class wizard and allows only the developer to select the most basic of options, including the following:

**Sample bean's Package.** This is the name of the package that the sample bean will reside. You can either create a new package by simply typing in the package, clicking on the drop-down list box to select from a list of commonly chosen packages already used in the current project, or clicking on the ellipses (three periods) and browsing to the package you want to use using the Package Browser.

```
package com.wiley.mastering.jbuilder;
```

**Sample bean's class name.** This is the name of the class that the sample bean will use. This will also be the name of the Java file because the bean class to be generated will be a public class.

```
public class FirstJavaServerPageBean {
```

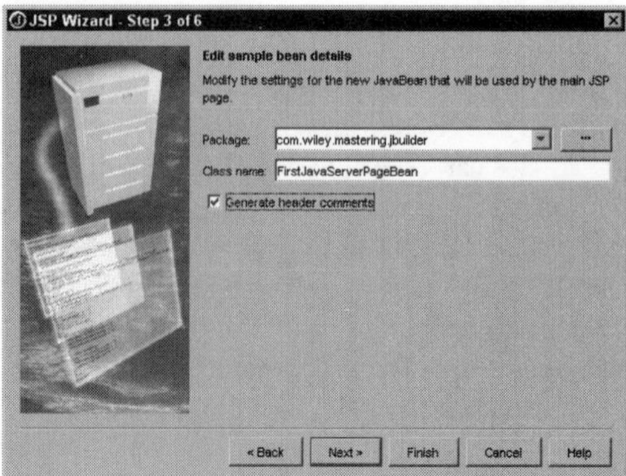


**Figure 17.3** Edit sample Bean details.

## HIDING JSPS IN THE WEB ARCHIVE'S WEB-INF DIRECTORY

**It is actually possible to hide Java Server Pages from outside access by creating them within the WEB-INF directory. The WEB-INF directory is not accessible from any outside request. This means that only other Java Server Pages and servlets can access any content located in the WEB-INF and its subdirectories. To create Java Server Pages in the WEB-INF directory, be sure to add the directory location to the name of the Java Server Page being created (WEB-INF/Jsp1.jsp). Only the Web container can assess files and resources located in the WEB-INF directory. This means that no external request can directly access any Java Server Page located in the WEB-INF directory. Typically, access is controlled by other Java Server Pages using the <jsp:include> and <jsp:forward> Standard Action tags or even from servlets that use the forward() and include() methods of the RequestDispatcher. It is common practice to create a servlet that controls access to many of the Java Server Pages in this manner. The following is an example on how this would look within a servlet:**

```
String path = "WEB-INF/Jsp1.jsp";
RequestDispatcher requestDispatcher =
context.getRequestDispatcher(path);
RequestDispatcher.forward(request,response);
```

**For JavaServer Pages, the <jsp:include> Standard Action tag will fetch the results of requesting the contents identified by the associated page or file attribute. The page= attribute will most likely be the URL of another Java Server Page, servlet, or some form of static content. The contents of the result will be inserted at the location of the include. Parameters can also be passed in using the <jsp:param> Standard Action tag.**

**Unlike the <jsp:include>, which will call an external resource and insert the resulting contents, the <jsp:forward> Standard Action tag will actually pass control to the external resource. If you decide to hide your Java Server Pages under the WEB-INF directory to prevent accidental browsing, you can use the forward Standard Action tag to access these hidden pages.**

**When using the <jsp:include> and <jsp:forward> Standard Action tags, you may want to pass additional parameters to the forwarded or included URL. To do this, you would use the <jsp:param> Standard Action tag. Each <jsp:param> will be accessible in the same manner in which parameters from an HTML's <form> and a URL's Query String are accessed.**

```
<jsp:param name="name" value="value" />
```

**Generate header comments.** Using the values defined in the project's Class JavaDoc Fields (located on the General tab of the Project Properties dialog), selecting this option will generate a Comment tag at the beginning of the sample bean's source code.

```
/**
 * <p>Title: </p>
 * <p>Description: </p>
 * <p>Copyright: Copyright (c) 2002</p>
 * <p>Company: </p>
```

```
 * @author not attributable
 * @version 1.0
 */
```

The <jsp:useBean> Standard Action tag will also be added to the Java Server Page based on the entries entered in this step.

```
<jsp:useBean id="firstJavaServerPageBeanId" scope="session"
class="com.wiley.mastering.jbuilder.FirstJavaServerPageBean" />
```

## Enter Additional Beans

Beyond just generating a sample bean, existing Java Beans can also be utilized in a Java Server Page. You can do the following:

**Add/remove bean.** If you already have a Java Bean in mind that you want to use in the Java Server Page, you can select this bean and add it to the list of beans to be accessible. When you select Add Bean, the Package Browser will display where you can either browse to a class in the classpath or you can search for a class in the classpath. Just as in adding a sample bean, the <jsp:useBean> tag will be added to the generated Java Server Page. After adding a bean, you can remove a bean from the list (Figure 17.4).

**Class.** This is the fully qualified package and class name of the Java Bean to be referenced.

**Id.** In the Java Server Page's Java code, a local reference or handle name will be available to the developer. You can edit what name will be assigned to the reference by setting the id property of the <jsp:useBean> Standard Action tag.

**Scope.** The scope defines where and how the reference for the Java Bean will be created.

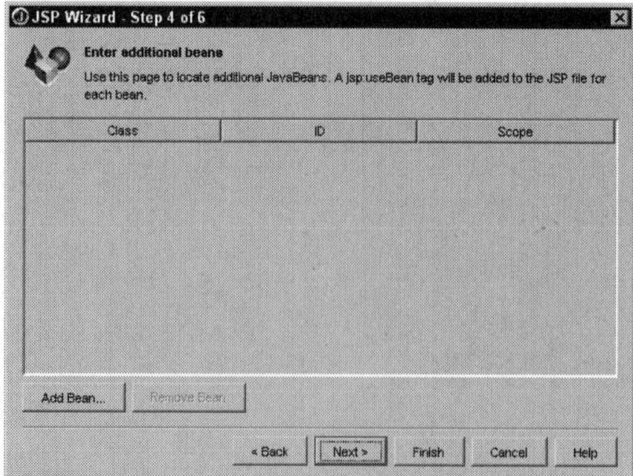


**Figure 17.4** Enter additional beans.

When you enter additional beans in the Java Server Page wizard, the idea is to abstract as much programming logic from the Java Server Page as possible. Most of the more complex coding activity should take place in the scope of the added Java Beans. The <jsp:useBean> Standard Action tag identifies a reference name that a particular instance of a class will be referred to throughout the Java Server Page's Java code. The id= attribute is the name of the reference that is to be defined. This handle is accessible by all Java code segments throughout the page. The scope= attribute can be set to page, request, session, or application. This attribute will determine the lifetime of the object instance. None of the Java Beans identified in the <jsp:useBean> Standard Action tag will actually be a member of the generated servlet class. If you examine the generated Java source code, you will notice that it is the PageContext that will manage all instances of these Java Beans. Setting the scope= to page will make the class instance available:

```
<jsp:useBean id="bean0" scope="page"
class="com.wiley.mastering.jbuilder.JavaBean0" />
pageContext.getAttribute("bean0",PageContext.PAGE_SCOPE);

<jsp:useBean id="bean1" scope="application"
class="com.wiley.mastering.jbuilder.JavaBean1" />
pageContext.getAttribute("bean1",PageContext.APPLICATION_SCOPE);

<jsp:useBean id="bean2" scope="session"
class="com.wiley.mastering.jbuilder.JavaBean2" />
pageContext.getAttribute("bean2",PageContext.SESSION_SCOPE);

<jsp:useBean id="bean3" scope="request"
class="com.wiley.mastering.jbuilder.JavaBean3" />
pageContext.getAttribute("bean3",PageContext.REQUEST_SCOPE);
```

The <jsp:setProperty> Standard Action tag is used in conjunction with the id= property set in the <jsp:useBean> Standard Action tag. Assuming that the bean identified in the <jsp:useBean> declaration is, in fact, a true JavaBean, there will be independent getter and setter methods for each of the private data members of the class. A quick way of accessing these getter and setter methods is through the use of the <jsp:setProperty> and <jsp:getProperty> Standard Action tags. The <jsp:setProperty> will call the setter method for the property= being identified, passing in the specified value= as the parameter:

```
<jsp:setProperty name="bean0" property="sample" value="value1"/>
```

Rather than code a value, it is also customary to pass in the value of one of the incoming parameter values that are typically defined in a <form> of a HTTP POST or in the query string of a HTTP GET:

```
<form method="post">
<input name="param1">
<jsp:setProperty name="bean1" property="sample" param="param1"/>
</form>
```

If the names of all the incoming parameters exactly match the properties of the Java Bean identified, an asterisk "*" can be used to set all the properties of the Java Bean using the values of all the matching parameter values. The Web container will actually generate the necessary servlet code to iterate through the parameters and evoke the same named property of the Java Bean:

```
<jsp:setProperty name="bean2" property="*"/>
```

The <jsp:getProperty> Standard Action tag is also used in conjunction with the id= property set in the <jsp:useBean> Standard Action tag. The <jsp:getProperty> will call the getter method and will retrieve the value of the property with the following code:

```
<jsp:getProperty name="bean3" property="sample" />
```

## Edit Error Page Details

Only accessible if the Generate error page option is selected in the first step, an additional HTML document will be generated that will be used as the result if an exception occurs while processing the request for the generated Java Server Page. The Error Page Details (Figure 17.5) can be input as follows:

**Error page's name.** This will be the name of the Java Server Page generated as the error page. The first selection in Step 1 enabled this accessibility of this step. When the Java Server Page is generated, the appropriate Error Page tag will be placed in the beginning of the Java Server Page. Error pages are not static HTML pages; rather, they are also Java Server Pages.

```
<%@ page isErrorPage="true" %>
<html>
<body>
<h1>Error page FirstJavaServerPage</h1>
<br>An error occured in the bean. Error Message is: <%=
exception.getMessage() %><br>
Stack Trace is : <pre><font color="red"><%
 java.io.CharArrayWriter cw = new java.io.CharArrayWriter();
 java.io.PrintWriter pw = new java.io.PrintWriter(cw,true);
 exception.printStackTrace(pw);
 out.println(cw.toString());
 %></font></pre>
<br></body>
</html>
```

**Error page's background.** The default is that no background color is set for the error page, but you can select the background color of the HTML of the generated error page.

```
<body bgcolor="#ffffc0">
```

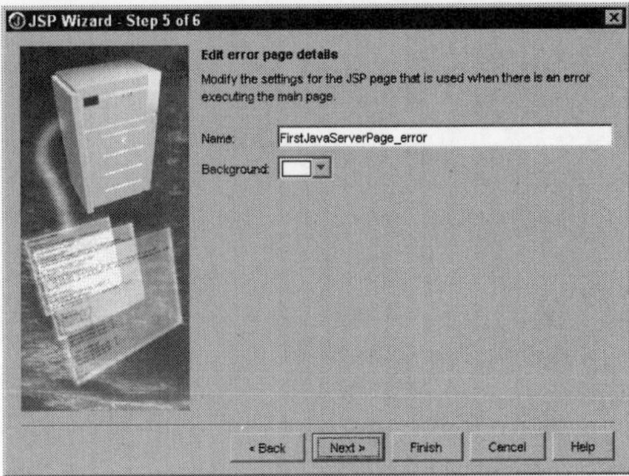


**Figure 17.5** Edit error page details.

## Define JSP Configuration

Runtime configurations are useful when running, debugging, or optimizing a given application's entry point (Figure 17.6). They are used to set up and run, debug, and optimize the Java applications created in JBuilder. The Java Server Page wizard can automatically create a Runtime configuration for the Java Server Page being created.

# Tag Libraries

Standard Actions do have some advantages over Java Server Pages, but everything that a Web application developer wants to do is not defined in such a standard set of actions. Each developer will most likely want to define his or her own set of tags to interact with. For this purpose, the Java Server Page specification has defined what is referred to as Tag Libraries.

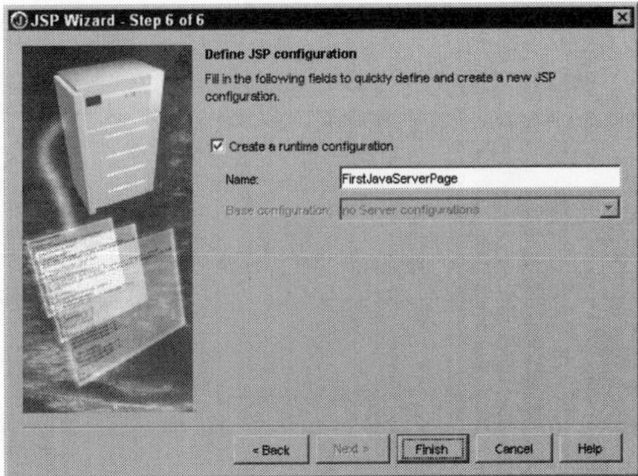


**Figure 17.6** Define JSP configuration.

With Tag Libraries, developers can pass in information to a specific Java Bean's properties and evoke code. By design, these custom Tag Libraries will have access to the same Response, Request, and Context objects that servlets and Java Server Pages have access to. Java Beans that are to be used as Custom Tag Libraries are also called Tag Handlers. These Tag Handlers will be referenced in the Java Server Page. There are two methods of creating Tag Handlers: implementing one of the Tag Handler interfaces and implementing an extension of one of the helper classes.

## Tag Handlers: Implement the Interface

Use the New Class wizard to create a new Java object and the New Test Case wizard to test the properties that were added using BeansExpress. Implementing one of the javax.servlet.jsp.tagext interfaces — Tag, IterationTag, BodyTag, or TryCatchFinally — makes these classes accessible to Java Server Pages as Tag Handlers. When using the Implement Interface wizard in this manner, the task of implementing the logic that goes into creating one of these interfaces rests entirely on the shoulders of the Tag Handler developer.

```
package com.wiley.mastering.jbuilder;

import javax.servlet.jsp.PageContext;
import javax.servlet.jsp.tagext.Tag;
import javax.servlet.jsp.JspException;

public class FirstTagInterface extends FirstJavaBean implements Tag {
  public void setPageContext(PageContext pc) {
    /**@todo Implement this javax.servlet.jsp.tagext.Tag method*/
    throw new java.lang.UnsupportedOperationException("Method
setPageContext() not yet implemented.");
  }
  public void setParent(Tag t) {
    /**@todo Implement this javax.servlet.jsp.tagext.Tag method*/
    throw new java.lang.UnsupportedOperationException("Method
setParent() not yet implemented.");
  }
  public Tag getParent() {
    /**@todo Implement this javax.servlet.jsp.tagext.Tag method*/
    throw new java.lang.UnsupportedOperationException("Method
getParent() not yet implemented.");
  }
  public int doStartTag() throws JspException {
    /**@todo Implement this javax.servlet.jsp.tagext.Tag method*/
    throw new java.lang.UnsupportedOperationException("Method
doStartTag() not yet implemented.");
  }
  public int doEndTag() throws JspException {
    /**@todo Implement this javax.servlet.jsp.tagext.Tag method*/
```

```
    throw new java.lang.UnsupportedOperationException("Method doEndTag()
not yet implemented.");
  }
  public void release() {
    /**@todo Implement this javax.servlet.jsp.tagext.Tag method*/
    throw new java.lang.UnsupportedOperationException("Method release()
not yet implemented.");
  }
}
```

## Tag Handlers: Extending the Support Class

If you already have a tested Java Bean that is being utilized by other classes, it might be best to extend one of the support classes and use delegation to access the existing properties and business functionality. The two dummy classes in the javax.servlet.jsp.tagext package that were created for this purpose are the TagSupport and BodyTagSupport support classes. These classes have already implemented the required methods of the IterationTag and BodyTag interfaces. All that is left for the developer is to choose which inherited methods to override and to implement the necessary delegation code. Use the Class wizard (see Figure 17.7) from the Object Gallery to extend the TagSupport class and generate the following code:

```
package com.wiley.mastering.jbuilder;

import java.io.*;
import javax.servlet.jsp.tagext.*;

public class FirstTagExtension
    extends TagSupport {
  FirstJavaBean firstJavaBean1 = new FirstJavaBean();
  public FirstTagExtension() {
    try {
      jbInit();
    } catch (Exception e) {
      e.printStackTrace();
    }
  }

  private void jbInit() throws Exception {
  }

  public String getFirstProperty() {
    return firstJavaBean1.getFirstProperty();
  }

  public void setFirstProperty(String firstProperty) {
```

```
        firstJavaBean1.setFirstProperty(firstProperty);
    }

    public int doStartTag() throws javax.servlet.jsp.JspException {
        javax.servlet.jsp.JspWriter out = this.pageContext.getOut();
        try {
            out.println("Value of FirstProperty is: " +
                        firstJavaBean1.getFirstProperty());
        } catch (IOException ex) {}
        return javax.servlet.jsp.tagext.Tag.SKIP_BODY;
    }
}
```

Choosing which method to override depends greatly on what you what to accomplish. The doStartTag(), doAfterBody(), and doEndTag() methods are a few options available. Using the Override Method wizard (see Figure 17.8) to select the appropriate method to override; the next step would be to implement the logic as follows:

```
    public int doStartTag() throws javax.servlet.jsp.JspException {
        /**@todo Implement this javax.servlet.jsp.tagext.Tag abstract
method*/
        throw new java.lang.UnsupportedOperationException("Method
doStartTag() not yet implemented.");
    }
```

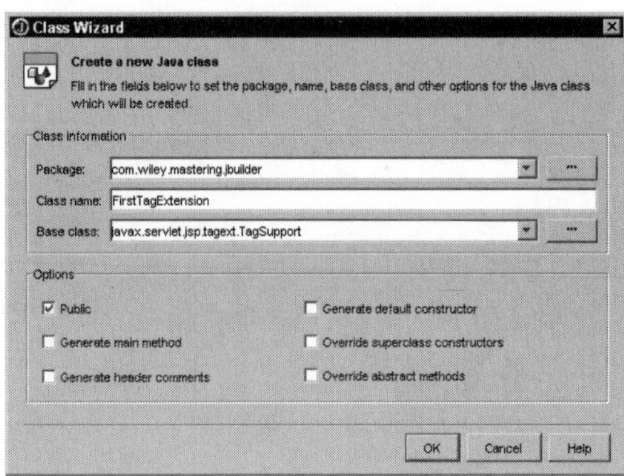


**Figure 17.7** Extend TagSupport class.

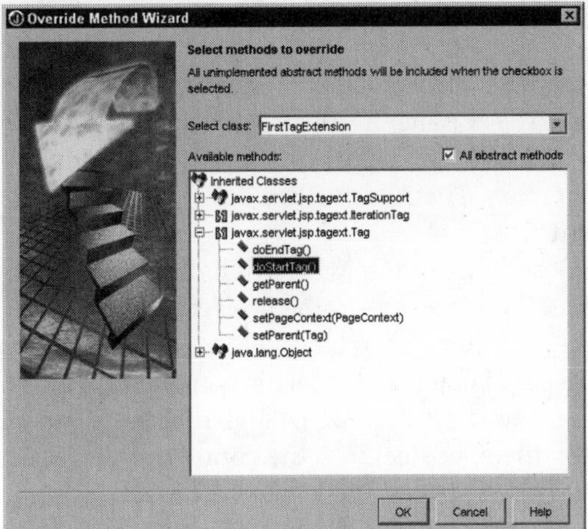


**Figure 17.8** Override doStartTag() method.

In the scope of the class that extends TagSupport, the PageContext is available. Through the PageContext attribute, the JspWrite is accessible, as well as the Servlet-Request, the ServletResponse, and the HTTPSession classes. Basically, the doStartTag() method can act as if it were a local method of the Java Server Page itself.

```
public int doStartTag() throws javax.servlet.jsp.JspException {
  javax.servlet.jsp.JspWriter out = this.pageContext.getOut();
  try {
    out.println("Value of FirstProperty is: " +
                firstJavaBean1.getFirstProperty());
  } catch (IOException ex) {}
  return javax.servlet.jsp.tagext.Tag.SKIP_BODY;
}
```

## Tag Library Descriptor: Creation and Validation

Depending on whether the Tag Library that you have created is to be utilized only by the current project you are working with or if multiple existing projects are to use this Tag Library, the location of the Tag Library Descriptor will change. If this is to be the only Web application that is to use the Tag Library, then create the Tag Library Descriptor file under the Web application's WEB-INF directory. When the Web archive is generated, all Tag Library Descriptors will be added to the WEB-INF directory.

On the other hand, if this Tag Library is to be used by other projects and perhaps even other developers, then you may want to consider creating a Java Archive using the Archive Builder. In this case, the Tag Library Descriptor file must be created under the source directory in a subdirectory of the root of the source directory titled META-INF and end in the .tld file extension.

## Create Tag Library Descriptor File for Basic Archives

Select "Add Files/Packages to Project" from the toolbar or the Project menu, or by right-mouse clicking on the Project node in the Project pane. If you are creating an archive for this Tag Library, be sure to add the Tag Library Descriptors to the META-INF directory of the root of the project's source directory. The Archive Builder will look in the project's source path for additional content.

To add the Tag Library's Tag Library Descriptor to the META-INF directory of the Java Archive, you must first create a META-INF directory in the project's source path. You will have to create this directory manually, using the New folder toolbar button located in the Add Files or Packages to Project dialog box. Once this is created, you can then add the Tag Library Descriptor to this newly created META-INF directory. When you create the archive, be sure to add this file specifically to the content of the basic archive you created.

## Create Tag Library Descriptor File for Web Applications

If you are adding the Tag Library Descriptor file to the Web application's WEB-INF Directory, no additional directory needs to be created. Add the Tag Library Descriptor file directly to the WEB-INF directory that already exists under the root directory of the Web application (see Figure 17.9). You will need to modify the Directory properties of the Web application to include regular content in WEB-INF and subdirectories. If you do not do this, the Tag Library Descriptor will not be added to the WEB-INF directory of the generated Web archive when you build the Web application.

## Edit Tag Library Descriptor

There are three main parts to a Tag Library Descriptor file:

- The header, which contains information pertaining to the type and format of the XML document itself using the <?xml/>, <!NOTATION>, and <!DOCTYPE> elements
- The root element <taglib/>, which defines the Tag Library as a whole
- The individual <tag/> elements, which define the implemented class as well as the accessible attributes of each Tag Handler

Making sure that the header is defined properly will ensure that the validation of the grammatical content is possible as follows:

```
<?xml version="1.0" encoding="ISO-8859-1" ?>
<!NOTATION WEB-JSPTAGLIB.1_2 PUBLIC--//Sun Microsystems, Inc.//DTD
JSP Tag Library 1.2//ENî>
<!DOCTYPE taglib
        PUBLIC "-//Sun Microsystems, Inc.//DTD JSP Tag Library 1.2//EN"
        "http://java.sun.com/j2ee/dtds/web-jsptaglibrary_1_2.dtd">
```

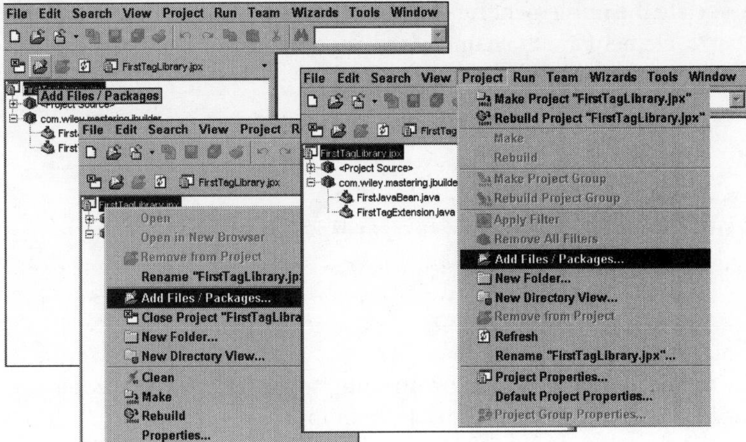


**Figure 17.9** Add file to project.

### Taglibrary

Looking at the DTD, the Tag Library itself primarily defines versioning information and a unique short name for the library itself:

```
<!ELEMENT taglib (tlib-version, jsp-version, short-name, uri?, display-
name?,small-icon?, large-icon?, description?, validator?, listener*,
tag+) >
```

Additional information can be defined such as the library's URI. All options for the <taglib/> root element are defined in detail in the comments of Java Server Page Tag Library Descriptor Document Type Definition file. For this example the following will suffice:

```
<taglib>
  <tlibversion>1.0</tlibversion>
  <jsp-version>1.2</jsp-version>
  <short-name>firsttaglibrary</short-name>
</taglib>
```

### Tag

Once the Tag Library Descriptor has been created, adding individual entries for each Tag Handler is next. Each Tag Handler will require a separate <tag/> element within the Tag Library Descriptor's <taglib/> tag. The definition for the tag is as follows:

```
<!ELEMENT tag (name, tag-class, tei-class?, body-content?, display-
name?, small-icon?, large-icon?, description?, variable*, attribute*,
example?) >
```

This is used to associate the implementing class with a name. The required elements of an individual <tag/> element are the name of the tag and the full class name of the Tag Handler.

Add tagclass to tag using the following code:

```
<tag>
  <name>firsttag</name>
  <tagclass>com.wiley.mastering.jbuilder.FirstTagExtension</tagclass>
</tag>
```

### Attribute

Within each <tag/>, there should be as many <attribute/> tags as there are properties in the implementing Tag Handler's class. The definition for the tag is as follows:

```
<!ELEMENT attribute (name, required? , rtexprvalue?, type?,
description?) >
```

Each getter/setter pairing needs only one <attribute/> tag. The only required element of the <attribute/> element is the canonical name of the individual property that is implemented on the Tag Handler, which can be generated using the following code:

```
<attribute>
  <name>FirstProperty</name>
</attribute>
```

## *Using Compound Code Templates*

Code templates can be set up and used to accelerate the development of Tag Library Descriptors. Through the use of a series of broken code templates, a more complex task can be accomplished without having to move the cursor around. Using the pipe "|" character in a given code template, the cursor's position at the completion of the code template can be controlled. In this manner, creating unfinished or incomplete code for the initial steps in a compound code template is necessary. To keep things simple and streamlined, it is often necessary to uniquely identify a given code template in three or four characters, using the description to help jog the memory. Once all code templates in a compound code template series have been completed, the code segment should be valid.

Add a TLDLibrary code template as follows:

```
<taglib>
  <tlibversion>1.0</tlibversion>
  <jsp-version>1.2</jsp-version>
  <short-name>|
</taglib>
```

Add a TLDName code template as follows:

```
  </short-name>
<tag>
  <name>
</tag>
```

Add a TLDClass code template as follows:

```
  </name>
  <tagclass>|</tagclass>
```

## *Validate the Tag Library Descriptor*

Regardless of which methods are used to create the Tag Handler and the Tag Library Descriptor, you can validate the Tag Library Descriptor file because it is an XML document. You can check this XML document to see whether it is well formed and to see whether it is grammatically valid. If there are syntactical errors in the Tag Library Descriptor, an Error folder will appear in the Structure pane listing all syntactical errors in the document. If, for instance, the first <taglib> tag was actually mistyped as <mytaglib>, you may notice a syntactical error listed in the Structure pane (see Figure 17.10), stating that the element type "mytaglib" must be terminated by the matching end tag "</mytaglib>".

To validate the Tag Library Descriptor file, you must have access to the Java Server Page Tag Library Descriptor Document Type Definition file (DTD) that is identified in the DOCTYPE of the Tag Library Descriptor. If you are connected to the Internet (or if you have a local copy of the DTD file on your host machine or local network), you can validate the format of the Tag Library Descriptor file you created by right-mouse clicking on the file in the Project pane and selecting Validate. If there are any errors, they will be displayed in the Message view (see Figure 17.11).

This will check to see whether the grammar of the tag structure that was utilized conforms to the specified DTD. When migrating from version 1.1 of the Java Server Page Tag Library Descriptor Document Type Definition to version 1.2, you will mainly notice that many of the tags have introduced a hyphen between words.

If you are not connected to the Internet, or if your Internet connection is quite slow, you could always point the DOCTYPE of the Tag Library:

```
<!DOCTYPE taglib
  PUBLIC "-//Sun Microsystems, Inc.//DTD JSP Tag Library 1.2//EN"
  "file:///JBuilder/extras/BorlandXML/example/j2ee/dtd/web-
jsptaglibrary_1_2.dtd">
```

**Figure 17.10** Well-formed XML error.

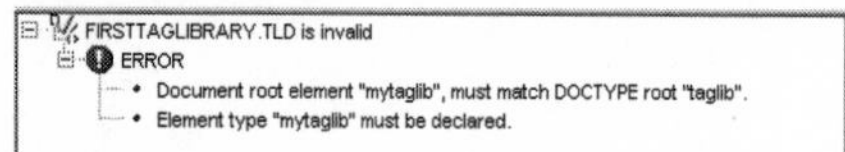


**Figure 17.11** Gramatical XML error.

## *Packaging Tag Libraries in Basic Archives*

The classes that make up a Tag Library do not have to reside in the WEB-INF/classes directory with their Tag Library Descriptor files in the WEB-INF directory. Rather, Tag Libraries can also be packaged into a single Java Archive and deployed in the WEB-INF/lib directory instead. When packaging Tag Libraries, you must also be sure to place the Tag Library Descriptor in the Java Archive's META-INF directory. Web containers will look in the META-INF directory of the Java Archives (see Figure 17.12) deployed in their respective WEB-INF/lib directories and make the Tag Libraries available to all Java Server Pages in that particular Web application.

## *Modifying the Web Application's Deployment Descriptor*

If you have added the Tag Library Descriptor to the Web applications WEB-INF directory (see Figure 17.13), you will also have to modify the web.xml Deployment Descriptor file of the Web application. A map needs to be created in the Web applications Deployment Descriptor.

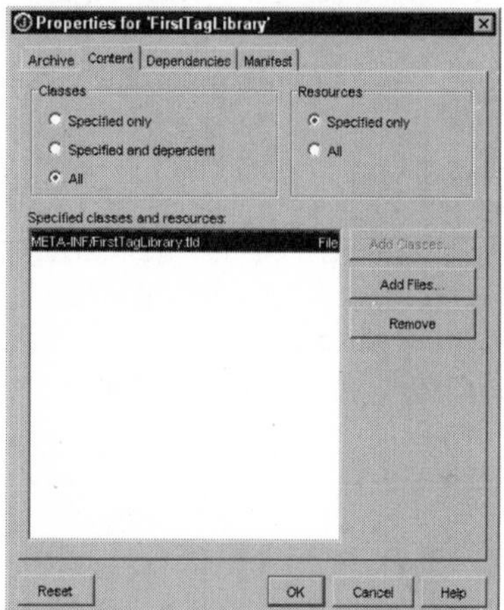


**Figure 17.12** Java Archive's META-INF directory content.

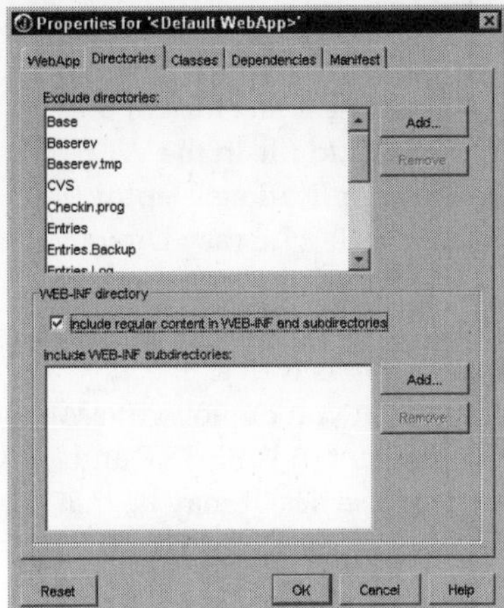


**Figure 17.13** Web archive's WEB-INF directory content.

## Tag Library Directive: Accessing Custom Tag Libraries from the Java Server Page

Java Server Pages know which Tag Libraries to communicate via Tag Library Directives. The Tag Library Directive is the part of the Java Server Page that establishes the tag prefix that will be used throughout the Java Server Page for which a particular Tag Library will be used. These directives are very similar to the <jsp:useBean> Standard Action tag also used by Java Server Pages. Only two properties, uri and prefix, need to be defined. The uri= property of the Tag Library Directive points to the definition in the Tag Library Descriptor or is a redirect to the web.xml file that contains the real URI to the Tag Library Descriptor or jar file. The prefix= property is used as a sort of local reference for the Java Server Page to use when accessing the various tags of the Tag Library.

```
<%@ taglib uri="/FirstUri" prefix="firstPrefix" %>
```

## Java Server Page Tag Library Compilation Errors

In the Web application, you can compile the Java Server Pages prior to deploying the Web archive to the Web container. This is particularly useful when working with Tag Libraries. Some Java Server Page compilation errors are specific to working with Tag Libraries. Not much can go wrong when compiling Java Server Pages that use Tag Libraries. The error is usually the URI, Tag Library Descriptor location, Tag Handler class name, or attribute name that was typed incorrectly in the Web applications Deployment Descriptor, the Tag Library Descriptor, or the Java Server Page itself. Deciphering the Java Server Page compilation error is usually a matter of tracking down where the erroneous setting is. Tomcat's Jasper Java Server Page compiler was used to produce the following compiler errors:

**"jsp1.jsp": org.apache.jasper.JasperException: File "/FirstUri " not found.** The .tld file containing the Tag Library Descriptors was not located by the Web container. If adding Tag Library Classes to the WEB-INF/classes directory of the Web application, make sure that there is a corresponding .tld file in the WEB-INF directory as well as the necessary entry in the Web applications Deployment Descriptor web.xml file. If both are not in place, the Tag Library Directive that you coded in your Java Server Page will not be valid. Also ensure that the URI that you used in the Tag Library Directive matches the URI that you specified in both the Web application's Deployment Descriptor as well as the Tag Library Descriptor. If you are getting this error only when you deploy your Web archive, make sure that you have "included regular content in WEB-INF and sub directories" on the Web applications Directories properties. It may be that the .tld file is not being included when the Web archive is being created.

**"jsp1.jsp": Unable to load class firsttag.** If you have created your Java Server Pages as you have created your Tag Handlers, it may be that you are trying to make or compile your Java Server Page prior to making or compiling the Tag Handler class itself. Also ensure that the name being specified for a particular prefix matches exactly the name of a tag identified for the Tag Library to which the prefix is pointing. If you are using a prebuilt Java Archive of Tag Handlers, make sure that the Java Archive has a Library defined and that the Library is part of the Project's Required Libraries and is "Always Included" as a Required Library in the Web application's dependencies.

**"jsp1.jsp": According to the TLD attribute FirstProperty is mandatory for tag firsttag.** The Tag Library Descriptor has identified an attribute that is mandatory. This means that all usage of this tag must set a value for this property prior to using the tag.

**"jsp1.jsp": Unable to find setter method for attribute: FirstProperty.** Properties are case sensitive and follow standard naming conventions for Java Beans. It is typical for the property to begin with a lowercase alpha character and for the setter method to use the uppercase of this alpha character. Make sure that the method implemented in the Tag Handler is using the proper setFirstProperty() naming convention and that the Tag Library Descriptor for the named tag specifies the proper firstProperty naming convention. It is also important to use the lowercase name in the Java Server Page as well.

## Summary

In this chapter we examined how JSPs are not only the inverse of a servlet from a development point of view, but also how JSPs are servlets from the Web container's point of view. We also examined how Standard Action tags can be utilized to interact with Java objects without having to write any Java code. We also took a look at how to develop custom tags that can communicate directly to the Tag Libraries that we created. In Chapter 18, "Developing with Struts," we see how the fundamentals of servlet and JSP technologies can be used together to create the model view controller architecture know as Struts.

CHAPTER

18

# Developing with Struts

Servlets lay the groundwork for all Java-based Web technologies. Java Server Pages extend the technology by providing a developer-friendly framework that allows the separation of the presentation layer from the reusable Java classes that are accessed via Standard Action tags or more extensively by using Tag Libraries, including a standard set of Tag Libraries that have been endorsed and accepted as the Java Standard Template Library.

Taking this to the next level, so to speak, would be to look for a framework based on the servlet technologies and that uses the flexibility introduced by Java Server Pages to implement a pattern of development common to user interface design. Though there are various event- and listener-based patterns associated with user interface design, it is the model view controller architecture that has been identified with the Java Foundation Classes (Swing) that would also make an excellent candidate for Web development as well. To that end, the Jakarta Project that is being managed by the Apache Software Foundation has devised a Web-based implementation of the model view controller architecture based on the Java Servlet and Java Server Pages specifications.

This chapter covers the following topics:

**Developing in the Struts Framework.** A basic understanding of the design principles of the Struts Framework is outlined. In addition, the use of the technologies provided by the Java Servlet and JSP specifications is discussed to emphasize the fact that the Struts Framework is a logical extension of these base technologies. A simple action is created to demonstrate the steps necessary to develop Web-based solutions based on the Struts Framework.

**HTML Form Processing.** Once an understanding of how to develop actions is mastered, one realizes that this is only half the equation. Web browsers need to send data to Web servers for processing. The <form> element in HTML provides a basic mechanism for sending this data. Struts provide an ActionForm specifically for creating easier access to the data sent from the browser to the server. Techniques on how to generate ActionForms from existing HTML code or how to generate JSPs from existing ActionForms are discussed.

**Creating a Struts 1.1 Library.** Struts is an evolving technology. Although JBuilder does not officially support Struts 1.1, some basic capabilities do exist. How to unlock these capabilities and develop Struts-based solutions using the latest builds is outlined.

# Developing in the Struts Framework

The Struts Framework is based on the model view controller design paradigm. This means that the underlying technology that Struts is based on will help the Web application developer separate even further his or her presentation code from the business logic and data access code. When moving from servlet development to Java Server Pages, one of the main differences was in the way that the Java program source code was separated from the user interface markup code. In a traditional servlet, a considerable amount of Java coding is dedicated to parsing together chunks of HTML code to create the user interface. Java Sever Pages help by initially inverting this world and allowing the Web application developer to insert Java source code in HTML. Standard actions could be used to interact with objects in the JVM, and the use of Tag Libraries helped separate even further HTML presentation code from Java source code.

How developers decide to take advantage of this opportunity to separate the presentation or view from the business logic and data access layer or model is up to each individual developer. Think of Struts as the conductor that steps in to take control and organize or coordinate the manner in which the Java source code is separated from HTML source code. The first step in allowing Struts to take control of the situation is to enable the Struts controller to handle all incoming requests by setting up a <servlet-mapping> in the Web application's Deployment Descriptor.

## Configure the Struts Controller for a Web Application

Web applications can be configured to use the Struts Framework when they are first created, or the struts configuration can be added to an existing Web application by modifying its properties. When creating a new Web application, you will notice a list of JSP/servlet Frameworks to choose from (see Figure 18.1). By selecting Struts 1.0, the name and the directory will be set to "struts" (unless it is already named). When finished, the appropriate Struts Tag Library entries will be added to the Deployment Descriptor for the Web application, and the Struts library will be added to the dependencies list of the Web application and set to Include All. In addition, a struts-config.xml file will be added to the WEB-INF directory of the Web application.

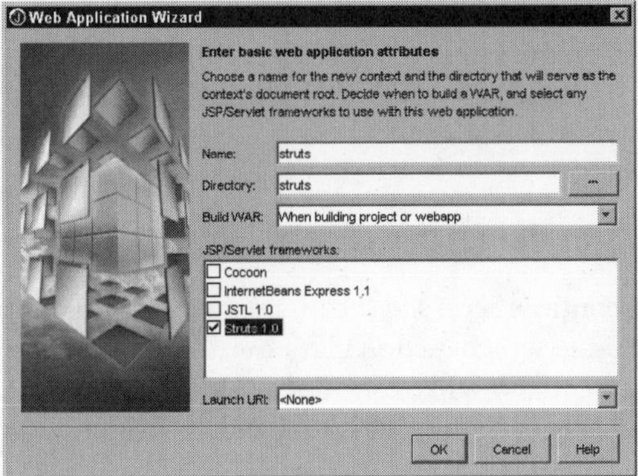


**Figure 18.1** Enter basic web application attributes.

With an existing Web application, you can add the Struts Framework to the Web application by modifying its properties (see Figure 18.2). In either case, not only have the Struts Tag Libraries been added to the Web application's Deployment Descriptor, but an Action Servlet has also been added that will respond to all incoming requests that are to be handled by the Struts Framework. This is made possible by creating a servlet mapping for all incoming requests in the Deployment Descriptor as follows:

```
<servlet>
  <servlet-name>action</servlet-name>
  <servlet-class>org.apache.struts.action.ActionServlet</servlet-class>
  <init-param>
    <param-name>debug</param-name>
    <param-value>2</param-value>
  </init-param>
  <init-param>
    <param-name>config</param-name>
    <param-value>/WEB-INF/struts-config.xml</param-value>
  </init-param>
  <load-on-startup>2</load-on-startup>
</servlet>
<servlet-mapping>
  <servlet-name>action</servlet-name>
  <url-pattern>*.do</url-pattern>
</servlet-mapping>
```

The org.apache.struts.action.ActionServlet is the Controller class that determines how to handle incoming requests. Extension mapping is used to register Apache's ActionServlet to handle all incoming requests that match the *.do extension. Taking charge of incoming requests is where Struts begins. It is the struts-config.xml file that is set up in the <init-param> that defines exactly what is to happen based on the information contained in the incoming HTTP requests. This HTTP request comes into the server and is converted to an HTTPServletRequest object, which is then passed on to the Servlet that is registered to handle requests based on the URI. In this case, an instance of the ActionServlet object will be created, and its doGet() or doPost() method will be evoked depending again on the information contained in the HTTP request. Based on the configuration information contained in the struts-config.xml file, an Action class's execute() method will be evoked.

## Control Access to the Model with the Action Wizard

In the Struts Framework, the Action class controls access to the business logic and data access code. The ActionServlet will determine which Action class to call based on the information in the struts-config.xml document and will evoke the execute() method of the Action class. The Action wizard on the Object Gallery's Web tab can be used to create a new instance of an Action class.

### *WebApp and Name for Action*

With this wizard (see Figure 18.3), you can choose from any Web application that has already been added to the project, or you can elect to create a new Web application. If you choose to add an Action class to a Web application that has not been configured to utilize the Struts Framework, it will be assumed that you intended to do this and the Action Class wizard will make the changes for you. The properties of the Web application will be modified, and the Struts 1.0 Framework will be selected; the necessary edits will be made to the web.xml file, and the Struts Library will be added to the dependencies. Most importantly, the struts-config.xml file will be added to the Web application's WEB-INF directory, and an entry will be made for the Action class.

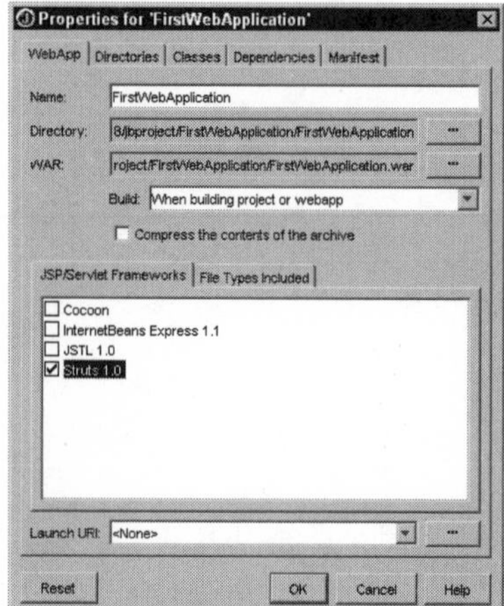


**Figure 18.2** Web application properties.

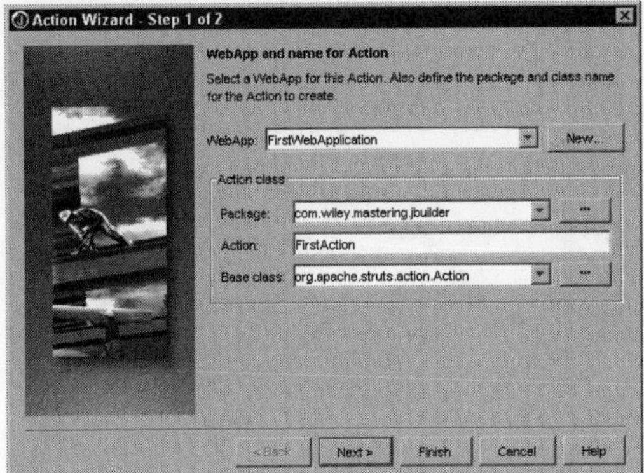


**Figure 18.3** WebApp and name for action.

The Action class is an extension of the org.apache.struts.action.Action class and will initially contain an implementation of the execute() method. In this method is where you will place the source code to control access to the business logic and data access code. The first step of the Action wizard will expect the following:

**Package.** The package name that will be used to create the Action class.

**Action.** The public name of the class and therefore the name of the .java file as well.

**Base class.** The base class from which the Action class will extend.

## *Configuration Information*

The ActionServlet class will use the information in the struts-config.xml file to determine which Action class's execute() method to evoke (Figure 18.4). This information will be added to the struts-config.xml file and has no effect on the generated Java source code.

Action Path is the name associated with the Action class that the ActionServlet will use to distinguish which execute() method to call. In the HTTP request, this is typically the name that has the *.do extension added to it. Therefore, the servlet mapping for *.do passes all incoming HTTP requests to the ActionServlet, and the Action Servlet looks at the Action Path preceding the *.do extension to determine which Action class to use.

Depending on how you decide to develop your Struts components, you may already have an ActionForm developed that you want to utilize for the Action class that you are developing. The optional ActionForm information that you enter will be added to the Action entry in the struts-config.xml file. If you have not created an ActionForm, you will be able to use the Struts Config Editor to add this information later:

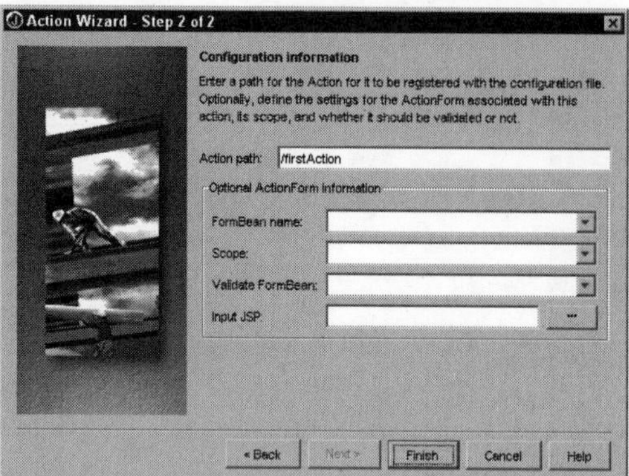


**Figure 18.4** Configuration information.

**FormBean name.** The name of the ActionForm class that is to be utilized whenever the Action class is called. An instance of this ActionForm call will be passed in as a parameter to the perform() method of the Action class.

**Scope.** The scope of the action can be set to either request or session.

**Validate FormBean.** ActionForms, along with having properties that correspond with a <form>'s field definitions, also have validate() methods that can be used to check the values of the properties prior to executing an Action's perform() method. The ActionServlet will evoke the validate() method of the FormBean if the value is set to true and will not if the value is set to false.

**Input JSP.** There are two views to consider for each Action and ActionForm that is created. The first view is obvious; it is the view that will be displayed when the Action has completed successfully. The second view, which is not as obvious, is the view that is used to call the Action in the first place. The Input JSP can be set to point to the URL of the Java Server Page or HTML document that originally called the Action class. If an error occurs when calling the ActionForm's validate() method, the ActionForm developer can create an instance of an ActionError object:

```
package com.wiley.mastering.jbuilder;

import org.apache.struts.action.*;
import javax.servlet.http.*;

public class FirstAction extends Action {
  public ActionForward perform(ActionMapping actionMapping, ActionForm
actionForm, HttpServletRequest httpServletRequest, HttpServletResponse
httpServletResponse) {
    /**@todo: complete the business logic here, this is just a
skeleton.*/
```

```
      throw new java.lang.UnsupportedOperationException("Method
  perform() not yet implemented.");
    }
  }
```

At a really basic level, the perform() method of the Action class is very similar to the service() method of a servlet. Just as the Web container uses the information in the web.xml file to determine which servlet's service method to evoke, the ActionServlet uses the struts-config.xml file to determine which Action's perform() method to evoke. Also similar to the servlet's service() method, theAction's perform() method is passed references to the HttpServletRequest and the HttpServletResponse objects. The difference is that the Action's perform() method also has a reference to an ActionForm and an ActionMapping object.

## HTML Form Processing

When you storyboard how the various views flow through the Web application from the end user's point of view, you will find that each view will have from zero to many different directions for the end user to choose. Each direction that the end user can take will be a navigation-only direction, or additional information will be collected and passed to the server for processing or storage.

When additional information is passed to the server, that information will go through several transformations before it becomes useful to the developer who is writing the business logic or data access logic. The first transformation will be managed by the Web container and will map raw text of an HTTP request to the attributes of a HttpServletRequest object. These attributes are then accessible through the HttpServletRequest object's API, as specified by the Java Servlet specification. Though this is helpful, many developers take the transformation one step further and use the attributes of the HttpServletRequest object to populate the attributes of domain-specific objects that have more meaning to the application being developed.

## ActionForm Wizard

ActionForm classes help collect information that is passed to the Web application via the HTTP request. There are two basic mechanisms for passing information into the Web application. The first, part of the URL itself, is called the Query String and is associated with GET requests. Query Strings are usually at the end of the URL, begin with a question mark (?), and contain name=value pairs of information separated by ampersands (&), as follows:

```
<a href="/struts/firstAction.do?name1=value1&name2=value2">First
Action</a>
```

The second mechanism by which information is passed into the Web application occurs when the name=value pairs of information are actually part of the message body and are associated with POST requests:

```
<form action="/firstAction.do" method="POST">
<input type="text" name="name1">
<input type="text" name="name2">
<input type="submit" name="Submit" value="Submit">
<input type="reset" value="Reset">
</form>
```

## *Web Application and Class Information for ActionForm*

You can choose from any Web application that has already been added to the project, or you can elect to create a new Web application. If you choose to add an ActionForm class to a Web application that has not been configured to utilize the Struts Framework, it will be assumed that you intended to do this and the ActionForm Class wizard will make the changes for you. The properties of the Web application will be modified, and the Struts 1.0 Framework will be selected, the necessary edits will be made to the web.xml file, and the Struts Library will be added to the dependencies. Most importantly, the struts-config.xml file will be added to the Web application's WEB-INF directory.

When you create a new ActionForm (see Figure 18.5), you can configure the package that it is to be named in as well as the name of the ActionForm class itself and the base class that it will extend:

**Package.** The package name that will be used to create the Action class.

**ActionForm.** The public name of the class and therefore the name of the .java file as well.

**Base class.** The base class from which the Action class will extend.

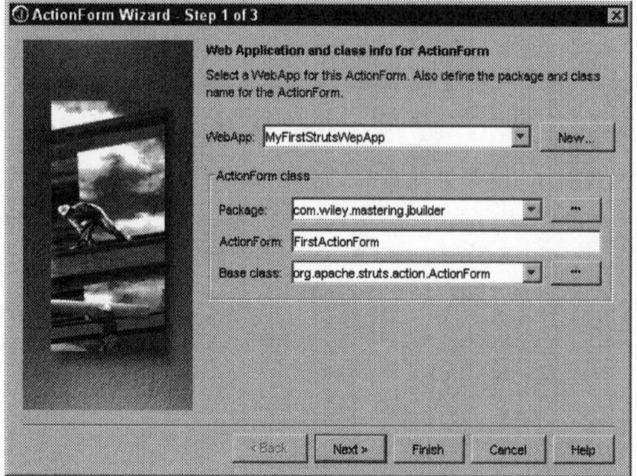


**Figure 18.5** Web Application and class information for ActionForm.

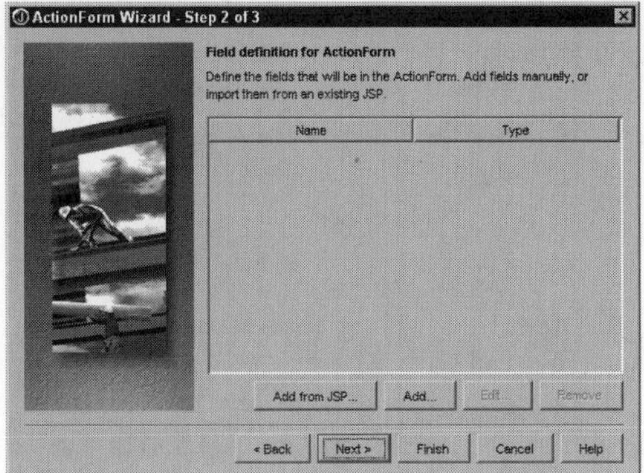


**Figure 18.6** Field definition for ActionForm.

## *Field Definition for ActionForm*

Defining the field definitions of an ActionForm is the whole point of having an ActionForm in the first place. The ActionForm wizard is a unique wizard in that it was designed to overlay existing ActionForms with new field definitions (see Figure 18.6). This means that you can use the ActionForm wizard to modify an existing ActionForm's field definitions. For instance, if you use the ActionForm wizard to create an ActionForm from an existing JSP or HTML document's <form>, and later you decide to add another JSP or HTML document's <form> to the same ActionForm, you can run the ActionForm wizard a second time and modify the existing ActionForm. It is important to note that the ActionForm wizard will read in the existing ActionForm's field definitions and add them to the list. If you delete the existing field definitions from the list, they will be removed from the ActionForm. These definitions will all turn into properties of the ActionForm with a getter and setter method for public access to each property:

**Name and type.** Manually adds field definitions by specifying their names and data types.

**Add from JSP.** Even though it claims to be able to read only the <html.form> of any Java Server Page that has been coded, you can also point to any JSP or HTML document in the Web application that has traditional <form> tags. The field definitions from the documents specified will be added to the Field Definition list.

## *Select Additional Options*

With the final step of this wizard (see Figure 18.7) , you can choose to modify the struts-config.xml while generating the ActionForm source code, or you can always use the Struts Config Editor to do the following:

**Add to struts-config.xml.** Selecting this option will modify the struts-config.xml file with the definition of the ActionForm class. This will not add the ActionForm to an existing Action. To add a new ActionForm to an existing Action, you will have to edit the struts-config.xml file using the Struts Config Editor.

**FormBean name.** A default name will initially be provided based on the class name of the ActionForm; this is the name that will be used in the struts-config.xml file.

**Create/replace reset() method body.** If you are overlaying an existing ActionForm, you can opt to replace the reset() method with a new reset() method. If you are creating a new ActionForm, this option will also generate the code for the reset() method. It is up to the developer to code the implementation of the reset() method.

**Clear validate() method body in original file.** This option should be selectable only if you are overlaying an existing ActionForm and the existing ActionForm has a validate() method already implemented. Selecting this option will overwrite the existing validate() method.

```
package com.wiley.mastering.jbuilder;

import org.apache.struts.action.*;
import javax.servlet.http.*;

public class FirstActionForm extends ActionForm {
  public ActionErrors validate(ActionMapping actionMapping,
HttpServletRequest httpServletRequest) {
    /**@todo: finish this method, this is just the skeleton.*/
    return null;
  }
  public void reset(ActionMapping actionMapping, HttpServletRequest
httpServletRequest) {
  }
}
```

Once a basic ActionForm has been created, one that was not created from an existing Java Server Page or HTML document that already contains a <form>, you can also add properties to the ActionForm using the BeansExpress Properties Editor.

## JSP from ActionForm wizard

If you have created an ActionForm, you can generate a Struts-compliant Java Server Page that will contain the <html:form> tag and necessary field definitions based on the properties of the ActionForm class.

**Figure 18.7** Select additional options.

## *WebApp, JSP, and ActionForm*

Select the Web application to which you want to add the Java Server Page, and edit the name of the Java Server Page (see Figure 18.8). You can browse the classes in the project to select the ActionForm class whose properties you wish to generate the <html:form> from. In addition, you can also select the Action that will be used in the form.

## *Tag Types for ActionForm Fields in JSP*

You cannot add any field definitions to the list (see Figure 18.9), but you can decide how the field will be utilized in the form — as text, password, or textfield. Additionally, you can elect not to use the field definition at all. This is particularly useful when using a single ActionForm to handle the field definitions from several Java Server Pages.

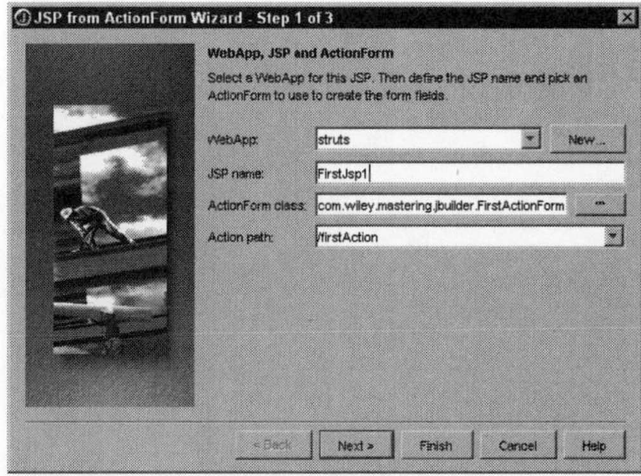


**Figure 18.8** WebApp, JSP and ActionForm.

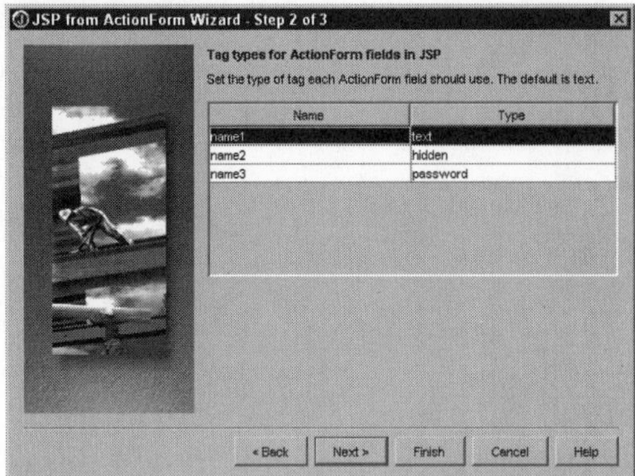


**Figure 18.9** Tag types for ActionForm fields In JSP.

## *Specify the Options for Creating This Strut's JSP*

The Struts Tag library also provides additional tags for processing the Java Server Page (see Figure 18.10). You can select which Java Server Pager you wish to implement:

```
<%@ taglib uri="/WEB-INF/struts-logic.tld" prefix="logic" %>
<%@ taglib uri="/WEB-INF/struts-template.tld" prefix="template" %>
<%@ taglib uri="/WEB-INF/struts-bean.tld" prefix="bean" %>
<%@ taglib uri="/WEB-INF/struts-html.tld" prefix="html" %>
<%@ page contentType="text/html; charset=windows-1252" %>
<html:html xhtml="true" locale="true">
<head>
<title>
FirstJsp1
</title>
<html:base/>
</head>
<body>
<h1>JBuilder Generated Struts JSP for ActionForm
com.wiley.mastering.jbuilder.FirstActionForm</h1>
<p>
<html:form action="/firstAction.do" method="POST">
<html:text property="name1"/>
<br>
<html:hidden property="name2"/>
<br>
<html:password property="name3"/>
<br>
<html:submit property="submit" value="Submit"/><br>
<html:reset value ="Reset"/>
</html:form>
</body>
</html:html>
```

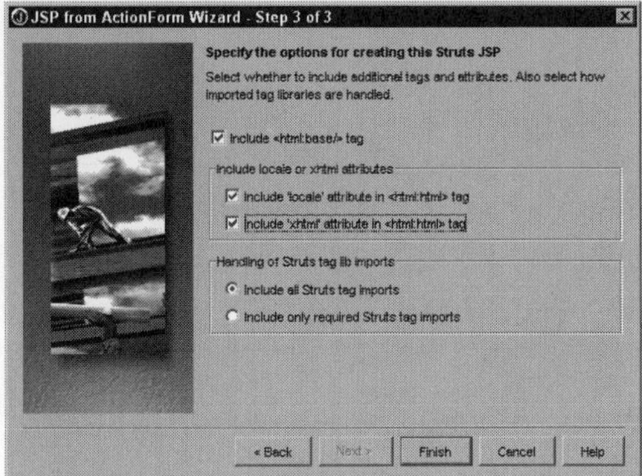


**Figure 18.10** Specify the options for creating this Strut's JSP.

# Creating a Struts 1.1 Library

Struts 1.1 is not officially supported because it is being beta tested. If you decide that you want to work with Struts 1.1, you will have to download the binary distribution from Apache's Jakarta Project and create a new library that points to the location where you installed the download. Include the appropriate jar files as part of the library's class definition. Depending on which version of Tomcat you are using and which version of the JDK you are targeting, the jar files you include could change. If you have downloaded the source and API documentation in JavaDoc form, you can set that up as well.

If you decide to configure this Struts 1.1 Library as *the* Struts Framework, you will have to disable the Struts 1.0 Framework by setting the Framework setting to None on the Struts 1.0 Libraries Framework tab. Only one library can be configured as "the" Struts Framework. If you do this, you will not include the additional Tag Library Descriptors that are now part of Struts 1.1. If you do have multiple libraries configured as Struts Framework, you will notice some weird behavior in the Web application. The best bet is to configure the library as a User Defined Tag Library. The only benefit that you will lose is the automatic adding of the struts-config.xml file in the WEB-INF directory of the Web application. This is no major loss because the file that is added is not exactly correct for using Struts 1.1. There is a new Data Type Definition (DTD) for Struts 1.1 that you will have to use in place of the version of the DTD that was used for Struts 1.0. Once you change the version of the DTD that you are using, the Struts Config Editor will come alive with all the new edits that are part of the Struts 1.1 Framework:

```
<?xml version="1.0" encoding="UTF-8"?>
<!DOCTYPE struts-config PUBLIC "-//Apache Software Foundation//DTD
Struts Configuration 1.0//EN"
"http://jakarta.apache.org/struts/dtds/struts-config_1_1.dtd">
<struts-config />
```

You can even manually add the Tiles Definition XML to the WEB-INF directory by creating a file named tiles-defs.xml:

```
<?xml version="1.0" encoding="ISO-8859-1" ?>
<!DOCTYPE tiles-definitions PUBLIC "-//Apache Software Foundation//DTD
Tiles Configuration//EN" "http://jakarta.apache.org/struts/dtds/tiles-
config.dtd">
<tiles-definitions>
```

## Summary

Struts development can become very addictive. It is very easy to get into a smooth rhythm when developing Actions and ActionForms. Depending on how you decide to initiate the development of a given Web site, we examined two different techniques for bringing <form> elements together with ActionForms. In the first scenario, ActionForms were created first, and the JSP was generated based on the fields in the ActionForm. In the second scenario, HTML and JSP <form> elements were utilized to generate ActionForms quickly. In both cases, Actions were easily associated with ActionForms using the Struts Configuration Editor.

PART

Six

# Enterprise Development with Enterprise JavaBeans

Where Part Five focused on the various Web-based technologies that make up the Enterprise Edition of Java 2 (J2EE), Part Six focuses on the Enterprise JavaBean (EJB) specification. JBuilder can develop to either the 1.1 or the 2.0 version of the EJB specification. Which version you want to use to depends on what is supported by the target application server you are using. The EJB 2.0 specification stipulates that all compliant EJB 2.0 containers must be equipped to support EJB 1.1 deployed modules. If your application server is compliant with EJB 2.0, you should also be able to develop and deploy EJB 1.1 code. This is particularly useful if you started developing with EJB 1.1, deployed some applications, and now want to take advantage of the features introduced in EJB 2.0. A key difference between EJB 1.1 and EJB 2.0 development in JBuilder is the introduction of the EJB 2.0 Designer.

This part consists of two chapters:

**Developing EJB 1.1.** Focusing on version 1.1 of the Enterprise JavaBean specification, Chapter 19 will outline the steps necessary to develop Enterprise JavaBeans compliant with the EJB 1.1 specification. In addition, Deployment Descriptor edits and configuration will be discussed for Session Beans and Entity Beans.

**Developing EJB 2.0.** Not only are there new capabilities in the EJB 2.0 specification, but JBuilder has also introduced a new way of developing EJBs with the EJB 2.0 Designer. Chapter 20 will cover the development of EJBs using all the features and capabilities of this designer.

CHAPTER

19

# Developing EJB 1.1

Sun Microsystems not only invented the Java programming language, but it also was instrumental in coming up with a distributed object framework. Beyond the basics of transferring streams of data from point A to point B on a given network, the Enterprise JavaBean (EJB) specification originally set out to define a set of capabilities that objects in a distributed system should have. As the job of providing the necessary infrastructure to support these basic sets of capabilities became more complex, additional supporting frameworks were birthed. The entire collection of technologies that were created for enterprise systems, now referred to as the Java 2 Enterprise Edition (J2EE), support a fundamental set of services that the EJB container now uses. The EJB container is responsible for making these services available to the components it manages, namely Enterprise JavaBeans. The lifecycle of each type of Enterprise JavaBean is also the responsibility of the Enterprise JavaBean container, just as the lifecycle of the servlet and the Java Server Page is the responsibility of the Web container. So what is an EJB?

There are two basic types of Enterprise JavaBeans in the 1.x version of the specification: Session Beans and Entity Beans. You could think of these two classifications of EJBs as a decoupling of the business methods from the attributes of what is traditionally referred to as a business object. Session Beans are primarily responsible for the implementation of application and business logic (workflow), and Entity Beans are responsible for the object-to-relational mapping of the business attributes and data. Given this, one may think that this breaks the business object concept and is a bad design, but this may not necessarily be true. Think of EJB as more of an implementation detail of the business model. When you get right down to the metal, the way that the most elegant objects within the Java Virtual Machine are executed within the registries of the central processing unit of a given machine for a given cycle is hardly distinguishable from the machine code compiled from the most procedural of function calls. Eventually, all designs turn into a series of ones and zeros.

So, what is the most elegant implementation that most effectively gets the job done for a given business requirement? How does the design of Enterprise JavaBeans lead to more effective execution of Java byte code within the Java Virtual Machine? It was noticed that most distributed systems aspired to certain design principles and offered a basic set of capabilities to each object within certain closed systems. There is typically a published interface that identifies the accessible methods of an object and a factory class that controls the access and construction of the object, as well as the implemented business logic of the object itself. Each Enterprise JavaBean will always have these three components: the Remote and Home interfaces and the Bean itself. When you want to create a new Enterprise JavaBean, all three Java source files also must be created.

# New Enterprise JavaBean 1.x

Before creating Enterprise JavaBeans, it is important that you determine the version of the EJB specification with which your particular EJB container complies. This will determine the type of EJB module to create as well as what types of Enterprise JavaBeans to create. Regardless of which server is configured, the wizards will all behave the same way. Choosing a server is also choosing an implementation of the EJB container and, therefore, the compliant version of the EJB specification. The Enterprise JavaBean 1.x wizard will generate the necessary code for the Remote and Home interfaces as well as the Bean class itself.

## Select EJB Module

Collections of Enterprise JavaBeans are packaged within a Java Archive and deployed to an EJB container for execution. This Java Archive also contains the required Deployment Descriptor that instructs the EJB container how to manage the Enterprise JavaBeans within the Java Archive as well as how to configure certain resources that are to be made available to the Enterprise JavaBeans. JBuilder manages each of these Java Archives in what is called an EJB module.

To create Enterprise JavaBeans compliant with the 1.x version of the specification, it is important that the EJB module was initially set up specifically for 1.x EJB development. It is not possible to mix 1.x and 2.x EJB in the same EJB module. The EJB module can have one and only one Deployment Descriptor and will produce one and only one EJB Java Archive. Each Deployment Descriptor within the Java Archive is validated against the Document Type Definition for each compliant version of the EJB specification. EJB containers themselves are to be backward compatible, but this means only that they can host both 1.x-compliant archives and 2.x-compliant archives. Depending on the application server selected, it may be possible to deploy both 1.x and 2.x Enterprise JavaBean archives. Likewise, projects can have multiple EJB modules, each with its own EJB Java archive, and each EJB module can, of course, have multiple Enterprise JavaBeans, again provided that all of the EJBs within a single module are compliant with the same version of the EJB specification.

Only EJB 1.x-compliant EJB modules should appear in this list. Likewise, only EJB modules that are already nodes of the project will show up in this list. If a 1.x-compliant EJB module does not exist, selecting the "New..." button can create one. If several 1.x-compliant EJB modules exist, one must be selected.

## Create a New Enterprise JavaBean Component

This is the main step of the 1.x wizard (see Figure 19.1). Here you will choose which type of Enterprise JavaBean you wish to create as well as establish the basic class information.

### *Class Information*

Class information is used to establish how the Enterprise JavaBean relates to existing packages and classes that have already been developed. Enter the following information for each Enterprise JavaBean you create:

**Package.** Though not necessary, it is a good idea to consider separating Enterprise JavaBeans by business function or by implemented design pattern. Each package name could contain groupings of related Enterprise JavaBeans:

```
package com.wiley.mastering.jbuilder;
```

**Class name.** This is the actual Java class name that will be used by the class that implements the core logic.

```
public class FirstStatelessSessionBean implements SessionBean {
```

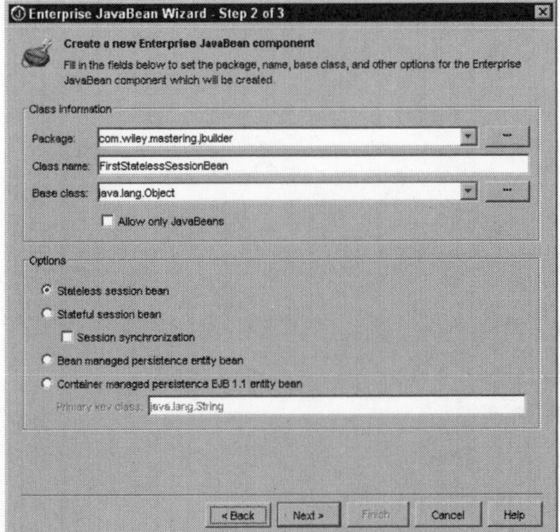


**Figure 19.1** Create a new Enterprise JavaBean component.

**Base class.** Because the Enterprise JavaBean, represented by the preceding class name, which is generated by the wizard, is an implementation of an existing javax.ejb.EntityBean, or javax.ejb.SessionBean interface, developers are free to extend preexisting classes. By clicking on the ellipses, the Find Classes dialog will appear to allow the developer to either browse or search the project's classpath for a particular class to extend. In all cases, the remote interface code that is generated will extend javax.ejb.EJBObject; the code is initially identical, regardless of the option selected. This is also true for the Home interface, which extends javax.ejb.EJBHome.

## Options

The *Stateless Session Bean*, which resembles a CORBA server, is probably the most common Enterprise JavaBean. Successive calls to Stateless Session Beans are not guaranteed to reach the same Enterprise Bean instance. In fact, if the load is particularly high, and if there are several clients accessing the same Stateless Bean, chances are more than likely that two successive calls from the client, even within the same scope of a single method, will not reach the same instance of the Enterprise Bean class running in the EJB container.

It is important to note that clients do not have direct handles to the implemented class running in the EJB container. Clients have access to the EJB container, and the EJB container is responsible for maintaining the lifecycle of the Enterprise Bean instance as well as delegating access to its methods. The following is the generated source code for the Session Bean's Bean class:

```
package com.wiley.mastering.jbuilder;

import java.rmi.*;
import javax.ejb.*;

public class FirstSessionBean implements SessionBean {
  SessionContext sessionContext;
  public void ejbCreate() {
  }
  public void ejbRemove() {
  }
  public void ejbActivate() {
  }
  public void ejbPassivate() {
  }
  public void setSessionContext(SessionContext sessionContext) {
    this.sessionContext = sessionContext;
  }
}
```

*Stateful Session Beans* are Enterprise Beans designed to maintain state, as long as the client retains the handle to the Remote interface. Once the client's reference to the

Remote Interface of a Stateful Session Bean goes out of scope, the EJB container is no longer responsible for maintaining the stateful information associated with the Session Bean. If it is necessary for successive calls within the scope of a single method on a client to access exactly the same instance of a Session Bean, then Stateful Session Beans should be used. It is also true that the Stateful Session Service can maintain the Stateful information of a Session Bean in a long-term repository (such as a relational database), but this is not a requirement for use. Do not think of successive calls from the user interface point of view. Using a Stateful Session Bean solely to retain data collected by the user interface for use in a future action by the user interface may not be in the best interest of the infrastructure. Consider retaining that information closer to the user interface or persisting it in the back-end data store or repository (database). The difference between a Stateful and Stateless Session Bean is not distinguishable in the source code; rather, it is a property that is set in the Deployment Descriptor:

```
<session-type>Stateful</session-type>
```

Only Stateful Session Beans should consider implementing the javax.ejb.SessionSynchronization interface. This should also be considered only where container-managed transactions are being used. This will add afterBegin(), beforeCompletion(), and afterCompletion() methods to the Enterprise Bean class. The intention of this interface is to give the Enterprise JavaBean developer the ability to perform work just after a transaction has begun, just before it is to complete, and after it has completed:

```
public void afterBegin() {
}
```

The afterBegin() method will be evoked some time shortly after a new transaction has been started and before the first business method is called. This method is executed in the scope of the transactional context:

```
public void beforeCompletion() {
}
```

The beforeCompletion() method will be evoked some time shortly after the last business method is evoked and just prior to the transaction being committed. Like the afterBegin() method, this method is also executed in the scope of the transactional context:

```
public void afterCompletion(boolean committed) {
}
```

The afterCompletion() method will be evoked after the transaction has completed. If the transaction was successful, the value of the committed parameter will be true. If the transaction was not successful, the value will be false.

Entity Beans are the object-oriented representation of information that is typically stored in relational databases. An Entity Bean's state is guaranteed to be maintained based on the state of the last successful transaction to create, update, or delete. The data that Entity Beans represent is meant to be used over relatively long periods of time.

This data is also meant to be shared by more than one client. There are two very different strategies for developing Entity Beans. *Bean Managed Persistence* should more likely be termed Developer Managed Persistence because it is the Entity Bean Developer that is responsible for developing the code necessary to persist the state of the Entity Bean. This usually involves the use of JDBC:

```
package com.wiley.mastering.jbuilder;

import java.rmi.*;
import javax.ejb.*;

public class FirstEntityBean implements EntityBean {
  EntityContext entityContext;
  public String ejbCreate() throws CreateException {
    /**@todo Implement this method*/
    return null;
  }
  public void ejbPostCreate() throws CreateException {
  }
  public void ejbLoad() {
  }
  public void ejbStore() {
  }
  public void ejbRemove() throws RemoveException {
  }
  public void ejbActivate() {
  }
  public void ejbPassivate() {
  }
  public void setEntityContext(EntityContext entityContext) {
    this.entityContext = entityContext;
  }
  public void unsetEntityContext() {
    entityContext = null;
  }
}
```

The EJB container will take care of most of the object relational mapping for the Entity Bean developer. All of the information that is required by the EJB container to manage the object to relational mapping for a Container-Managed Persistence Entity (CMP) Bean is stored within the Deployment Descriptor. The EJB 1.x Entity Bean Modeler wizard does a more effective job of creating CMP Entity Beans based on existing database tables that are accessible via an existing JDBC driver.

Primary Keys contain the unique information that is used to locate a single instance of an Entity Bean. This class could be as simple as a java.lang.String object, or it could be a new class that you create. It is important that this class implements the java.io.Serializable interface:

```
package com.wiley.mastering.jbuilder;

import java.io.*;

public class FirstPrimaryKey implements Serializable {

  public String key;

  public FirstPrimaryKey() {
  }

  public FirstPrimaryKey(String key) {
    this.key = key;
  }
  public boolean equals(Object obj) {
    if (this.getClass().equals(obj.getClass())) {
      FirstPrimaryKey that = (FirstPrimaryKey) obj;
      return this.key.equals(that.key);
    }
    return false;
  }
  public int hashCode() {
    return key.hashCode();
  }
}
```

## Set EJB Interface Names

Prior to actually generating the Java source code and editing the Deployment Descriptor, the individual names of each of the components can be modified (see Figure 19.2). The naming convention that is utilized by default uses the class name established in the previous step as the Enterprise Bean class, replaces "Bean" with "Home" for the Home Interface class, and removes both "Bean" and "Home" for the Remote Interface class. This affects both the generated Java source code and the initial XML code that is added to the Deployment Descriptor as follows:

```
<session>
 <ejb-name>FirstStatelessSessionBean</ejb-name>
 <home>com.wiley.mastering.jbuilder.FirstStatelessSessionBeanHome</home>
 <remote> com.wiley.mastering.jbuilder.FirstStatelessSession</remote>
 <ejb-class>
com.wiley.mastering.jbuilder.FirstStatelessSessionBean</ejb-class>
 <session-type>Stateless</session-type>
 <transaction-type>Container</transaction-type>
</session>
```

You can enter the following information using the Deployment Descriptor Editor:

**Enterprise Bean class: <ejb-class>.** This is the class that the EJB container will access to evoke the implemented application and business logic that the Enterprise JavaBean developer has written. The EJB container also maintains the lifecycle of this class.

**Home Interface class: <home>.** The Home interface defines all of the methods to create, remove, and find Enterprise JavaBeans. Clients that want to access the Enterprise Bean class must first obtain a reference to its Home Interface class. The client, through a standard Java naming and directory lookup using the defined JNDI name, can discover the Home interface.

**Remote Interface class: <remote>.** The Remote Interface class defines the methods that are accessible to the calling client. Clients do not access Enterprise Bean classes directly. Where this gets a bit confusing is when you notice that the Enterprise Bean class does not implement the Remote Interface class. It is easy to see the relationship between the Home and Remote interfaces. It is the responsibility of the EJB container to delegate access to the Enterprise Bean class via the Remote Interface class that the client is using. Clients do not communicate directly with the Enterprise Bean class; clients communicate with the EJB container.

**Bean name: <ejb-name>.** This name is used by the Deployment Descriptor and the EJB container. It has no meaning to the Java source code of the Home, Remote, or Bean classes. This will be the name that is displayed in the Project pane under the EJB module. Clicking on this name in the Project pane will go to the Deployment Descriptor Editor for the Bean.

**JNDI name.** Each application server can set up the JNDI tree differently. The JNDI name that is entered here will be used in the container-specific Deployment Descriptor. This is the registered name that clients will use to look up the Home Interface class.

**Generate headers.** Using the values defined in the project's class JavaDoc fields (located on the General tab of the Project properties), selecting this option will generate a Comment tag at the beginning of the Sample Bean's source code:

```
/**
 * <p>Title: </p>
 * <p>Description: </p>
 * <p>Copyright: Copyright (c) 2002</p>
 * <p>Company: </p>
 * @author not attributable
 * @version 1.0
 */
```

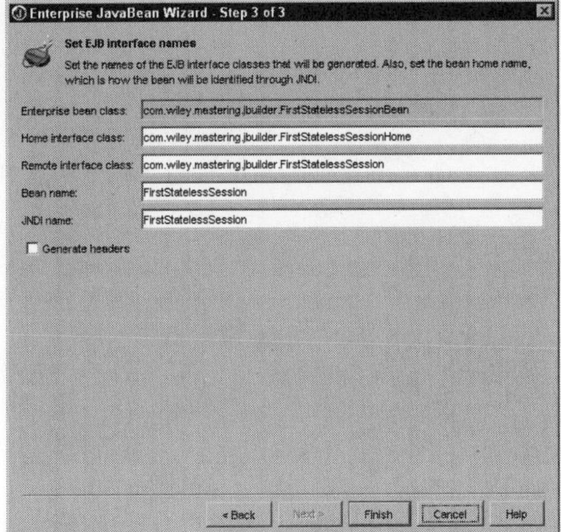


**Figure 19.2** Set EJB interface names.

# Deployment Descriptor Editor

A list of all EJBs that are part of the EJB module is displayed in the Project pane (see Figure 19.3) under the EJB module node. Double-clicking on each node will open the Deployment Descriptor Editor for that particular Enterprise JavaBean. Once the Deployment Descriptor Editor is open, you will notice that there are several tabs: General, Environment, EJB Reference, Resource Reference, Security Role Reference, and Properties. Each tab configures various behaviors and settings that the EJB container is to manage for the Enterprise JavaBean when it is deployed.

## General Tab

Similar to the "Set EJB Interface Names" step of the new Enterprise JavaBean 1.x wizard, the General tab is where the developer would set the various classes that make up this particular Enterprise JavaBean. For the most part, if the wizard was used to create the Enterprise JavaBean, there will be few reasons to modify the settings on the General tab. If, however, any of the class names or packages were refactored, renamed, or migrated, it will be necessary to update the information in the Deployment Descriptor to use the new names. There are also differences in the General tab for Session Beans and Entity Beans, including the following:

**Bean class <ejb-class>.** This is the Enterprise Bean class that the EJB container will access to evoke the implemented application and business logic that the Enterprise JavaBean developer has written. The EJB container also maintains the lifecycle of this class.

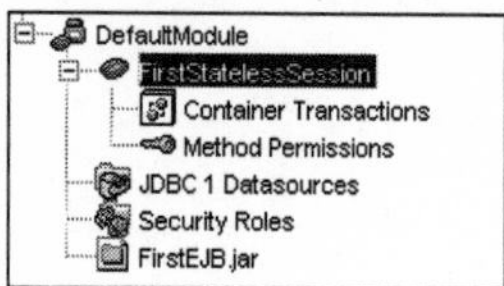


**Figure 19.3** Project pane.

**Home interface <home>.** This class defines all the methods to create, remove, and find Enterprise JavaBeans. Clients that want to access the Enterprise Bean class must first obtain a reference to its Home Interface class. The client, through a standard Java naming and directory lookup using the defined JNDI name, can discover the Home interface.

**Remote interface <remote>.** This class defines the methods that are accessible to the calling client. Clients do not access Enterprise Bean classes directly. Where this gets a bit confusing is when you notice that the Enterprise Bean class does not implement the Remote Interface class. It is easy to see the relationship between the Home and Remote interfaces. It is the responsibility of the EJB container to delegate access to the Enterprise Bean class via the Remote Interface class that the client is using. Clients do not communicate directly with the Enterprise Bean class; clients communicate with the EJB container.

**Home JNDI name.** Each application server can set up the JNDI tree differently. The JNDI name that is entered here will be used in the container-specific Deployment Descriptor. This is the registered name that clients will use to look up the Home Interface class.

**Description.** This optional information is useful only to the developer and is meaningless to the EJB container. You can enter descriptive information that could be displayed on a console's screen depending on the target application's EJB container.

**Small and large icon.** Also meant for use in deployment consoles as well as development tools, the Enterprise JavaBean Developer can set both a small and a large icon similar to those used by graphical Java Beans that are added to the Component Palette in the Swing Designer.

## *Session*

The following information is only visible when viewing the Deployment Descriptor for Session Beans:

**Session Type.** In the new Enterprise JavaBean 1.x wizard, it appeared that two different types of Java source code were chosen to be generated. What was actually being determined was how to set this particular property in the Deployment Descriptor. The <session-type> property can be set to either Stateful or Stateless (Figure 19.4).

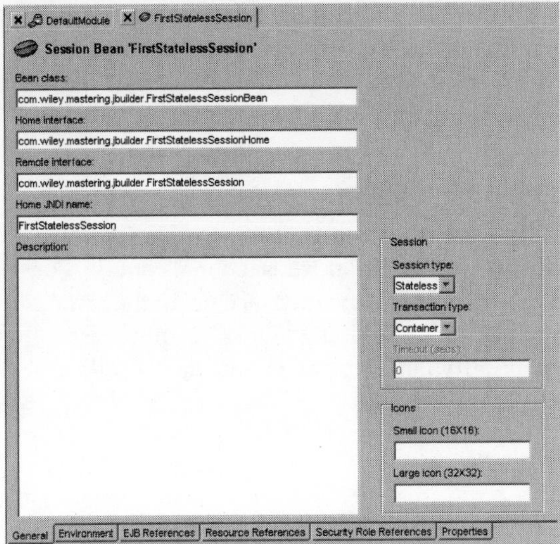


**Figure 19.4** General properties.

**Transaction type <transaction-type>.** This can be set to either Bean or Container. The default value is Container. It is also assumed that if implementing the SessionSynchronization interface in Stateful Session Beans, that container-managed transactions are used. If Bean-managed transactions are desired, then the Session Bean developer is responsible for creating an instance of a javax.transaction.UserTransaction and managing the transaction programmatically. A third option would be for the calling client to create the UserTransaction and handle the transactional programming from the client side.

**Timeout.** Only editable for Stateful Session Beans, this property controls the lifetime that a Stateful Session Bean will remain in a passive state. The EJB container is responsible for managing the lifecycle of all Enterprise JavaBeans and may remove any Stateful Session Beans after their timeout is reached. Any successive calls from the client will result in a java.rmi.NoSuchObjectException. This is a requirement for all compliant EJB containers.

## *Entity*

The following information is only visible when viewing the Deployment Descriptor for Entity Beans:

**Persistence type.** Similar to Stateful and Stateless Session Beans, there is not much difference between the base implementation of a Bean-Managed Persistence Entity Bean and a Container-Managed Persistence Entity Bean. The differences do become more obvious once all the necessary persistence logic is added to the Bean-Managed Persistence Entity Beans, of course. But again, it is primarily the Deployment Descriptor that determines if a given Entity Bean's attributes are to be Container Managed or Bean Managed.

**Primary Key class.** All Entity Beans are to have a Primary Key class that can uniquely identify a specific instance of a given Entity Bean. Think of this as a unique object that is used as a key in a hashtable.

**Reentrant.** Developers can control how many clients can access an Entity Bean at a given point in time within the scope of a particular transactional context. For two calls to be made to a given Entity Bean's remote interface using the same transactional context while a previous call is still doing "work" is quite rare. This is typically possible only when Entity Beans engage in the use of callbacks to the client.

## Environment

Environment variables (see Figure 19.5) can be established in the Deployment Descriptor and accessed using the JNDI API just as resources are used in more traditional Java programming. You can Add, Remove, and Remove All properties on the Environment page of the Deployment Descriptor Editor as follows:

**Description.** This optional information is useful only to the developer and is meaningless to the EJB Container. You can enter descriptive information that could be displayed on a console's screen depending on the target EJB container.

**Property.** This is the name that will be used to look up the instance of the type of property in order to return the value. Think of this as a sort of String Key value or a JNDI name that will be used.

**Value.** This is the actual value that will be returned by the instance of the type of property that is looked up.

**Type.** Values can be of many types. Typically only the object equivalent of Java's basic types are used.

To access information, set up in the Environment settings of a given Enterprise JavaBean; the developer can write JNDI code to access the environment context and retrieve the value of the property accordingly:

```
javax.naming.Context initCtx = new javax.naming.InitialContext();
javax.naming.Context myEnv =
(javax.naming.Context)initCtx.lookup("java:comp/env");
java.lang.Integer someNumber =
(java.lang.Integer)myEnv.lookup(-SomeNumberî);
```

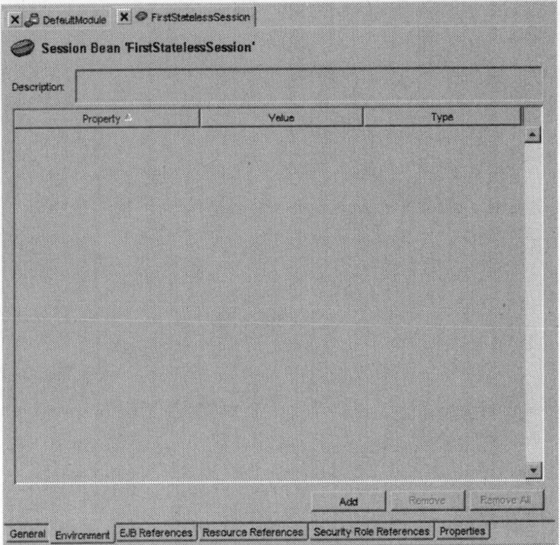


**Figure 19.5** Environment settings.

## EJB Reference

There are times when one Enterprise JavaBean will want to call on another Enterprise JavaBean. In all such cases an EJB Reference (see Figure 19.6) must be established for each such call. You can Add, Remove, and Remove All properties on the EJB Reference page of the Deployment Descriptor Editor.

The description is optional information. It is useful only to the developer and is meaningless to the EJB container. You can enter descriptive information that could be displayed on a console's screen depending on the target EJB container.

The name will be used locally by the Enterprise JavaBean to perform the lookup. For calls to other EJBs, it is the accepted practice to preface the name with an ejb/ prior to establishing a unique name. Think of this as a layer of indirection; the ejb/LocalSecondStatelessSession name will be directed to the SecondStatelessSession JNDI name. It is the EJB container's responsibility to provide all access to external resources; this includes other EJBs. This code within the EJB that establishes this EJB Reference would look something like this:

```
javax.naming.Context context = new javax.naming.InitialContext();
java.lang.Object object =
context.lookup("java:comp/env/ejb/SecondStatelessSession");
com.wiley.mastering.jbuilder.SecondStatelessSessionHome home =
(com.wiley.mastering.jbuilder.SecondStatelessSessionHome)
javax.rmi.PortableRemoteObject.narrow(object,
com.wiley.mastering.jbuilder.SecondStatelessSessionHome.class);
com.wiley.mastering.jbuilder.SecondStatelessSession
secondStatelessSession = home.create();
```

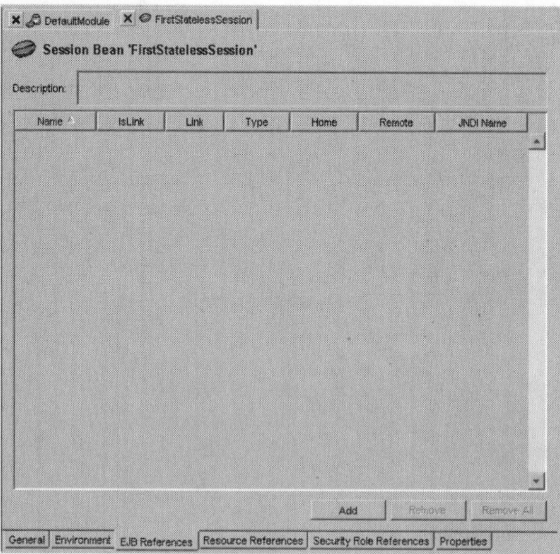


**Figure 19.6** EJB Reference.

## *EJB Is in a Java Archive Deployed to the Same EJB Container*

If you check the IsLink property, the Type, Home, Remote, and JNDI Name selection boxes are no longer accessible. Instead, the Deployment Descriptor looks at other Enterprise JavaBeans that are already defined in the Deployment Descriptor; these beans and only these beans are selectable in the Link selection box. The Type, Home, and Remote settings are set based on the information already defined in the Deployment Descriptor for the Enterprise JavaBean selected. The JNDI name is no longer necessary because the EJB container will not be asked to make a remote call or use the registered JNDI naming service to look up a reference to the Enterprise JavaBean.

Instead, the IsLink setting is letting the EJB container know that the Enterprise JavaBean is already located within the container and is already being managed within the same EJB container as the calling Enterprise JavaBean. Where this gets a little more confusing is when multiple EJB archives are to be deployed to the same EJB container. Although it is true that the same EJB container will manage Beans in each archive, and depending on the container's implementation, they may also both share the same class loader, JBuilder does not know that this is the intention of the developer. Therefore, only Enterprise JavaBeans defined in the same EJB module are visible in the list.

## *EJB Is in a Different Java Archive Deployed to a Different EJB Container*

Other than selecting an Enterprise JavaBean that is already defined in the same EJB module, the other option is to set the necessary properties to access an Enterprise JavaBean that is running in another EJB container somewhere on the network. Here you select the type of Enterprise JavaBean that you wish to access, either a Session Bean or an Entity Bean. Again, this selection box is accessible only when Enterprise JavaBeans are being defined that are not part of the EJB module and therefore not to be part of the EJB archive that the EJB module is to create (IsLink is not selected). The Home and Remote Interface classes are selected and set and should correspond to the classes that are defined in conjunction with the JNDI name that is defined. The developer will use code that will already assume the Home and Interface class and will perform a JNDI lookup based on the name.

In the Deployment Descriptor, the developer can modify the actual JNDI name that the Enterprise JavaBean is bound to without having to modify the source code. This could be useful if a different JNDI name is used for test and production. This way, the same compiled class can be accessed by a test JNDI name, and a separately running instance on the same network can be accessed by a production JNDI name. Switching from test to production can take place without editing the source code and without rebuilding the project and repackaging the EJB archive.

## Resource References

Resource references are used to make various external resources available to Enterprise JavaBeans being managed by the EJB container (Figure 19.7). In general, all resources that an Enterprise JavaBean will need to perform its implemented logic must be registered with the EJB container in some manner. There are Environment objects, EJB references, and Resource references. All are looked up via a JNDI name. Some of these resources are accessible only locally and have only one JNDI name bound to them; others have their own local JNDI name that the Enterprise JavaBean uses as well as their own JNDI name. The most common type of Resource reference used is, of course, a DataSource. You can Add, Remove, and Remove All properties on the Resource Reference page of the Deployment Descriptor Editor as follows:

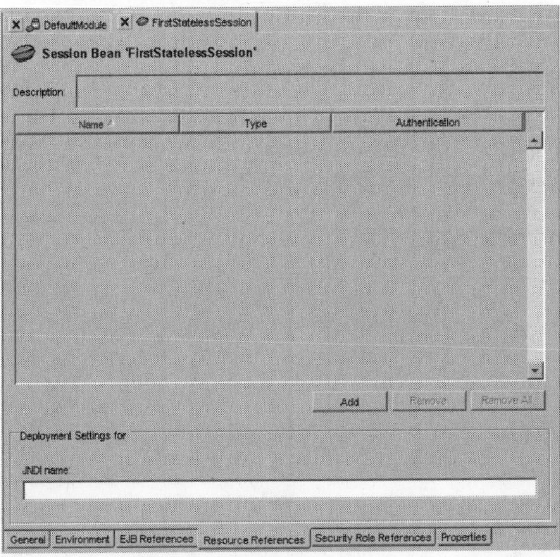


**Figure 19.7** Resource references.

**Description.** This optional information is useful only to the developer and is meaningless to the EJB container. You can enter descriptive information that could be displayed on a console's screen depending on the target application server.

**Name.** This is the name that will be used locally by the Enterprise JavaBean to perform the lookup. For calls to external resources like DataSource, it is the accepted practice to preface the name with a jdbc/ prior to establishing a unique name for the local DataSource. This is also a layer of indirection because the DataSource must be bound to the naming service and the name used by the Enterprise JavaBean must be a separate name. Only Container Managed Persistence Entity Beans need this type of resource to be defined. The EJB container will lookup this reference and establishes a connection. Bean Managed Persistence Entity Beans and Session Beans will need to look up these resources and obtain connections programmatically. The code that establishes this type of JDBC connection would look something like this:

```
javax.naming.Context context = new javax.naming.InitialContext();
javax.sql.DataSource dataSource = (javax.sql.DataSource)ctx.lookup
("java:comp/env/jdbc/LocalFirstDataSource");
java.sql.Connection conn = dataSource.getConnection();
```

**Type.** There are several different types of resources that can be defined in the Deployment Descriptor. DataSources are probably the most widely used.

**Authentication.** Can be set to wither container or application.

## Summary

In this chapter we looked at the development steps necessary to create Enterprise JavaBeans that are compliant with the EJB 1.1 specification. JBuilder employs the use of wizards to generate the Home, Remote, and Bean classes for both Session Beans and Entity Beans. In Chapter 20, "Developing EJB 2.x," we not only see some of the new technology features that are introduced in the updated EJB 2.0 specification, but we also look at how JBuilder solves the problem of not being able to go back and use a wizard on existing code by using a new two-way EJB 2.0 Designer.

CHAPTER

20

# Developing EJB 2.x

As the EJB specification evolved, so did the tools used to create Enterprise JavaBeans. One of the biggest changes introduced in the 2.0 version of the Enterprise JavaBean specification was in the area of Entity Beans. With EJB 1.x development, JBuilder provided a series of wizards and code generators as well as a Deployment Descriptor Editor to help J2EE developers create their Enterprise applications. The limitation of this RAD approach is true of all code-generation productivity wizards: What happens after the code is initially generated?

One may think that using a UML design tool could help with creating Enterprise JavaBeans, but this just does not seem to be true. To start, the relationships between the Remote interface, Home interface, and the Bean implementation class itself are not exactly represented by a "has a" or an "is a" relationship. It is actually the EJB container that is responsible for managing the relationship between an Enterprise JavaBeans Remote interface and the lifecycle of the implemented Bean class. This is also true of the relationships between two Entity Beans. It is the column of the relational database tables defined in the Deployment Descriptor that actually defines the nature of the relationship between two Entity Beans. In fact, so much of the relationships between Enterprise Beans are dependent on information in the Deployment Descriptor, it is almost impossible to solely depend on a purely object-oriented class diagram based on UML to manage the development of Enterprise JavaBeans within the J2EE framework.

Just as developers do not use UML modelers to create graphical user interfaces (for instance, JFrame has a JPanel, JPanel has a JButton, JPanel has a JTextField, and so on), it does not make sense for Enterprise Java developers to rely on UML modelers to developer their Enterprise JavaBeans. Given the limitations of solely using code generators, and the limitations of depending on UML modelers to graphically develop Enterprise JavaBeans, it is only natural that an EJB Designer was considered.

This chapter looks at the following EJB technologies:

**EJB 2.0 Designer.** With the EJB Designer, developers can work on laying the foundation that they will use to create their EJB applications. With Container-Managed Persistence Entity Beans, the developer may never need to modify the source code or the Deployment Descriptor outside of the Designer. With other Enterprise JavaBeans like Session Beans, the two-way nature of the EJB 2.0 Designer will help make tedious modifications easier with the visual designer.

**EJB Test Client.** Once development has reached a point where it is time to test the business logic that has been implemented in the various EJBs contained within a given EJB module, the EJB Test Client can be used to generate the test code necessary to evoke the various remote methods. JUnit can be used as a testing framework.

**EJB Deployment Descriptor.** Most of the Deployment Descriptor edits are now handled by the EJB Designer. The EJB module still owns the Deployment Descriptor and other layout files that the Designer now uses.

**DataSources.** Accessing databases through the use of DataSources, the EJB Designer can either generate design time schema definitions of existing databases or use the fields of the various Entity Beans to create a new schema that can, in turn, be used to generate the Data Definition Language to create a database.

# EJB 2.0 Bean Designer

There are actually two ways to access the EJB 2.0 Bean Designer. From the Object Gallery, you can select the new EJB 2.0 Designer wizard, which will prompt you for the name of the existing EJB module that will contain EJB 2.0 Enterprise JavaBeans. If there are no EJB modules in the project that are set to develop version EJB 2.0 Enterprise JavaBeans, you can click on the New button to create one. You must first ensure that the server that you have selected for the project is capable of supporting EJB 2.0.

It is not possible to change the version of EJBs that an EJB module was created to develop after the EJB module was established. If an EJB 1.x module was created by mistake, then a new EJB 2.0 module must be created. By default, when an EJB 2.0 module is created, and the module is opened (by double-clicking on the module's name in the Project pane), the EJB 2.0 Bean Designer is open, even if you did not create an EJB 2.0 Bean Designer. This is the other way to access the EJB 2.0 Bean Designer: by creating one from the Object Gallery, or by creating a new EJB 2.0-compliant EJB module and double-clicking on the EJB module name in the project pane. The two-way tool nature of the various editors in the EJB Designer ensures that edits outside the Designer are in sync with any changes or edits made within the Designer. The EJB Designer is a graphical way to edit both the Java source code and the Deployment Descriptor for each Enterprise Bean in the EJB module.

Once the EJB 2.0 Bean Designer is open, you will notice a toolbar along the top of the Designer (see Figure 20.1); there are technically no more wizards involved in the creation of EJB within that particular EJB module, at least not in the traditional sense of a wizard. This is where you will begin to work with the Designer. Here you will Create, Delete, and View the source code of EJBs as well as Create and Import Database Schemas and Control Design Time views of the EJBs you are working on. Alternatively, you can also right-mouse click anywhere within the EJB Designer, and a menu will pop up, giving you access to the same functionality (see Figure 20.2).

## Create EJB

You have the ability to create CMP or BMP Entity Beans, Session Beans, and Message Driven Beans. The principle is the same, and except where there are specific differences between the 1.1 and the 2.0 versions of the EJB specification, the generated source code and deployment descriptor edits are basically the same. The added ability you now have is that you can go back and modify the settings and properties you could only set when the wizard was first used. Within the EJB Designer, you have the full two-way tool capability to modify source and Designer.

### *Container Managed Persistence Entity Bean*

There are two different types of Entity Beans. Container Managed Persistence (CMP) is where the EJB container is responsible for generating all of the necessary Structured Query Language (SQL) code used to persist the object's attributes to the Java Database Connectivity (JDBC) DataSource. Most often, it is the case that a given vendor's CMP engine is optimized to persist only the delta between the previous state of the Entity Bean and the new state of the Entity Bean. CMP engines should also be optimized to make the fewest remote procedure calls (RPCs).

With CMP Entity Beans, there are two basic design approaches to take. One is where the attributes and class relationships are defined by an existing database table structure, and the other is where the attributes and class relationships define a new database table structure. Deciding which way to go will determine how to utilize the EJB Designer. If the CMP Entity Bean is to be developed first, then use the Designer's toolbar or popup menu to create the Entity Bean. This will give you an empty shell to which you can quickly add field and methods.

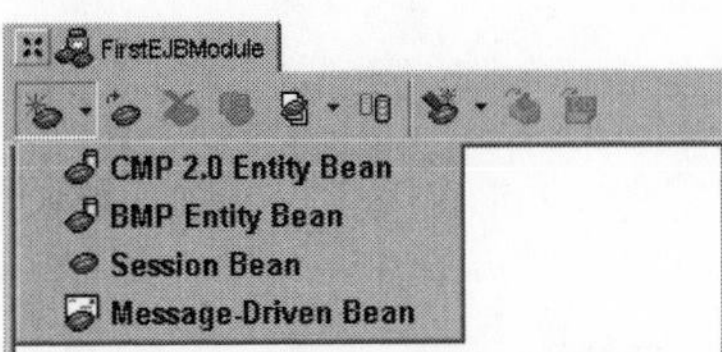


**Figure 20.1** EJB Designer toolbar.

**Figure 20.2** EJB Designer popup menu.

### Bean Properties

When you first create a new CMP Entity Bean, a Properties dialog will appear in the Designer (see Figure 20.3), where you can edit configuration settings of the Bean at design time. This is a change from the one-way wizards of EJB 1.1 development. Use this dialog to enter the following information:

**Bean name: <ejb-name>.** This name is used by the Deployment Descriptor and the EJB container. It has no meaning to the Java source code of the Home, Remote, or Bean classes. This will be the name that is displayed in the Project pane under the EJB module. Clicking on this name in the Project pane will bring out the Deployment Descriptor Editor for the Bean. This name is also accessible from the Classes and Packages dialog. You can also change this name on the Classes and Packages dialog.

**Abstract schema name.** Defined for each Entity Bean, the value of the abstract schema name must be unique within the ejb-jar file and therefore unique within the Deployment Descriptor for a given EJB module. This name will be used in the specification of EJB QL queries. Most likely, this name will be set to the same name as the Bean name, but that is not a requirement.

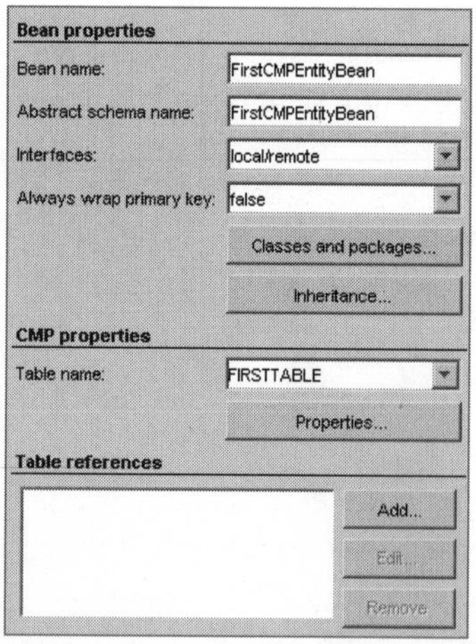

**Figure 20.3** CMP Entity Bean properties.

**Always wrap primary key.** If there is only one field that makes up the Primary Key for a given CMP Entity Bean, and that field is an implementation of an Object class in the java.lang.* package (String, Double, Short, Long, Float, Integer, and so on), you have the choice of using this class as the Primary Key class or having the EJB Designer "wrap" the class in another class that has an implementation of an object in the java.lang.* package as one of its properties. Setting this value to true will force the creation of a new Primary Key class. Setting this value to false will allow one of the Object classes in the java.lang.* package to be used as the Primary Key class if only one field is used to make up the primary key.

### Interfaces

With the introduction of EJB 2.0, the choice you make during development as to which interface your Enterprise JavaBeans subscribe to affects the actual code you develop. This architectural change that forces a developer to make a decision that should not be made until deployment time is largely due to limitations in certain vendors' communications layer. Beans that were co-located within the same Java Virtual Machine were making remote procedure calls to each other. This decision will affect the interface options that the methods and fields you implement can choose from as well as the generated classes that are named in the Classes and Packages dialog:

**Remote.** If the Enterprise JavaBeans you are developing are to be accessed by an external client or other Enterprise JavaBeans running within a separate EJB container running in a different partition or on a separate server, then you will want to use the Remote interface.

**Local.** If the Enterprise JavaBeans you develop are to be accessed only by other beans within the EJB container and are most likely packaged within the same EJB archive file (therefore all part of the same EJB module), then you will want to use the Local interface.

**Local/Remote.** If you are not sure, or if you are sure that your Enterprise JavaBean will be accessed locally by other Enterprise JavaBeans co-located in the same Java Virtual Machine as well as by clients and other Enterprise JavaBeans running in an external Java Virtual Machine, then you should select to support both Local and Remote interfaces.

### Classes and Packages

You can almost use the designer too much and forget that actual code is being generated and updated. You can initially set the Class and Package names of the generated source code (see Figure 20.4). If you change this after developing and working on this and other code within the project, and come back to change the classes and packages for a particular JavaBean, you will most likely break some other piece of code. This does not work as the UML refactoring works, nor does it work like a global search and replace. What this will do is update both the source code and the Deployment Descriptor, which is something that the UML refactoring cannot do. The Classes and Packages options are as follows:

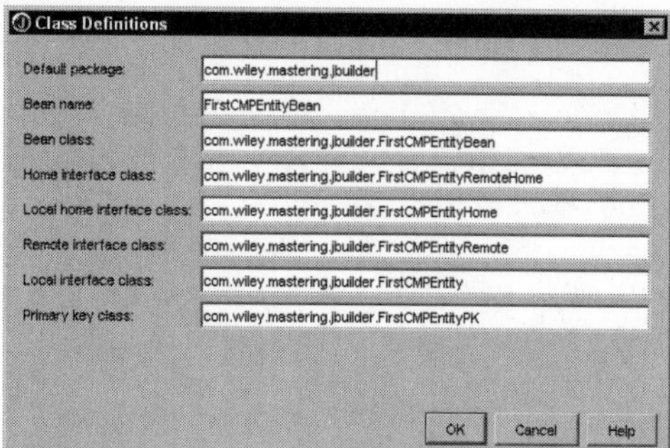


**Figure 20.4** CMP Entity Bean class definitions.

**Default package.** Although not necessary, it is a good idea to consider separating Enterprise JavaBeans by business function or by implemented design pattern. Each package name could contain groupings of related Enterprise Beans.

```
package com.wiley.mastering.jbuilder;
```

**Bean name: <ejb-name>.** This name is used by the Deployment Descriptor and the EJB container. It has no meaning to the Java source code of the Home, Remote, or Bean classes. This will be the name that is displayed in the Project pane under the EJB module. Clicking on this name in the Project pane will bring up the Deployment Descriptor Editor for the Bean. If you change the Bean name here, it will also change the Bean name on the Beans Properties page.

**Bean class: <ejb-class>.** This is the Enterprise Bean class that the EJB container will access to evoke the implemented application and business logic that the Enterprise JavaBean developer has written. The EJB container also maintains the lifecycle of this class.

```
package com.wiley.mastering.jbuilder;

import javax.ejb.*;

abstract public class FirstCMPEntityBean implements EntityBean {
  EntityContext entityContext;
  public java.lang.String ejbCreate(java.lang.String untitledField1)
throws CreateException {
    setUntitledField1(untitledField1);
    return null;
  }
  public void ejbPostCreate(java.lang.String untitledField1) throws
CreateException {
    /**@todo Complete this method*/
  }
  public void ejbRemove() throws RemoveException {
    /**@todo Complete this method*/
  }
```

```
  public abstract void setUntitledField1(java.lang.String
untitledField1);
  public abstract java.lang.String getUntitledField1();
  public void ejbLoad() {
    /**@todo Complete this method*/
  }
  public void ejbStore() {
    /**@todo Complete this method*/
  }
  public void ejbActivate() {
    /**@todo Complete this method*/
  }
  public void ejbPassivate() {
    /**@todo Complete this method*/
  }
  public void unsetEntityContext() {
    this.entityContext = null;
  }
  public void setEntityContext(EntityContext entityContext) {
    this.entityContext = entityContext;
  }
}
```

**Home interface class: <home>.** This class defines all the methods to create, remove, and find Enterprise JavaBeans. Clients that want to access the Enterprise Bean class must first obtain a reference to its Home Interface class. The client, through a standard Java naming and directory lookup using the defined JNDI name, can discover the Home interface.

```
package com.wiley.mastering.jbuilder;

import javax.ejb.*;
import java.util.*;
import java.rmi.*;

public interface FirstCMPEntityRemoteHome extends javax.ejb.EJBHome {
  public FirstCMPEntityRemote create(String untitledField1) throws
CreateException, RemoteException;
  public FirstCMPEntityRemote findByPrimaryKey(FirstCMPEntityBeanPK
pk) throws FinderException, RemoteException;
}
```

**Local home interface class.** A major difference between the EJB 1.x and the EJB 2.x specification is in the area of Local versus Remote classes. Local Home Interface classes are accessed only by other Enterprise JavaBeans within the same deployed JAR and therefore are managed by the same EJB container.

```
package com.wiley.mastering.jbuilder;

import javax.ejb.*;
import java.util.*;

public interface FirstCMPEntityHome extends javax.ejb.EJBLocalHome {
  public FirstCMPEntity create(String untitledField1) throws
CreateException;
  public FirstCMPEntity findByPrimaryKey(String untitledField1) throws
FinderException;
}
```

**Remote interface class: <remote>.** This class defines the methods that are accessible to the calling client. Clients do not access Enterprise Bean classes directly. Where this gets a bit confusing is when you notice that the Enterprise Bean class does not implement the Remote Interface class. It is easy to see the relationship between the Home and Remote interfaces. It is the responsibility of the EJB container to delegate access to the Enterprise Bean class via the Remote Interface class that the client is using. Clients do not communicate directly with the Enterprise Bean class; clients communicate with the EJB container.

```
package com.wiley.mastering.jbuilder;

import javax.ejb.*;
import java.util.*;
import java.rmi.*;

public interface FirstCMPEntityRemote extends javax.ejb.EJBObject {
  public String getUntitledField1() throws RemoteException;
}
```

**Local interface class.** A major difference between the EJB 1.x and the EJB 2.x specifications is in the area of Local versus Remote classes. Local Interface classes are accessed only by other Enterprise JavaBeans within the same deployed JAR and therefore are managed by the same EJB container.

```
package com.wiley.mastering.jbuilder;

import javax.ejb.*;
import java.util.*;

public interface FirstCMPEntity extends javax.ejb.EJBLocalObject {
  public String getUntitledField1();
}
```

**Primary key class.** When developing a CMP Entity Bean, a Primary Key class will be created if more than one field is set as being part of the Primary Key, or if you have decided to always wrap the Primary Key in the Bean properties. The Primary Key is to be created by the client and passed in to the findByPrimaryKey() method of the Entity Bean's Home interface. The Primary Key is typically a combination of fields that can uniquely identify a single instance of the Entity Bean. If a database is used, the field or fields that make up the Primary

Key for the Entity Bean are likely the same database table columns that make up the Primary Key or Index for that table. Just as important as it is that the field or combination of fields results in a unique combination, it is important that the equals() and hashCode() methods of the Primary Key Class function properly:

```
package com.wiley.mastering.jbuilder;

import java.io.*;

public class FirstCMPEntityBeanPK
    implements Serializable {

  public String untitledField1;

  public FirstCMPEntityBeanPK() {
  }

  public FirstCMPEntityBeanPK(String untitledField1) {
    this.untitledField1 = untitledField1;
  }

  public boolean equals(Object obj) {
    if (obj != null) {
      if (this.getClass().equals(obj.getClass())) {
        FirstCMPEntityBeanPK that = (FirstCMPEntityBeanPK) obj;
        return ( ( (this.untitledField1 == null) &&
                  (that.untitledField1 == null)) ||
                (this.untitledField1 != null &&
                 this.untitledField1.equals(that.untitledField1)));
      }
    }
    return false;
  }

  public int hashCode() {
    return untitledField1.hashCode();
  }
}
```

## Inheritance

Similar to the Base class of the 1.x Java Bean wizard, this allows the developer to extend the Bean Class from an existing implementation or abstract class. Because the Enterprise JavaBean, represented by the preceding Bean class, is an implementation of an existing javax.ejb.EntityBean, or javax.ejb.SessionBean interface, developers are free to extend preexisting classes. By clicking on the ellipses, the Find Classes dialog will appear to allow the developer to either browse or search the project's classpath for a particular class to extend. In all cases, the remote interface code that is generated will extend javax.ejb.EJBObject and is initially identical code regardless of the option selected. This is also true for the Home interface, which extends javax.ejb.EJBHome.

## CMP Properties

Container Managed Persistence Entity Beans have additional properties that are configured in the Deployment Descriptor and that instruct the EJB container how to manage the individual CMP Entity Beans. These properties are specific to each server. How these properties are configured can affect the behavior and performance of the EJB container.

## Table References

Each CMP Entity Bean will have a primary table that is used to map its attributes for persistence. If you are creating the CMP Entity Bean first, you can edit the table name to be the table name that will be used when the Schema is generated. Once the Schema is generated, you can produce the Data Definition Language (DDL) that will have all of the SQL needed to create the necessary tables to support the CMP Entity Beans you have created in the Designer. Before you use a table reference, you must first define a table name. You have two choices: You can either create a separate CMP Entity Bean and establish a relationship between the two Entity Beans, or you can add a table reference to an existing CMP Entity Bean and establish a table reference to make the columns of the referenced table accessible to the persisted fields of the first CMP Entity Bean. You can add tables to the table references list, and their columns will become available on the individual field's drop-down list of column name choices. When you do add a new table to the Reference table list (see Figure 20.5), a dialog will pop up asking which fields in the corresponding database tables are to use to link the two tables together. This is the same mechanism that is used when establishing relationships between two different CMP Entity Beans.

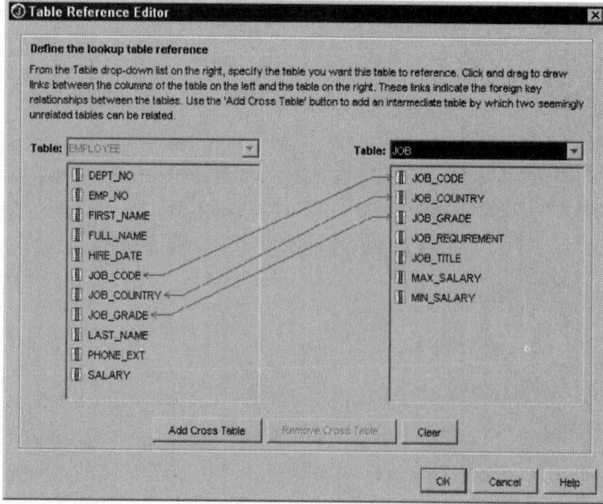


**Figure 20.5** Table references.

## Bean Managed Persistence Entity Bean

As mentioned, there are two different types of Entity Beans; Bean Managed Persistence (BMP) is where the Entity Bean developer is responsible for writing all of the JDBC code necessary to persist the attributes of a given Entity Bean. Once you start developing BMP Entity Beans, you will most likely start identifying some utility classes, perhaps as simple as requesting a DataSource from a connection pool, and you will eventually begin to realize that much of the BMP code you write is very repetitive and similar. You will look for patterns in your BMP code style and try to abstract out certain responsibilities to your ever-increasing BMP utility class framework to make BMP development a little easier.

Once you begin deploying your BMP Entity Beans, performance will become an issue. You will also start looking for areas of your reusable BMP utility class framework to enhance the overall performance of your persistence logic. Eventually your BMP persistence solution will very closely resemble a CMP engine. This is not to say that there are not any good reasons to use BMP Entity Beans.

If you do decide to switch from a Container Managed Persistence Entity Bean to a Bean Managed Persistence Entity Bean by changing the persistence type on the General tab of the Deployment Descriptor Editor for the Entity Bean, all of the CMP 2.0 edits that were applied to the Deployment Descriptor (containing the object-to-relational mapping data for each of the fields) will be lost.

### Bean Properties

Bean Managed Persistence Entity Beans have a similar look to them when compared to Container Managed Persistence Entity Beans. Because most of the work of persisting the fields of the BMP Entity Bean is the responsibility of the developer and not the EJB container, you need to set less information when developing BMP Entity Beans. This is apparent in the Designer by the decrease in the number of properties that exist. You can modify the following properties from within the EJB Designer:

**Bean name: <ejb-name>.** This name is used by the Deployment Descriptor and the EJB container. It has no meaning to the Java source code of the Home, Remote, or Bean classes. This will be the name that is displayed in the Project pane under the EJB module. Clicking on this name in the Project pane will bring out the Deployment Descriptor Editor for the Bean. This name is also accessible from the Classes and Packages dialog. You can also change this name in the Classes and Packages dialog.

**Always wrap primary key.** Just as with CMP Entity Beans, JBuilder can generate the Primary Key class for Bean Managed Persistence Entity Beans. This makes sense because the format of the generated code of the Primary Key is based solely on the fields that make up the Entity Bean and are not dependent on the Deployment Descriptor of the EJB container. As with CMP Entity Beans, if there is only one field that makes up the Primary Key for a given BMP Entity Bean, and if that field is an implementation of an Object class in the java.lang package (String, Double, Short, Long, Float, Integer, etc.), you have the choice of using this class as the Primary Key class or having the EJB Designer "wrap" the class in another class that has an implementation of an Object in the java.lang package as one of its properties. Setting this value to true will force the creation of a new Primary Key class. Setting this value to false will allow one of the Object classes in the java.lang package to be used as the Primary Key class if only one field is used to make up the Primary Key.

### Interfaces

With the introduction of EJB 2.0, the choice you make at development time as to which interface your Enterprise JavaBeans subscribe to has an impact on the actual code you develop. This architectural change that forces a developer to make a decision that should not be made until deployment time is largely due to limitations in certain vendors' communications layer. Beans that were co-located within the same Java Virtual Machine were making remote procedure calls to each other. This decision will affect the interface options that the methods and fields you implement can choose from as well as the generated classes that are named in the Classes and Packages dialog:

**Remote.** If the Enterprise JavaBeans you are developing are to be accessed by an external client or other Enterprise JavaBeans running within a separate EJB container running in a different partition or on a separate server, then you will want to use the Remote interface.

**Local.** If the Enterprise JavaBeans you develop are to be accessed only by other beans within the EJB container and are most likely packaged within the same EJB Archive file (therefore all are part of the same EJB module), then you will want to use the Local interface.

**Local/Remote.** If you are not sure, or if you are sure that your Enterprise JavaBean will be accessed locally by other Enterprise JavaBeans co-located in the same Java Virtual Machine as well as by clients and other Enterprise JavaBeans running in an external Java Virtual Machine, then you should select to support both Local and Remote interfaces.

### Classes and Packages

You can almost use the Designer too much and forget that actual code is being generated and updated. You can initially set the Class and Package names of the generated source code. If you change this after developing and working on this and other code within the project, and if you come back to change the classes and packages for a particular JavaBean, you will most likely break some other piece of code. This does not work as the UML refactoring works, nor does it work like a global search and replace. What this will do is update both the source code and the Deployment Descriptor, which is something that the UML refactoring cannot do. The Classes and Packages options are as follows:

**Default package.** Although not necessary, it is a good idea to consider separating Enterprise JavaBeans by business function or by implemented design pattern. Each package name could contain groupings of related Enterprise Beans.

```
package com.wiley.mastering.jbuilder;
```

**Bean name: <ejb-name>.** This name is used by the Deployment Descriptor and the EJB container. It has no meaning for the Java source code of the Home, Remote, or Bean classes. This will be the name that is displayed in the Project pane under the EJB module. Clicking on this name in the Project pane will bring up the Deployment Descriptor Editor for the Bean. If you change the Bean name here, it will also change the Bean name on the Beans Properties page.

**Bean class: <ejb-class>.** This is the Enterprise Bean Class that the EJB container will access to evoke the implemented application and business logic that the Enterprise JavaBean developer has written. The EJB container also maintains the lifecycle of this class.

```
package com.wiley.mastering.jbuilder;

import javax.ejb.*;

public class FirstBMPEntityBean implements EntityBean {
  EntityContext entityContext;
  java.lang.String untitledField1;
  public java.lang.String ejbCreate() throws CreateException {
    return null;
  }
  public void ejbPostCreate() throws CreateException {
    /**@todo Complete this method*/
  }
  public void ejbRemove() throws RemoveException {
    /**@todo Complete this method*/
  }
  public java.lang.String getUntitledField1() {
    return untitledField1;
  }
  public java.lang.String ejbFindByPrimaryKey(java.lang.String
untitledField1) throws FinderException {
    /**@todo Complete this method*/
    return null;
  }
  public void ejbLoad() {
    /**@todo Complete this method*/
  }
  public void ejbStore() {
    /**@todo Complete this method*/
  }
  public void ejbActivate() {
  }
```

```
    public void ejbPassivate() {
    }
    public void unsetEntityContext() {
      this.entityContext = null;
    }
    public void setEntityContext(EntityContext entityContext) {
      this.entityContext = entityContext;
    }
  }
```

**Home interface class: <home>.** This class defines all the methods to create, remove, and find Enterprise JavaBeans. Clients that want to access the Enterprise Bean class must first obtain a reference to its Home Interface class. The client, through a standard Java naming and directory lookup using the defined JNDI name, can discover the Home interface.

```
package com.wiley.mastering.jbuilder;

import javax.ejb.*;
import java.util.*;
import java.rmi.*;

public interface FirstBMPEntityRemoteHome extends javax.ejb.EJBHome {
  public FirstBMPEntityRemote create() throws CreateException,
RemoteException;
  public FirstBMPEntityRemote findByPrimaryKey(String untitledField1)
throws FinderException, RemoteException;
}
```

**Local home interface class.** A major difference between the EJB 1.x and the EJB 2.x specification is in the area of Local versus Remote classes. Local Home Interface classes are accessed only by other Enterprise JavaBeans within the same deployed JAR and therefore are managed by the same EJB container.

```
package com.wiley.mastering.jbuilder;

import javax.ejb.*;
import java.util.*;

public interface FirstBMPEntityHome extends javax.ejb.EJBLocalHome {
  public FirstBMPEntity create() throws CreateException;
  public FirstBMPEntity findByPrimaryKey(String untitledField1) throws
FinderException;
}
```

**Remote interface class: <remote>.** This class defines the methods that are accessible to the calling client. Clients do not access Enterprise Bean classes directly. Where this gets a bit confusing is when you notice that the Enterprise Bean class does not implement the Remote Interface class. It is easy to see the relationship between the Home and Remote interfaces. It is the responsibility of the EJB container to delegate access to the Enterprise Bean class via the Remote Interface class that the client is using. Clients do not communicate directly with the Enterprise Bean class; clients communicate with the EJB container.

```
package com.wiley.mastering.jbuilder;

import javax.ejb.*;
import java.util.*;
import java.rmi.*;

public interface FirstBMPEntityRemote extends javax.ejb.EJBObject {
  public String getUntitledField1() throws RemoteException;
}
```

**Local interface class.** A major difference between the EJB 1.x and the EJB 2.x specification is in the area of Local versus Remote classes. Local Interface classes are accessed only by other Enterprise JavaBeans within the same deployed JAR and therefore are managed by the same EJB container.

```
package com.wiley.mastering.jbuilder;

import javax.ejb.*;
import java.util.*;

public interface FirstBMPEntity extends javax.ejb.EJBLocalObject {
  public String getUntitledField1();
}
```

**Primary key class.** When developing a CMP Entity Bean, a Primary Key class will be created if more than one field is set as being part of the Primary Key, or if you have decided to always wrap the Primary Key in the Bean properties. The Primary Key is to be created by the client and passed in to the findByPrimaryKey() method of the Entity Bean's Home interface. The Primary Key is typically a combination of fields that can uniquely identify a single instance of the Entity Bean. If a database is used, the field or fields that make up the Primary Key for the Entity Bean are likely the same database table columns that make up the Primary Key or Index for that table. Just as important as it is that the field or combination of fields results in a unique combination, it is important that the equals() and hashCode() methods of the Primary Key class function properly.

```
package com.wiley.mastering.jbuilder;

import java.io.*;

public class FirstBMPEntityBeanPK
    implements Serializable {

  public String untitledField1;

  public FirstBMPEntityBeanPK() {
  }

  public FirstBMPEntityBeanPK(String untitledField1) {
```

```
      this.untitledField1 = untitledField1;
    }

    public boolean equals(Object obj) {
      if (obj != null) {
        if (this.getClass().equals(obj.getClass())) {
          FirstBMPEntityBeanPK that = (FirstBMPEntityBeanPK) obj;
          return ( ( (this.untitledField1 == null) &&
                     (that.untitledField1 == null)) ||
                   (this.untitledField1 != null &&
                    this.untitledField1.equals(that.untitledField1)));
        }
      }
      return false;
    }

    public int hashCode() {
      return untitledField1.hashCode();
    }
  }
```

### Inheritance

Similar to the Base Class of the 1.x Java Bean wizard, this allows the developer to extend the Bean Class from an existing implementation or abstract class. Because the Enterprise JavaBean, represented by the preceding Bean class is an implementation of an existing javax.ejb.EntityBean, or javax.ejb.SessionBean interface, developers are free to extend preexisting classes. By clicking on the ellipses, the Find Classes dialog will appear to allow the developer to either browse or search the project's classpath for a particular class to extend. In all cases, the generated remote interface code that is generated will extend javax.ejb.EJBObject and is initially identical code regardless of the option selected. This is also true for the Home interface, which extends javax.ejb .EJBHome.

## *Session Bean*

The only real difference between Stateful and Stateless is actually in the Deployment Descriptor. The generated source code for both Session Beans is the same. Left-clicking on the Session Bean in the Designer will bring up the Bean Properties Editor.

### Bean Properties

The Bean Properties for the Session Bean (see Figure 20.6) affect not only the Java source code but also the Deployment Descriptor for the Session Bean being edited. The two-way tool nature of the Bean Properties Editor in the EJB Designer ensures that edits outside of the Designer are in sync with any changes or edits made within the Designer.

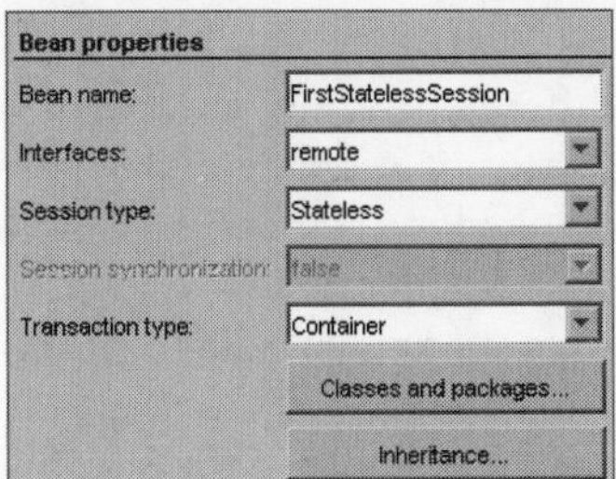


**Figure 20.6** Session Bean properties.

The Bean name (<ejb-name>) is used by the Deployment Descriptor and the EJB container. It has no meaning to the Java source code of the Home, Remote, or Bean classes. This will be the name that is displayed in the Project pane under the EJB module. Clicking on this name in the Project pane will bring out the Deployment Descriptor Editor for the Bean. This name is also accessible from the Classes and Packages dialog.

## Interfaces

With the introduction of EJB 2.0, the choice you make at development time as to which interface your Enterprise JavaBeans subscribe to has an impact on the actual code you develop. This architectural change that forces a developer to make a decision that should not be made until deployment time is largely due to limitations in certain vendors' communications layer. Beans that were co-located within the same Java Virtual Machine were making remote procedure calls to each other. This decision will affect the interface options that the methods and fields you implement can choose from as well as the generated classes that are named in the Classes and Packages dialog, including the following:

**Remote.** If the Enterprise JavaBeans you are developing are to be accessed by an external client or other Enterprise JavaBeans running within a separate EJB container running in a different partition or on a separate server, then you will want to use the Remote interface.

**Local.** If the Enterprise JavaBeans you develop are to be accessed only by other beans within the EJB container and are most likely packaged within the same EJB Archive file (therefore all are part of the same EJB module), then you will want to use the Local interface.

**Local/Remote.** If you are not sure, or if you are sure that your Enterprise JavaBean will be accessed locally by other Enterprise JavaBeans co-located in the same Java Virtual Machine as well as by clients and other Enterprise JavaBeans running in an external Java Virtual Machine, then you should select to support both Local and Remote interfaces.

### Stateful or Stateless

The appropriate use of Stateful Session Beans seems to differ depending on what it is you want to accomplish. With Stateless Session Beans, you are not guaranteed that two successive calls, even from the same client, are going to evoke the same instance. It is the responsibility of the EJB container to determine how to best allocate resources and respond to incoming requests. With Stateful Session Beans, successive calls from the same client are guaranteed to evoke the same instance as long as the remote reference is maintained. Once the remote reference goes out of scope, the instance of the Stateful Session Bean is lost. Use the EJB Designer to select and set the following information:

**Session type.** This is where you choose between a Stateful and a Stateless Session Bean. If a Stateful Session Bean is chosen, the Session Synchronization edit field will be enabled.

**Session synchronization.** Only Stateful Session Beans should consider implementing the javax.ejb.SessionSynchronization interface. Likewise, this should also be considered only where container managed transactions are being used. This will add an afterBegin(), beforeCompletion(), and afterCompletion() method to the Enterprise Bean class. The intention of this interface is to give the Enterprise JavaBean developer the ability to perform work just after a transaction has begun, just before it is to complete, and after it has completed.

```
public void afterBegin() {
}
```

The afterBegin() method will be evoked sometime shortly after a new transaction has been started and before the first business method is called. This method is executed within the scope of the transactional context.

```
public void beforeCompletion() {
}
```

The beforeCompletion() method will be evoked sometime shortly after the last business method is evoked and just prior to the transaction being committed. Like the afterBegin() method, this method is also executed within the scope of the transactional context.

```
public void afterCompletion(boolean committed) {
}
```

The afterCompletion() method will be evoked after the transaction has completed. If the transaction was successful, the value of the committed parameter will be true. If the transaction was not successful, the value will be false.

**Transaction type.** This can be set to either Bean or Container. The default value is Container. It is also assumed that, if implementing the SessionSynchronization interface in Stateful Session Beans, container managed transactions are used. If Bean managed transactions are desired, then the Session Bean developer is responsible for creating an instance of a javax.transaction.UserTransaction and managing the transaction programmatically. A third option would be for the calling client to create the usertransaction and handle the transactional programming from the client side.

### Classes and Packages

The default package is not necessary, but it is a good idea to consider separating Enterprise JavaBeans by business function or by implemented design pattern. Each package name could contain groupings of related Enterprise Beans.

```
package com.wiley.mastering.jbuilder;
```

The Bean name (<ejb-name>) is used by the Deployment Descriptor and the EJB container. It has no meaning to the Java source code of the Home, Remote, or Bean classes. This will be the name that is displayed in the Project pane under the EJB module. Clicking on this name in the Project pane will bring out the Deployment Descriptor Editor for the Bean. If you change the Bean name here, it will also change the Bean name on the Beans Properties page.

The Bean class (<ejb-class>) is the Enterprise Bean class that the EJB container will access to evoke the implemented application and business logic that the Enterprise JavaBean developer has written. The EJB container also maintains the lifecycle of this class.

```
package com.wiley.mastering.jbuilder;

import javax.ejb.*;

public class FirstStatelessSessionBean implements SessionBean {
  SessionContext sessionContext;
  public void ejbCreate() throws CreateException {
    /**@todo Complete this method*/
  }
  public void ejbRemove() {
    /**@todo Complete this method*/
  }
  public void ejbActivate() {
    /**@todo Complete this method*/
  }
  public void ejbPassivate() {
    /**@todo Complete this method*/
  }
  public void setSessionContext(SessionContext sessionContext) {
    this.sessionContext = sessionContext;
  }
}
```

The Home Interface class (<home>) defines all the methods to create, remove, and find Enterprise JavaBeans. Clients that want to access the Enterprise Bean class must first obtain a reference to its Home Interface class. The client, through a standard Java naming and directory lookup using the defined JNDI name, can discover the Home interface.

```
package com.wiley.mastering.jbuilder;

import javax.ejb.*;
import java.util.*;
import java.rmi.*;

public interface FirstStatelessSessionHome extends javax.ejb.EJBHome {
  public FirstStatelessSession create() throws CreateException,
RemoteException;
}
```

A major difference between the EJB 1.x and the EJB 2.x specification is in the area of Local versus Remote classes. Local Home Interface classes are accessed only by other Enterprise JavaBeans within the same deployed JAR and therefore are managed by the same EJB container.

```
package com.wiley.mastering.jbuilder;

import javax.ejb.*;
import java.util.*;
import untitled22.*;

public interface FirstStatelessSessionLocalHome extends
javax.ejb.EJBLocalHome {
  public FirstStatelessSessionLocal create() throws CreateException;
}
```

The Remote Interface class (<remote>) defines the methods that are accessible to the calling client. Clients do not access Enterprise Bean classes directly. Where this gets a bit confusing is when you notice that the Enterprise Bean class does not implement the Remote Interface class. It is easy to see the relationship between the Home and Remote interfaces. It is the responsibility of the EJB container to delegate access to the Enterprise Bean class via the Remote Interface class that the client is using. Clients do not communicate directly with the Enterprise Bean class; clients communicate with the EJB container.

```
package com.wiley.mastering.jbuilder;

import javax.ejb.*;
import java.util.*;
import java.rmi.*;

public interface FirstStatelessSession extends javax.ejb.EJBObject {
}
```

A major difference between the EJB 1.x and the EJB 2.x specification is in the area of Local versus Remote classes. Local Interface classes are accessed only by other Enterprise JavaBeans within the same deployed JAR and therefore are managed by the same EJB container.

```
package com.wiley.mastering.jbuilder;

import javax.ejb.*;
import java.util.*;

public interface FirstStatelessSessionLocal extends
javax.ejb.EJBLocalObject {
}
```

### Inheritance

Similar to the Base class of the 1.x Java Bean wizard, this allows the developer to extend the Bean class from an existing implementation or abstract class. Because the Enterprise JavaBean, represented by the preceding Bean class, is an implementation of an existing javax.ejb.EntityBean, or javax.ejb.SessionBean interface, developers are free to extend preexisting classes. By clicking on the ellipses, the Find Classes dialog will appear to allow the developer to either browse or search the project's classpath for a particular class to extend. In all cases, the generated remote interface code that is generated will extend javax.ejb.EJBObject and is initially identical code regardless of the option selected. This is also true for the Home interface, which extends javax.ejb.EJBHome.

## Import Enterprise JavaBeans

Assuming that there is additional EJB source code in your project's source path that is not already part of the existing EJB module that you are working with, you can add EJBs to the Designer and therefore to the EJB module without having to create a new Enterprise JavaBean. Using the dialog that is provided (see Figure 20.7), you can use the class browser to search for the Bean class, and Remote and Home Interface classes as well as the following:

**Bean name: <ejb-name>.** This name is used by the Deployment Descriptor and the EJB container. It has no meaning to the Java source code of the Home, Remote, or Bean classes. This will be the name that is displayed in the Project pane under the EJB module. Clicking on this name in the Project pane will bring out the Deployment Descriptor Editor for the Bean. If you change the Bean name here, it will also change the Bean name on the Beans Properties page.

**Bean type.** You must specify what type of Enterprise JavaBean is being imported so that the necessary Deployment Descriptor fields can be created. You can choose CMP 2.0, BMP, Session, or Message-Driven.

**Bean class: <ejb-class>.** This is the Enterprise Bean class that the EJB container will access to evoke the implemented application and business logic that the Enterprise JavaBean developer has written. The EJB container also maintains the lifecycle of this class.

**Home interface class: <home>.** This class defines all the methods to create, remove, and find Enterprise JavaBeans. Clients that want to access the Enterprise Bean class must first obtain a reference to its Home Interface class. The client, through a standard Java naming and directory lookup using the defined JNDI name, can discover the Home interface.

**Local home interface class.** A major difference between the EJB 1.x and the EJB 2.x specification is in the area of Local versus Remote classes. Local Home Interface classes are accessed only by other Enterprise JavaBeans within the same deployed JAR and therefore are managed by the same EJB container.

**Remote interface class: <remote>.** This class defines the methods that are accessible to the calling client. Clients do not access Enterprise Bean classes directly. Where this gets a bit confusing is when you notice that the Enterprise Bean class does not implement the Remote Interface class. It is easy to see the relationship between the Home and Remote interfaces. It is the responsibility of the EJB container to delegate access to the Enterprise Bean class via the Remote Interface class that the client is using. Clients do not communicate directly with the Enterprise Bean class; clients communicate with the EJB container.

**Local interface class.** A major difference between the EJB 1.x and the EJB 2.x specification is in the area of Local versus Remote classes. Local Interface classes are accessed only by other Enterprise JavaBeans within the same deployed JAR and therefore are managed by the same EJB container.

**Primary key class.** When developing a CMP Entity Bean, a Primary Key class will be created if more than one field is set as being part of the Primary Key, or if you have decided to always wrap the Primary Key in the Bean properties. The Primary Key is to be created by the client and passed in to the findByPrimaryKey() method of the Entity Bean's Home interface. The Primary Key is typically a combination of fields that can uniquely identify a single instance of the Entity Bean. If a database is used, the field or fields that make up the Primary Key for the Entity Bean are likely the same database table columns that make up the Primary Key or Index for that table. Just as important as it is that the field or combination of fields result in a unique combination, it is important that the equals() and hashCode() methods of the Primary Key class function properly.

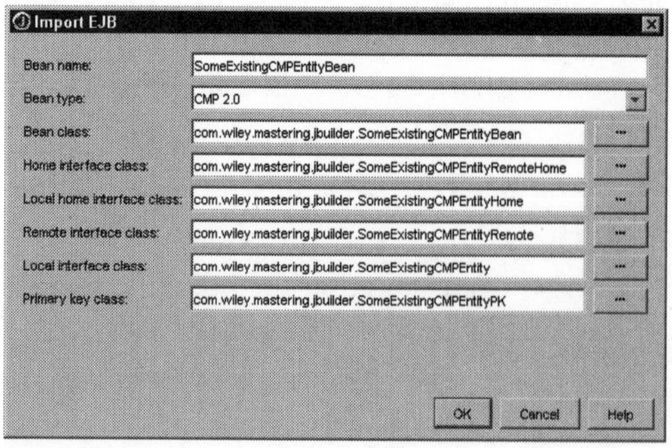

Import EJB
Bean name: SomeExistingCMPEntityBean
Bean type: CMP 2.0
Bean class: com.wiley.mastering.jbuilder.SomeExistingCMPEntityBean
Home interface class: com.wiley.mastering.jbuilder.SomeExistingCMPEntityRemoteHome
Local home interface class: com.wiley.mastering.jbuilder.SomeExistingCMPEntityHome
Remote interface class: com.wiley.mastering.jbuilder.SomeExistingCMPEntityRemote
Local interface class: com.wiley.mastering.jbuilder.SomeExistingCMPEntity
Primary key class: com.wiley.mastering.jbuilder.SomeExistingCMPEntityPK
OK Cancel Help

**Figure 20.7** Import EJB dialog.

## Delete Selected Enterprise JavaBeans

Inside of the EJB Designer, you can select one or several enterprise JavaBeans. You will be able to tell which Enterprise JavaBeans have been selected based on the color of the border. If your JBuilder settings are still set to the default, a black border signifies an Enterprise JavaBean that is not selected, and a red border signifies an Enterprise JavaBean that is selected. You can delete EJBs from the Designer and from the EJB module in this manner. When you delete a selected EJB, this not only removes the selected EJB from the EJB module, it also deletes the associated source code from the project's source path.

## Adding Methods and Fields

Once you have created your Enterprise JavaBean, you will want to start working on it by adding methods, fields, and ejbCreate methods, as well as establishing relationships with other CMP Entity Beans and developing Finder methods to help locate specific instances of an Entity Bean or collections of related Entity Beans. Most of the editors for each of the Enterprise JavaBeans are the same.

### *Add and Delete Methods*

Typically most business methods would be added to Session Beans, and Session Beans will be used as Facades to access Entity Beans. The properties of the method (see Figure 20.8) are as follows:

**Method name.** This is the name of the method.

**Return type.** You can use the class browser to select the Object class that will be the return type for this method.

**Input parameters.** Type out the parameter list as it would appear in the Java source code. For instance, if you were to pass in a String with a handle named param1, you would type java.lang.String param1. If you have multiple input parameters, separate them with a comma, just as you would when directly editing the source code.

**Interface.** If the Enterprise JavaBean is only local or only remote, you can choose between none or either Local or Remote interfaces.

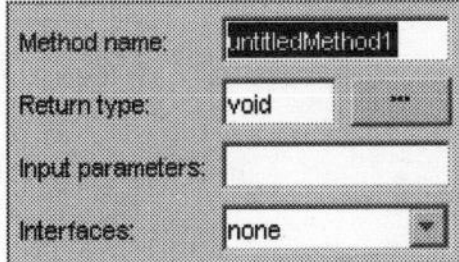


**Figure 20.8** Method Editor.

## *Add and Delete Fields*

You should be adding fields to CMP Entity Beans only if you have created the CMP Entity Bean prior to creating the database table, or if you are adding a table reference to an existing CMP Entity Bean that was generated from an existing database table's DataSource information. It is important that either the table name and/or the table reference has been established that contains the database column to which this field is to be persisted. The properties of the fields (see Figure 20.9) are as follows:

**Field name.** This will be the name of the field. When using the BeansExpress Properties wizard to develop Java Beans and EJB 1.x Entity Beans, it became customary to use a lowercase alpha character to begin the name of a given field.

**Type.** Any class can be used as the type for the field, but remember that the CMP engine must map the field to a corresponding database field type.

**Is persisted.** This property is not accessible if the field is part of the Primary Key. There must be at least one field in a CMP Entity Bean, and at least one field must be used in the Primary Key. All Primary Key fields must be persisted. This property is visible only for CMP Entity Beans.

**Is primary key.** If only one field is a Primary Key, then it could be the Primary Key class as well. If multiple fields comprise the Primary Key, then all fields will be wrapped into a single class that will be the Primary Key class for the CMP Entity Bean. If you have elected to always wrap the Primary Key in the Bean Properties, then a separate Primary Key class will be created even if just one field is a Primary Key field. Once a field is set to be part of the Primary Key, it must be set as a persisted field. This property is visible for Entity Beans.

**In ejbCreate().** Entity Beans can have several ejbCreate() methods. Typically these methods vary by the number of parameters they accept. Most likely all parameters that are passed into an Entity Beans Create Statement map to one of the fields of the Entity Bean. This property is visible for Entity Beans.

**Getters and Setters.** Here you can determine if an Entity Bean's fields are read only or have write access to the client that is using them. You can further refine access to an Entity Bean's fields by having only the Local interface allow write access, while the Remote interface has only read access.

**Column name.** Each field in a CMP Entity Bean maps back to a column in a relational database table. This property is visible only for CMP Entity Beans.

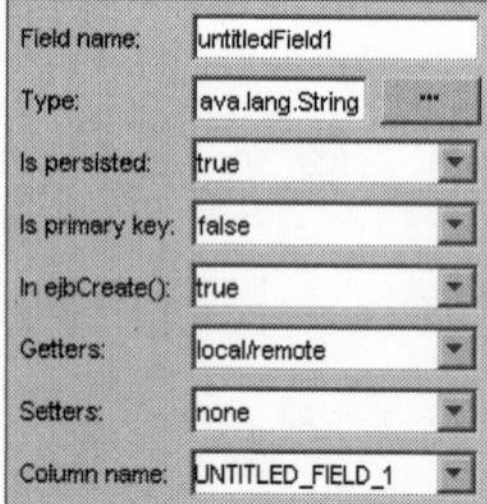


**Figure 20.9** Entity Bean Field Editor.

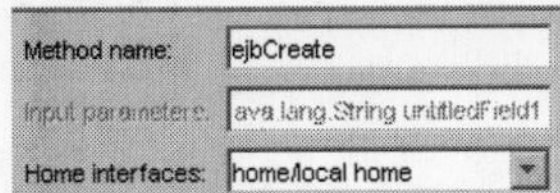


**Figure 20.10** ejbCreate Method Editor.

## *Add and Delete ejbCreate() Methods*

Not all Enterprise JavaBeans need to be created the same way. It is possible to overload the ejbCreate() method and provide several distinctly different ways of creating the same class of Enterprise JavaBean. Creating ejbCreate() methods is very similar to creating any other method, except that ejbCreate() methods do not have return types. Session Beans can have only one ejbCreate method, whereas Entity Beans can have several. The properties of the ejbCreate() method (see Figure 20.10) are as follows:

**Method name.** Because you are creating multiple ejbCreate() methods for an Entity Bean, you should enter a unique method name.

**Input parameters.** Type out the parameter list as it would appear in the Java source code. For instance, if you were to pass in a String with a handle named param1, you would type java.lang.String param1. If you have multiple input parameters, separate them with a comma just as you would when directly editing the source code.

**Home interface.** If you have chosen to support both Local and Remote interfaces, you can choose between including the ejbCreate() method on the local home, the remote home, or both.

## *Add and Delete Finder Methods*

All Entity Beans can be found by their Primary Keys. By default, a findByPrimaryKey() method will be added to each Entity Bean. You can control which fields are used in the findByPrimaryKey() method by making that field part of the Primary Key. The findByPrimaryKey() is meant to produce a unique result and therefore will return a single instance of the Entity Bean. If you would like to return a collection of Entity Beans that all share a similar characteristic, then you can create a specific finder method (see Figure 20.11) for that purpose. The following finder information can be modified from within the EJB Designer:

**Finder name.** This is the method name for the Finder.

**Return type.** For Finder methods, the return type is either a bean instance or a java.util.Collection. The Container will return several Entity Beans based on the input parameter, or the container will return a single instance. If the Query that is used does not return a single instance, and if the return type is set to return a bean instance, then the EJB container will most likely return the first bean instance that the query provides.

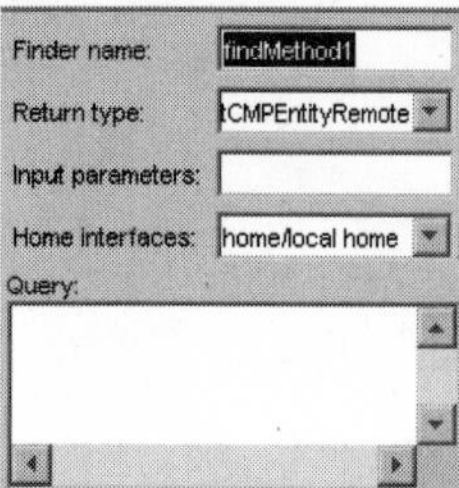


**Figure 20.11** Finder Method Editor.

**Input parameters.** Type out the parameter list as it would appear in the Java source code. For instance, if you were to pass in a String with a handle named param1, you would type java.lang.String param1. If you have multiple input parameters, separate them with a comma, just as you would when directly editing the source code.

If you decide to use the refactoring tool to change the parameters that are being passed into the method you have created, you will notice that its interface has been modified to none in the EJB Designer. You will need to reset the Interface setting and regenerate interfaces. You will also have to ensure that all of the code successfully builds. This includes successfully creating a JAR file and passing the verify test. If you do not wish to build a JAR and verify that JAR each time you build the project's source code, you can change the EJB module's properties. If the project does not build successfully, the refactor will fail. If the build does complete successfully, you will see the following in the Message view:

```
WARNING: You are refactoring an EJB file. This may require that you
change some source code and the deployment descriptor by hand. We
recommend using the EJB Designer for most refactoring scenarios.
```

**Home interface.** Depending on whether the Entity Bean supports Local, Remote, or both interfaces, you may or may not have a choice to make here. If only a Local interface is supported by this Entity Bean, then only Local will be a choice. If both Local and Remote interfaces are supported, then you will be able to choose between Local, Remote, or both interfaces. This allows the developer to create Finder methods that are accessible only by local Enterprise JavaBeans and separate Finder methods that are accessible only remotely.

**Query.** This is where you type in the Enterprise JavaBean Query Language statement.

## *Add and Delete Relationships*

Unique to CMP Entity Beans, rather than create a reference table that will allow you to expose the columns of other tables as attributes of a given Entity Bean, you may want that second table to have its own Entity Bean that can be accessed independently. In this case, you would want to create a relationship between the two Entity Beans. To create a relationship, right-click on the Bean that you want to create the relationship for (see Figure 20.12), and drag the mouse to the Entity Bean with which you want to create the relationship.

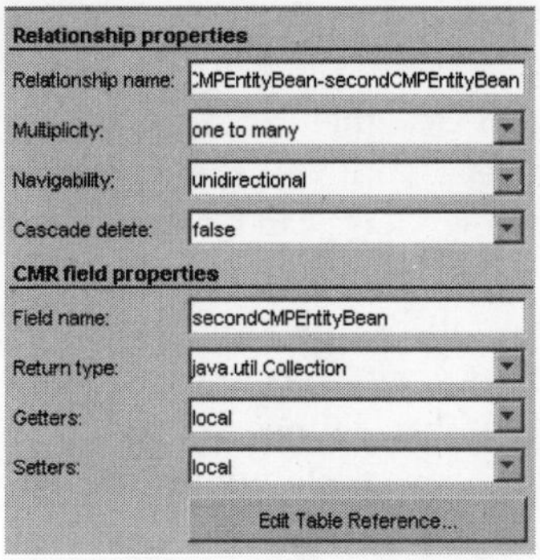

**Figure 20.12** CMP relationships.

## View Bean Source

This will take you to the Java source code of the Bean class itself. This Bean class is where you will implement any specific code for the methods that you have added to the Bean. You should be able to manage the Home and Remote interfaces through the Designer, and you should rarely have to edit their source code directly. If you make changes to the Bean class, you may need to regenerate the Bean's Interface classes.

## Regenerate Interfaces

If you have made significant changes to the Enterprise JavaBean by directly editing the source code of the Bean class, you may forget to make all of the necessary changes to the related Interface classes as well. And because there is no direct relationship between a Bean class and its Remote or Home Interface classes, a rebuild of the project may not catch this discrepancy, especially if you are not always creating the JAR file when building the project or if you have elected not to verify compliance after building JAR in the properties of the EJB module.

## Views

Views do not directly affect either the Java code or the Deployment Descriptor. Views are a way to organize the EJBs that are part of an EJB module. If there are more than 10 to 20 EJBs in a single module, the EJB Designer could get a little complicated. The EJB designer is not like a UML view; you will be able to see all the EJBs of a given EJB module, regardless of class or package. The commonality between the EJBs from the designer's point of view is the Deployment Descriptor.

You may want to organize the EJBs that you are working with by business function, Bean type, or possibly by implemented design pattern. For instance, you may have one or more views dedicated to only Entity Beans, another view for all Stateless Session Facades, and yet another for all Enterprise JavaBeans that deal with state tax calculation, for instance. Fundamentally, there are two types of Actions you can take for views and EJBs within views. One type of Action deals with the management of the views themselves, and the other deals with the management of the contents with views.

## New, Delete, or Rename View

Creating a view will create a tab at the bottom of the EJB Designer. Each tab that is added actually adds a new <view> tag to the ejb-modeler-layout.xml file. Even the Default view has its own <view> tag associated with it. New views can be created, or existing views can be deleted or renamed. Renaming a view does not have any effect on the Beans within that view. When you delete a view, all Bean shortcuts will be moved to the leftmost or default view, even if the leftmost view is no longer named Default. What is actually happening is that all of the XML that defines the layout of EJBs within the deleted view is being copied to the first view node within the ejb-modeler-layout.xml file.

```
<view>
  <name>Entity Beans</name>
</view>
```

## Move, Copy, or Remove Selection

Working with EJBs within a view, you can move an EJB's shortcut from one view to another. You can also copy an EJB's shortcut to another view. This allows you to see an EJB in several different views. For instance, you may want to view your Stateless Session Facades all in one view, and you may also want to view them within a separate view along with the Entity Beans to which they delegate access. To move multiple EJBs, you can use the mouse to drag and select multiple EJBs at the same time. You will visually be able to notice which EJBs are selected by looking at their border. Using the default color scheme, their border will be red if they are selected and black if they are not selected.

It is important to note that removing an EJB from a view does not remove the EJB from the Deployment Descriptor and therefore does not remove the EJB from the EJB module. You have removed the EJB only from the view or from all views. You should not be able to remove the final shortcut for a given EJB. This means that each EJB within an EJB module must exist on at least one view. If, for some reason, an EJB is still part of the Deployment Descriptor and is therefore still part of the EJB module, but it is not in any view, you could just add the necessary XML to the ejb-modeler-layout.xml file manually.

```
<ejb>
  <name>FirstStatelessSessionBean</name>
  <x>425</x>
  <y>225</y>
  <width>131</width>
  <height>91</height>
</ejb>
```

### Arrange EJBs

When working in the EJB Designer, you may want to have the graphical representations of the EJBs realign themselves.

### Find EJB from Search Menu

When using the EJB Designer, you will notice an option on the Search menu that appears only when you are in the EJB Designer. You can search for an EJB by name. This is particularly useful when you have multiple EJBs spread across several different views.

## EJB Test Client

Most of the client code that will be written to access a deployed Enterprise JavaBean is very similar. In all cases, the external client will work primarily with the Home and Remote interfaces of the Bean. For this reason, Enterprise JavaBeans that implement the Local Home and Local interfaces will not be accessible by EJB test clients. The JNDI lookup code will, in most cases, look like the following initialize() method:

```
public void initialize() {
  try {
    //get naming context
    Context context = new InitialContext();
    //look up jndi name
    Object ref = context.lookup("FirstSessionBean");
    //look up jndi name and cast to Home interface
    firstSessionHome = (FirstSessionHome)
PortableRemoteObject.narrow(ref, FirstSessionHome.class);
  }
  catch(Exception e) {
    e.printStackTrace();
  }
}
```

There are three basic types of test clients that will be built around the initialize() method: Application, JUnit, and Cactus.

## Application

Applications are the only client that can generate a main() method. Applications can have their own runtime configurations. All three types of EJB test clients are very similar (see Figure 20.13). Only the Application class can run on its own. When creating an application, the following information is required:

**EJB name.** Initially only Enterprise JavaBeans that are part of the currently open project will be selectable. You can also point to external EJB Archive files and even directories that contain Enterprise JavaBeans to expand this list.

**From project, JAR, or directory.** The test client that is to be generated can read the remote interface of any Enterprise JavaBean in the currently open project, or you can select an existing JAR or directory in which the bean is located. Once you point to an external EJB Archive or directory containing EJBs, the list of EJB names will expand.

**Package, class name, and base class.** The EJB test client that you create does not have to belong to the same package to which the existing Enterprise JavaBeans belong. Select the base class from which the EJB test client is to extend and choose the name of the class.

**Generated code options.** When all options are not selected, you will generate a test client with only the initialize() method. Additionally, you can add header comments and logging information. The logging information will print out a message to the standard out, which, in turn, is displayed in the JBuilder's Message view. The logged message will include such information as the name of the method that was called and how long the method took to execute.

**Create a Runtime configuration.** Each EJB test application that is created can become its own Runtime configuration.

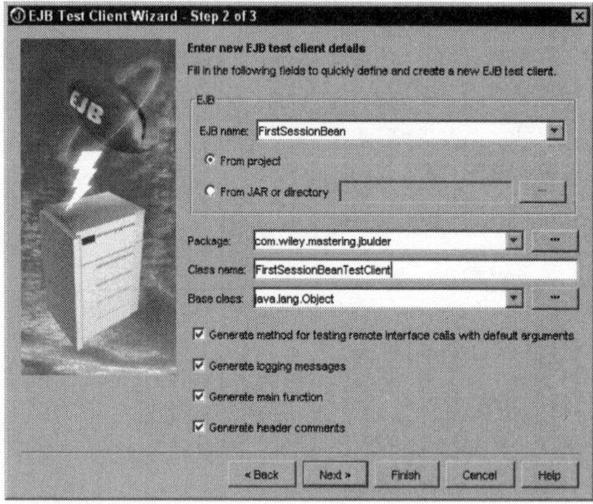


**Figure 20.13** Enterprise JavaBean Test Client wizard.

## JUnit

The main difference that the JUnit has over the application is that the base class that is generated is an extension of the junit.framework.TestCase Class. The other major difference is that EJB test clients that are JUnit test clients cannot have their own main() methods. When you configure a Runtime configuration for JUnit, you can choose the type of test runner you want to use. It is common to want to generate a new EJB test client over to an existing test client when the interface of an Enterprise JavaBean changes. This can cause problems when you modify the generated class after using the wizard. It is possible to generate an EJB test client application and then create a separate JUnit test case from the Object Gallery's Test tab that uses the EJB test client. In this situation, the EJB test client application can be generated over and over, again and again, without writing over any test code. That is, of course, if the only changes that have been made to the remote interface were the addition of methods and not the removal or changing of a method's parameter or return type.

## Cactus

An extension to JUnit, Cactus is a way to proxy access to your EJBs through a Web application. Like the JUnit EJB test client, the Cactus EJB test client is very similar to the code generated when creating an application EJB test client. Once the project is configured properly to use Cactus, Cactus EJB test client can be created. The main difference between the JUnit test client and the Cactus test client is that the JUnit test client extends junit.framework.TestCase, whereas the Cactus test client extends org.apache.cactus.ServletTestCase, a descendant of the junit.framework.TestCase.

### *Configure the Project for Cactus*

When using Cactus for testing your Enterprise JavaBeans, you must ensure that you have set up the integration between the deployed Web application and the EJB module properly. With Cactus, there will actually be a Java Server Page deployed to a Web container that is being used as a proxy to access the Enterprise JavaBeans that you have deployed to an EJB container. It is equally important that the Web application that is to be utilized for testing has all of the necessary JUnit and Cactus libraries deployed and configured. To assist in this part of the setup, the EJB Test Client wizard has a Configure Project for Cactus button that will be accessible only when you choose to test your application using Cactus. This will walk you through the necessary steps to configure a Web application for Cactus.

## EJB Deployment Descriptor

From time to time, you may feel the need to edit the various XML files of the EJB module directly and not use the Deployment Descriptor Editor. When you do this, you may be surprised to find out that the EJB module does not manage the XML files of an Enterprise JavaBeans Archive individually. Instead, all of the relevant .xml files located in the META-INF directory of the archive are all located within the EJB module's .ejbgrpx file. You can access what appears to be each file individually, but what is actually happening is that you are editing the .ejbgrpx file that was created by the EJB Module wizard. There are not too many differences between the Deployment Descriptor in EJB 1.1 and the Deployment Descriptor in EJB 2.0. For the most part, you will make most of the edits to the Deployment Descriptor in the EJB Designer directly. There are two new files that are maintained by the EJB module because of the EJB Designer; these are the modeler-schema and the modeler-layout XML files, as described here:

- ejb-jar.xml is the actual Deployment Descriptor that is compliant with the EJB 2.0 specification.
- ejb-borland.xml is the vendor-specific portion of the Deployment Descriptor as allowed by the specification.
- ejb-modeler-schema.xml is the schema that was created for the DataSources from either an existing database or the fields of Entity Beans within the Designer.
- ejb-modeler-layout.xml controls which Enterprise JavaBeans appear on which views and where they are placed within the view.

You can edit the Beans Deployment Descriptor settings using the Deployment Descriptor Editor. This menu item is provided as a quick and easy way to access this information. Alternatively, you can also double-click on the Bean's name in the Project pane under the EJB module that it is part of.

## DataSources

DataSources are similar to database connections. From the EJB 2.0 Bean Designer's point of view, a DataSource contains the Schema information for the tables and columns that are used to map the fields of CMP 2.0 Entity Beans. You can create a Schema from newly created Entity Beans, or you can import an existing Schema from an existing connection using a JDBC driver. When you create a new EJB module that is compliant with the EJB 2.0 specification, you will notice that the EJB module is added to the Project pane (see Figure 20.14), the Designer is visible in the Content pane, and the DataSource viewer is visible in the Navigation pane.

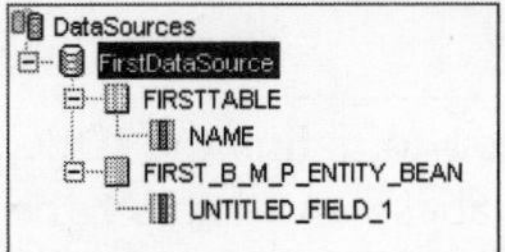


**Figure 20.14** DataSources.

# Create Schema from Selection

After creating a single Entity Bean or a collection of Entity Beans, you can generate a Schema based on the table names, reference table names, and the column names in the Entity Beans. The first time you use this capability, assuming you have not imported or created a Schema already, you will be prompted to name a new DataSource.

If a DataSource already exists, you will not be prompted; it will be assumed that you will want to add the information to the existing DataSource's Schema. If multiple DataSources exist, you will be prompted to choose which DataSource you want to add the Schema to. So, if you have an existing DataSource that points to an existing database, and if you want to create a new Schema for a new DataSource, create the new DataSource first; otherwise, the Schema will be automatically added to the existing DataSource.

While creating Entity Beans, you could also be editing the table names, reference table names, and the column names for all of the new Entity Beans you are creating. When you are finished, you can then select these Entity Beans and generate a Schema. This Schema should then be used to generate the Data Definition Language that contains the create table SQL that you can use to create the required table structure to support the Entity Beans you have been working on. If you forget to name all of the table names, reference table names, and column names for all of the fields in all of the Entity Beans you have created, or if you are creating Bean Managed Persistence Entity Beans that do not have access to such properties, the EJB 2.0 Bean Designer will create the table and column names for you.

# Import Schema from Database

JBuilder creates a Schema from an existing JDBC database connection. Right-mouse click on the DataSources node in the Navigation pane to bring up the menu items that will allow you to either import or add a new DataSource. The Schema file that is created and that the Designer uses is actually kept with the Deployment Descriptor files. You can view and edit this file named ejb-modeler-schema.xml from the EJB DD Source tab.

### Database Schema Provider

The Database Schema Provider (see Figure 20.15) will allow you to define the JDBC connection properties that will be used to connect to the database and extract the necessary information to create the Schema that will be used in the EJB 2.0 Bean Designer, including the following:

**All schemas.** If the username and password you use to establish a logon to the database allow you to view more than just one Schema, typically the Schema assigned to a particular user account, you can display multiple Schemas' tables and views.

**Views.** By default, views will not appear. Check this option if you wish to display views in addition to tables.

**Driver.** Specify the full class name of the JDBC Drive class that will be used to connect to the database.

**URL.** The database URL that will be used to establish a connection.

**Username.** This is the username used to logon to the database.

**Password.** This is the password used to logon to the database.

**JNDI name.** This is the JNDI name that the EJB container will use to bind the DataSource.

## Add DataSource

If you do not have an existing database that you are using for the Enterprise JavaBeans that you are creating, you can simply create a new, empty DataSource.

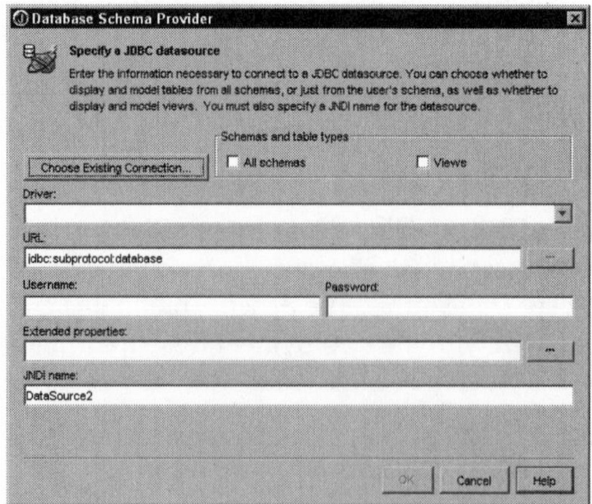


**Figure 20.15** Database Schema Provider dialog.

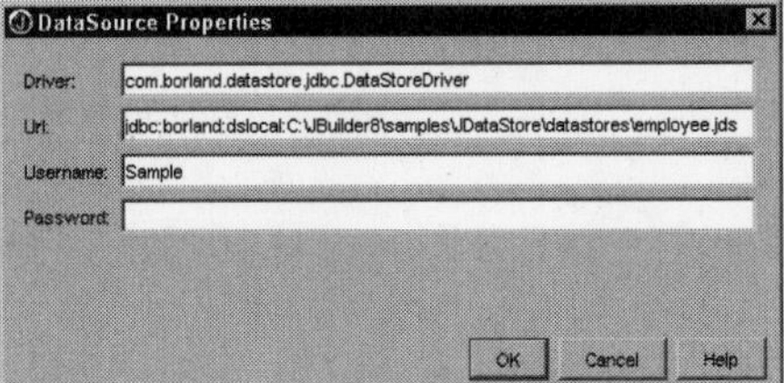


**Figure 20.16** DataSource Properties.

# Working with DataSources

Once a DataSource is established, you can export the DataSource to an SQL file containing the DDL necessary to create the database table structure that the DataSource represents (see Figure 20.16). You can also edit the DataSource properties to point to a different database server containing another instance, perhaps a test versus production instance of the database you are working with, or you can refresh the DataSource's Schema if the table structure has changed.

## *Export to SQL DDL*

The Schema that you have either created from the Entity Beans you have created or from the database you are working from can be exported in the form of a Data Definition Language file that can be used to create (or recreate, as the case may be) the tables that the Schema represents. This is a one-way path, meaning that you could create the DataSource Schema, generate the DDL, use the DDL in the database pilot to create the table structures, modify the DataSource properties, and refresh the DataSource from the database.

## *Edit DataSource Properties*

If you have imported the Schema from an existing database, then the DataSource properties (see Figure 20.17) should already be set for you. On the other hand, if you have created the Schema from scratch, and if you now want to point it to a new database instance, you can edit the properties and point the DataSource at a new database instance. You can also edit existing DataSource properties to change from a test to a production database prior to deploying a finished EJB module. The DataSource properties are as follows:

**Driver.** Specify the full class name of the JDBC Driver class that will be used to connect to the database.

**URL.** This is the database URL that will be used to establish a connection.

**Username.** This is the username used to logon to the database.

**Password.** This is the password used to logon to the database.

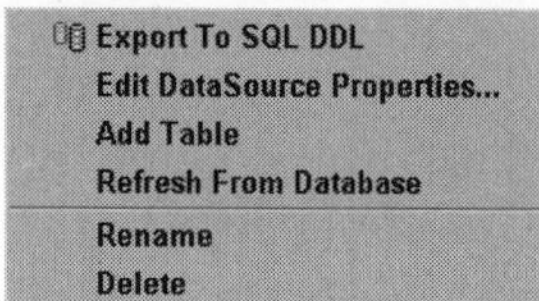


**Figure 20.17** Working with DataSources.

### Add Table

When working with CMP 2.0 reference tables, it is sometimes useful to add a new table to the DataSource Schema prior to editing the Bean's properties. Otherwise, when you go to generate the Schema, the Designer will not know if your intention was to use the reference table or the primary table.

### Refresh from Database

It is often the case that database table structures change during the development process. When this happens, you may need to refresh a DataSources Schema from the updated database information.

### Rename or Delete DataSource

If the original DataSource name that was entered needs to be changed, or if you no longer need the DataSource defined for this particular EJB module, you can either rename the DataSource or delete it entirely.

## Working with Tables

A given DataSource will have from one to many tables defined. Each table can be used to generate an Entity Bean. Additionally, you can add columns to tables and even rename and delete tables from the DataSource it belongs to (see Figure 20.18).

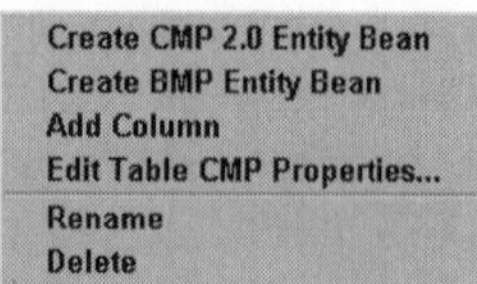


**Figure 20.18** Working with tables.

### Create CMP 2.0 Entity Bean

To create a CMP 2.0 Entity Bean in the Designer, first choose from which table you want to create the Entity Bean, then right-mouse click on that table and create the Entity Bean. If you select several tables, several Entity Beans will be created. If your intention was to create a single Entity Bean from several tables, decide which table is to be the master table and create a single Entity Bean for that table. Then go into the Entity Bean's properties, and add a reference table. Once the reference table is added, you can add the addition fields manually, setting their column to point to the reference table.

### Create BMP Entity Bean

To create a BMP Entity Bean in the Designer, first choose from which table you want to create the Entity Bean, then right-mouse click on that table and create the Entity Bean. If you select several tables, several Entity Beans will be created. For BMP Entity Beans for which you wish to create a single Entity Bean from several tables, decide which table is to be the master table, create a single Entity Bean for that Table, go into the Entity Bean's properties, and add the addition fields manually.

### Add Column

You can add columns to the DataSources Schema for the table. This does not have a direct effect on the actual table structure. This is mainly useful when developing Entity Beans and setting their fields' Columns properties to the column names for a given table. Once the table has all of the necessary columns to support the Entity Beans you are creating, you can generate the DDL and create the tables in the database that you are planning to use.

### Rename and Delete Table

You can rename the tables that are part of a DataSource as well as delete the table entirely. It is important to note that renaming and deleting tables in a particular DataSource will not automatically be reflected in the Entity Beans that have already specified this table's name in their CMP table or their reference table definitions. You will have to go back and modify these settings manually.

## Working with Columns

Drilling down one more layer, you can also work with a given table's columns (see Figure 20.19). You can change their properties, rename a column, and even delete a column from a table.

Edit Column Properties...
Edit Column CMP Properties...
Rename
Delete

**Figure 20.19** Working with columns.

You can rename the individual columns of a table or delete the columns entirely. Just as with tables, if you delete or rename a column, the corresponding column names used in the individual fields for the Entity Beans will not be modified automatically. You will have to edit these changes manually in the Designer.

## Summary

In this chapter we have seen how a two-way designer can be used to quickly lay the foundation necessary for constructing complex Enterprise JavaBean applications. Once a collection of EJBs has been created, EJB test clients can be utilized to test for the expected results and zero in on any problem areas quickly. We have also seen that with the use of DataSources, CMP Entity Beans can be quickly generated from existing database connections. If BMP is to be used, the Schema can quickly be generated from the fields of the Entity Beans, and a new database can be created using the Data Definition Language that results.

# PART Seven

# Distributed Computing with RMI, CORBA and Web Services

By now you should have read about the latest, hottest topics on J2EE development with JSP, servlets, and Enterprise JavaBeans. In Part Seven, we will discuss pre-EJB technologies, like RMI and CORBA, followed by the post-EJB technology that is Web services. This part focuses on how JBuilder works and integrates with the development environment for RMI, CORBA, and Web services applications.

Part Seven includes three chapters:

**RMI Development with JBuilder.** Chapter 21 discusses how JBuilder facilitates development with RMI.

**CORBA Development with JBuilder.** Chapter 22 discusses how JBuilder facilitates development with CORBA.

**Web Services Development with JBuilder.** In Chapter 23, you will learn to consume and construct Web services with the Apache Axis toolkit and Borland application server. JBuilder provides wizards to create Web services from any Java class and EJB components. Also, the chapter shows the Web Services Explorer for searching and publishing Web services to a UDDI registry.

CHAPTER

21

# RMI Development with JBuilder

Remote Method Invocation (RMI), Common Object Request Broker Architecture (CORBA), and Java 2 Enterprise Edition (J2EE) together make up the Java server-side architecture. This chapter (as well as Chapter 22, "CORBA Development with JBuilder") focuses on how JBuilder facilitates development with RMI and CORBA.

RMI was first introduced in JDK 1.1, and it was highly and widely accepted by the Java community for its ease of use and its considerable performance in all Java distributed object applications (Figure 21.1). An RMI application contains both a server component and a client component. The server component generates and maintains its objects, which are also called *remote objects*. The server component registers local references to those remote objects to a directory service, which is RMIRegistry — a bootstrap naming service provided by JDK. The RMIRegistry is an implementation of the java.rmi.registry.Registry interface and the java.rmi.registry.LocateRegistry class. It provides a bootstrap service for retrieving and registering objects by names. When the client application obtains a remote reference to one of the remote objects in the registry, the client application is able to make invocations to the remote object's methods. This RMI mechanism is enabled using a Java interface that extends java.rmi.Remote package. Each server component owns an interface, which has contractual services that enable remote invocations. RMI uses object serialization as a key mechanism to marshal and unmarshal parameters from components to components.

This chapter introduces the JBuilder environment for developing RMI applications. First, we take a brief look at how to configure RMI options in JBuilder. Then, we review the RMI development process in order to follow how JBuilder assists in developing RMI applications.

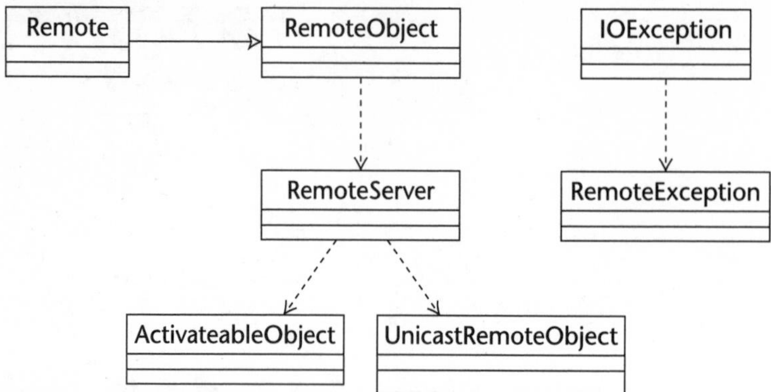


**Figure 21.1** RMI Object model view.

# Configuring RMI in JBuilder

This section shows you how to configure RMI options in the JBuilder environment. Typically, you should see an RMIRegistry item under JBuilder Tools menu (see Figure 21.2). If you do not see it, use the Configure Tools dialog box to add RMIRegistry to JBuilder's Tools menu. The RMIRegistry items that you add can run externally from JBuilder, or they can run as a service within JBuilder (see Figure 21.3). To display this dialog box, choose Tools | Configure Tools.

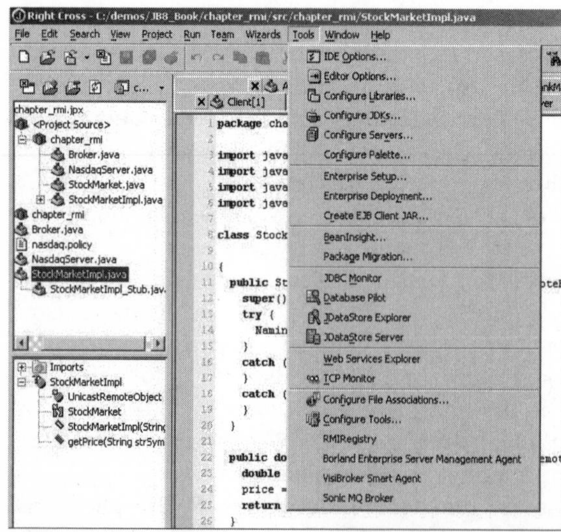


**Figure 21.2** RMIRegistry configuration.

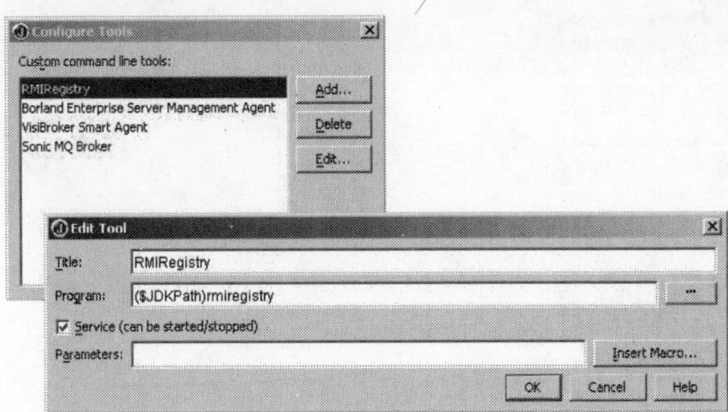


**Figure 21.3** Create RMI registry item.

JBuilder provides a Properties Settings for its Java files. You can open the Properties dialog box for a Java file by right-clicking on a .java file in the Project pane and selecting Properties. When this Generate RMI stub/skeleton option is selected and the project is compiled, the stub and skeleton files will be generated.

# RMI Development Process

The RMI development process consists of the following steps:

1. **Define an interface for the server component.** First we need to define a remote object interface. Per the RMI specification (http://java.sun.com/j2se/1.4.1/docs/api/java/rmi/package-summary.html), the remote interfaces must be declared public and extend the java.rmi.Remote interface. The interface will declare each of the methods provided by the services for remote invocation later. Each method must throw a java.rmi.RemoteException.
2. **Implement the interface.** When the interface is defined, we will write a class that implements the interface. The class is designed to fulfill all methods and their signatures declared in the interface.
3. **Generate RMI stub/skeleton.** RMI Stub and Skeleton class files are generated by compiling the .java source files using *rmic* compiler in the JDK. A stub is defined as a client-side proxy for a remote object. The stub is responsible for forwarding remote invocation calls to the server-side dispatcher, which is called a skeleton. A skeleton communicates with the actual remote object implementation. JBuilder handles this step automatically for you when you have the Generate RMI stub/skeletons enabled in the java node properties.
4. **Create a server.** The server program constructs an instance of the remote object implementation. The server then binds that instance to a name referenced by an RMIRegistry. The RMIRegistry is a simple model of a name server that allows remote clients to get a reference to a remote object. It is typically used for bootstrapping the communication.

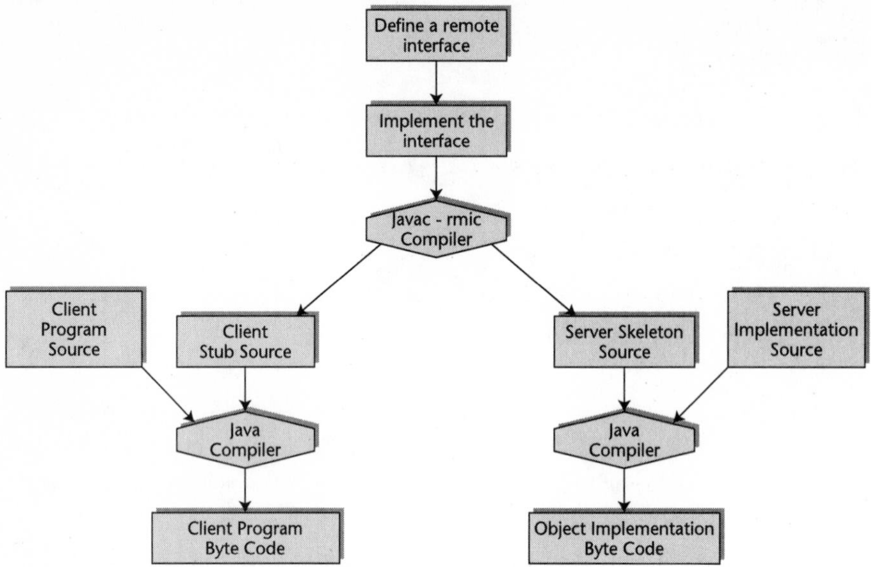


**Figure 21.4** RMI development process.

5. **Create a client.** The client program mainly gets a reference to the remote object from the RMIRegistry. After obtaining the remote object reference, the client can invoke any public method of the remote methods on the server's remote object.
6. **Write an RMI policy file.** The policy file is used to set access permission at the method level for the Java application environment, specifically a Policy class that is defined in the java.security package.

# Building the RMI Application

In this section, we follow the RMI development steps (Figure 21.4) with JBuilder to build an RMI application; those steps involve writing Java codes for interfaces and implementation classes, generating Stub and Skeleton class files from the implementation classes, writing Java codes for a remote service host program and RMI client program, and installing and running the RMI application. Those steps are described as follows:

1. Create a JBuilder project, and name it: rmi_stockmarket.
2. Create a remote interface, and define its methods. Use New Class wizard [Choose File | New Class] to create an interface named *StockMarket* that extends the base interface of java.rmi.Remote. Then edit the file *StockMarket.java* with the following code:

```
// StockMarket.java
package chapter_rmi;
```

```
import java.rmi.Remote;
import java.rmi.RemoteException;

public interface StockMarket extends Remote { // line 4
  double getPrice(String strSymbol) throws RemoteException; // line 5
}
```

In Line 4, *StockMarket* is defined as an RMI interface; therefore, it must extend the java.rmi.Remote interface. In line 5, the method *getPrice(String strSymbol)* throws a RemoteException because the RMI specification calls for each invokable method to raise a java.rmi.RemoteException when there is a remote communication error.

3. Create an implementation for the remote interface. Use the New Class wizard [Choose File | New Class] to construct a class named *StockMarketImpl* that extends java.rmi.server.UnicastRemoteObject. Then use the Implement Interface wizard to implement the StockMarket interface. Then edit the file *StockMarketImpl.java* with the following code:

```
// StockMarkerImpl.java
package chapter_rmi;

import java.rmi.server.UnicastRemoteObject;
import java.rmi.RemoteException;
import java.rmi.Naming;
import java.net.MalformedURLException;
import java.util.Random;

class StockMarketImpl extends UnicastRemoteObject
                              implements StockMarket //line 8
{
  public StockMarketImpl(String strName) throws RemoteException {
    super(); // line 12
    try {
      Naming.rebind(strName, this); // line 14
    }
    catch (MalformedURLException ex) {
      ex.printStackTrace();
    }
    catch (RemoteException ex) {
      ex.printStackTrace();
    }
  }

  public double getPrice(String strSymbol) throws RemoteException{
    double price;
    Random random_generator =
        new Random(System.currentTimeMillis());
```

```
    price =
(double)strSymbol.length()*random_generator.nextDouble()*10.0; //line
24
    return price;
  }
}
```

In line 8, the StockMarketImpl class extends java.rmi.UnicastRemoteObject and implements the interface StockMarket. By extending UnicastRemoteObject, the StockMarketImpl is enabled to use RMI's default sockets-based transport for its remote object communication. If you choose to extend a remote object from any class other than UnicastRemoteObject, please refer to the RMI specification for more information: http://java.sun.com/j2se/1.4/docs/guide/rmi.

In line 12, to export the remote object, *StockMarketImpl* needs to invoke the parent constructor super() method, which is a no-argument constructor of java.rmi.server.UnicastRemoteObject.

In line 14, note that the StockMarketImpl constructor accepts a string as an input parameter. Naming.rebind(strName, this) is used to bind the given name to a reference for the remote object. This rebinding will replace any existing binding by the specified name.

In line 24, a sample implementation of getPrice() method returns a random double as a value of a given symbol.

4. Generate the RMI stub and skeleton using *rmic* compiler. Right-mouse click on StockMarketImpl.java. Select "Properties"; you should see the Properties form for StockMarketImpl.java. Check the box Generate RMI stub/skeleton, and click the OK button on the Build | RMI/JNI table (see Figure 21.5). The Generate RMI stub/skeleton option generates Java codes for remote method invocation communication transparently. This allows code on the client side to invoke a method on a remote object on the server side.

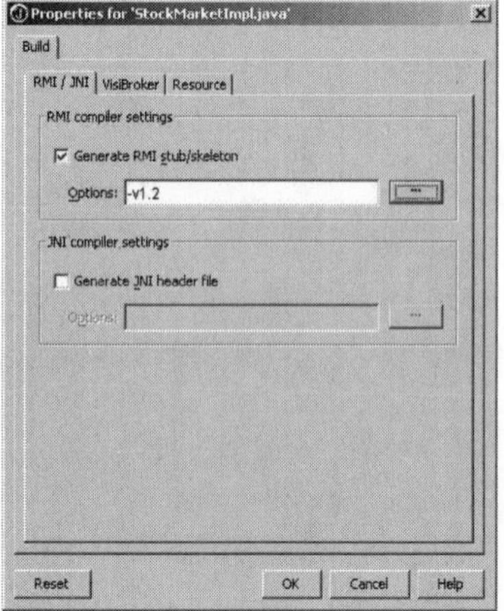


**Figure 21.5** RMIC configuration.

There are additional option settings for rmic compiler, as shown in Figure 21.6.

1. Right-mouse click on StockMarketImpl.java. Select "Make"; JBuilder will generate stub and skeleton for the StockMarket interface by invoking the configured *rmic* compiler.
2. Expand StockMarketImpl.java node; you should see that the file StockMarketImpl_stub.java has been generated.
3. Create a server program that constructs an instance of the StockMarketImpl class. Use New Class wizard [Choose File | New Class] to create a class named *NasdaqServer* with a main method and no constructor. Then edit the file *NasdaqServer.java* with the following code:

```
// NasDaqServer.java
package chapter_rmi;

import java.rmi.RMISecurityManager;
import java.util.Date;
import java.rmi.RemoteException;

public class NasdaqServer {
  public static void main(String[] args) {
    try {
      System.setSecurityManager( new RMISecurityManager() ); // Line
11
      StockMarketImpl nasdaqServer = new StockMarketImpl("NASDAQ");
      System.out.println("NASDAQ is up at " +  new Date().toString()
);
    }
    catch (RemoteException ex) {
       ex.printStackTrace();
    }
  }
}
```

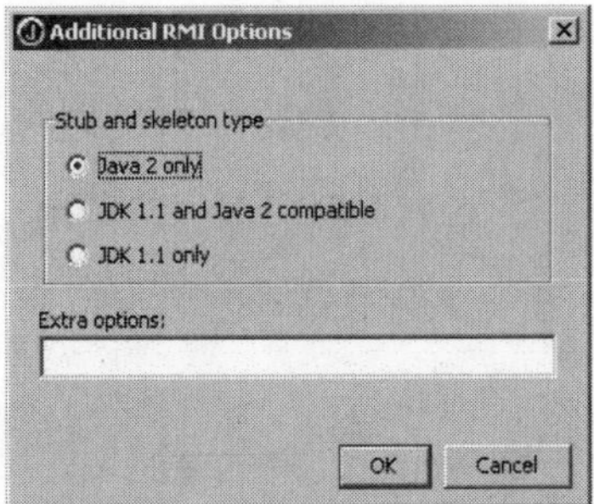


**Figure 21.6** Additional option settings for rmic.

In lines 10-11, the server sets a new system-level RMISecurityManager; then it instantiates an instance of the StockMarketImpl class, specifying a name "NASDAQ". Behind the scene, the StockMarketImpl implementation registers its remote object with the RMIRegistry. Indeed, the remote object is made available to remote clients as "// <server name or IP address >:<service port number>/ NASDAQ".

4. Create a client that connects to the server object. Use the New Class wizard [Choose File | New Class] to create a class named *Broker* with a main method but no default constructor. Then edit the file *Broker.java* with the following code:

```
// Broker.java
package chapter_rmi;

import java.rmi.*;
import java.net.*;

public class Broker {
  public static void main (String[] args) {
    try {
      System.setSecurityManager (new RMISecurityManager ());
      StockMarket nasdaq = (StockMarket)

java.rmi.Naming.lookup("//localhost:1099/NASDAQ"); //Line 11
      System.out.println ("Market price of BORLAND is " +
                          nasdaq.getPrice ("BORL"));
    } catch (RemoteException ex) {
      ex.printStackTrace ();
    } catch (NotBoundException ex) {
      ex.printStackTrace ();
    } catch (MalformedURLException ex) {
      ex.printStackTrace ();
    }
  }
}
```

**RMISECURITYMANAGER**

**RMISecurityManager extends the java.lang.SecurityManager class. The RMISecurityManager is used to install an example security manager for use by RMI applications. If an RMI application does not have SecurityManager installed, the RMI class loader will not allow any classes downloaded from remote locations.**

**In general, RMISecurityManager enables RMI applications to implement a security policy that sets what operations can be allowed or disallowed to perform based on the security policy.**

In line 11, in order to contact a remote RMI server, the RMI client must obtain a reference to the server. The java.rmi.Naming.lookup() method is used to initially obtain references to remote servers. A typical remote reference URL is //host:port/<server>, which includes a server host name and port number that allow RMI clients to communicate to the server virtual machine. When an RMI client has a remote reference, the client will use the host name and port provided in the reference to open a socket connection to the remote server.

Note that the RMI default port is set to 1099. Remember to specify the port number in the remote reference URL if a server creates a registry on a port other than the default. For example, a port number can be supplied in the reference URL as "//localhost:14400/NASDAQ".

5. Write an RMI policy file. Choose Add Files/Packages, and enter *nasdaq.policy* in the File Name field. Click OK to create the file. In this example, nasdaq.policy is saved to <C:\Demos\JB8_Book\chapter_rmi>. Double-click the file nasdaq .policy to open it in the editor. Enter the following code:

```
grant {
  permission java.net.SocketPermission  "*:1024-65535", "accept,
connect, listen";
};
```

Note that this policy is used for demonstration purpose only. The policy file gives global permission to anyone from anywhere to listen on unprivileged ports. And it should not be used in a production environment. Visit http://java.sun.com/j2se/1.4/docs/guide/security/PolicyFiles.html#FileSyntax for more information on the Java policy file and its syntax.

When the coding for the StockMarket example is done, the project should have the following files:

- **StockMarket.java.** Contains codes for the remote interface definition.
- **StockMarket Impl.java.** Contains codes for the remote object implementation.
- **NasdaqServer.java.** Contains codes for the RMI server side.
- **Broker.java.** Contains codes for the RMI client.
- **nasdaq.policy.** Contains permission information.

6. Create run configurations for the NASDAQ server and the RMI client program. Use the New Configuration wizard [Choose Run | Configuration] to create run configurations for both the RMI server and client programs.

VM parameters for the NASDAQ Server Run configuration are as follows:

- Djava.rmi.server.codebase=file:C:\Demos\JB8_Book\chapter_rmi\classes\.
- Djava.security.policy=file:C:\Demos\JB8_Book\chapter_rmi\nasdaq.policy.

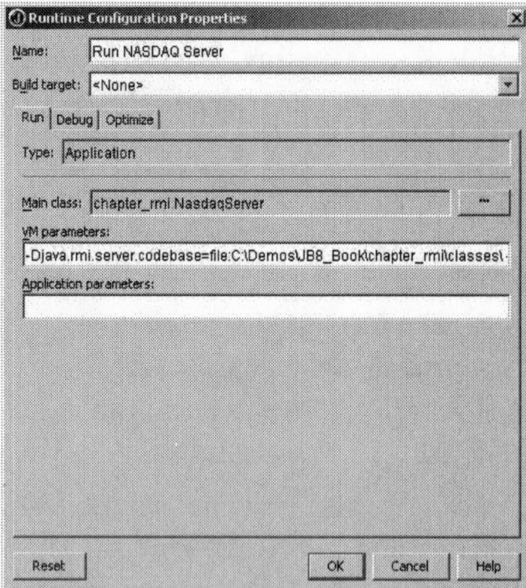


**Figure 21.7** Set up server run configuration.

- The URL is set with the system property java.rmi.server.codebase for clients to download the stub classes. Note that the backslash "\" is required after the class, and no space can be used in the class name and its path.

VM parameters for the Broker client run configuration are as follows:

- Djava.security.policy=file:C:\Demos\JB8_Book\chapter_rmi\ nasdaq.policy.
- Start RMIRegistry by selecting Tools | RMIRegistry.

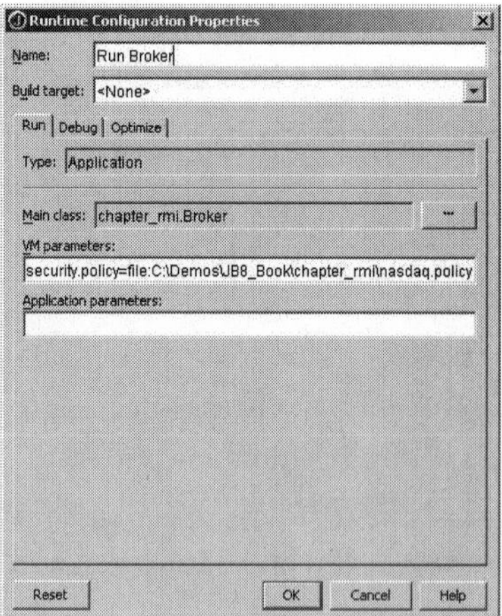


**Figure 21.8** Set up client run configuration.

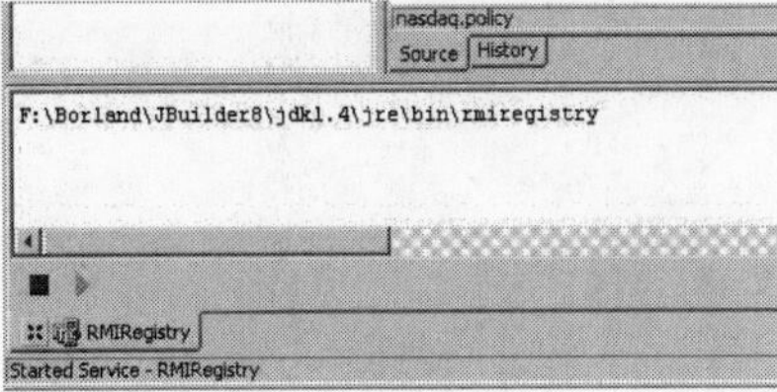


**Figure 21.9** RMIRegistry running in the Message pane.

7. Run RMI server (see Figure 21.10). When the NASDAQ server is started, the NASDAQ server Message pane should display a message in the following format:
   - NASDAQ is up at Mon Aug 12 03:05:35 EDT 2002.
   - When the Broker runs, the Broker Message pane should display a message in the following format:

     ```
     Market price of BORLAND is 21.981286069775898
     ```

# RMI Deployment

The RMI application can be deployed to a location on a server or client machine where the application will be executed. JBuilder provides a wizard to assist the deployment process. JBuilder's Archive Builder automatically and selectively collects necessary Java classes, resources, and libraries and then archives these files to a compressed format as ZIP or JAR file. In this example, we use JBuilder Archive Builder to construct a server archive JAR file and a client archive JAR file.

To set up the client archive, as shown in Figure 21.10, follow these steps:

1. Open Wizards | Archive Builder.
2. Set the Archive type to Basic, then click Next.
3. Set the Name field to an archive node name (for example, ClientArchive) and the file (C:\Demos\JB8_Book\chapter_rmi\deploy\Broker.jar), then click Next.
4. Set Include required classes and known resources. Click Add File and select nasdaq.policy from the RMI project directory.
5. Click Add Class and select Broker, StockMarket, and StockMarketImpl_Stub from chapter_rmi package.
6. Click Finish.

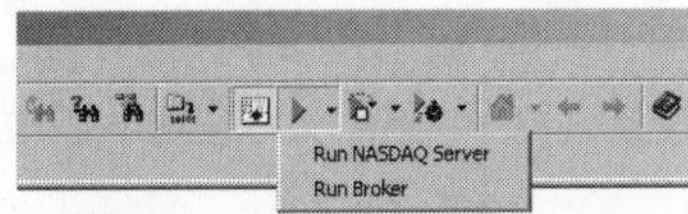


**Figure 21.10** Project run configuration.

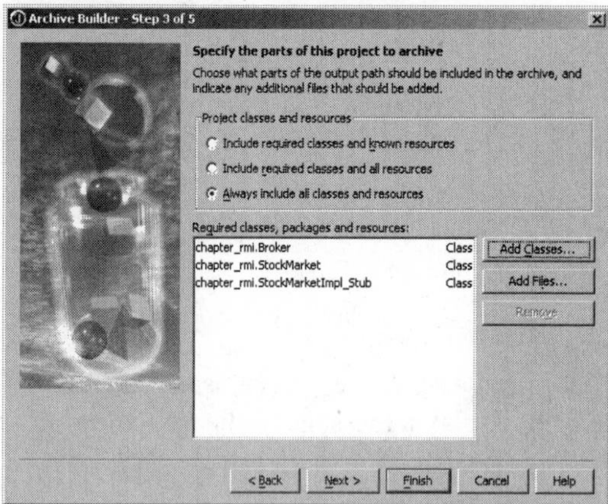


**Figure 21.11** Add classes to client archive.

To set up the server archive, as shown in Figure 21.11, follow these steps:

1. Open Wizards | Archive Builder.
2. Set the Archive type to Basic, then click Next.
3. Set the Name field to an archive node name (for example, ServerArchive) and the file (e.g., C:\Demos\JB8_Book\chapter_rmi\deploy\NasDaqServer.jar), then click Next.
4. Set Include required classes and known resources. Click Add File and select nasdaq.policy from the RMI project directory.
5. Click Add Class and select NasDaqServer, StockMarket, and StockMarketImpl from chapter_rmi package.
6. Click Finish.

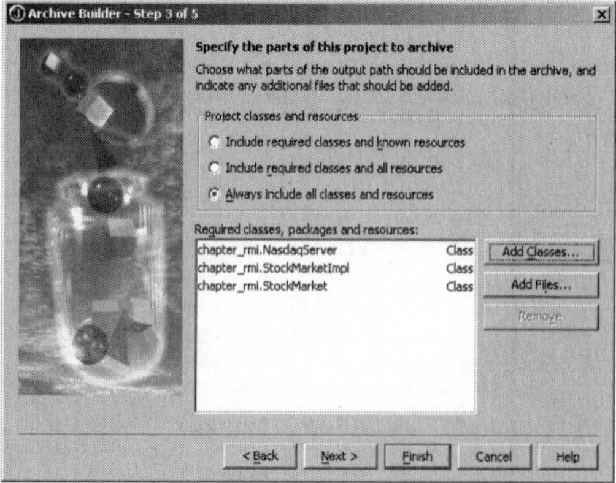


**Figure 21.12** Add classes to server archive.

You can start the server and client application by using the commands listed here:

- To start the server application: "java -cp Broker.jar -Djava.security.policy=c:\demos\JB8_Book\chapter_rmi\nasdaq.policy -Djava.rmi.server.codebase=file: c:\demos\JB8_Book\ chapter_rmi\rmi_stockmarket\Broker.jar rmi_stockmarket.NasdaqServer"
- To start the client application: "java -cp Broker.jar -Djava.security.policy=c:\demos\JB8_Book\chapter_rmi\nasdaq.policy -Djava.rmi.server.codebase=file: c:\demos\JB8_Book\ chapter_rmi\rmi_stockmarket\Broker.jar rmi_stockmarket.Broker"

## Summary

The JBuilder development environment provides an easy approach to create RMI distributed applications. After having the RMI interface defined, JBuilder generates many necessary stub and skeleton files for the application. Then you can just code your business logic without going through generating the required RMI files. The JBuilder approach also utilizes the CORBA development process, which we discuss in Chapter 22.

CHAPTER

# 22

# CORBA Development with JBuilder

CORBA is a standard for developing distributed systems with the concentration in object-oriented methodology. It is platform, programming language, and implementation neutral. To get started with CORBA, we recommend that you visit the OMG Web site for many CORBA tutorials and white papers: www.omg.org/gettingstarted/corbafaq.htm.

The chapter gives a brief introduction to CORBA and its development process. We assume that you are familiar with the CORBA framework in this chapter. The objective is to help you understand how to use JBuilder to implement CORBA applications for both client-side and server-side applications. The chapter walks you through different approaches to enable the CORBA applications, such as using object reference via the file system, using Borland VisiBroker ORB development tools, or using CORBA Naming Services.

While reading this chapter, you may need to refer back to Chapter 15, "Server and Service Configuration," for information on setting up the CORBA environment with JBuilder.

## Overview of CORBA

Before we get into what and how JBuilder works with distributed application development using CORBA, the following section offers some basic information about CORBA: the IDL interface, Object Request Broker, and some CORBA common services.

## The IDL Interface

Similar to RMI technology, CORBA starts with an interface. RMI uses Java as the interface language, whereas CORBA uses its own language called the Interface Definition Language (IDL). IDL is a contract that defines the server's services and shows how clients should send requests for the services that implement the defined interfaces. Here is an IDL example:

```
module FirstCorbaApp  // Module defines namespace that corresponds
closely to a Java package.
{
  interface HelloWorld   // An IDL interface declares a set of
operations, exceptions, and attributes
{
   attribute string objectID;
     string sayHelloWorld();
     oneway void exit();
  };
};
```

After we define the interface, we need to compile the interface based on our selected implementation language. For example, if we select Java as our implementation language, we will run the interface through an IDL-to-Java compiler. The IDL compiler is provided by any ORB vendor. This compilation process will produce the IDL stubs, skeletons, and many other support classes. JBuilder should activate the appropriate IDL compiler automatically when you run a make on the IDL file.

## Object Request Broker

The Object Request Broker (ORB) can be viewed as the network plumbing facility. It is a collection of libraries and network resources that is integrated with end-user applications, allowing CORBA client applications to locate and utilize server objects. It uses Internet Inter-ORB Protocol (IIOP) as its communication protocol over TCP/IP. An ORB connects a client application with the targeted server. It enables "the plumbing" transparently; that is, the client program does not know whether the targeted server resides on the same computer or on a remote node in its network (see Figure 22.1). The client program passes the server's name and the server's interface to the ORB, which then locates the server, dispatches the request, and delivers the result. The ORB uses the subordinate source files generated by the IDL compiler to facilitate the communication process and to provide accurate marshaling of the IDL data types, as defined in the CORBA specification.

Currently, Borland VisiBroker 5.1 is a CORBA 2.4-compliant ORB implementation.

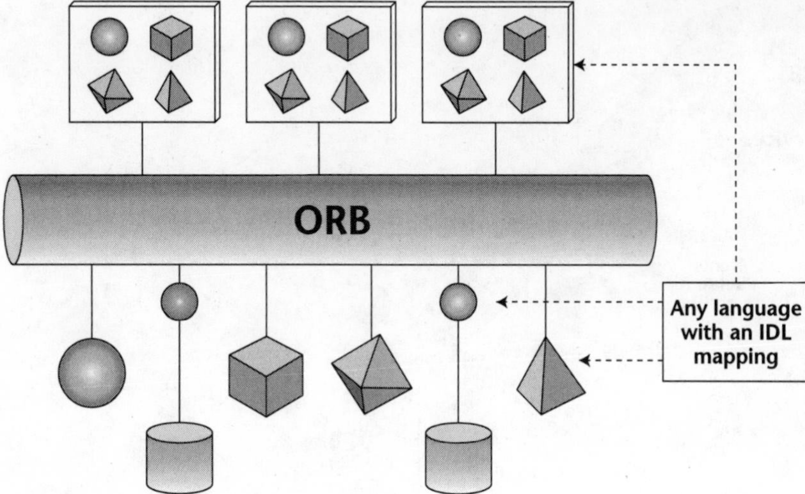


**Figure 22.1** CORBA as a middleware.

## Common Services

In addition to the core ORB functionality, the Object Management Group has introduced a set of services that provide additional capabilities to the CORBA framework (see Figure 22.2). These services include the following:

**CORBA Naming Service (or COS Naming).** This is a name-to-object association directory called a name binding. CORBA servers register object names to COS Naming; CORBA clients look up references by name via COS Naming.

**CORBA Event Service (or COS Event).** This service enables asynchronous communications between CORBA objects. COS Event uses the channel approach to orchestrate multiple suppliers' communication with multiple consumers asynchronously. Event channels are standard CORBA objects, and communication with an event channel is accomplished using standard CORBA requests via a push model or a pull model.

**CORBA Notification Service.** This extends the existing COS Event Service by adding industrial required capabilities, which are defined as typed data structure, event filtering, quality of service, and event repository.

**CORBA Object Transaction Service (OTS).** This service brings transaction capabilities to CORBA objects. The service is essential to developing reliable distributed applications addressing the business problems of commercial transaction processing.

**CORBA Security Service.** This enables CORBA systems security, including confidentiality, integrity, accountability, and availability characteristics.

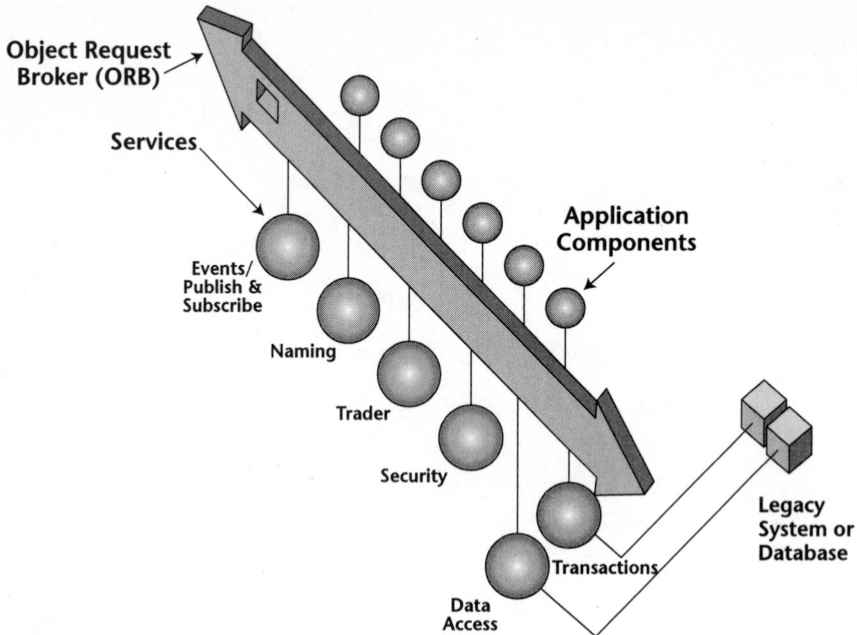


**Figure 22.2** Common services.

These popular services are implemented by Borland VisiBroker, which is included with JBuilder Enterprise. Ten additional services are Collection Service, Concurrency Service, Externalization Service, Licensing Service, Life Cycle Service, Property Service, Query Service, Relationship Service, Time Service, and Trading Object Service. You can find more information on these services at www.omg.org.

## CORBA Development Process

Similar to the RMI development process, the CORBA development process contains a series of steps to define the server object interface, create server object implementation, register server objects, and implement client-side component (see Figure 22.3):

1. **Define an IDL interface for server object component.** CORBA objects must have an IDL interface. The IDL interface defines an object type along with its operations, exceptions, and typed attributes.

**NOTE An IDL interface can inherit from one or more other interfaces. Syntax for IDL is closely similar to Java or C++ syntax, and IDL has appropriate mappings for each programming language. IDL can be translated to a selected programming language by using an IDL-to-specific-language compiler. For the example in this chapter, we will use Borland VisiBroker idl2java compiler.**

2. **Generate CORBA stub, skeleton, and supporting files.** CORBA Stub and Skeleton class files are generated by compiling the IDL. Similar to RMI, a stub is defined as a client-side proxy for a remote object. Stubs are responsible for forwarding remote invocation calls to the server-side dispatcher, which is also called a skeleton. Skeletons directly communicate with the actual remote object implementation. Supporting files include helper classes and holder classes, which are object management and object marshaling utilities.
3. **Implement the interface.** Typically, the IDL compiler generates an implementation file for the interface. The naming convention for the implementation class is the actual interface name suffixed by "Impl." For example, if the interface name is Nasdaq, the IDL compiler will generate a file name NasdaqImpl. This step fulfills the business logic for all methods and their signatures, declared in the interface.
4. **Create a server program.** A server application offers one or more CORBA objects to client applications. The server program must complete the following tasks: initialize the Object Request Broker, create a Portable Object Adapter (POA) with its appropriate policies, construct the servant object, activate the Object Adapter, and signal its ready state to receive requests. Since OMG released the CORBA 2.3 specification, many ORB vendors have implemented the POA architecture in replacement of the deprecated Basic Object Adaptor (BOA).
5. **Create a client program.** The client program uses the generated stubs, obtains server object references, and invokes any of the IDL methods on the server's object.

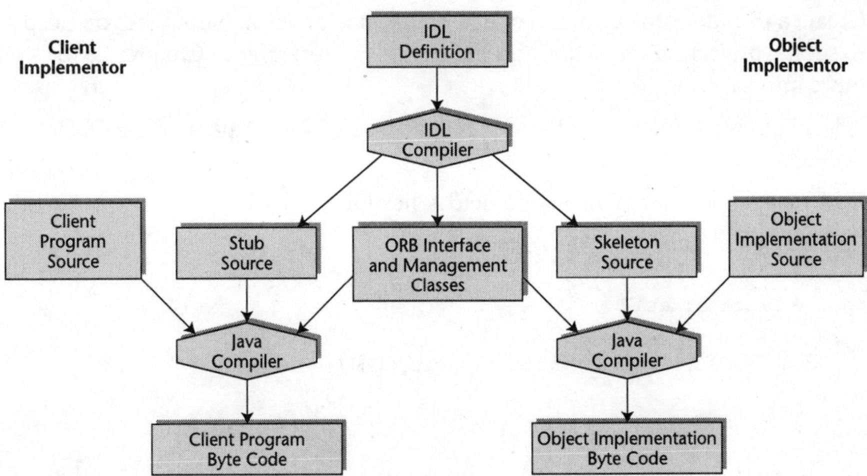


**Figure 22.3** CORBA development process.

**WHAT IS THE POA?**

**Per the CORBA specification (www.omg.org), the specification defines a Portable Object Adapter that can be used for most ORB objects with conventional implementations. The intent of the POA is to provide an Inter-ORBs interoperable Object Adapter, which intercepts a client request and identifies the object that satisfies the client request. The object is then invoked, and the response is returned to the client. Also, the POA is designed to offer portability on the server side to achieve a minimum of rewriting needed to deal with different vendors' implementations.**

# Building a CORBA Application

This section covers how to apply the CORBA development process to creating a distributed application using JBuilder and the VisiBroker ORB. JBuilder Enterprise Edition ships with a development version of Borland Enterprise Server (BES), which includes the VisiBroker product. Those steps involve defining an IDL interface; generating Stub, Skeleton, and support class files from the IDL; writing Java codes for the object service; writing the server and client program; and building and running the CORBA application.

## Define the IDL Interface

We will use the same StockMarket example as we illustrated in Chapter 21 and implement the example using the CORBA approach.

1. Create a JBuilder project, and name it: corba_stockmarket. Note that you need to set the project server to Borland Enterprise Server; refer to Chapter 15 for more information.
2. Select File | New, then select Sample IDL from the CORBA page of the Object Gallery.
3. Enter nasdaq.idl in the File Name field. Click OK.
4. Edit nasdaq.idl with the following code:

```
module StockMarket {
  interface Nasdaq {
    double getPrice(in string ticketSymbol);
  };
};
```

The *nasdaq.idl* defines a Nasdaq object, on which a client can invoke the *getPrice()* operation with a string argument and return a double result. In addition to the type, IDL, the parameters are specified by *in, out* or *inout* attributes; these attributes identify whether the value will be passed from client object to server object, or from server object to client object, or bidirectional across client object and server object.

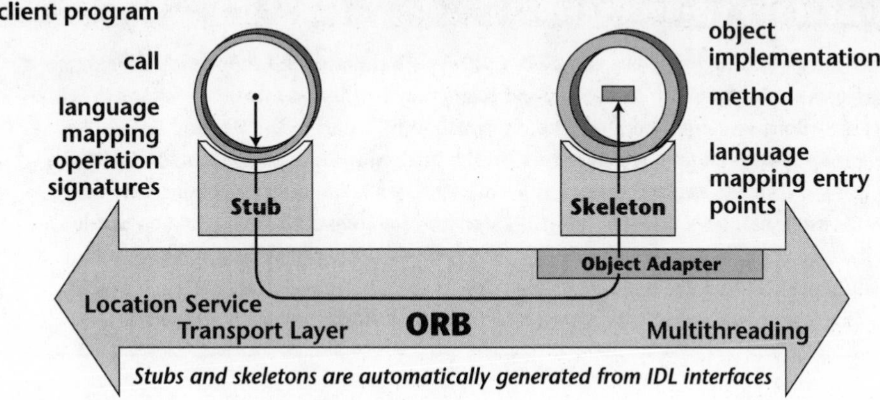


**Figure 22.4** Role of the ORB in the CORBA system.

To edit the IDL compiler settings, you can open the Properties dialog box by right-mouse clicking on nasdaq.idl file in the Project pane and selecting Properties. The dialog box in Figure 22.5 will be displayed. The box includes the following options:

**Package.** When this option is set to a specified package, codes are generated accordingly and stored under the specified package name.

**Strict portable code generation.** When this option is selected, compiled codes are generated strictly to be compliant with the CORBA specification. This means that any vendor-specific code will not be generated.

**Generate example implementation.** When this option is selected, the IDL compiler will generate example implementation classes.

**Generate comments.** When this option is selected, the IDL compiler will insert comments in the generated codes.

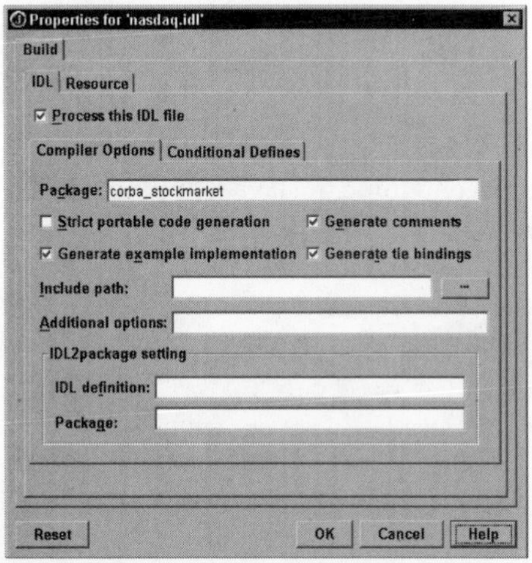

Properties for 'nasdaq.idl'
Build
IDL | Resource
☑ Process this IDL file
Compiler Options | Conditional Defines
Package: corba_stockmarket
☐ Strict portable code generation ☑ Generate comments
☑ Generate example implementation ☑ Generate tie bindings
Include path:
Additional options:
IDL2package setting
IDL definition:
Package:
Reset OK Cancel Help

**Figure 22.5** IDL compiler dialog box.

**WHAT IS THE VISIBROKER ORB?**

**The VisiBroker ORB provides a complete CORBA ORB runtime and supporting development environment for building, deploying, and managing distributed Java applications that are open, flexible, and interoperable. The VisiBroker ORB is part of the Borland Enterprise Server AppServer Edition, which comes "in the box" with JBuilder. Objects built with the VisiBroker ORB are easily accessed by Web-based applications that communicate using OMG's Internet Inter-ORB Protocol (IIOP) standard for communication between distributed objects through the Internet or through local intranets (see Figure 22.4). In addition, VisiBroker ORB provides implementation of key CORBA common services such as COS Naming, COS Event, COS Notification, OTS, and COS Security Service.**

**Generate tie bindings**. When this option is selected, the IDL compiler will generate CORBA _tie classes for CORBA skeletons. For more information on the CORBA tie mechanism, see http://info.borland.com/techpubs/books/bes/htmls/DevelopersGuide5/DevelopersGuide/tie.html#3373.

**Include path**. If the IDL file includes other IDL files, you must select a directory that contains those included IDL files:

```
Example:
#include MutualFundMarket.idl
module StockMarket {
  interface Nasdaq {
    double getPrice(in string ticketSymbol);
  };
};
```

**Additional options.** You can use this field to set additional IDL compiler options.

**IDL2package**. This puts definitions in the scope of IDL into the specified Java package.

**Conditional Defines.** This tab adds conditional IDL compilation parameters; i.e., #define name def.

## IDL Compilation

When *nasdaq.idl* is compiled, a directory structure containing the Java mappings for the IDL declarations is created (see Figure 22.6 and Table 22.1).

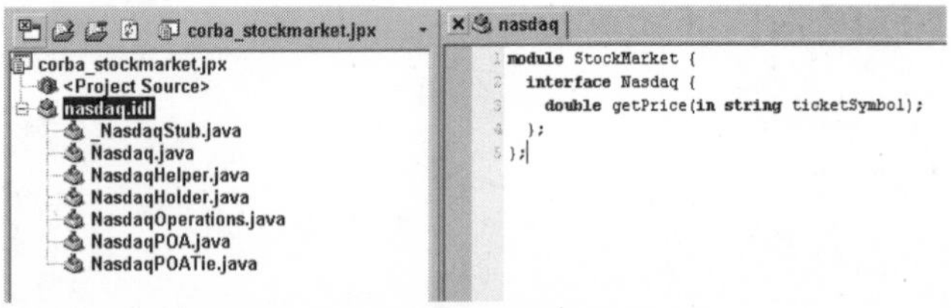

**Figure 22.6** Generated Stub/Skeleton classes.

**Table 22.1** Generated Files

| FILE | FUNCTION |
|---|---|
| _NasDaqStub.java | Is stub code for the NasDaq object on the client side. |
| NasDaq.java | Declares the NasDaq interface. |
| NasDaqHelper.java | Declares the NasDaqHelper class, which defines helpful utility methods. |
| NasDaqHolder.java | Declares the NasDaqHolder class, which provides a holder for passing the NasDaq object. |
| NasDaqOperations.java | Declares the method signatures defined in the NasDaq interface in the nasdaq.idl file. |
| NasDaqPOA.java | Is the POA servant code (implementation base code) for the NasDaq object implementation on the server side. |
| NasDaqPOATie.java | Used to implement the NasDaq object on the server side using the CORBA tie mechanism. |

## Create a Server Application

JBuilder provides a wizard to construct an application that has a complete default implementation for a CORBA server. To open this wizard, choose File | New, select the CORBA tab of the Object Gallery, and then select the CORBA Server Application (see Figure 22.7).

Following this two-step wizard, you will construct a visible server application with a log GUI and object counter GUI. You can later modify the generated server application to meet your requirements. In addition, this wizard will create a new Runtime configuration for running the CORBA Server Application.

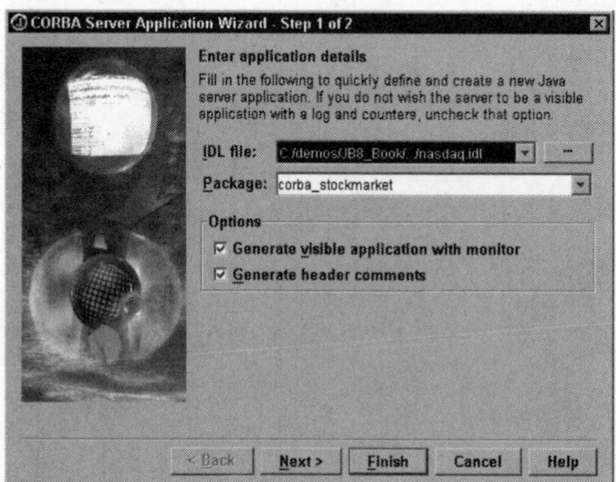


**Figure 22.7** CORBA Server Application wizard.

The wizard generates the following files:

- *NasdaqImpl.java* provides default implementation for the server side of a CORBA. This file can also be generated using the *CORBA Server Interface wizard*. Our next step is to provide business logic for this implementation.
- *StockMarketServerApp.java* is a CORBA Server Application.
- *ServerResources.java* contains server application strings for localization.
- *ServerFrame.java* is a server application frame that is the container for the Server Monitor.
- *ServerMonitor.java* maintains the server log and is the container for all the Server Monitor pages.
- *ServerMonitorPage.java* implements a Server Monitor page to display interface counters.

Reviewing the generated server application codes (*StockMarketServerApp.java*), we see that the JBuilder wizard has taken care of all major tasks: initializing the Object Request Broker, creating a Portable Object Adapter with its appropriate policies, constructing the servant object, activating the Object Adapter, and signaling its ready state to receive requests. The only necessary step for us is to implement the business logic for the Nasdaq object (see Source 22.1).

```
// StockMarketServerApp.java

package corba_stockmarket;

import corba_stockmarket.StockMarket.server.*;
import javax.swing.UIManager;
import java.awt.*;
import org.omg.PortableServer.*;

public class StockMarketServerApp {

  private boolean packFrame = false;


  public StockMarketServerApp() {
    ServerFrame frame = new ServerFrame();

    if (packFrame)
      frame.pack();
    else
      frame.validate();

    Dimension screenSize = Toolkit.getDefaultToolkit().getScreenSize();
    Dimension frameSize = frame.getSize();
    if (frameSize.height > screenSize.height)
```

**Source 22.1** StockMarketServerApp.java.

```
      frameSize.height = screenSize.height;
    if (frameSize.width > screenSize.width)
      frameSize.width = screenSize.width;
    frame.setLocation((screenSize.width - frameSize.width) / 2,
(screenSize.height - frameSize.height) / 2);
    frame.setVisible(true);
  }

  public static void main(String[] args) {
    try  {

UIManager.setLookAndFeel("com.sun.java.swing.plaf.windows.WindowsLookAnd
Feel");

//UIManager.setLookAndFeel(UIManager.getSystemLookAndFeelClassName());

//UIManager.setLookAndFeel("javax.swing.plaf.metal.MetalLookAndFeel");

//UIManager.setLookAndFeel("com.sun.java.swing.plaf.motif.MotifLookAndFe
el");

//UIManager.setLookAndFeel("com.sun.java.swing.plaf.windows.WindowsLookA
ndFeel");
    }
    catch (Exception ex) {
    }
    new StockMarketServerApp();

    try {
      java.util.ResourceBundle res =
java.util.ResourceBundle.getBundle("corba_stockmarket.StockMarket.server
.ServerResources");
      String name;

      //(debug support)System.getProperties().put("vbroker.agent.debug",
"true");
      //(debug support)System.getProperties().put("vbroker.orb.warn",
"2");
      if (System.getProperties().get("vbroker.agent.port") == null) {
        System.getProperties().put("vbroker.agent.port", "14000");
      }
      if (System.getProperties().get("org.omg.CORBA.ORBClass") == null)
{
        System.getProperties().put("org.omg.CORBA.ORBClass",
"com.inprise.vbroker.orb.ORB");
      }
      if (System.getProperties().get("org.omg.CORBA.ORBSingletonClass")
== null) {
```

**Source 22.1** *(continued)*

```
        System.getProperties().put("org.omg.CORBA.ORBSingletonClass",
"com.inprise.vbroker.orb.ORB");
      }

      org.omg.CORBA.ORB orb = org.omg.CORBA.ORB.init(args,
System.getProperties());

      POA poaRoot =
POAHelper.narrow(orb.resolve_initial_references("RootPOA"));

      name = "Nasdaq";
      org.omg.CORBA.Policy[] NasdaqPolicies = {
        poaRoot.create_lifespan_policy(LifespanPolicyValue.PERSISTENT)
      };
      POA poaNasdaq = poaRoot.create_POA(name + "_poa",
                                         poaRoot.the_POAManager(),
                                         NasdaqPolicies);
      poaNasdaq.activate_object_with_id(name.getBytes(), new
NasdaqImpl());
      ServerMonitor.log(ServerResources.format(res.getString("created"),
"StockMarketServerApp.java Nasdaq"));

      poaRoot.the_POAManager().activate();
      ServerMonitor.log(ServerResources.format(res.getString("isReady"),
"StockMarketServerApp.java StockMarket"));
      orb.run();
    }
    catch(Exception ex) {
      System.err.println(ex);
    }
  }
}
```

**Source 22.1** *(continued)*

# Object Implementation

Open and edit *NasDaqImpl.java* with the following changes to *the getPrice()* method:

```
// NasdaqImpl.java
package corba_stockmarket.StockMarket.server;

import java.sql.*;
import java.util.*;
```

```
import java.math.*;

import org.omg.PortableServer.*;


public class NasdaqImpl extends corba_stockmarket.StockMarket.NasdaqPOA
{
  private String _name = "Nasdaq";
public static ServerMonitorPage monitor = null;
  public java.util.Random randomGenerator =
            new java.util.Random(System.currentTimeMillis());

  private void init() {
    if (monitor == null) {
      monitor = ServerMonitor.addPage(this, "Nasdaq");
      monitor.showObjectCounter(true);
    }
    monitor.updateObjectCounter(1);

  }

  public NasdaqImpl(java.lang.String name, java.lang.String
creationParameters) {
    this._name = name;
    init();
  }

  public NasdaqImpl(java.lang.String name) {
    this._name = name;
    init();
  }

  public NasdaqImpl() {
    init();
  }

// For demonstration purpose, we use a fake implementation of getPrice()
method that returns a random double as a value of a given symbol.

  public double getPrice(String ticketSymbol)  {
    double price;
    price =
(double)ticketSymbol.length()*randomGenerator.nextDouble()*10.0;
    ServerMonitor.log("(" + _name + ") NasdaqImpl.java getPrice()");
    return price;
  }
}
```

Figure 22.8 shows the NasDaqImpl class in a UML format.

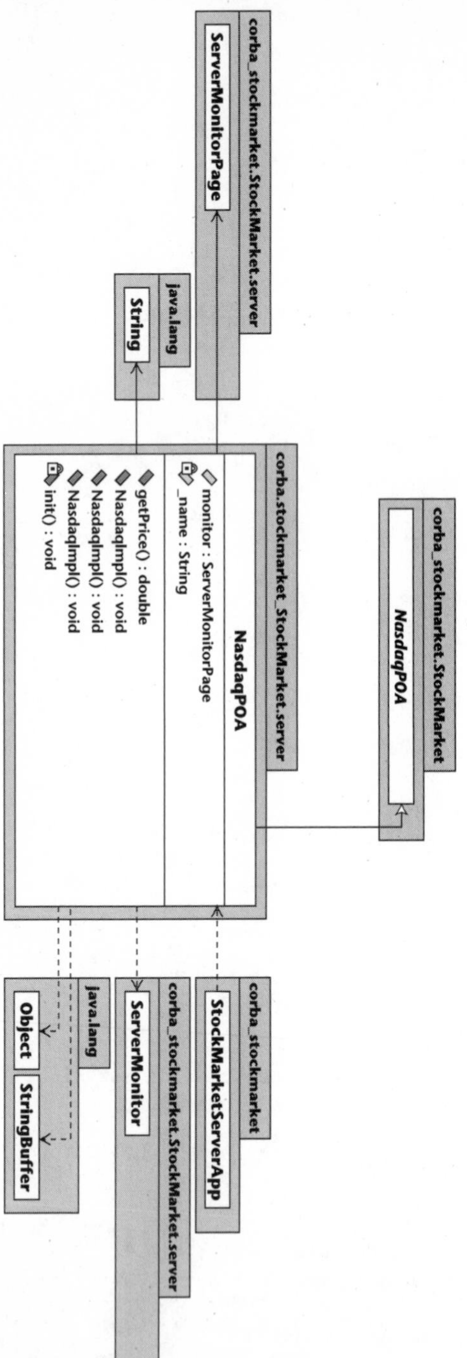


**Figure 22.8** NasDaqImpl UML view.

## Create a Client Application

A typical CORBA client program performs the following tasks:

- Initializes the ORB.
- Obtains an object reference to the CORBA server.
- Invokes the server's remote methods.

The object reference contains a structure for CORBA server's host machine/IP address, the port on which the host server is listening on for requests. Following is an example of an object reference content:

```
Interoperable Object Reference:
  Type ID: IDL:omg.org/CosNaming/NamingContextExt:1.0
  Contains 1 profile.
  Profile 0-IIOP Profile:
    version: 1.2
    host: 192.168.0.190
    port: 3717
    Object Key: ServiceId[service=/CONTEXT_POAnamingservice,id={1 bytes:
[2]},key_string=%00PMC%00%00%00%04%00%00%00%1a/CONTEXT_POAnamingser
vice%00%20%20%00%00%00%012]
    VB Capability component:
    ORB_TYPE Component: VBJ 4.x
    Code Sets Component: native char codeset:ISO 8859_1
conversion_code_sets:, native wchar codeset:ISO UTF-16
conversion_code_sets:
```

CORBA client programs obtain object references from a factory object, the naming service, or a string that was specially created from an object reference. The example in this chapter shows you how a client locates a server via VisiBroker SmartAgent.

To best assist in building the CORBA application, JBuilder provides a wizard to generate a client interface that is a wrapper of CORBA service calls for the client side. The client interface is generated as a Java Bean format, which can be utilized in any client-side applications. When a client-side application constructs this bean and invokes methods in this bean, this bean will connect to an ORB and execute the server's methods.

### WHAT IS THE SMART AGENT?

**VisiBroker Edition's Smart Agent (osagent) is a dynamic, distributed directory service that provides facilities used by both client programs and object implementations. A Smart Agent must be started on at least one host within your local network. When your client program invokes bind() on an object, the Smart Agent is automatically consulted. The Smart Agent locates the specified implementation so that a connection can be established between the client and the implementation. The communication with the Smart Agent is completely transparent to the client program. See http://info.borland.com/techpubs/books/bes/htmls/DevelopersGuide5/DevelopersGuide/smrtagnt.html#.**

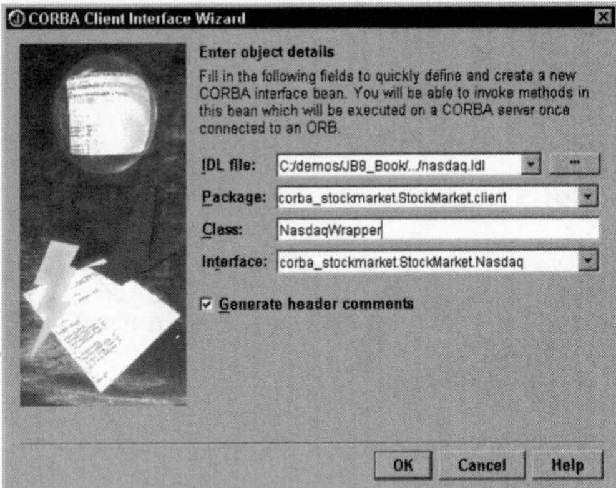


**Figure 22.9** CORBA Client Interface wizard.

To open this wizard, select File | New, select the CORBA tab of the Object Gallery, then select CORBA Client Interface and click OK. The dialog box shown in Figure 22.9 will appear.

Select nasdaq.idl in the current project from the drop-down list to create the CORBA interface bean, which is named as NasdaqWrapper under *Class* field. Change the package name for the generated file to *corba_stockmarket.StockMarket.client*. The *Interface* field reflects a list of interfaces associated with the provided file. In this case, nasdaq.idl is provided, and the *corba_stockmarket.StockMarket*.NasDaq Interface is selected (see Source 22.2).

```
// NasdaqWrapper.java
package corba_stockmarket.StockMarket.client;

import java.awt.*;
import org.omg.CORBA.*;

public class NasdaqWrapper {
  private boolean bInitialized = false;
  private corba_stockmarket.StockMarket.Nasdaq _nasdaq;
  private com.borland.cx.OrbConnect orbConnect1;
  private String _name = "Nasdaq";

  public NasdaqWrapper() {
    try {
      jbInit();
    }
    catch (Exception ex) {
      ex.printStackTrace();
    }
  }
  private void jbInit() throws Exception {
```

**Source 22.2** NasdaqWrapper.java.

```
  }

  public boolean init() {
    if (!bInitialized) {
      try {
        org.omg.CORBA.ORB orb = null;
        if (orbConnect1 != null) {
          orb = orbConnect1.initOrb();
        }
        if (orb == null) {
          orb = org.omg.CORBA.ORB.init((String[])null,
System.getProperties());
        }
        _nasdaq = corba_stockmarket.StockMarket.NasdaqHelper.bind(orb,
"/" + _name + "_poa", _name.getBytes());
        bInitialized = true;
      }
      catch (Exception ex) {
        ex.printStackTrace();
      }
    }
    return bInitialized;
  }

  public corba_stockmarket.StockMarket.Nasdaq getCorbaInterface() {
    return _nasdaq;
  }

  public void setCorbaInterface(corba_stockmarket.StockMarket.Nasdaq
intf) {
    _nasdaq = intf;
  }

  public com.borland.cx.OrbConnect getORBConnect() {
    return orbConnect1;
  }

  public void setORBConnect(com.borland.cx.OrbConnect orbConnect) {
    this.orbConnect1 = orbConnect;
  }

  public double getPrice(String ticketSymbol)  {
    init();
    return _nasdaq.getPrice(ticketSymbol);
  }
}
```

**Source 22.2** *(continued)*

*NasdaqWrapper* code uses the CORBA express component, which contains CORBA connection classes. The *OrbConnect* class is a non-UI bean that resolves a given name to a CORBA object without using the VisiBroker ORB root context extension to the Naming Service. The *OrbConnectBeanInfo* class provides descriptive information so that the UI Designer will be more useful when inspecting an instance of that object.

Next, create a simple Java program to use *NasDaqWrapper* bean. Use the New Class wizard (Choose File | New Class) to construct a class named *NonGuiClient*. Then edit the file *NonGuiClient.java* with the following codes:

```
// NonGuiClient.java
package corba_stockmarket.StockMarket.client;

public class NonGuiClient {

  public static void main(String[] args) {
     NasdaqWrapper myCorbaInterface = new NasdaqWrapper();
     System.out.println("Price of BORL = " +
                    myCorbaInterface.getPrice("BORL"));
  }
}
```

## Run the Applications

In order to run both server and client applications, you need to start the VisiBroker SmartAgent, which is a VisiBroker-specific object location service. When you used Tools | Configure Server to set up the Borland Enterprise Server in the previous chapter, your CORBA settings were automatically set up for you at the same time. You can see your current settings on the CORBA page of the Tools | Enterprise Setup dialog box. Also, a command to start the Smart Agent was added to the Tools menu item. To start the VisiBroker ORB Smart Agent, choose Tools | VisiBroker Smart Agent. For Windows users, note that running osagent will add an icon to the taskbar, and it does not have to be restarted every time you restart the client or server.

To start the server implementation, right-mouse click the file StockMarketServerApp.java in the Project pane. Choose Run. From the drop-down menu, choose Use Server Application. The application will display the GUI shown in Figure 22.10.

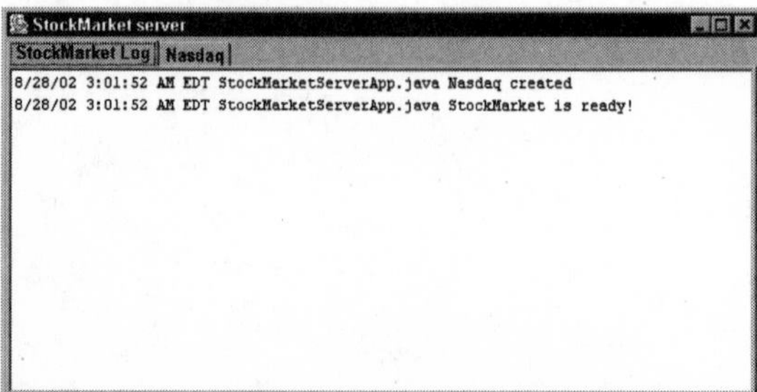


**Figure 22.10** StockMarket server application.

To start the *NonGuiClient*, right-mouse click the file *NonGuilClient.java* in the Project pane. Choose Run. From the drop-down menu, choose Use Server Application. The JBuilder Message pane should display a similar result.

```
Price of BORL = 20.768581150166604
```

The server GUI will update its message, as shown in Figure 22.11.

## Building a GUI Client with a CORBA Client Interface

*NasdaqWrapper* is a nonvisual bean, and it can be used in client CORBA applications. This section explores how to connect a GUI application, a reference, and a CORBA client interface that was built earlier. The Use CORBA Interface wizard provides information on using CodeInsight in the Source pane, helping the UI designer connect the necessary pieces.

The next step is to create a new application by clicking the File | New menu item, selecting the Application icon, and clicking the OK button. This will display a three-step dialog that will help create the Java GUI application:

1. Define a package name and an application class name (see Figure 22.12).
2. Enter a name for the application's frame (see Figure 22.13).
3. Select to create a Runtime configuration (see Figure 22.14).

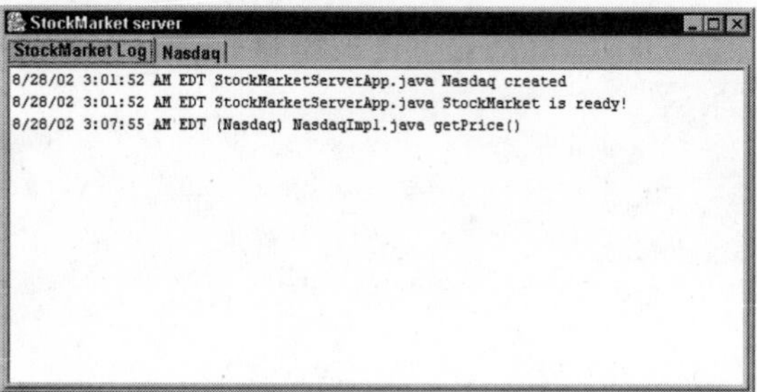


**Figure 22.11** StockMarket server application update.

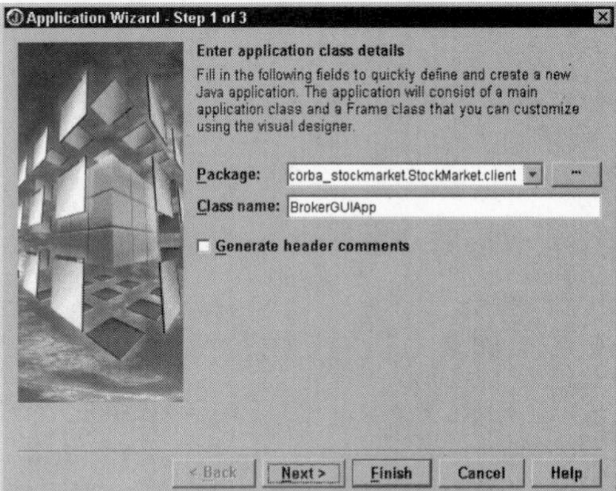


**Figure 22.12** Step 1 – Enter names for the package and application class file.

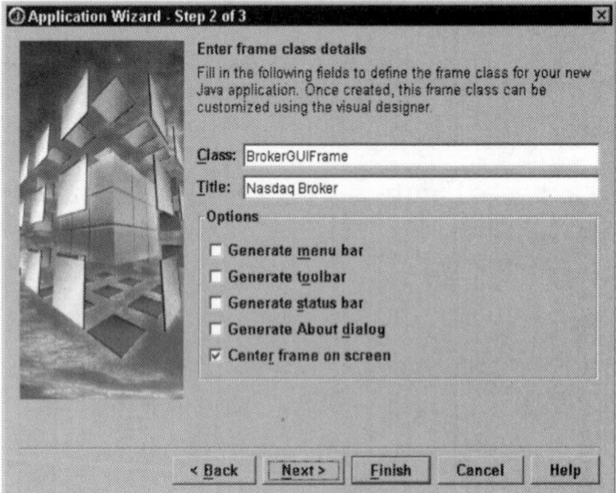


**Figure 22.13** Step 2 – Enter frame class details.

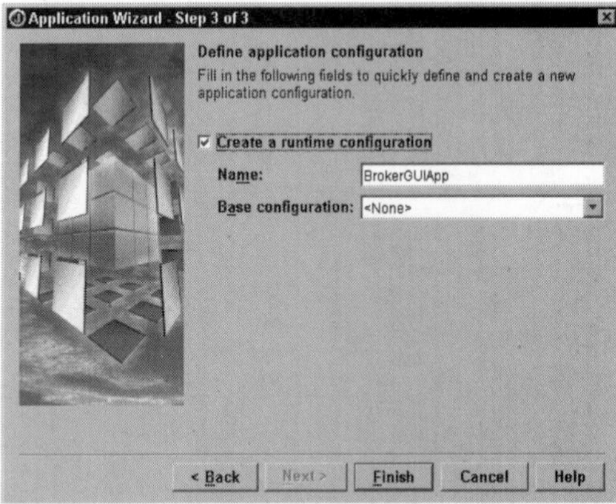


**Figure 22.14** Step 3 – Create a Runtime configuration.

By default, the JBuilder Content pane should have BrokerGUIFrame.java opened (see Source 22.3).

```
// BrokerGUIFrame.java
package corba_stockmarket.StockMarket.client;

import java.awt.*;
import java.awt.event.*;
import javax.swing.*;

public class BrokerGUIFrame extends JFrame {
  private JPanel contentPane;
  private BorderLayout borderLayout1 = new BorderLayout();

  //Construct the frame
  public BrokerGUIFrame() {
    enableEvents(AWTEvent.WINDOW_EVENT_MASK);
    try {
      jbInit();
    }
    catch(Exception e) {
      e.printStackTrace();
    }
  }
  //Component initialization
  private void jbInit() throws Exception  {

//setIconImage(Toolkit.getDefaultToolkit().createImage(BrokerGUIFrame.cl
ass.getResource("[Your Icon]")));
    contentPane = (JPanel) this.getContentPane();
    contentPane.setLayout(borderLayout1);
    this.setSize(new Dimension(400, 300));
    this.setTitle("Nasdaq Broker");
  }
  //Overridden so we can exit when window is closed
  protected void processWindowEvent(WindowEvent e) {
    super.processWindowEvent(e);
    if (e.getID() == WindowEvent.WINDOW_CLOSING) {
      System.exit(0);
    }
  }
}
```

**Source 22.3** BrokerGUIFrame.java.

We connect this GUI application to a CORBA client interface using the Use CORBA Interface wizard. Select Wizards | Use CORBA Interface to display a two-step dialog (see Figure 22.15 and Figure 22.16):

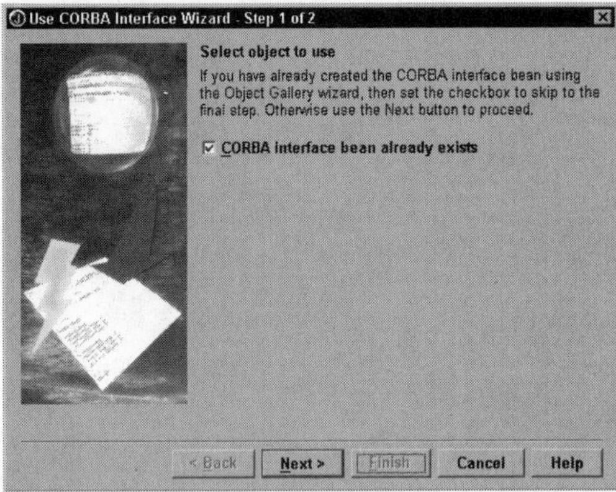


**Figure 22.15** CORBA Interface wizard, Step 1.

1. Select an existing CORBA interface bean.
2. Select the CORBA Interface Bean class, and set a field name as an instance variable for that class.

On completing the wizard, JBuilder will insert *myCorbaInterface* as a private variable and instantiate a new instance NasdaqWrapper() in BrokerGUIFrame.java file.

```
private NasdaqWrapper myCorbaInterface = new NasdaqWrapper();
```

Let's design a simple GUI, as shown in Figure 22.17. The GUI includes a jGetQuote-Button for command, a jResultLabel for output, jTicketSymbolTextField for input, and three other labels that show static texts: "NASDAQ BROKER GUI", "Stock Symbol", and "Last Sale At:", respectively.

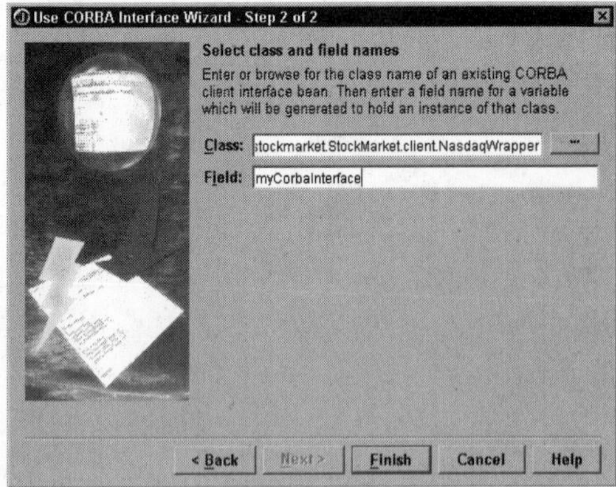


**Figure 22.16** CORBA Interface wizard, Step 2.

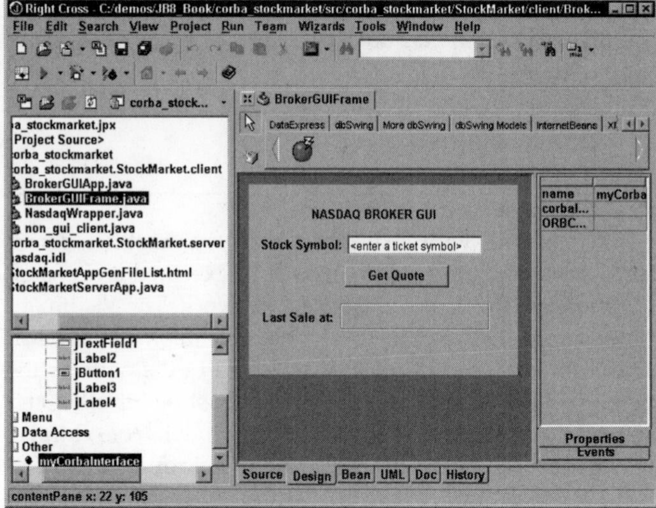


**Figure 22.17** BrokerGUIFrame designer.

Double-click on the Get Quote button, and add this code to the source.

```
void jGetQuoteButton_actionPerformed(ActionEvent e) {
      jResultLabel.setText(
String.valueOf(myCorbaInterface.getPrice(jTicketSymbolTextField.getText(
))));
}
```

To run the BrokerGUIApp, select Run|Run Project and pick BrokerGUIApp (see Figure 22.18).

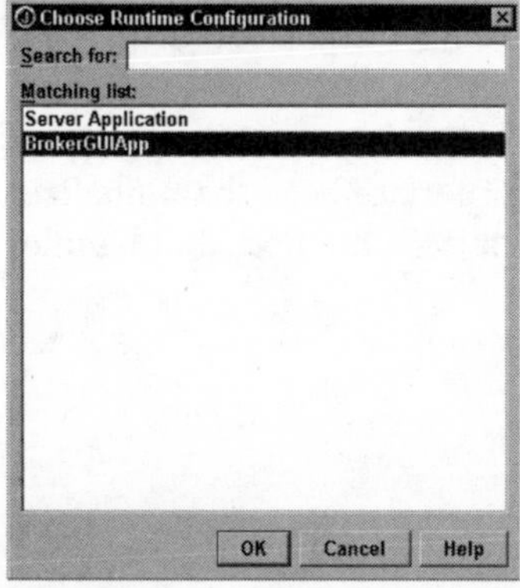


**Figure 22.18** Select a run configuration.

The BrokerGUIApp will display the simple GUI (see Figure 22.19), which is designed in the previous step. Enter a symbol to look up its quote. For example, enter "BORL" for Stock Symbol, and click the Get Quote button.

# Deploying the Application

In order to deploy applications developed with VisiBroker ORB, you must first set up a runtime environment on the host where the application is to be executed and ensure that the necessary support services are available on the local network. The VisiBroker ORB libraries and packages must be installed on the host where the deployed application is to execute. The location of these libraries must be included in the path for the application's environment. Also, a Java Runtime Environment must be installed and configured on the host. See http://info.borland.com/techpubs/books/bes/htmls/DevelopersGuide5/DevelopersGuide/envsetup.html# for more information on setting up VisiBroker deployment.

The CORBA application can be deployed to a location on a server or client machine where the application will be executed. JBuilder provides a wizard to assist the deployment process. JBuilder's Archive Builder automatically collects necessary Java classes, resources, and libraries, then archives these files to a compressed format as ZIP or JAR files.

# Summary

This chapter provides a brief tutorial on the basic concepts and design of a CORBA application with JBuilder using Borland VisiBroker ORB. The JBuilder provides an integrated environment for developing CORBA-based distributed applications. After defining object interfaces in IDL, JBuilder generates client stub routines and server servant (or skeleton) code. To help implement the server object, the CORBA Server Application wizard constructs a server program that initializes the ORB, creates the POA, creates the servant object, activates the servant object, activates the POA manager and the POA, and prepares to receive requests. To help implementing the client program, JBuilder provides a wizard to construct a CORBA client interface bean that initializes the ORB, binds to the server object, invokes the server object's method, and handles exceptions.

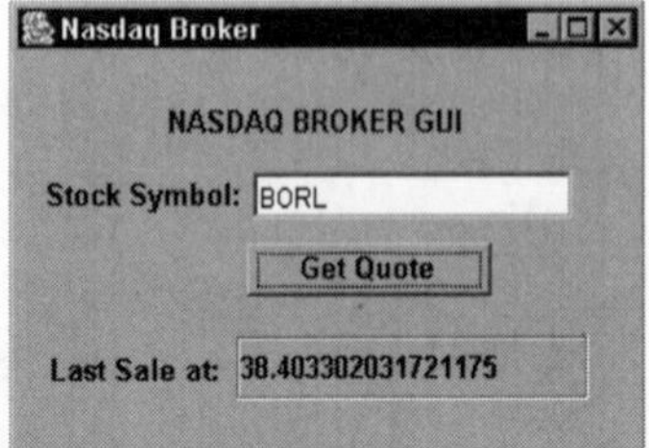


**Figure 22.19** BrokerGUI application.

In the next chapter, we discuss how to extend various Java distributed technologies like RMI and CORBA into the newly emerging Web services for a true Internet platform for server-to-server or service-to-service communication. This will allow the developer to write server applications using standardized XML messaging technology that openly communicate with other servers, regardless of platform, hardware, or language.

CHAPTER

23

# Web Services Development with JBuilder

Web Services holds the promise of interoperability across software components, applications, platforms, programming languages, and organizations. Web Services is a Web-centric architecture that can describe, publish, locate, and invoke Web service applications over the network using standardized XML messaging technology. The framework is built up by leading-edge technologies like Simple Object Access Protocol (SOAP); Web Services Description Language (WSDL); and Universal Discovery, Description, and Integration (UDDI). These new technologies integrate with existing computing frameworks like CORBA, J2EE, COM/DCOM, and CGI.

The chapter does not provide yet another introduction to the Web Services framework — we assume that you are familiar with Web Services and its offerings. Our objective is to help you understand how to use JBuilder to implement Web Services applications for both consumer-side and provider-side applications. This chapter presents an introduction to Web Services technology, including the benefits of Web Services and how easy it is to facilitate Web Services using JBuilder. This chapter includes a practical tutorial for understanding the concept of Web Services and how to apply it in Java application. Also, this chapter discusses Web Services and J2EE integration.

## Web Services Orientation

At the W3C Web Services Architecture Group, we found a definition of a Web service as follows:

*A Web service is a software application identified by a URI, whose interfaces and binding are capable of being defined, described, and discovered by XML artifacts, and supports direct interactions with other software applications using XML-based messages via Internet-based protocols. (W3C — www.w3.org/TR/2002/WD-ws-arch-20021114/)*

A distributed software component is defined as a software service that contains a self-described service interface, implements a set of tasks that are published to the world, and builds on top of a standard transportation protocol. In combination with the W3C definition of Web service, a Web service is actually a distributed software component that is invoked from any programming language and any platform, and across a network. The service interface offered to the public is described in an XML-based language called Web Services Description Language (WSDL). A published Web service registers and describes itself in a Universal Discovery, Description, and Integration (UDDI) server so that one business can locate other businesses' Web services and build applications to suit their customers' needs via a transportation protocol like Simple Object Access Protocol (SOAP).

## Benefits of Web Services

From the definition of the Web service and its supporting technology, here are a few key messages that the Web service promises:

**Interoperability.** The communication between Web services components is designed to be 100 percent platform and language independent. A universal data format XML-based WSDL document is used to describe the interface and illustrate the service over a standard network protocol. Web services written in any language can run on any platform. For example, a consumer application written using C++ and running on Windows could request a service from a component written in Java and running on Linux.

**Business integration.** The Web services framework is designed to ease the integration across business in a rapid manner. Finding and discovering services are operated dynamically as new services are made available from the service broker. Binding and evoking services are on-demand 24 x 7 operations. This means that the framework forms a self-configured, adaptive, and robust integrated system.

**Simplicity.** Loosely coupled and coarse-grained characteristics are the two most-mentioned characteristics to reduce complexity for doing Web services. Service requesters and providers are not tied to each other. They communicate via well-defined interfaces that contain information necessary for them to interact with each other. That enables Web service implementation to integrate many systems at a corporate level to provide large business services in a coarse-grained manner.

**Industrial standard.** Many major companies are supporting Web services and their underlying technologies. For example, Borland is going full speed at Web services by providing tools and frameworks across platforms and languages to make it easy to develop, deploy, and manage Web service components.

## Web Services Architecture

The Web Services Architecture view is based on three operations of typical Web services: to publish, to find, and to bind. First, the Web services must be published or have registered its services with a so-called Service Broker. This publish operation is handled by a Service Provider. The Service Broker then makes the Web services available for the "Service Requestor" to access by communicating with the Service Broker to find the Web services. A Service Broker role is to help Service Providers and Service Requestors locate each other. The Service Requestor is now able to bind and invoke a particular Web service on demand via the Simple Object Access Protocol (SOAP). Services deployed by service providers are described using the Web Services Description Language (WSDL). A Service Requestor uses the Universal Discovery, Description, and Integration (UDDI) APIs to request the required services from the Service Broker. The conceptual view is described in Figure 23.1.

## Web Services Technologies

In order to publish, describe, locate, and evoke a Web service, Web services use the following core technologies.

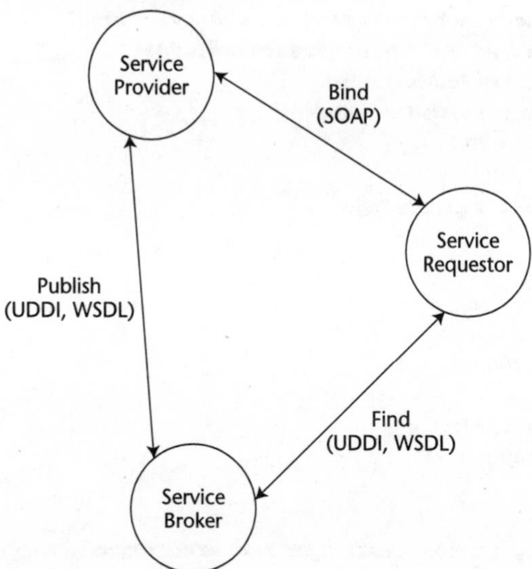


**Figure 23.1** Conceptual view of Web Services.

## Universal Description, Discovery, and Integration

The first step to connect to the Web service is to locate that business with the needed services. Universal Description, Discovery, and Integration (UDDI) is the mechanism to browse and query for a particular service. UDDI can be viewed as a "yellow page" for the published Web services. The programmable UDDI API is used to discover the service interface and semantics reference to the service. Web service providers can register and describe their services in the UDDI registry. And Web service consumers can query the registry to find the Web services and to locate information needed to interoperate with those services. UDDI registry is a Web service itself. Developers can use SOAP messaging to communicate with the registry in support of publishing, editing, browsing, and searching for information.

## Web Services Description Language

The Web Services Description Language (WSDL) specification is an XML-based document that describes the interfaces, semantics, and location information for a Web service. WSDL semantics contains structured information for a Web service: input/output parameters, return data type, and service protocol used in the binding process. In short, WSDL describes the what-how-where aspect of the Web service.

Following is the WSDL definition for the FedEx Tracker service (www.xmethods.net/sd/2001/FedExTrackerService.wsdl):

```
<?xml version="1.0" ?>
<definitions name="FedExTrackerService"
targetNamespace="http://www.xmethods.net/sd/FedExTrackerService.wsdl"
xmlns:tns="http://www.xmethods.net/sd/FedExTrackerService.wsdl"
xmlns:xsd="http://www.w3.org/2001/XMLSchema"
xmlns:soap="http://schemas.xmlsoap.org/wsdl/soap/"
xmlns="http://schemas.xmlsoap.org/wsdl/">
<message name="statusRequest">
  <part name="trackingNumber" type="xsd:string" />
  </message>
<message name="statusResponse">
  <part name="return" type="xsd:string" />
  </message>
<portType name="FedExTrackerPortType">
<operation name="getStatus">
  <input message="tns:statusRequest" />
  <output message="tns:statusResponse" />
  </operation>
  </portType>
<binding name="FedExTrackerBinding" type="tns:FedExTrackerPortType">
  <soap:binding style="rpc"
transport="http://schemas.xmlsoap.org/soap/http" />
```

```
<operation name="getStatus">
  <soap:operation soapAction="urn:xmethodsFedEx#getStatus" />
<input>
  <soap:body use="encoded" namespace="urn:xmethodsFedEx"
encodingStyle="http://schemas.xmlsoap.org/soap/encoding/" />
  </input>
<output>
  <soap:body use="encoded" namespace="urn:xmethodsFedEx"
encodingStyle="http://schemas.xmlsoap.org/soap/encoding/" />
  </output>
  </operation>
  </binding>
<service name="FedExTrackerService">
  <documentation>Provides access to a variety of FedEx delivery status
information</documentation>
<port name="FedExTrackerPort" binding="tns:FedExTrackerBinding">
  <soap:address
location="http://services.xmethods.net:80/perl/soaplite.cgi" />
  </port>
  </service>
  </definitions>
```

This service allows access to FedEx tracking information. Method service takes in a FedEx tracking number and returns the latest status from FedEx Tracking System. Following is the definition of the FedEx tracking service:

```
METHOD: getStatus()   INPUT: trackingNumber (xsd:string)  OUTPUT:
xsd:string
```

## Simple Object Access Protocol

Simple Object Access Protocol (SOAP) uses XML technology to provide a simple and lightweight distributed protocol for exchanging information between software components. XML is used because of its universal data format, programming language-neutrality, and extensibility. From the W3C specification, SOAP consists of three parts: an envelope that defines a framework for describing what is in a message and how to process it, a set of encoding rules for expressing instances of application-defined data types, and a convention for representing remote procedure calls and responses, shown in Figure 23.2. Therefore, SOAP defines a simple mechanism to support a variety of lower-level protocols, such as HTTP(S), SMTP, TCP, and others. The SOAP message contains application semantics by providing a modular packaging model and encoding mechanisms for encoding data within modules. This is the mobile characteristic that allows SOAP to be used in different messaging systems.

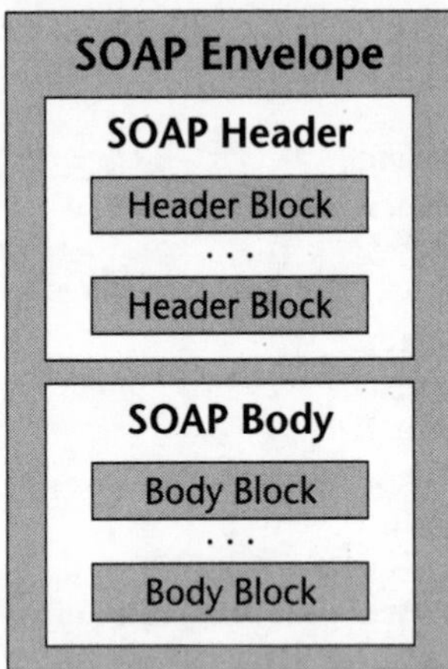


**Figure 23.2** SOAP message structure.

Following is an example of a simple SOAP message sent over HTTP requesting the current status of a FedEx package:

```
POST /FedexTrack HTTP/1.1
Host: www.fedex.com
Content-Type: text/xml; charset="utf-8"
Content-Length: nnnnn
SOAPAction: "urn:fedex-track-services"

<SOAP-ENV:Envelope
        xmlns:SOAP-ENV="http://schemas.xmlsoap.org/soap/envelope/"
        SOAP-
ENV:encodingStyle="http://schemas.xmlsoap.org/soap/encoding/">
    <SOAP-ENV:Body>
        <m:GetLastTrackInfo xmlns:m="Some-URI">
            <id>18973</id>
        </m: GetLastTrackInfo>
    </SOAP-ENV:Body>
</SOAP-ENV:Envelope>
```

## *Apache eXtensible Interaction System (Axis)*

Axis (http://xml.apache.org/axis) stands for Apache eXtensible Interaction System. The name does not have a link to SOAP; however, Apache Axis is the actual implementation of the next-generation Apache SOAP 3.0 engine. It uses a Simple API for XML (SAX, the Simple API for XML) streaming model to achieve modularity, flexibility, and performance enhancement over SOAP 2.0 implementation. More than just a SOAP engine, Axis has additional supports, such as a stand-alone server model, a servlet-able server for the Tomcat engine, full support for the Web Service Description Language (WSDL), and utilities for generating Java classes from WSDL (see Figure 23.3).

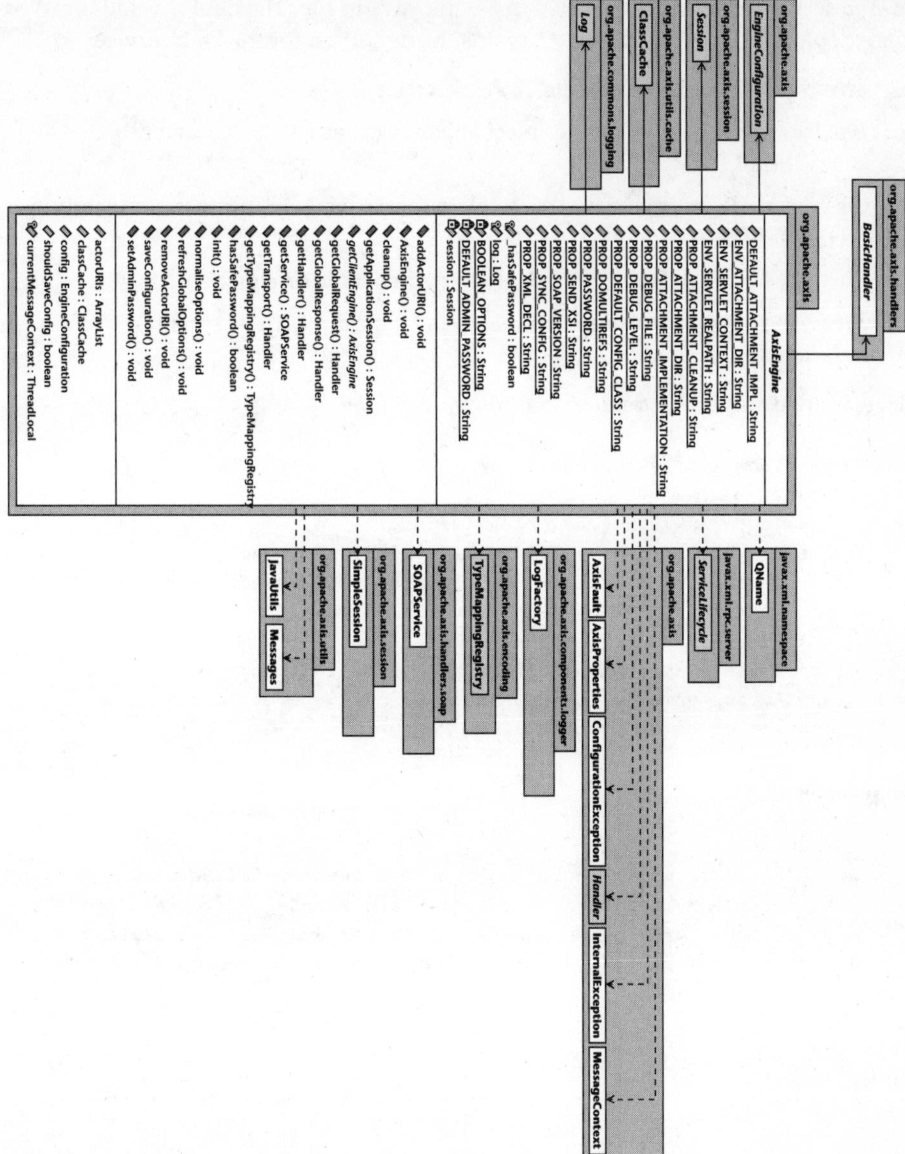


**Figure 23.3** Apache Axis engine in the UML view.

The Axis engine is the main gate to the SOAP processor. The engine interacts with the AxisHandlers to link Axis to the back-end components. Axis engine dispatches incoming SOAP Web service requests to "Web service providers." Axis supports RPC/Java-type providers and EJB-type providers. Additional providers can be implemented as add-ons to the Axis engine. For example, Borland Enterprise Server supports Axis with an additional CORBA provider for the Borland VisiBroker component.

The Web service provider is specified in a deploy.wsdd file. The deploy.wsdd is a Web service deployment descriptor that contains the definition for the Web service:

- *Service Name* defines the name of the service.
- *Provider* specifies the provider mechanism, such as java:RPC, java:EJB, or java:VISIBROKER.
- *Class Name* defines the name of the class that is loaded when a request arrives on this service.
- *AllowedMethods* defines methods that are invokable on this class.
- *Type Mapping* defines types that map to a Java class with its serializer and deserializer information.

Here is an example of a deploy.wsdd file:

```
<?xml version="1.0" encoding="UTF-8"?>
<deployment
    xmlns="http://xml.apache.org/axis/wsdd/"
    xmlns:ns="http://bean.jbuilder.mastering.wiley.com"
    xmlns:java="http://xml.apache.org/axis/wsdd/providers/java">
  <service name="ProfileManager" provider="java:RPC">
      <parameter name="className"
value="com.wiley.mastering.jbuilder.bean.ProfileManager"/>
      <parameter name="allowedMethods" value="getProfile "/>
      <parameter name="scope" value="Request"/>

  <typeMapping
    xmlns:ns="http://bean.jbuilder.mastering.wiley.com"
    qname="ns:ProfileBean"
    type="java:com.wiley.mastering.jbuilder.bean.ProfileBean"
    serializer="org.apache.axis.encoding.ser.BeanSerializerFactory"
    deserializer="org.apache.axis.encoding.ser.BeanDeserializerFactory"
    encodingStyle="http://schemas.xmlsoap.org/soap/encoding/"
  />

  </service>
</deployment>
```

# Using Web Services with JBuilder

There are four steps involved in developing Web services in JBuilder.

1. Construct the Web service business logic.
2. Package implementation files into a Web services deployable archive. Regarding the Java language, the archive will contain .class file and the Web service deployment descriptor.
3. Deploy the archive to the SOAP server. We talk about Apache Axis SOAP server and the JBuilder deployment tool for Web services in a later section.

4. Generate client access stubs. This step is necessary for developing client applications to consume the Web services. The generated client stubs will facilitate the communication with the Web service.

Before getting into each step, we discuss how to obtain and install the Borland Web Services Kit with JBuilder.

## Borland Web Services Kit Installation

JBuilder 8 has incorporated the Borland Web Services Kit for Java with its installation. *You can skip this portion if you have JBuilder 8.*

If you use a previous version of JBuilder, you need to download the Borland Web Services Kit for Java at www.borland.com/products/downloads/download_jbuilder.html. The download server will send you a Borland Web Services Kit license key via your registered email address. The license key comes as a text file, and you need to save the text file into your home directory. For example, if you run Windows 2000/XP, your home directory is C:\Documents and Settings\<username>. If you run Unix or Linux, the home directory could be /user/<username> or /home/<username>.

When installing the Web Services Kit, make sure that you extract the contents of the archive for your platform into a temporary directory, and then run the installer from that directory. If you try to run the installer directly from your archive file, you may encounter problems where you are not prompted for the registration wizard. In this case, the Web services functionality is disabled in JBuilder.

Follow these steps to install the Borland Web Services Kit for Java:

1. Unzip the webservices3_kit.zip into a temp directory.
2. Run wsk_install.exe to start the installation. Click Next to continue.
3. Read and accept the license agreement when prompted. Click Next to continue.
4. Review your selected options. Click Install to finalize the installation.
5. Click Done when the installation program is completed.

## JBuilder Web Services Features

JBuilder supports these toolkits for developing Web services: Apache Axis, Apache SOAP 2, Borland Enterprise Server, WebLogic, and WebSphere Application Server. It provides three Web services wizards, which are available on the Web Services page of the Object Gallery (File | New), as shown in Figure 23.4:

- *Web Services Configuration wizard* is for configuring your project for Web services. The wizard is used to create a SOAP-enabled Web application that hosts the Web services server locally.
- *Export as a Web Service wizard* is used for exporting Java classes and EJBs as Web services.
- *Import a Web Service wizard* is used for importing Web services from a WSDL or an EAR to generate Java classes for Web services consumer applications.

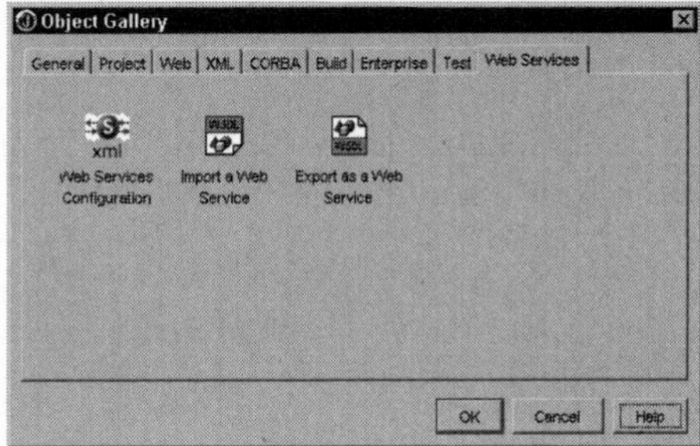


**Figure 23.4** Wizards for Web services.

JBuilder also provides additional tools for Web services development:

- *Web Services Explorer* (formerly known as UDDI Explorer) is used for browsing and publishing your Web services. You can use the Explorer to browse to WSDL documents and import them, browse to WSIL documents, publish businesses and services, and monitor UDDI SOAP messages.
- *TCP Monitor* is used for monitoring SOAP requests and responses between the Web services peer components. The TCP Monitor can also be used for debugging JSP and servlet applications.

# Constructing Web Services

The following sections introduce you to the first experience with Web services. The sections are tutorial-like sessions that take you, step–by–step, through how to construct Web services applications in JBuilder. You need to configure your project working with an application server. This chapter uses Borland Enterprise Server in its examples. Refer to Chapter 15, "Server and Service Configuration," for information on how to set up an application server in JBuilder.

## *Consuming Existing Web Services*

XMethods (www.xmethods.net) is one of the most popular sites for learning and playing with Web services. XMethods lists more than 200 services on its home page. Each service includes a short overview definition and a full description of how to use the service. Note that the XMethods services are made available for your personal, noncommercial use and demonstration purposes only. In this example, we build a client application consuming AltaVista's famous Babelfish service, shown in Figure 23.5. BabelFish is a translation service that can translate a text of up to 150 words in length from one language to another language.

To start the tutorial, let's click on the BabelFist service. The XMethods server will display detailed contents of the BabelFish service, as shown in Figure 23.6. On the page, you can access the BabelFish service's methods, parameters and their associated SOAPAction, method Namespace URI, and endpoint URL.

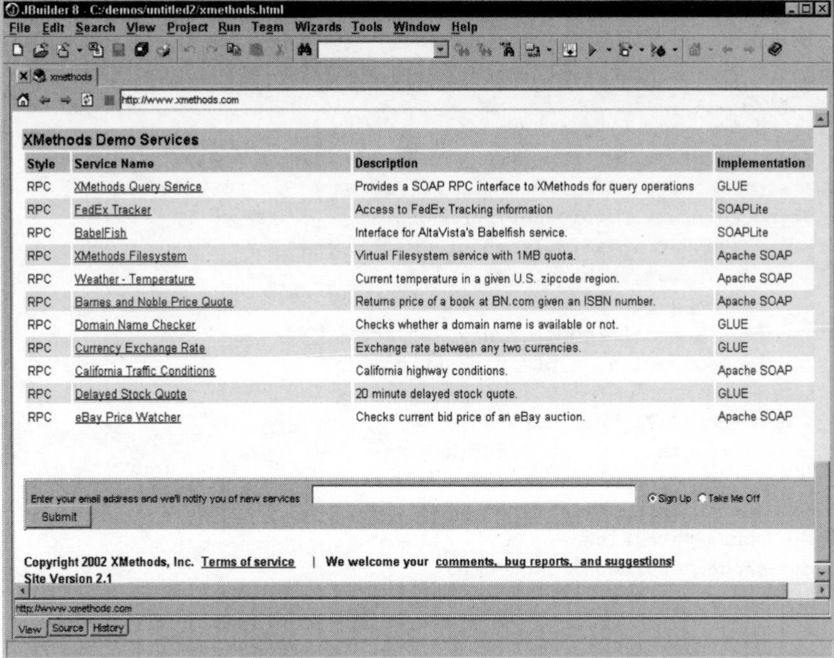


**Figure 23.5** XMethods demo services.

Copyright 2002, XMethods, Inc.

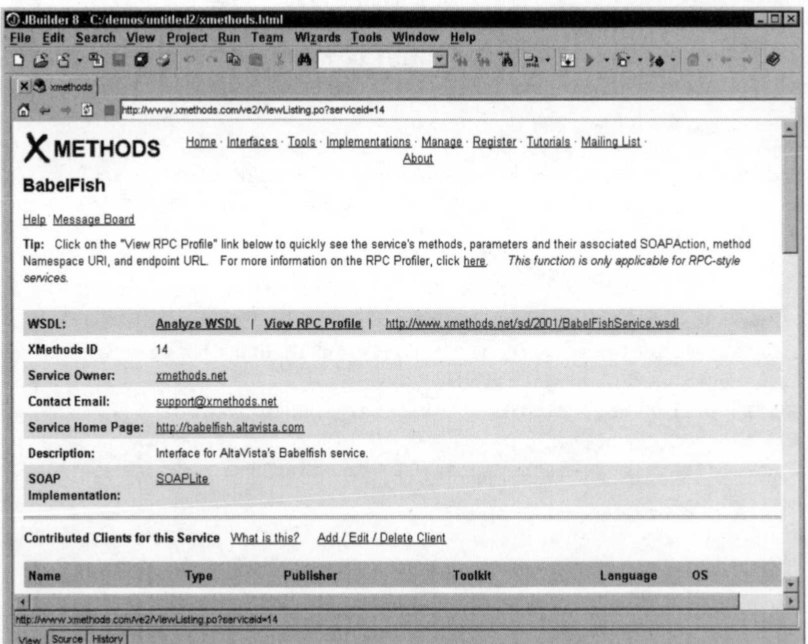


**Figure 23.6** Detailed Information for the BabelFish service.

Copyright 2002, XMethods, Inc.

The BabelFish WSDL file shown here can be found at www.xmethods.net/sd/2001/BabelFishService.wsdl:

```
<?xml version="1.0" ?>
<definitions name="BabelFishService"
xmlns:tns="http://www.xmethods.net/sd/BabelFishService.wsdl"
targetNamespace="http://www.xmethods.net/sd/BabelFishService.wsdl"
xmlns:xsd="http://www.w3.org/2001/XMLSchema"
xmlns:soap="http://schemas.xmlsoap.org/wsdl/soap/"
xmlns="http://schemas.xmlsoap.org/wsdl/">
<message name="BabelFishRequest">
  <part name="translationmode" type="xsd:string" />
  <part name="sourcedata" type="xsd:string" />
  </message>
<message name="BabelFishResponse">
  <part name="return" type="xsd:string" />
  </message>
<portType name="BabelFishPortType">
<operation name="BabelFish">
  <input message="tns:BabelFishRequest" />
  <output message="tns:BabelFishResponse" />
  </operation>
  </portType>
<binding name="BabelFishBinding" type="tns:BabelFishPortType">
  <soap:binding style="rpc"
transport="http://schemas.xmlsoap.org/soap/http" />
<operation name="BabelFish">
  <soap:operation soapAction="urn:xmethodsBabelFish#BabelFish" />
<input>
  <soap:body use="encoded" namespace="urn:xmethodsBabelFish"
encodingStyle="http://schemas.xmlsoap.org/soap/encoding/" />
  </input>
<output>
  <soap:body use="encoded" namespace="urn:xmethodsBabelFish"
encodingStyle="http://schemas.xmlsoap.org/soap/encoding/" />
  </output>
  </operation>
  </binding>
<service name="BabelFishService">
  <documentation>Translates text of up to 5k in length, between a
variety of languages.</documentation>
<port name="BabelFishPort" binding="tns:BabelFishBinding">
  <soap:address
location="http://services.xmethods.net:80/perl/soaplite.cgi" />
  </port>
  </service>
</definitions>
```

## BABELFISH USAGE

**The BabelFish service defines its method, input, and output format as follows:**

***METHOD*: BabelFish**

***INPUT* :**

**translationmode(xsd:string)**

**sourcedata (xsd:string) which is the text to be translated.**

***OUTPUT***

**return (xsd:string) which is the translated text.**

**Available translationmodes include the following:**

| TRANSLATION | TRANSLATIONMODE |
|---|---|
| English → French | "en_fr" |
| English → German | "en_de" |
| English → Italian | "en_it" |
| English →Portugese | "en_pt" |
| English → Spanish | "en_es" |
| French → English | "fr_en" |
| German → English | "de_en" |
| Italian → English | "it_en" |
| Portugese → English | "pt_en" |
| Russian → English | "ru_en" |
| Spanish → English | "es_en" |

### Using the Import a Web Service Wizard

Let's create a JBuilder project called ConsumerApplication. The next step is to use the JBuilder utility to create a proxy from the BabelFish WSDL file by importing the WSDL file. Open the Web Services page of the Object Gallery by doing File | New and selecting the Import a Web Service icon. JBuilder will display a series of wizard dialogs.

First, we need to select an available Web Service toolkit for a specific wizard of that toolkit. In this example, we select Apache AXIS as the toolkit we will use. Enter the URL for the BabelFish service (see Figure 23.7).

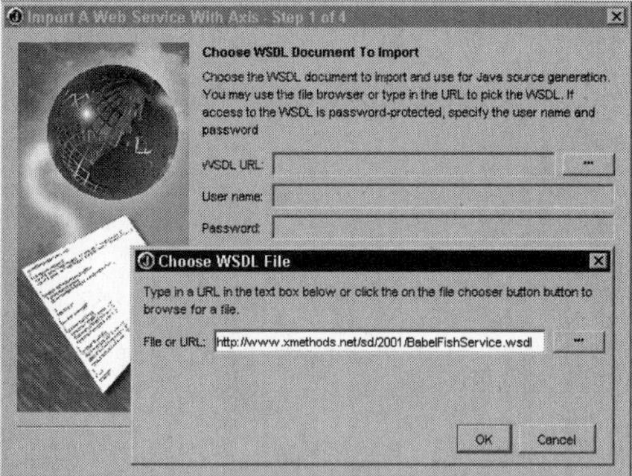


**Figure 23.7** Choose the WSDL to import.

In Step 2, we select server-side code generation options (see Figure 23.8). Check Generate server-side classes to have Java source generated from the imported WSDL. JBuilder provides two choices for server-side implementation on importing the WSDL file. We can choose to implement the service as a Java class or an Enterprise Session Bean. Depending on what we choose, the wizard will add steps to complete the implementation. Deploy scope options are to define how instances of the service will be created. The Request option indicates that there is one instance per request. The Session option indicates that there is one instance per authenticated session. And the Application option indicates that there is one instance being shared among requests.

Check the Generate skeleton classes option when you want to generate the Skeleton class to encapsulate an implementation for the server. When the option is checked, the Skeleton class shows the meta data for methods and parameters. When the option is unchecked, deploy.wsdd shows the meta data for methods and parameters.

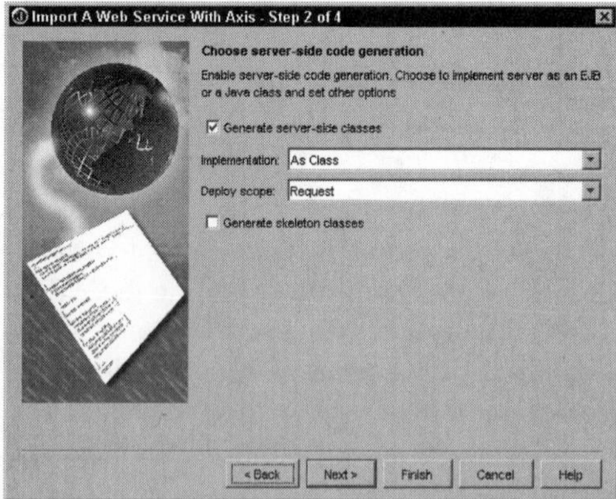


**Figure 23.8** Select server-side code generation options.

Step 3 is to set output options for the generated classes (see Figure 23.9). A package name is required for the package options. If you want to use an existing package, you can select an available package from the drop-down list or use the ellipses button to browse to a package in the project. When the Use this package globally for all types option is checked, all the generated Java source will be located in the same package. And later, you do not need to customize the namespace mapping that is used for packages.

The Type version option allows us to select a particular type mapping. In this case, there are two choices: SOAP 1.2 and SOAP 1.1 style type mappings. For more information on SOAP type mappings, you can visit the following link: www.w3.org/2000/XP/Group.

When the Overwrite any existing Bean types option is checked, existing bean types of the same name will be overwritten with new generated Java sources. Next, generate the declared type mapping in separate Helper classes. The Generate JUnit test case option generates a JUnit test case to test the Web service immediately. In this example, we check Generate JUnit test case and Generate wrapped style types options. The Generate wrapped style types option is used to determine whether to generate a Java class for the WSDL complex type. When this option is checked, the wrapped style types are used as individual parameters, and no Java classes are being generated for the complex type. Otherwise, all complex types in the WSDL will be generated to Java classes.

Check the Generate code for all elements even if not referenced option if you want to have nonreferenced elements in the WSDL being generated to Java classes. Finally, the Ignore imports and use only the immediate WSDL document option is used to bypass code generation for the import statements in the WSDL and the associated schema within the WSDL. Click the Next button to advance to Step 4.

The final step is to edit the namespace mapping that is used for many packages. This step is useful for organizing multiple Web services components in the same project. Click Finish to complete the Import WSDL wizard. JBuilder then generates the files listed in Table 23.1.

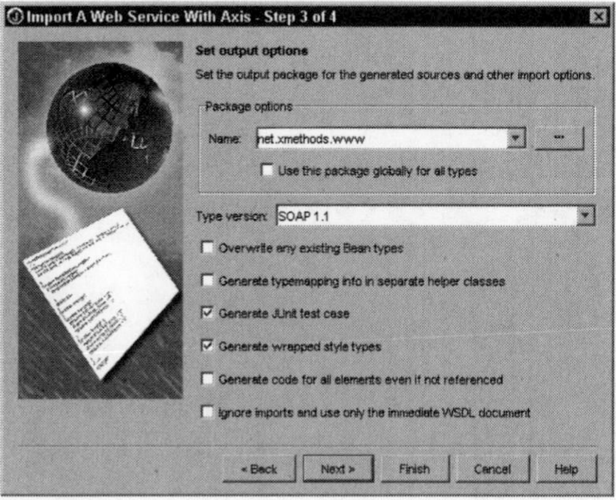


**Figure 23.9** Configure Output Options dialog.

**Table 23.1** Generated Files from Import WSDL Wizard

| GENERATED FILES | DESCRIPTIONS |
|---|---|
| BabelFishBindingImpl.java | This class implements the BabelFish portType interface. |
| BabelFishBindingStub.java | This local proxy class represents binding to a remote BabelFish Web service. |
| BabelFishPortType.java | This interface represents BabelFish portType in the WSDL. |
| BabelFishService.java | This service interface defines a get method for the BabelFish port listed in the service element of the WSDL. Also, it defines a factory class to get the BabelFish stub instance. |
| BabelFishServiceLocator.java | This class extends BabelFishService.java and defines the port address to locate the implementation of BabelFishService. |
| BabelFishServiceTestCase.java | This is the JUnit test case for testing the Web service. |

### Use the Generated JUnit Test Case

We can make use of the generated JUnit test case to test the Web service immediately. Let's edit the generated JUnit test case by adding a few lines of code to fulfill the test case:

```
package net.xmethods.www;
import junit.framework.*;

public class BabelFishServiceTestCase extends TestCase {
    public BabelFishServiceTestCase(java.lang.String name) {
        super(name);
    }
    public void test1BabelFishPortBabelFish() {
        BabelFishPortType binding;
        try {
            binding = new BabelFishServiceLocator().getBabelFishPort();
        }
        catch (javax.xml.rpc.ServiceException jre) {
            if(jre.getLinkedCause()!=null)
                jre.getLinkedCause().printStackTrace();
            throw new AssertionFailedError("Exception caught:"+ jre);
        }
        assertTrue("binding is null", binding != null);

        try {
```

```
            java.lang.String value = null;
            java.lang.String text = "Hello, how are you?";
            java.lang.String mode = "en_fr";
            value = binding.babelFish(mode, text);
            System.out.println(text + " is translated to: " + value);
        }
        catch (java.rmi.RemoteException re) {
            throw new AssertionFailedError("Exception caught:" + re);
        }
    }
}
```

The output from running the test case is as follows:

```
Hello, how are you? is translated to: bonjour, comment allez-vous?
```

## Build a Simple GUI Application

We can build a simple Swing GUI to do more tests for the BabelFish Web services. Go to File | New and select Application. Choose "ConsumerApplication" as the application name and "ConsumerFrame" as the application frame. JBuilder should generate a ConsumerApplication.java and ConsumerFrame.java file and make ConsumerFrame.java active in the Content pane. Click on the Design tab to go to the Design view for ConsumerFrame and add a couple of buttons and text fields, as shown in Figure 23.10.

The changes in the GUI result in the code changes in ConsumerFrame.java. Double-click on the Go! button and add the boldface code from Source 23.1 into the jButton1_actionPerformed() method of the ConsumerFrame.java.

```
package com.wiley.mastering.jbuilder.webservices;

import java.awt.*;
import java.awt.event.*;
import javax.swing.*;
import net.xmethods.www.*;

public class ConsumerFrame extends JFrame {
  JPanel contentPane;
  JLabel jLabel1 = new JLabel();
  JLabel jLabel2 = new JLabel();
  JTextField jTextField1 = new JTextField();
  JLabel jLabel3 = new JLabel();
  JTextField jTextField2 = new JTextField();
  JTextField jTextField3 = new JTextField();
  JButton jButton1 = new JButton();

  //Construct the frame
  public ConsumerFrame() {
```

**Source 23.1** ConsumerFrame.java. *(continued)*

```
    enableEvents(AWTEvent.WINDOW_EVENT_MASK);
    try {
      jbInit();
    }
    catch(Exception e) {
      e.printStackTrace();
    }
  }
  //Component initialization
  private void jbInit() throws Exception  {
    contentPane = (JPanel) this.getContentPane();
    jLabel1.setEnabled(true);
    jLabel1.setFont(new java.awt.Font("Dialog", 1, 16));
    jLabel1.setBorder(BorderFactory.createRaisedBevelBorder());
    jLabel1.setHorizontalAlignment(SwingConstants.CENTER);
    jLabel1.setText("BabelFish Translator");
    jLabel1.setBounds(new Rectangle(75, 21, 223, 61));
    contentPane.setLayout(null);
    this.setSize(new Dimension(400, 300));
    this.setTitle("BabelFish Client");
    jLabel2.setText("Enter Your Text:");
    jLabel2.setBounds(new Rectangle(45, 98, 84, 30));
    jTextField1.setText("");
    jTextField1.setBounds(new Rectangle(46, 125, 308, 35));
    jLabel3.setText("Translate To:");
    jLabel3.setBounds(new Rectangle(45, 174, 83, 26));
    jTextField2.setText("");
    jTextField2.setBounds(new Rectangle(46, 208, 307, 46));
    jTextField3.setText("en_fr");
    jTextField3.setBounds(new Rectangle(112, 178, 92, 21));
    jButton1.setBounds(new Rectangle(216, 178, 73, 22));
    jButton1.setText("Go!");
    jButton1.addActionListener(new
ConsumerFrame_jButton1_actionAdapter(this));
    contentPane.add(jLabel1, null);
    contentPane.add(jLabel2, null);
    contentPane.add(jTextField1, null);
    contentPane.add(jLabel3, null);
    contentPane.add(jTextField2, null);
    contentPane.add(jTextField3, null);
    contentPane.add(jButton1, null);
  }
  //Overridden so we can exit when window is closed
  protected void processWindowEvent(WindowEvent e) {
    super.processWindowEvent(e);
    if (e.getID() == WindowEvent.WINDOW_CLOSING) {
      System.exit(0);
    }
```

**Source 23.1** *(continued)*

```
  }

  void jButton1_actionPerformed(ActionEvent e) {
    net.xmethods.www.BabelFishPortType binding = null;
    try {
      binding = new BabelFishServiceLocator().getBabelFishPort();
      java.lang.String translatedText = null;
      java.lang.String text = jTextField1.getText();
      java.lang.String mode = jTextField3.getText();
      translatedText = binding.babelFish(mode, text);
      jTextField2.setText(translatedText);
    }
    catch (javax.xml.rpc.ServiceException jre) {
      jre.printStackTrace();
    }
    catch (java.rmi.RemoteException re) {
      re.printStackTrace();
    }
  }
}

class ConsumerFrame_jButton1_actionAdapter implements
java.awt.event.ActionListener {
  ConsumerFrame adaptee;

  ConsumerFrame_jButton1_actionAdapter(ConsumerFrame adaptee) {
    this.adaptee = adaptee;
  }
  public void actionPerformed(ActionEvent e) {
    adaptee.jButton1_actionPerformed(e);
  }
}
```

**Source 23.1** *(continued)*

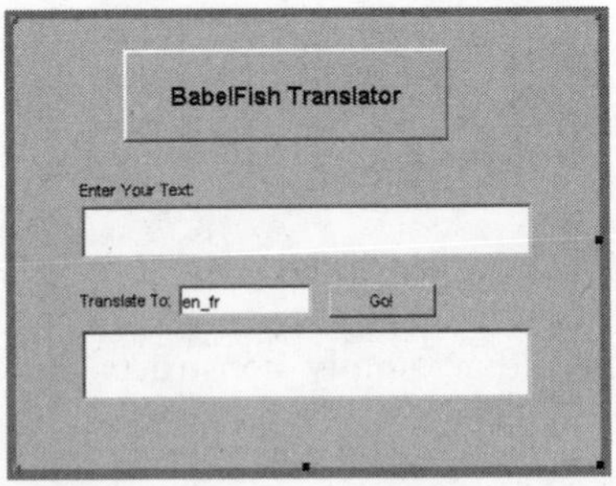

**Figure 23.10** Form Design view for ConsumerFrame.

Compile the whole project and run the ConsumerApplication. Now, you can enter a text line and click the Go! button to see the translated text.

## Generating Web Services from a Java Component

This section explores the use of the Export as a Web Service wizard to generate a Web service from an already existing Java class in your project. Usually the Java class is a Java Bean type class. In case you work with a non–Java Bean type class, you need to implement and provide custom serializers and deserializers for the client-side stubs.

### Create Sample Java Bean

To start, let's create a new JBuilder project called javabean2webservice and add two new Java classes, ProfileBean.java and ProfileManager.java in to the project.

The ProfileBean has two string properties and their getters and setters. To simplify the example, the ProfileBean constructor takes in a string personID and sets a personName to the combination of "Borland_" + the personID:

```
package com.wiley.mastering.jbuilder.bean;

public class ProfileBean {

  private String personID;
  private String personName;
  public ProfileBean( String personID) {
this.personID = personID;
// This step is to obtain personName from the given personID.
// In this example, we just return a sample "Employee_" + personID
// for demonstration purpose.
    this.personName = "Employee_" + personID;
  }
  public String getPersonID() {
    return personID;
  }
  public void setPersonID(String personID) {
    this.personID = personID;
  }
  public String getPersonName() {
    return personName;
  }
  public void setPersonName(String personName) {
    this.personName = personName;
  }
}
```

ProfileManager implements a getProfile() method that simply constructs and returns a new ProfileBean object with a personID:

```
package com.wiley.mastering.jbuilder.bean;

public class ProfileManager {
  public ProfileManager() {
  }
  public ProfileBean getProfile(String personID){
    return new ProfileBean( personID);
  }
}
```

Later, we will export ProfileManager with its getProfile() method as a Web service.

## Configure the Web Service Application

Next, we configure the project for Web services before exporting the ProfileManager as a Web service:

1. Use the Web Application wizard (File | New, Web, Web Application) to create a new WebApp called mywebservice.
2. If the project uses an Enterprise application server, then we need to create an EAR file by using the EAR wizard (File | New, Enterprise, EAR). In this example, enter "Profile" as the EAR's name.
3. Use the Web Services Configuration wizard (File | New, Web Services, Web Services Configuration) to configure the project for Web service (see Figure 23.11). Select Profile for the EAR file in the project and select mywebservice for a WebApp in the project.

JBuilder integrates with three Web services toolkits: Apache Axis, Apache SOAP 2, and WebLogic. In the example, we select an Apache Axis toolkit for the project.

Step 2 (see Figure 23.12) of the wizard is to set up a Web services server run-configuration. Click Finish to complete the wizard and configure the project for Web services.

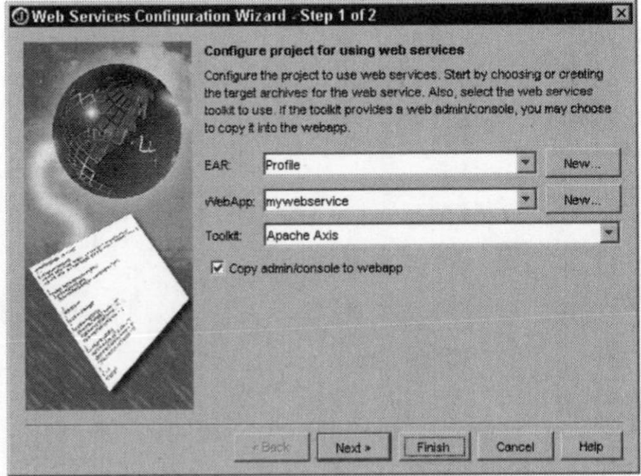


**Figure 23.11** Web Services Configuration wizard – Step 1.

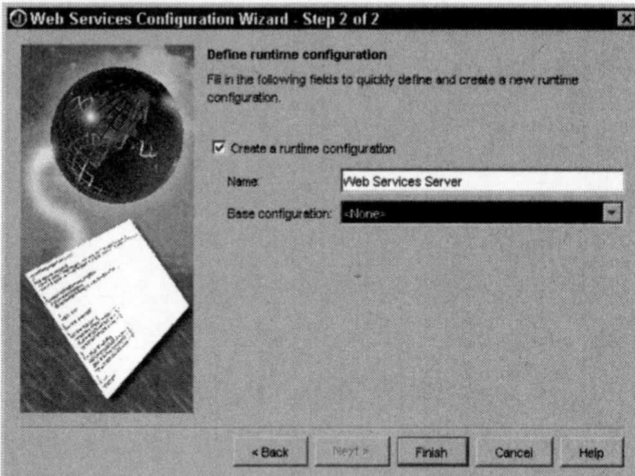


**Figure 23.12** Web Services Configuration wizard – Step 2.

### Using Export as a Web Service Wizard

To export ProfileManager as a Web service, right-mouse click on the ProfileManager .java and select the Export as a Web service option. The wizard will export Profile-Manager to a Web service component.

In this very first step, if you select Generate client stubs, the wizard will add two additional steps to configure the output options of the client stubs. We do not need to generate the client stubs in this example; therefore, we will go through only five steps instead of seven steps.

Scope options define how instances of the service will be created. *Request option* indicates that there is one instance per request. *Session option* indicates that there is one instance per authenticated session. *Application option* indicates that there is one instance being shared among requests.

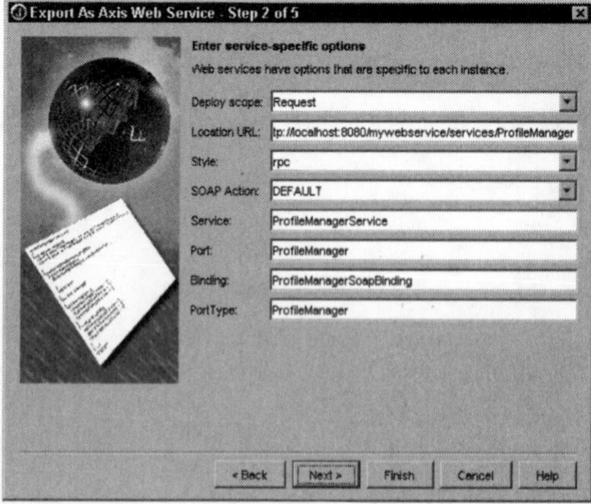


**Figure 23.13** Setting service-specific options.

Location shows the URL address of the Web service. The URL will be set to the location attribute of the <wsdlsoap:address> element in the WSDL file, for example:

```
<wsdlsoap:address
location="http://localhost:8080/mywebservice/services/ProfileManager"/>
```

Apache Axis supports these styles: rpc, document, and wrapped. They are all mapped to an RPC provider. When a style is selected, it is set to the binding style in the WSDL document. For example:

```
<wsdlsoap:binding style="rpc"
transport="http://schemas.xmlsoap.org/soap/http"/>
```

SOAP Action sets a soapAction name for the operation in the WSDL. Default for the soapAction is set to " ", and it reflects in the WSDL as follows:

```
<wsdlsoap:operation soapAction=""/>
```

Service is a service name set to the <service> element in the generated WSDL file, as follows:

```
<wsdl:service name="ProfileManagerService">
```

Port is a port name set to the <port> element in the generated WSDL file. Binding is a binding name set to the <binding> element in the generated WSDL file. For example:

```
      <wsdl:port binding="intf:ProfileManagerSoapBinding"
name="ProfileManager">

         <wsdlsoap:address
location="http://localhost:8080/mywebservice/services/ProfileManager"/>

      </wsdl:port>
```

PortType is a port type name set to the <portType> element in the generated WSDL file; for example:

```
   <wsdl:portType name="ProfileManager">

      <wsdl:operation name="getProfile" parameterOrder="personID">

         <wsdl:input message="intf:getProfileRequest"
name="getProfileRequest"/>

         <wsdl:output message="intf:getProfileResponse"
name="getProfileResponse"/>

      </wsdl:operation>

   </wsdl:portType>
```

The next step is to set the output options for the generated WSDL, as shown in Figure 23.14.

This step of the wizard configures output options to generate the interfaces and implementations of the service. Select one of the following modes when generating WSDL:

- Select the Interface and Implementation mode to generate both the interface and implementation parts of the WSDL.
- Select the Interface Only mode to generate only the interface portion of the WSDL.
- Select "Implementation Only" mode to generate only the implementation portion of the WSDL.
- Select the Interface and Implementation in Separate Files mode to generate both the interface and implementation parts of the WSDL into separate Java source files. This selection will enable the Output Impl file and Import URL options. The Output Impl file option contains the name of the file for the WSDL implementation. The Import URL option contains a URL location to the interface WSDL file.
- For the Output file option, enter the pull path and name of the WSDL file.

The next step is to select what business methods are to be exposed in the Web service from the hierarchy Tree view (see Figure 23.15). You can expose one or more methods in the class, or you can expose all available methods in the class. In this example, only the getProfile() method is exposed to the Web service. By default, inherited packages and classes are excluded from the Web service; however, you can include inheritance exposure by checking the Enable inheritance option. You can use the Add/Remove button to exclude or include additional packages and classes.

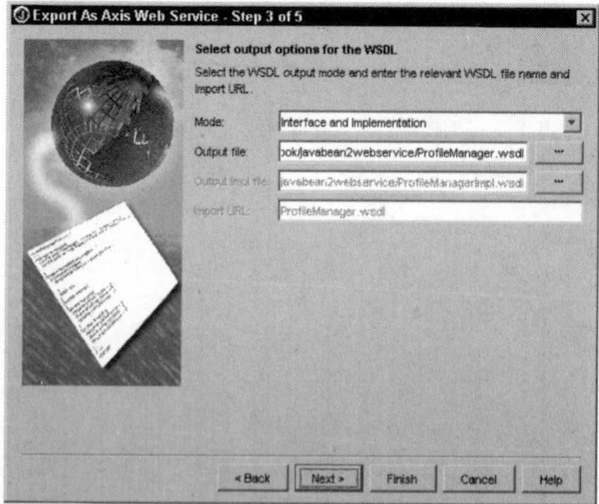


**Figure 23.14** Select output options for the WSDL.

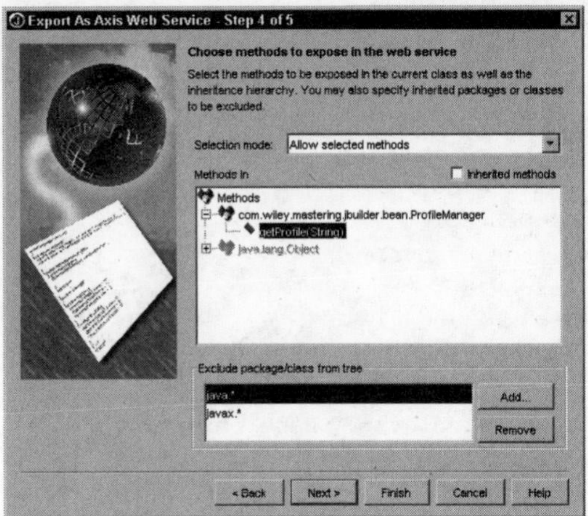


**Figure 23.15** Select methods to expose in the web service.

The last step is to enter custom namespace mapping for the packages. This step is useful for organizing multiple Web services components in the same project. Click Finish to complete the Export as a Web Service wizard.

After completing the wizard, you can explore the Project pane to see that JBuilder generated a Web service deployable archive in .war format; which is mywebservice .war (see Figure 23.16). You also see the javabean2webservice.ear file, which can be deployable to any J2EE application server supporting Web service deployment. In this example, we deploy the .EAR file into Borland Enterprise Server.

The selected Apache Axis toolkit generated the deploy.wsdd and server-config.wsdd. The two files contain information describing what, where, and how to access the Web service. Source 23.2 shows the server-congfig.wsdd.

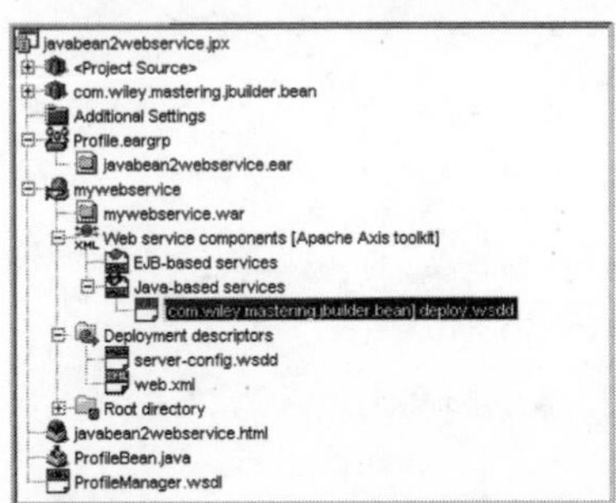


**Figure 23.16** Project pane view.

```
<?xml version="1.0" encoding="UTF-8"?>
<deployment xmlns="http://xml.apache.org/axis/wsdd/"
xmlns:java="http://xml.apache.org/axis/wsdd/providers/java">
 <globalConfiguration>
  <parameter name="adminPassword" value="admin"/>
  <parameter name="attachments.implementation"
value="org.apache.axis.attachments.AttachmentsImpl"/>
  <parameter name="sendXsiTypes" value="true"/>
  <parameter name="sendMultiRefs" value="true"/>
  <parameter name="sendXMLDeclaration" value="true"/>
  <requestFlow>
   <handler type="java:org.apache.axis.handlers.JWSHandler">
    <parameter name="scope" value="session"/>
   </handler>
   <handler type="java:org.apache.axis.handlers.JWSHandler">
    <parameter name="scope" value="request"/>
    <parameter name="extension" value=".jwr"/>
   </handler>
  </requestFlow>
 </globalConfiguration>
 <handler name="LocalResponder"
type="java:org.apache.axis.transport.local.LocalResponder"/>
 <handler name="URLMapper"
type="java:org.apache.axis.handlers.http.URLMapper"/>
 <handler name="RPCDispatcher"
type="java:org.apache.axis.providers.java.RPCProvider"/>
 <handler name="Authenticate"
type="java:org.apache.axis.handlers.SimpleAuthenticationHandler"/>
 <handler name="MsgDispatcher"
type="java:org.apache.axis.providers.java.MsgProvider"/>
 <service name="ProfileManager" provider="java:RPC">
  <parameter name="allowedMethods" value="getProfile "/>
  <parameter name="scope" value="Request"/>
  <parameter name="className"
value="com.wiley.mastering.jbuilder.bean.ProfileManager"/>
  <typeMapping
deserializer="org.apache.axis.encoding.ser.BeanDeserializerFactory"
encodingStyle="http://schemas.xmlsoap.org/soap/encoding/"
qname="ns1:ProfileBean"
serializer="org.apache.axis.encoding.ser.BeanSerializerFactory"
type="java:com.wiley.mastering.jbuilder.bean.ProfileBean"
xmlns:ns1="http://bean.jbuilder.mastering.wiley.com"/>
 </service>
 <service name="AdminService" provider="java:MSG">
  <parameter name="allowedMethods" value="AdminService"/>
  <parameter name="enableRemoteAdmin" value="false"/>
  <parameter name="className" value="org.apache.axis.utils.Admin"/>
  <namespace>http://xml.apache.org/axis/wsdd/</namespace>
```

**Source 23.2** Server-Config.wsdd.

```
  </service>
  <service name="Version" provider="java:RPC">
   <parameter name="allowedMethods" value="getVersion"/>
   <parameter name="className" value="org.apache.axis.Version"/>
  </service>
  <transport name="http">
   <requestFlow>
    <handler type="URLMapper"/>
    <handler type="java:org.apache.axis.handlers.http.HTTPAuthHandler"/>
   </requestFlow>
  </transport>
  <transport name="local">
   <responseFlow>
    <handler type="java:org.apache.axis.transport.local.LocalResponder"/>
   </responseFlow>
  </transport>
</deployment>
```

**Source 23.2** *(continued)*

## Deploy the Web Service Application

In this example, we use the Apache Axis toolkit shipped with Borland Enterprise Server to host the Web services. When configuring the project for Web service development, we did select a Web Services Server run configuration in the previous discussion. Let's review the settings of the Web Services Server run configuration. Do Run | Configuration, and select Web Services Server to edit its settings (see Figure 23.17).

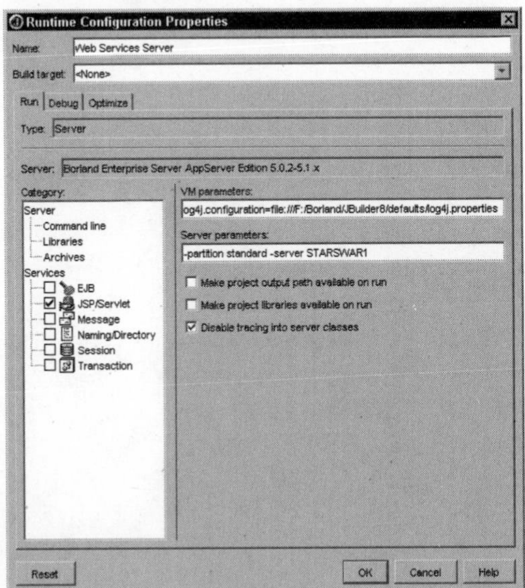


**Figure 23.17** Web Services Server run configuration.

**Figure 23.18** Start Web Services Server.

Note that we select to run only JSP/servlet service because we do not need other services in this example. Let's start the Web Services Server, as shown in Figure 23.18.

After the Web Services Server launched, the archive files are deployed to the server. The JBuilder Content pane will display the Axis entry Web page, as shown in Figure 23.19.

From this page, you can view a list of deployed services in the Axis server or validate the local installations' configuration. The validation process will examine the webapp-deployed files and verify the included libraries. Also, the process will list all system properties and class loader information. Click on the View link to display a list of deployed services in the browser.

You can see that a ProfileManager (wsdl) link takes you to the ProfileManager.wsdl. Then you can import the ProfileManager.wsdl to build the consumer-side application for the Web service, as discussed in the previous session. We use a different approach to discover the Web services via the Web Service Explorer.

## Discovering Web Services with the Web Service Explorer

Let's leave the Web Service Server running and create a new project called testwebservice. When you have a new project activated in JBuilder, do Tools|Web Services Explorer. Click on WSDL Servers, create a new server, and name it mywebservice (see Figure 23.20).

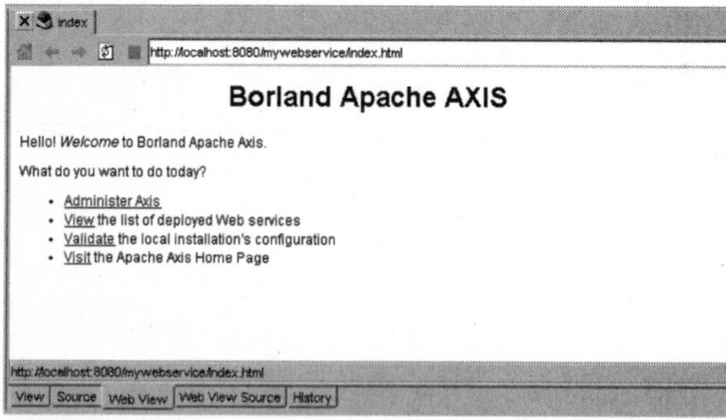


**Figure 23.19** Apache Axis Start page.

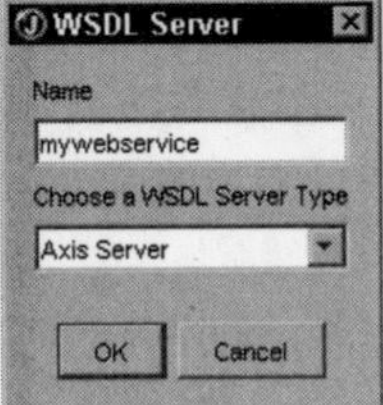


**Figure 23.20** Create a new WSDL server.

Enter http://localhost:8080/mywebservice/servlet/AxisServlet for the service port URL, as shown in Figure 23.21.

When we click on the Display Services button, we will see the list of services available for the MyWebService WSDL server.

Now, we can import the ProfileManager service to build the consumer application. Select the ProfileManger, and click on the Import WSDL icon, which is the last button located above the WSDL servers. JBuilder will take you through the Import a Web Service wizard, as discussed in the previous section. When completing the import WSDL steps, we edit ProfileManagerServiceTestCase.java before running the test (Source 23.3).

```
/**
 * ProfileManagerServiceTestCase.java
 *
 * This file was auto-generated from WSDL
 * by the Apache Axis WSDL2Java emitter.
 */

package localhost;

public class ProfileManagerServiceTestCase extends
junit.framework.TestCase {
    public ProfileManagerServiceTestCase(java.lang.String name) {
        super(name);
    }
    public void test1ProfileManagerGetProfile() {
        localhost.ProfileManager binding;
        try {
            binding = new
localhost.ProfileManagerServiceLocator().getProfileManager();
        }
        catch (javax.xml.rpc.ServiceException jre) {
```

**Source 23.3** ProfileManagerServiceTestCase.java. *(continued)*

```
            if(jre.getLinkedCause()!=null)
                jre.getLinkedCause().printStackTrace();
            throw new junit.framework.AssertionFailedError("JAX-RPC
ServiceException caught: " + jre);
        }
        assertTrue("binding is null", binding != null);

        try {
            com.wiley.mastering.jbuilder.bean.ProfileBean value = null;
            // set customerID as a current time in milli-second
            String customerID =
String.valueOf(System.currentTimeMillis());
            // invoke getProfile() from the web service to get
ProfileBean
            // object.
            value = binding.getProfile(customerID);
            System.out.println("GetProfile(): " +
value.getPersonName());
        }
        catch (java.rmi.RemoteException re) {
            throw new junit.framework.AssertionFailedError("Remote
Exception caught: " + re);
        }
    }
}
```

**Source 23.3** *(continued)*

This is a sample output from running the test case:

```
GetProfile(): Employee_1037844915846
```

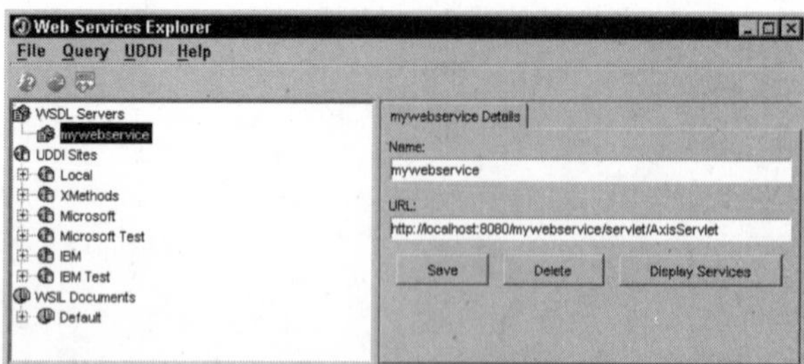


**Figure 23.21** MyWebService WSDL server.

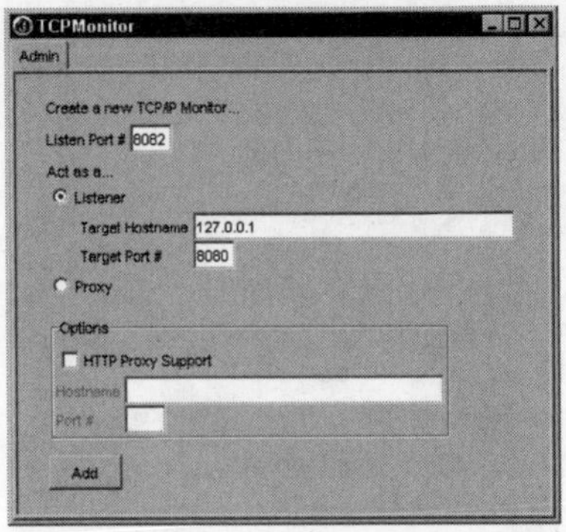

**Figure 23.22** Add the TCP Monitor listening port.

### Monitoring Web Service with TCP Monitor

The Axis toolkit includes the TCP Monitor listening over a connection to help monitor and debug any of the SOAP envelopes when the SOAP envelopes are transported through the monitor. To start the TCP Monitor, select Tools | TCP Monitor (see Figure 23.22).

You need to create a new port for the TCP Monitor to listen to. Figure 23.22 shows that port 8082 is selected for the listening port, the forwarding listener is set to host 127.0.0.1, and 8080 to the destination port. Click the Add button to activate the new TCP/IP Monitor. A new page is added into the TCP Monitor GUI (see Figure 23.23).

The client application needs to use the listening port of TCP Monitor to send and receive its messages. In this example, the listening port is 8082, and we need to edit the ProfileManagerServiceLocator.java to redirect the messages to the listening port 8082. Open ProfileManagerServiceLocator.java, and locate the following line:

```
    // Use to get a proxy class for ProfileManager

private final java.lang.String ProfileManager_address =
"http://localhost:8080/mywebservice/servlet/AxisServlet/ProfileManager";
```

Then change the port from 8080 to 8082 (see Source 23.4).

```
/**
 * ProfileManagerServiceLocator.java
 *
 * This file was auto-generated from WSDL
 * by the Apache Axis WSDL2Java emitter.
 */
```

**Source 23.4** ProfileManagerServiceLocator.java. *(continued)*

```
package localhost;

public class ProfileManagerServiceLocator extends
org.apache.axis.client.Service implements
localhost.ProfileManagerService {

    // Use to get a proxy class for ProfileManager
    private final java.lang.String ProfileManager_address =
"http://localhost:8082/mywebservice/servlet/AxisServlet/ProfileManager";

    public java.lang.String getProfileManagerAddress() {
        return ProfileManager_address;
    }

    // The WSDD service name defaults to the port name.
    private java.lang.String ProfileManagerWSDDServiceName =
"ProfileManager";

    public java.lang.String getProfileManagerWSDDServiceName() {
        return ProfileManagerWSDDServiceName;
    }

    public void setProfileManagerWSDDServiceName(java.lang.String name)
{
        ProfileManagerWSDDServiceName = name;
    }

    public localhost.ProfileManager getProfileManager() throws
javax.xml.rpc.ServiceException {
       java.net.URL endpoint;
        try {
            endpoint = new java.net.URL(ProfileManager_address);
        }
        catch (java.net.MalformedURLException e) {
            return null; // unlikely as URL was validated in WSDL2Java
        }
        return getProfileManager(endpoint);
    }

    public localhost.ProfileManager getProfileManager(java.net.URL
portAddress) throws javax.xml.rpc.ServiceException {
        try {
            localhost.ProfileManagerSoapBindingStub _stub = new
localhost.ProfileManagerSoapBindingStub(portAddress, this);
            _stub.setPortName(getProfileManagerWSDDServiceName());
            return _stub;
```

**Source 23.4** *(continued)*

```
        }
        catch (org.apache.axis.AxisFault e) {
            return null;
        }
    }

    /**
     * For the given interface, get the stub implementation.
     * If this service has no port for the given interface,
     * then ServiceException is thrown.
     */
    public java.rmi.Remote getPort(Class serviceEndpointInterface)
throws javax.xml.rpc.ServiceException {
        try {
            if
(localhost.ProfileManager.class.isAssignableFrom(serviceEndpointInterfac
e)) {
                localhost.ProfileManagerSoapBindingStub _stub = new
localhost.ProfileManagerSoapBindingStub(new
java.net.URL(ProfileManager_address), this);
                _stub.setPortName(getProfileManagerWSDDServiceName());
                return _stub;
            }
        }
        catch (java.lang.Throwable t) {
            throw new javax.xml.rpc.ServiceException(t);
        }
        throw new javax.xml.rpc.ServiceException("There is no stub
implementation for the interface:  " + (serviceEndpointInterface == null
? "null" : serviceEndpointInterface.getName()));
    }

    /**
     * For the given interface, get the stub implementation.
     * If this service has no port for the given interface,
     * then ServiceException is thrown.
     */
    public java.rmi.Remote getPort(javax.xml.namespace.QName portName,
Class serviceEndpointInterface) throws javax.xml.rpc.ServiceException {
        java.rmi.Remote _stub = getPort(serviceEndpointInterface);
        ((org.apache.axis.client.Stub) _stub).setPortName(portName);
        return _stub;
    }

    public javax.xml.namespace.QName getServiceName() {
```

**Source 23.4** *(continued)*

```
        return new
javax.xml.namespace.QName("http://localhost:8080/mywebservice/servlet/Ax
isServlet/ProfileManager", "ProfileManagerService");
    }

    private java.util.HashSet ports = null;

    public java.util.Iterator getPorts() {
        if (ports == null) {
            ports = new java.util.HashSet();
            ports.add(new javax.xml.namespace.QName("ProfileManager"));
        }
        return ports.iterator();
    }
}
```

**Source 23.4** *(continued)*

Rebuild the *testwebservice* project, and run the ProfileManagerServiceTestCase to interact with the Web service and view the SOAP requests and responses in the TCP Monitor (see Figure 23.23).

The TCP Monitor can have multiple listener ports in different pages by adding new listening ports. The SOAP messages can be edited and resent to view new requests and responses through the TCP Monitor. In addition, requests and responses can be saved to a file for later use.

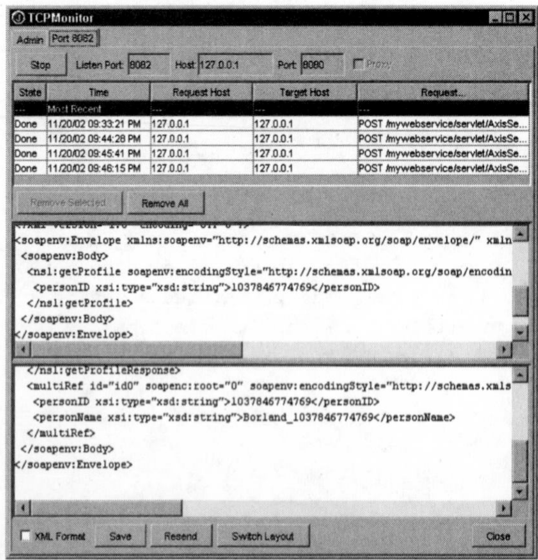


**Figure 23.23** TCP Monitor in action.

## *Generating Web Services from an EJB Component*

To create Web services from EJBs, follow these steps:

1. Generate a WSDL file that is used by clients for invoking the service using the Axis tool: Java2WSDL.
2. Create the EJB deployable JAR file using your targeted application server's toolkit.
3. Create the Web service deployable WAR. This process involves generating the client stubs for the EJB, packaging the client stubs into WEB-INF/lib directory of the WAR, creating a Web services deployment descriptor (deploy.wsdd) file, providing the JNDI name of the bean and the class name of the home interface, and creating server-config.wsdd using Axis utilities.

JBuilder eliminates these steps in its well-designed wizard. It automatically exports the EJBs as Web services, so there is no extra work required for this process. When you have your EJB application implemented, you run the Web Services Configuration wizard to configure your project for Web services. Immediately, you see that the stateless Session Beans, with their exposed business methods to remote interface, are automatically made available to the server as Web services. You can later edit the Web service deployment node to add or remove any business methods as you desire.

### Create New Project, New EJB, and New WebApp

Let's create a new project called nasdaq_ejb and configure the Borland Enterprise Server as your targeted server. (Project | Project Properties, Server Tab, and select Borland Enterprise Server 5.x).

This section will not cover how to create and implement an EJB application. Refer to Chapter 20 and Chapter 21 for how to work with EJB applications. In this example, we build two session beans: one named NasdaqSession and the other named Enterprise1 (see Figure 23.24).

The NasdaqSession has getQuote() as its exposed method. Enterprise1 has getTimeStamp() as its exposed method.

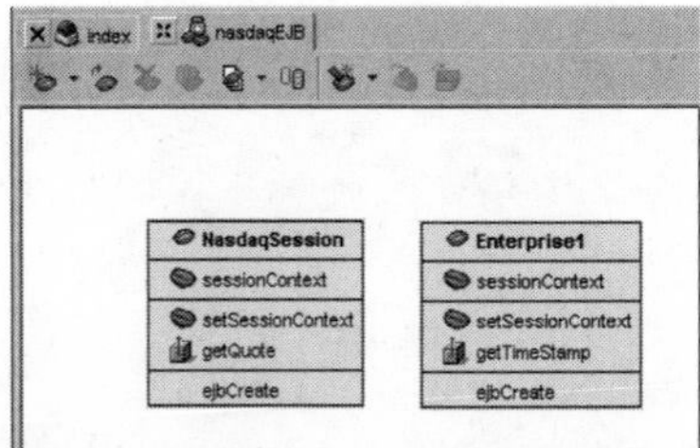


**Figure 23.24** EJB Designer with two Session Beans.

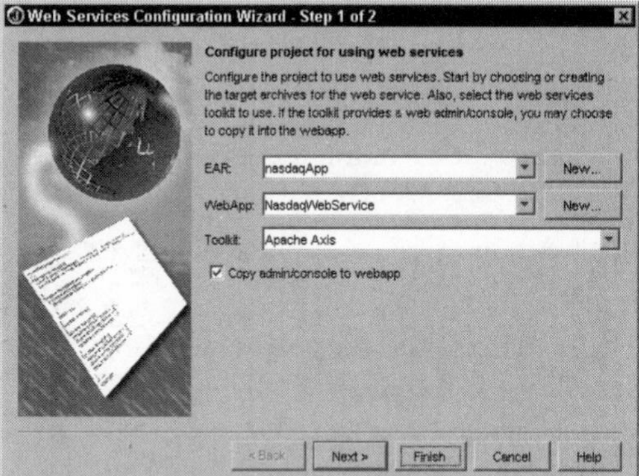


**Figure 23.25** Configure NasdaqWebService.

Here are the implementations of the two exposed methods:

```
public String getQuote(String ticketSymbol) {
  // Return fake value of the ticket sysmbol.
    return String.valueOf(ticketSymbol.length()*10);
}

public String getTimeStamp() {
  // Return System milli-sencond
    return String.valueOf(System.currentTimeMillis());
}
```

The next step is to use the Configure Web Service Application wizard, as discussed in the previous section for how to set up a Web service application. Let's call the Web service application NasdaqWebServiceApp (see Figure 23.25).

Upon completing the Web Services Configuration wizard, the nasdaq_ejb Project pane will be updated with the new Web service component, as shown in Figure 23.26.

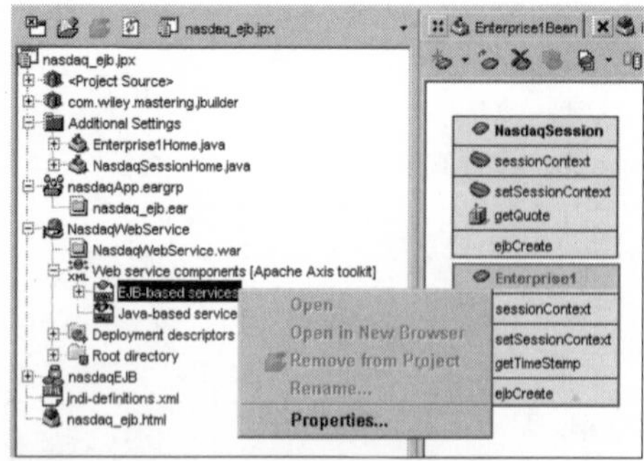


**Figure 23.26** Updated Project pane.

As seen in Figure 23.26, JBuilder automatically exports the NasdaqSession and Enterprise1 stateless session EJB as Web services. You can see that their exposed business methods to the remote interface are defined in the Web service deployment descriptor. You can later edit the Web service deployment node to add or remove any business methods. Right-mouse-click on the EJB-based services item under Web service component node, as shown in Figure 23.26. Then select Properties. The Properties dialog GUI shown in Figure 23.27 will be displayed.

In this example, we expose only the NasdaqSession bean by checking on the item. The Web service deploy.wsdd is instantly updated with new changes:

```
<?xml version="1.0" encoding="UTF-8"?>
<deployment xmlns:java="http://xml.apache.org/axis/wsdd/providers/java"
xmlns="http://xml.apache.org/axis/wsdd/">
    <documentation>[JBUILDER marker begin 1037888029500 JBUILDER marker
end]</documentation>
    <service name="NasdaqSession" provider="java:EJB">
        <documentation>JBUILDER should auto generate this entry:
YES(YES/NO)</documentation>
        <parameter name="beanJndiName" value="NasdaqSession"/>
        <parameter name="homeInterfaceName"
value="com.wiley.mastering.jbuilder.NasdaqSessionHome"/>
        <parameter name="allowedMethods" value="getQuote"/>
    </service>
</deployment>
```

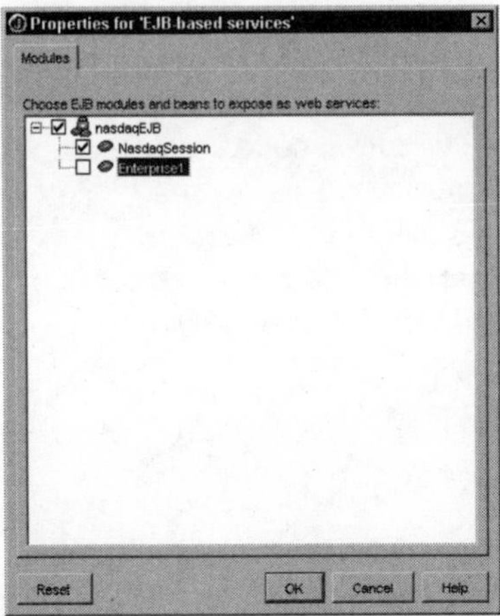


**Figure 23.27** EJB-based Web services properties.

The essential parameters for the EJB-based Web services are as follows:

- *beanJndiName* indicates the name of the bean in JNDI.
- *homeInterfaceName* shows a fully specified class of the EJB home interface. This class will be included in the WAR file.
- *allowedMethods* are exposed methods from the EJBs. Those methods can be invoked on this EJB through the Web services. If there are more than two exposed methods, they are separated by spaces. For example:

```
<parameter name="allowedMethods" value="getQuote getCompanyInfo
getLastestNew"/>
```

Those listed methods are available for remote invocation.

Note that the EJB-based deploy.wsdd uses Java:EJB as the Web service provider. The Java:EJB provider understands that the class serving the Web service is an EJB. Therefore, as a Web service request arrives, the EJB provider looks up the bean name in the JNDI initial context, locates the home class, creates an instance of the bean, and invokes the specified method using reflection on the EJB stub. The process requires that the actual EJB be deployed to an EJB container before a client can access it. A J2EE EAR file can contain both EJB-based Web services and the EJB component in one single archive to ease the deployment process.

**WEB SERVICES FROM A CORBA COMPONENT**

**Depending on what Object Request Broker you use, there could be a different approach to generate Web services from a CORBA component. Borland Enterprise Server (BES) by nature is a CORBA-based application server. The BES partition for Web services supports Java:RPC, Java:EJB, and Java:VISIBROKER service providers. We have talked about Java:RPC and Java:EJB in a few sections. In order for the Java:VISIBROKER provider to work properly, the class serving the Web service must be a Visibroker CORBA component. This component can be either C++ or a Java component. When a Web service SOAP request arrives, Java:VISIBROKER provider will initialize the ORB, bind to the name specified to get a CORBA object, invoke the specific method on the CORBA object, and return the result. You must have a VisiBroker server started before the Web service can locate the CORBA object. Let's take a look at the following IDL:**

```
// StockModule.idl
module StockModule {
  interface Quote {
    string getStatus();
    string getQuote (in string arg);
    long getDelay(in long interval);
  };
};
```

When we apply idl2java on StockModule.idl, we will get a set of stubs and skeleton. We are interested in a generated file, called StockOperations.java. And here is the equivalent deploy.wsdd, generated by using Java2WSDL on StockOperations interface.

```
<deployment
   xmlns="http://xml.apache.org/axis/wsdd/"
   xmlns:ns="http://borland.com"
   xmlns:java="http://xml.apache.org/axis/wsdd/providers/java">
  <service name=" Quote" provider="java:VISIBROKER">
     <parameter name="className"
value="com.wiley.mastering.jbuilder.QuoteModule. Quote"/>
     <parameter name="allowedMethods" value="getStatus getQuote getDelay"/>
     <parameter name="locateUsing" value="osagent"/>
     <parameter name="objectName" value="StockName"/>

  </service>
</deployment>
```

This deploy.wsdd shows that we will use OSAgent to locate the CORBA object by object name. Here are different examples of deploy.wsdd that use other location services.

```
<!-- Using poa object and OSAgent -->
     <parameter name="locateUsing" value="osagent"/>
     <parameter name="objectName" value=" StockName2"/>
     <parameter name="poaName" value="/quote_poa"/>

 <!-- Using naming service -->
     <parameter name="locateUsing" value="nameservice"/>
     <parameter name="objectName" value="USA/Virginia/Leesburg/StockName"/>

<!-- Using ior and corbaname with host:port -->
     <parameter name="locateUsing" value="ior"/>
     <parameter name="objectName" value="corbaname::192.168.1.120:9999#
USA/Virginia/Leesburg/StockName "/>
     -->
```

When packaging the deployment file, the CORBA stub must be packaged as part of the WAR file.

In contrast to the Web Services Server run configuration in Figure 23.17, we select to run the server with all available J2EE services, which include EJB, JSP/Servlet, Message, Naming/Directory, Session, and Transaction services. Now you can start the Web Services Server and import the wsdl to build the consumer application for that EJB-based Web service, as we discussed in the previous section.

## Web Service Packaging

Generally, a Web service component is packaged in a WAR format. One WAR can include multiple Web services. And multiple WAR files can be deployed into any Web service container. Each Web services WAR file contains one Deployment Descriptor named server-config.wsdd in the WEB-INF directory. The server-config.wsdd file provides Web service configuration information, such as the name of the Web service, the provider type, and any corresponding Java classes and exposed methods.

### Common Structure of a Web Service WAR File

Following is a typical component structure of a Web service WAR:

- WEB-INF/web.xml.
- WEB-INF/server-config.wsdd.
- WEB-INF/web-borland.xml. This is a vendor-specific Deployment Descriptor.
- WEB-INF/classes/. Java classes corresponding to your Web services are located in this directory and common Web services toolkit libraries.
- WEB-INF/lib/. JAR files corresponding to your Web services are located in this directory.

Index.html and other JSP pages launch the Web services. Figure 23.28 shows an Apache Axis WAR structure.

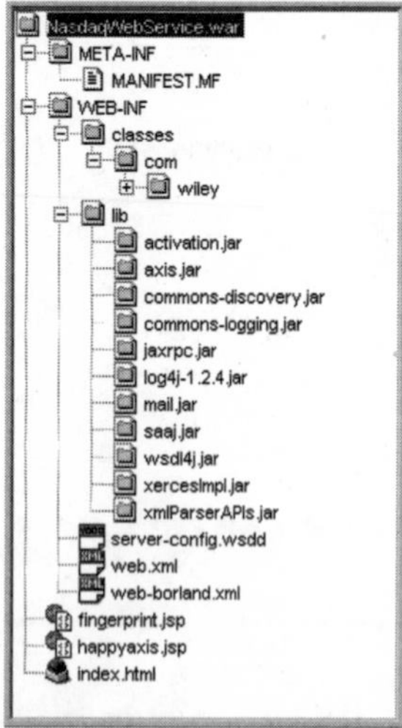


**Figure 23.28** Common structure of a Web service WAR.

## Summary

This chapter introduces the basic concepts and design of a Web service application with JBuilder using Web Service wizards. This includes a review of the steps to do the following:

- Generate Java code from WSDL
- Generate WSDL from Java code, using a UDDI Explorer
- Use TCP Monitor to review request and response SOAP messages, then deploy Web services using Tomcat and the Apache Axis implementation of the SOAP standard with Borland Enterprise Server
- Generate Web services from a Session Bean in a J2EE application

# Index

## C

## Q



## R

## T

## U



## V



## W

## X



## Z